Enjoy Learning Chinese Characters

Discover their Hidden Meanings

Authors Kun Ho Park & Kyung Yong Kong
Translation Young Youp Hwang & Jennifer Jean Lim
with Babel Korea Corp.
Design Sang Hee Kim, Jae Kyoung Shim and Dae Han Youn
Illustration Jae Young Lee
Editor Kyung Yong Kong

Publisher
KONG & PARK, Inc.
4F, 22, Samil-daero 15-gil, Jongno-gu, Seoul, 110-111 Korea
Registration No. 300-2008-82 (September 2nd, 2008)
Tel +82_2_565_1531
Fax +82_2_3445_1080
www.kongnpark.com

Second Edition 2013

ISBN 978-89-97134-09-0

Distributed by

America & Europe
KONG & PARK, Inc.
4F, 22, Samil-daero 15-gil, Jongno-gu, Seoul, 110-111 Korea
Tel +82_2_565_1531 Fax +82_2_3445_1080 info@kongnpark.com
www.kongnpark.com

Asia, Oceania & Africa
Pan Asia Publishing Pte Ltd
Raffles City P O Box 677 Singapore 911723
Tel +65_6316_1788/ +65_9660_1088 Fax +65_6291_0500 pa@panasiabooks.com
www.panasiabooks.com

Printed in Korea

ENJOY LEARNING CHINESE CHARACTERS

Discover their Hidden Meanings

Kun Ho Park · Kyung Yong Kong

KONG & PARK, Inc

Contents

Nature 396

Introduction

Because Chinese characters are commonly known as pictograms, most Chinese learners wonder if they can possibly learn thousands of characters. Some give up altogether and choose to learn only Pinyin, the romanized form of Chinese characters and so their use of the language becomes very limited. However, considering that the people who devised the Chinese language and most of the people who write and speak it every day are not geniuses, we have found a shortcut, an easier way, that would help people appreciate and learn the Chinese characters. This book has been written to share that secret with you!

Countries that still use Chinese characters in their vocabulary are China (including Taiwan, Hong Kong and Singapore), Korea and Japan. China, for obvious reasons, uses it most often. The simplified characters are used in China and Singapore, whereas Taiwan and Hong Kong use the original complicated characters. Japan uses a mix of both. Korea has her own alphabet Hangul, but up to 60% of the vocabulary has borrowed meaning from Chinese characters. Therefore, if you don't know them, it is very hard for you to understand their true meanings. For these reasons, many researches on Chinese characters have been carried out mostly in China, Korea and Japan. We have taken into account the opinions of scholars from these three countries and shortlisted 3,500 characters, which outnumbers the 2,633 characters in the HSK Level 1-6 characters list. This book contains 1,160 characters that explain about the most frequently-used 856 characters including 623 characters in the HSK Level 1-3 list.

Chinese characters are based on inscriptions found on bones and tortoise carapaces used in the 14th and 12th century B.C. centuries. In the 6th and 7th centuries, they were said to have been passed on to nations in the Korean peninsula at that time, and then passed on to Japan. All languages change with time and Chinese was no exception. The usage of Chinese characters in Korea and Japan retain the original form and meaning of when they were passed on, so it was very helpful to have the input of scholars from the three countries.

This book is an attempt to compile the opinions of scholars from these three countries, and the authors' personal interpretations of the inscriptions on bronze, bones and tortoise carapaces to explain the origin of the characters. The authors' aim is to help our readers understand the characters, not to become scholars in their own right. But that does not mean this book is a pet project. It is intended to help readers further understand the meanings of all Chinese characters.

PARK, Kun Ho
朴乾晧

KONG, Kyung Yong
孔卿镕

User Guide

To learn Chinese characters much more easily, one must understand how they came to be. This book will introduce you to the characters about people, life and nature.

Characters about people

- Human body : Though different in color and size, we share the same physical characteristics. Most characters are based on human physical attributes.
- Person : Many basic characters depict the form of certain human postures, such as 'standing man,' 'crouching man,' 'kneeling man.'
- Title : From unborn baby to elderly man, and from slave to king.

Characters about life

- War : The history of man might as well be the history of war. Many Chinese characters are related to war, which influenced life greatly.
- Necessities of life : Characters related to the necessities of life.
- Agriculture : Farming is an occupation that produces food, the most essential element for human existence. It has a long association with the survival of mankind.

Characters about nature

- Animals : They can be categorized into 'land animals,' 'other animals' and 'animal by-products.'
- Natural scenery : Characters about mountains, minerals, water, greenery and trees are the most-used Chinese characters.
- Heavenly bodies : The characters about the sun, moon and stars are combined with other characters, contributing to produce another meaning.
- Miscellaneous : Numbers and signs.

By finding out how these Chinese characters were initially developed, and later by and repeatedly using the same basic characters in more complicated ones, you will be able to dissect the complicated ones and appreciate the story each of them tell. If you practice reading and writing these characters repeatedly, your Chinese ability will improve surprisingly fast. Furthermore, if you come across new characters not listed in this book, you can guess what their pronunciation would be and what they mean.

Structure of the content

To gain the most from this book, you will need to understand the structure of the content of this book and the intention of the editors. The contents of this book can be divided into two parts, the diagram and the explanation.

The Diagram

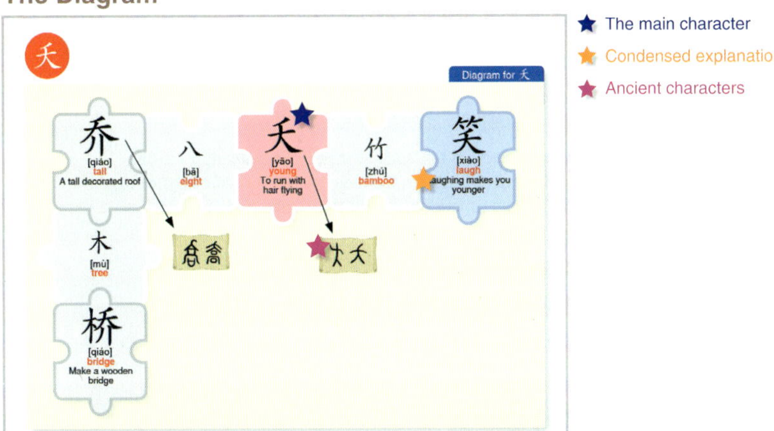

★ The main character : These may not be part of the 200 radicals that the scholars have identified. But remember that a character doesn't have to be a radical to have an important meaning within another, more complicated, character. In essence, radicals are only used to categorize characters and are seldom used other than when one is looking a character up in a dictionary. So, because they are of little importance, this book does not list radicals. By the time you are done reading, you will be able to dissect each Chinese Character into the basic components, and with this information you can look them up in a Chinese dictionary.

Condensed explanation : Read the short explanation, and you will be able to understand how a certain Chinese character was originally developed. In the latter part of the book, you will find some Chinese characters appearing in a diagram without much explanation about them. That is because these characters would have already been explained and therefore a short introduction should be enough to have you guess the origin and meaning of it. When you go back to reread about a certain character, the short introduction and diagram will be enough to jog your memory.

Ancient characters : In order to help the readers to better understand the characters in current use, the ancient characters such as the inscriptions on bones and tortoise carapaces, bronze inscriptions and seal characters have been listed in this book. These ancient characters will help the readers to clearly understand the hidden meanings of the Chinese characters by simple storytelling of each character.

The main body

16

16c

号 hào

name; number

mouth 口 [kǒu] + skillful 丂 [kǎo]

It takes much skill(丂) to remember one's name so you can call out(口) to him from within a crowd. But, when there are too many people to call everyone's name, it's easier to use numbers, which is why this character is now also a quantifier.

* "丂" depicts an artisan making something with skill or wit.

一百多号人。Over a hundred people. - 223 134a 222d 16c 63

16d

听 tīng

hear

mouth 口 [kǒu] + ax 斤[118] [jīn]

Taking an ax(斤) to someone's mouth(口) is a harsh way of saying one must listen carefully.

听见[tīngjiàn] hear - 13
听说[tīng/shuō] be told; hear of - 72d
听写[tīngxiě] dictate; dictation - 169a

- Quick reference number
- Character explained
- Dissection
- Stroke order
- Explanations and footnotes
- Vocabulary
- Examples

★ Quick reference number : Each character in this book has its own quick reference number. This is to aid you in searching for a specific character you do not know or cannot remember. Use them to go back to a certain word or character that appears on another page.

★ Character explained : Each character in blue is on the HSK Level 1-3 word list. Each in blue with an extra line is on the HSK Level 1-3 list, not only as part of a word but more often as a character alone. Each in grey is not on the HSK Level 1-3 list, but since it is a basic character or in the process of developing from the basic to the HSK Level 1-3, they are also worth remembering. Making use of this division will help you prepare for the HSK exam.

★ Dissection : This explains which basic characters are brought together to make the complicated one. It is also helpful to check how the Pinyin of one affects that of the other. As the epilogue states, most characters not mentioned in this book take the Pinyin of a character it is composed of. Also, there is nothing to worry if the shape of a character changes when it becomes part of another. That change was made over centuries, according to what the people thought would look better.

★ Stroke order : There's a rule to the stroke order when writing a Chinese character. Left to right, top to bottom. When two strokes meet, write the horizontal stroke first, then the vertical. Follow the stroke order in this book and your Chinese characters will look balanced. It should help if you try to recall the smaller components of each character when writing.

★ Explanations and footnotes : This is the most important part of this book. These explain how a character is made. In some cases, the ancient version of the same character is provided to aid understanding.

★ Vocabulary : Those (+words) in black are on the HSK Level 1-3 word list. Those in grey are not, but will help in understanding the usage. Any collocations with a slash (/) between each word can either be joined together or separated.

★ Examples : When the usage of the character explained is hard to find in the word lists, we have provided extra usage examples to enhance your understanding of the given character.

People

People

Human body

When the ancient Chinese first came up with the shapes that later became the basis of the present Chinese characters, it would have been much easier for them to use something associated with their bodies. Everything from the top of the head to the tip of the toes is depicted in a character.

1. The head can also symbolize a leader.
2. A face has ears, eyes, a nose and a mouth.
3. Which part of the body would be used to describe emotions like happiness, anger, sadness and joy? It's "心 [xīn]," the character meaning 'heart.'
4. Which body part is used the most? It's our hands, which is what differentiates us from animals. Of all body parts, the character for 'hand' is used the most as part of a more complicated character.
5. The second most used body part is 'foot,' which is also part of many characters.

Person

Many characters in this category describe people, not just body parts. Whereas some mean 'a person,' others now entail a different meaning.

1. Explanations on how the meaning of "人," 'a person,' influences a character.
2. Some characters look like "大," a man with arms and legs splayed out.
3. 'Standing man, crouching man, kneeling man,' and how they change a character's meaning.

Title

Any dictionary will tell you that humans are a social species. In this section, we will find out how titles and class are inflected in various characters.

1. Some characters describe the class one is born into.
2. There is also the social class the separates kings from commoners. As there are many more subjects than kings, there are many more characters about subjects, too.

亠

Diagram for 交

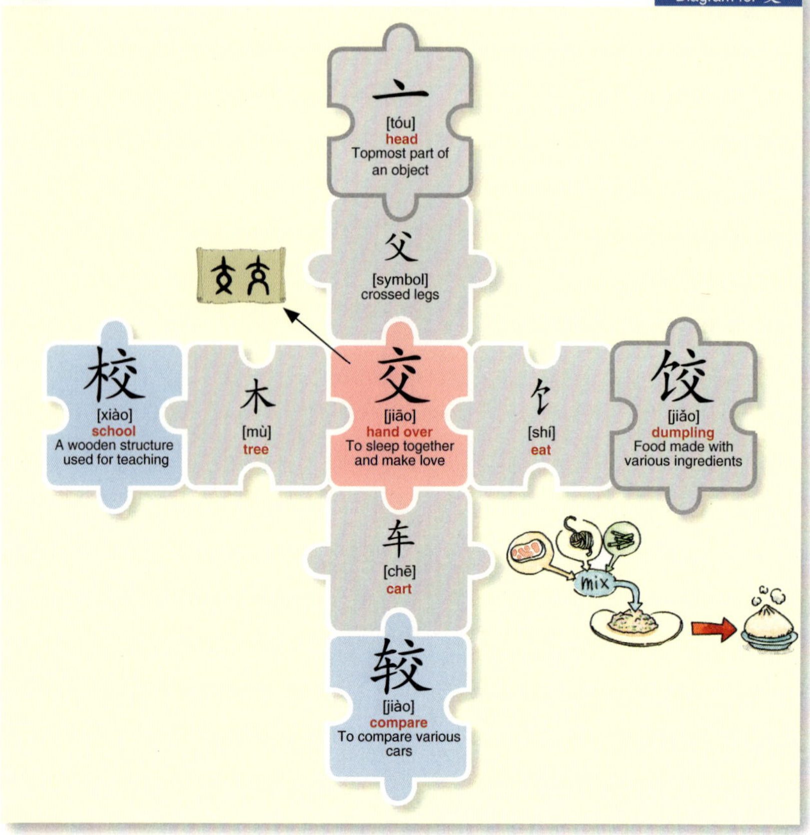

1

1 丶 亠

亠 tóu

head

The ‘head’ of a person or animal, the ‘roof’ of a building, the ‘upper part’ of an object.

1a 丶 亠 亣 六 ㄊ 交

交 jiāo

hand over

head 亠 [tóu] + crossed legs 父 [symbol]

When you see an image of two people(亠) with legs crossed/mixed(父) to make love, this character means 'associate with.' For a man and woman to be in this posture, it also indicates they are in love with each other and reciprocate each other's feelings.

* The character that looks like "father 父[98][fù]" is a pictorial image of crossed legs and has nothing to do with the word. Remember, just because they have the same shape doesn't mean they have the same meaning.

交付[jiāofù] hand over; pay - 41
交换[jiāohuàn] exchange; swap - 68d
交流[jiāoliú] exchange; interchange - 202a
外交[wàijiāo] diplomacy; foreign affairs - 222a

1b ノ ㇇ 饣 饣 饣 饣 饣 饺 饺

饺 jiǎo

dumpling

eat 饣=食[137][shí] + mix/hand over 交 [jiāo]

Dumplings are made by mixing(交) various ingredients to make the stuffing, then separately kneading dough to make the skin, wrapping some stuffing in a piece of skin, then cooking them to eat(饣).

饺子[jiǎozi] dumpling (with meat and vegetable stuffing) - 95

1c 一 𠂉 𠂉 车 车 车 车 车 较 较

较 jiào

compare

cart 车[124][chē] + mix/hand over 交 [jiāo]

Out of an assortment of(交) cars(车), they are comparing which one is better.

* Even in ancient China, they compared cars or carts to judge who was better off.

比较[bǐjiào] compare - 88a

1d 一 十 才 木 木 木 木 木 校 校

校 xiào

school

tree 木[210][mù] + hand over 交 [jiāo]

A school is a structure made with wood(木) where teachers and students get together to exchange(交) knowledge.

* An example of an old wooden Chinese structure would be the Forbidden City.

学校[xuéxiào] school - 95a
校长[xiàozhǎng] schoolmaster; principal - 102

1

京

Diagram for 京

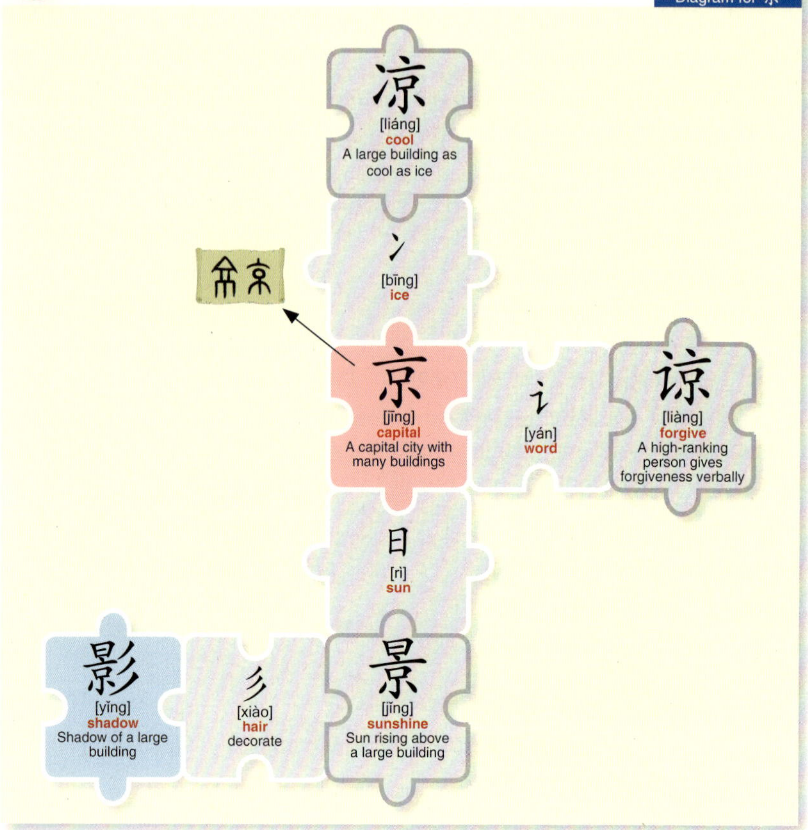

2

2

丶 亠 亠 亡 宁 亨 京 京

京 jīng

capital

head 亠[1] [tóu] + structure of a building 小 [symbol]

Symbolizing the shape of a high-rise building(小) with a roof(亠), it means something high or large. It also means a large city, like the capital of a nation.

* This character is associated with a building, so "亠" is the roof and the rest is the actual structure. It has nothing to do with "mouth 口[16][kǒu]" or "small 小[235][xiǎo]."

北京 [Běijīng] Beijing; Peking - 88c

2a　丶 冫 冫 冫 冫 冫 冫 凉 凉 凉

凉 liáng

cool

ice 冫[206] [bīng] + large/capital 京 [jīng]

A large building(京) with a high ceiling and thick walls is cool like ice(冫), even in the summer.

凉快[liángkuai] pleasantly cool - 28d

2b　丶 讠 讠 讠 讠 讠 讠 讠 谅 谅

谅 liàng

forgive

word 讠=言[22] [yán] + large/capital 京 [jīng]

Words(讠) of a high-ranking official living in a large building(京) has the power to forgive/pardon.

原谅[yuánliàng] excuse; forgive - 201d

2c　丨 冂 日 日 旦 早 早 昌 畧 景 景 景

景 jǐng

sunshine

sun 日[218] [rì] + large/capital 京 [jīng]

The sun(日) shines over a large building(京).

风景[fēngjǐng] scenery; landscape - 213c

2d　丨 冂 日 日 旦 早 早 昌 畧 景 景 景 景' 影 影

影 yǐng

shadow

sunshine 景 [jǐng] + decorate/hair 彡[8] [shān]

When the sun shines(景), buildings cast shadows(彡). Shadows are also used in photographs and movies.

* "Hair 彡" describes the shadow.

电影[diànyǐng] film; movie - 157a　　影响[yǐngxiǎng] influence; affect - 150a

2

高

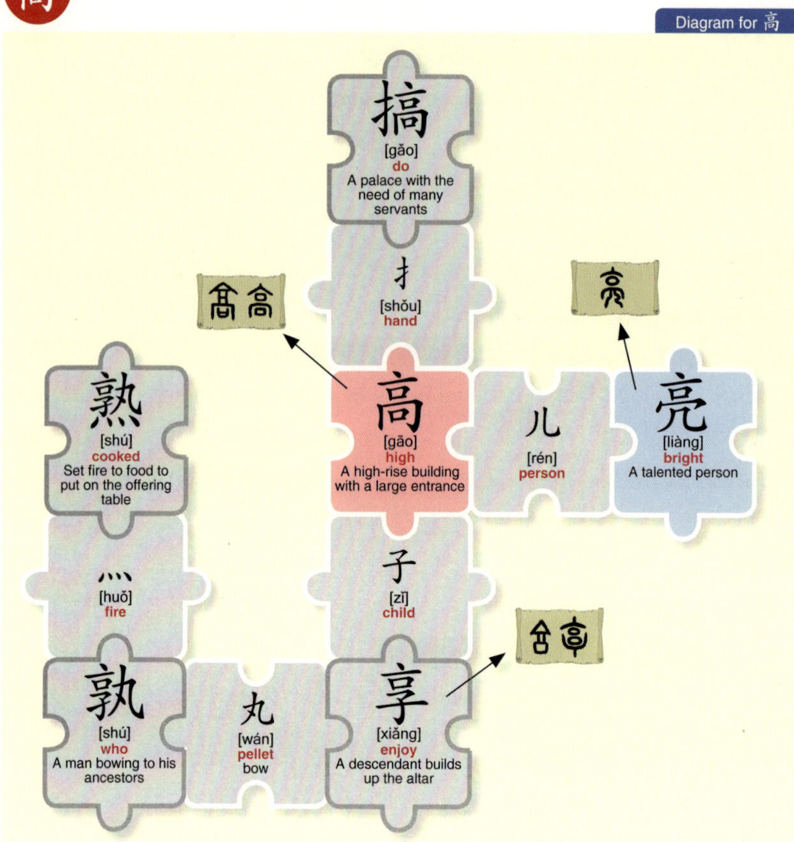

3

3

高
gāo

high

The shape of a large palace with a high and large entrance(口[16]) for people to enter and exit through. Means 'high.'

* As this character is about a building, "亠[1][tóu]" is the roof.

高兴[gāoxìng] glad; happy - 43d	提高[tígāo] raise, improve - 54c
高度[gāodù] altitude; high degree - 143b	高尚[gāoshàng] noble; lofty - 150b
高涨[gāozhǎng] upsurge - 102b	

3a 一 丨 扌 扌 扩 扩 扩 护 护 搞 搞 搞 搞

搞 gǎo

do

hand 扌=手[31][shǒu] + high 高 [gāo]

There is much to do in a tall(高) and large palace like the Forbidden City, which requires several hands(扌) on board to help.

搞鬼[gǎo/guǐ] play tricks - 155a　　搞好了吗? Is it done? - 3a 96c 168a 176a

3b 丶 亠 亠 亡 亩 产 高 亭 亮

亮 liàng

bright

high 高 [gāo] + person 儿[71][rén]

A person with talent or beauty(儿) that rises high(高) above all others shines brightly far and wide.

* The lower half of "高" was omitted to make the character look more presentable.

漂亮[piàoliang] pretty; beautiful - 126e　　月亮[yuèliang] moon - 221

3c 丶 亠 亠 亡 亩 亨 享 享

享 xiǎng

enjoy

high 高 [gāo] + child 子[95][zǐ]

To help ancestors to enjoy their life, the descendants(子) build up and decorate a high(高) altar for offerings.

* There are two kinds of offerings in the Chinese custom. One is to the gods and the other is to one's ancestors. "享" is an offering meant for ancestors.

享福[xiǎng/fú] enjoy a happy life - 126i

3d 丶 亠 亠 亡 亩 亨 享 享 孰 孰 孰

孰 shú

who

enjoy 享 [xiǎng] + bow/pellet 丸[230c][wán]

Who is the one bowing(丸) at the ancestral shrine, which is pleasing to the ancestors(享)?

* A man in the deep bowing posture is crouching on the floor, curled up like "丸," a ball.

3

3e 丶 亠 亠 亣 古 亨 享 享 孰 孰 孰 孰 熟 熟 熟

熟 shú

cooked; ripe

who 孰 [shú] + fire 灬=火[158][huǒ]

To impress dead ancestors, one(孰) has to make an offering or cook the ancesto's favorite meal over a fire(灬). Of course, all fruit offered has to be ripe.

* The Chinese really do offer the deceased's favorite foods, as well as the usual set offerings.

成熟[chéngshú] ripe; mature - 114a   熟练[shúliàn] skilled; practised; proficient - 132g

亥

Diagram for 亥

4

4

丶 亠 亡 亥 亥 亥

亥 hài

bone

This character takes the shape of an animal's skeleton. When coupled with other characters, it means 'bone, frame.'

* "亠[1] [tóu]" is the top of the head, because this character is about an animal.

4a

丶 亠 亡 亥 亥 亥 亥 刻

刻 kè

carve

bone 亥 [hài] + knife 刂=刀[119] [dāo]

Like the inscriptions on bones and tortoise carapaces, this character depicts an image of using a knife(刂) to carve words or pictures on a bone(亥). In the ancient days, the Chinese divided one day into 100'刻[kè],' so now '刻' also means 'moment, a quarter (of an hour).'

* Bone and tortoise carapace carvings: Ancient writing was found carved on dried tortoise carapaces and cattle shoulder bones, estimated to have been written in the 14th century B.C. They are said to be the origin of the current Chinese characters.

立刻[lìkè] immediately; at once - 79
深刻[shēnkè] deep; profound - 202c
时刻[shíkè] time; hour; moment - 42d

4

4b

丶 讠 讠 讠 讠 讠 该 该

该 gāi

should

word 讠=言[22] [yán] + bone 亥 [hài]

Literally meaning 'a bone(亥) within a word(讠),' it is a lesson or warning that should be heeded.

应该[yīnggāi] should; ought to; must - 143c

4c

了 了 子 孑 孑 孑 孩 孩 孩

孩 hái

child

child 子[95] [zǐ] + bone 亥 [hài]

The bones(亥) of a young child(子) can be felt under the skin, because young children are yet to gain much fat and muscle.

孩子[háizi] child - 95
小孩儿[xiǎoháir] child; kid - 235 71

4d

丨 ㄇ 口 口` 口亠 口亡 口亥 口亥 咳

咳 ké

cough

mouth 口[16][kǒu] + bone 亥 [hài]

Unlike talking or breathing, coughing(口) is so hard on the body that the whole frame(亥) shakes.

* In this character, "口" is the mouth through which the cough exits the body.

咳嗽[késou] cough; tussis - 211b

亡

Diagram for 亡

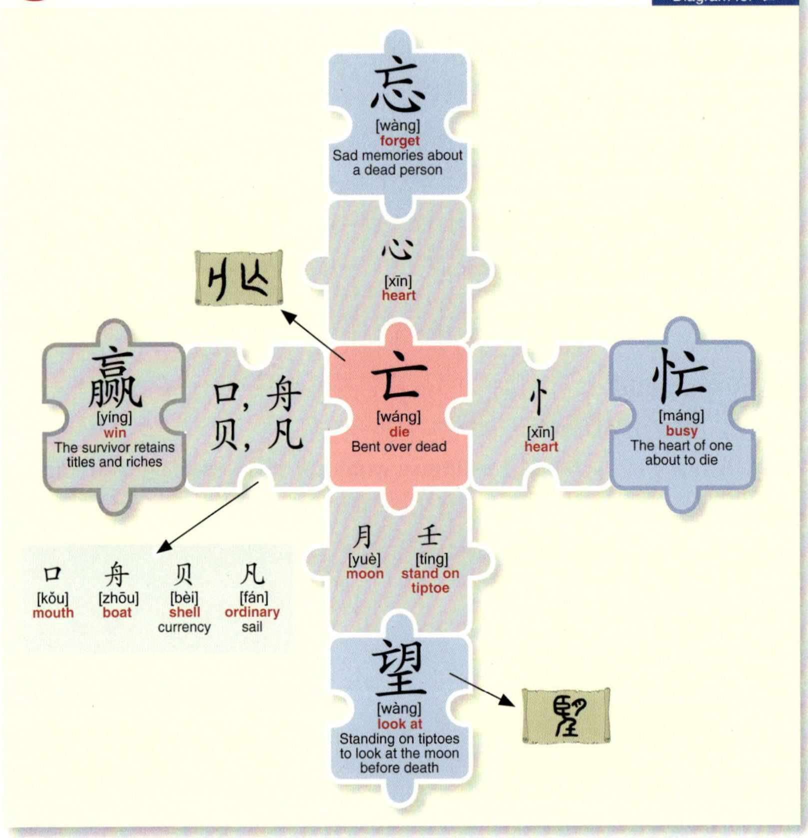

5

5 丶 亠 亡

亡 wáng die

A person(亠) who usually stands up straight(丨) is considered hunched over and dead(乚) due to old age or sickness.

* "亠[1][tóu]" signifies the top of the body, the head.

死亡[sǐwáng] die - 30a

5a 丶 亠 亡 亡 忘 忘 忘

忘 wàng forget

die 亡 [wáng] + heart 心[28][xīn]

Memories of a dead(亡) loved one breaks the heart(心), so it's best to forget.

忘记[wàngjì] forget - 82b

5b 丶 丶 忄 忄 忙 忙

忙 máng busy

heart 忄=心[28][xīn] + die 亡 [wáng]

A person about to die(亡) has a 'busy heart(忄)' because there is little time and so much to do.

* The "亡" in "忘[5a]" is at the top, which signals it's a memory that has to be forgotten. "忙" has "亡" in front of "忄" which means the mental state of someone about to die.

帮忙[bāng/máng] help - 209b   急忙[jímáng] hurriedly; hastily - 36f

5c 丶 亠 亡 亡 切 切 胡 胡 望 望 望

望 wàng look at

die 亡 [wáng] + moon 月[221][yuè] + stand on tiptoe 王→𡈼[105][tíng]

A man who is about to die(亡) away from home misses his family and his home and stands tiptoe(𡈼) to look at the same moon(月) they will be seeing in the night sky.

* The ancient character suggests that the character "king 王[108][wáng]" originally meant "stand on tiptoe(𡈼)."

希望[xīwàng] hope; wish - 131d   愿望[yuànwàng] desire; wish - 201e

5

5d

赢 yíng **win** = die 亡 [wáng] + mouth 口[16] [kǒu] + boat 月→舟[125] [zhōu] + currency/shell 贝[186] [bèi] + sail/ordinary 凡[213b] [fán]

A ship(舟) with a sail(凡) signifies going to war. A man who is victorious is one who did not die(亡), lives to tell the tale(口) and has gained riches(贝).

* "口" is used to speak and eat, so is often used to signify a live person.
* "Moon 月[221] [yuè]" used with other characters to form yet another, more complicated character, often takes the meaning of "meat 肉[192] [ròu]." But sometimes it can mean "boat 舟 [zhōu]."

这场比赛谁赢了? Who won the game? - 133a 152a 88a 206d 178b 5d 168a

页

Diagram for 页

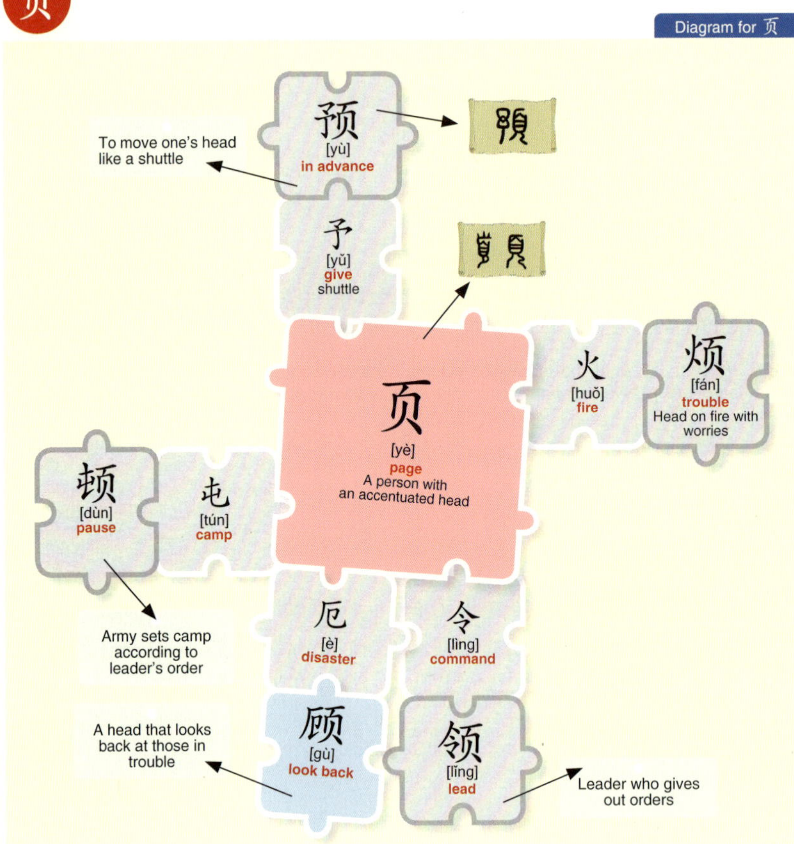

6

一 丆 丆 百 页 页

页 yè

page

A head(一) above a person's(人[63]→"person 儿[71][rén]") legs and face(冂) put together to mean 'head.' This character is also used to indicate pages of a book.

6a

マ マ 予 予 予 予 预 预 预 预

预 yù

in advance

shuttle/give 予[168b][yǔ] + head/page 页 [yè]

When weaving with a loom, the weft yarn that goes horizontally is woven through the vertical warp yarn with a flying shuttle(予). This character means a man's head(页) or thoughts are moving to and fro as fast as a shuttle to think of many options in advance so he can plan ahead.

* "予" is the shape of the flying shuttle used in weaving.

预习 [yùxí] prepare lessons before class - 182a

预备 [yùbèi] prepare - 56a

6

6b

丶 丷 火 火 火 火 灯 灯 烦 烦

烦 fán

trouble

fire 火[158][huǒ] + head/page 页 [yè]

Anyone with a head(页) on fire(火) would be in much trouble.

麻烦 [máfan] troublesome; inconvenient - 212a

6c

丿 人 人 今 令 令 令 邻 领 领 领

领 lǐng

lead

command 令[86][lìng] + head/page 页 [yè]

The head(页) of a team who leads and gives orders(令).

领导 [lǐngdǎo] lead; leader - 7b

本领 [běnlǐng] ability; capability; skill - 210a

6d 一 厂 𠂆 厄 厄 厄 厄 厄 顾 顾

顾 gù

look back

disaster 厄[85a] [è] + head/page 页 [yè]

The head(页), the leader has to look back and look after those who are in danger(厄).

* "厄" is the shape of a person(㔾[85]) crouching at the bottom of a cliff(厂[148]).

照顾[zhàogù] give consideration to; look after - 120c　顾客[gùkè] customer; client - 57b

6e 一 エ 口 屯 屯 屯 屯 顿 顿 顿

顿 dùn

pause; <quantifier>

camp 屯 [tún] + head/page 页 [yè]

The leader(页) orders his army to take a break, pause to eat while his men set the camp(屯). Each time an army sets camp, they cook and eat, so this character became a measure word, a quantifier of 'meals (number of), times (number of scoldings).'

* "屯" is the shape of a plant with roots deep in the ground, which is similar to the stakes driven into the ground to hold up the tents or tether the animals to.

一顿早饭。One setting of breakfast. - 223 6e 218e 148b
我被他批评了一顿。I got a scolding from him. - 113b 130a 84b 88b 122a 168a 223 6e

7

首

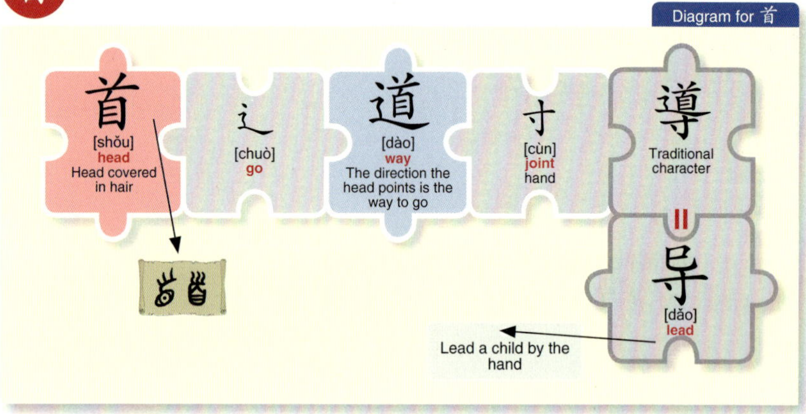

7 丶 丷 䒑 䒑 丷 𦣻 首 首 首

首
shǒu

head

A person's face(自) with hair(䒑) on top to mean a head.

* In this character, "self 自[26][zì]" is the nose, which is the boldest feature on one's face.

首都[shǒudū] capital; metropolitan - 101a　首先[shǒuxiān] first - 71d

7a 丶 丷 䒑 䒑 丷 𦣻 首 首 首 首 道 道

道
dào

way; moral; <quantifier>

head 首 [shǒu] + go 辶[61][chuò]

The direction the head(首), the leaders goes(辶) is the way his men must follow. This character also means morals, because it's the way one must go, the right way. It's also a quantifier for long items.

知道[zhīdào] know; realize - 111c　街道[jiēdào] street; road; way - 60c
道理[dàoli] principle; reason - 108b　道路[dàolù] road; way; path - 57a
走道[zǒudào] sidewalk; pavement - 53c　一道河。One stretch of river. - 223 7a 17d

7

7b ㇇ ㇇ 巳 巳 导 导

导
dǎo

lead

unborn child 巳[92][sì] + hand/joint 寸[40][cùn]

Leading a young child(巳) by the hand(寸) so the child will not fall down.

* The traditional character(導) depicts someone leading another by the hand(寸) along the right road(道[7a]).

辅导[fǔdǎo] give guidance in study or training; tutor - 124a
领导[lǐngdǎo] lead; leader - 6c　半导体[bàndǎotǐ] semiconductor - 175b 29b

8

8 彡 shàn hair

丿 彡 彡

The soft hair on a plant or a person. Hair on the head keeps one warm, hair elsewhere is more decorative than functional. Characters that include this character have something to do with decorations or the act of decorating.

8a

丿 彡 彡 彡 须 须 须 须 须

须 xū

must

hair 彡 [shàn] + head/page 页[6][yè]

All men were expected to grow hair on their faces(页) like mustaches(彡) or beards.

* "页" is also often used to mean 'face.'

必须[bìxū] must; have to; necessary - 28b

8b

彩 彩 彩 彩 彩 彩 彩 彩 彩 彩 彩

彩 cǎi

color

pick 采[33d][cǎi] + decorate/hair 彡 [shàn]

To take the leaves(采) of a tree or plant and create different colors to dye material or clothes for decoration(彡) purposes.

精彩[jīngcǎi] brilliant; splendid; wonderful - 135b 彩色[cǎisè] multicolored; color - 68f

8c

参 参 参 参 参 参 参 参

参 cān

take part in

accessory 厶 [symbol] + person/big 大[74][dà] + decorate/hair 彡 [shàn]

When taking part in a party, a noble lady(大) decorates(彡) her hair with an accessory(厶).

* The traditional character(參) takes the shape of decorations(厽) in the hair(dark and bushy 㐱 [zhěn]) to attend a party or a function.

参加[cānjiā] take part in; participate in - 159g 参观[cānguān] visit; look around - 13b

8d

产 产 产 产 产 产

产 chǎn

give birth to

stand 立[79][lì] + cliff 厂[148][ān]

A man standing(立) on top of a cliff(厂) signifies a hero who has survived many trials. A mother who gave birth always wishes that her child will become such a person.

* The traditional character(產) is a combination of "man of virtue and ability 彦[8e][yàn]" and "be born 生[208][shēng]."

生产[shēngchǎn] produce - 208

8

8e

丶 亠 亣 亣 立 产 产 彦 彦

彦 yàn

man of virtue and ability

give birth to 产 [chǎn] + hair 彡 [shàn]

A mother bears(产) a child hoping he will become a hero, and he does grow old enough to have a beard(彡) and learn along the way, which means he is a 'man of virtue and ability.'

8f

丶 亠 亣 亣 立 产 产 彦 彦 彦 彦 彦 颜 颜 颜

颜 yán

face

man of virtue and ability 彦 [yàn] + head/page 页[6] [yè]

Virtuous men who were respected(彦) grew long beards(彡). The part of one's head(页) with long strands of hair is one's face.

颜色[yánsè] color; countenance - 68f

8

而

Diagram for 而

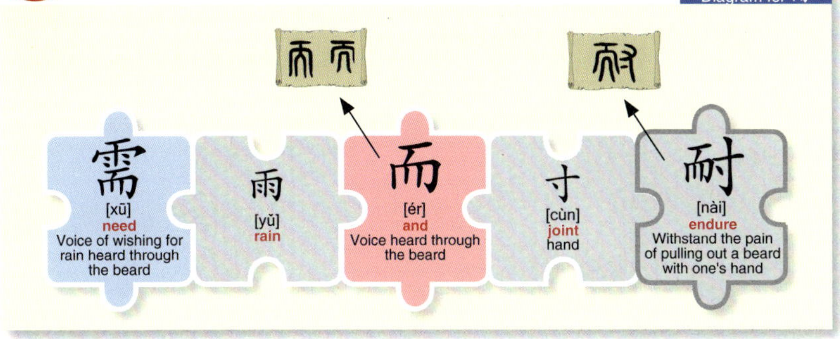

9

一 丆 丆 丙 丙 而

而 ér

and; as well as

This character originally meant the beard under the nose. When a man with a beard speaks, it sounds like the sound is coming from between the strands of facial hair, which is why now it's used to mean "and, as well as."

9

而且[érqiě] not only … but (also); and that - 224

9a

一 丆 丆 丙 丙 而 而一 耐 耐

耐 nài

endure

beard/and 而 [ér] + hand/joint 寸[40][cùn]

To endure the pain of having one's beard(而) pulled out by hand(寸) for being disobedient.

9b

一 ㇀ 𠂉 ...需

需 xū

need

rain 雨[205][yǔ] + beard/and 而 [ér]

In the ancient times of a drought, the only thing men could do was pray to the gods for rain. This character depicts the leader endlessly demanding for rain (雨) through his beard(而) out of need for water.

需要[xūyào] need - 170b

面

Diagram for 耳

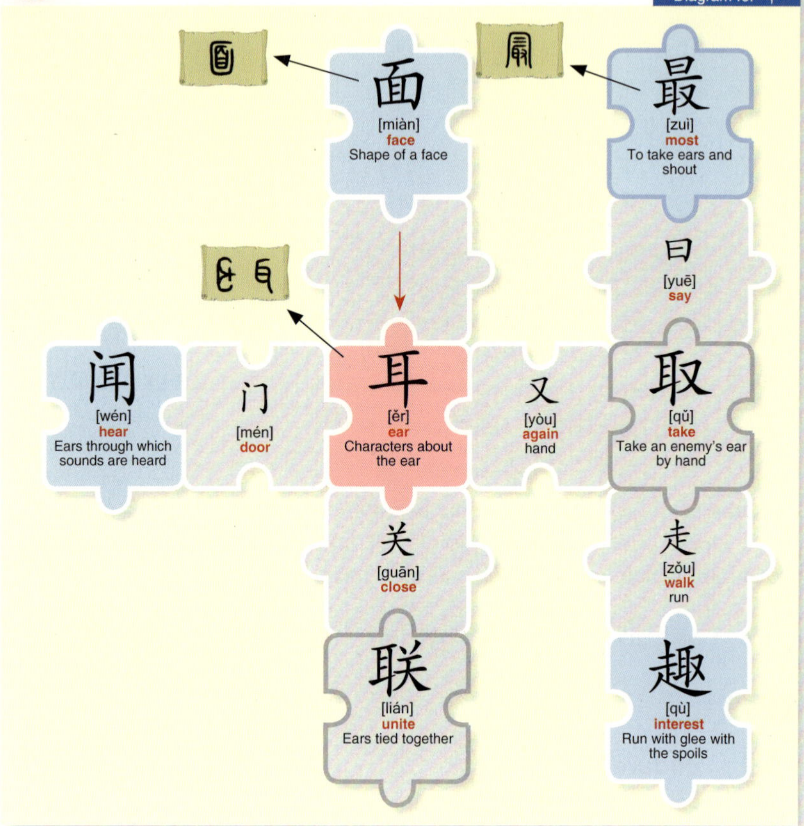

10

10

一 ア ア 丙 丙 而 而 面 面

面 miàn

face; flour

The shape of a face with an eye(目[11]) and a nose(自[26]). Regardless of the meaning, the pronunciation is identical to that of powdered grain, especially flour, and came to mean 'flour or noodles.'

后面[hòumiàn] back; rear; later - 18d
前面[qiánmian] front; ahead - 221a
见面[jiàn/miàn] meet; see - 13
面包[miànbāo] bread - 47
面条[miàntiáo] noodles - 56c
方面[fāngmiàn] aspect; side; field - 160
面条儿[miàntiáor] noodles - 56c 71

10a

一 丆 丌 丌 耳 耳

耳 ěr

ear

Shaped like a human's ear.

耳朵[ěrduo] ear - 210j

10b

一 丆 丌 丌 耳 耳 耵 取

取 qǔ

take

ear 耳 [ěr] + hand/again 又[34] [yòu]

Victorious soldiers took the ears(耳) of their fallen enemies and carried them in their hands(又).

* This depicts the old custom where the ears of the fallen enemies were taken(取) back as prizes.

取得[qǔdé] acquire - 40b	采取[cǎiqǔ] adopt; take - 33d
取消[qǔxiāo] cancel - 235d	争取[zhēngqǔ] strive for; fight for - 36a

10c

丨 口 日 日 旦 早 早 早 早 旱 昂 最

最 zuì

most

say 曰[48a] [yuē] + take 取 [qǔ]

Victorious soldiers who have taken(取) the ears of their fallen enemies are in the most greatest of moods and shouting(曰) and cheering.

* "Say 曰 [yuē]" is one speaking, with his tongue(一) coming out of his mouth(口[16]).
* "曰" is said to be a variation of "hood 冃[11e] [mào]," meaning the best prize of all is to take(取) the head(冃) of the opposing leader.

最近[zuìjìn] recently; lately - 118a	最初[zuìchū] first; prime; initial - 119c
最后[zuìhòu] last; final - 18d	最好[zuìhǎo] best - 96c

10d

一 十 土 キ 卡 赱 走 走 起 趄 趄 趄 趄 趣 趣

趣 qù

interest

run/walk 走[53c] [zǒu] + take 取 [qǔ]

The victorious soldiers have taken(取) the spoils and are running(走) home with a cheerful heart because their main interests are the spoils.

兴趣[xìngqù] interest - 43d

10

10e 一 丅 𠃌 ... 联

联 lián

unite

ear 耳 [ěr] + close 关[45] [guān]

The ears(耳) the soldiers brought back are tied(关) to be connected together.

* "关" is the shape of a lock tied up so it can't be undone.

联系 [liánxì] contact; connect - 132b
联邦 [liánbāng] federation; union - 209a
联合 [liánhé] unite; combine - 65a

10f 丶 冂 门 门 问 问 闻 闻 闻

闻 wén

hear; smell

door 门[145] [mén] + ear 耳 [ěr]

10

As people go through doors(门), sounds are heard through the ears(耳). 'Sound' and 'smell' are all external stimuli, and in Chinese, share the same pronunciation, which is why this character means both.

新闻 [xīnwén] news - 103b

目

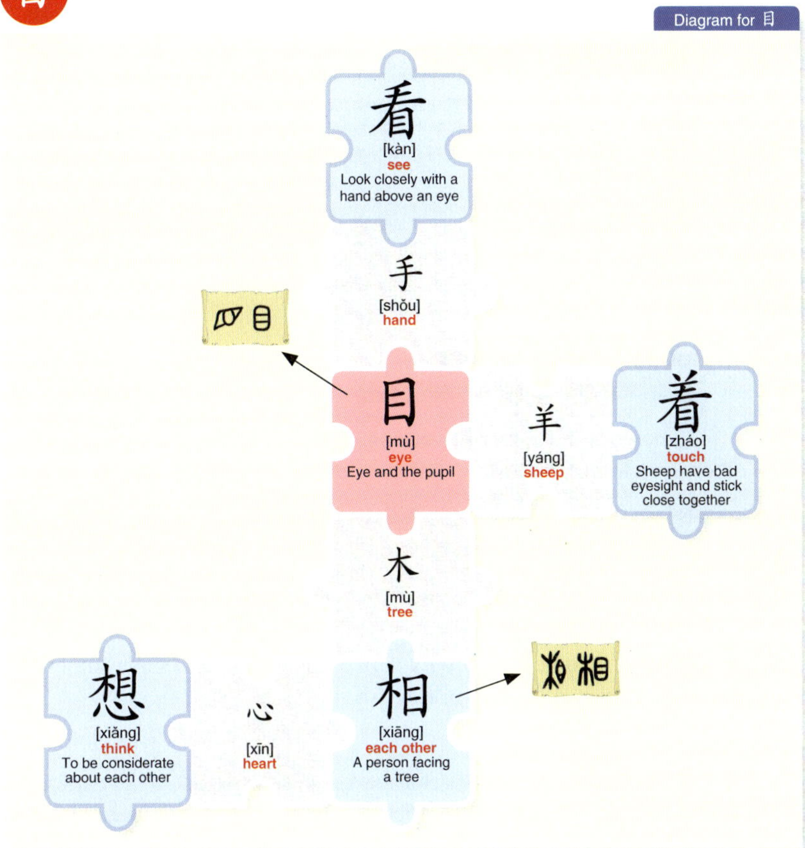

11

11

丨 冂 月 月 目

目 mù — **eye**

The shape of an eye with a pupil.

节目 [jiémù] program (TV, radio) - 85g	目前 [mùqián] at present; at the moment - 221a
目的 [mùdì] purpose; aim; goal - 46b	题目 [tímù] title; subject; topic - 54d

11a

看 kàn

see

hand 手[31] [shǒu] + eye 目 [mù]

To put a hand(手) above an eye(目) to look at something closely.

看见[kànjiàn] catch sight of; see - 13
看病[kàn/bìng] see a patient; treat - 81a
看电视。Watch TV. - 11a 157a 13c
好看[hǎokàn] good-looking - 96c
难看[nánkàn] ugly - 34h
看天气。Observe the weather. - 11a 74b 204

11b

着 zháo/zhe

touch / <postposition>

sheep 𦍌→羊[171] [yáng] + eye 目 [mù]

Sheep(羊), known to have terrible eyesight(目), stick close enough to touch each other so as to not get lost.

* Sheep are actually so nearsighted, they can't tell a cliff from a forest.

着急[zháo/jí] worry; feel anxious - 36f
上不着天，下不着地。Cannot reach the skies, or reach the ground.
- 223f 223a 11b 74b, 223g 223a 11b 84a

As a postposition, it comes(着) after a verb or an adjective to show something is in progress, similar to '…ing' in English.

接着[jiēzhe] catch; continue - 96i
他正穿着衣服。He is putting on his clothes. (Continuation of action) - 84b 54 25a 11b 130 34b
我到家时大门开着。When I got home, the door was opened. (Continuation of status)
- 113b 112b 174a 42d 74 145 43a 11b

11c

相 xiāng/xiàng

each other / appearance

tree 木[210] [mù] + ear 目 [mù]

A man is standing in front of a tree(木) and looking(目) at it to see if it is good to cut down for timber. The character shows a man and a tree facing each other.

* Trees provide us with food and wood, and we in turn plant and care for them. We have taken care of each other since the beginning of time.

相同[xiāngtóng] identical; same - 149b
互相[hùxiāng] mutual; each other - 146
相信[xiāngxìn] believe - 22a

A man standing in front of a tree(木) to look(目) at it, is checking the outward appearance.

照相机[zhàoxiàngjī] camera - 120c 213a   照相[zhào/xiàng] take a picture - 120c

11d 一 十 才 木 木 札 相 相 相 相 相 想 想 想

想 xiǎng

think

each other 相 [xiāng] + heart 心[28] [xīn]

People in love think of each other(相) and miss them in their hearts(心).

思想[sīxiǎng] thought; thinking; idea - 28a

目

Diagram for 目

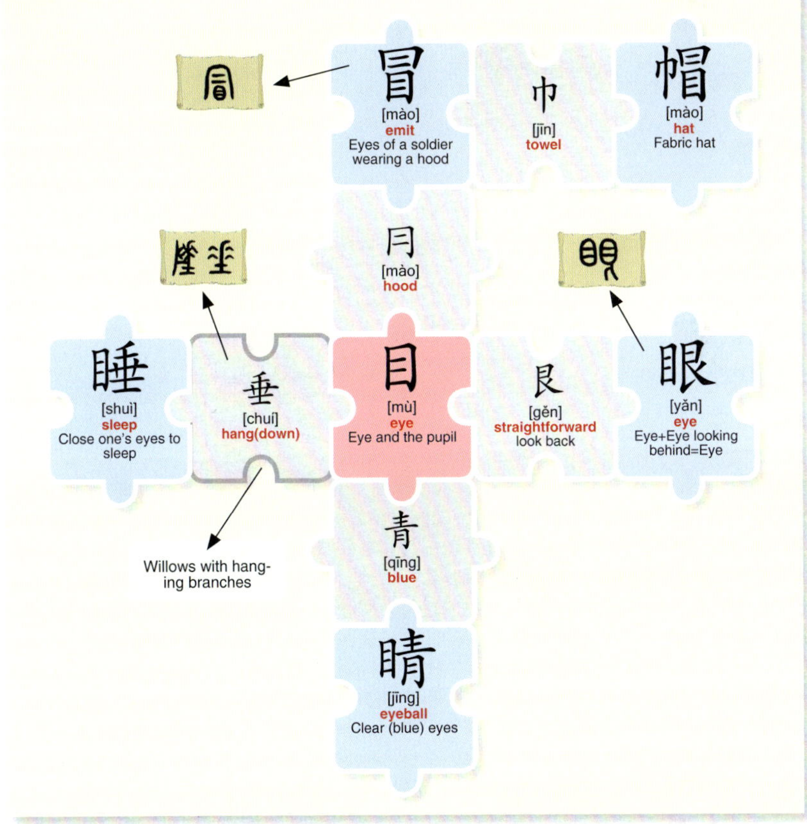

11

11e

冒 mào

emit; risk

hood 冃[28e][mào] + eye 目 [mù]

The eyes(目) of a soldier wearing a hood(冃) to go to war emits ferociousness. This character also means 'to risk the danger of going to war.'

* "冃" is the hood worn on one's head.

感冒[gǎnmào] catch cold; influenza - 114d

11f

帽 mào

hat

towel 巾[131][jīn] + emit 冒 [mào]

When a hood worn above one's eyes(冒) came to mean "emit or risk," the Chinese added "巾" meaning 'fabric' to make a character meaning 'hat.'

帽子[màozi] cap; hat - 95

11g

眼 yǎn

eye

eye 目 [mù] + look back/straightforward 艮[14][gěn]

"目" meaning 'eye' and "艮" meaning 'backwards' were put together to mean 'eye' but with a different pronunciation.

眼睛[yǎnjing] eye - 11h 眼镜[yǎnjìng] eyeglasses - 21e
眼前[yǎnqián] at present; at the moment - 221a

11h

睛 jīng

eyeball

eye 目 [mù] + blue 青[135][qīng]

When water is clear and deep it looks green(青), and when one's eyes(目) are that clear, one can see the pupils.

* When the sun's rays hit water, lights in the red spectrum are absorbed and the blues are reflected back. That is why clear, deep waters shine blue.

眼睛[yǎnjing] eye - 11g

11i 一 二 千 千 千 乖 垂 垂

垂 chuí hang (down)

A tree(木[210]) with branches and leaves hanging far enough to reach the ground (土[152]).

垂直[chuízhí] perpendicular; vertical - 12

11j 丨 冂 冃 月 目 目' 目' 盰 盰 睡 睡 睡 睡

睡 shuì sleep

eye 目 [mù] + hang(down) 垂 [chuí]

When the eyelids of someone's eyes(目) are hanging down(垂), it means he is asleep. This character shows someone asleep with his eyes(目) closed(垂)

睡觉[shuì/jiào] sleep; go to bed - 13a

12

直

Diagram for 直

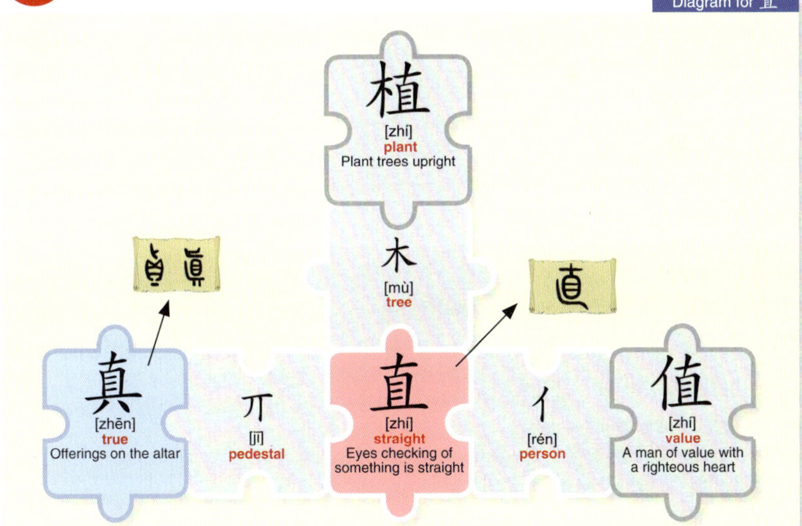

12

一 十 十 方 冇 直 直 直

直 zhí

straight

A carpenter or artisan takes a piece of wood(一) and uses his eyes(目[11][mù]) to see if it is horizontally and vertically(十) straight.

一直[yīzhí] straight; continuously - 223
垂直[chuízhí] perpendicular; vertical - 11i
直接[zhíjiē] direct; immediate - 96i

12a

一 十 才 木 木 朴 朾 栯 植 植 植 植

植 zhí

plant

tree 木[210][mù] + straight 直 [zhí]

Planting trees(木) upright(直) so they grow well.

种植[zhòngzhí] plant; grow - 232c

12b

12

丿 亻 亻 仁 仕 佶 佶 佶 值 值

值 zhí

value

person 亻[70][rén] + straight 直 [zhí]

Being rich or learned doesn't necessarily mean that you are a valued friend. A truly valuable person(亻) is one with a straight, honest(直) heart.

值得[zhíde] be worth - 40b

12c

一 十 十 方 冇 直 直 直 真 真

真 zhēn

true

straight 直 [zhí] + pedestal 丌[44][jī]

Flawless(直) offerings are placed on an altar(丌) to the gods, and with their blessings, the humans hope to learn the truth.

* The "丌" shape is the pedestal.

* The ancient character depicts the gods using cutlery(匕[88]) to eat the food offered up in bronze pot or cooker with legs(鼎-败; refer to 186g) and then sharing their wisdom and truth with the humans in return.

认真[rènzhēn] earnest; serious - 63a
真正[zhēnzhèng] genuine; true; real - 54

见

Diagram for 见

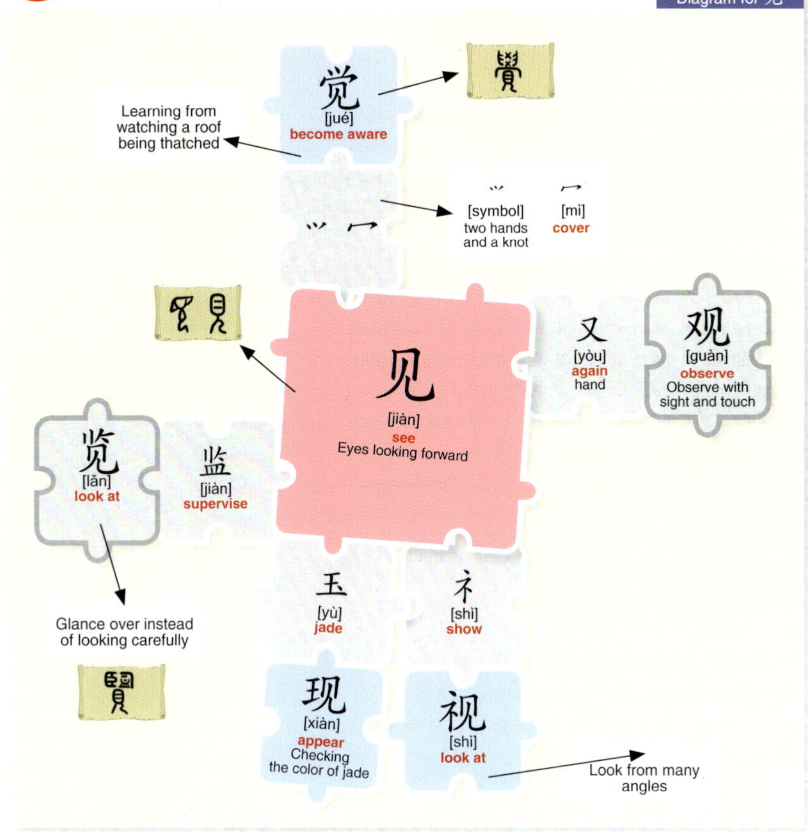

13

13

丨 冂 贝 见

见 jiàn **see**

A man(儿[71]) with open eyes(冂→目[11]) and looking straight means he is staring forward.

* The traditional character(見) is a combination of an eye(目) and a person(儿).

看见[kànjiàn] catch sight of; see - 11a
见面[jiàn/miàn] meet; see - 10
意见[yìjiàn] opinion; idea; view - 21b
再见[zàijiàn] good-bye; see you again - 149a
听见[tīngjiàn] hear - 16d

丶 丷 丷 ⺍ 𭕄 ⺌ 常 觉 觉

13a

觉 jué/jiào

become aware; feel / sleep

two hands and a knot ⺍ [symbol] + cover 冖[169] [mì] + see 见 [jiàn]

A young boy watches(见) the adults tie straw together(⺍) to cover a roof (冖), and 'becomes aware of (realizes or learns) the wisdom of daily life from the adults.'

* The traditional character(覺) looks more complicated. The simplified character "觉" has three dots (⺍) at the top, which signify a pair of hands(臼[95a]) and a knot(㐅). One can learn much from watching(見) a pair of hands(臼) used to tie(㐅) bundles of straw to thatch a roof(冖).

觉得[juéde] feel; sense - 40b

The imagery of a child watching(见) and learning from adults tie(⺍) bundles of straw to cover a roof(冖) was also considered waking up from one's sleep to see the world.

睡觉[shuì/jiào] sleep; go to bed - 11j

13b

フ 又 对 双 观 观

观 guàn

observe

hand/again 又[34] [yòu] + see 见 [jiàn]

Using hands(又) to touch, and eyes to see(见) an object. It means to observe closely.

参观[cānguān] visit; look around - 8c
观察[guānchá] observe - 126b
观众[guānzhòng] audience; spectator; viewer - 63h
乐观[lèguān] optimistic; sanguine - 212c

13

13c

丶 ラ 才 礻 礻 初 初 视

视 shì

look at

show 礻=示[126] [shì] + see 见 [jiàn]

Not only to see(见) with one's eyes but to learn from the gods' point of view (礻). When looking at something, one must be able to see all sides of it.

* "礻" is an altar to depict the gods showing something in return for an offering.

电视[diànshì] television; TV - 157a
监视[jiānshì] keep watch on; surveillance - 107a
重视[zhòngshì] attach importance to - 151a

13d 一 二 千 王 玑 玑 玑 现

现 xiàn

appear; present

jade 王→玉[198][yù] + see 见 [jiàn]

When holding the jade(玉) object under the sun to see(见) the purity and check the value, the sun's reflection causes many colors to appear on the jade. Because the brightness of the sun changes the reflection on the jade(玉) when it's held up against the sun to be checked(见), it also became to mean 'the present.'

* When it becomes part of a more complicated character, "玉" often loses the dot(丶) to look like "king 王[108][wáng]."

现在[xiànzài] now; at present - 32a	出现[chūxiàn] appear; emerge; turn up - 167a
发现[fāxiàn] find; discover - 34f	表现[biǎoxiàn] show; express - 130b
实现[shíxiàn] realize; achieve - 75a	现代[xiàndài] modern times - 110c

13e 丨 丨丨 丨丿 丨𠂉 丨𠂉 丨𠂉 览 览 览

览 lǎn

look at

supervise 监[107a][jiàn] + see 见 [jiàn]

Back when there were no mirrors, people(𠂉 →人[63]) poured water(丶) into a bowl (皿[125b]) to look at(刂→臣[106]) reflections of their faces and that character became "监." Add to this the "见" character, which means 'to look straight at,' and it means 'look.'

* "Subject 臣 [chén]" is the image of someone looking with eyes wide open.
* "Vessel 皿 [mǐn]" is a plate or bowl in which food is served.
* The traditional character(覽) is a combination of "supervise 監 [jiàn]" and "see 見 [jiàn]."

展览[zhǎnlǎn] exhibit; show; display - 90a	游览[yóulǎn] go sightseeing - 161b

13

艮

Diagram for 艮

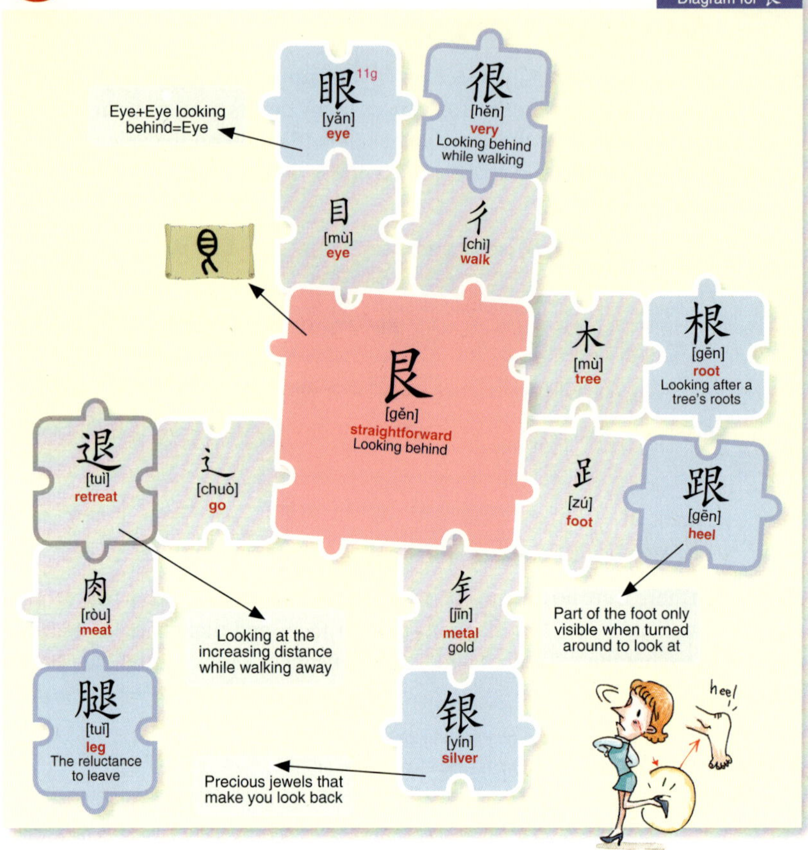

14

14

艮 gěn

straightforward; tough

The opposite of "look 见[13][jiàn]," which means 'to look straight at.' "艮" is the shape of someone turning to look behind and means 'look back.' To turn one's head to look behind after bring asked for a favor is a gesture of refusal, so this character came to mean 'straightforward or tough personality.'

14a ノ ノ 彳 彳 彳 彳 很 很 很

很 hěn

very

walk 彳[60] [chì] + look back/straightforward 艮 [gěn]

Turning to look back(艮) while walking forward(彳) means one is very reluctant to leave something behind.

得很[dehěn] very (much, good etc.) - 40b
很好 very good - 14a 96c

14b 一 十 才 木 村 村 村 相 相 根

根 gēn

root

tree 木[210] [mù] + look back/straightforward 艮 [gěn]

A tree(木) needs to be looked after(艮) until its root firmly attaches into the soil. This character is also a quantifier used to count the number of long things like roots.

根据[gēnjù] based on; according to - 90h
根本[gēnběn] root; fundamental - 210a
一根草。a stalk of grass - 223 14b 207a

14c 丶 口 口 早 早 足 足 跙 跙 跙 跟 跟 跟

跟 gēn

heel; follow; and

foot ⻊=足[52] [zú] + look back/straightforward 艮 [gěn]

The heel is the part of the foot(足) that one can see only by turning one's head to look behind(艮). To be able to see one's heel all the time means you are following him. It also came to mean 'and.'

跟前[gēnqián] near; in front of - 221a
英国跟中国的文化。Britain and China's culture. - 77a 20a 14c 232a 20a 46b 133 70a

14d ノ ⺈ 𠂉 乍 钅 钌 钌 钌 钽 钽 银

银 yín

silver

gold/metal 钅=金[199] [jīn] + look back/straightforward 艮 [gěn]

Silver used to be prized more than gold because it was harder to find in the natural state and was very hard to purify. To find a metal(钅) as precious as silver means one has to keep looking everywhere, including behind(艮) himself.

银行[yínháng] bank - 60b

14

14e

退 tuì

retreat

look back/straightforward 艮 [gěn] + go 辶[61][chuò]

"辶" is a character combined with "road(彳[60])" and "foot(止[53])." Therefore, the meaning of 'to look back(艮) to the road while walking(辶)' focuses on the increasing distance and came to mean 'step back or retreat.'

14f

腿 tuǐ

leg

meat 月[221]→肉[192][ròu] + retreat 退 [tuì]

A hesitating person reluctant to leave(退) has a hard time bidding farewell. One's legs carry the most burden as it is the body part(肉) that has to walk away.

* When "moon 月 [yuè]" becomes part of a character, it takes the meaning of "meat 肉."

鸡大腿 chicken drumstick - 177a 74 14f

15

良

Diagram for 良

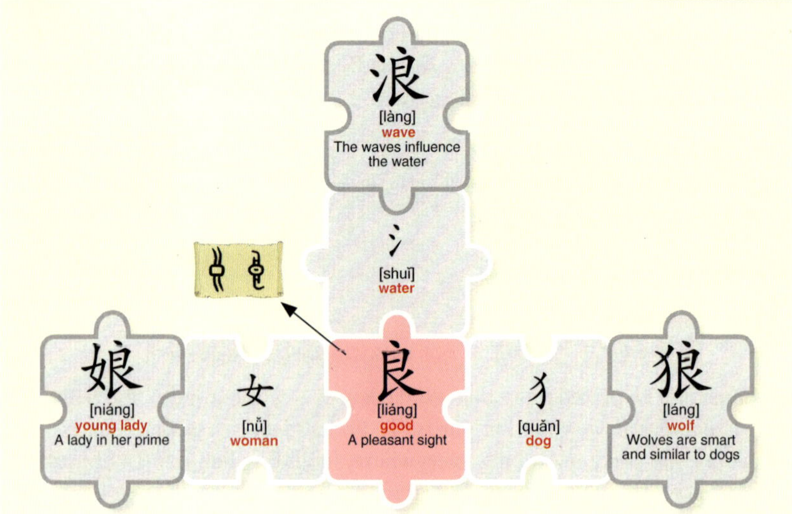

15

丶 ㇇ ㇇ ㇇ 户 艮 良

良 liáng good

The long corridor of a palace or a well-maintained castle wall is always good to see.

* Has no correlation with "straightforward 艮 [gěn]."

良好[liánghǎo] good; fine - 96c

15a

丶 丶 氵 氵 氵 氵 氵 浪 浪 浪

浪 làng wave

water 氵[202] [shuǐ] + good 良 [liáng]

Waves or ripples have a good(良) effect on water(氵). A popular Korean proverb goes "stagnant water will rot." Waves or ripples are nature's way of showing that water is alive and moving. Plankton is said to rely on the currents and waves to move around.

风浪[fēnglàng] wind and waves; storm - 213c

15

15b

丿 犭 犭 犭 犭 犭 犭 狼 狼 狼

狼 láng wolf

dog 犭[173] [quǎn] + good 良 [liáng]

Wolves(犭) are smart and possess a keen(良) sense of what to do. Native Americans used to revere wolves for their loyalty and cunningness.

* "犭" means the animal looks like or is similar in size to a dog.

15c

㇛ 女 女 女 女 女 女 娘 娘 娘

娘 niáng young lady

woman 女[96] [nǚ] + good 良 [liáng]

The best(良) time in a woman's(女) life is when she is a young lady. All women want to look young, so this character is used as an honorific when addressing an older lady like one's mother or aunt.

姑娘[gūniang] young woman; young lady - 19c

我娘刚回来了。My mother just came home. - 113b 15c 165b 20d 212d 168a

口

16

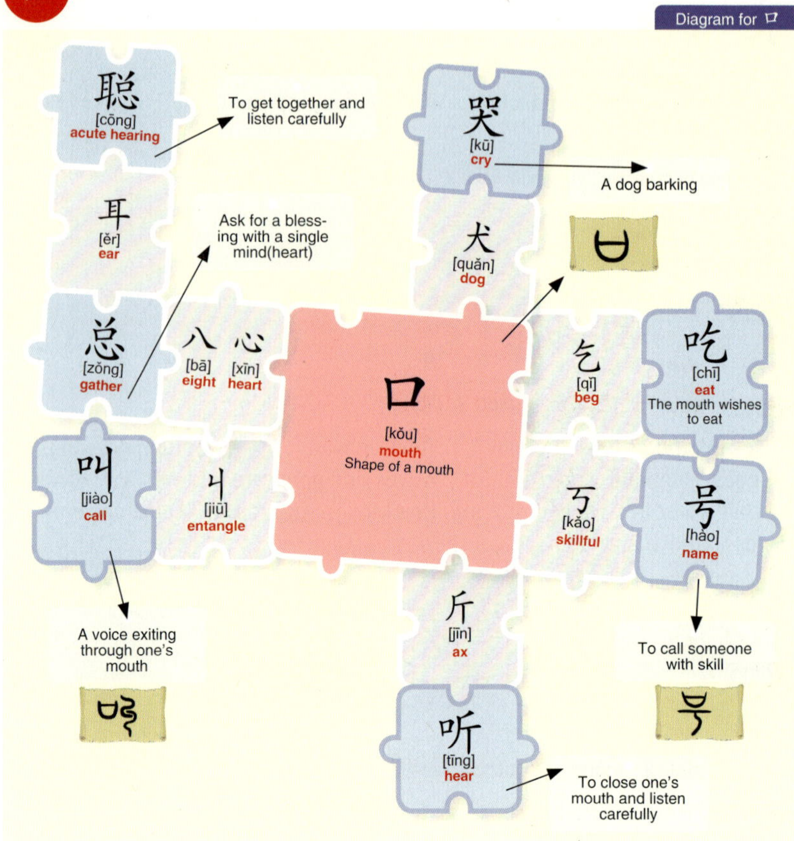

16 丨 冂 口

口 kǒu **mouth**

The shape of a mouth. When used as part of another character, it describes an action done with a mouth, like 'eat, speak, cry.' But there are characters out there that look like "口" but have nothing to do with it.

* Chinese characters have changed over the centuries. Therefore, there exist numerous characters which look similar but originate from different sources of characters. Just because the two characters look same, it doesn't necessarily mean that they have the same meaning.

口语 [kǒuyǔ] spoken language - 226c　　门口 [ménkǒu] entrance; doorway - 145

16a

丶 口 口 吅 吅 吅 哭 哭 哭 哭

哭 kū

cry

shout 吅 [xuān] + dog 犬[172] [quǎn]

A dog(犬) barks(吅) when it senses something is wrong.

* "吅" is she shape of two mouths(口) and means 'to strongly assert one's opinion.'

你为什么哭呢? Why are you crying? - 69a 159c 231a 93a 16a 90c

16b

丶 口 口 口' 口𠂉 吃

吃 chī

eat

mouth 口 [kǒu] + beg 乞[83a] [qǐ]

Directly translated, it means the mouth(口) is asking for(乞) something to eat.

* "乞" is the shape of a person(𠂉 →人[63]) crouching or bowing(乙[83]) to ask or beg.

好吃[hǎochī] tasty; delicious - 96c

16c

丶 口 口 旦 号

号 hào

name; number

mouth 口 [kǒu] + skillful 丂 [kǎo]

It takes much skill(丂) to remember one's name so you can call out(口) to him from within a crowd. But, when there are too many people to call everyone's name, it's easier to use numbers, which is why this character is now also a quantifier.

* "丂" depicts an artisan making something with skill or wit.

一百多号人。Over a hundred people. - 223 134a 222d 16c 63

16d

丶 口 口 口' 叮 叮 听

听 tīng

hear

mouth 口 [kǒu] + ax 斤[118] [jīn]

Taking an ax(斤) to someone's mouth(口) is a harsh way of saying one must listen carefully.

听见[tīngjiàn] hear - 13

听说[tīng/shuō] be told; hear of - 72d

听写[tīngxiě] dictate; dictation - 169a

16

16e

丨 ㄇ 口 口ㄴ 叫

叫 jiào

call; cry

mouth 口 [kǒu] + entangle 丩[50e] [jiū]

To call someone, you use your mouth(口) to make a sound(丩). Air from the lungs travel through the vocal cords(丩) and come out through the mouth(口). It can also mean 'bark,' the sound an animal makes.

* "丩" is the shape of a vine curling itself around and up a tree trunk.

叫做[jiàozuò] be called - 19b

16f

丶 丷 丷 并 台 台 总 总 总

总 zǒng

gather

eight 丷→八[229] [bā] + mouth 口 [kǒu] + heart 心[28] [xīn]

This character depicts a scene where many people are gathered together unified with one heart(心) to ask for(口) the gods' blessings(八). Because people usually want to be blessed all the time, this character came to mean 'always, anyway, at least.'

16

* "八" is the shape of 'blessings coming down from the sky.'

总是[zǒngshi] always - 54b
总结[zǒngjié] summary - 104b
总理[zǒnglǐ] premier; prime minister - 108b

16g

一 丅 丌 丌 ㄏ 耳 耳 耳' 耳' 耳' 耳' 耳' 聪 聪 聪

聪 cōng

acute hearing

ear 耳[10a] [ěr] + gather 总 [zǒng]

To receive divine blessings from the God, we must follow what is taught by Him. For receiving God's blessings, we have to get together(总) and give an acute hearing(耳) to what God teaches us.

聪明[cōngmíng] intelligent; bright; clever - 218h

可

Diagram for 可

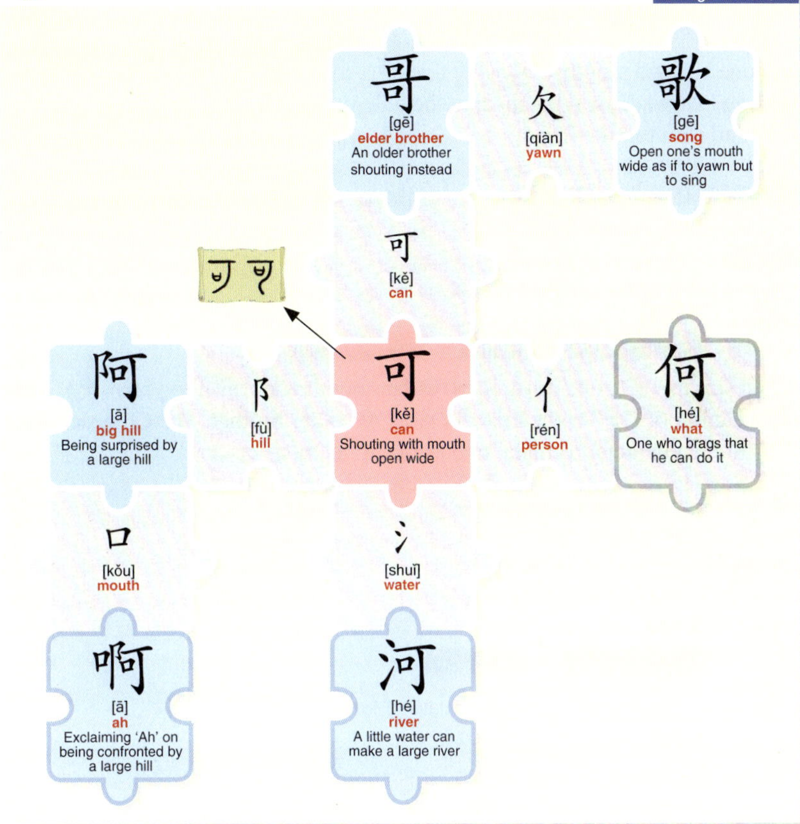

17

17

可 kě

can

mouth open wide 丁 [symbol] + mouth 口[16] [kǒu]

Shouting with one's mouth(口) wide open(丁) means one is not shy and can do something or ask for the approval of something. It also means 'but, yet' because despite shouting about it, one has to try to see if it is possible.

可能[kěnéng] possible; can; may - 89b
可爱[kě'ài] lovable; lovely - 34e
可怕[kěpà] fearful; dreadful; horrible - 134c
可以[kěyǐ] can; may - 63j
可是[kěshì] but; yet - 54b

17a

哥 gē

elder brother

can 可 [kě] + can 可 [kě]

Not one but two mouths(口) wide open(丁) to shout(可＋可) originally meant 'to sing.' Nowadays, it means that the elder brother is the one who gets to pull rank and shout in the house.

哥哥[gēge] possible; can; may

17b

歌 gē

song

song/elder brother 哥 [gē] + yawn 欠[23][qiàn]

When singing(哥), one must open his/her mouth wide, as if to yawn(欠). After the meaning of "哥" went from 'to sing' to 'older brother,' the Chinese added "欠" to the character to make one to mean 'to sing.'

唱歌[chànggē] sing a song - 218d

17c

何 hé

what

person 亻[70][rén] + can 可 [kě]

A person(亻) boastfully saying he can(可) do whatever it takes.

任何[rènhé] any; whatever - 105a 如何[rúhé] how - 96g

17d

河 hé

river

water 氵[202][shuǐ] + can 可 [kě]

A little water(氵) gathers to make a stream, and a few streams can(可) make a river.

一条河。One river - 223 56c 17d

17e

阿 ā

big hill

hill 阝[147][fù] + can 可 [kě]

A man who bragged that he could(可) do something is confronted with an obstacle such as a hill(阝) and is taken aback. A big hill is enough to shock anyone who wasn't expecting an obstacle to be in his way.

阿姨[āyí] auntie - 109e

17f

丨 口 口 口一 口阝 口阝一 口阝一 口阝一 口阝口 啊

啊 ā/a

ah; oh / <modal particle>

mouth 口[16] [kǒu] + big hill 阿 [ā]

When "阿" came to mean 'a large hill,' the Chinese needed another character to use as when protesting or showing shock or awe. So they added a mouth (口).

啊，又下了大雪。Ah, it's snowing again. - 17f 34 223g 168a 74 205a

This character is sometimes used at the end of a sentence to indicate surprise or question.

你看，外面天气多好啊。Look, the weather's great out. - 69a 11a 222a 10 74b 204 222d 96c 17f
你去不去啊？Are you going out, huh? - 69a 94 223a 94 17f

18

奇

Diagram for 奇

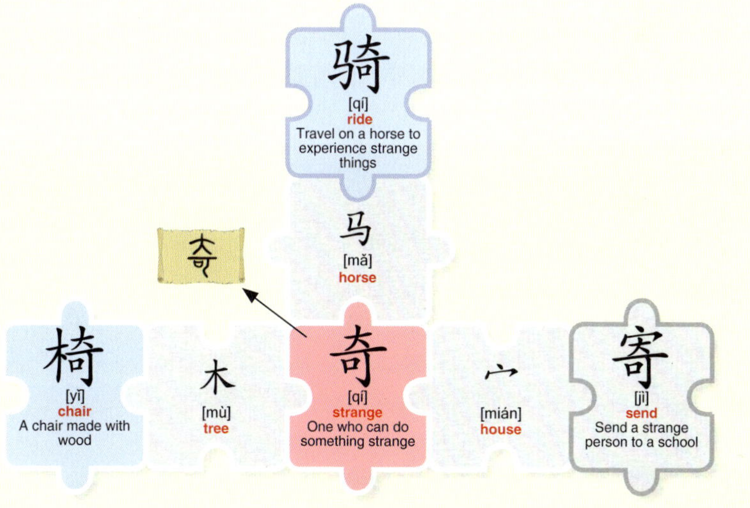

18

一 ナ 大 太 夲 夻 奆 奇

奇 qí

strange

person/big 大[74][dà] + can 可[17][kě]

A person(大) who can(可) carryout strange activities, but which others cannot.

奇怪[qíguài] strange; odd - 152f　　好奇[hàoqí] curious - 96c

18a

㇆ 马 马 马一 马ナ 马大 马太 马夲 马夻 马奆 骑

骑 qí

ride (an animal or bike)

horse 马[176][mǎ] + strange 奇 [qí]

Depicts a man who rides a horse(马) to travel and see strange(奇) things he cannot see in his hometown.

妈妈骑马。Mother rides a horse. - 176b 176b 18a 176

我每天骑自行车上班。I ride a bicycle to work every day. - 113b 97a 74b 18a 26 60b 124 223f 119f

18

18b

丶 丶 宀 宀 宀 宊 宎 宎 寄 寄 寄

寄 jì

send

house 宀[141][mián] + strange 奇 [qí]

Persons who can do strange(奇) things that others cannot are sent to a school (宀) to develop their skills.

寄信 send a letter - 18b 22a

18c

一 十 才 木 木一 木ナ 木大 木太 木夲 木夻 木奆 椅

椅 yǐ

chair

tree 木[210][mù] + strange 奇 [qí]

Strangely(奇), unlike other animals, humans stand on two feet and walk, where wooden(木) chairs became a very useful tool which changed their lives forever.

椅子[yǐzi] chair - 95

司

Diagram for 司

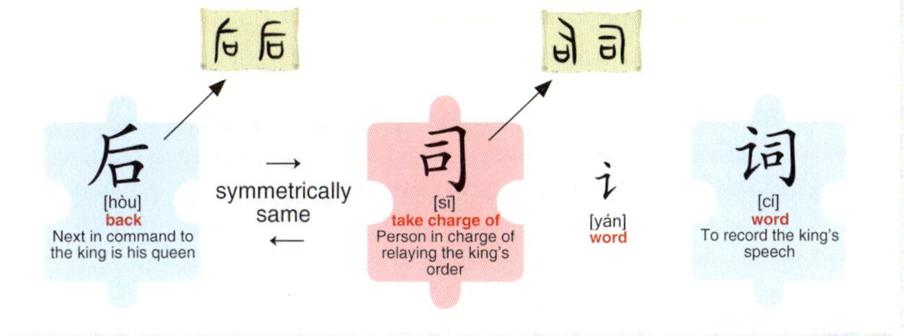

18d

后 hòu

back; later

person 𠂆→人[63] [rén] + mouth 口[16] [kǒu]

This character used to denote 'king' and was a combination of one who gives orders(𠂆→人) and a mouth(口) with which the order was imparted. Nowadays, it means "queen 王后 [wánghòu]," the king's wife. As she is second in command, this character came to mean 'after, later.'

- 后面[hòumiàn] back; rear; later - 10
- 以后[yǐhòu] after; later - 63j
- 最后[zuìhòu] last; final - 10c
- 然后[ránhòu] then; after that; afterwards - 158e
- 后边[hòubiān] back; rear; behind - 61a

18e

司 sī

take charge of

person ㇆→人[63] [rén] + mouth 口[16] [kǒu]

This character is the mirror image version of "back 后 [hòu]" and depicts a mouth giving the order(口) and a servant(㇆→人) who will relay it.

- 公司[gōngsī] corporation; company - 93b
- 司机[sījī] driver ; chauffeur - 213a

18f

丶 讠 订 订 订 词 词

词 cí

word

word 讠=言[22] [yán] + take charge of 司 [sī]

When the king gives an order or a speech(讠), the servant on duty(司) records it, and so this character came to mean 'word.'

词语[cíyǔ] words; expressions; terms - 226c　　词典[cídiǎn] dictionary; lexicon - 217a
生词[shēngcí] new word - 208

19

古

Diagram for 古

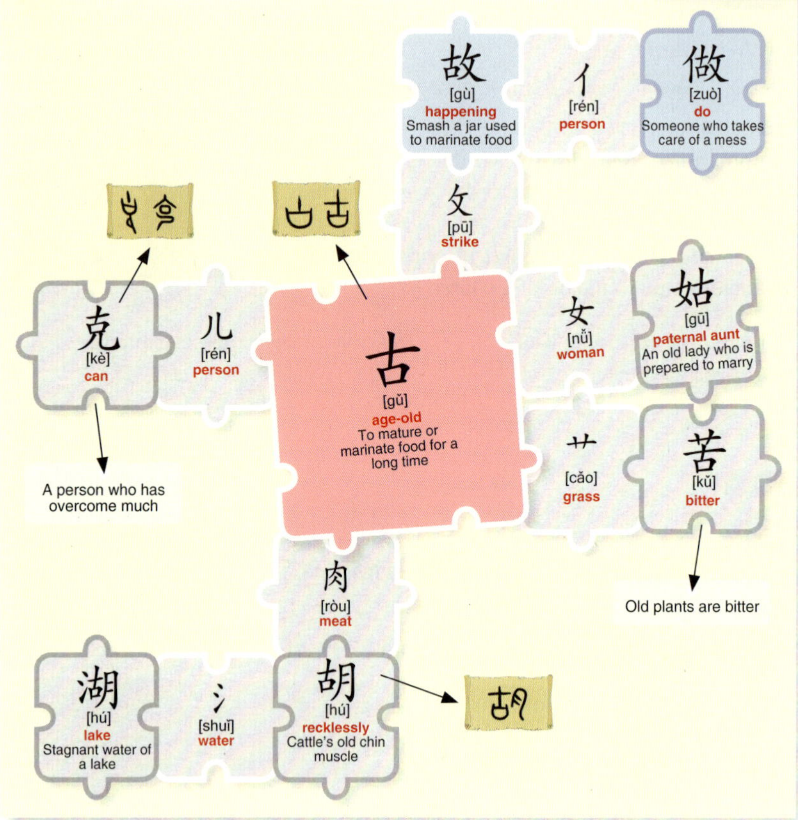

19 一 十 十 古 古

古 gǔ **age-old**

To put food in a jar(口) and tighten the lid with a heavy stone(十) on top of it, to marinate or ripen the food for a long time.

* In this character, "口" has nothing to do with 'mouth.' Here, it's the shape of a container.

古代[gǔdài] ancient times - 110c

19a 一 十 十 古 古 古 古 故 故

故 gù **happening**

age-old 古 [gǔ] + strike 攵[50] [pū]

In the olden days, when there were no refrigerators, if someone smashed(攵) a pot that was used to store food for a long period of time(古), it was considered as a terrible happening because there were only few ways to preserve food.

故事[gùshi] story; tale - 36d　　故意[gùyì] intentionally; willfully - 21b

19b 丿 亻 亻 亻 仕 估 估 估 估 做 做

做 zuò **do**

person 亻[70] [rén] + happening 故[gù]

A person(亻) who does cleansing or taking care of an incident(故).

叫做[jiàozuò] be called - 16e

19c 𡿨 女 女 女 女 女 姑 姑

姑 gū **paternal aunt**

woman 女[96] [nǚ] + age-old 古 [gǔ]

An old(古) woman(女) in this instance means a woman of marriageable age, a woman who is physically ready to be married. This character usually means aunt, father's sister, or sister-in-law or mother-in-law.

姑娘[gūniang] young woman; young lady - 15c

19

19d 一 ⺊ 艹 艹 芏 苲 苦 苦

苦 kǔ

bitter

grass 艹[207] [cǎo] + age-old 古 [gǔ]

Old(古) plants(艹) usually mean medicinal herbs, which are naturally bitter. "Good medicines are bitter to the taste but good for your body" is a well-known saying.

* In traditional Chinese medicine, herbs(艹) were dried so they could be kept for longer(古).

辛苦[xīnkǔ] hard; toilsome - 103 痛苦[tòngkǔ] pain - 81c

19e 一 十 十 古 古 古 胡 胡 胡

胡 hú

recklessly

age-old 古 [gǔ] + meat 月[221] → 肉[192] [ròu]

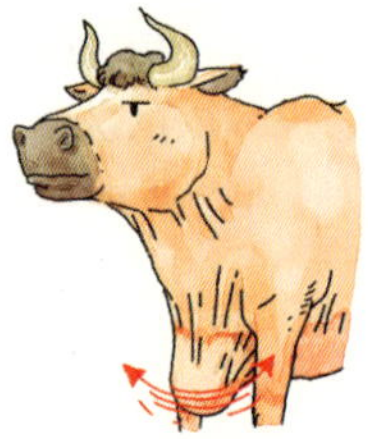

Literally translated, it means 'old(古) meat(肉).' The flabby neck muscle of an old ox hangs loose and shakes uncontrollably.

* "Moon 月 [yuè]" combined with other characters means 'meat(肉).'

胡乱[húluàn] carelessly - 24e

19

19f 丶 丶 氵 氵 汁 汁 沽 沽 沽 湖 湖 湖

湖 hú

lake

water 氵[202] [shuǐ] + neck muscle/recklessly 胡 [hú]

Water(氵) that is like the flabby skin of an old cow(胡) is like a lake. A lake's water does not flow, but ripples with the wind, very much like how the flabby skin, even though it is part of the cow, moves on its own.

19g 一 十 十 古 古 吉 克

克 kè

can

age-old 古 [gǔ] + person 儿[71] [rén]

A strong person(儿) who has overcome many hurdles over a period of time(古) can do anything. Because of the similar pronunciation, this character came to signify 'grams.'

克服[kèfú] surmount; overcome - 34b

囗

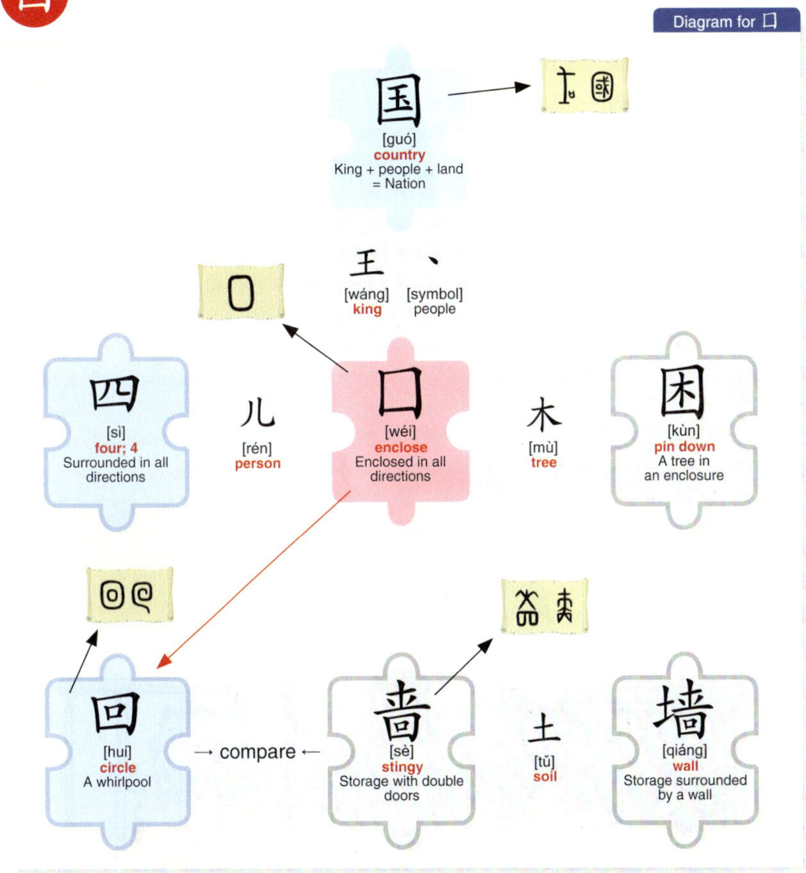

20

20

囗 wéi

enclose

To be enclosed in all directions by something like a castle wall.

* This character has the same shape as "mouth 口[16][kǒu]," but is much larger and encircles other characters.

20a

丨 冂 冂 冃 冃 国 国 国

国 guó

country; nation

enclose 口 [wéi] + king 王[108][wáng] + people 丶 [symbol]

A king(王), people(丶), and a boundary(口) makes a nation. These are the three basic components of a country.

* The traditional character(國) is a combination of people(口[16]), land(一), a spear(戈[113]) and a boundary(口).

中国 [Zhōngguó] China - 232a
外国 [wàiguó] foreign country - 222a
国王 [guówáng] king - 108
国家 [guójiā] country; state; nation - 174a
祖国 [zǔguó] mother country; one's country - 126j

20b

丨 冂 冃 冃 闲 困 困

困 kùn

pin down

enclose 口 [wéi] + tree 木[210][mù]

To enclose a tree(木) or a person within a frame(口) means to imprison or shut in.

20

困难 [kùnnan] difficulty; difficult - 34h

20c

丨 冂 冂 四 四

四 sì

four; 4

enclose 口 [wéi] + person 儿[71][rén]

A person(儿) surrounded(口) from all four directions.

四分之一 one-fourth (1/4); a quarter - 20c 119a 83d 223

20d　丨 冂 冋 冋 回 回

回 huí

circle; time

A body of water whirling in circles in the same place. This character came to mean 'number of times an action takes place.'

* This character has nothing to do with "enclose 囗 [wéi]" or "mouth 口[16][kǒu]".

回答[huídá] reply; answer - 65b
回来[huílái] return; come back - 212d
回去[huíqù] return; go back - 94
看一回。Look (at something) one time. - 11a 223 20d

20e　一 十 土 圭 圭 亠 啬 啬 啬 啬 嗇

嗇 sè

stingy

double lid 䒑, 十 [symbol] + storage 回 [symbol]

A stingy owner stores his grains in a storage room(回) with double doors(䒑, 十) so no one can steal from him.

* The character for storage(回) looks like "circle 回 [huí]," but it symbolizes sacks of grains piled in layers.

20f　一 十 土 圵 圵 圵 圵 坴 坴 墙 墙 墙 墙 墻

墻 qiáng

wall

soil 土[152][tǔ] + stingy 嗇 [sè]

A stingy(嗇) man guards his storage room by building a wall with soil(土).

20

21

音

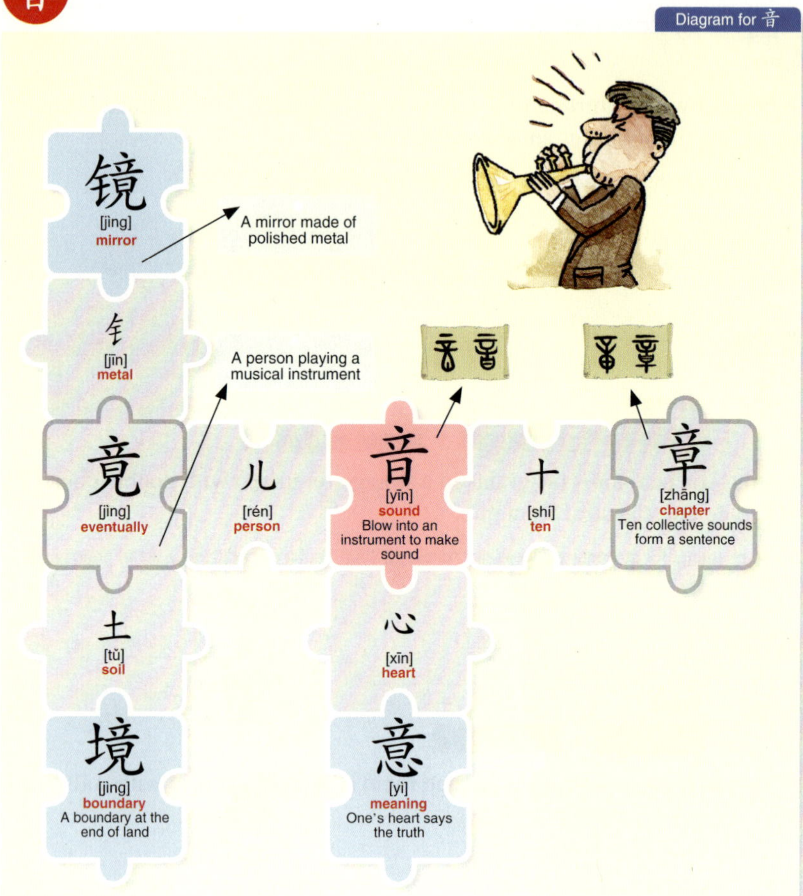

21 丶 亠 亠 立 立 产 音 音 音

音 yīn **sound**

Ancient Chinese text shows that "word 言[22][yán]" and "sound 音" have something to do with blowing into an instrument. At first they were used interchangeably until "音" came to stress sound and "言" was used to stress context.

* The upper part of "立" looks like "stand 立[79][lì]" but is unrelated.

声音[shēngyīn] voice; sound - 104d
音乐[yīnyuè] music - 212c
录音[lù/yīn] sound recording - 203a

21a

丶 亠 亠 立 立 产 音 音 音 音 章

章 zhāng

chapter

sound 音 [yīn] + ten 十[231] [shí]

Many(十) sounds(音) make a sentence and many sentences make phrases and paragraphs.

* Ancient characters show that a sharp tool like an awl or a gimlet(辛[103]) was used to draw tattoos, which is how this character came be mean 'writing.' A lot of writing makes a sentence or a chapter.

文章[wénzhāng] article; essay - 133

21b

丶 亠 亠 立 立 产 音 音 音 音 意 意 意

意 yì

meaning

sound 音 [yīn] + heart 心[28] [xīn]

What the heart(心) says(音) is what one really means to say.

意思[yìsi] meaning - 28a
满意[mǎnyì] satisfied - 64e
同意[tóngyì] agree - 149b
愿意[yuànyì] be willing; be ready - 201e
注意[zhùyì] pay attention to; take note of - 233e
没意思[méiyìsi] boring; uninteresting - 117f 28a
意见[yìjiàn] opinion; idea; view - 13
意义[yìyì] meaning; significance - 233a
有意思[yǒuyìsi] significant; meaningful - 39c 28a
主意[zhǔyi] plan; idea - 233c

21c

丶 亠 亠 立 立 产 音 音 音 音 竟

竟 jìng

eventually

instrument/sound 音 [yīn] + person 儿[71] [rén]

This character describes a person(儿) who is playing a musical instrument (音), such as a trumpet. Even if someone knows how to make a sound from the instrument, we cannot conclude that he is very good at playing musical instruments. In that context, this letter means 'eventually or finish' because the ability of a player of a musical instrument should eventually reach a certain level of competence if the player is considered to be good at it.

21

21d

一 十 土 圤 圹 圹 圹 垆 垆 培 培 培 境 境

境 jìng

boundary

soil 土[152][tǔ] + finish/eventually 竟 [jìng]

This character signifies 'boundary' because it means a finishing(竟) line or place of a certain land(土). At the same time, it indicates a spacious 'place' which is defined by its boundary. It can also refer to a 'situation' of a certain separated place.

环境[huánjìng] environment; circumstances - 108c

21e

丿 𠂉 𠂉 𠂉 钅 钅 钅 钅 钅 铲 铲 锫 锫 锫 镜 镜

镜 jìng

mirror; lens

metal 钅 = 金[199][jīn] + eventually 竟 [jìng]

In ancient times, mirrors were made of silver or copper(金). To make a mirror, the surface of the metal(钅) was polished such that a face could eventually(竟) be looked at. During the 12th–13-th centuries, the mirror was made of glass, and the meaning of lens was derived from this character.

21

眼镜[yǎnjìng] eyeglasses - 11g

言

Diagram for 言

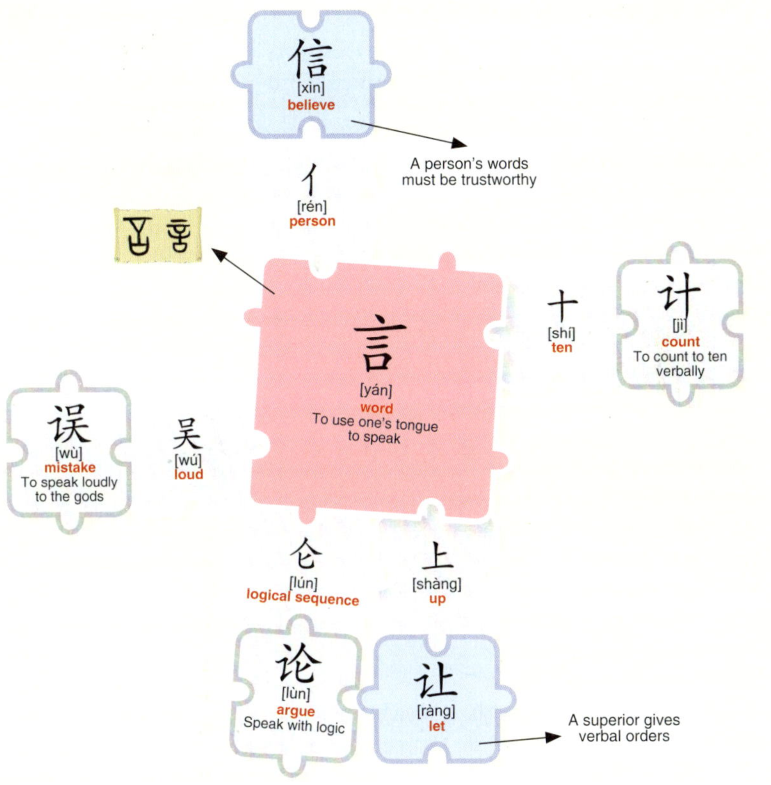

22

22

丶 亠 亠 亖 亖 言 言

言 yán

word

To speak a word in earnestness by sticking one's tongue out of one's mouth (口[16]). When used as a radical, it becomes "讠."

语言 [yǔyán] language - 226c　　发言 [fā/yán] speak; make a statement (speech) - 34f

22a

丿 亻 亻 亻 亻 亻 亻 信 信

信 xìn

believe; letter

person 亻[70] [rén] + word 言 [yán]

Anything a person(亻) says(言) must be trustworthy. A letter, which is a person's(亻) written word (言) must also mean what it says.

相信 [xiāngxìn] believe - 11c
信封 [xìnfēng] envelope - 40e

22b

丶 讠 讠 计

计 jì

count

word 讠=言 [yán] + ten 十[231] [shí]

To count up to ten(十) verbally, with words(讠).

计划 [jìhuà] plan; project - 119g
设计 [shè/jì] plan; design - 117e
计算 [jìsuàn] count - 43b

22

22c

丶 讠 讠 讠 让

让 ràng

let; give ground

word 讠=言 [yán] + up 上[223f] [shàng]

A widely used causative verb, it means someone higher up(上) gave a verbal order(讠) to make someone 'do' something. It also means 'to give way or to offer' food to someone higher up(上) by saying(讠) so.

22d

丶 讠 讠 讠 论 论

论 lùn

argue

word 讠=言 [yán] + logical sequence 仑 [lún]

To use logic(仑) when speaking(讠) means 'to argue or discuss.'

* The traditional character of "仑" is "侖" and means a lot of books(冊[217]) are gathered together (亼[65]).

讨论 [tǎolùn] discuss; talk over - 40g
争论 [zhēnglùn] dispute - 36a

22e ` 讠 讠 讠 讠 讠 讠 误 误

误 wù — mistake

word 讠=言 [yán] + loud 吴 [wú]

A human being speaking(讠) in a loud voice(吴) to the gods is making a mistake because it is wrong to do so.

* "吴" shows a person looking up at the sky(天[74b]) and opening his mouth(口[16]) wide to shout.

错误[cuòwù] wrong; mistake; error - 199b 误会[wùhuì] misunderstand; mistake - 66c

欠

Diagram for 欠

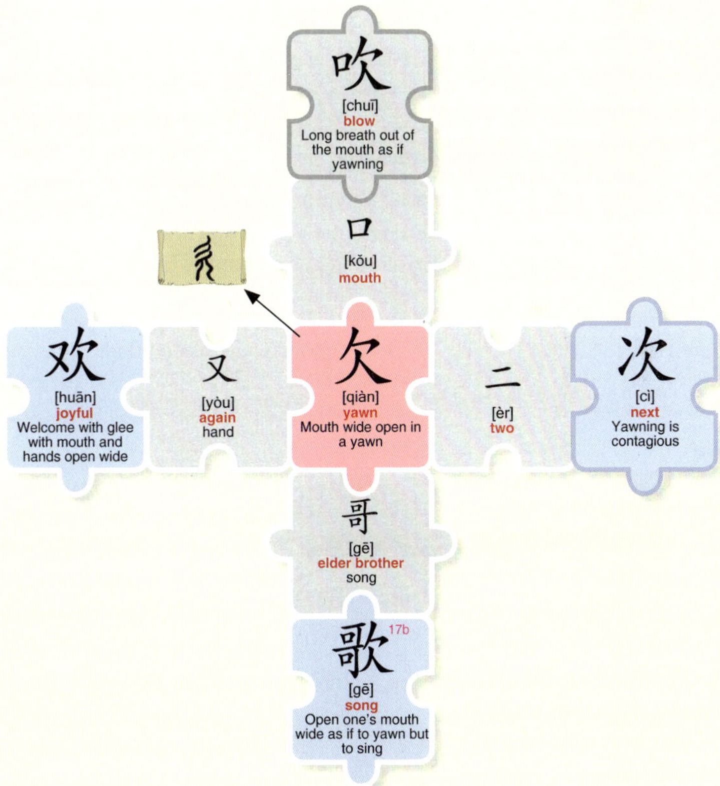

23

23

23

丿 𠂊 𠂊 欠

欠
qiàn

yawn

A person(人[63]) opening his mouth wide to yawn.

23a

丨 ㄇ 口 口' 口𠂊 口𠂊 吹

吹
chuī

blow

mouth 口[16][kǒu] + yawn 欠 [qiàn]

To breath in as if yawning(欠), then exhaling through the mouth(口) to blow on an instrument.

他把火给吹着了。He blew the fire out. - 84b 92b 158 65d 23a 11b 168a

23b

丶 冫 冫' 冫𠂊 冫𠂊 次

次
cì

next

two 二[226][èr] + yawn 欠 [qiàn]

Many animals yawn, but contagious yawning is only found in human beings and a few species of primates. This character means that after one person yawns (欠), it moves on to the next, the second(二) person. It is also used to count numbers of actions.

其次[qícì] next; secondly - 44
第二次 the second time - 109b 226 23b
8次列车 No. 8 train - 23b 30b 124

23c

フ 又 又' 又𠂊 对 欢

欢
huān

joyful

hand/again 又[34][yòu] + yawn 欠 [qiàn]

To welcome someone joyfully with mouth open as if yawning(欠) and arms or hands(又) open wide.

喜欢[xǐhuan] like; enjoy - 140a
欢迎[huānyíng] welcome - 87a
欢送[huānsòng] see off; send off - 45a

舌

Diagram for 舌

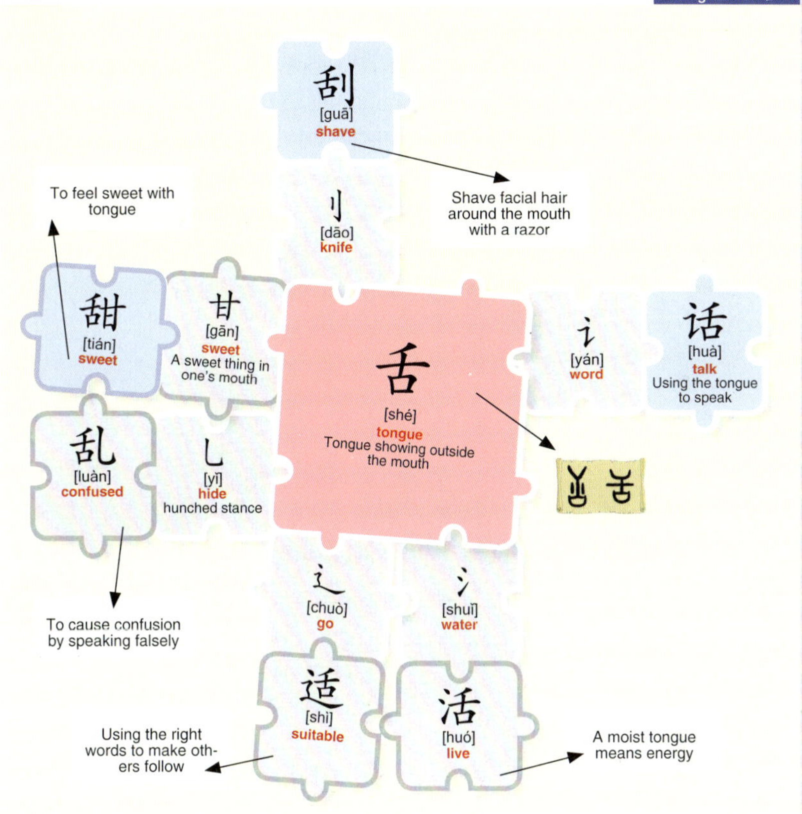

24

舌
shé

tongue

This character came to mean tongue because it's the shape of a tongue (千) sticking out of a mouth(口[16][kǒu]).

丿 二 千 千 舌 舌 刮 刮

24a

刮 guā

shave; blow (of the wind)

tongue 舌 [shé] + knife 刂=刀[119] [dāo]

The character for knife(刂) was added to "舌" to signify the shaving action. Although The traditional character has nothing to do with the wind, because of the similar pronunciation, it came to mean 'blow (of the wind).'

* This character is easier to remember if you remember that "舌" is a tongue hanging out of a mouth (口) and a razor(刂) is being used to shave the facial hair.

刮风[guāfēng] blow (of the wind) - 213c
我每天早上刮脸。I shave every morning. - 113b 97a 74b 218e 223f 24a 67d
首尔的夏天常刮东南风。A southeasterly wind often blows through Seoul in the summer. - 7 69 46b 56e 74b 150c 24a 211 231b 213c

丶 讠 讠 讠 讠 讠 话 话

24b

话 huà

talk

word 讠=言[22] [yán] + tongue 舌 [shé]

To speak or to say something(讠), one needs to use his tongue(舌).

打电话[dǎdiànhuà] make a (phone) call - 31c 157a
说话[shuō/huà] speak; talk - 72d
普通话[pǔtōnghuà] Mandarin (common speech of the Chinese language) - 79g 166b
电话[diànhuà] telephone - 157a
会话[huìhuà] conversation; dialogue - 66c
讲话[jiǎng/huà] speak; talk - 228a
谈话[tán/huà] conversation; talk - 158c
笑话[xiàohua] joke; jest - 78a

丶 丶 氵 氵 氵 汗 汗 活 活

24c

活 huó

live; work

water 氵[202] [shuǐ] + tongue 舌 [shé]

When a person's tongue(舌) is moist with water(氵), it means one is healthy and alive. Because it means that one can move actively, it also came to mean 'work.'

* The small bumps on the tongue(舌) are able to excrete fluid(氵), so the tongue of a healthy and energetic person is always moist.

活动[huódòng] activity - 159d
生活[shēnghuó] live; life - 208

24

24d

丿 二 千 千 舌 舌 舌 活 适

适 shì

suitable

tongue 舌 [shé] + go 辶[61] [chuò]

To make other people follow the road(辶) you have taken, you must use your tongue(舌) wisely. By saying the most suitable words(舌) at the right time, you can make others follow(辶) you.

合适[héshì] suitable - 65a　　舒适[shūshì] comfort; comfortable - 168d

24e

丿 二 千 千 舌 舌 乱

乱 luàn

confused

tongue 舌 [shé] + hunched stance/hide 乚[83e] [yǐ]

To have a crooked(乚) tongue(舌) means you said something wrong and caused confusion.

* "乚" doesn't mean much, and can be translated in many ways.

胡乱[húluàn] carelessly - 19e
家里很乱The house is very messy. - 174a 151 14a 24e
现在的社会是很乱。Society these days is very muddled up. - 13d 32a 46b 126h 66c 54b 14a 24e

24

24f

一 十 廿 廿 甘

甘 gān

sweet

This character depicts the image of holding a sweet thing(-) in one's mouth(廿→口[16]) without swallowing it.

24g

丿 二 千 千 舌 舌 舌 甜 甜 甜 甜

甜 tián

sweet

tongue 舌 [shé] + sweet 甘 [gān]

This character symbolizes a tongue(舌), an organ of human body through which one can feel the taste of sweetness(甘).

牙

Diagram for 牙

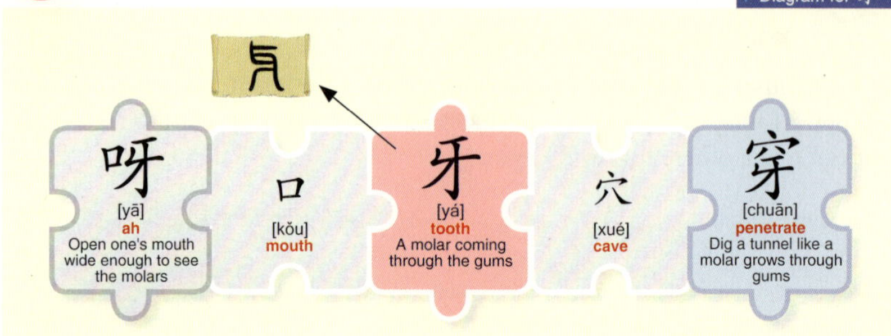

25 — 一 二 于 牙

牙 yá — **tooth**

A molar is a tooth that grows in the innermost corners of the mouth.

刷牙 [shuāyá] brush one's teeth - 90i

25

25a — 丶 丶 宀 穴 穴 空 空 穿 穿

穿 chuān — **penetrate; wear**

cave 穴[142][xué] + tooth 牙 [yá]

One digs a tunnel or a cave(穴) like a molar(牙) penetrates the gums. Squirming around in clothes while trying to figure out where your arms and legs go has a similar imagery, so this character came to mean 'to wear (clothes or socks).'

她从不穿绿色的衣服。She never wears green. - 84c 63g 223a 25a 132j 68f 46b 130 34b

25b — 丨 ㄇ 口 口一 口二 吁 呀

呀 yā/ya — **ah; oh / <modal particle>**

mouth 口[16][kǒu] + tooth 牙 [yá]

This character means 'ah, oh' because that's the sound one makes when one's mouth(口) is open wide enough to see the molars(牙).

When the sentence ends in 'a, e, i, o, ü,' '啊[17f]' was used instead to close the sentence.

自

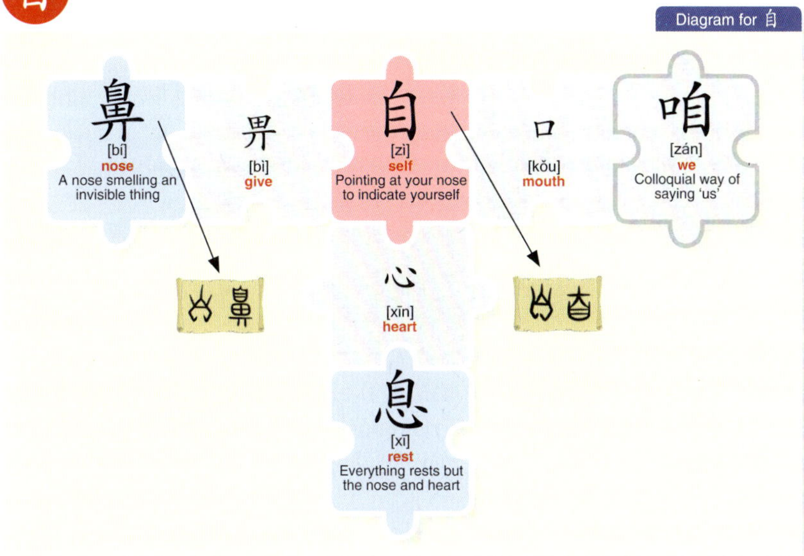

26

自 zì

self

The nose is the most prominent feature of a face. When someone points to indicate himself or herself, they usually point at his own nose.

* A nose appears in a lot of sayings or proverbs about pride or arrogance. This is more proof on how a nose can mean oneself.

自行车[zìxíngchē] bicycle - 60b 124
自卑[zìbēi] feel oneself inferior - 215b
自由[zìyóu] freedom - 156
自己[zìjǐ] oneself - 82
自我[zìwǒ] oneself; self; ego - 113b

26a

咱 zán

we

mouth 口[16] [kǒu] + self 自 [zì]

The colloquial plural form of myself(自) is us, with an added mouth(口).

咱们[zánmen] we - 145a

26b

ノ 亻 冂 白 白 自 自 息 息 息

息 xī

rest; news

nose/self 自 [zì] + heart 心[28] [xīn]

A nose(自) and heart(心) are organs about breathing and work until one breaths his last breath. When only the nose and heart are moving, it means one is resting. It also means that information keeps coming in endlessly.

休息[xiūxi] rest - 70c　　消息[xiāoxi] news - 235d

26c

ノ 亻 冂 白 白 自 自 鼻 鼻 鼻 鼻 鼻 鼻 鼻

鼻 bí

nose

The character, "self 自 [zì]" is a character borrowed from the image of nose. Its meaning is derived from its original meaning by adding a phonetic element "畀[bì]."

* The character, "give 畀 [bì]" shows an image where a steamer(田) is placed on a stand(丌[12c]) with a hole through which steam comes up from its bottom. This suggests emphasis on the function of nose that can smell an invisible thing like steam.

* Out of Its ancient letter, the stroke of "steamer 田" is different from "field 田[154] [tián]."

鼻子[bízi] nose - 95

26

身

Diagram for 身

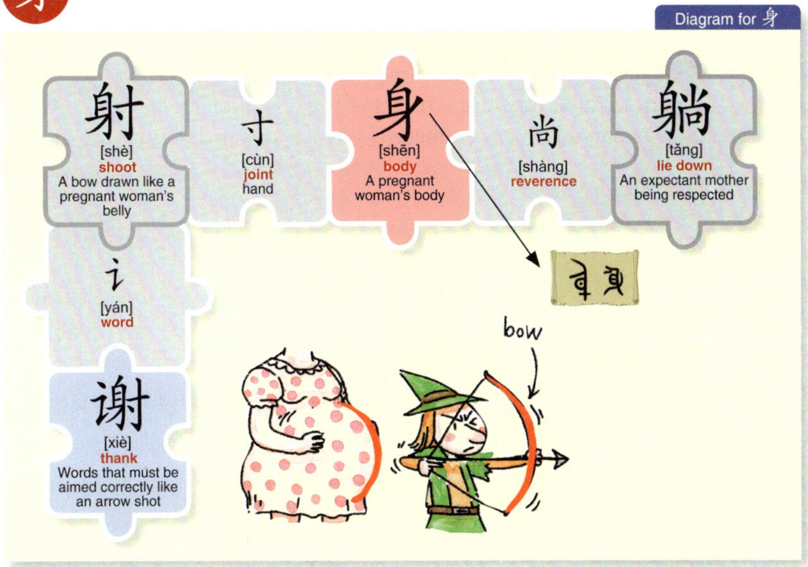

27

身 shēn — body

A side profile of a pregnant woman's body.

身体[shēntǐ] body; health - 29b　　身边[shēnbiān] at (by) one's side - 61a

27a

躺 tǎng — lie down

pregnant woman/body 身 [shēn] + reverence 尚[150b] [shàng]

A pregnant woman(身) who deserves everyone's care and respect(尚) gets to lie down.

地上躺着四个人。
Four people are lying on the floor. - 84a 223f 27a 11b 20c 63b 63

27b

丿 亻 冂 自 自 身 身 身 射 射

射
shè

shoot

pregnant woman/body 身 [shēn] + hand/joint 寸[40] [cùn]

To shoot an arrow, one must draw the bow back with one's hand(寸). When done, the bow is curved, like a pregnant woman's side profile(身).

注射[zhùshè] inject; get a shot - 233e

27c

丶 讠 讠 讠 讠 讠 讠 讠 讠 讠 谢 谢

谢
xiè

thank

word 讠=言[22] [yán] + shoot 射 [shè]

A word(讠) of thanks has to be aimed well, like an arrow shot(射) at a target. It is of no use when said at the wrong time or without sincerity.

谢谢[xièxie] thanks; thank you

感谢[gǎnxiè] thank - 114d

27

心

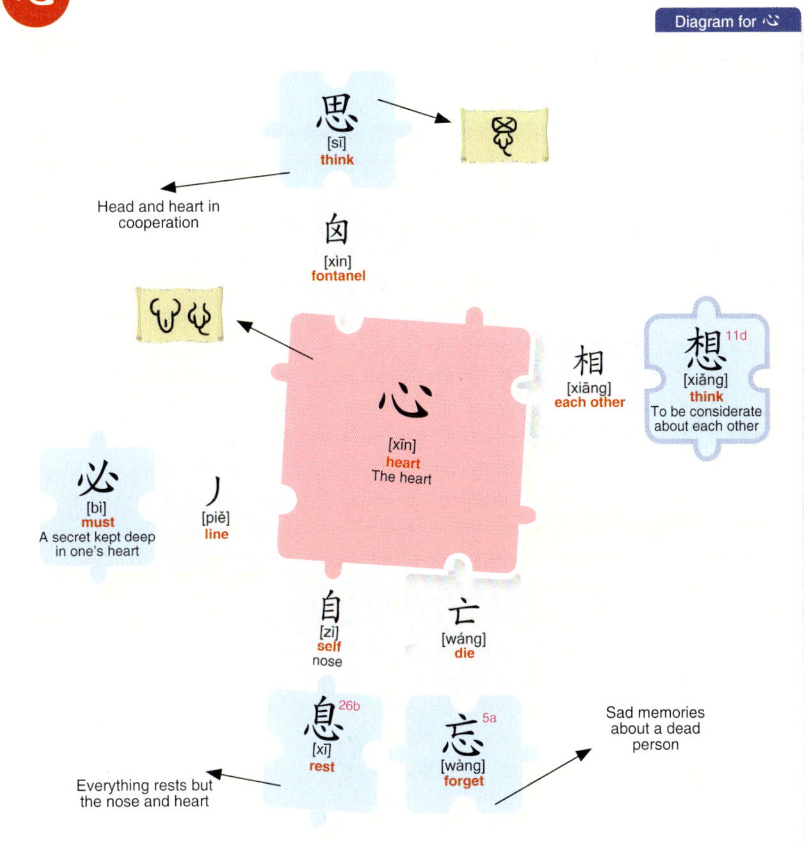

28

28

心 xīn

heart

This is what a heart is said to look like. It means 'heart,' but in other characters it symbolizes emotion or characteristics.

担心[dān/xīn] worry; anxious - 31g
放心[fang/xīn] set one's mind (heart) at rest - 50a
关心[guānxīn] concern; interest; attention - 45
小心[xiǎoxīn] be careful - 235
点心[diǎnxin] snack; refreshment - 127d
心情[xīnqíng] mood - 135d
细心[xìxīn] careful; attentive - 132h

28a

思 sī

think

head/fontanel 田[154] → 囟[132h] [xìn] + heart 心 [xīn]

A thought is something you have when your head(囟) works alongside your heart(心). The ancient Chinese thought it was about reason(囟) and emotion (心).

* Ancient characters are proof that "field 田 [tián]" is a simplified version of "囟." The dot on the top is the hole in the top of a baby skull, before the bones fuse.

意思[yìsi] meaning - 21b
没意思[méiyìsi] boring; uninteresting - 117f 21b
思想[sīxiǎng] thought; thinking; ideau - 11d
有意思[yǒuyìsi] significant; meaningful - 39c 21b

28b

必 bì

must

heart 心 [xīn] + line 丿[234] [piě]

28

A secret buried(丿) deep within one's heart(心) must be kept.

* "丿" has no specific meaning and can be interpreted differently.

必须[bìxū] must; have to; necessary - 8a

忄

Diagram for 忄

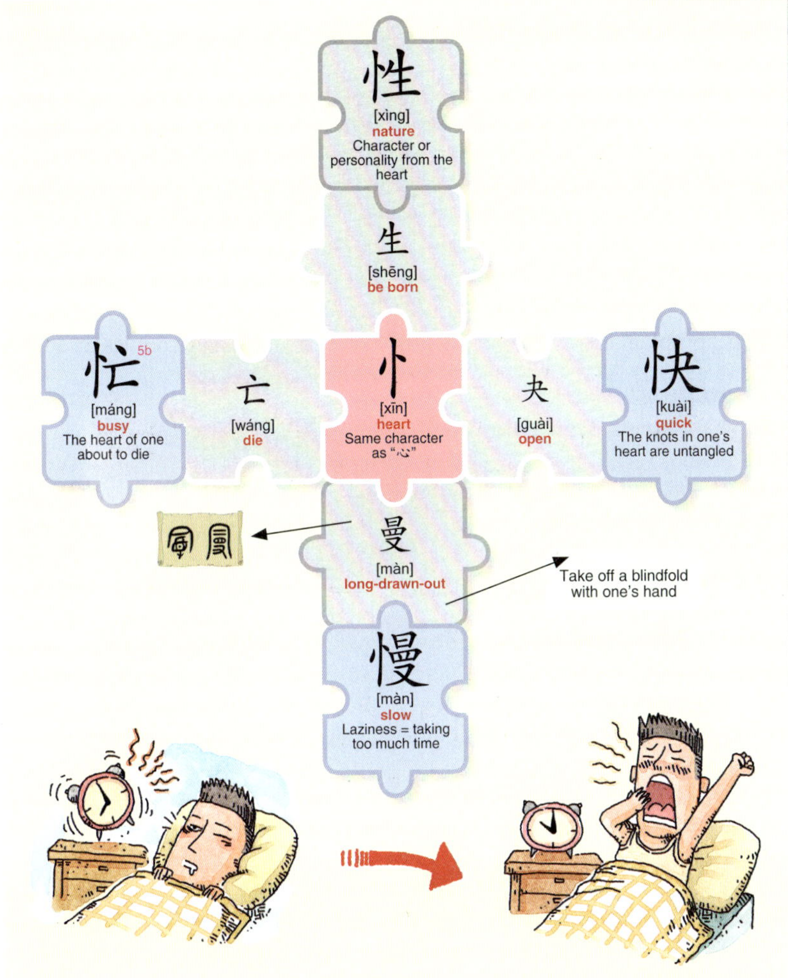

28

28

忄
xīn

heart

"忄" is the same character as "heart 心 [xīn]," but takes this shape when used as a radical and placed on the left of a character.

28c　丶 丷 忄 忄 忄 性 性 性

性 xìng

nature

heart 忄=心 [xīn] + be born 生[208] [shēng]

Something that comes out of(生) one's heart(忄) is that person's nature.

个性[gèxìng] individuality - 63b

28d　丶 丷 忄 忄 忄 快 快

快 kuài

quick; pleased

heart 忄=心 [xīn] + open 夬[76] [guài]

When a problem is solved, one's heart(忄) feels free(夬) and troubles disappear instantaneously. This character also came to mean 'pleased.'

快乐[kuàilè] happy; joyful; cheerful - 212c
凉快[liángkuai] pleasantly cool, - 2a
痛快[tòngkuài] very happy; delighted; joyful - 81c
愉快[yúkuài] cheerful; pleasant - 221c

28e

曼 màn

long-drawn-out

hood 曰→冃[11e] [mào] + eye 罒→目[11] [mù] + hand/again 又[34] [yòu]

Picture a hand(又) taking off a hood(冃) that was used to cover someone's eyes(目). It takes a while for that person to grow accustomed to the light, which is how this character came to mean 'take time.'

* There's a protein called rhodopsin in the retina. When hit with light, rhodopsin has a chemical reaction and releases energy which make us see. When one steps suddenly into a bright light, rhodopsin dissolves to release energy in a short burst, which is why we are blinded temporarily. But after a while, the rhodopsin dissolves and we recover.

28f

慢 màn

slow

heart 忄=心 [xīn] + long-drawn-out 曼 [màn]

A lazy(忄) person who is slow all the time takes a while(曼) to wake up.

* "心" is all about emotion or characteristics and means lazy.

我的表慢五分钟。My watch is five minutes slow. - 113b 46b 130b 28f 226a 119a 232b

28

骨

Diagram for 骨

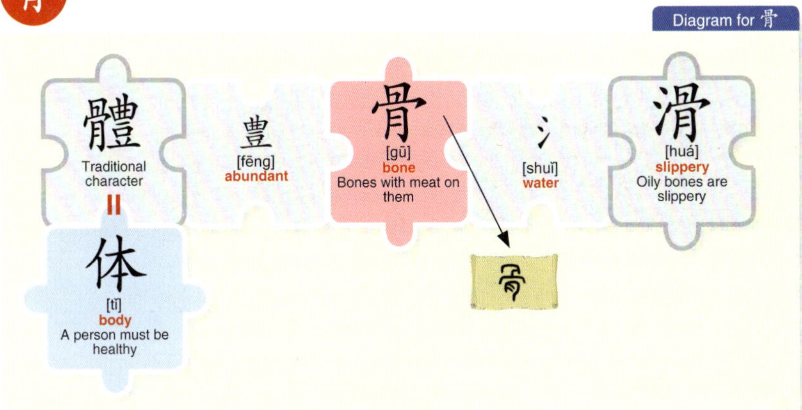

29

骨 gū

bone

Bones(冎) with meat(月) are still bones. "冎 [guǎ]" means bones with out the surrounding meat. 29

* "Moon 月[221][yuè]" as part of another character usually means "meat 肉[192][ròu]."

骨头[gǔtou] bone - 75

29a

滑 huá

slippery

water 氵[202][shuǐ] + bone 骨 [gū]

When there is water(氵) on the bone(骨) it means the meat is oily. Oily bones are slippery.

滑冰[huá/bīng] ice skating - 206a

29b ノ 亻 仁 什 休 休 体

体
tǐ

body

person 亻[70][rén] + root 本[210a][běn]

"To lose a fortune is to lose a lot. To lose one's health is to lose all." The root (本) of a person(亻) is his healthy body.

* The traditional character(體) portrayed a body with bones(骨) and plentiful(豊→丰[209]) flesh.

身体[shēntǐ] body; health - 27
全体[quántǐ] all; entire - 63f
尸体[shītǐ] corpse; dead body - 90
体育[tǐyù] sports; physical education - 192b
半导体[bàndǎotǐ] semiconductor - 175b 7b

30

歹

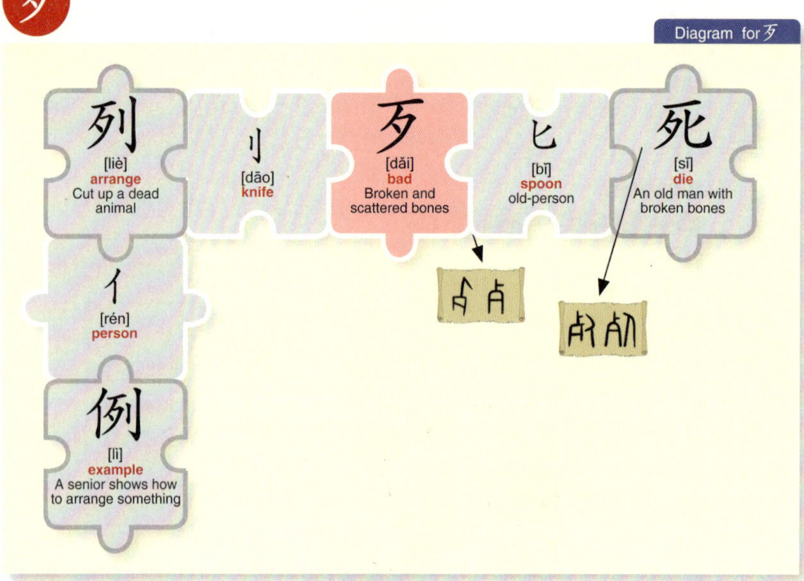

30 一 丆 歹 歹

歹 dǎi **bad**

Broken bones with no flesh on them. When used on its own, this character means 'bad,' and used alongside another character it means 'death and disaster.'

30a 一 丆 歹 歹 歹 死

死 sǐ **die**

broken bone/bad 歹 [dǎi] + old-person/spoon 匕[88] [bǐ]

Broken bones(歹) and an old man(匕) can only mean 'death.'

* "匕" is another character meaning person(人[63]), but the crooked angle means 'old person.'

死亡[sǐwáng] die - 5
他什么时候死了? When he died? - 84b 231a 93a 42d 111b 30a 168a

30b 一 丆 歹 歹 歹 列

列 liè **arrange**

dead/bad 歹 [dǎi] + knife 刂=刀[119] [dāo]

Using a knife(刂) to cut up a dead(歹) animal and arrange the pieces.

排列[páiliè] arrange - 181a

30c 丿 亻 亻 亻 亻 亻 亻 例

例 lì **example**

person 亻[70] [rén] + arrange 列 [liè]

There are rules as to how one must cut up and arrange(列) pieces of a carcass. This character shows a senior(亻) giving a demonstration.

例如[lìrú] for example; for instance - 96g

30

手

Diagram for 手

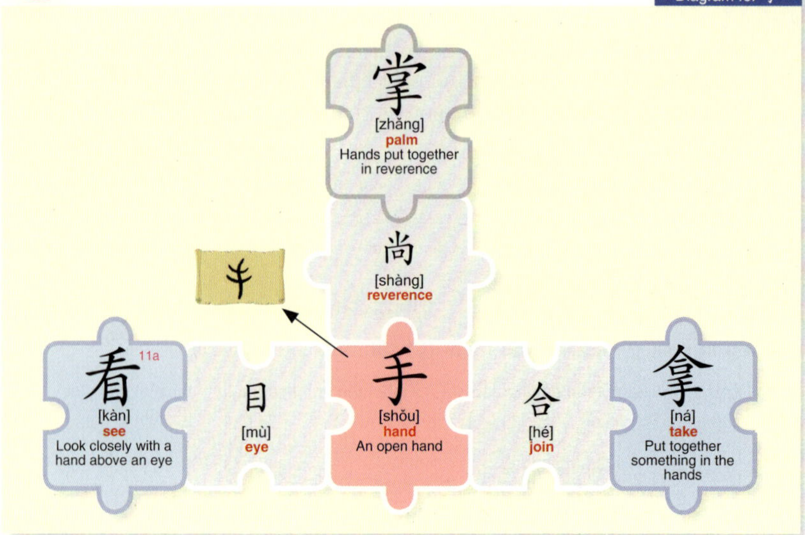

31

31 一 二 三 手

手 shǒu — **hand**

A hand with five outstretched fingers.

手表[shǒubiǎo] wrist watch - 130b
手机[shǒujī] cell phone; mobile phone - 213a
洗手间[xǐshǒujiān] restroom; toilet - 71e 145c
握手[wò/shǒu] shake hands - 90f
手段[shǒuduàn] means; measure; method - 117a
手续[shǒuxù] procedure; process - 75e
手指[shǒuzhǐ] finger - 89a

31a 丨 丨丨 丷 ⺌ 尚 尚 尚 尚 尚 堂 堂 掌

掌 zhǎng — **palm**

reverence 尚 150b [shàng] + hand 手 [shǒu]

To show one's reverence(尚), like when praying or bowing to gods, people usually hold their palms(手) together.

掌握[zhǎngwò] grasp; master - 90f
鼓掌[gǔ/zhǎng] clap one's hands - 51b

31b

拿 ná

take

join 合[65a] [hé] + hand 手 [shǒu]

To take up(合) in one's hand(手) means to hold something.

他手里拿的是什么? What is he holding in his hand? - 84b 31 151 31b 46b 54b 231a 93a

手

Diagram for 扌

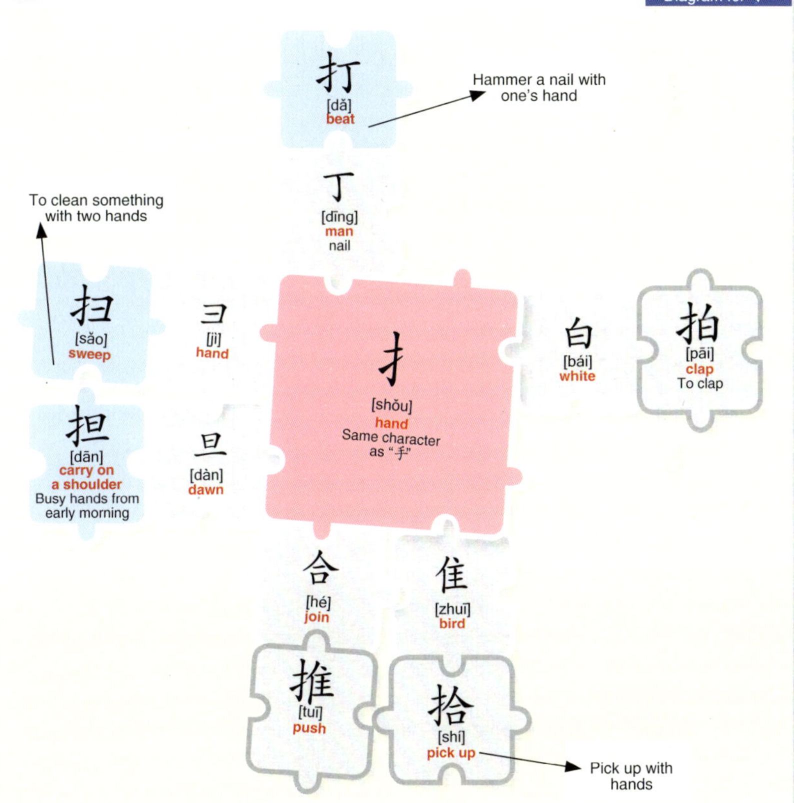

31

31

一 扌 扌

扌 shǒu

hand

This is the same character as "hand 手 [shǒu]." Whereas "手" is an independent character or used in the center of a more complicated character, "扌" is a radical that comes on the left.

31c

一 扌 扌 扌 打

打 dǎ

beat

hand 扌=手 [shǒu] + nail/man 丁[225][dīng]

Using one's hand(扌) to hold a hammer and hit a nail(丁).

打电话[dǎdiànhuà] make a (phone) call - 157a 24b
打篮球[dǎlánqiú] play basketball - 107c 198b
打扫[dǎsǎo] sweep; clean - 31h
打算[dǎsuan] plan - 43b
打败[dǎ/bài] defeat; beat - 186g
打倒[dǎdǎo] overthrow; down with - 112c

31

31d

一 扌 扌 扌 扌 拍 拍 拍

拍 pāi

clap; take (a photograph)

hand 扌=手 [shǒu] + white 白[134][bái]

To hit or clap one's hands(扌) together to make a noise which sounds a lot like "白 [bái]."

* It might be easier to remember this character if you imagine taking a photo. You need hands(扌) to hold the camera and press a button(扌) as well as a white(白) light, a flash.

拍手 handclap - 31d 31
拍电影 shoot a film - 31d 157a 2d

31e

一 扌 扌 扌 扌 扌 拎 拾 拾

拾 shí

pick up

hand 扌=手 [shǒu] + join 合[65a][hé]

"Hold 拿[31b][ná]" is the image of using one's hand(手) to get(合) something placed above. "拾" is the image of someone using his hand(扌) to pick up or to collect something(合) from the ground.

收拾[shōushi] gather up; put in order; tidy - 50e

31f 一 † 扌 扌 扌 扌 扌 扌 扌 推 推

推 tuī

push

hand 扌=手 [shǒu] + bird 隹[178] [zhuī]

A mother bird lightly pushes her young(隹) one with a wing(扌) to see if it is ready to leave the nest.

推动 [tuīdòng] push forward - 159d

推车。Push the car. - 31f 124

31g 一 † 扌 扌 扣 扣 担 担

担 dān

carry on a shoulder

hand 扌=手 [shǒu] + dawn 旦[218a] [dàn]

Right from the dawn i.e. very early morning(旦) when the sun rises above the horizon, one starts to use one's hands(扌) busily. This character derives its meaning 'to shoulder, take on' from the image of a person who is charged with heavy responsibilities on his or her shoulders.

担心 [dān/xīn] worry; anxious - 28

31

31h 一 † 扌 扫 扫 扫

扫 sǎo

sweep

hand 扌=手 [shǒu] + hand 彐[36] [jì]

This character symbolizes a person who is busy sweeping or cleaning the floor with a broom.

* The stroke on the right side of its traditional character(掃) shows an image that someone is holding a broom or mop made of cloth(巾[131]) on his or her hands(彐).

打扫 [dǎsǎo] sweep; clean - 31c

才

Diagram for 才

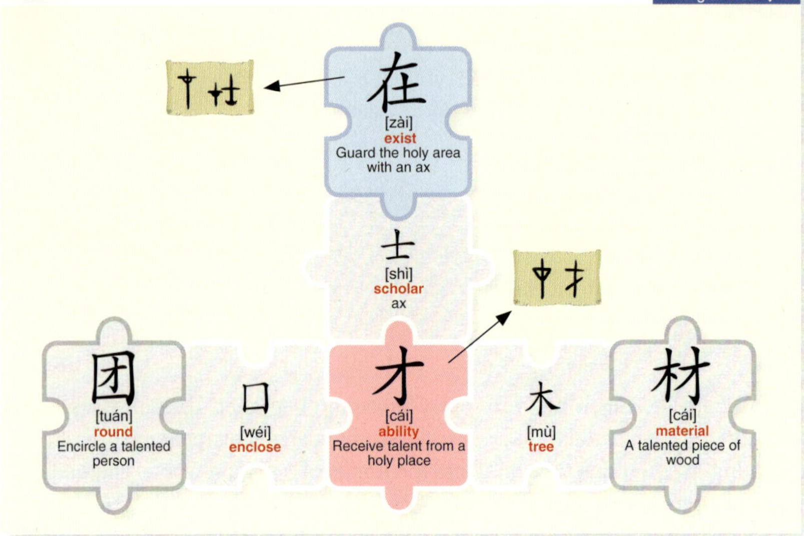

32

32

一 十 才

才 cái

ability

In the ancient times, it seems the people carved marks(丿) on wooden sticks (十) to point out the holy places. By entering such places, one could receive gifts, talents, abilities from the gods. But it was hard to reach such areas, so this character also meant that the time had passed, as well as 'just now, barely.'

刚才 [gāngcái] just now; a moment ago - 165b   人才 [réncái] person of ability - 63

32a

一 ナ 𠂇 𡉀 在 在

在 zài

exist

ability 才 [cái] + ax/scholar 土[152]→士[104][shì]

To guard a holy place with an ax(士) meant that a god capable of bestowing gifts or talents(才) was present.

* The left side of "在" stems from "才," and the right side means ax "士," not "soil 土 [tǔ]."

现在[xiànzài] now; at present - 13d　　正在[zhèngzài] in process of; in course of - 54

32b　一 十 才 木 木 村 材

材 cái

material

tree 木[210][mù] + ability 才 [cái]

A talented(才) piece of wood(木) means lumber that is good to be used as building material.

材料[cáiliào] material - 164b

32c　丨 冂 冃 冃 团 团

团 tuán

round

enclose 囗[20][wéi] + ability 才 [cái]

To encircle(囗) talented(才) people so that they can unite and cooperate.

* The traditional character(團) shows a hand(寸[40]) used to coil thread around something round, like a flying shuttle(専[zhuān]), to accentuate the round, encircling imagery.

团结[tuánjié] unite; rally - 104b

32

爪

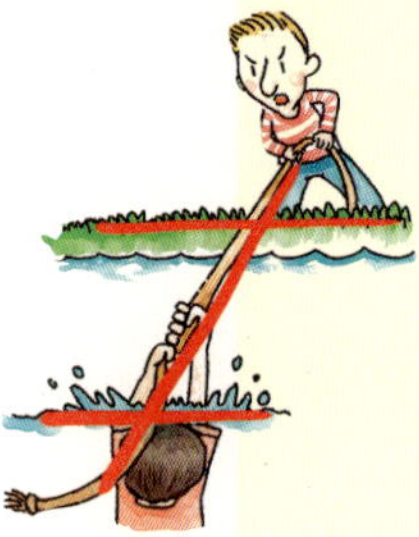

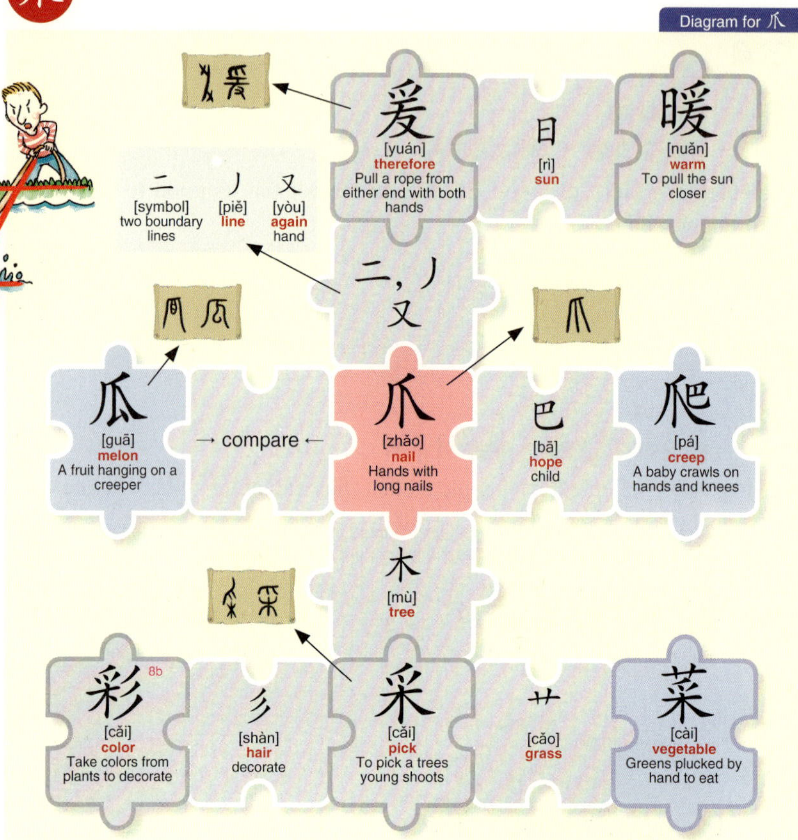

33

33 丿 厂 爪 爪

爪
zhǎo

nail

This character depicts a hand with long fingernails trying to grasp something. When used as part of another character, it means 'hand' and sometimes changes into "爫."

* The ancient character shows that despite the slightly different shape, it means the same as "hand 手[31][shǒu]."

33a

丿 𠂆 𠂇 𠂈 爫 爫 乎 爰 爰

爰 yuán

therefore

hand/nail 爫=爪 [zhǎo] + two boundary lines 二 [symbol] + line 丿[234][piě] + hand/again 又[34][yòu]

The hand(爫) of someone by the water(一) and the hand(又) of someone in the water(一) are tied together with a rope(丿). It's the image of someone trying to pull a drowning person to shore. The meaning gradually changed to 'therefore.'

* "丿" doesn't mean anything specific and can be translated differently depending on the character.

33b

丨 冂 日 日 日' 日'' 日''' 日爫 日爫 日爫 日乎 日爰 暖

暖 nuǎn

warm

sun 日[218][rì] + pull/ therefore 爰 [yuán]

If you pull(爰) the sun(日) closer to you, now how warm would that be!

暖和 [nuǎnhuo] warm; nice and warm - 139a

33c

丿 厂 𠂆 爪 爬 爬 爬 爬

爬 pá

creep

hand/nail 爪 [zhǎo] + child/hope 巴[92a][bā]

A young child(巴) is crawling on his hands(爪) and knees.

* "巴" is the shape of a fat baby.

爬山 [páshān] mountain climbing - 195

33d

丿 𠂆 𠂇 𠂈 爫 乎 采 采

采 cǎi

pick

hand/nail 爫 = 爪 [zhǎo] + tree 木[210][mù]

To pick a tree's(木) young shoots, tea leaves, or fruit by hand(爫).

33e

一 十 卄 艹 艹 艹 苎 苎 苹 茱 菜

菜 cài

vegetable

grass 艹[207][cǎo] + pick 采 [cǎi]

Vegetables are plants(艹) that are picked by hand(采), which is true because most edible vegetation can be picked by hand.

33

菜单[càidān] menu; bill of fare - 231c   白菜[báicài] Chinese cabbage - 134

33f   ㇒ 𠂆 𠂋 瓜 瓜

瓜 guā **melon**

This character symbolizes a fruit hanging on creeping plants. It is commonly used to describe any kind of melon or gourd.

* The shape of the character is similar to that of "nail 爪 [zhǎo]," but its meaning is different.

西瓜[xīguā] watermelon - 170

又

34

Diagram for 又

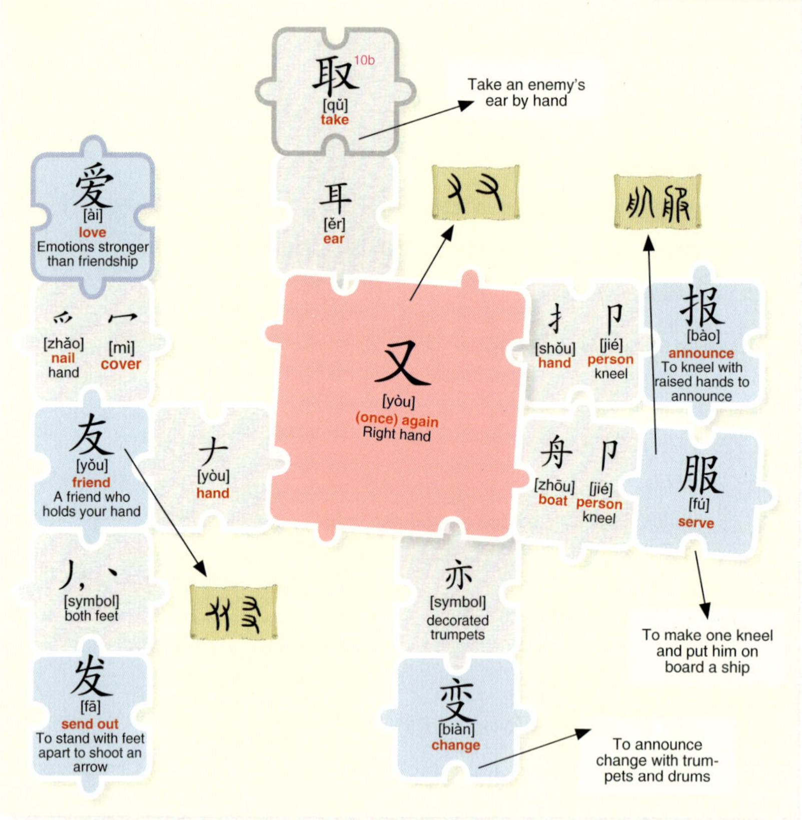

34 ㇇ 又

又 yòu (once) again

When the character was first created, it meant 'right hand,' but because most people are right-handed and use it for most chores, it came to mean 'again.' When used as part of a more complicated character, it's better to think it means 'hand.'

34a 一 扌 扌 扌 护 报 报

报 bào announce

hand 扌=手[31] [shǒu] + kneel/person 卩[85] [jié] + hand/again 又 [yòu]

To use your hand(又) to force someone to kneel(卩), then raise your hand(扌) to announce that you have a conquered. It came to mean newspaper, because that's how announcements are made now.

* "卩" is the shape of a man on his knees.

报纸[bàozhǐ] newspaper - 99a
报告[bàogào] inform; report - 175d
报名[bào/míng] enroll; enlist; enter one's name - 222c
画报[huàbào] illustrated magazine; pictorial - 167c

34b 丿 刀 月 月 月 肌 服 服

服 fú serve; clothes

boat 月[221] →舟 [zhōu] + kneel/person 卩[85] [jié] + hand/again 又 [yòu]

You force(又) a man to kneel(卩) and keep him in your ship(舟). To take someone on board meant you made him serve you, and to differentiate such people from your original crew, you made them wear special clothes.

* The "moon 月 [yuè]" in the ancient version of the "服" character is actually "舟."

衣服[yīfu] clothes - 130
服务员[fúwùyuán] service staff - 159f 186h
舒服[shūfu] comfortable - 168d
服务[fúwù] serve - 159f
克服[kèfú] surmount; overcome - 19g

34

34c

丶 亠 亣 亣 亦 亦 亦 变

变 biàn

change

decorated trumpets 亦 [symbol] + hand/again 又 [yòu]

When there was a huge change, like the coronation of a new king, the men blew trumpets(亦) with tassels and beat drums with their hands(又).

* The traditional character(變) is the shape of someone blowing into a wind instrument(言[22]/refer to 21) with tassels(絲[132a]) and beating a drum(攵[50]).

变化[biànhuà] change - 70a	变成[biànchéng] turn into; change into - 114a
改变[gǎibiàn] change - 50b	

34d

一 ナ 方 友

友 yǒu

friend

hand ナ[39][yòu] + hand/again 又 [yòu]

Two overlapping hands(ナ, 又) means 'cooperation.' A friend is someone who offers a hand when one is in need.

朋友[péngyou] friend - 192a	友好[yǒuhǎo] close friend - 96c
友谊[yǒuyì] friendship - 224e	小朋友[xiǎopéngyǒu] children - 235 192a

34e

一 ㇀ ㇀ ㇀ 爫 爫 爫 爱 爱 爱

爱 ài

love

hand/nail 爫 =爪[33][zhǎo] + cover 冖[169][mì] + friend 友 [yǒu]

Love is an emotion that tempts you to touch your lover's(友) private areas(冖) with your hands(爫).

爱好[ài/hào] to be fond of; interest; hobby - 96c	可爱[kě'ài] lovable; lovely - 17
爱人[àiren] spouse - 63	爱情[àiqíng] love (between man and woman); affection - 135d
热爱[rè'ài] ardently love - 158f	

34f

㇀ ナ 步 发 发

发 fā/fà

send out / hair

both feet ノ, 丶 [symbol] + hand ナ[39][yòu] + hand/again 又 [yòu]

A man with both feet(ノ+丶) apart, a bow in one hand(ナ) and a spear in another(又). This character came to mean 'to send' because both arrows and spears travel through the air.

* The traditional character(發) shows a man with both feet apart(癶[59]) to shoot a bow(弓[109]) and throw a spear(殳[117]).

发烧[fā/shāo] have a fever; have a temperature - 158b
发现[fāxiàn] find; discover - 13d
出发[chūfā] set out; start off - 167a
发生[fāshēng] happen; occur; arise - 208
发展[fāzhǎn] develop; grow - 90a

Although the tone is different, it can mean 'hair' because of the similar pronunciation.

头发[tóufa] hair - 75
理发[lǐ/fà] haircut; hairdressing - 108b

又

34

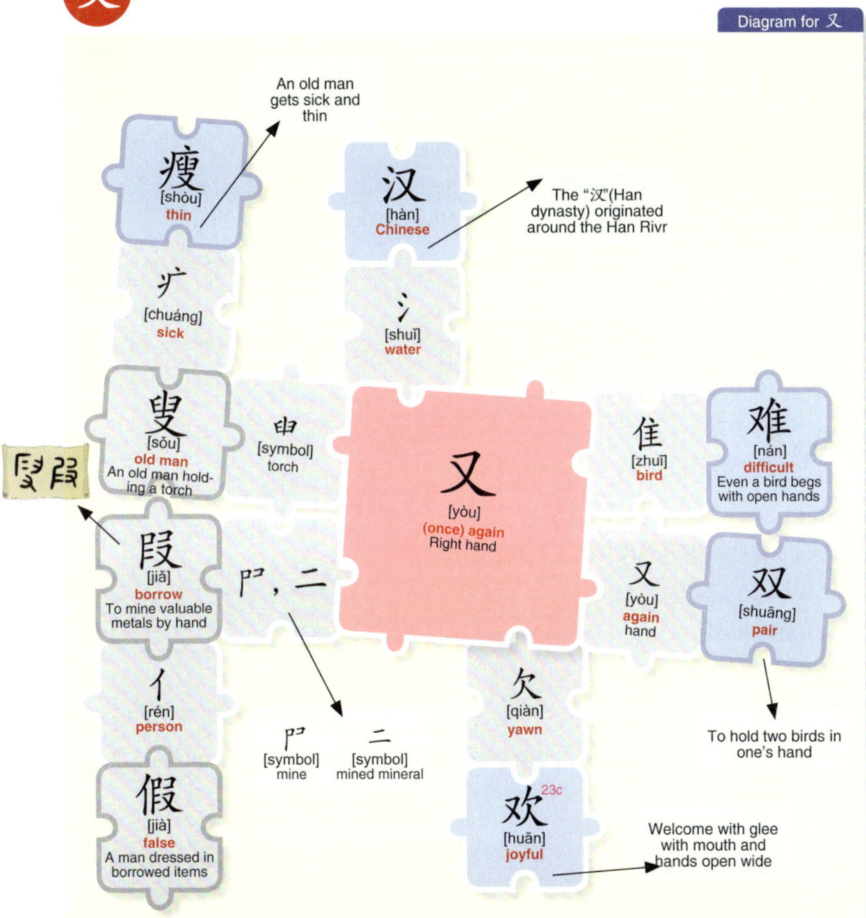

34g 丶 冫 氵 汈 汉

汉 hàn

Chinese

water 氵[202] [shuǐ] + hand/again 又 [yòu]

This character signifies the Hanshui River(汉江[hànjiāng]), the largest tributary of the Chang River(长江[chángjiāng]). The Han "汉" originated from around this river and established what is widely accepted to be the present Chinese culture.

* It's easier to remember this character if you think of a body of water(氵) near which the "汉" people built the present Chinese culture with their hands(又).

汉语[hànyǔ] Chinese (language) - 226c　　汉字[hànzì] Chinese character - 95b

34h ㇇ 又 又' 对 对 对 对 对 难 难

难 nán

difficult

hand/again 又 [yòu] + bird 隹[178] [zhuī]

Even a small bird that can fly(隹) is begging with outstretched hands(又) because of the drought and the difficulties the famine caused.

34

* The traditional character(難) describes land with yellow soil(堇[jǐn]), so parched that there's nothing even for the birds(隹) to eat.

难过[nánguò] have a hard time - 40f　　困难[kùnnan] difficulty; difficult - 20b

难看[nánkàn] ugly - 11a

34i ㇇ 又 刄 双

双 shuāng

pair

hand/again 又 [yòu] + hand/again 又 [yòu]

To hold a pair of birds in both hands(又+又).

* The traditional character(雙) has one hand(又) holding two birds(隹[178]).

双方[shuāngfāng] both sides; both parties - 160

34j ㇆ ㇆ 尸 尸 尸 尸 尸 叚 叚

叚 jiǎ

borrow

mine 𠃜 [symbol] + mined mineral 二 [symbol] + hand/again 又[34] [yòu]

This character seems to describe a man's hand(又) mining valuable metals

(二) in a mine(𠃊). There's a philosophical interpretation to this character that says the metals are only borrowed from nature.

* Because Chinese characters have changed over the centuries, sometimes it's hard to decipher the exact meaning.

34k

丿 亻 亻 亻 亻 亻 亻 亻 亻 假 假

假 jiǎ/jià false / vacation

person 亻[70] [rén] + borrow 叚 [jiǎ]

A man(亻) well-dressed in jewels borrowed(叚) from nature. A beauty that comes from dressing up with borrowed items is considered fake. Also, a vacation is defined as a temporary break on borrowed(叚) time, taken by a man (亻) who has a job.

放假[fàng/jià] have a holiday or vacation - 50a
寒假[hánjià] winter vacation - 206b
请假[qǐng/jià] ask for leave - 135c

34l

叟 sǒu old man

torch 臼 [symbol] + hand/again 又 [yòu]

This letter symbolizes an old man who has poor eye sight and is searching for something in every nook and corner with a torch(臼) in his hands(又).

34m

丶 亠 广 疒 疒 疒 疒 疒 疒 疒 疒 疒 瘦 瘦

瘦 shòu thin; emaciated

sick 疒[81] [chuáng] + old man 叟 [sǒu]

This letter shows the image of an old man(叟) who is struck with illness(疒) and becomes very thin like a person of spare frame.

34

史

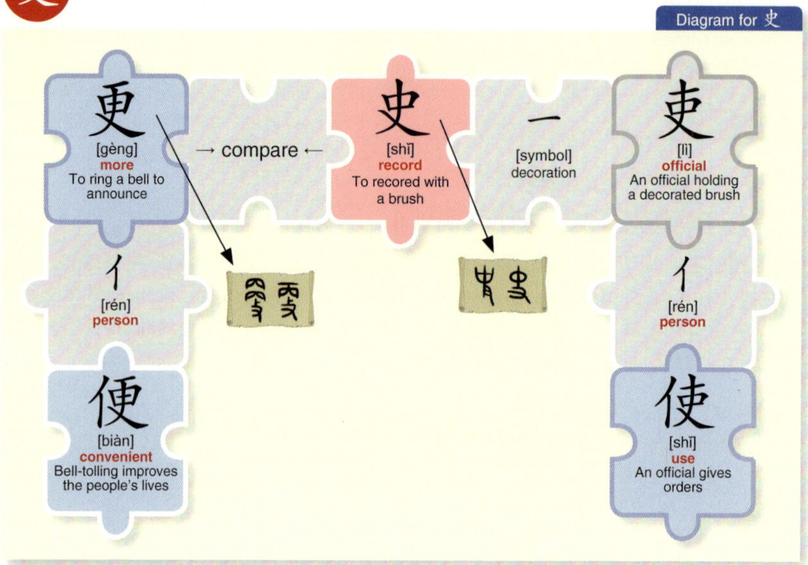

35

35

丨 冂 口 中 史

史 shǐ — history

Writing by holding a brush in hand(㕚→"又[34][yòu]") is how a government official writes when recording facts. And such facts become history.

历史[lìshǐ] history - 159j

35a

一 丆 丙 百 吏 吏

吏 lì — official

decoration 一 [symbol] + brush in hand/history 史 [shǐ]

"吏" is a hand holding a brush with a decoration(一). "史[shǐ]" is an official taking records, but "吏" is a man holding a special brush and therefore a high-ranking official.

35b

使 shǐ

use; make

person 亻[70] [rén] + official 吏 [lì]

A government official(吏) can 'use' his subordinate(亻) and make him do as he bids.

使用 [shǐyòng] make use of; use - 166　　大使馆 [dàshǐguǎn] embassy - 74 193c

35c

更 gèng

more

strike 攴→攵[50] [pū] + say 曰[10c] [yuē]

At the start of every hour, the governmental office rang a bell(攴→攵) to announce(曰) the time. Each time the bell was rung, a prayer was chanted to wish for more blessings for a better life.

* The "曰" shape in The ancient character is a bell(曰→丙) that has been hung up.

更加 [gèngjiā] still more - 159g

35

35d

便 biàn/pián

convenient / cheap

person 亻[70] [rén] + sound of the bell/more 更 [gèng]

The bell(更) helped people(亻) tell the time and follow a schedule, which made things more convenient.

方便 [fāngbiàn] convenient - 160

Back when there were no refrigerators, the bell(更) announcing the end of the trading day told people(亻) that food could be bought at a cheaper price.

便宜 [piányi] cheap; inexpensive - 224d

彐

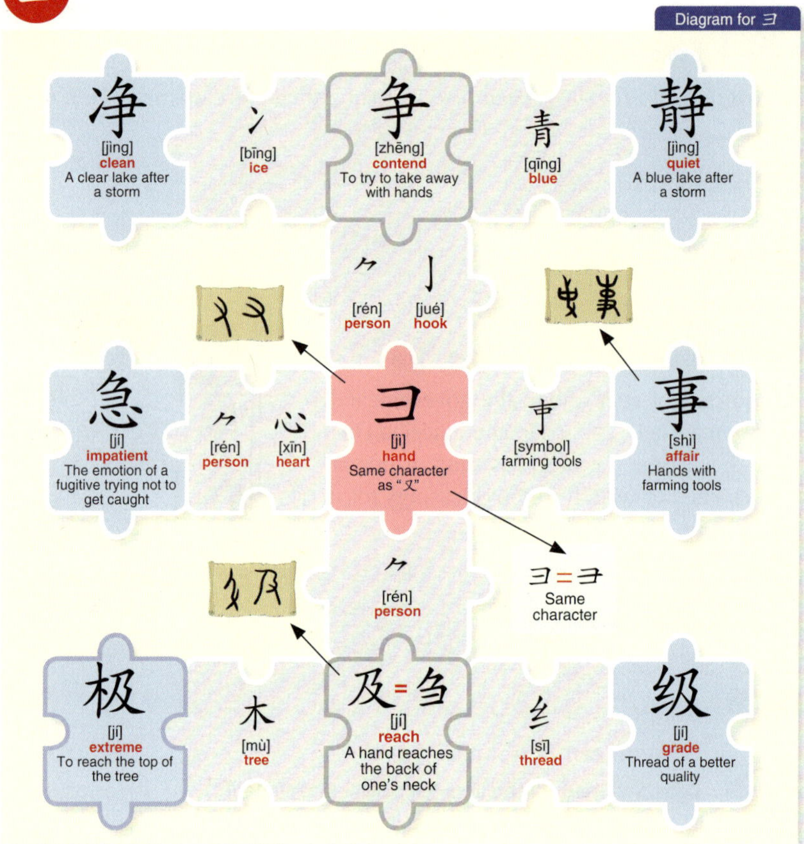

36

36

㇇ ㇌ 彐

彐
jì

hand

Ancient records show this is the same character as "hand 又[34][yòu]" that also means 'hand.'

36a

丿 ⺈ ⺈ 刍 刍 争

争
zhēng

contend

person ⺈[68][rén] + hand 彐 [jì] + hook 亅[168][jué]

A person(⺈) is holding something(亅) which another person is contending and trying to take away by hand(⺕).

* The traditional character(爭) shows two hands(爫[33], ⺕) trying to take something(亅).
* "亅" is called a hook because it looks like one, but can be interpreted in many ways.

斗争[dòuzhēng] fight; struggle - 164　　争论[zhēnglùn] dispute - 22d

36b

丶 冫 冫 冫 冫 冫 冫 净

净 jìng

clean

ice 冫[206] [bīng] + contend 争 [zhēng]

Figuratively speaking, a storm is the heavens in a fight(争). After it passes, the water in a lake is usually as clear as a sheet of ice(冫).

* The traditional character(淨) depicts a clear body of water(氵) after a storm(爭).

干净[gānjìng] clean; neat and tidy - 121

36c

一 = 丰 丰 丰 青 青 青 青 青 静 静 静 静

静 jìng

quiet

blue 青[135] [qīng] + contend 争 [zhēng]

After a storm(争) passes, the sky becomes blue(青) and calm as a lake.

* The blue color of water is a reflection of the sunlight. The clearer the sky and calmer the water, the bluer the water is.

安静[ānjìng] quiet; peaceful - 96a　　平静[píngjìng] calm; tranquil - 122

36d

一 ㄱ 彐 彐 ... 事

事 shì

affair

farming tools 亊 [symbol] + hand ⺕ [jì]

In an agricultural society, working with farming tools(亊) like rakes and spades in their hands(⺕) was a common affair.

事情[shìqing] affair; matter; thing - 135d　　故事[gùshi] story; tale - 19a
同事[tong/shì] colleague; work together - 149b　　事件[shìjiàn] event; incident - 175a

36

36e

丿 乃 及

及 jí

reach; and

person 𠂆 → ⺈[68] [rén] + hand/again 又[34] [yòu]

Someone's hand(又) is about to reach the back of a man(⺈) who is running away. With time, this character came to mean 'and.'

及时 [jíshí] timely; in time - 42d

36f

丿 ⺈ ⺈ 刍 刍 刍 急 急 急

急 jí

impatient

person ⺈[68] [rén] + hand ⺕ [jì] + heart 心[28] [xīn]

This character describes the impatience(心) of a man(⺈) running as fast as he can to avoid getting caught(⺕). 刍 = 及

着急 [zháo/jí] worry; feel anxious - 11b　　急忙 [jímáng] hurriedly; hastily - 5b

36g

𠃋 纟 纟 纠 纫 级

级 jí

grade

thread 纟[132] [sī] + reach 及 [jí]

A character made to record which grade a bundle of thread(纟) had reached (及), high, average or low.

年级 [niánjí] grade; year - 121a　　初级 [chūjí] elementary; primary; junior - 119c

36

36h

一 十 才 木 朳 极 极

极 jí

extreme

tree 木[210] [mù] + reach 及 [jí]

To reach(及) the top of a tree(木) meant that one had reached one's goal, 'the end, the extreme.'

…极了 [jíle] extremely - 168a　　极其 [jíqí] most; extremely - 44

聿

Diagram for 聿

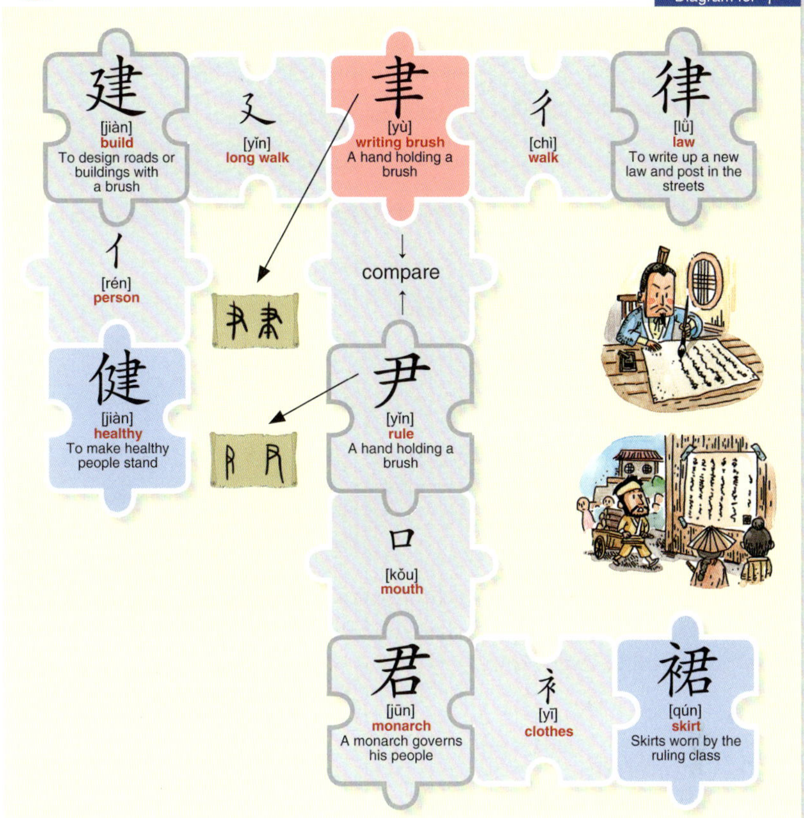

37

37

ㄱ ⺕ ⺕ ⺕ 肀 聿

聿 yù — writing brush

A hand(彐[36][jì]) holding a brush(⺗), which corresponds to a fountain pen in the present day.

37a

丿 彡 彳 彳 彳 彳 彳 徨 律

律 lǜ — law

walk 彳[60][chì] + writing brush 聿 [yù]

To write out a new law with a brush(聿) so that people walking(彳) in the streets could read them.

37b ㇇ ⺕ ⺕ ⺕ 聿 聿 津 建

建 jiàn

build

writing brush 聿 [yù] + long walk 廴[62] [yǐn]

"廴" means a narrow and winding road while "聿" is a brush. To build roads (廴) or buildings, they needed a brush(聿) to design them first.

建设[jiànshè] build; construct - 117e 建立[jiànlì] build; set up; establish - 79

37c ノ 亻 亻 亻 亻 亻 亻 律 健 健

健 jiàn

healthy

person 亻[70] [rén] + build 建 [jiàn]

If people(亻) can stand up(建), it means they are healthy.

健康[jiànkāng] health; healthy - 38b 健壮[jiànzhuàng] healthy and strong; robust - 214b

37d ㇇ ⺕ ⺕ 尹

尹 yǐn

rule

37

This character gives us the image of a hand(彐[36]) that holds a brush like "聿 [yù]." In ancient times, the ruling class used the letters, therefore, they came to mean 'to control or to govern.'

37e ㇇ ⺕ ⺕ 尹 尹 君 君

君 jūn

monarch

rule 尹 [yǐn] + mouth 口[16] [kǒu]

Among the ruling class, a 'monarch' is a person who controls(尹) his people with his words(口).

37f 丶 ㇇ 礻 礻 礻 衤 衤 衤 衤 裙 裙 裙

裙 qún

skirt

clothes 衤=衣[130] [yī] + monarch 君 [jūn]

In order to create the character 'skirt,' the meaning of "clothes 衤 [yī]" and the sound of "monarch 君 [jūn]" are combined.

* For easy understanding of this character, let us remind ourselves that the ruling class people(君), unlike the commoners, used to wear skirts(衤) and continued to do so in the modern times in China.

裙子[qúnzi] skirt - 95

隶

Diagram for 隶

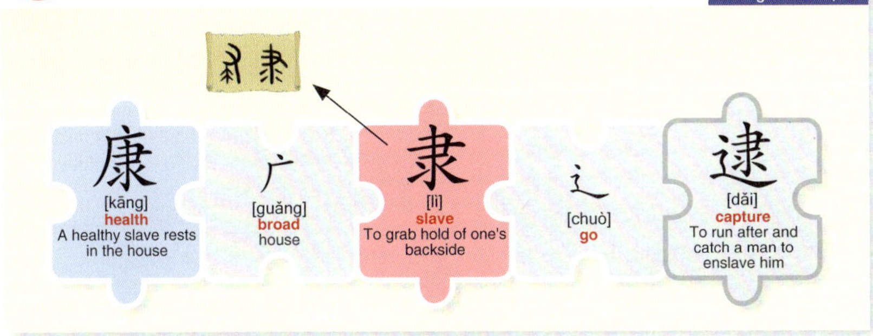

38

㇇ ⺕ ⺕ 肀 肀 肀 隶 隶

隶 lì

slave

To grab and hold(⺕) of the backside(氺) of an enemy who is on the run and make him your slave.

* The ancient character shows a hand(⺕) holding on to an animal's tail(氺).

奴隶[núlì] slave - 96e

38a

㇇ ⺕ ⺕ 肀 肀 肀 隶 隶 逮 逮 逮

逮 dǎi

capture

slave 隶 [lì] + go 辶[61] [chuò]

To run after(辶) an enemy, catch and enslave(隶) him.

逮捕[dàibǔ] arrest; apprehend - 166d

38b

丶 亠 广 户 户 户 庐 庚 唐 康 康

康 kāng

health

house/broad 广[143] [guǎng] + slave 隶 [lì]

A slave(隶) who worked hard all day gets to rest comfortably in the house (广), so they can retain their health.

* "广" is the shape of a large house with one wall torn down.

健康[jiànkāng] health; healthy - 37c

十

Diagram for 十

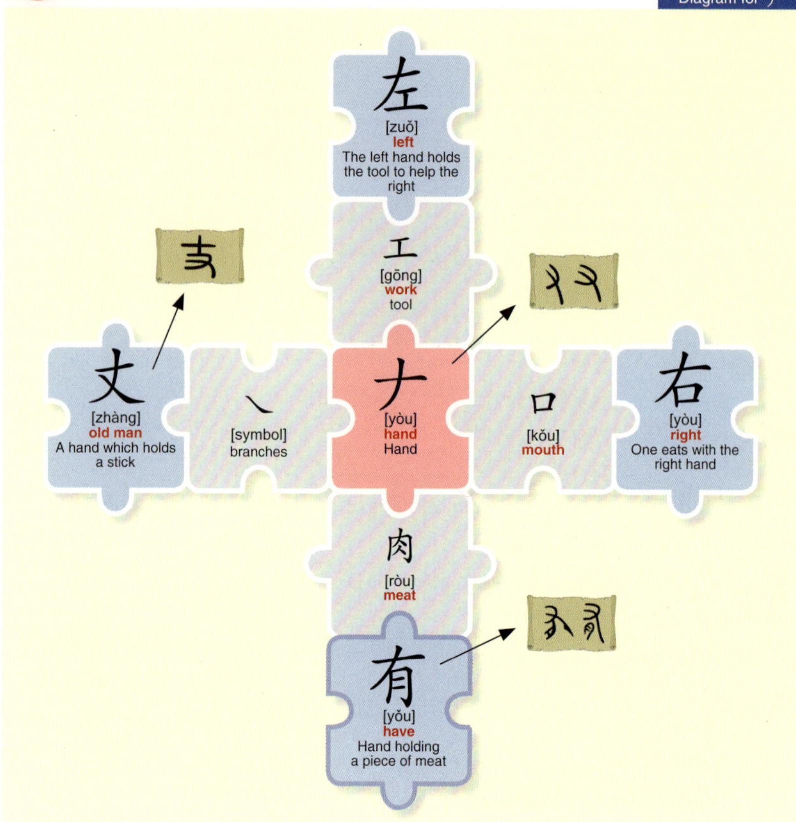

39

39 一 十

十 yòu **hand**

"十," "又[34][yòu]" and "彐[36][jì]" are all different shapes but ancient texts say they all mean 'hand.'

39a 一 十 ナ 左 左

左 zuǒ **left**

hand 十 [yòu] + tool/work 工[200][gōng]

A hand(ナ) holding a tool(エ). It means 'left' because that's the hand that holds the tool to help the right hand do the work.

左边[zuǒbian] the left side - 61a　　左右[zuǒyòu] the left and right sides - 39b

39b 一ナ大右右

右 yòu

right

hand ナ [yòu] + mouth 口[16][kǒu]

The hand(ナ) that helps the mouth(口). In other words, it's the 'right' hand used to eat. Of course, some people are left-handed, but in China most people use chopsticks with their right hand.

右边[yòubian] the right side - 61a　　左右[zuǒyòu] the left and right sides - 39a

39c 一ナ大有有有

有 yǒu

have; exist

hand ナ [yòu] + meat 月[221]→肉[192][ròu]

A hand(ナ) holding meat(肉), which is a sacrifice. It came to mean 'have, exist.'

* "Moon 月 [yuè]" as part of another character means "肉."

有名[yǒumíng] famous; well-known - 222c
所有[suǒyǒu] own; possess; have - 144a
有时候[yǒushíhou] between times; occasionally - 42d 111b
有意思[yǒuyìsi] significant; meaningful - 21b 28a
没有[méiyǒu] not have - 117f
有的[yǒude] some - 46b
有些[yǒuxiē] some - 88h

39d 一ナ丈

丈 zhàng

old man

hand ナ [yòu] + branches ㇏ [symbol]

This character depicts the image of an old man who is holding a stick(㇏) in his hand(ナ). It is a form of address for certain male relatives by marriage.

丈夫[zhàngfu] husband - 74a

寸

Diagram for 寸

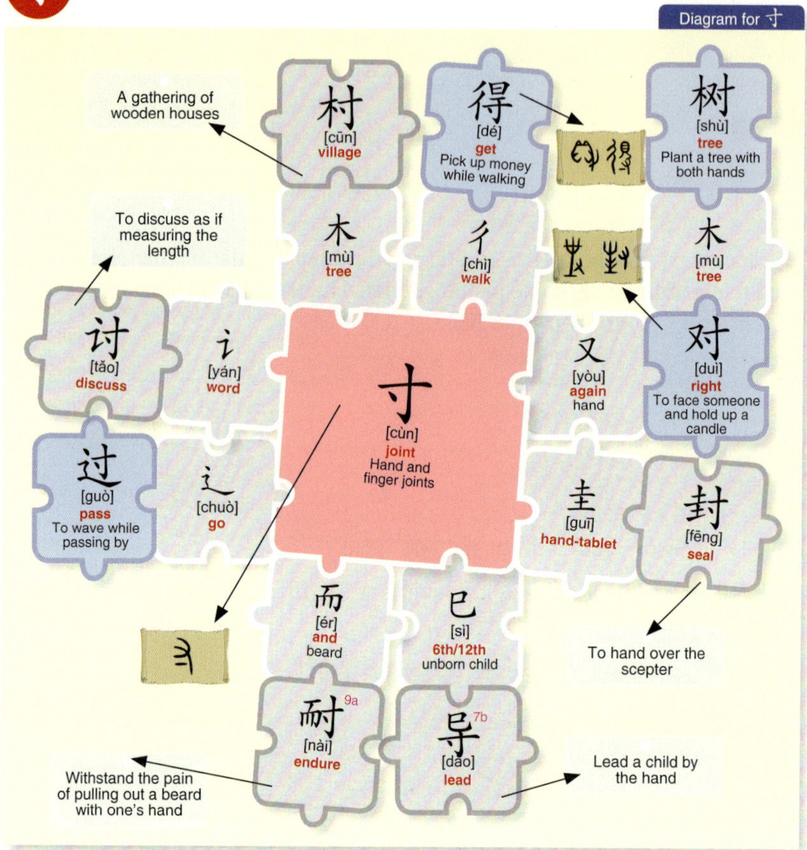

40

40	一 十 寸

寸 cùn **joint**

One presents gifts and offerings with one's 'hand.' The dot in the character means joint but is also used as a measurement of length.

* Most ancient cultures, regardless of location, used body parts to measure length.

* This character is 3.33 centimeters, 1/10 of a "尺[chǐ]."

尺寸[chǐcun] measurement; size - 91

40a 一 十 才 木 木一 村 村

村 cūn

village

tree 木[210][mù] + hand/joint 寸 [cùn]

This character depicts a village with many houses built by hand(寸) with wood(木).

* The Forbidden City is China's most famous wooden construction

农村[nóngcūn] farm village; rural area - 130c　　村庄[cūnzhuāng] village; hamlet - 143d

40b 丿 彡 彳 彳 彳 彳 彳 彳 得 得 得

得 dé/de/děi

get / <structural particle> / need

walk 彳[60][chì] + currency/shell 旦[218a]→贝[186][bèi] + hand/joint 寸 [cùn]

To pick up by hand(寸) and therefore obtain seashells(旦→贝), used as money, while walking(彳).

* "Dawn 旦 [dàn]" was originally a seashell(贝).

得到[dédào] get; obtain; gain - 112b　　取得[qǔdé] acquire - 10b

When used after a verb, it means to obtain(得) permission.

觉得[juéde] feel; sense - 13a　　记得[jìde] remember - 82b
得很[dehěn] very (much, good etc.) - 14a　　懂得[dǒngde] understand - 151b
吃得了。I can eat. - 16b 40b 168a
这双鞋穿得上。These shoes can be worn. - 133a 34i 153b 25a 40b 223f

Wherever you go(彳), one needs money(旦→贝) on hand(寸).

40

40c フ 又 又一 对 对

对 duì

right; to···

hand/again 又[34][yòu] + hand/joint 寸 [cùn]

Two persons are holding up candles with their hands(又, 寸) to talk to each other to see if they have the right person whom they have been looking for. It came to mean 'to···' by its image 'facing toward each other or face-to-face.'

* The traditional character(對) shows the candle on the left.

对不起[duìbuqǐ] I'm sorry - 223a 53d　　反对[fǎnduì] oppose - 148a
对象[duìxiàng] target; object - 174b
对。为什么不早点这么做呢? Right! Why didn't you do it like this earlier? - 40c 159c 231a 93a 223a 218e 127d 133a 93a 19b 90c

40

40d 一 十 才 木 权 权 权 树 树

树 shù

tree

tree 木[210][mù] + hand/again 又[34][yòu] + hand/joint 寸 [cùn]

One is planting a tree(木) with two hands(又, 寸).

树林[shùlín] wood; grove - 212 树木[shùmù] tree - 210

40e 一 十 土 圭 圭 圭 圭 封 封

封 fēng

seal

hand-tablet 圭[153][guī] + hand/joint 寸 [cùn]

A king is handing(寸) his servant a sealed letter of appointment and a scepter (圭) to award a title. This character is used to count the number of sealed items, such as letters.

* "圭" is a decoration of sorts that the king's subjects held whenever in his presence.

信封[xìnfēng] envelope - 22a 一封请柬。One letter of invitation. - 223 40e 135c 211c

40f 一 寸 寸 讨 讨 过

过 guò/guo

pass / <postposition>

hand/joint 寸 [cùn] + go 辶[61][chuò]

To wave a hand(寸) while passing on the road(辶).

When used after a verb, it means that an action has been done, or there was a certain experience in the past.

过去[guò/qù] in the past; formerly - 94
经过[jīngguò] pass; go through - 132e
难过[nánguò] have a hard time - 34h
过来[guòlái] come over - 212d
通过[tōngguò] pass; pass through - 166b
我已经吃过饭了。I have already eaten. - 113b 82a 132e 16b 40f 148b 168a
去年我去过英国。I have been to England. - 94 121a 113b 94 40f 77a 20a

40g 丶 讠 讠 讨 讨

讨 tǎo

discuss

word 讠=言[22][yán] + joint 寸 [cùn]

During a discussion, you do not speak whatever you desire to. You speak(讠) carefully, after considerations and carefully measuring(寸) what to say.

讨论[tǎolùn] discuss; talk over - 22d

付

Diagram for 付

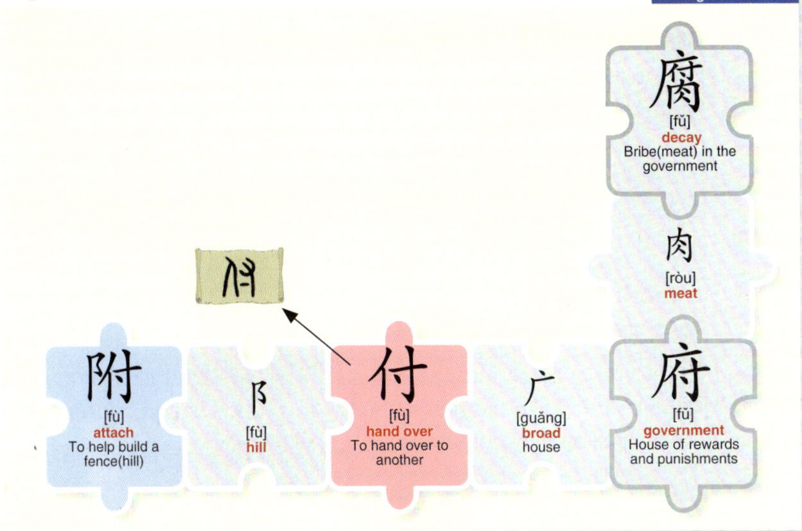

41

丿 亻 仁 付 付

付 fù **hand over**

person 亻[70][rén] + hand/joint 寸[40][cùn]

To hand over something to another person(亻) by hand(寸).

交付[jiāofù] hand over; pay - 1a

41a

丶 亠 广 广 庁 庁 府 府

府 fǔ **government**

house/broad 广[143][guǎng] + hand over 付 [fù]

A government house(广) hands out rewards(付) as well as punishments(付).

＊"广" is the shape of a house with one wall torn down, because that open space was where the official sat.

政府[zhèngfǔ] government - 50f

41b 丶 亠 广 广 广 庁 府 府 府 府 腐 腐 腐 腐

腐 fǔ

decay

government 府 [fǔ] + meat 肉[192] [ròu]

The government(府) is the center of power, and when meat(肉) is offered as a bribe, it is a sign of corruption.

豆腐 [dòufu] bean curd - 140

41c 阝 阝 阝 阝 阝 附 附

附 fù

attach; approach

hill 阝[147] [fù] + hand over 付 [fù]

To build a hill(阝) or a fence for protection, the less powerful needed to offer or add(付) their services to the rich and powerful. They had to approach the corrupt officials just so they could survive.

* The Forbidden City is China's most famous wooden construction

附近 [fùjìn] vicinity; nearby - 118a

41

寺

Diagram for 寺

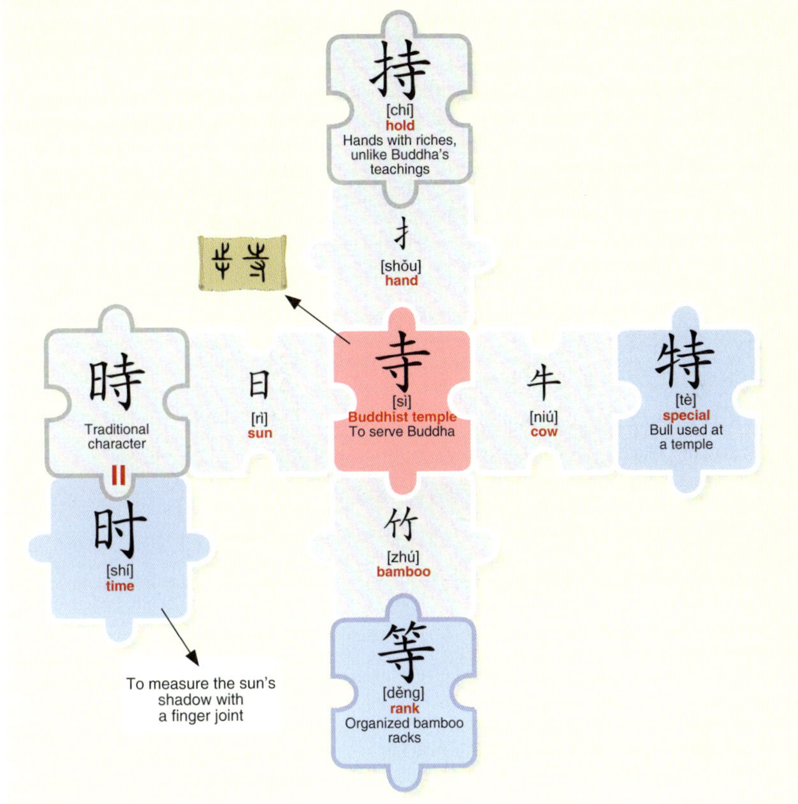

42

一 十 土 圭 寺 寺

42

寺 sì

Buddhist temple

foot/stop 土[152]→止[53][zhǐ] + hand/joint 寸[40][cùn]

To serve as one's feet(土→止) and hands(寸). At first it was used to describe an office of the king, but it became 'temple' after Buddhism was brought into China.

* "Soil 土 [tǔ]" is a variation of "止," the shape of a foot.

42a

一 扌 扌 扌 扌 扌 扌 持 持

持 chí

hold

hand 扌=手[31] [shǒu] + temple 寺 [sì]

A famous Buddhist teaching goes, "You come with nothing, you leave with nothing." One must never covet material possessions. But unlike those teachings taught at a temple(寺), some hands(扌) crave riches, so this character came to mean 'to keep or hold.'

坚持[jiānchí] persist in; stick to; adhere to - 106c　　支持[zhīchí] support - 51

42b

丿 𠂉 牛 牛 牛 牜 牪 牲 特 特

特 tè

special

cow 牛[175] [niú] + temple 寺 [sì]

Buddhists do not kill animals or eat meat. When a bull(牛) is offered to a Buddhist temple(寺), it is considered as a special offering.

* The people offered a bull of best quality as a sacrifice.

42

特别[tèbié] special; especially - 119e
特点[tèdiǎn] characteristic; distinguishing feature - 127d

42c

丿 𠂉 𠂉 ⺮ ⺮ ⺮ 竺 竺 笙 笙 等 等

等 děng

rank; wait

bamboo 竹[216] [zhú] + temple 寺 [sì]

In temples(寺), Buddhist teachings were written on slices of bamboo(竹) and organized according to importance or level of difficulty. This character also came to mean to wait in line, like neatly stacked bamboo.

* The Chinese used bamboo(竹) to make books before paper was invented.

平等[píngděng] equal; equality - 122
等车。Wait for a train. - 42c 124

42d

丨 冂 月 日 日一 时 时

时 shí

time

sun 日[218] [rì] + joint 寸[40] [cùn]

The length of the shadow on a sun(日) dial was measured by a finger joint (寸) to tell the time.

* The traditional character(時) tells us that the local office(寺) rang a bell to tell the people the time, based on the sun(日)dial.

时候 [shíhou] time; moment - 111b
时间 [shíjiān] time; hour - 145c
小时 [xiǎoshí] hour - 235
同时 [tóngshí] at the same time - 149b
有时候 [yǒushíhou] between times; occasionally - 39c 111b

廾

Diagram for 廾

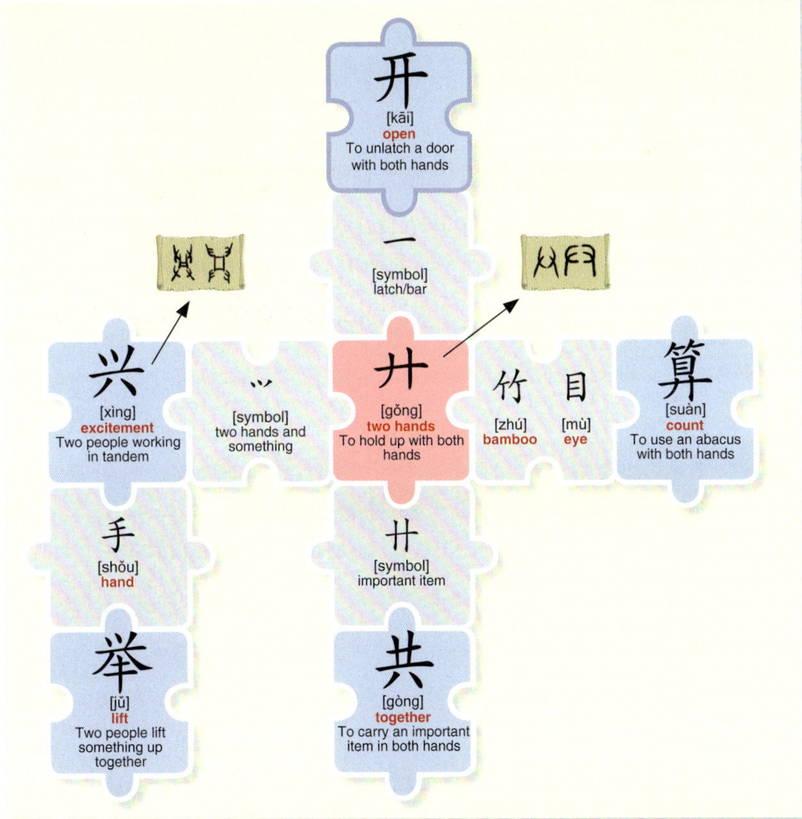

43

43

43 一 ナ 廾

廾 gǒng

two hands

The shape of two hands holding something up wards. The character changes shape when used as part of another character.

43a 一 二 于 开

开 kāi

open

latch/bar 一 [symbol] + two hands 廾 [gǒng]

Using two hands(廾) to push up a latch(一) and open the gate.

开始[kāishǐ] begin; start - 93f
离开[líkāi] leave; depart from - 194a
开玩笑[kāiwánxiào] joke; make fun of - 198a 78a
开学[kāi/xué] school opens; term begins - 95a

43b ノ ト ケ 𠂉 竹 竹 竹 笞 笞 笞 管 筸 算 算

算 suàn

count

bamboo 竹[216] [zhú] + eye 目[11] [mù] + two hands 廾 [gǒng]

Using both hands(廾) to flick bamboo(竹) abacus beads(目) to calculate.

* The abacus came into Asia from Europe around 500 B.C. and the Chinese used bamboo to make them.

打算[dǎsuan] plan - 31c
计算[jìsuàn] count - 22b

43c 一 十 卄 廾 共 共

共 gòng

together

important item 卄 [symbol] + two hands 廾 [gǒng]

To bring two hands(廾) together to carry something important(卄).

* "廾" is shaped like a "one 一[223] [yī]" above an "eight 八[229] [bā]," for aesthetic reasons.

公共汽车[gōnggòngqìchē] bus - 93b 204a 124
一共[yīgòng] altogether - 223
公共[gōnggòng] public - 93b

43d 丶 丷 ⺍ 业 兴 兴

兴 xìng

excitement

two hands and something ⺍ [symbol] + two hands 廾 [gǒng]

To hold something(丶) together, two hands above(丷) and two hands below (廾). It describes two people cheerfully working together.

* The traditional character(興) can be broken down into "same 同[149b][tóng]," "both hands 臼[13a][jiù]" and "廾." It's the cheerfulness of two people(臼, 廾) working together(同).
* If "廾[gǒng]" are the hands facing up, "臼[jiù]" are the two hands facing down.

高兴[gāoxìng] glad; happy - 3 兴趣[xìngqù] interest - 10d

43e 丶 丷 ⺍ 业 兴 兴 兴 举 举

举 jǔ

lift

excitement 兴 [xìng] + hand 扌→手[31][shǒu]

"兴[xìng]" came to mean 'excitement' because it depicts two hands working together, so the Chinese added another hand(手) to accentuate the lifting action.

* Compared to The traditional character(舉), the shape of the hand(手) has changed to "扌"

举行[jǔxíng] hold; stage - 60b

44

其

Diagram for 其

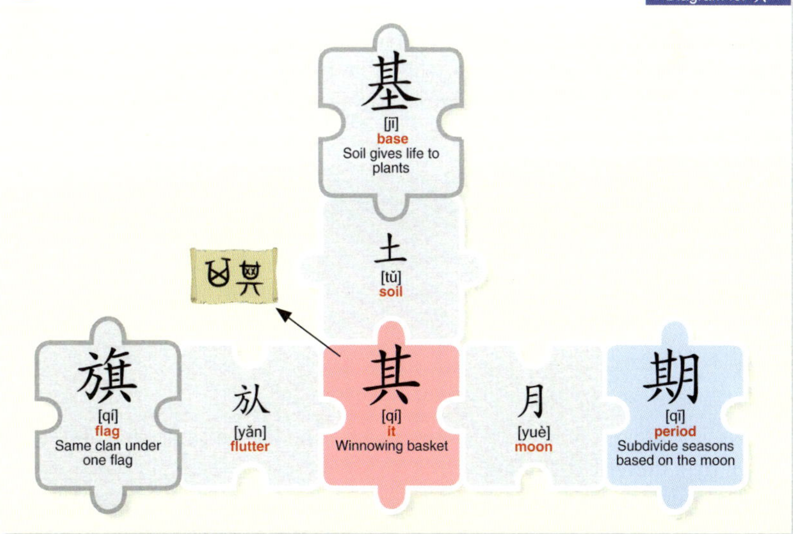

44

44 其 qí — it

一 十 廾 廿 甘 甘 其 其

The shape of a winnowing basket used to sort grain is leaning against a stand (丌[12c]). The character took the meaning of 'it' because that's how people referred to the grain.

* The "丌[jī]" part is the pedestal on which items can be placed.

其实[qíshí] actually; in fact - 75a
其他[qítā] other; else - 84b
尤其[yóuqí] especially; particularly - 80a
极其[jíqí] most; extremely - 36h

44a 基 jī — base

一 十 廾 廿 甘 甘 其 其 其 基 基

winnowing basket/it 其 [qí] + soil 土[152] [tǔ]

Grain that is winnowed(其) is grown from the soil(土).

基本[jīběn] basic - 210a
基础[jīchǔ] base; foundation - 167b

44b 期 qī — period

一 十 廾 廿 甘 甘 其 其 期 期 期 期

winnowing basket/it 其 [qí] + moon 月[221] [yuè]

Before taking grains to winnow(其), farmers checked the moon(月) to ascertain the seasonal period. In Asia where the lunar calendar is still often used, the moon(月) is an important factor when judging the right time or period to sow and harvest.

星期[xīngqī] week - 208b
星期日[xīngqīrì] Sunday - 208b 218
长期[chángqī] long term (period) - 102
短期[duǎnqī] short term (period) - 111d

44c 旗 qí — flag

丶 亠 方 方 方 方 方 旂 旃 旃 旃 旗 旗 旗

flutter 㫃[161] [yǎn] + winnowing basket/it 其 [qí]

People who share winnowed(其) grains lived under the same flag and that is shown by a fluttering(㫃) flag.

红旗[hóngqí] red flag; red banner - 132i

关

Diagram for 关

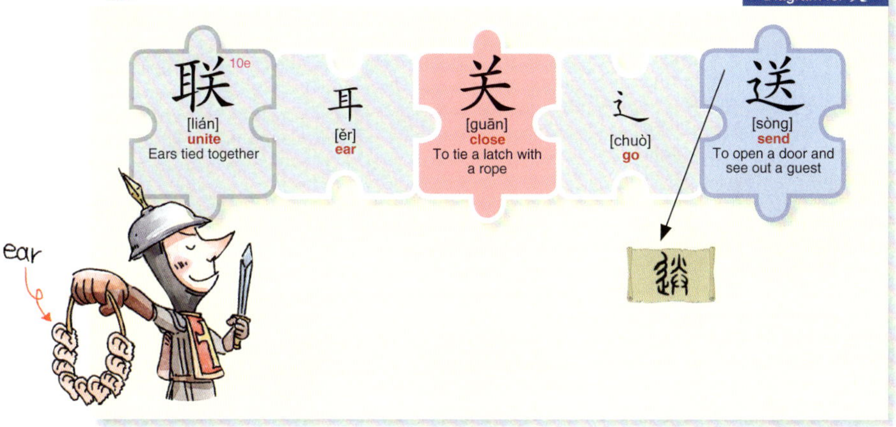

45

丶 丷 丷 兰 关 关

关 guān **close**

If "open 开[43a][kāi]" is two hands(廾[43]) pushing up a latch(一), "关 [guān]" is someone closing a gate and tying it with a rope.

* The traditional character(關) shows a tied-up(丱[symbol]) rope(thread 絲[132a][sī]).

没关系[méiguānxi] it doesn't matter - 117f 132b　关系[guānxì] relation - 132b
关心[guānxīn] concern; interest; attention - 28　关于[guānyú] concerning; regarding - 121d
海关[hǎiguān] customhouse; customs - 97b

45

45a

丶 丷 丷 兰 关 关 关 送 送

送 sòng **send**

close 关 [guān] + go 辶[61][chuò]

To let a guest leave, one must open the closed(关) door so the guest can go out(辶).

* The ancient character shows a person holding up a light or fire(火[158]) with both hands(廾[43]), sending off the guest who is leaving(辶).

欢送[huānsòng] see off; send off - 23c

勹

46

Diagram for 勹

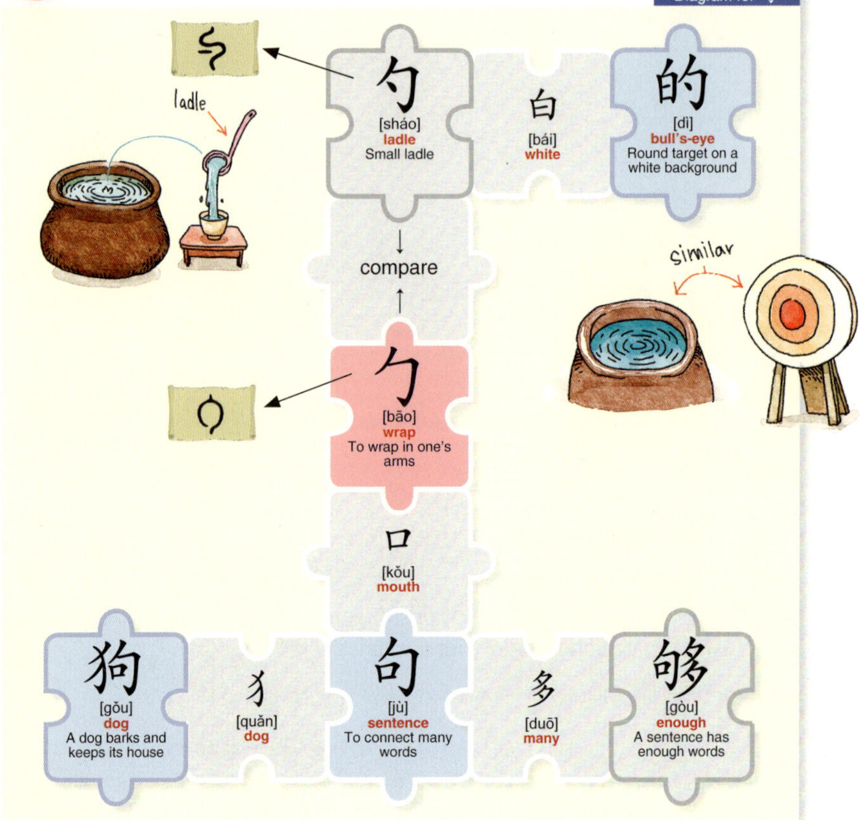

46 丿 勹

勹 bāo	**wrap**

The shape of a pregnant woman or a woman holding a child wrapped in her arms.

46a 丿 勹 勺

勺 sháo	**ladle**

A small ladle used to serve wine from a jar.

* The ancient character shows that it has nothing to do with the "wrap 勹 [bāo]" character.

46b ノ 亻 亣 白 白 白' 的 的

的 dì/de

bull's-eye / <structural particle>

white 白[134] [bái] + ladle 勺 [sháo]

Round ripples shaped like a shooting target form when a ladle(勺) is used to serve wine. Most targets are drawn on white(白) backgrounds so they are visible from a distance.

When this character is used as an independent unit in "Rebus (phonetic loan) script," it functions as a structural particle placed after an attributive(定语), and links the relationship between the modifier and modified.

别的[biéde] other; else - 119e 有的[yǒude] some - 39c
① 'Noun+的+noun.' - 我的父亲。My father. - 113b 46b 98 103a
② 'Verb+的+noun.' - 唱的歌。The song being sung. - 218d 46b 17b
③ 'Adjective+的+noun.' - 漂亮的小姐。Pretty lady. - 126e 3b 46b 235 224a

46c ノ 勹 勹 句 句

句 jù

sentence

wrap 勹 [bāo] + mouth 口[16] [kǒu]

To wrap(勹) the mouth(口) with both arms is an analogical way of saying a sentence is many words(口) brought together(勹).

46

句子[jùzi] sentence - 95

46d ノ 勹 勹 句 句 句' 句' 句' 够 够 够

够 gòu

enough

sentence 句 [jù] + many 多[222d] [duō]

A good sentence(句) does not repeat the same word but the many(多) words must make enough sense.

能够[nénggòu] can; be able to - 89b

46e ノ 犭 犭 犭' 犳 犳 狗 狗

狗 gǒu

dog

dog 犭[173] [quǎn] + sentence 句 [jù]

A faithful dog(犭) keeps barking(句) at a stranger to protect his owner's house.

包

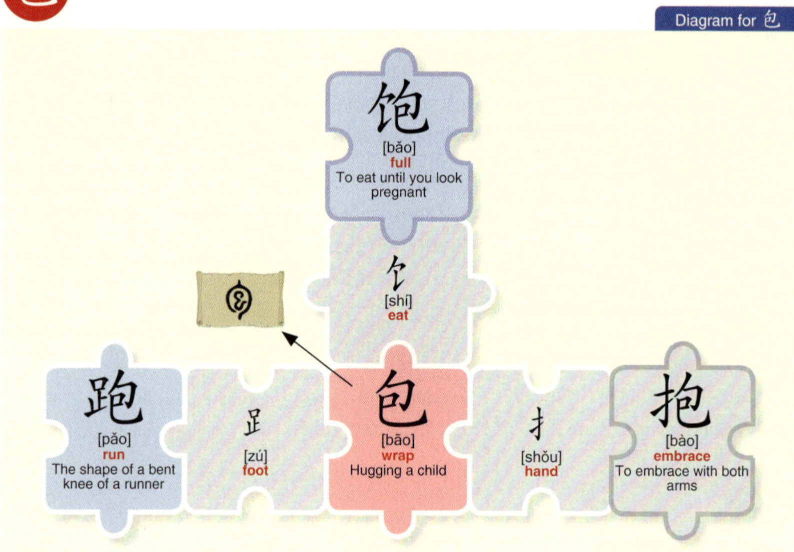

47

47 丿 勹 勺 句 包

包 bāo

wrap

wrap 勹[46][bāo] + unborn child 巳[92][sì]

The shape of a pregnant woman hugging(勹) her unborn child(巳) in her belly, or wrapping(勹) the child(巳) in her two arms.

面包[miànbāo] bread - 10
包含[bāohán] contain; embody; include - 66a
书包[shūbāo] schoolbag; satchel - 232d

47a 丿 𠂊 饣 饣 饣 饣 饣 饱

饱 bǎo

full

eat 饣=食[137][shí] + wrap 包 [bāo]

To be 'full' means you eat(饣) so much that you look like a woman who has a child inside(包) her.

我吃饱了。I ate, so I am full. - 113b 16b 47a 168a

47b 一 十 扌 扌 扚 扚 抱 抱

抱 bào

embrace

hand 扌=手[31][shǒu] + wrap 包 [bāo]

To embrace a child with both arms(扌) as closely as a child is contained(包) in its mother's womb.

母亲抱着孩子。A mother is carrying a child in her arms. - 97 103a 47b 11b 4c 95
一抱衣服。An armful of clothes. - 223 47b 130 34b

47c 丶 口 口 ⻊ ⻊ ⻊ ⻊ ⻊ 趵 趵 跑 跑

跑 pǎo

run

foot ⻊=足[52][zú] + wrap 包 [bāo]

Your arm bends at the elbow when you embrace(包) something with your arms(扌[31]). When you run, your knee moves the same way and your leg(足) bends as if to hug(包) something.

跑步[pǎo/bù] run; march at the double - 53a 逃跑[táopǎo] run away; escape - 129b

48

匃

Diagram for 匃

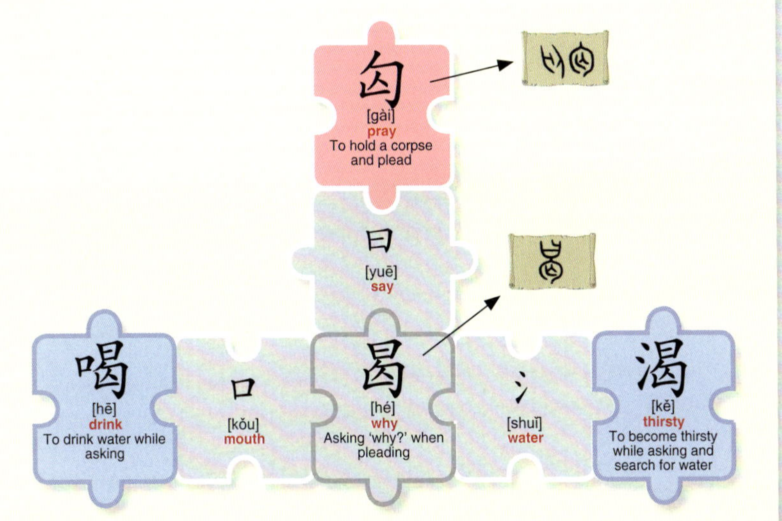

48

丿 勹 勹 勺 匃

匃 gài

pray

wrap 勹[46][bāo] + die 亾→亡[5][wáng]

The shape of a man hugging(勹) a dead person(亡), praying to the gods let him live.

* In ancient characters, "亾" and "亡" are the same character.

48a

丨 冂 日 曰 旦 曷 曷 曷 曷

曷 hé

why

say 曰[10c][yuē] + pray 匃 [gài]

When a family member dies, anyone would shout(曰) and plead(匃) to the gods, asking why they allowed such a thing to happen.

* Ancient characters show that "曰" is not "sun 日[218][rì]" but the shape of someone talking.

48b

丶 丶 氵 氵 沪 沪 沪 沪 渴 渴 渴 渴

渴 kě

thirsty

water 氵[202][shuǐ] + why 曷 [hé]

A person pleading 'Why?(曷)' becomes thirsty and searches for water(氵) to drink.

渴望。To wish earnestly. - 48b 5c

48c

丨 冂 口 口 口 口 口 口 喝 喝 喝 喝

喝 hē

drink

mouth 口[16][kǒu] + why 曷 [hé]

A person pleading 'Why?(曷)' opens his mouth(口) wide to drink water.

请喝杯水。Have a drink of water. - 135c 48c 223b 201

勿

Diagram for 勿

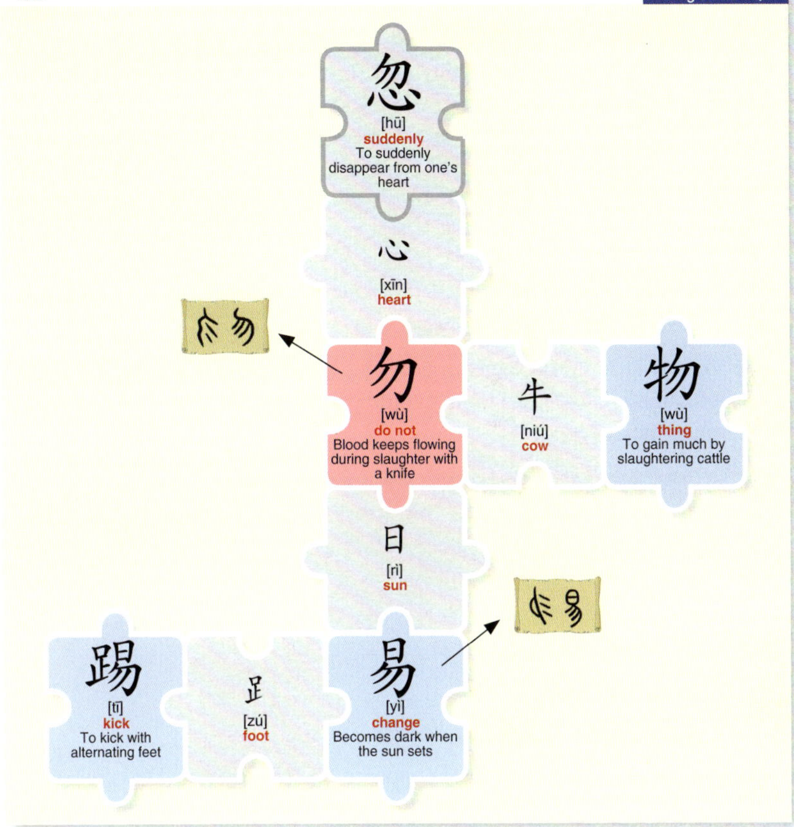

49

49 丿 勹 勺 勿

勿 wù

do not

flowing blood 丿 [symbol] + knife 刀[119] [dāo]

Ancients text suggest it is a description of a slaughtering knife(刀) and flowing blood(丿). Using a knife(刀) to draw blood(丿) is never ideal, so it came to mean 'do not.'

* When "勿" is used to describe inanimate objects, "丿" is the shape of a flying banner or haze.

49a ノ 勹 勺 勿 㔾 忽 忽 忽

忽 hū

suddenly

do not 勿 [wù] + heart 心[28][xīn]

Thoughts and feelings have no physical form and disappear(勿) from one's heart(心) suddenly.

忽然[hūrán] suddenly - 158e

49b ノ 𠂉 牛 牛 𤘅 牞 物 物

物 wù

thing

cow 牛[175][niú] + kill with knife/do not 勿 [wù]

In the ancient agricultural society, cattle(牛) was a valuable possession. When one was slaughtered(勿), the family could gain meat and leather, and purchase other things they needed.

* "勿" describes blood(丿) flowing when the animal is killed with a knife(刀[119]).

动物[dòngwù] animal - 159d
物理[wùlǐ] innate laws of things; physics - 108b
礼物[lǐwù] gift; present - 126g
食物[shíwù] food - 137

49

49c 丨 ㄇ 日 日 旦 㫃 易 易

易 yì

change; easy

sun 日[218][rì] + haze/do not 勿 [wù]

When the sun(日) sets, a haze(勿) appears on the horizon. Day changes to night in a second. Because the sun(日) disappears beyond the horizon fast, this character came to mean 'easy.'

容易[róngyì] easy - 196a

49d 丨 ㄇ 口 ㄗ 𧾷 𧾷 足 跀 跀 跀 跀 跀 踢 踢 踢

踢 tī

kick

foot 𧾷=足[52][zú] + change 易 [yì]

To change(易) feet and kick with the right(𧾷) then the left(𧾷).

踢足球[tīzúqiú] play football - 52 198b
我们的小孩们在踢足球。Our kids are playing football. - 113b 145a 46b 235 4c 145a 32a 49d 52 198b

攵

Diagram for 攵

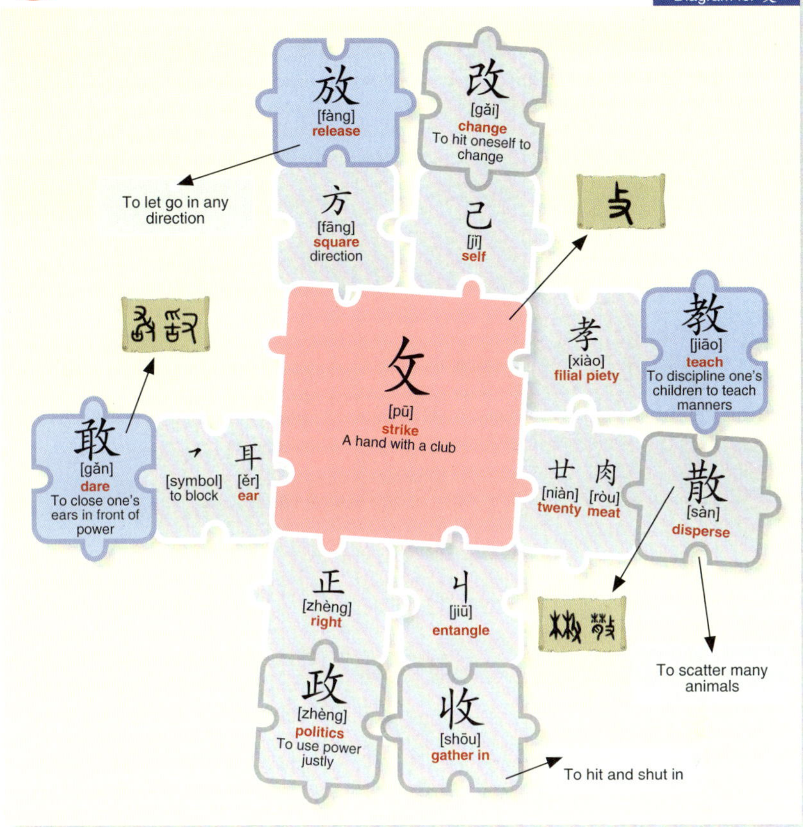

50

50

攵
pū

strike

This character means 'strike' because it is a hand(又[34]) holding a club(丨).

* It is always a hand that beats or whips.

50

50a

丶 亠 亍 方 方 方 放 放

放 fàng

release

direction/square 方[160] [fāng] + strike 攵 [pū]

To whip(攵) and then release a prisoner so he can go in any direction(方) he chooses.

放心 [fàng/xīn] set one's mind (heart) at rest - 28
放假 [fàng/jià] have a holiday or vacation - 34k
解放 [jiěfàng] liberate - 175c

50b

乛 ㇆ 己 己 己 改 改

改 gǎi

change

self 己[82] [jǐ] + strike 攵 [pū]

To change the world, one must first whip(攵) oneself(己) to change for the better.

改变 [gǎibiàn] change - 34c
改革 [gǎigé] reform; reformation - 189b

50c

一 十 土 耂 耂 孝 孝 孝 孝 教 教

教 jiāo/jiào

teach / religion; teach

filial piety 孝[100b] [xiào] + strike 攵 [pū]

If one teaches his/her child with an appropriate amount of discipline(攵), the child will be filial(孝).

* "攵" means discipline because it's the shape of a hand holding a stick.

我教她骑自行车。I taught her to ride a bicycle. - 113b 50c 84c 18a 26 60b 124

Religion is the best teaching.

教室 [jiàoshì] classroom - 112a
教育 [jiàoyù] education - 192b
教师 [jiàoshī] teacher - 131e
教员 [jiàoyuán] teacher - 186h

50d

一 十 廾 廾 艹 昔 昔 昔 昔 昔 散 散

散 sàn

disperse

twenty 廿→龷[143b] [niàn] + meat 月[221] → 肉[192] [ròu] + strike 攵 [pū]

To hit(攵) and scatter twenty(龷) animals(肉) with a stick because they are ruining the crops.

* In ancient texts, "forest(林[212])" describes hitting(攵) with a stick. When one hits a fruit tree with a stick, the fruits fall and scatter.
* "廿" is two "ten 十[231][shí]" characters written to overlap.
* When "moon 月 [yuè]" is part of another character, it means "肉."

散步[sàn/bù] take a walk - 53a

50e

丨 丩 丩' 丩⺧ 收 收

收 shōu

gather in

entangle 丩[16e][jiū] + strike 攵 [pū]

Figuratively speaking, something that is tangled up(丩) means 'something is unruly and needs to be straightened out.' Discipline(攵) is needed to gather things in order and set things right.

* "丩" is the shape of a vine wrapped around a tree.

收拾[shōushi] gather up; put in order; tidy - 31e   收入[shōurù] income - 63e

50f

一 丅 下 正 正 正' 正⺧ 政 政

政 zhèng

politics

right 正[54][zhèng] + strike 攵 [pū]

Politics is power(攵) that should be used justly(正) to improvize the nation and its people.

* "攵" is a hand(又[34]) holding a stick(丨), which symbolizes power that gives the right to punish others.

政府[zhèngfǔ] government - 41a   政治[zhèngzhì] politics - 93e

50g

⺈ 工 干 千 千 千 耳 耳' 耳⺧ 敢 敢

敢 gǎn

dare

to block ⺈ [symbol] + ear 耳[10a][ěr] + strike 攵 [pū]

To block(⺈) one's ears(耳) and dare to face something, even when faced with power(攵).

* The ancient character shows that someone grasps, with his two hands(又[34], 攵), 'fortune(卜[127]),' which is the top part of "occupy 占[127a][zhān]," in order to adamantly challenge God with its force.

敢问。Dare to ask. - 50g 145b

50

支

Diagram for 支

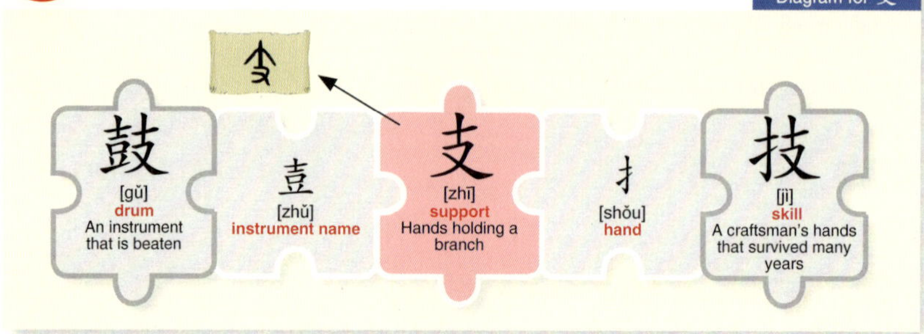

51

支 zhī

support

This character means 'branch' and the ancient texts show a hand(又[34][yòu]) hold-
ing a split branch(十). It also means 'support' because it is the shape of a hand
(又) propping up a branch(十). As it is also the shape of a hand(又) holding a
51 baton(十), it means 'counter used to quantify armies or music.'

支持[zhīchí] support - 42a　　一支歌。One song. - 223 51 17b

51a

技 jì

skill

hand 扌=手[31][shǒu] + support 支 [zhī]

When you see a building that has withstood(支) centuries, you can feel the craftsman's touch(扌) and 'skill and talent.'

技术[jìshù] technique; skill; art - 210f　　技术员[jìshùyuán] technician - 210f 186h

51b

鼓 gǔ

drum

instrument name 壴[140a][zhǔ] + branch/support 支 [zhī]

"壴" is a musical instrument(十) on an altar(豆[140]), which describes an instrument played during ancestral rites. Of those instruments(壴), this points to one played with a branch(支), a 'drum.'

* "Bean 豆 [dòu]" is the shape of a high altar or a ceremonial container.

足

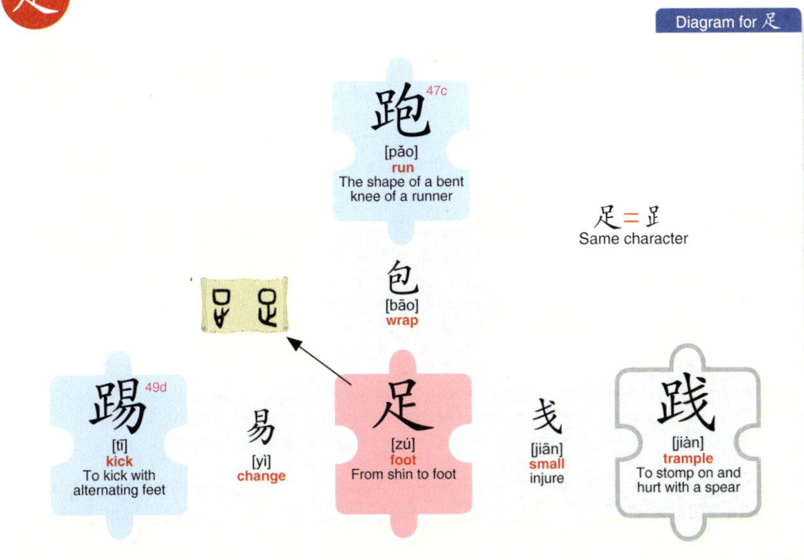

52

52

足 zú

foot

This character means 'foot,' but it refers to the shin, calf, ankle, and foot.

踢足球[tīzúqiú] play football - 49d 198b
足球[zúqiú] soccer; football - 198b
满足[mǎnzú] satisfied; content - 64e

52a

践 jiàn

trample; carry out

foot ⻊=足 [zú] + injure/small 戋[115][jiān]

This character means 'to carry out' a mission because it describes an army stomping on the enemy with their feet(⻊) and harming others with spears (戋).

* "戋" is the shape of two spears(戈[113]) piled together and means 'little volume,' but also means 'to injure.'

实践[shíjiàn] practice; fulfill - 75a

止

Diagram for 止

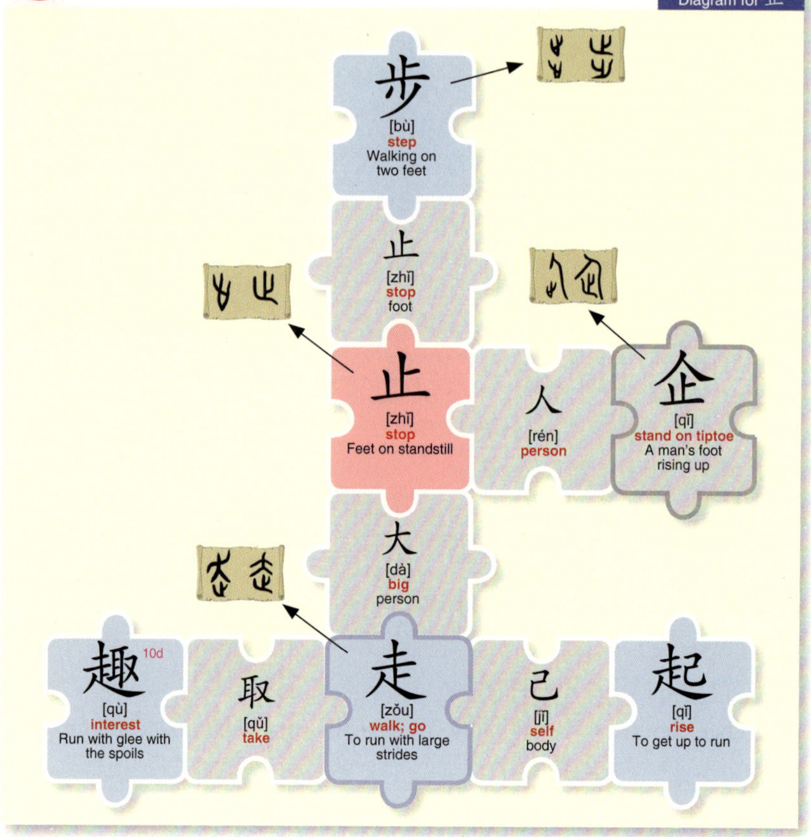

53

53 丨 ⺊ 𣥂 止

止 zhǐ

stop

This character is the shape of a foot that is waiting to move, but because it is not moving at the moment, it means 'stop.'

停止[tíngzhǐ] stop; halt - 225b

53a

丨 ⺊ 𣥂 止 步 步 步

步 bù

step

foot/stop 止 [zhǐ] + foot/stop 少 → 止 [zhǐ]

Two feet(止, 止), the left(止) and the right(止) on the move, walking.

跑步[pǎo/bù] run; march at the double - 47c　散步[sàn/bù] take a walk - 50d
初步[chūbù] first step; initial - 119c

53b

丿 人 个 个 企 企

企 qǐ

stand on tiptoe

person 人[63] [rén] + foot/stop 止 [zhǐ]

A person's(人) foot(止) rising up to get going.

企图[qǐtú] attempt; seek; try - 206f

53c

一 十 土 キ 牛 走 走

走 zǒu

walk; go

person/big 土[152] → 大[74] [dà] + foot/stop 止 [zhǐ]

This character describes a person(大) running with two feet(止), arms moving rapidly and means 'to walk, to go.'

* The ancient character shows that "soil 土 [tǔ]" means 'person(大).'

走道[zǒudào] sidewalk; pavement - 7a

53d

一 十 土 キ 牛 走 走 起 起 起

起 qǐ

rise

run/walk 走 [zǒu] + body/self 己[82] [jǐ]

An athlete raising his body(己) to run(走) as soon as the signal is given.

对不起[duìbuqǐ] I'm sorry - 40c 223a　起床[qǐ/chuáng] get up; rise - 143a
一起[yīqǐ] in the same place; together - 223　起来[qǐlái] stand up; sit up - 212d

53

正

54

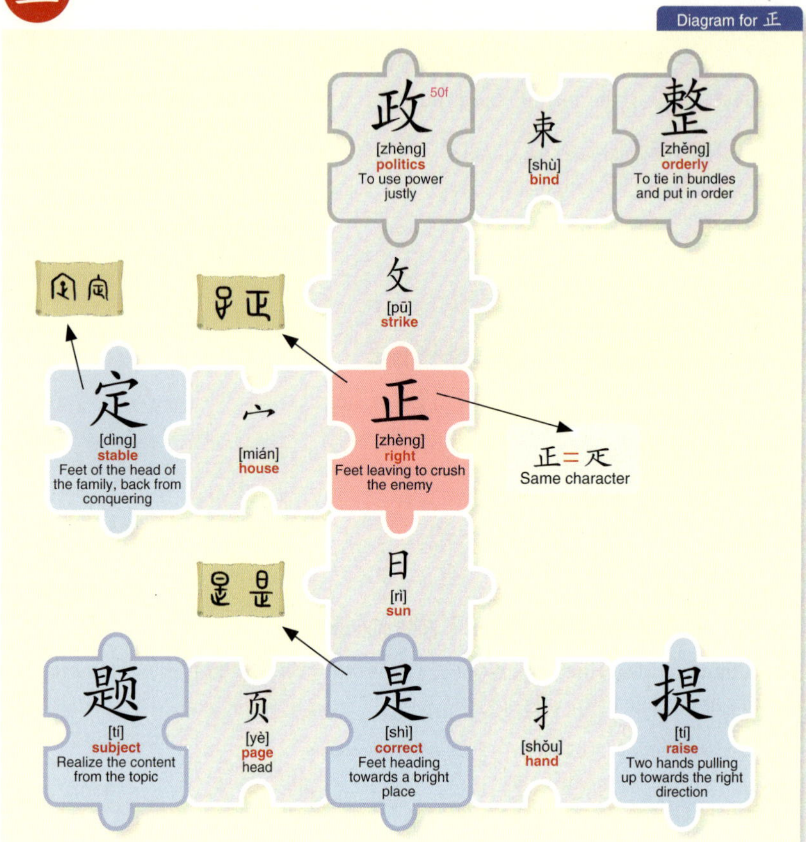

54 一 丅 下 正 正

正 zhèng

right

enemy camp 一 [symbol] + foot/stop 止[53] [zhǐ]

This character describes that the feet(止) of soldiers are off to attack the enemy(一) and means 'to conquer.' To do so is the 'right' thing.

* The ancient character shows ' feet(止) facing a castle(口[20]).'

正在[zhèngzài] in process of; in course of - 32a 真正[zhēnzhèng] genuine; true; real - 12c
正确[zhèngquè] exactness; correct - 191a

54a

一 ｢ ｢ ｢ 市 亩 束 束 束 敕 敕 敕 整 整 整 整

整 zhěng

orderly; whole

bind 束[221a][shù] + strike 攵[50][pū] + right 正 [zhèng]

To tie wood in bundles(束) and tap the ends(攵) so they are easy to carry means to put in order, which is the right(正) thing to do. As bundles of wood become one, it also means 'whole.'

整齐[zhěngqí] orderly; neat; even - 133b　　整个[zhěnggè] whole - 63b

54b

丨 冂 日 日 旦 早 早 是 是

是 shì

correct; this

sun 日[218][rì] + conquer/right 正 [zhèng]

Feet heading out to conquer(正) are facing the sun(日). To head towards the light means it is the right thing to do. One must always try to do 'this,' the right thing.

* The lower part is the same shape as "foot 疋[55][shū]," but the stroke at the top(一) makes it different from "正."

但是[dànshì] but; however - 218b　　还是[háishì] still; nevertheless - 61b
总是[zǒngshì] always - 16f　　可是[kěshì] but; yet - 17
要是[yàoshì] if; suppose; in case - 170b

54

54c

一 十 扌 扌 扣 扣 扣 押 捍 捍 捍 提

提 tí

raise

hand 扌=手[31][shǒu] + correct 是 [shì]

The shape of hands(扌) pulling up or raising something in the correct(是) direction.

提高[tígāo] raise, improve - 3

54d

丨 冂 日 日 旦 早 早 是 是 是 是 是 题 题 题

题 tí

subject

correct 是 [shì] + head/page 页[6][yè]

To be able to tell the contents of a book accurately(是), the subject is written at the head(页), the front of it.

问题[wèntí] question; problem - 145b　　题目[tímù] title; subject; topic - 11

54e 丶 丷 宀 宀 宁 宇 宇 定

定 dìng

stable

house 宀[141] [mián] + conquer/right 正 [zhèng]

Feet that went out to conquer(正) are now heading home(宀). When the head of the family comes home, stability returns.

* Part of this character is the same shape as “foot 疋[55] [shū],” but the stroke at the top(一) makes it different from “正.”

决定[juédìng] decide - 76a
一定[yīdìng] fixed; established; regular - 223
坚定[jiāndìng] firm; steadfast - 106c

54

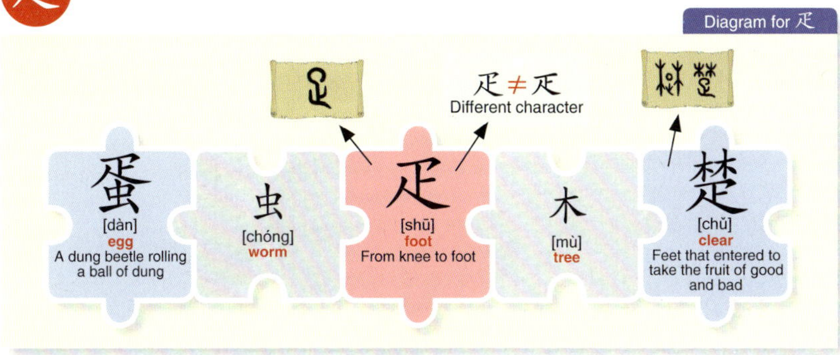

55

疋 shū

foot

It describes the knee to the end of the 'foot.'

55a

楚 chǔ

clear; pain

tree 木[210][mù] + tree 木 [mù] + foot 疋 [shū]

The shape of Eve's feet(疋) as she walked between two trees(林) to get to the tree of the knowledge of good and bad(木) from the tree of life(木), something God had clearly ordered her not to touch. Eating the fruit did not improve man's life like the snake said it would. Genesis 3:18 says the ground is full of 'thorns and thistles,' which means it inflicts pain.

* Why is it Eve's feet? The character for "forbid 禁 [jìn]" means that God(示[126]) forbid her from touching the two trees(林), and "greedy 婪 [lán]" means Eve, the woman(女[96]), desired what they (林) had to offer.

清楚[qīngchu] clear; understand - 135a   苦楚[kǔchǔ] suffering; misery - 19d

55b

蛋 dàn

egg

foot 疋 [shū] + worm 虫[184][chóng]

A dung beetle(虫) rolling a ball of dung larger than itself with its feet(疋) signifies an 'egg.'

鸡蛋[jīdàn] (hen's) egg - 177a   蛋糕[dàngāo] cake - 171d

The Holy Scriptures
禁
The Tree of Life
The Tree of the Knowledge of Good and Bad
The God
楚
婪
The God

夂

Diagram for 夂

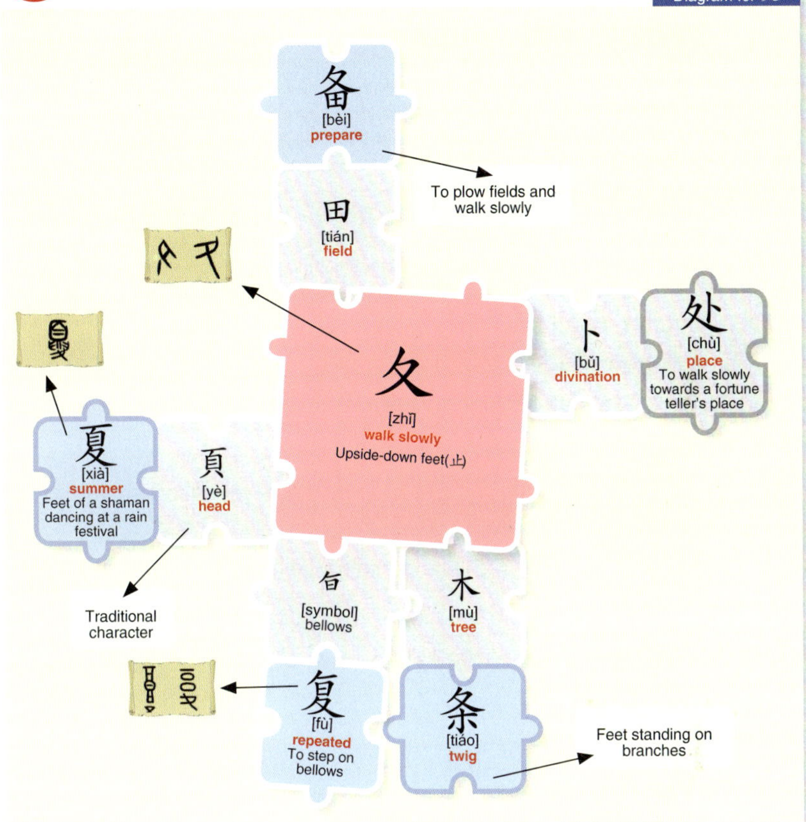

56

丿 ㄅ 夂

56

夂 zhǐ

walk slowly

Upside-down feet(止[53]) because someone pulled a man down from behind. When one is being stopped from walking at normal speed, one has to 'walk slowly or fall behind others.'

56a

丿 ㇇ 夂 夂 各 各 备 备

备 bèi

prepare

walk slowly 夂 [zhǐ] + field 田[154] [tián]

A farmer walking slowly(夂) behind an ox-drawn plow, preparing his field (田) for the next year.

准备[zhǔnbèi] prepare - 178c
设备[shèbèi] equipment; facility - 117e
预备[yùbèi] prepare - 6a

56b

丿 ㇇ 夂 处 处

处 chù/chǔ

place / dwell

walk slowly 夂 [zhǐ] + divination 卜[127] [bǔ]

A fortune teller walking slowly(夂) towards an auspicious place to tell fortunes(卜).

好处[hǎochu] advantage; benefit - 96c
到处[dàochù] everywhere - 112b
坏处[huàichu] harm; disadvantage - 152d

56

Once one has walked slowly(夂) about and found a place to tell fortunes(卜), one can decide to live there.

处理[chǔlǐ] handle - 108b

56c

丿 ㇇ 夂 夂 各 条 条

条 tiáo

twig

foot/walk slowly 夂 [zhǐ] + tree 木[210] [mù]

Feet(夂) carefully stepping on twigs to climb a tree(木). This character is also used to count long and thin objects or living things like branches.

* To signify a man climbing a tree, the inverted shape of a foot "夂" was used.

面条[miàntiáo] noodles - 10
面条儿[miàntiáor] noodles - 10 71
条件[tiáojiàn] condition; qualification - 175a
三条河。Three streams of rivers. - 223e 56c 17d

56d

丿 ㇒ 𠂉 𠂊 ⺈ 旨 复 复 复

复 fù

repeated

bellows 旨 [symbol] + foot/walk slowly 夂 [zhǐ]

Ancient texts show that this character originally took the shape of a foot(夂) stepping on bellows(畐). Bellows inflate and deflate repeatedly.

复习 [fùxí] review - 182a
复杂 [fùzá] complicated - 230b
复印 [fùyìn] duplicate; copy - 87b

56e

一 丆 丆 丙 百 百 頁 頁 夏 夏

夏 xià

summer

head 頁 → 页[6](simplified)[yè] + foot/walk slowly 夂 [zhǐ]

Some say this character describes a shaman(頁) with wildly dancing feet(夂). Of all the rites, the most important was to pray for rain, so in the Eastern Zhou (东周, 770~256 BC) Dynasty, this character came to mean 'summer.'

* "頁" the top part of "夏 [xià]," is the shaman dancing in a long-sleeved outfit and shows both hands (臼[43d]). When a shaman is dancing in a trance, the feet look like they are upside down, which is why "夂" was used.

夏天 [xiàtiān] summer - 74b

56

各

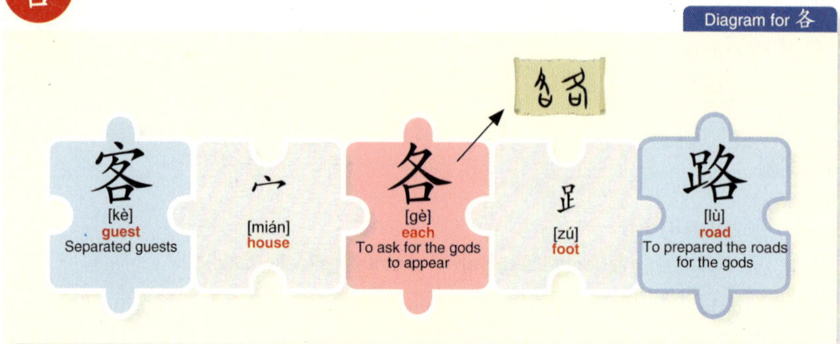

57 丿 ク 夂 夂 各 各

各 gè

each; every

foot/walk slowly 夂 [zhǐ] + mouth 口[16][kǒu]

If "止[53][zhǐ]" is a foot facing upwards, "夂" is a foot facing downwards. So "各" is a mouth(口) begging the gods for help and feet(夂) facing the mouth. Everyone wishes(口) that the gods would come(夂) and help them.

57

各种[gèzhǒng] every kind - 232c

57a 丨 口 口 早 早 足 足 足 𧾷 跄 路 路 路

路 lù

road

foot ⻊=足[52][zú] + each 各 [gè]

A combination of "各," means that all people wish for the gods to come and help, and "足," means that the gods are coming. To welcome the gods, one must prepare the roads.

道路[dàolù] road; way; path - 7a   马路[mǎlù] street; road - 176

57b 丶 丶 宀 宀 宀 安 安 客 客

客 kè

guest

house 宀[141][mián] + each 各 [gè]

Men together in one house(宀) but separated(各) is 'a guest.'

不客气[búkèqi] impolite; you're welcome - 223a 204   客人[kèrén] guest - 63
客气[kèqi] polite; courteous - 204   乘客[chéngkè] passenger - 88d

舛

Diagram for 舛

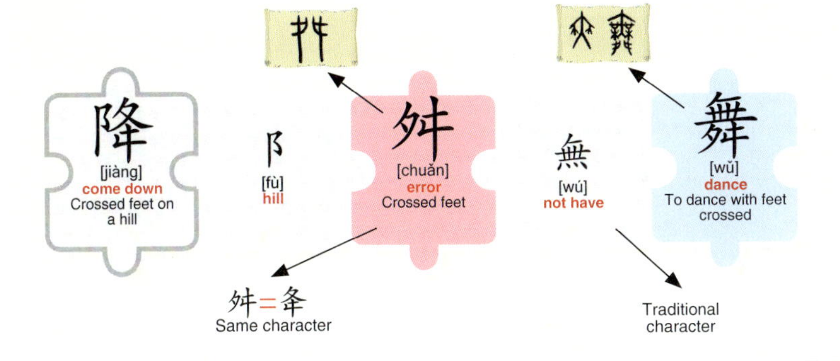

58

舛 chuǎn

error

The character on the left, "evening 夕[222][xī]," is a variation of the downward-turned foot "夂[56][zhǐ]." The character on the right is a shape of a foot(㐄→止[53]), and when used together it means 'error,' because feet should face the same direction, not be crossed. 58

58a

舞 wǔ

dance

not have 無→无[80c](simplified)[wú] + crossed feet/error 舛 [chuǎn]

"無" is the shape of a shaman holding a sacred object like feathers and dancing in a trance, so fast that the feet are only visible as four dots(灬). When this character took the meaning of 'non-existant,' the Chinese added "舛," to mean two crossed feet to dance.

* Even now in China, shamans dance with swords decorated with feathers or tassels.

跳舞[tiào/wǔ] dance - 129a

鼓舞[gǔwǔ] inspire; hearten; stimulate - 51b

58b

降 jiàng

come down

hill 阝[147][fù] + crossed feet/error 舛 [chuǎn]

Feet crossed(舛) on top of a hill(阝). When this happens, you will fall down.

癶

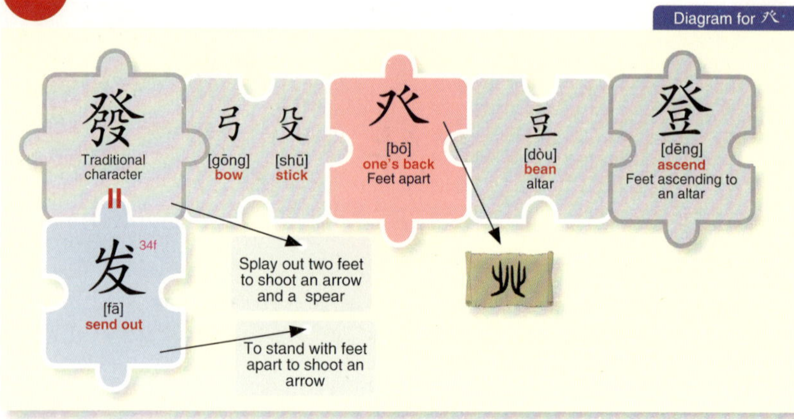

59　　　　フ ヲ ヺ ヺ' 癶

癶
bō

one's back; splay

59 Two feet splayed apart or upward means 'to part.' When this character is included, think of feet.

59a　　　　フ ヲ ヺ ヺ' 癶 癶 癶 昝 昝 昝 登 登

登
dēng

ascend

two feet/one's back 癶 [140] [bō] + altar/bean 豆 [dòu]

Two feet(癶) ascending to a high altar(豆) to offer a sacrifice to the gods.

* "豆" is a high altar or a ceremonial vessel.

登记[dēngjì] register; check in; enter one's name - 82b

彳

Diagram for 彳

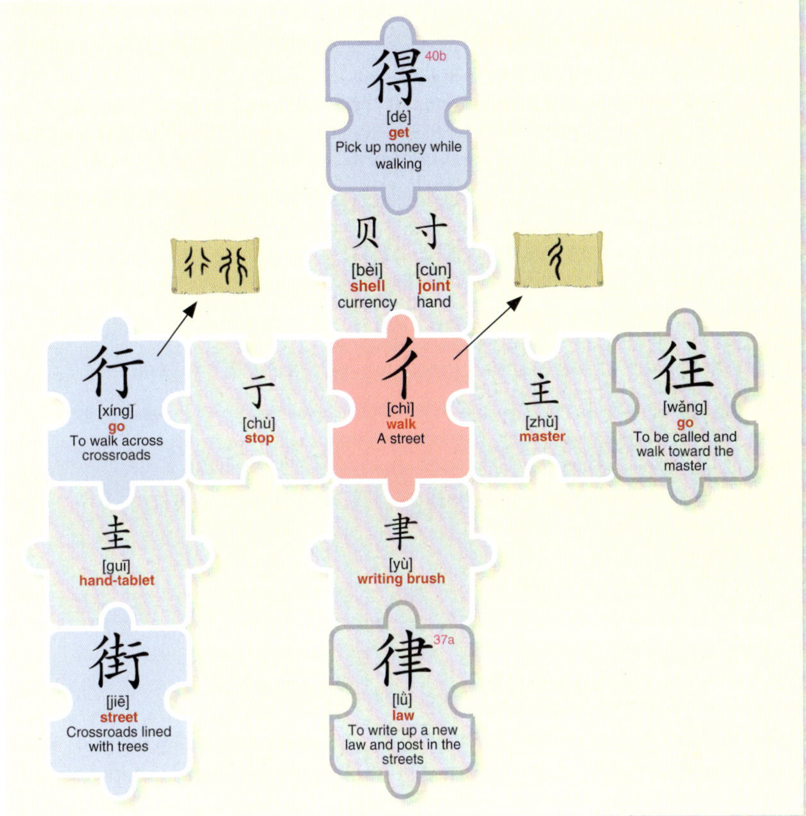

60

60

ノ 彡 彳

彳 chì **walk**

The left side of "go 行[60b][xíng]," which is a crossroad. It means 'road, walk.'

* We can tell this character is association with feet from the meanings 'road' and 'walk.'

60a

丿 彡 彳 彳' 彳' 彳' 往 往

往 wǎng

go; toward

walk 彳 [chì] + master 主[233c][zhǔ]

To be summoned and walk(彳) toward one's master(主). The pronunciation comes from The traditional character of "主," which is "king 王[108][wáng]."

你往南，我往北。You go south and I go north. - 69a 60a 231b, 113b 60a 88c

60b

丿 彡 彳 彳 彳 行

行 xíng

go; walk

walk 彳 [chì] + stop 亍 [chù]

Taking the shape of a crossroad, this character means 'to go, walk.'

* "彳" is the left of the crossroad, "亍" is the right. Neither character(彳, 亍) is used on its own.

自行车[zìxíngchē] bicycle - 26 124
行李箱[xínglǐxiāng] suitcase; trunk (boot) - 95c 216a
进行[jìnxíng] progress; advance - 228b
举行[jǔxíng] hold; stage - 43e
银行[yínháng] bank - 14d
旅行[lǚxíng] travel - 63i

60

60c

丿 彡 彳 彳 彳 彳 彳 彳 彳 彳 彳 街

街 jiē

street

crossroads/go 行 [xíng] + hand-tablet 圭[153][guī]

This character means 'street' because a crossroad(行) lined with trees looks just like king's men standing in rows holding their ceremonial scepters(圭).

* "圭" is a decorative plaque or scepter that the king's subjects carried for ceremonies.

街道[jiēdào] street; road; way - 7a
大街[dàjiē] avenue; street; main street - 74

辶

Diagram for 辶

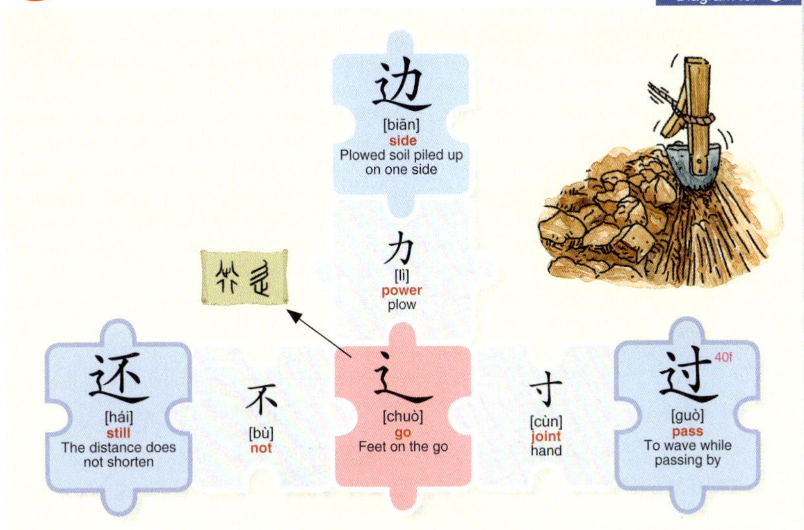

61

61

丶 辶 辶

辶 chuò **go**

The ancient character shows a combination of "crossroad/go 行[60b][xíng]" and "foot/stop 止[53][zhǐ]," which means 'a road describing distance,' or 'to go.'

61a

㇆ 力 力 边 边

边 biān **side**

plow/power 力[159][lì] + go 辶 [chuò]

A furrow is made when a plow(力) passes(辶), and soil pushed to one side piles up.

* "力" is the shape of a plow.

旁边[pángbiān] lateral; side - 160b
左边[zuǒbian] the left side - 39a
北边[běibiān] north side - 88c
后边[hòubian] back; rear; behind - 18d
南边[nánbian] south side - 231b
上边[shàngbian] upside - 223f
西边[xībiān] west side - 170
右边[yòubian] the right side - 39b
一边[yìbiān] one side - 223
东边[dōngbiān] east side - 211
里边[lǐbian] inside - 151
前边[qiánbiān] in front; ahead - 221a
外边[wàibian] outside - 222a
下边[xiàbian] below; under - 223g
一边…一边…[yībiān...yībiān...] two actions taking place simultaneously - 223
(他们一边工作一边学习。They work and learn at the same time.) - 84b 145a 223 61a 200 234b 223 61a 95a 182a

一 丆 不 不 不 还 还

还
hái/huán

still / go (come) back

not 不[223a] [bù] + road/go 辶 [chuò]

When "辶" is used about a road, it's about the distance. This describes the situation when one is on the road(辶), but the distance is still not(不) decreasing.

还是 [háishi] still; nevertheless - 54b

When one is on the road(辶) but is not(不) getting anywhere, there is a high chance he will turn back.

还东西。To return something. - 61b 211 170

61

廴

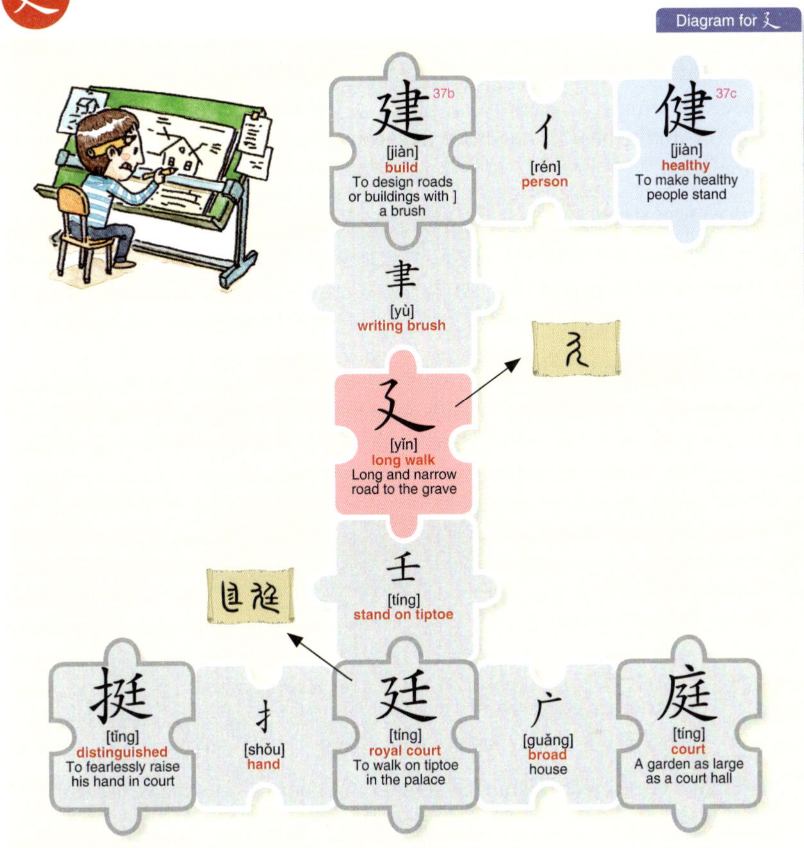

62

62

廴 yǐn

long walk

This character describes a long and narrow road to the king's tomb, to mean 'a long walk, a narrow road.'

* King's tombs contain many treasures and artifacts, so they were designed to be reached only by a long and narrow road. Think of a man walking carefully.

62a

丿 二 千 壬 廷 廷

廷 tíng

royal court

stand on tiptoe 壬[105][tíng] + long walk 廴 [yǐn]

Subjects walking(廴) carefully on tiptoe(壬) in court. "壬" is the shape of a foot(止[53]) with the heel lifted above the ground and also gives the character its pronunciation.

* "壬" is the same shape as "9th/10th 壬[105][rén]," but a completely different character.

62b

丶 亠 广 广 庐 庄 庄 庭 庭

庭 tíng

court; hall

house/broad 广[143][guǎng] + royal court 廷 [tíng]

In the olden days, most large Asian houses had a yard without walls within the house. The meaning 'yard, hall' originated from it being a large space like a court(廷) within a house(广).

* "广" is the shape of a house with one wall taken down.

家庭[jiātíng] family - 174a

62

62c

一 寸 扌 扌 扌 扌 扌 挺 挺

挺 tǐng

distinguished; very

hand 扌=手[31][shǒu] + royal court 廷 [tíng]

A distinguished subject raising his hand(扌) in court(廷) to speak his mind. It also implies that it is a very difficult thing to do.

我们都挺喜欢他的。We all like him very much. - 113b 145a 101a 62c 140a 23c 84b 46b

PEOPLE | PERSON | "人"

人

Diagram for 人

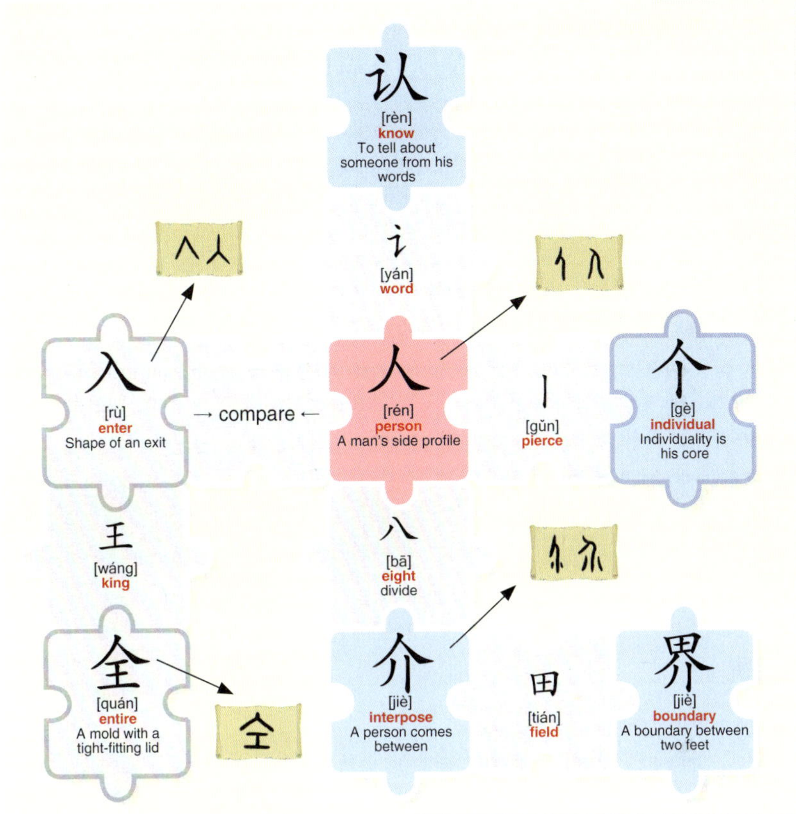

63

63

丿 人

人 rén

person

The side profile of a person, and means 'man.'

男人[nánrén] man - 159a	女人[nǚrén] woman - 96
别人[biérén] other people; others - 119e	客人[kèrén] guest - 57b
爱人[àiren] spouse - 34e	夫人[fūren] lady; madam; Mrs. - 74a
工人[gōngrén] worker; workman - 200	人们[rénmen] people - 145a
人民[rénmín] the people - 99c	

63

63a

` 讠 讠 认

认
rèn

know

word 讠=言[22] [yán] + person 人 [rén]

One can know a lot about a person(人) from his accent and what he says(讠).

认识 [rènshi] recognize; know - 179b
认为 [rènwéi] think; consider - 159c
认真 [rènzhēn] earnest; serious - 12c

63b

丿 人 个

个
gè

individual; <quantifier>

person 人 [rén] + pierce 丨[232] [gǔn]

Every person has a personality, a character(个性) that sets him apart from others. As that is the core of a person(人), adding a stroke(丨) in the middle gave the meaning 'individually.' Now this character is used to count objects.

* " 丨 " is 'the center, the middle.'

那个 [nàge] that one - 147e
这个 [zhège] this one - 133a
个性 [gèxìng] individuality - 28c
哪个 [nǎge] which - 147f
整个 [zhěnggè] whole - 54a

63c

丿 人 个 介

介
jiè

interpose; introduce

person 人 [rén] + divide/eight 八[229] [bā]

A person(人) interjects into something that is divided in two(八) to solve a problem or to introduce others.

介绍 [jièshào] introduce; present - 120a

63d

丨 冂 冂 田 田 罒 臾 界 界

界
jiè

boundary

field 田[154] [tián] + interpose 介 [jiè]

"田 [tián]" is a ditch dividing two rice paddies and means 'rice paddy, farming land.' This character is the boundary between(介) two fields(田).

世界 [shìjiè] world - 207f

63e 丿 入

入 rù

enter

The entrance to a cave or mud hut. It means 'to enter.'

* It is a radical but no one is sure of the origin. Not to be confused with "person 人 [rén]."

深入[shēnrù] go deep into - 202c

63f 丿 入 亼 仒 仝 全

全 quán

entire

enter 入 [rù] + king 王[108] [wáng]

A mold with a body(王) and lid(入) that fits the mold completely.

* Regardless of the shape, "王" is the container and "入" is the lid.
* The ancient character(仝) describes a mold used to make farming tools(work 工[200] [gōng]) and its lid(口).

全部[quánbù] whole; entire - 79f
全体[quántǐ] all; entire - 29b
完全[wánquán] perfect; complete; entire - 73a
安全[ānquán] safe; secure - 96a

63

人

Diagram for 从

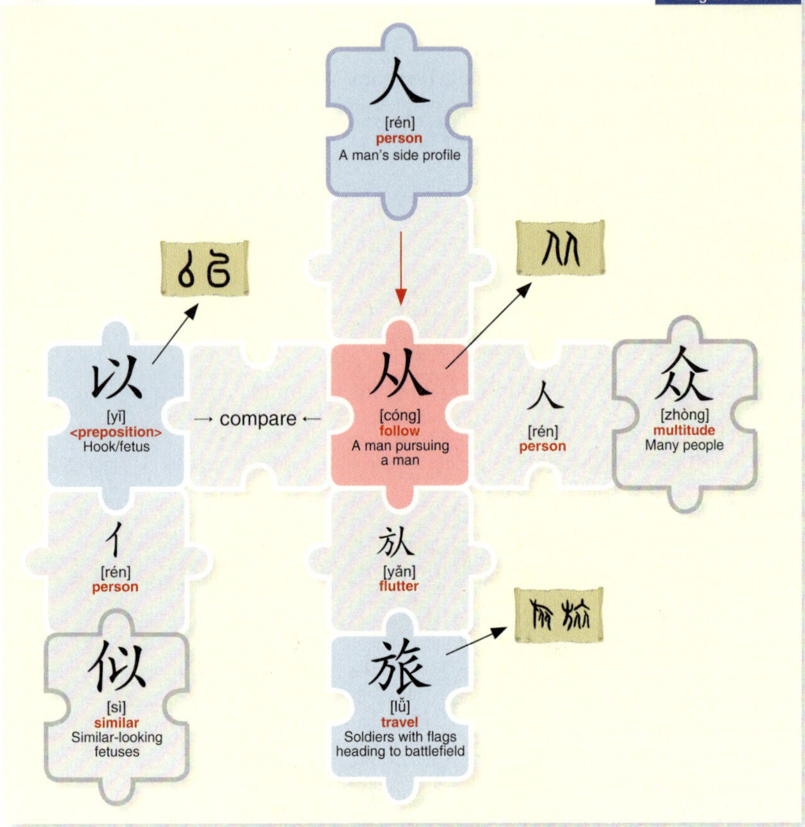

63

63g 丿 人 从 从

从 cóng

follow; from

person 人 [rén] + person 人 [rén]

The ancient character shows two people(人人), one(人) running after the other(人). It is also used as a preposition meaning 'from,' 'for how long.'

从…到…[cóng···dào···] from···to - 112b 从前[cóngqián] before; formerly - 221a

63h

众 zhòng

multitude

person 人 [rén] + follow 从 [cóng]

Three overlapping "人" means many people.

观众[guānzhòng] audience; spectator; viewer - 13b

63i

旅 lǚ

travel

flutter 方→㫃[161][yǎn] + two people/follow 𠂆→从 [cóng]

'Two men(从) under a fluttering(㫃) flag' describes 'soldiers heading to war.' It came to mean 'travel' because soldiers fight away from home.

旅游[lǚyóu] trip; travel - 161b
旅行[lǚxíng] travel - 60b

63j

以 yǐ

<preposition>

Some say it's a hook, some say it's a fetus. Farming begins with plowing the fields and life begins as a fetus. This character is a preposition describing the cause or means of an action.

* The present character has something that looks like "person 人 [rén]" on the right but not in the ancients texts.

可以[kěyǐ] can; may - 17
所以[suǒyǐ] so; therefore - 144a
以后[yǐhòu] after; later - 18d
以前[yǐqián] before; formerly - 221a
以为[yǐwéi] think; believe; consider - 159c
除了…以外[chúle...yǐwài] except for; but for - 147a 168a 222a

63

63k

似 sì

similar

person 亻[70][rén] + fetus/preposition 以 [yǐ]

A person(亻) added to "以," a plow or a fetus. Regardless of who it is(亻), newborn babies(以) all look too similar to tell apart.

相似[xiāngsì] resemble; be similar - 11c

内

Diagram for 内

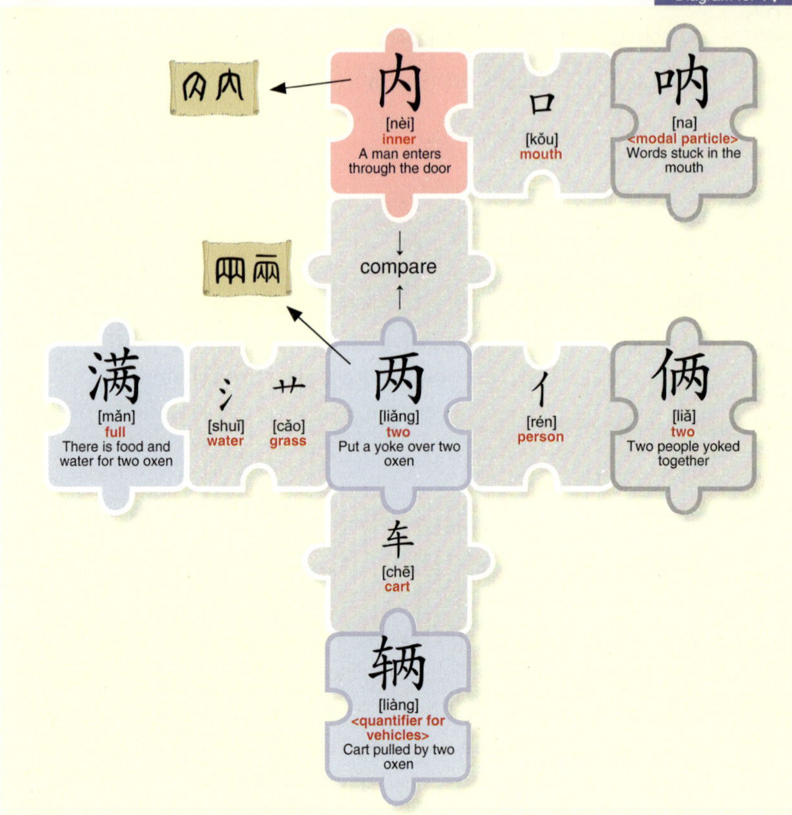

64

64 丨 冂 内 内

内 nèi

inner

entrance 冂 [symbol] + person 人[63][rén]

A man(人) goes inside through the entrance(冂).

内容[nèiróng] content; substance - 196a

内部[nèibù] inside; interior - 79f

64a 丨 ㄇ 口 叼 叼 呐 呐

呐 na

modal particle

mouth 口[16][kǒu] + inner 内 [nèi]

When words(口) are stuck inside(内), it means 'one is stuttering.' But it is also used at the end of a sentence to add coyness to the conversation, which makes it sound colloquial.

* Same usage as "哪[147f][na]." (天[74b]呐！= 天啊！- oh my god!)

谢谢您呐。Thank you. - 27c 27c 69b 64a
你们得小心呐。You need to be careful. - 69a 145a 40b 235 28 64a

64b 一 厂 冂 丙 丙 两 两

两 liǎng

two

yoke 丆 [symbol] + hooked up 冂 [symbol]

To put(冂) a yoke(丆) over two oxen to plow the field.

* A yoke - A curved wooden bar put over a horse or an ox's neck.

* This character is included here because of the part that looks like a person(人[63]), but the meaning has nothing to do with people.

他比我大两岁。He is my senior by two years. - 84b 88a 113b 74 64b 195a

64c 丿 亻 亻 亻 仃 仴 俩 俩 俩

俩 liǎ

two

person 亻[70][rén] + two 两 [liǎng]

This character means 'two' because it's about two(两) people(亻) being connected to a yoke. This character meaning two(两) already mentions it's about people(亻), so a counter is unnecessary. "两" has the same meaning 'two,' but a counter is needed.

你俩吃饭了吗? Have you two eaten? - 69a 64c 16b 148b 168a 176a

64

64d 一 𠃋 𠃋 车 车一 车丆 车丙 车丙 辆 辆 辆

辆 liàng

<quantifier for vehicles>

cart 车[124][chē] + two 两 [liǎng]

Two(两) oxen or horses pulling the same cart(车). This character is used to count vehicles of transportation.

三辆自行车。Three bicycles. - 223e 64d 26 60b 124

64e 丶 丶 氵 氵一 氵十 氵廾 氵芏 氵芏 满 满 满 满 满

满 mǎn

full

water 氵[202][shuǐ] + grass 艹[207][cǎo] + two 两 [liǎng]

It means 'full' because there is enough water(氵) and grass(艹) to feed the two (两) horses or oxen.

满意[mǎnyì] satisfied - 21b　　满足[mǎnzú] satisfied; content - 52

64

亼

Diagram for 合

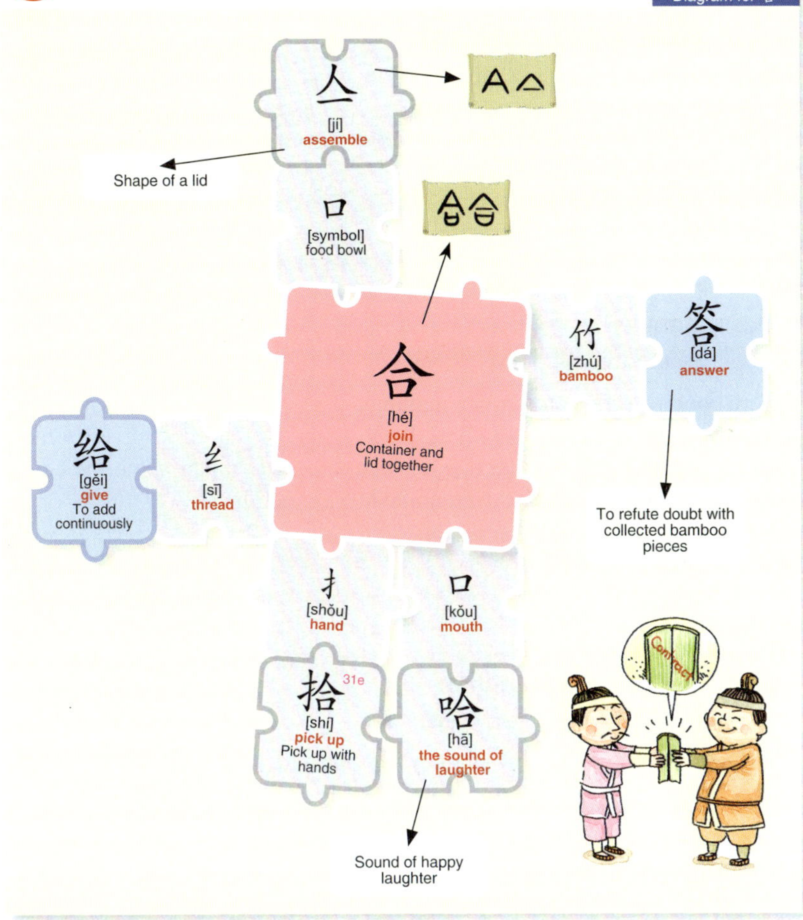

65

65

丿 人 亼

亼
jí

assemble

A container and its lid must be assembled or kept together.

* This character is listed here because of the "person 人[63][rén]" component, not the meaning.

65

65a

丿 人 亼 亽 合 合

合 hé

join

assemble 亼 [jí] + food bowl 口 [symbol]

The lid(亼) and the bowl(口) are joined together.

* Some say that this character describes the time when man spoke one language(口[16]) in one community(亼) before the Tower of Babel had been built. - Genesis 11:1-9

合适[héshì] suitable - 24d　　集合[jíhé] gather; assemble - 178a

65b

丿 𠂉 ⺮ ⺮ ⺮ 竹 竺 笂 笞 答 答 答

答 dá

answer

bamboo 竹[216][jí] + join 合 [hé]

Before paper was invented, when making a deal the Chinese wrote on a piece of bamboo(竹) and broke it in half. Later, when they needed to verify facts, they joined the pieces together(合). When there was doubt about the conditions, the bamboo(竹) pieces were joined(合) to get the answer.

回答[huídá] reply; answer - 20d　　答应[dāying] answer; reply; respond - 143c

65c

丨 冂 口 口丿 叭 哈 哈 哈 哈

哈 hā

the sound of laughter

mouth 口[16][kǒu] + join 合 [hé]

"口" and "合" combined together to record the sound of laughter.

* The sound of laughter(口) brings(合) happiness.

哈哈[hāhā] (an onomatopoeia for laughing)

65d

乚 乡 纟 纟丿 纵 纵 给 给 给

给 gěi

give; to; for

thread 纟[132][sī] + join 合 [hé]

Thread(纟) is used to connect something, so this character has the meaning of adding up(合) with continuous provision of materials. It also has the prepositional meaning of 'to, for.'

给予[jǐyǔ] give - 168b　　把这本书给她。Give her the book. - 92b 133a 210a 232d 65d 84c

给儿子讲故事。Talk to the son. - 65d 71 95 228a 19a 36d

亼

Diagram for 今

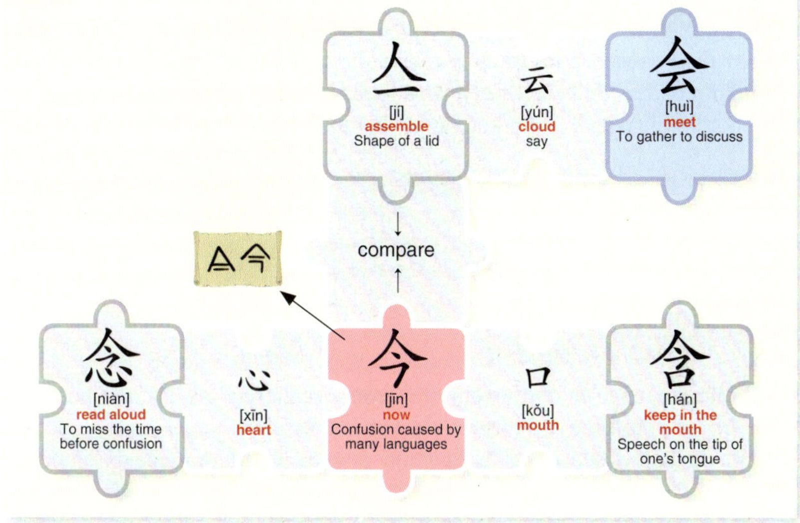

66

丿 人 亼 今

66

今 jīn

now

assemble 亼[65][jí] + to be broken ㇇ [symbol]

Before they built the Tower of Babel, man used one language(口[16]) which made the human beings unite as a single community(亼). But when the tower was built, God became angry with them, and broke(㇇) the languages so they couldn't communicate. Such an important incident changed history, so this character means 'now.' - Genesis 11:1-9

* "㇇" is the shape of a broken "mouth 口 [kǒu]" and symbolizes that one language was broken into many.

今天[jīntiān] today - 74b
今年[jīnnián] this year - 121a
至今[zhìjīn] up to now - 112

66a 丿 人 𠆢 今 今 含 含

含 hán

keep in the mouth

confused language/now 今 [jīn] + mouth 口[16] [kǒu]

When God caused confusion(今) with the languages, people spoke(口) but could not understand each other. This looks like speech(口) on the tip of one's tongue, 'in the mouth,' not knowing what to say.

包含[bāohán] contain; embody; include - 47

66b 丿 人 𠆢 今 今 念 念 念

念 niàn

miss; thought

confused language/now 今 [jīn] + heart 心[28] [xīn]

With the language in confusion(今), people scattered, but in their hearts(心) they missed the time they were one community. The ancestors recorded this and made their descendants 'read aloud' so they wouldn't make the same mistake.

留念[liúniàn] accept(keep) as a souvenir - 87d
概念[gàiniàn] concept; conception - 80f
纪念[jìniàn] commemorate - 82c
想念[xiǎngniàn] long to see again; miss - 11d

66

66c 丿 人 𠆢 亼 会 会

会 huì

meet; can

assemble 亼[65] [jí] + say/cloud 云[227] [yún]

To discuss(云) an issue, people must gather(亼) or meet. When people gather (亼) and discuss(云), good ideas or solutions are obtained, so seemingly impossible things can be done.

会议[huìyì] meeting; conference - 233b
机会[jīhuì] chance; opportunity - 213a
一会儿[yīhuìr] a little while - 223 71
会话[huìhuà] conversation; dialogue - 24b
社会[shèhuì] society - 126h
晚会[wǎnhuì] soiree; evening party - 68b
宴会[yànhuì] banquet; feasty - 96b
你会说英语吗? Do you speak English? - 69a 66c 72d 77a 226c 176a

佥

Diagram for 佥

67

67

丿 人 亼 亼 佥 佥 佥

佥 qiān

all

assemble 亼[65] [jí] + many people 𭕄 [symbol]

Many people(𭕄) are all gathered(亼) in one place.

* The traditional character(僉) shows many people(人[63] 人) all gathered(亼) in one place and speaking(口[16] 口).

67

67a 阝 阝 阝 阶 阶 阶 险 险 险

险 xiǎn

danger

hill 阝[147][fù] + all 佥 [qiān]

A hill(阝) that is in everybody's(佥) way is a large mountain or obstacle, which is where the meaning 'danger' comes from.

危险[wēixiǎn] dangerous - 68e

67b 一 十 木 木 杉 杉 枪 枪 检 检 检

检 jiǎn

check up

tree 木[210][mù] + all 佥 [qiān]

All(佥) the people are checking the trees(木) to see if they are good building material.

检查[jiǎnchá] inspect; examine - 224c

67c 马 马 马 马 驴 驴 验 验 验 验

验 yàn

test

horse 马[176][mǎ] + all 佥 [qiān]

All(佥) the people are testing the horses(马) by making them run and jump.

* Part of the character "check up 检[67b][jiǎn]" is a tree(木), which is a plant on which tests can be run. But a horse is an animal whose build and movement cannot be tested in a lab. Remember the difference.

经验[jīngyàn] experience - 132e　　试验[shìyàn] experiment; test; trial - 110b

67d 丿 月 月 月 肞 肞 脍 脍 脸 脸 脸

脸 liǎn

face

meat 月[221] → 肉[192][ròu] + all 佥 [qiān]

Of all(佥) the parts of one's body(肉), the face is the most memorable.

* "Moon 月 [yuè]" means "肉" when part of another character.

你每天都要洗脸。Wash your face every day. - 69a 97a 74b 101a 170b 71e 67d
他很要脸。He thinks much of saving face. - 84b 14a 170b 67d

⺈

Diagram for ⺈

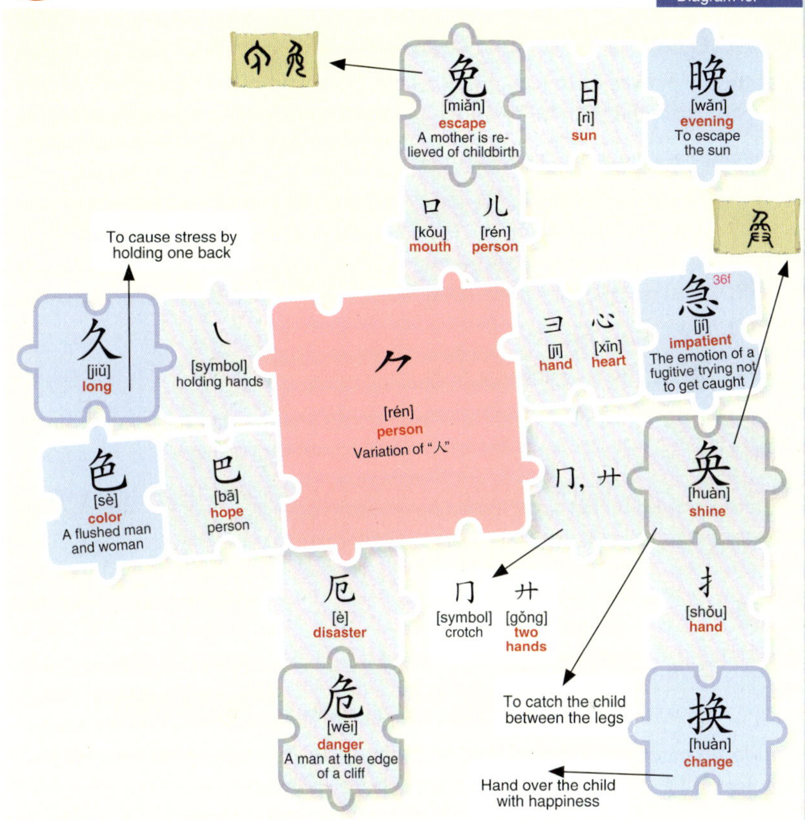

68

68 ノ ⺈

⺈ rén

person

Has a different shape but means the same as "person 人[63] [rén]." But it sometimes is used to give a different meaning to a character. The same shape doesn't necessarily mean that it always has the same meaning.

68

68a

丿 𠂊 𠂊 𠂊 𠂊 免 免

免 miǎn

escape

person 𠂊 [rén] + mouth 口[16] [kǒu] + person 儿[71] [rén]

A mother(𠂊) gives birth to a child(儿) from her womb(口). It signifies she has 'escaped' from the pain, or from the guilt of not being able to bear children.

* In the past, not being able to have children was reason for divorce in China.

不免[bùmiǎn] unavoidable - 223a

68b

丨 冂 日 日 日' 日⺈ 日⺈ 晚 晚 晚 晚

晚 wǎn

evening; late

sun 日[218] [rì] + escape 免 [miǎn]

To escape(免) the sun(日) means it is evening. As the day has ended, it also means late.

晚上[wǎnshang] (in the) evening; (at) night - 223f
晚饭[wǎnfàn] supper; dinner - 148b
晚会[wǎnhuì] soiree; evening party - 66c
夜晚[yèwǎn] night - 222b

68c

丿 𠂊 𠂊 𠂊 𠂊 奂 奂

奂 huàn

shine

person 𠂊 [rén] + crotch 冂 [symbol] + two hands 大→廾[43] [gǒng]

A midwife catches the child with both hands(廾) from between the mother's (𠂊) legs(冂). For a woman, childbirth is the most amazing miracle, a 'shining' accomplishment.

68d

一 十 扌 扌 扌 扌 扌 扌 换 换

换 huàn

change

hand 扌=手[31] [shǒu] + shine 奂 [huàn]

With her hands(扌), the midwife hands over the child to the mother who is shining(奂) with happiness. As she is now a mother, this character signifies change.

兑换[duìhuàn] exchange - 72c
交换[jiāohuàn] exchange; swap - 1a

68e

丿 ⺈ ⺈ 产 产 危

危
wēi

danger

person ⺈ [rén] + disaster 厄[85a] [è]

A man(⺈) standing dangerously at the edge of a cliff, where 'falling' means certain disaster(厄).

* "厄" is the shape of a man hunched(㔾[85]) at the edge of a cliff(厂[148]).

危险[wēixiǎn] dangerous - 67a　　危机[wēijī] crisis; crunch - 213a

68f

丿 ⺈ ⺈ ⺈ 色 色

色
sè

color

person ⺈ [rén] + person/hope 巴[92a] [bā]

One person(⺈) on top of another(巴) making love. As they will both be flushed, this character means 'color.'

* "巴" is a fat baby and means 'person.'

颜色[yánsè] color; countenance - 8f　　彩色[cǎisè] multicolored; color - 8b

68

68g

丿 ク 久

久
jiǔ

long; for a long time

person ⺈ [rén] + holding hands ㇏ [symbol]

The shape of a person(⺈) pulling someone else back(㇏). When one is being stopped from walking at normal speed, it takes 'a long time.'

不久[bùjiǔ] soon; before long - 223a　　好久[hǎojiǔ] for a long time; long - 96c

尔

Diagram for 尔

69

尔 ěr

you

person 𠆢[68] [rén] + small 小[235] [xiǎo]

Any man wants to be better than another. This character says 'you' are a smaller(小) person(𠆢). It also means 'this, that.'

69a

69

你 nǐ

you

person 亻[70] [rén] + you 尔 [ěr]

When "尔" became a demonstrative pronoun, the Chinese added "亻" to stress the meaning of 'you.'

你们[nǐmen] you (plural) - 145a
你会说英语吗? Do you speak English? - 69a 66c 72d 77a 226c 176a

69b

您 nín

you (formal)

you 你 [nǐ] + heart 心[28] [xīn]

The Chinese added "心" to make a more polite version of 'you(你).' One must have the heart(心) to respect and honor someone else.

谢谢您，先生。Thank you, sir. - 27c 27c 69b, 71d 208

亻

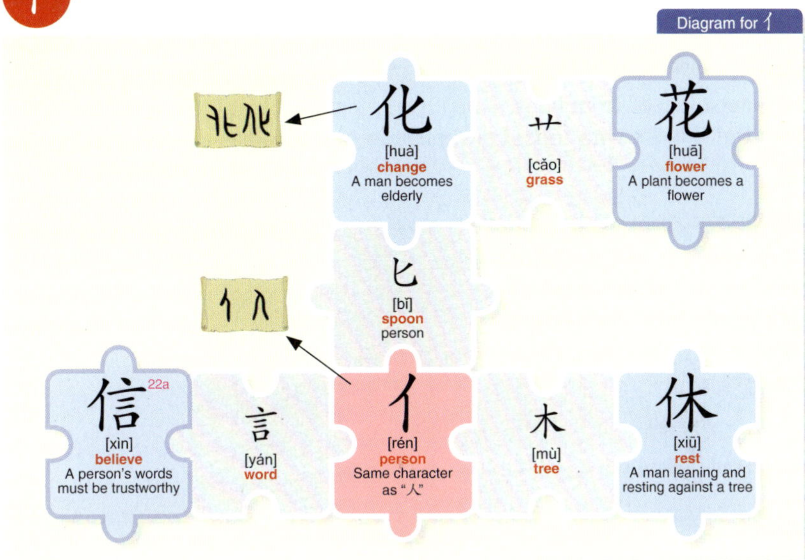

70

70 丿 亻

亻 rén **person**

It looks different, but it is the same character for "person 人[63][rén]." This shape is only taken when it's on the left of a more complicated character.

70a 丿 亻 亻' 化

化 huà **change**

person 亻[rén] + person/spoon 𠤎→匕[88][bǐ]

A man standing(亻) and a man upside down(匕). A person(亻) is born a baby but dies an old man(匕), which means everything changes.

变化[biànhuà] change - 34c	文化[wénhuà] culture - 133
化学[huàxué] chemistry - 95a	化石[huàshí] fossil - 197

70b 一 十 艹 艹 芢 花 花

花 huā

flower; spend

grass 艹[207] [cǎo] + change 化 [huà]

As a person goes from baby to an elderly person, plants(艹) change(化) into beautiful flowers with time. For a plant to bloom, it has to 'spend' time and energy.

花园[huāyuán] garden - 73c
鲜花[xiānhuā] fresh flower; flower - 185a
雪花[xuěhuā] snowflake - 205a

70c 丿 亻 仁 什 付 休

休 xiū

rest

person 亻 [rén] + tree 木[210] [mù]

A person(亻) leaning against a tree(木) to rest.

休息[xiūxi] rest - 26b

70

儿

Diagram for 儿

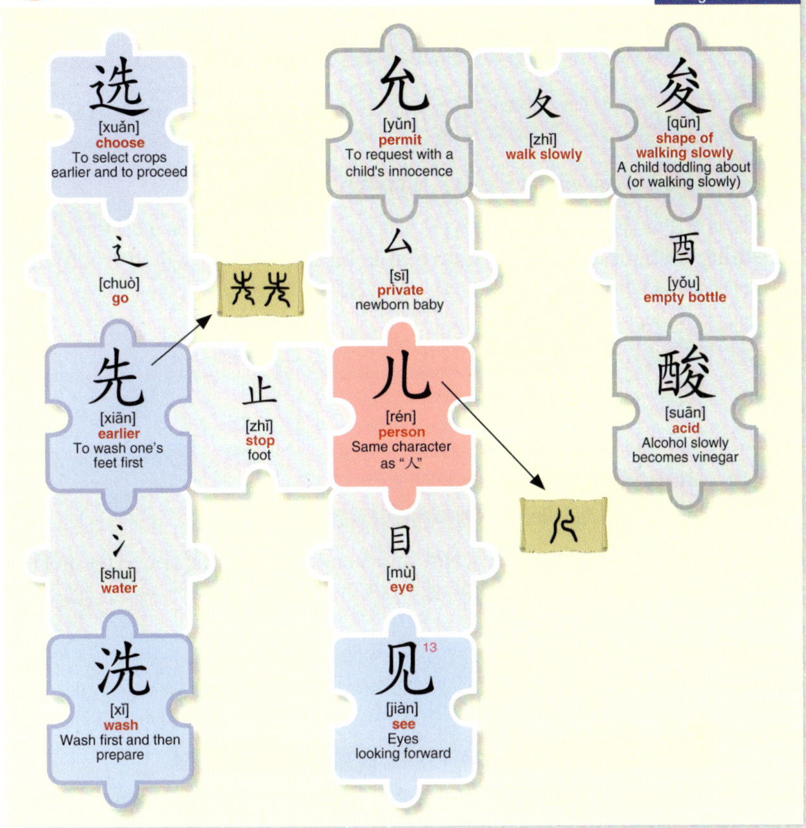

71

丿 儿

儿 rén/ér — person / child, son

The ancient character shows that it is the same character as "person 人[63][rén]" and means the same thing, 'person.'

The traditional character(兒) shows a young person(儿) whose skull bones have not fused(臼). It means 'child, son.'

儿子[érzi] son - 95	女儿[nǚér] daughter - 96
一会儿[yīhuìr] a little while - 223 66c	画儿[huàr] picture - 167c

71

面条儿[miàntiáor] noodles - 10 56c
玩儿[wánr] play - 198a
小孩儿[xiǎoháir] child; kid - 235 4c
一点儿[yīdiǎnr] a bit; a little - 223 127d
一块儿[yīkuàir] at the same place; together - 223 76b

71a

厶 厶 允 允

允 yǔn

permit

newborn baby/private 厶[93][sī] + person 儿 [rén]

A person(儿) as in a newborn baby(厶), a young person. When a child asks for something without an ulterior motive, it is hard to say no, which is why this character means 'to permit.'

允许[yǔnxǔ] permit; allow - 121c

71b

厶 厶 允 允 夋 夋 夋

夋 qūn

shape of walking slowly

child/permit 允 [yǔn] + walk slowly 夂[56][zhǐ]

71 A child(允) that is learning to walk, and hence is walking slowly(夂). This character accentuates the meaning of 'walking slowly.'

71c

一 厂 丙 丙 两 酉 酉 酉 酉 酉 酉 酉 酸 酸

酸 suān

acid

empty bottle 酉[162][yǒu] + shape of walking slowly 夋 [qūn]

Alcohol(酉) slowly ferments to give off the acidic taste. The slow process is likened to a child walking slowly(夋).

* When alcohol(酉) ferments(夋), it becomes more intoxicating and acidic.

这些苹果不熟，是酸的。These apples are not ripe; they are acidic.
- 133a 88h 122b 210g 223a 3e, 54b 71c 46b

71d

丿 ㇐ 屮 生 生 先

先 xiān

earlier

foot/stop 㞢→止[53][zhǐ] + person 儿 [rén]

Before entering a sacred place, a person(儿) must first wash his feet(止).

* "止" is the shape of a foot and means 'foot.'

先生[xiānsheng] teacher - 208　　首先[shǒuxiān] first - 7

71e　丶 丶 氵 氵 氵 汁 沙 洗 洗

洗 xǐ

wash

water 氵[202] [shuǐ] + earlier 先 [xiān]

To enter into where the altar is, one must first(先) wash with water(氵) and prepare for the service.

洗手间[xǐshǒujiān] restroom; toilet - 31 145c　　洗澡[xǐ/zǎo] have a bath; wash - 180b

71f　丿 𠂉 ⺧ 生 先 先 洗 选 选

选 xuǎn

choose

earlier 先 [xiān] + go 辶[61] [chuò]

To select the best parts of the crops harvested earlier(先), and to proceed(辶) to an alter.

选择[xuǎnzé] select; choose - 123d

71

兄

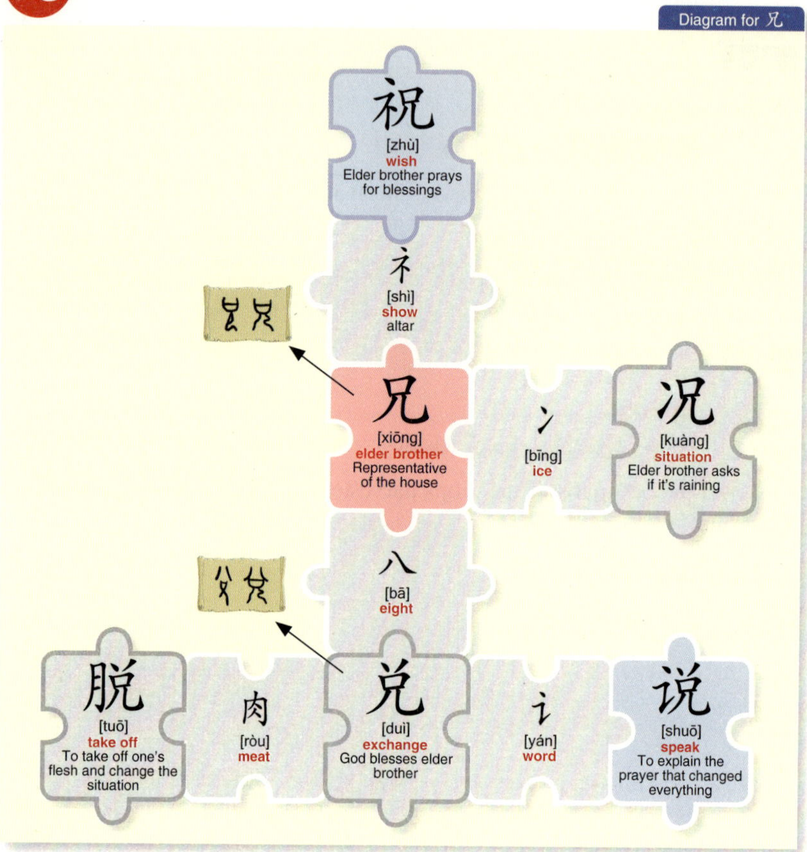

72

72 丶 ㄇ 口 尸 兄

兄 xiōng

elder brother

mouth 口[16][kǒu] + person 儿[71][rén]

A person(儿) with a large mouth(口). This is the person(儿) who speaks up (口) when discussing family matters and means 'elder brother.'

弟兄[dìxiong] brothers - 109a 兄弟[xiōngdì] brothers - 109a

72a 丶 ⺀ 礻 礻 礻 祀 祀 祀 祝

祝 zhù

wish

altar/show 礻=示[126][shì] + elder brother 兄 [xiōng]

As representative of the family, the elder brother(兄) goes to the altar(礻) to pray for his wish to come true.

＊ "礻" is the shape of the altar or pedestal.

祝你健康。I wish for your health. - 72a 69a 37c 38b

72b 丶 冫 冫 冫 冫 冫 况

况 kuàng

situation

ice 冫[206][bīng] + elder brother 兄 [xiōng]

The elder brother(兄) who was praying for rain(冫→氵) during the drought is enquiring with someone about the situation.

＊ The traditional character(況) shows that "water 氵[202][shuǐ]" changed to "冫."

情况[qíngkuàng] circumstances; situation - 135d

72c 丶 丷 丷 丷 丷 兑 兑

兑 duì

exchange

eight 丷 → 八[229][bā] + elder brother 兄 [xiōng]

God is touched by the brother's(兄) prayer and sends down(八) blessings in the form of rain, which changes the situation.

＊ The "八" in this character describes 'blessings coming down from the heavens.'

兑换[duìhuàn] exchange - 68d

72d 丶 讠 讠 讠 讠 讠 讠 说 说

说 shuō

speak

word 讠=言[22][yán] + exchange 兑 [duì]

The elder brother who changed the situation(兑) explains in words(讠) how he prayed.

说话[shuō/huà] speak; talk - 24b
说明[shuōmíng] explain; illustrate - 218h
听说[tīng/shuō] be told; hear of - 16d
你在说什么? What are you saying? - 69a 32a 72d 231a 93a

72

72e

丿 刀 月 月 月' 月'' 月'' 月'' 月'' 月'' 脱

脱 tuō

take off

meat 月[221] → 肉[192] [ròu] + exchange 兑 [duì]

Thanks to the gods' blessings, he has escaped the pain of the flesh(肉) and changed(兑) his life.

* Nirvana(解脱) is one of Buddhism's main teachings and is about putting down(兑) the flesh(月 = 肉) to achieve enlightenment.
* When "moon 月 [yuè]" is used as part of another character it means "肉."

脱离 [tuōlí] break away; secede - 194a

脱毛。Hair falls out. - 72e 188

脱帽。To take off the hat. - 72e 11f

72

元

Diagram for 元

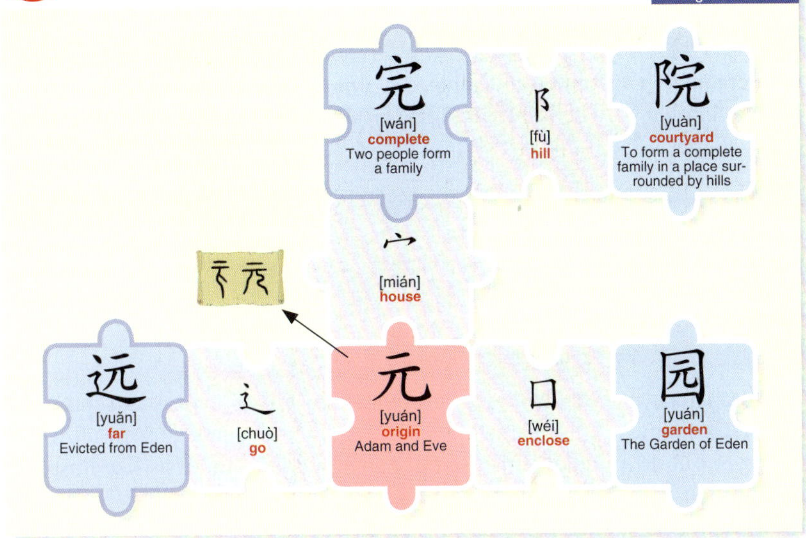

73 — 一 二 テ 元 — 73

元 yuán

origin

two 二[226] [èr] + person 儿[71] [rén]

The Bible says that two(二) people(儿), Adam and Eve, were the origin of all people. These two(二) people(儿) were our ancestors. This character also refers to 'China's monetary unit.'

公元[gōngyuán] Anno Domini (A.D.) - 93b   元旦[yuándàn] New Year's day - 218a

73a 丶 丿 宀 宀 宀 宁 完

完 wán

complete

house 宀[141] [mián] + origin 元 [yuán]

God created(元) people by forming Eve out of Adam's rib and told them to form a family(宀). The last living form God created to complete creation was Eve. - Genesis 2: 21~24

完成[wánchéng] complete - 114a 完全[wánquán] perfect; complete; entire - 63f

73b 阝 阝 阝 阝 阝 阝 院 院 院

院 yuàn

courtyard

hill 阝[147] [fù] + complete 完 [wán]

God prepared a place called Eden, surrounded by hills(阝), for Adam and Eve's perfect(完) family. This character means 'a home surrounded by a wall with a countyard in the middle.' It is used to name public institutions like hospitals or courthouses.

医院[yīyuàn] hospital - 111a 学院[xuéyuàn] college - 95a

73

73c 丨 冂 冂 冃 冃 园 园

园 yuán

garden

enclose 口[20] [wéi] + origin 元 [yuán]

Adam and Eve, the origin(元) of mankind, were given a garden called Eden to live in(口).

* The traditional character(園) supports the Bible verse that says in the Garden of Eden, where Adam and Eve resided(口), God gave them 'long leather clothes(long clothes 袁 [yuán]) to wear.'- Genesis 3: 21

公园[gōngyuán] park; public garden - 93b 花园[huāyuán] garden - 70b

73d 一 二 テ 元 元 沅 远

远 yuǎn

far

origin 元 [yuán] + go 辶[61] [chuò]

Adam and Eve, the origin(元) of mankind were expelled from the Garden of Eden and had to leave(辶) Eden for eating the forbidden fruit of good and evil. To them, Eden was a place so far away, they could never return. - Genesis 3: 24

永远[yǒngyuǎn] forever - 201a

大

Diagram for 大

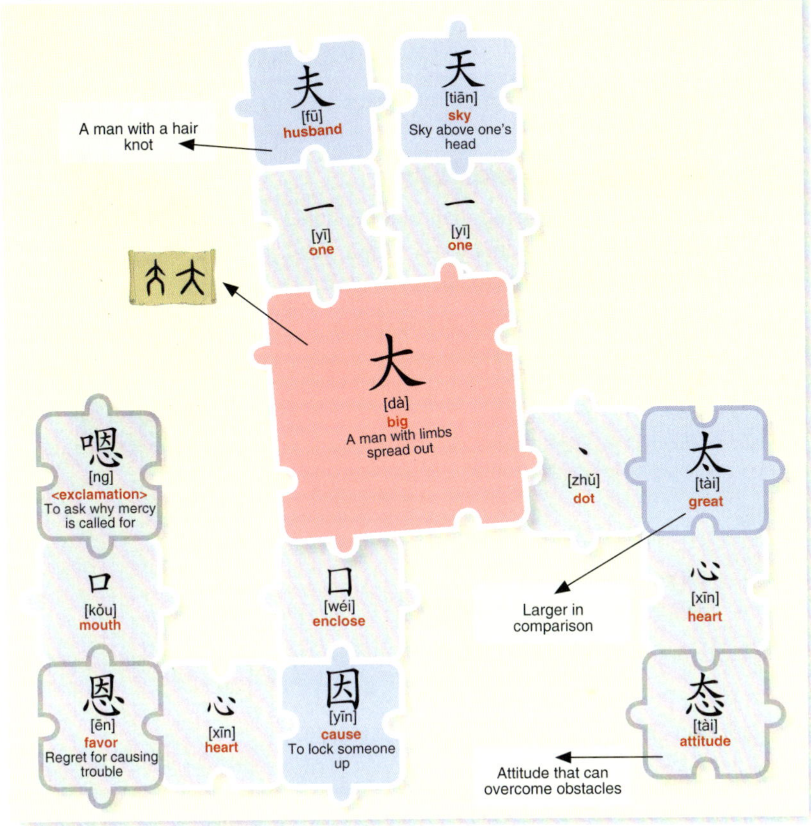

74

74 一 ナ 大

大 dà/dài **big / doctor**

A person(人[63][rén]) with four limbs spread out(一). This character is just another form of 'person.'

大家[dàjiā] great master; authority - 174a
大概[dàgài] general idea; broad outline - 80f
大声[dàshēng] loud; loudness - 104d
大学[dàxué] university; college - 95a
伟大[wěidà] great; mighty - 190a

Although the original meaning 'big' still remains, in some cases it also means 'doctor.'

大夫[dàifu] doctor - 74a

74a

一 二 夫 夫

夫 fū

husband

one 一[223][yī] + person/big 大[dà]

In the ancient China, a married man tied his hair up on the top of his head. A man(大) with a hair knot(一) therefore means 'husband.'

* "一" symbolizes the hair knot and has no extra meaning.

丈夫[zhàngfu] husband - 39d
夫人[fūren] lady; madam; Mrs. - 63
大夫[dàifu] doctor - 74

74b

一 二 チ 天

74

天 tiān

sky

one 一[223][yī] + person/big 大 [dà]

The sky is high above our heads and is described with "一" above a person (大).

* "一"symbolizes the sky and has no extra meaning.

今天[jīntiān] today - 66
天气[tiānqì] weather - 204
半天[bàntiān] half of the day - 175b
冬天[dōngtiān] winter - 206e
夏天[xiàtiān] summer - 56e
明天[míngtiān] tomorrow - 218h
昨天[zuótiān] yesterday - 234c
春天[chūntiān] spring - 218i
秋天[qiūtiān] autumn; fall - 139b

74c

一 ナ 大 太

太 tài

great; too; very

big 大 [dà] + dot 丶[233][zhǔ]

"大" with a dot(丶) stresses the size and means 'great, too, very.'

太阳[tàiyáng] the sun - 147b
太太[tàitai] Mrs; madame

74d 一 ナ 大 太 太 太 态 态

态 tài

attitude

great 太 [tài] + heart 心[28] [xīn]

This character describes the attitude of a person who has the heart(心) to overcome large(太) obstacles.

* The traditional character(態) shows the heart(心) of a person who is capable(能[89b]) of doing anything.

态度 [tàidu] manner; bearing - 143b

74e 丨 冂 冂 冃 闩 因

因 yīn

cause

enclose 口[20] [wéi] + person/big 大 [dà]

A person(大) is arrested and taken to prison(口) because there is a reason (cause) for him to be locked up there.

* “大” means ‘person.’

因为 [yīnwèi] because - 159c

因此 [yīncǐ] therefore; hence; for this reason - 88g

74

74f 丨 冂 冂 冃 闩 因 因 恩 恩 恩

恩 ēn

favor

cause 因 [yīn] + heart 心[28] [xīn]

The heart(心) of a man who sinned and caused(因) himself to be locked up. One who has such regrets wishes for favor.

恩人 [ēnrén] benefactor - 63

74g 丨 冂 口 叫 叩 叩 叩 呣 咽 咽 嗯 嗯 嗯

嗯 ng

<exclamation>

mouth 口[16] [kǒu] + favor 恩 [ēn]

Questioning and asking(口) why mercy(恩) is needed is a serious action, so this character shows surprise or exclamation.

嗯? 你刚才说什么? Huh? What did you say? - 74g? 69a 165b 32 72d 231a 93a

头

Diagram for 头

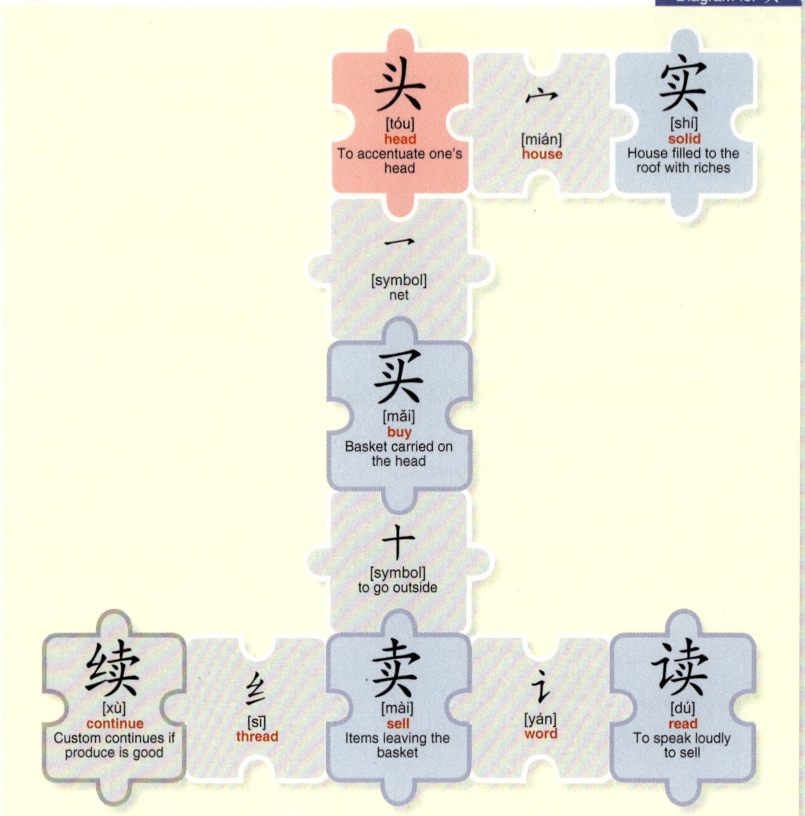

75

75 丶 丷 ⺀ 头 头

头 tóu

head; hair

dot 丶[233][zhǔ] + dot 丶[zhǔ] + person/big 大[74][dà]

Two dots(丶) on a man's(大) head means 'head, hair.'

头发[tóufa] hair - 34f	钟头[zhōngtóu] hour - 232b
骨头[gǔtou] bone - 29	

75a

丶 丷 宀 宀 宀 宀 实 实

实 shí

solid; fruit; real

house 宀[141] [mián] + head 头 [tóu]

A house(宀) filled to the head(头), the topmost part, with riches. This character came to mean fruit, and because one tree can only bear one kind of fruit, it also means 'real.'

其实 [qíshí] actually; in fact - 44
实践 [shíjiàn] practice; fulfill - 52a
结实 [jiēshi] solid; sturdy; fruition - 104b
确实 [quèshí] certain; true - 191a
实现 [shíxiàn] realize; achieve - 13d

75b

乛 乛 乛 买 买 买

买 mǎi

buy

net 乛 [symbol] + head 头 [tóu]

To buy items and put them in the basket(乛) on your head(头).

* The traditional character(買) shows one buying items with money(貝 → 贝[186]) and putting them in the basket(罒[165]).

买卖 [mǎimai] buying and selling - 75c

75c

一 十 士 卉 卉 卖 卖 卖

卖 mài

sell

to go outside 十 [symbol] + buy 买 [mǎi]

To take out(十) items from the basket and sell them for more money than you bought(买) them with.

* The traditional character(賣) shows items from the basket(罒[165]) being handed out(土 → 出[167a]) for money(貝 → 贝[186]).

买卖 [mǎimai] buying and selling - 75b

75d

丶 讠 讠 讠 讠 讠 讠 讠 读 读

读 dú

read

word 讠=言[22] [yán] + sell 卖 [mài]

To use words(讠) and read from a list of items to sell(卖).

读书 [dúshū] read; study - 232d
读者 [dúzhě] reader - 101

75

75e

续 xù

continue

thread 纟[132][sī] + sell 卖[mài]

One must sell(卖) good products for a good price if he desires continuous(纟) commercial transaction.

* Thread(纟) means connections or continuity.

继续[jìxù] continue - 132d
连续[liánxù] continue - 124c
手续[shǒuxù] procedure; process - 31

76

夬

Diagram for 夬

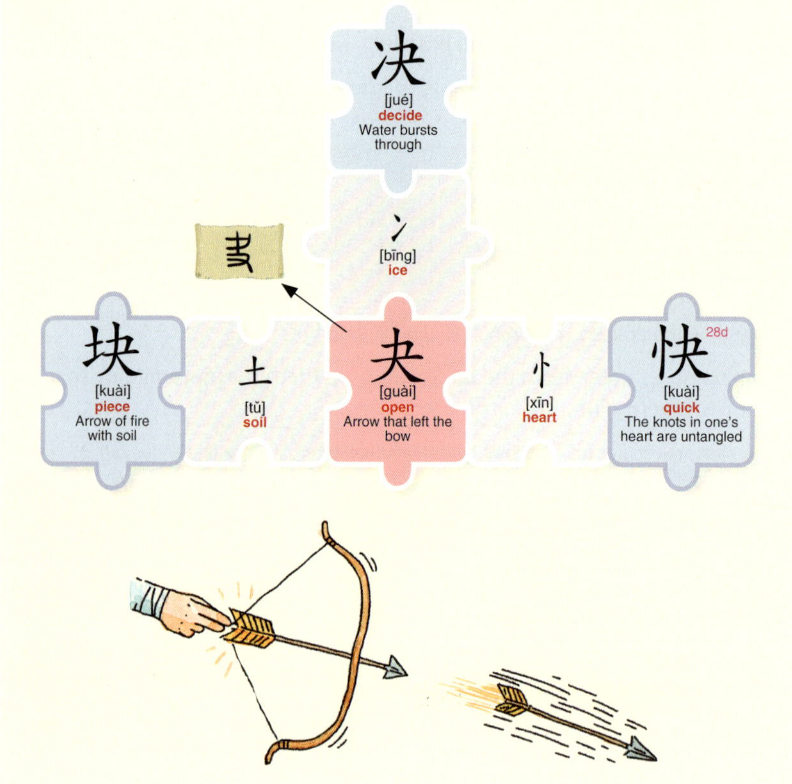

76　　ㄱ ㅋ 夬 夬

夬 guài

open; release

hand ヨ[36][jì] + arrow 矢[111][shǐ]

A hand(ヨ) fitting the notch of the arrow(矢) into the bowstring. An arrow flies, which is where this character got its meaning of 'open, release.'

* Notch of arrow: The part at the end of the arrow that fits into the bowstring.

76a　　丶 冫 冫 汩 決 决

决 jué

decide

ice 冫[206][bīng] + open 夬 [guài]

When a timely decision provides a permanent solution to a persistent problem, it can be said that 'everything works out like water(冫→氵[202]) bursting through (夬).'

* The traditional character(決) shows that "water 氵 [shuǐ]" changed to "冫."

解决[jiějué] solve - 175c　　决定[juédìng] decide - 54e

76b　　一 十 土 扌 圵 坱 块

块 kuài

piece

soil 土[152][tǔ] + open 夬 [guài]

A flying(夬) arrow lit with fire appears like a ball of fire in the sky. With the character for soil(土) added, it means 'piece, lump.'

一块儿[yīkuàir] at the same place; together - 223 71

76

央

Chart for 央

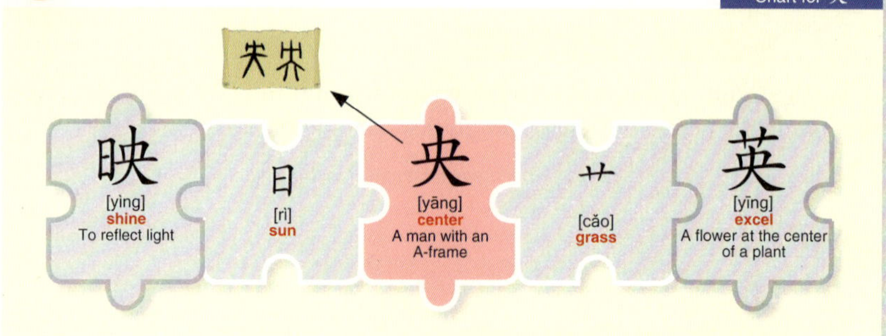

77

央 yāng

center

A-frame 冂 [symbol] + person/big 大[74] [dà]

A man(大) carrying an A-frame(冂) in the center of his back to carry heavy things.

77 中央[zhōngyāng] center; central government - 232a

77a

英 yīng

excel; English

grass 艹[207] [cǎo] + center 央 [yāng]

The center(央) of any plant(艹) is the flower, because it's beautiful and is used to multiply. The meaning of 'flower, excel' comes from that. This character is used in the Chinese name for Great Britain, the land 'where the sun never set.'

英语[yīngyǔ] English (language) - 226c

77b

映 yìng

shine

sun 日[218] [rì] + center 央 [yāng]

To reflect the sun(日) with a mirror and light the middle(央).

反映[fǎnyìng] reflect; mirror - 148a

夭

Diagram for 夭

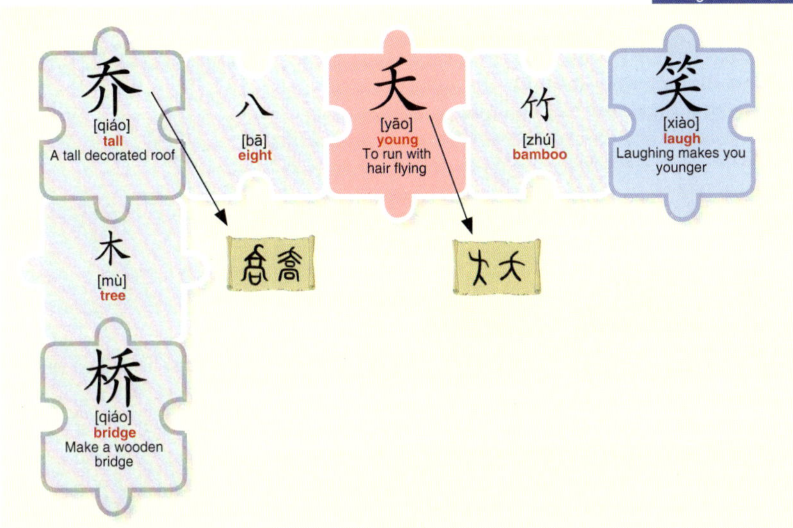

78

78

丿 二 千 夭

夭 yāo

young

line 丿[234][piě] + person/big 大[74][dà]

A man(大) running energetically with hair flying(丿) is a young man.

* "丿" has no set meaning and can be interpreted in many ways.

78a

笑

笑 xiào

laugh

bamboo 竹[216][zhú] + young 夭 [yāo]

A popular Chinese saying goes, "One laugh makes you younger, one frown makes you older." When you laugh, you appear younger(夭) and will live longer (竹) too.

* Bamboo(竹) lives for many years, stays green all year round, and has the same pronunciation as "wish 祝[72a][zhù]," so is a symbol of longevity and is often used to pray with.

开玩笑[kāiwánxiào] joke; make fun of - 43a 198a　　笑话[xiàohua] joke; jest - 24b

78b

一 二 チ 夭 乔 乔

乔 qiáo

tall

young 夭 [yāo] + eight 八[229] [bā]

"夭" is the decoration on the highest part of the roof. In China, it's usually the corner that takes the "八" shape.

* The traditional character(喬) shows the roof of a high(高[3]) building decorated with "夭."

78c

一 十 才 木 木' 木ˊ 杧 桥 桥 桥

桥 qiáo

bridge

tree 木[210] [mù] + tall 乔 [qiáo]

To construct a wooden(木) bridge higher(乔) than the water level so people can cross.

立交桥[lìjiāoqiáo] viaduct; overpass - 79 1a

78

立

Diagram for 立

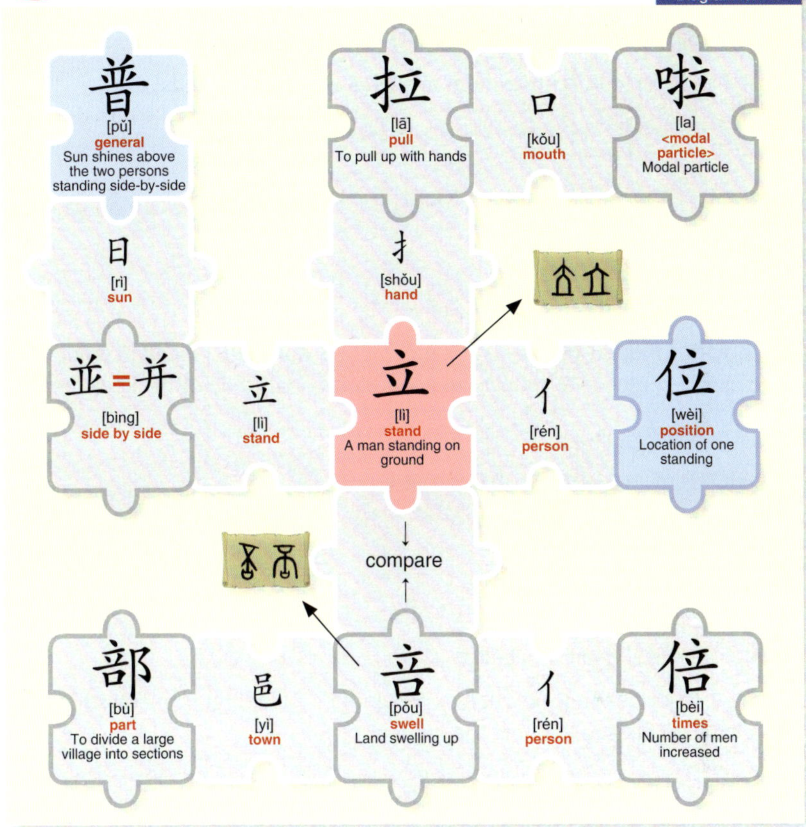

79

79

立
lì

stand

丶 亠 亣 立 立

A man(大[74][dà]) standing with two feet firmly on the ground(一).

立刻[ikè] immediately; at once - 4a
独立[dúlì] stand alone; independence - 173a
建立[jiànlì] build; set up; establish - 37b

79

79a

一 ㇏ 扌 扌 扩 扩 拉 拉

拉 lā

pull

hand 扌=手[31] [shǒu] + stand 立 [lì]

To use hands(扌) to pull up an item in such a way that it stands(立).

半拉[bànlǎ] half - 175b

79b

丨 ㄇ 口 口 叶 吖 吖 吖 啦 啦 啦

啦 la

<modal particle>

mouth 口[16] [kǒu] + pull 拉 [lā]

"拉 [lā] with a mouth(口)" as a modal particle is normally placed in front of or at the end of sentence to reflect the good mood or attitude of the speaker.

* "啦" is a combination of "了[168a] [le]" and "啊[17f] [a]" and takes both meanings.

该来的都来啦。Those who had to attend are all here. - 4b 212d 46b 101a 212d 79b

79c

丿 亻 亻 仁 仁 位 位

位 wèi

position

person 亻[70] [rén] + stand 立 [lì]

The location or position of where a person(亻) is standing(立) shows his title. This character is used to count the number of people.

单位[dānwèi] unit - 231c
地位[dìwèi] position, standing - 84a
座位[zuòwèi] seat; place - 152c
三位客人。Three guests. - 223e 79c 57b 63

79d

丶 亠 亠 立 立 产 音 音

咅 pǒu

swell

A part of land swelling up in a round shape(口) because plants are coming up (立) from the ground.

* This character has nothing to do with "mouth 口[16] [kǒu]" or "stand 立[79] [lì]."

79e

丿 亻 亻 亻 亻 亻 位 倍 倍 倍

倍 bèi

times

person 亻[70][rén] + swell 咅 [pǒu]

This character means 'times' because it signifies that the number of people (亻) have increased(咅).

这条街道比那条短四倍。This street is four times shorter than that one. - 133a 56c 60c 7a 88a 147e 56c 111d 20c 79e

79f

丶 亠 亠 亠 立 产 音 咅 部 部

部 bù

part

swell 咅 [pǒu] + town 阝[147] → 邑[92d][yì]

A village(邑) that has swelled(咅) or grown has to be divided into parts for better maintenance.

* When "hill 阝 [fù]" is on the right side of a character, it means "邑."

部分[bùfen] part; section - 119a
全部[quánbù] whole; entire - 63f
内部[nèibù] inside; interior - 64
干部[gànbù] cadre - 121
北部[běibù] north - 88c

79g

丶 丷 丷 丷 丷 丷 丷 並 並 普 普 普

普 pǔ

general

side by side 並=并[123][bìng] + sun 日[218][rì]

This character portrays the image of the sun(日) shining above two persons standing(立) side-by-side(並). The Sun(日) shines and disseminates its light to everybody, and, therefore, the meaning of 'general' is derived out of it.

* The character, "並[bìng]" describes two persons who are standing(竝) side-by-side.

普通话[pǔtōnghuà] Mandarin (common speech of the Chinese language) - 166b 24b

79

尢

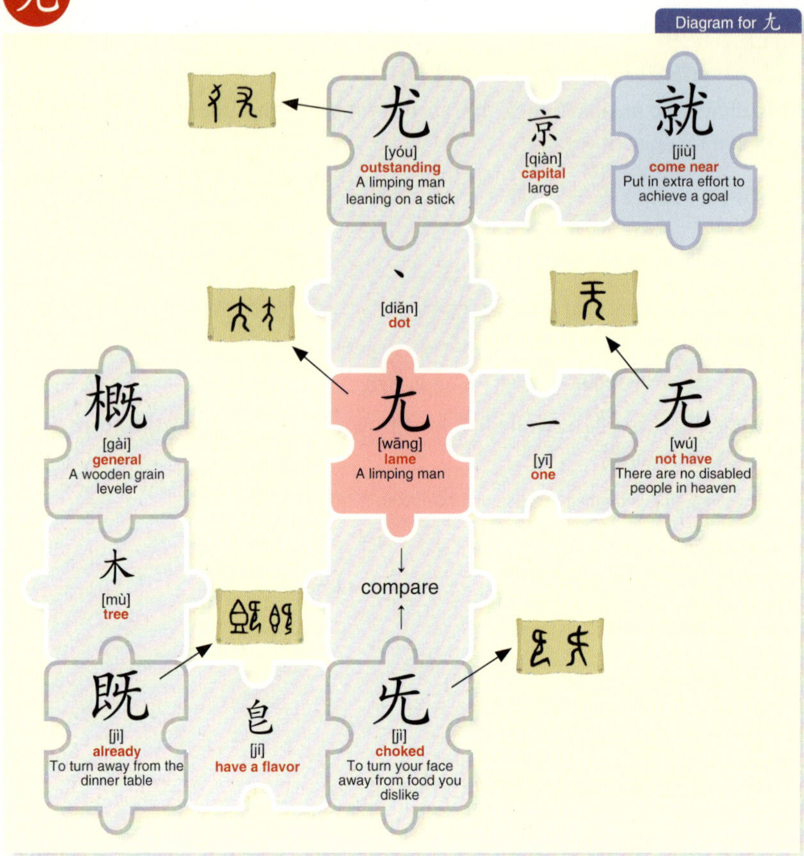

80

80

一 ナ 尢

尢 wāng **lame**

"Big 大[74][dà]" is the shape of an adult standing with arms spread. One leg of the character is hook-shaped(㇄), showing he's lame.

* "尢" is not used as a separate character in simplified Chinese.

80a

一 ナ 尢 尤

尤 yóu

outstanding

lame 尢 [wāng] + dot 丶[233] [diǎn]

A limping man(尢) with a cane(丶) will stand out.

尤其[yóuqí] especially; particularly - 44

80b

丶 亠 亡 亣 古 亨 亨 京 京 就 就 就

就 jiù

come near; at once

large/capital 京[2] [jīng] + outstanding 尤 [yóu]

This character shows a physically challenged person(尤) who puts in extra effort to get closer to achieving a large goal(京). It also means that one must immediately action one's plans to achieve his/her goal.

* "京" is the shape of a large building, so includes the meaning 'large.'

一…就…[yī...jiù...] as soon as; directly - 223

成就[chéngjiù] achievement; accomplishment - 114a

我很快就回来。I'll be back soon. - 113b 14a 28d 80b 20d 212d

80

80c

一 二 于 无

无 wú

not have

one 一[223] [yī] + lame 尢 [wāng]

There are no disabled people(尢) in heaven(一).

* The traditional character(無) means 'non existant' because it describes a shaman dancing so fast that his feet are only visible as four dots(灬), which looks like he has none. A simplified form(无) adapted from the ancient character.

毫无[háowú] not in the least - 188b

80d

一 二 于 旡

旡 jì

choked

The shape of someone turning his face away at the sight of food he dislikes. It means 'be choked, be fed up.'

* The ancient text was a description of a person sitting down and turning his head away.

80e ㇇ ㇇ ㇌ 㔾 艮 艮 㔾 旡 既

既 ji

already

have a flavor 艮 → 皀[jì] + turn face away/choke 旡 [jì]

A man who has already eaten to his full capacity at a party will turn away(旡) from the dinner table(皀) that his wife has set.

* The "皀" in the traditional character(旣) is the shape of a bowl of rice.

既然[jìrán] now that - 158e

80f 一 十 才 木 朩 朩 朩 朩 根 根 椤 概 概

概 gài

general; approximate

tree 木[210][mù] + already 既 [jì]

This character, meaning a wooden(木) grain leveler, takes its pronunciation from "既". In the olden days, when grain merchants leveled the grains, instead of leveling the whole measuring, they stopped just before reaching the end of leveling. So this character came to mean 'general, approximately.'

80

* In China a wooden(木) grain leveler is used to level out measures of grain, but everyone already (既) knew that one should give a little bit extra.
* Grain leveler – It's a stick-like took used to level out the grain scooped into a measuring bowl.

大概[dàgài] general idea; broad outline - 74 　 概念[gàiniàn] concept; conception - 66b

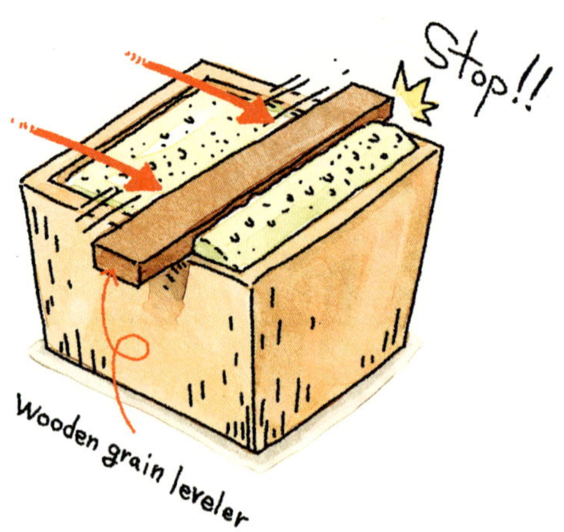

Diagram for 疒

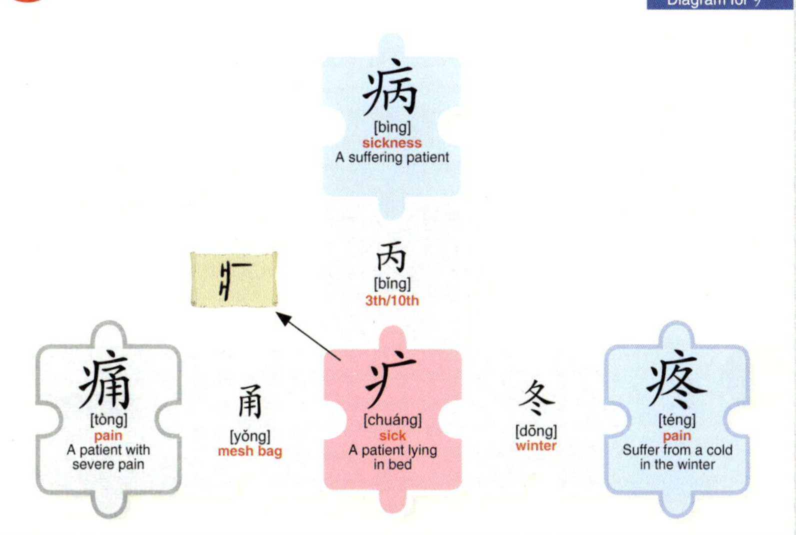

81 丶 亠 广 疒 疒 81

疒 chuáng **sick**

A patient(head 亠[1] [tóu]) is sick and is lying in bed(piece of wood 丬[214] [qiáng]).

81a 丶 亠 广 疒 疒 疒 疒 病 病 病

病 bìng **sickness**

sick 疒 [chuáng] + 3th/10th 丙 [bǐng]

Because "疒" cannot be used as a separate character, the Chinese added "丙," the third out of the ten calendar signs and adopted the pronunciation to make the character for 'sickness.'

生病 [shēng/bìng] get sick - 208	看病 [kàn/bìng] see a patient; treat - 11a

81b 丶 亠 广 疒 疒 疒 疒 疼 疼 疼

疼 téng **pain**

sick 疒 [chuáng] + winter 冬[206e] [dōng]

A man sick with a cold(疒) during winter(冬).

他疼得大叫起来。He roared with pain. - 84b 81b 40b 74 16e 53d 212d

81c 丶 亠 广 广 疒 疒 疒 疒 疒 病 痛 痛

痛 tòng

pain

sick 疒 [chuáng] + mesh bag 甬[166a] [yǒng]

A sick(疒) man suffering from pain that feels like wind seeping through a net (甬).

痛快[tòngkuài] very happy; delighted; joyful - 28d | 痛苦[tòngkǔ] pain - 19d

82

己

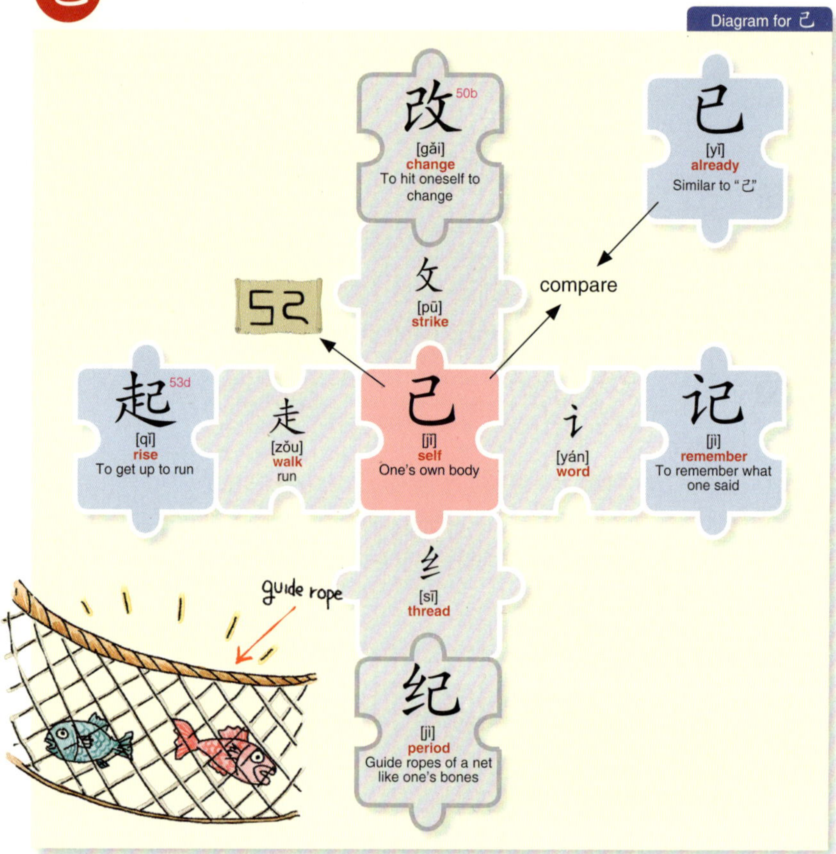

82 ㄱ ㅋ 己

己 jǐ self

We cannot tell what "己" originally meant, by its ancient character. But, nowadays it means 'body, self.'

* It looks similar to "unborn child 巳[92][sì]" and "already 已[82a][yǐ]," but the three are completely different.

自己[zìjǐ] oneself - 26

82a ㄱ ㅋ 已

已 yǐ already

It looks almost identical to "self 己 [jǐ]," but this character has a slightly longer side stroke on the left. All we know is that this character now means "already 已经[132e][yǐjing]."

已经[yǐjīng] already - 132e

82b 丶 讠 讠 讠 记

记 jì remember; write down

word 讠=言[22][yán] + self 己 [jǐ]

One must remember what words(讠) you(己) spoke. This character also means to record so as to not forget.

记得[jìde] remember - 40b 忘记[wàngjì] forget - 5a

82c 𠃋 𠃋 纟 纟 纟 纪

纪 jì period; discipline

thread 纟[132][sī] + body/self 己 [jǐ]

A skeleton is a frame and helps maintain the shape of one's body(己). A fishing net has something similar called a guide rope, a thick rope(纟) that goes around the net to retain its shape. That is why this character means a period, because such frames need to be in regular intervals to be effective. Also, society needs rules to stay in working form.

年纪[niánjì] age - 121a 纪律[jìlǜ] discipline - 37a 世纪[shìjì] century - 207f

82

83

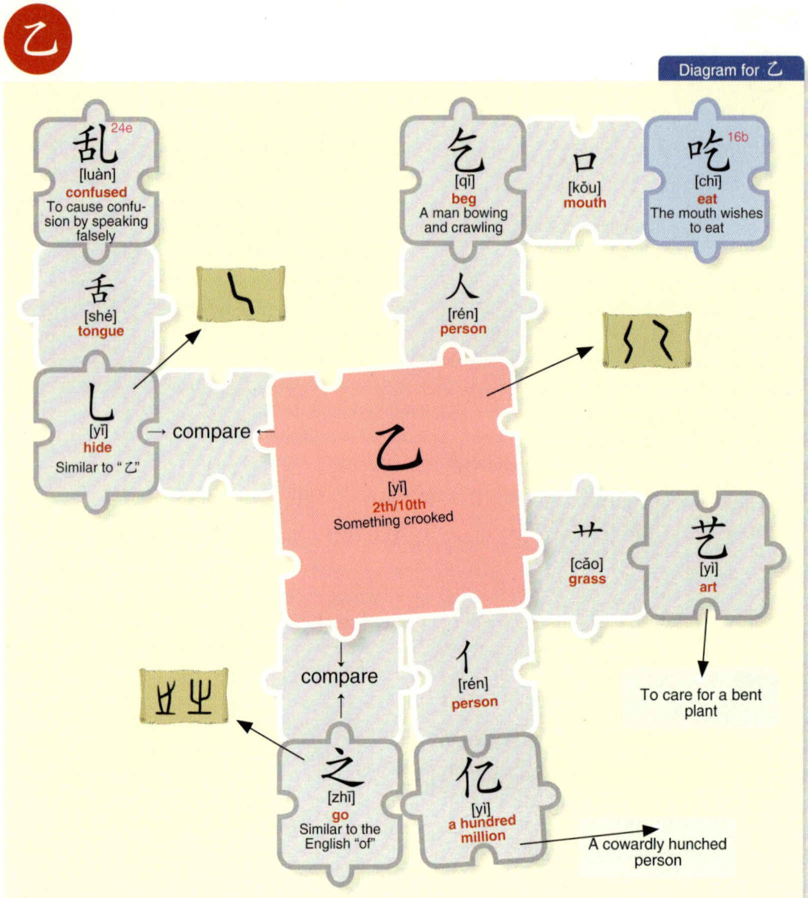

乙 yǐ **2th/10th**

In the spring, new buds and sprouts emerge, crooked and curved at first. This character is also the shape of someone cowering and begging. It's also the second out of the ten calendar signs.

83a

丿 𠂉 乞

乞 qǐ

beg

person 𠂉 → 人[63][yán] + hunched stance/2th 乙 [yǐ]

A man(人) is hunched over(乙) in a cowardly posture to beg.

乞求[qǐqiú] beg for - 203b

83b

一 十 艹 艺

艺 yì

art

grass 艹[207][cǎo] + hunched stance/2th 乙[yǐ]

This character describes someone looking after a plant(艹) that is growing haphazardly and crooked(乙). Attending to such a plant requires enormous effort and is a skilful art.

文艺[wényì] literature and art -133 艺术[yìshù] art -210f

83c

丿 亻 亿

亿 yì

a hundred million

person 亻[70][rén] + hunched stance/2th 乙 [yǐ]

A popular saying goes, "One can see into the water but never into a person's mind." Even if a person(亻) is hunched over(乙) in a cowardly posture, it will be hard to see into his mind. Equally hard to grasp is the numerical amount this character represents, a hundred million.

* The traditional character(億) explains that a man's(亻) thoughts or plans(意[21b]) are hard to understand.

亿万[yìwàn] hundreds of millions(too numerous to count) - 194d

83d

丶 ㇇ 之

之 zhī

go; of

Although it looks similar to "乙 [yǐ]," this character depicts a foot(止[53]) stepping on ground(一) to go somewhere. It has the same usage as '的[46b].' Usually used in documents then conversations, it has a similar usage to 'of' in English.

之间[zhījiān] between; among - 145c

83

⺃ yǐ **hide**

It is never used as a separate character and looks similar to "乙[yǐ]," the second out of the ten calendar signs, and it means 'to hide.' But when used as part of another character, instead of adding any meaning, it just represents 'something crooked.'

* It's considered a radical like "乙."

84

也

Diagram for 也

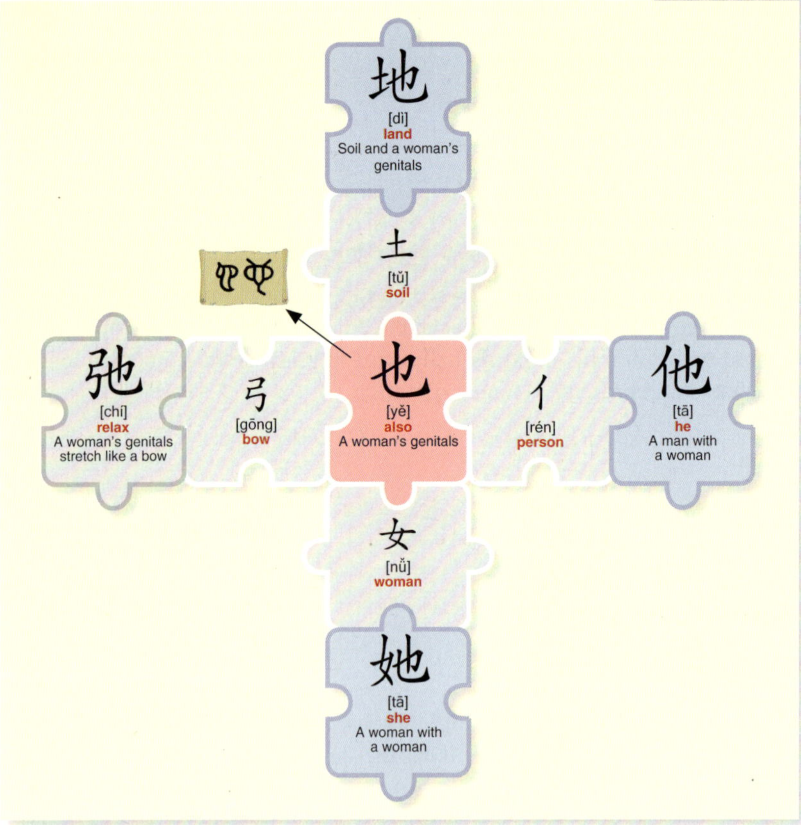

84 　　　　　　　　　　　　　　　　　　　　　　　　　　　　乛 乜 也

也
yě

also; too

It's said to be the shape of a woman's genitals. When used on its own, it means 'also, too.'

* This character is listed here because the radical of "也" is "2th/10th 乙[83][yǐ]."

连…都(也)…[lián...dōu(yě)...] even…is/does… - 124c 101a
也许[yěxǔ] perhaps; maybe - 121c

84a 　　　　　　　　　　　　　　　　　　　　　　　　　　　一 十 土 圴 坤 地

地
dì/de

land / <structural particle>

soil 土[152][tǔ] + female genitals/also 也 [yě]

Soil or the land is where the food chain begins and is the basis of all life forms. This character is formed with soil(土) which most ground is made of, and a woman's genitals(也).

地方[dìfang] area; place - 160
地图[dìtú] map - 206f
地球[dìqiú] the earth - 198b
地铁[dìtiě] subway; metro - 199d
地带[dìdài] zone; region; belt - 131b
地位[dìwèi] position; standing - 79c

When used as a structural particle, the pronunciation of "地" changes and signals that the word in front modifies the word that comes after.

我非常地难过。I am struggling a lot. - 113b 181 150c 84a 34h 40f

84

84b

丿 亻 仆 仲 他

他 tā

he

person 亻[70] [rén] + female genitals/also 也 [yě]

A person(亻) beside a woman's genitals(也) means 'him, that person.' It also means that a man(亻) and a woman(也) have different characters.

* In this character, it's better to think that "也" just means 'woman.'

其他[qítā] other; else - 44　　他们[tāmen] they - 145a

84c

㇛ 女 女 如 妕 她

她 tā

she

woman 女[96] [nǚ] + female genitals/also 也 [yě]

A woman(也) with another woman(女). To make a character meaning 'that woman' and to differentiate it from "he 他 [tā]," the Chinese added the character of a woman(女) instead of a man(亻).

她们[tāmen] they (female) - 145a

84

84d

㇆ ㇆ 弓 弔 弛 弛

弛 chí

relax

bow 弓[109] [gōng] + female genitals/also 也 [yě]

A woman's genitals(也) stretch like a bow(弓) when she gives birth, so this character came to mean 'relax.'

卩

Diagram for 卩

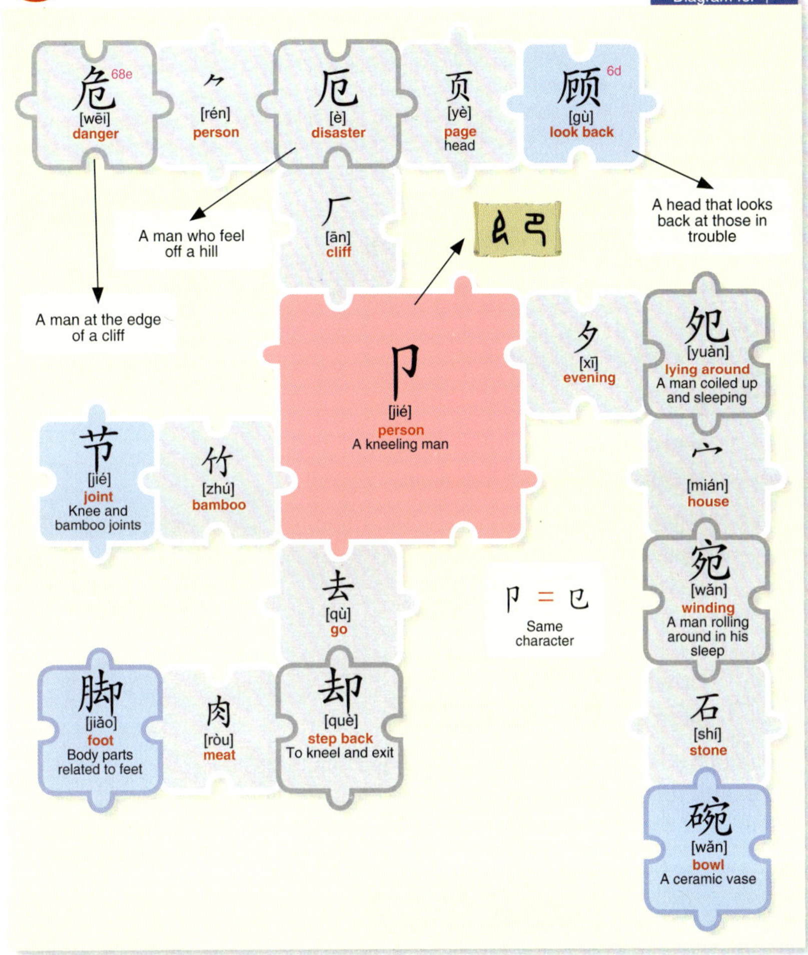

85

85

ㄱ 卩

卩
jié

person

A person crouching in a deep bow or a person who is kneeling.

85a 一 厂 𠂆 厄

厄 è

disaster

cliff 厂[148] [ān] + person 㔾=卩 [jié]

A person(㔾) who met a disaster by falling off a cliff(厂).

85b ノ ク 夕 夗 夗

夗 yuàn

lying around

evening 夕[222] [xī] + person 㔾=卩 [jié]

A person(㔾) hunched up in the evening(夕) sometimes 'lies around' before falling asleep.

85c 丶 丶 宀 宀 宀 宛 宛 宛

宛 wǎn

winding

house 宀[141] [mián] + lying around 夗 [yuàn]

A person rolling around in his sleep(夗) at home(宀) looks like something is being 'wound up.'

85

85d 一 丆 不 石 石 石 石 矿 矿 砂 砂 碗 碗

碗 wǎn

bowl

stone 石[197] [shí] + winding 宛 [wǎn]

To roll up(宛) clay into the shape of a bowl and fire it in a kiln until it is as hard as a stone(石). This character is also used to count the number of plates or bowls.

* China was the first East Asian country to develop ceramic wares.

那男孩今天早上吃了三碗米饭。The boy ate three bowls of rice this morning.
- 147e 159a 4c 66 74b 218e 223f 16b 168a 223e 85d 138 148b

85e 一 十 土 去 去 却 却

却 què

step back; but

go 去[94] [qù] + kneel/person 卩 [jié]

A man who lost a battle kneels(卩) and steps back to leave(去). Because all warriors are reluctant to lose, this character came to mean 'but.'

* "卩" is the shape of a man kneeling down.

冷却[lěngquè] cool down - 86b

85f 丿 月 月 月 月⁻ 月⁺ 月土 月去 月去 脚 脚

脚 jiǎo

foot

meat 月[221] → 肉[192] [ròu] + go 去[94] [qù] + kneel/person 卩 [jié]

To kneel(卩) or walk away(去) involves feet, so the character "meat 肉" is added to signify it's a body part.

* "Moon 月 [yuè]" means "肉" when used as part of another character.

85g 一 十 艹 节 节

节 jié

joint; festival

bamboo 艹[207] → 竹[216] [zhú] + kneel/person 卩 [jié]

The kneeling character(卩) and the character for bamboo(竹) were put together to mean 'joint.' It also means 'festival' because such anniversaries come round at regular intervals.

* The traditional character(節) shows that the top of "节" is not "grass 艹 [cǎo]" but bamboo(竹).

节目[jiémù] program (TV, radio) - 11　节日[jiérì] festival; holiday - 218
季节[jìjié] season; time - 139e　春节[chūnjié] Spring Festival (Chinese New Year) - 218i

85

卩

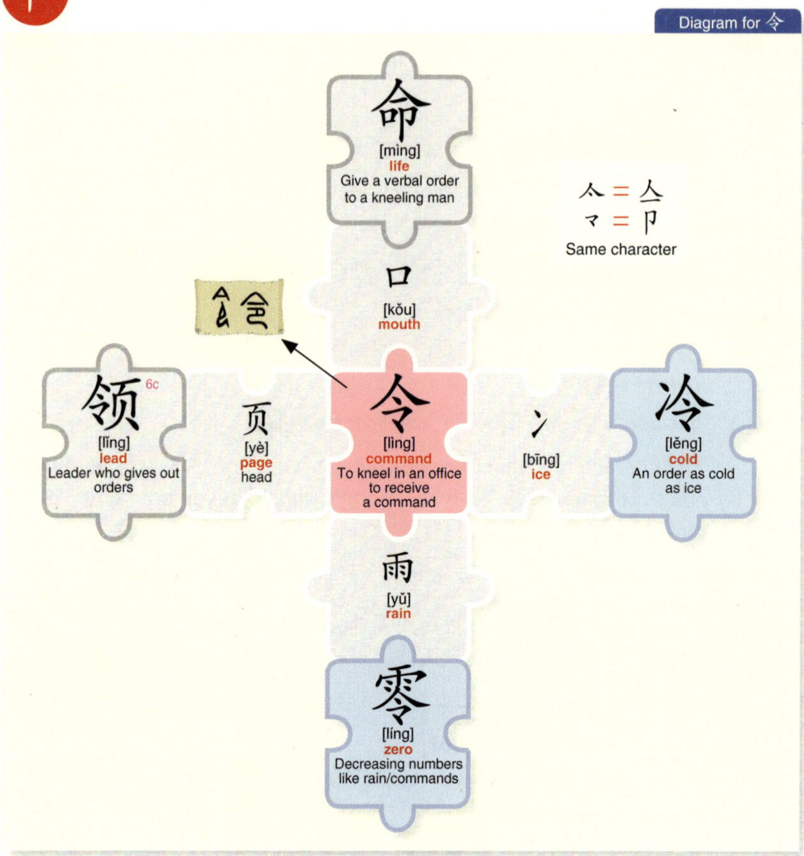

86

86 丿 人 亼 今 令

令 lìng

command

assemble 亼[65] [jí] + person 卩 [jié]

A man kneeling(卩) in an office, the seat of power(亼), to receive a command.

86a 丿 人 亼 亼 合 合 合 命

命 mìng

life; order

command 令 [lìng] + mouth 口[16] [kǒu]

To give a command(令) verbally(口) in an office to a kneeling man. To disobey the order of a powerful man meant certain death, so this character also means 'life.'

命令[mìnglìng] order; command - 86a 生命[shēngmìng] life - 208

86b

丶 冫 冫 冫 冫 冷 冷

冷 lěng

cold

ice 冫[206] [bīng] + command 令 [lìng]

However softly put, a command(令) or an order is always as cold as ice(冫).

寒冷[hánlěng] cold; frigid - 206b 冷却[lěngquè] cool down - 85e

外面太冷了。It's too cold outside. - 222a 10 74c 86b 168a

86c

一 ㄏ 冖 币 币 雨 雨 雨 雨 雰 雰 零 零

零 líng

zero; 0

rain 雨[205] [yǔ] + command 令 [lìng]

Commands(令) come from top down, just like rain(雨) from the sky. When you count down from a large number, you are bound to reach zero.

* The ordinary people in the ancient world did not use "zero." However, "zero" first used in India, was the best invention for scientists and rulers, because they needed to express as large of numbers as possible. Thus, just like rain(雨) falling down from the sky, it may be assumed that the number "zero," originating in this country run by the Gods, was passed down to rulers who commanded(令) that it be used.

零钱[língqián] small change - 115a

86

卩

87

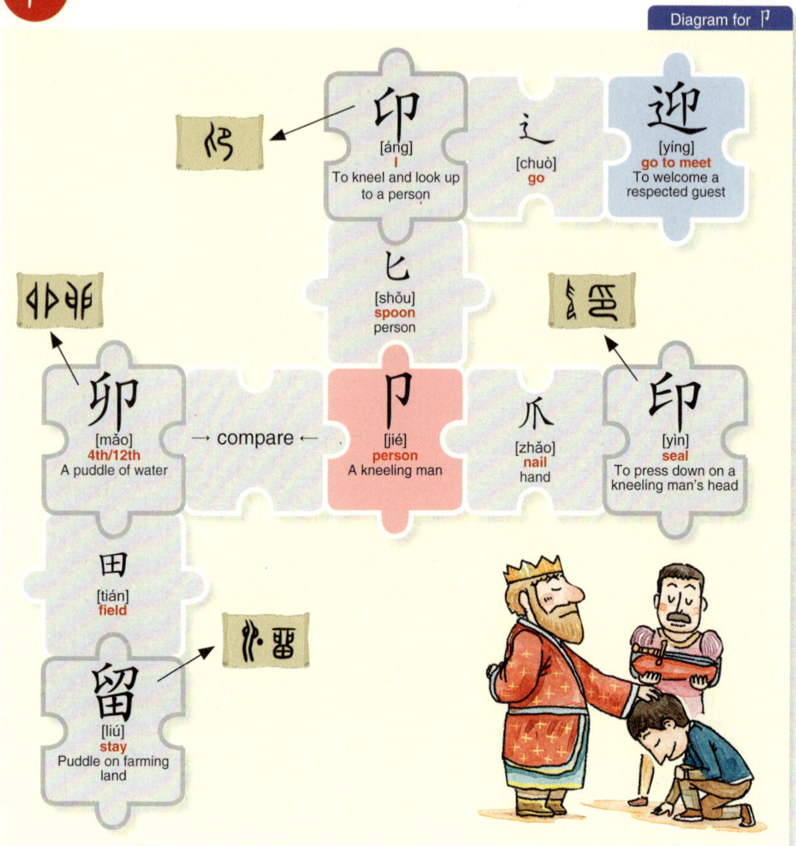

87

卬 áng

I

person/spoon ⺊→匕[88] [bǐ] + kneel/person 卩[85] [jié]

A kneeling(卩) person looking up to a person standing up(匕). As all people wish they are respected, this character came to mean 'me.'

87a

迎 yíng

go to meet

look up/I 卬 [áng] + go 辶[61] [chuò]

A man going out(辶) to welcome a guest who is much respected(卬).

欢迎[huānyíng] welcome - 23c　　迎接[yíngjiē] meet; welcome; greet; receive - 96i

87b

ノ 丆 F 巨 印

印 yìn

seal; print

hand/nail ⺈→爪[33][zhǎo] + kneel/person 卩[85][jié]

As an act of acceptance, the Chinese gently placed a hand(爪) on the head of a kneeling man(卩). This character means 'seal, print.'

复印[fùyìn] duplicate; copy - 56d

87c

ノ 𠂉 𠂎 卯 卯

卯 mǎo

4th/12th

This character depicts a long puddle by the side of a field or a rice paddy, and is the fourth sign of the Chinese zodiac.

* Ancient characters show that despite looking like "person 卩[85][jié]," the two characters have no connections.

87

87d

ノ 𠂉 𠂎 卯 卯 卯 留 留 留 留

留 liú

stay; study abroad

puddle/4th 卯 [mǎo] + field 田[154][tián]

To water one's farming land(田), the puddle(卯) always has to have excess water. This character also means 'to study abroad.'

* Ancient characters show that the top of this character is a variation of "卯[mǎo]."

留念[liúniàn] accept (keep) as a souvenir - 66b
留学生[liúxuéshēng] student studying abroad - 95a 208

匕

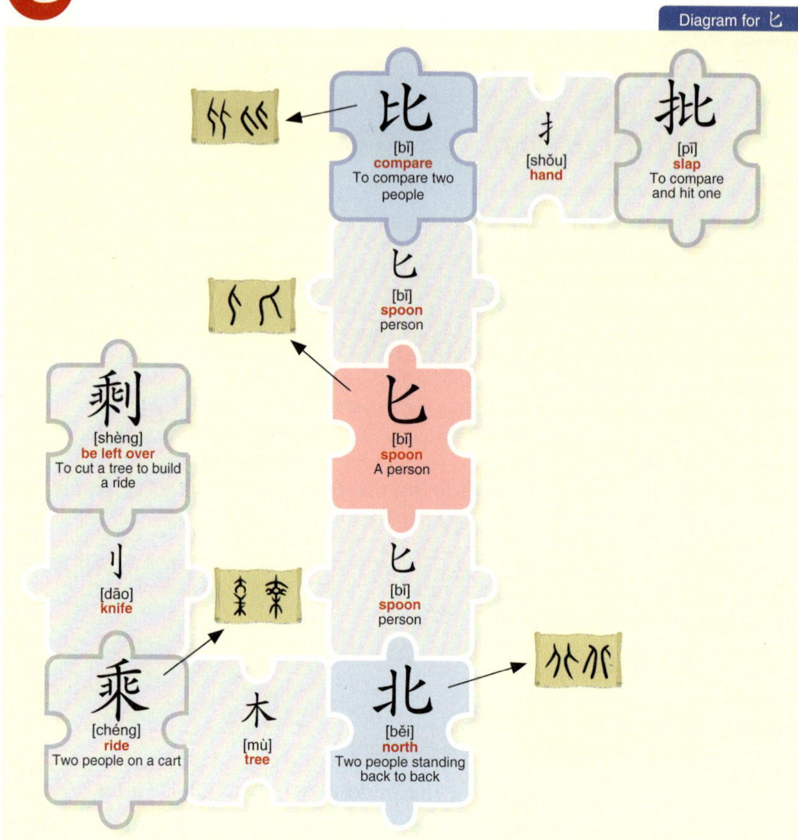

88

88 ノ 匕

匕 bǐ

spoon

It means 'spoon,' but is more often used to mean 'person.' Ancient texts explain that because it looks like a mirrored "person 人[63][rén]," it also means 'the elderly,' a frail person.

88a

一 ト ヒ 比

比 bǐ

compare

person/spoon 匕 [bǐ] + person/spoon 匕 [bǐ]

To compare the height or build of two people(匕) facing the same direction.

比较[bǐjiào] compare - 1c
比赛[bǐsài] match; contest; game - 206d

88b

一 十 扌 扌 扌 扌 批

批 pī

slap; criticize

hand 扌=手[31] [shǒu] + compare 比 [bǐ]

To criticize means to compare two people(比) and hit or slap(扌) the one that is below par.

批评[pīpíng] criticize; criticism - 122a

88c

丨 十 丬 丬 北

北 běi

north

person/spoon 匕 [bǐ] + person/spoon 匕 [bǐ]

Two people(匕) standing facing away from each other means 'to turn one's back on.' People prefer to face the light and build houses facing south, so this character came to mean 'north,' the direction one faces when their back is turned to the south.

北京[Běijīng] Beijing; Peking - 2
北方[běifāng] north; northern region - 160
北边[běibiān] north side - 61a
北部[běibù] north - 79f

88

88d

一 二 千 千 千 千 乖 乖 乘 乘

乘 chéng

ride

tree 禾[139] →木[210] [mù] + person/spoon 匕 [bǐ] + person/spoon 匕 [bǐ]

Two people(匕) riding on a wooden(木) cart. In the olden days, most of the things one could ride, like carts or carriages, were made of wood(木).

* Ancient characters show that "rice plant 禾 [hé]" is a variation of "tree 木."

乘客[chéngkè] passenger - 57b

88e

剩 shèng

be left over; remain

ride 乘 [chéng] + knife 刂=刀[119] [dāo]

To build a ride(乘) like a cart or a carriage, one must take a knife(刂) to cut off unwanted leaves and branches from the wood. That is how this character now means 'leftovers, remainders.'

剩饭。Leftover rice. - 88e 148b

88

匕

Diagram for 匕

88f 丶 丷 宀 宀 它

它 tā

it

house 宀[141] [mián] + old-person/spoon 匕 [bǐ]

This character means 'it' because it describes a weak old man(匕) who stays at home(宀) doing nothing but being a burden to others. It is also used when referring to objects.

* "匕" is the mirrored character of person(人[63]) and means 'an elderly person.'

它们[tāmen] they (thing) - 145a　　其它[qítā] other; the others - 44

88g 丨 ⺊ 卜 止 止 此

此 cǐ

this

stop 止[53] [zhǐ] + old-person/spoon 匕 [bǐ]

A weak old man(匕) stops walking(止) and instead uses only what he can reach. This character means 'this,' item that is close by.

因此[yīncǐ] therefore; hence; for this reason - 74e

88

88h 丨 ⺊ 卜 止 止 此 此 此 些

些 xiē

some; a few; a little

this 此 [cǐ] + two 二[226] [èr]

Where there are only two(二) of a certain item within arm's reach(此), there are only 'some, a few, a little.'

那些[nàxiē] those - 147e　　一些[yìxiē] some; a few; a little - 223

有些[yǒuxiē] some - 39c　　这些[zhèxiē] these - 133a

旨

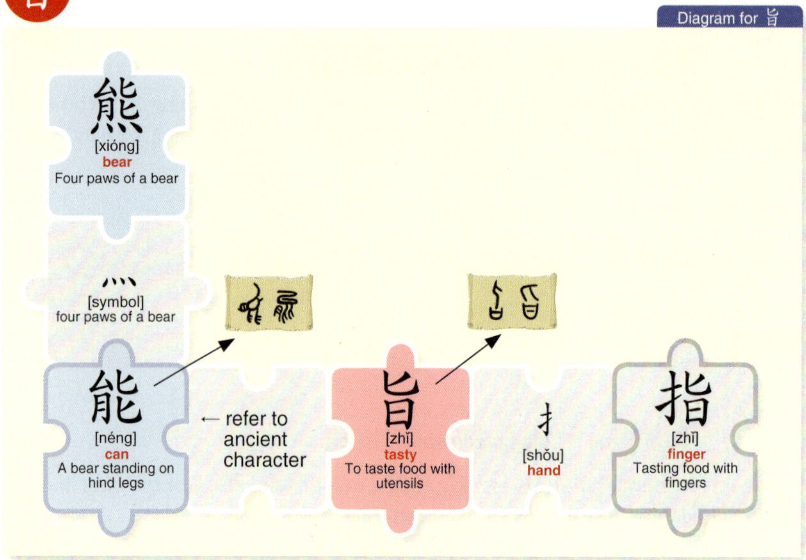

89

89 旨 zhǐ

丿 匕 匕 旨 旨 旨

tasty; purpose

spoon 匕[88] [bǐ] + bowl 日 [symbol]

To taste food in a bowl(日) with cutlery(匕). Some people use fingers to taste food, so this character came to mean 'finger.' Fingers are also used to point out a direction or a goal, so this character also means 'purpose.'

* The ancient text explains "旨" is a spoon(匕) hovering over a bowl(日).

89a 指 zhǐ

一 亅 扌 扌 扌 扌 指 指 指

finger; point

hand 扌=手[31] [shǒu] + purpose 旨 [zhǐ]

After "旨" came to mean 'purpose,' the Chinese added a hand(扌) to stress the meaning of 'finger.' This character also means 'to point.'

手指 [shǒuzhǐ] finger - 31　　指示 [zhǐshì] indicate; point out - 126

89b

能 néng

can

bear 㒸 [symbol] + bear's foot 匕 [symbol]

A bear(㒸) standing on its hind legs with its front paws(匕+匕) held high. A bear is very strong and for it to pose as if to attack means that one can do anything.

* The ancient character describes a bear(㒸) posing to attack prey with its front paws(匕+匕).

可能 [kěnéng] possible; can; may - 17
能干 [nénggàn] able; capable; competent - 121
能力 [nénglì] ability; capacity; capability - 159
能够 [nénggòu] can; be able to - 46d

89c

熊 xióng

bear

can 能 [néng] + four paws of a bear 灬 [symbol]

The pictogram of the character was created to mean bear "can 能 [néng]," and four paws(灬) were added to reinforce its original meaning 'bear.'

熊猫 [xióngmāo] panda; bearcat - 154d

89

尸

90

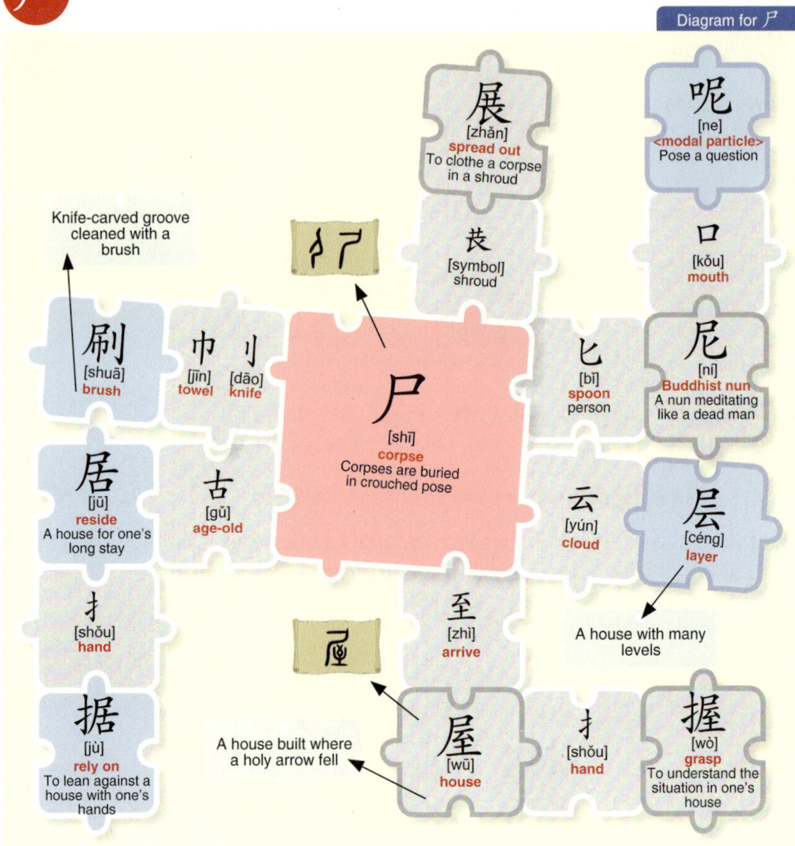

90

尸 shī **corpse**

This character describes a person crouching in a sitting position but with only the feet on the ground. Because people were buried in that posture, this character means 'corpse.' The ancient Chinese believed in an afterlife, so the biers used to transport corpses were made to look like houses and people were buried with some of their possessions. Which is why this character sometimes means house.

* Qin Shi Huang's(秦始皇, 259-210 BC) tomb is a good example of how the Chinese prepared a house within a tomb to prepare for the afterlife.

尸体[shītǐ] corpse; dead body - 29b

90a ㇕ ㇕ 尸 尸 尸 屈 屈 展 展 展

展 zhǎn

spread out

corpse 尸 [shī] + shroud(衣[130]) 㠭 [symbol]

A shroud(㠭) has been spread out to clothe the corpse(尸) in.

发展[fāzhǎn] develop; grow - 34f   展览[zhǎnlǎn] exhibit; show; display - 13e

90b ㇕ ㇕ 尸 尸 尼

尼 ní

Buddhist nun

corpse 尸 [shī] + person/spoon 匕[88][bǐ]

This character means 'Buddhist nun' because a person(匕) in deep meditation resembles a corpse(尸).

* Buddhism was imported from India and the Sanskrit word for a Buddhist nun is 'bhiksuni,' which in Chinese became "比丘尼[bǐqiūní]."

90

90c 丨 ㇕ 口 口㇕ 口㇕ 叩 叩 呢

呢 ne

<modal particle>

mouth 口[16][kǒu] + nun 尼 [ní]

A Buddhist nun(尼) moving her mouth(口) to quietly read a text is 'whispering.' But now this character us used at the end of a sentence to mark a question.

你为什么不去呢? Why aren't you going? - 69a 159c 231a 93a 223a 94 90c

90d ㇕ ㇕ 尸 尸 屈 层 层

层 céng

layer

house/corpse 尸 [shī] + cloud 云[227][yún]

A cloud(云) is layered because different clouds form at different altitudes. This character depicts a house(尸) with many floors.

我的新家在第十六层。My new house is on the sixteenth floor.
- 113b 46b 103b 174a 32a 109b 231 229a 90d

90e ㇇ ㇇ 尸 尸 尸 层 层 屋 屋

屋 wū

house

house/corpse 尸 [shī] + arrive 至[112] [zhì]

In ancient China, when building a house(尸), they shot a specially decorated arrow and built the house in the spot where the arrow landed(至).

* "至" is the actual shape of a decorated sacred arrow(矢[111]) stuck upside down in the ground (一).

屋子[wūzi] room - 95　　同屋[tóngwū] roommate - 149b

90f 一 十 扌 扌 扌 护 护 护 握 握 握 握

握 wò

grasp

hand 扌=手[31] [shǒu] + house 屋 [wū]

One always has more authority and sense of security in one's own house. One usually understands how things are at home(屋), so it is easier to grasp(扌) control of the situation.

握手[wò/shǒu] shake hands - 31　　掌握[zhǎngwò] grasp; master - 31a

90

90g ㇇ ㇇ 尸 尸 尸 尸 居 居

居 jū

reside

house/corpse 尸 [shī] + age-old 古[19] [gǔ]

This character symbolizes a house(尸) where one can live for the longest period(古) of time right from the time of his or her birth.

邻居[línjū] neighbor - 147g

90h 一 十 扌 扌 扌 护 护 护 据 据 据

据 jù

rely on

hand 扌=手[31] [shǒu] + reside 居 [jū]

It must be a safe and comfortable place if anybody can reside(居) in it for a long time. This character illustrates the image of a person's hands(扌) leaning against such a house.

根据[gēnjù] based on; according to - 14b

90i

㇇ ㇇ 尸 尸 启 届 刷 刷

刷 shuā

brush

corpse 尸 [shī] + towel 巾[131] [jīn] + knife 刂=刀[119] [dāo]

This character depicts the image of a dead body(尸) that is cleaned with cloth (巾) before being buried. Later on, a knife(刂) is added to this letter which came to mean 'to brush–clean' a knife-carved groove for making such a character.

* In the earlier days, printing was done in such a way that the surface of all letters carved in wooden block was first evenly brushed(刷) with ink and then the papers were printed.

刷牙 [shuāyá] brush one's teeth - 25 印刷 [yìnshuā] print - 87b

尺

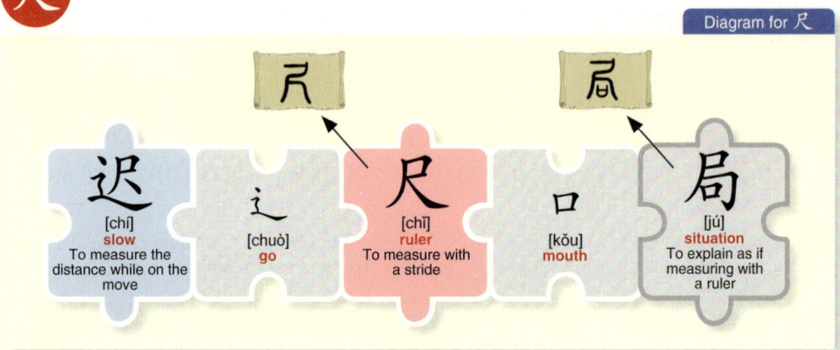

91 ㄱ コ 尸 尺

尺 chǐ ruler

To draw a line(丿[234]) between a person's(尸[90]) legs to measure the distance. It was a common way to measure distances, so this character means 'ruler, a unit of length.' One foot is 30.5 centimeters, about a third of a meter.

91 * "Corpse 尸 [shī]" is a crouching man, so in essence it means 'person.'

91a ㄱ コ 尸 月 局 局 局

局 jú situation; office

ruler 尺 [chǐ] + mouth 口[16] [kǒu]

An official verbally(口) describes the situation as if measuring(尺) the facts. This character also means office, because that is where official business takes place.

邮局 [yóujú] post office - 147d　　局长 [júzhǎng] director - 102

91b ㄱ コ 尸 尺 ˋ尺 讠尺 迟

迟 chí slow

ruler 尺 [chǐ] + go 辶[61] [chuò]

To move slowly because one is on the road(辶) with the purpose of measuring(尺) the distance and the strides have to be uniform.

* The traditional character(遲) is a large bull or rhino(犀[xī]) walking slowly along the road(辶).

迟到 [chídào] be late; arrive late - 112b

巳

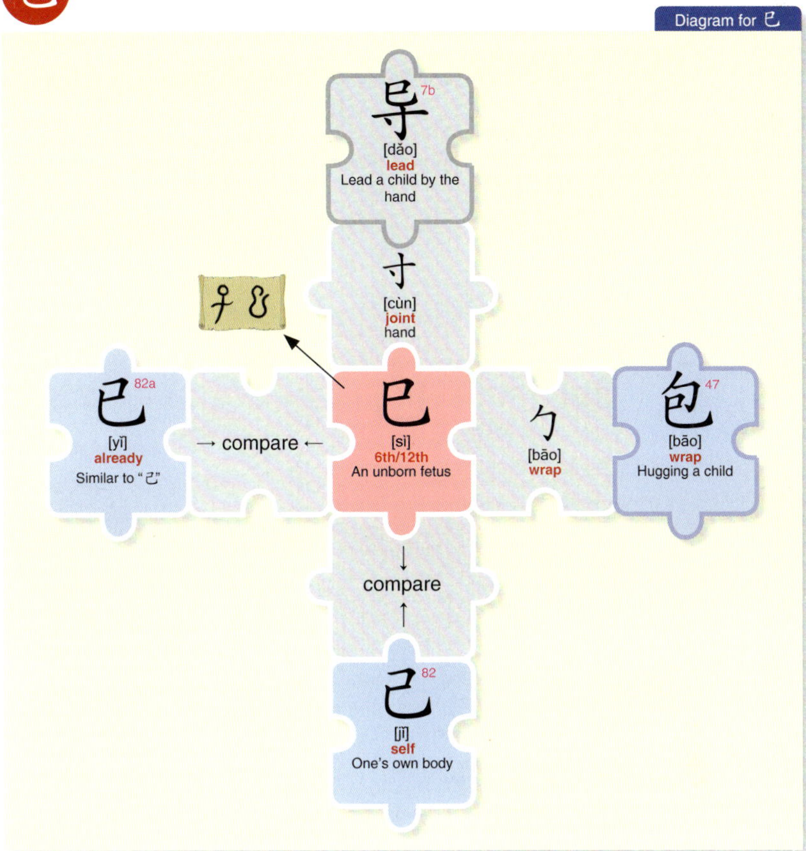

92

ㄱ ㄱ 巳

巳 sì

unborn child; 6th/12th

A fetus still in the mother's womb, or a newborn baby. It's the sixth out of the twelve Chinese zodiac signs.

92

巴

Diagram for 巴

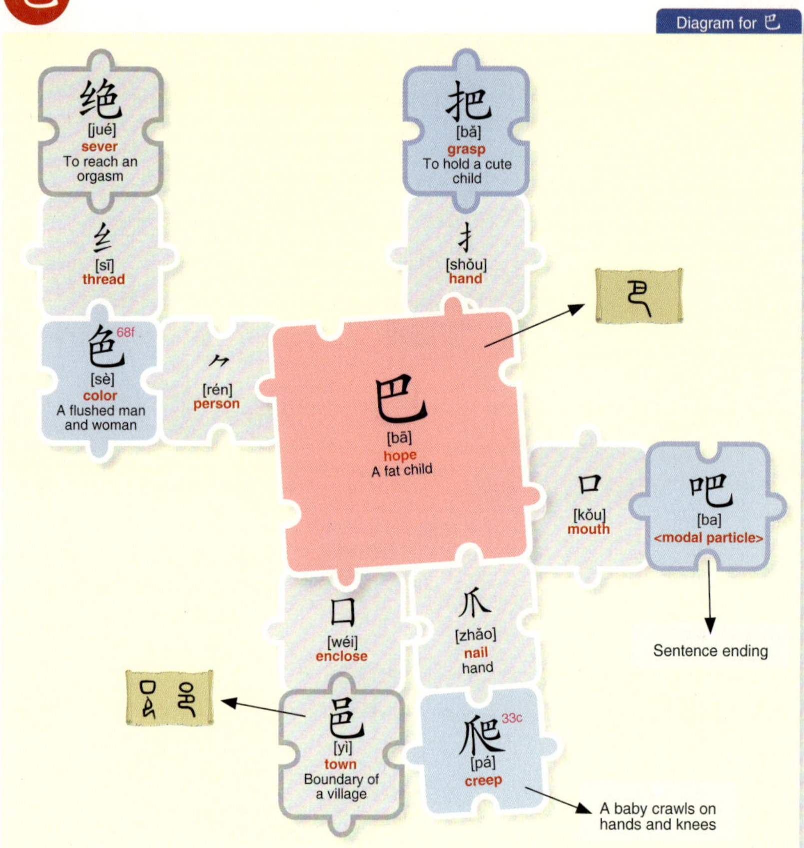

92a

巴 bā — hope; cling to

If "巳[sì]" is a fetus or a newborn baby, "巴" is a baby with more weight that can be considered a person. It signifies the wish that one wishes their children to be healthy. As it is a child(巳) that has gained weight(巴), it also means 'to stick.'

嘴巴[zuǐba] cheek; mouth - 191b

92b 一 扌 扌 扌 扌 扌 把

把 bǎ

grasp; <preposition>

hand 扌=手[31][shǒu] + child/hope 巴 [bā]

To hold a cute child(巴) with one's hands(扌). It came to mean the measure word of items that can be held in one hand or a handful of something. When used as a preposition, it takes the 把+object+verb structure and stresses the action of the verb.

把门开着! Keep the door open! (The object "door 门" comes in front of the verb "to open 开着" and accentuates(把) the meaning.) - 92b 145 43a 11b

92c 丨 口 口 口 口 口 吧

吧 ba

<modal particle>

mouth 口[16][kǒu] + child/hope 巴 [bā]

It was used to describe a child(巴) in an argument(口) but now it is used at the end of a sentence to stress a command or question.

* When a character with "口" does not imply speaking or eating, which is what a mouth(口) is for, it is mostly used as a modal particle.

你想想吧。ou think about it. - 69a 11d 11d 92c
他们是中国人吧? Are they Chinese? - 84b 145a 54b 232a 20a 63 92c

92d 丨 口 口 另 另 吕 邑

邑 yì

town

enclose 囗[20][wéi] + person/hope 巴 [bā]

The boundary(囗) surrounding a town where people(巴) live. When it is on the right of a more complicated character, it takes the shape of "hill 阝[147][fu]."

* When "阝[fu]" is on the left it means 'hill,' when it's on the right it means 'town(邑).'

92e 丿 纟 纟 纟 纟 纟 纟 绝 绝

绝 jué

sever; extremely

thread 纟[132][sī] + person ⺈[68][rén] + person/hope 巴 [bā]

When a person(⺈) is on top of another person(巴) to have intercourse(色) and the ecstasy reaches a climax, the 'severity, extremity' could be likened to the second before a length of thread(纟) snaps.

* "Color 色[68f][sè]" is a depiction of a person(⺈) on top of another(巴) to have sexual intercourse.

绝对[juéduì] absolute - 40c

92

ム

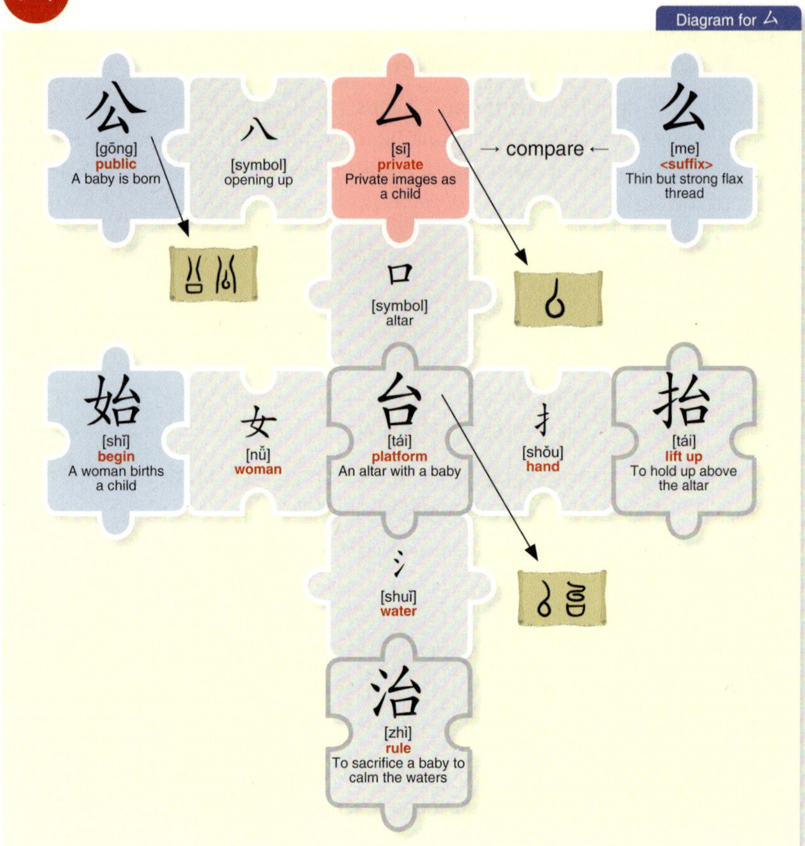

93

93 ム private

ㄥ ム

ム sī

private

We can't be sure what this ancient character meant, but if we consider the meanings of all the characters that include "ム," it seems to mean 'a newborn baby.' Such images are for private viewing.

93a

丿 ㄥ 么

么 me

<suffix>

The thread(幺→幺→糸[132]) made from flax fibers. It looks thin and flimsy but it's actually strong and becomes even stronger when wet, which is why it's used to make thick ropes. Because it's stronger than it looks, when used as a suffix, it poses a question.

* The traditional character(麼) shows a thread(幺→幺→糸) made of flax(麻[212a]) fibers.

什么 [shénme] what - 231a
怎么 [zěnme] how - 234d
怎么样 [zěnmeyàng] how - 234d 171a
为什么 [wèishénme] why - 159c 231a
多么 [duōme] how; what - 222d
那么 [nàme] that way; like that - 147e
这么 [zhème] this way; like this - 133a

93b

丿 八 公 公

公 gōng

public

opening up 八 [symbol] + newborn baby/private 厶 [sī]

The womb opens(八) and a fetus(厶) is born. It means that a baby is now a member of the public and no longer under the sole protection of its mother.

* The "eight 八[229][bā]" part of "公" is the shape of something opening up.

公共汽车 [gōnggòngqìchē] bus - 43c 204a 124
公斤 [gōngjīn] kilogram (kg) - 118
公司 [gōngsī] corporation; company - 18e
办公室 [bàngōngshì] office - 159b 112a
公园 [gōngyuán] park; public garden - 73c
公里 [gōnglǐ] kilometre (km) - 151
公共 [gōnggòng] public - 43c
公元 [gōngyuán] Anno Domini (A.D.) - 73

93

93c

𠃋 厶 台 台 台

台 tái

platform

newborn baby/private 厶 [sī] + altar 口 [symbol]

A newborn baby(厶) is on the altar(口) to be offered up as a sacrifice.

* Although there's no proof of this, some say it's the shape of a baby(厶) speaking(口[16][kǒu]) in baby talk.

舞台 [wǔtái] stage; arena - 58a

93d 一 十 扌 扌 扌 拧 抬 抬

抬 tái

lift up

hand 扌=手[31] [shǒu] + platform 台 [tái]

To lift up a baby with both hands(扌) above the altar(台) to sacrifice to the gods.

请抬起头来，看黑板。Please raise your head and look at the blackboard. - 135c 93d 53d 75 212d, 11a 158d 148c

93e 丶 丶 氵 氵 氵 氵 治 治

治 zhì

rule

water 氵[202] [shuǐ] + platform 台 [tái]

Whenever there was a drought or a flood, the people offered a baby on the altar(台) to calm or rule the waters(氵). The Chinese believed the gods had power over natural phenomena.

政治 [zhèngzhì] politics - 50f

93

93f 𡿨 女 女 女 女 女 始 始

始 shǐ

begin

woman 女[96] [nǚ] + newborn baby/platform 台 [tái]

This character proves that the chicken comes before the egg. It shows a woman (女) giving birth to a child(台), which signaled the beginning of a life.

* "台" is the shape of a baby(厶) speaking(口[16] [kǒu]) in baby talk.

开始 [kāishǐ] begin; start - 43a

去

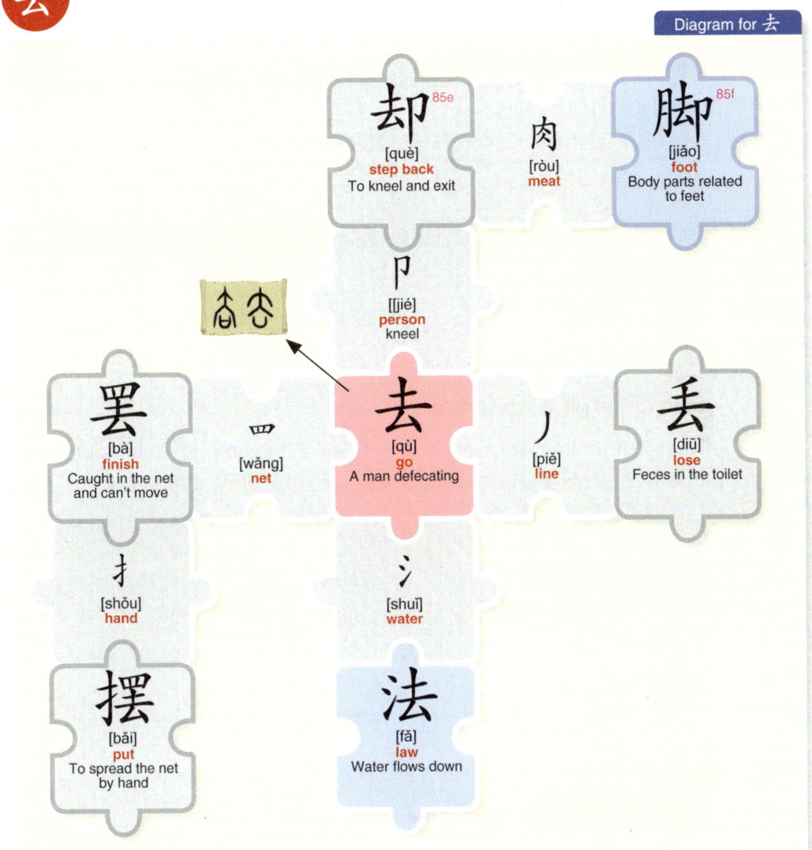

94

94

一 十 土 去 去

去 qù

go

person 土→大[74][dà] + night-soil jar 厶→凵 [symbol]

A man(大) sitting above a toilet(凵) to defecate(㚎). Because feces exits the body, this character came to mean ‘to go.’

* The “厶[93][sī]” in “去” does not mean ‘private’ or ‘fetus.’ Same shape doesn't always translate to same meaning.

去年[qùnián] last year - 121a
出去[chūqù] go out; get out - 167a
进去[jìnqù] go in; get in; enter - 228b
下去[xiàqù] go down; descend - 223g
过去[guòqù] in the past; formerly - 40f
回去[huíqù] return; go back - 20d
上去[shàngqù] go up; upward - 223f

94a

丿 二 千 壬 丟 丟

丟 diū

lose; throw

line 丿 [234] [piě] + go 去 [qù]

If "去→厺" is a man defecating, "丿" is the feces. It must be thrown out, which is why this character also means 'to lost, to throw.'

* "丿" has no meaning and can be interpreted in many ways.

上午我的自行车丢了。I lost my bicycle in the morning. - 223f 121b 113b 46b 26 60b 124 94a 168a

94b

丶 丶 氵 氵 汁 注 法 法

法 fǎ

law

water 氵 [202] [shuǐ] + go 去 [qù]

It is a natural phenomenon for water(氵) to flow(去) from high to low altitudes. For people to live in harmony, there are laws that must be adhered to.

* For water(氵) to go(去), it has to flow.

办法[bànfǎ] method; means; way - 159b
方法[fāngfǎ] method; means; way - 160
法律[fǎlǜ] law; statute - 37a
法语[fǎyǔ] French (language) - 226c
语法[yǔfǎ] grammar; syntax - 226c

94

94c

丶 冖 冖 罒 罒 罒 罒 罒 罢 罢

罢 bà

finish

net 罒=网 [165] [wǎng] + go 去 [qù]

This character came to mean 'stop, finish' because it describes someone caught in a net(罒) and not being able to go(去) anywhere.

罢工[bà/gōng] strike; walk out - 200

94d

一 十 扌 扌 扌 扌 扌 扌 扌 押 押 摆 摆

摆 bǎi

put; arrange

hand 扌=手 [31] [shǒu] + caught in the net/finish 罢 [bà]

One must 'put, arrange' a net by hand(扌) to catch(罢) an animal.

把书摆在桌子上。Put the book on the table - 92b 232d 94d 32a 128b 95 223f

子

Diagram for 子

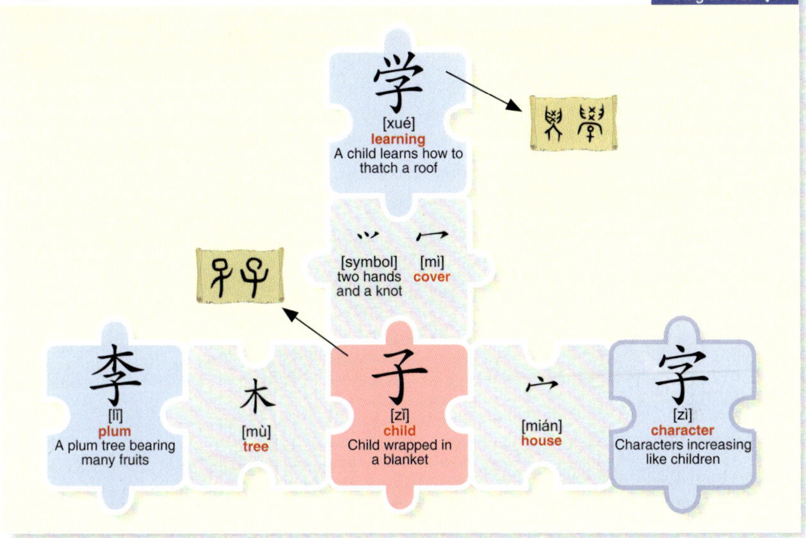

95

フ 了 子

95

子 zǐ/zi

child / suffix

A child wrapped in a blanket means 'sons and daughters,' but more often 'son' than 'daughter' because Confucianism caused parents to prefer sons.

This character is also used as a meaningless suffix.

杯子[bēizi] cup; glass - 223b
椅子[yǐzi] chair - 18c
孩子[háizi] child - 4c
鼻子[bízi] nose - 26c
句子[jùzi] sentence - 46c
裤子[kùzi] pants; trousers - 124e
盘子[pánzi] tray; plate - 125c
本子[běnzi] book; notebook - 210a
饺子[jiǎozi] dumpling (with meat and vegetable stuffing) - 1b
橘子[júzi] orange; tangerine - 116b
袜子[wàzi] socks; stockings - 210c
样子[yàngzi] appearance; shape - 171a

儿子[érzi] son - 71
桌子[zhuōzi] table; desk - 128b
妻子[qīzi] wife - 96l
电子邮件[diànzǐyóujiàn] E-mail - 157a 147d 175a
筷子[kuàizi] chopstick - 216b
帽子[màozi] cap; hat - 11f
裙子[qúnzi] skirt - 37f
日子[rìzi] day; date - 218
屋子[wūzi] room - 90e

95

95a

丶 丷 丷 丷 丷 学 学 学

学 xué

learning

two hands and a knot ⺍ [symbol] + cover 冖[169] [mì] + child 子 [zǐ]

A boy(子) watching and learning from the adults who were thatching a roof (冖) with their hands(⺍).

* The upper part of The traditional character(學) is "学," with three dots(⺍), a pair of hands(臼[13a]) and a knot(㐅). The boy(子) learns from watching men cover a roof(冖) with bundles(㐅) of hay using their hands(臼).

同学[tóngxué] be in the same school - 149b
学生[xuésheng] student - 208
学习[xuéxí] study; learn - 182a
学校[xuéxiào] school - 1d
数学[shùxué] mathematics - 138c
大学[dàxué] university; college - 74
化学[huàxué] chemistry - 70a
开学[kāi/xué] school opens; term begins - 43a
科学[kēxué] science - 164a
留学生[liúxuéshēng] student studying abroad - 87d 208
上学[shàng/xué] go to school - 223f
文学[wénxué] literature - 133
文学家[wénxuéjiā] Trecentist; litterateur - 133 174a
学院[xuéyuàn] college - 73b
中学[zhōngxué] middle school - 232a

95b

丶 丶 宀 宀 字 字

字 zì

character; word

house 宀[141] [mián] + child 子 [zǐ]

Just like the number of children(子)in a household(宀) increase, new characters are made. Chinese characters are mostly pictograms and one character usually means one thing, so new characters have to be made to reflect the changing times. In comparison, the alphabet has changed much less.

名字[míngzi] name - 222c
字典[zìdiǎn] dictionary - 217a
汉字[hànzì] Chinese character - 34g
数字[shùzì] numeral - 138c

95c

一 十 才 木 本 李 李

李 lǐ

plum

tree 木[210] [mù] + child 子 [zǐ]

This character illustrates the characteristics of a plum tree(木) that bears many fruits(子).

行李箱[xínglǐxiāng] suitcase; trunk (boot) - 60b 216a

女

Diagram for 女

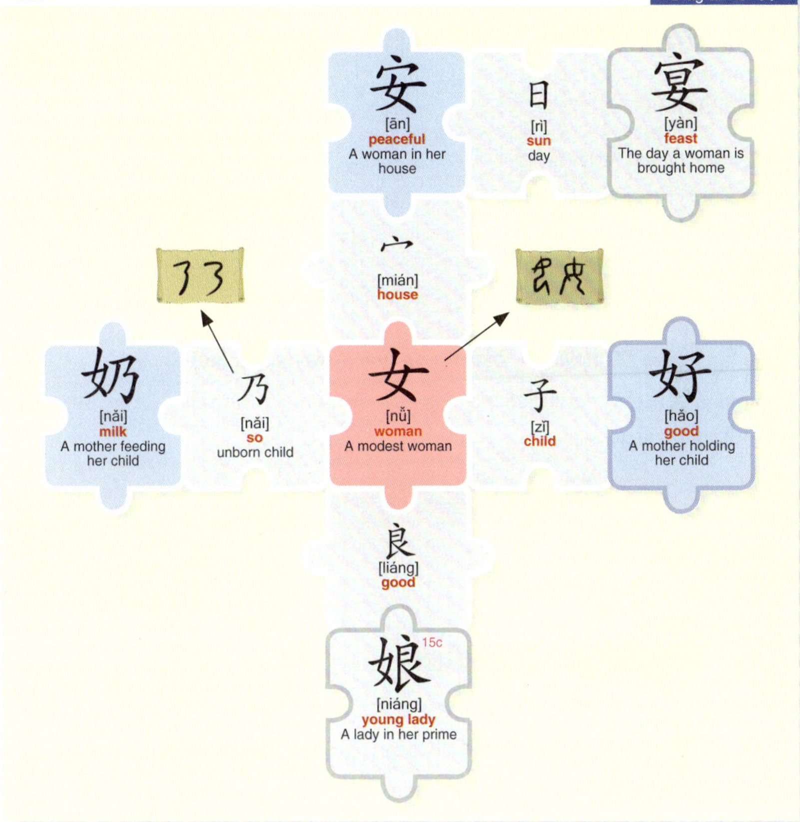

96

96

く 女 女

女 nǚ

woman

A woman sitting with her hands on her knees.

女儿[nǚér] daughter - 71	女人[nǚrén] woman - 63

96

96a

丶 ⺊ 宀 宁 安 安

安 ān

peaceful

house 宀[141] [mián] + woman 女 [nǚ]

A woman(女) is relatively weaker than man, so she feels peaceful and safe when at home(宀).

安静[ānjìng] quiet; peaceful - 36c
安排[ānpái] arrange - 181a
安全[ānquán] safe; secure - 63f

96b

丶 ⺊ 宀 宀 宁 官 宫 宴 宴 宴

宴 yàn

feast

house 宀[141] [mián] + day/sun 日[218] [rì] + woman 女 [nǚ]

To hold a feast to celebrate bringing a woman(女) home(宀) on the man's wedding day(日).

宴会[yànhuì] banquet; feast - 66c

96c

㇛ 女 女 女' 好 好

好 hǎo

good

woman 女 [nǚ] + child 子[95] [zǐ]

It's always a 'good' thing for a mother(女) to hold her child(子).

好吃[hǎochī] tasty; delicious - 16b
爱好[ài/hào] to be fond of; interest; hobby - 34e
好处[hǎochu] advantage; benefit - 56b
好看[hǎokàn] good-looking - 11a
好像[hǎoxiàng] seem; be like - 174c
问好[wèn/hǎo] send one's regards to - 145b
友好[yǒuhǎo] close friend - 34d
只好[zhǐhǎo] have to; be forced to - 179

96d

㇛ 女 女 奶 奶

奶 nǎi

milk

woman 女 [nǚ] + unborn child/so 乃 [nǎi]

A mother(女) holding her new baby(乃) in her arms to feed milk.

* The ancient character of "so 乃 [nǎi]" is the shape of a fetus.

牛奶[niúnǎi] (cow's) milk - 175
奶奶[nǎinai] grandmother; grandma

女

Diagram for 女

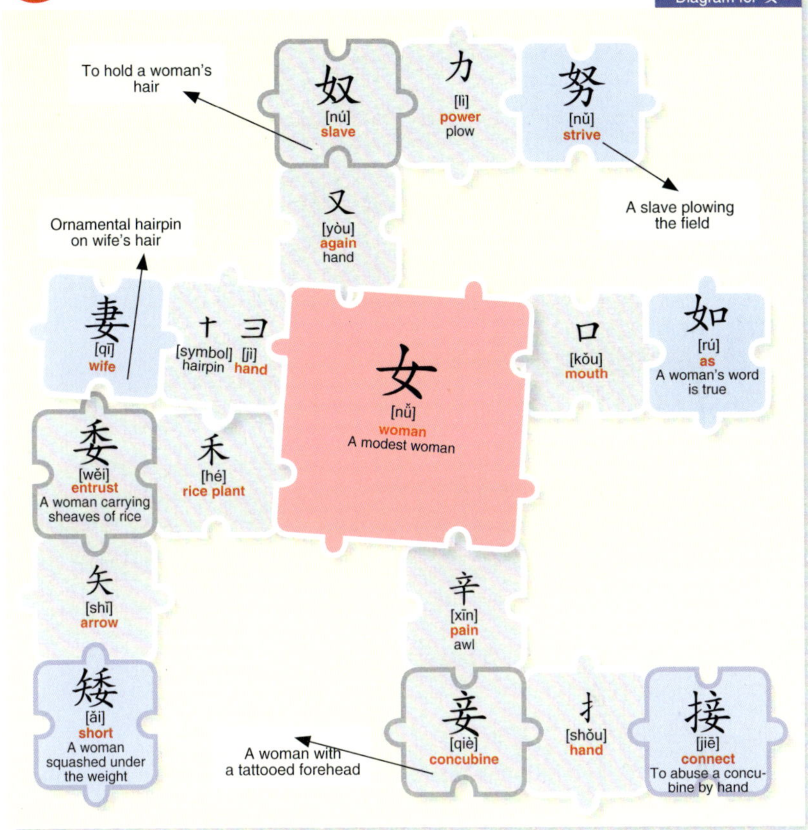

96

96e

奴 nú	**slave**

woman 女 [nǚ] + hand/again 又[34] [yòu]

When being mistreated, a female(女) slave is held(又) by her hair.

奴隶[núlì] slave - 38

96

96f

ㄑ 女 女 奴 奴 努 努

努 nǔ

strive

slave 奴 [nú] + plow/power 力[159] [lì]

A slave(奴) working hard in the field plowing(力).

* The Chinese word "努力 [nǔlì]" means to work as hard as a slave(奴) who is putting much strength (力) into his work.

努力 [nǔ/lì] try hard; strive - 159

96g

ㄑ 女 女 如 如 如

如 rú

as

woman 女 [nǚ] + mouth 口[16] [kǒu]

This character got the 'just like~' meaning because what a woman(女) says (口) is closer to the truth.

如果 [rúguǒ] if; in case; in the event of - 210g
不如 [bùrú] not as good as; not equal to - 223a
例如 [lìrú] for instance; for example - 30c
如何 [rúhé] how - 17c

96h

丶 亠 亠 立 立 妾 妾 妾

妾 qiè

concubine

awl/pain 立[79] → 辛[103] [xīn] + woman 女 [nǚ]

To use an awl(辛) to tattoo a woman's(女) forehead and make her a man's slave or a concubine. In ancient China, female(女) prisoners or the wives and daughters of dead criminals were tattooed on the forehead with an awl(辛) and taken as slaves or concubines.

* The upper part of "妾," The ancient character has nothing to do with "stand 立 [lì]."

96i

一 十 扌 扌 扩 扩 护 护 挃 接 接

接 jiē

connect; receive

hand 扌=手[31] [nǔ] + concubine 妾 [qiè]

To tease a concubine(妾) with one's hand(扌) means to have an heir to succeed the family name, or to 'receive' her servitude.

接着 [jiēzhe] catch; continue - 11b
接近 [jiējìn] be close to; near; approach - 118a
迎接 [yíngjiē] meet; welcome; greet; receive - 87a
直接 [zhíjiē] direct; immediate - 12

96j

丿 二 千 千 禾 禾 委 委

委 wěi

entrust

rice plant 禾[139] [hé] + woman 女 [nǚ]

A woman(女) carrying sheaves of rice(禾) on her head is a woman being entrusted with her duty and helping out during the busy harvest.

委员 [wěiyuán] committee member - 186h

96k

丿 𠂉 𠂉 ⺈ 矢 矢 矢 矢 矢 矢 矮 矮 矮

矮 ǎi

short

arrow 矢[111] [shǐ] + entrust 委 [wěi]

A woman carrying sheaves of rice on her head(委) hunches over and becomes shorter, and this is likened to a short arrow(矢).

在我们的花园里有一棵矮苹果树。There is a dwarf apple tree in our garden.
- 32a 113b 145a 46b 70b 73c 151 39c 223 210h 96k 122b 210g 40d

96l

一 ㄱ 彐 彐 ⺕ 妻 妻 妻

妻 qī

wife

hairpin 𠆢 [symbol] + hand 彐[36] [jì] + woman 女[96] [nǚ]

This character symbolizes a married woman(女) who has her ornamental hairpin(𠆢) on her hair to do or keep up(彐) in a chignon.

* In ancient China, only married women tied up their hair with an ornamental hairpin.

妻子 [qīzi] wife - 95

96

母

Diagram for 母

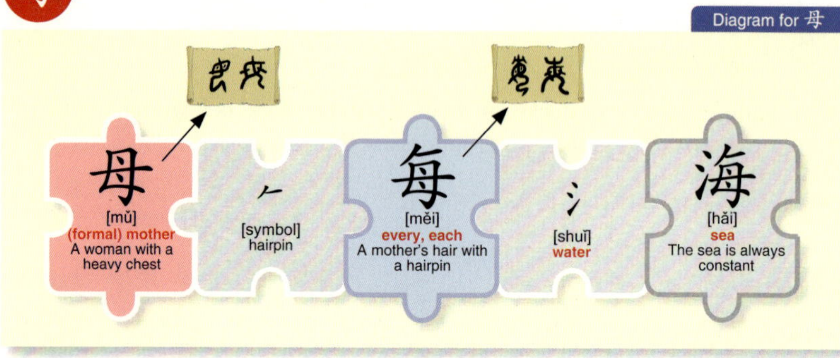

97

母 mǔ — (formal) mother

Skew the "woman 女[96][nǚ]" character to the side, add two dots(丶, 丶) to accentuate breastfeeding, and the character means 'mother.'

97 母亲[mǔqīn] mother - 103a

97a

每 měi — every, each

hairpin 𠂉 [symbol] + mother 母 [mǔ]

A mother(母) usually pulls her hair up with a hairpin(𠂉), which is why this character means 'every, each.'

* "𠂉" is not a person but a zanzi(簪子), a traditional Asian hairpin that is stuck through a woman's hair. In ancient China, only married women tied up their hair with one.

每周末 every weekend - 97a 154a 210b

97b

海 hǎi — sea

water 氵[202][shuǐ] + every 每 [měi]

The sea never overflows or dries up and always(每) maintains the same water (氵) level.

海关[hǎiguān] customhouse; customs - 45

父

Diagram for 父

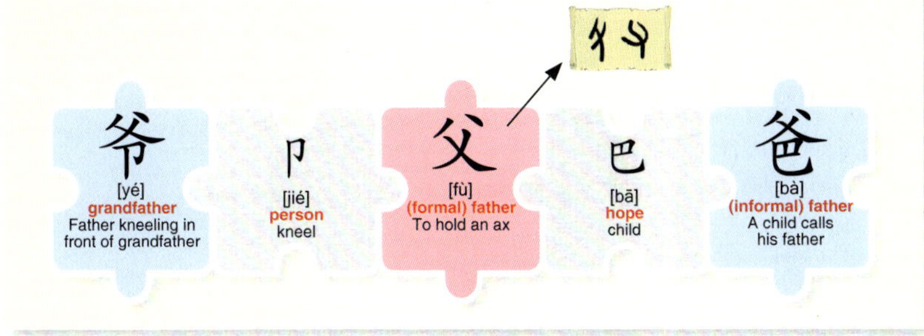

98 ノ ハ ク 父

父 fù

(formal) father

A father holding a hammer or a stick in his hand(又[34]) to hunt for the family.

父亲 [fùqīn] father - 103a

98a ノ ハ ク 父 父 父 父 爸

爸 bà

(informal) father

father 父 [fù] + child/hope 巴[92a] [bā]

A young child(巴) calling out to his father(父) would say 'dad.'

* "巴" is a baby with more weight, a child.

爸爸 [bàba] papa; dad; daddy; father

98b ノ ハ ク 父 父 爷

爷 yé

grandfather

father 父 [fù] + kneel/person 卩[85] [jié]

A grandfather is someone a father(父) would kneel(卩) to.

* "卩" is the shape of a kneeling man.

爷爷 [yéye] grandfather

氏

Diagram for 氏

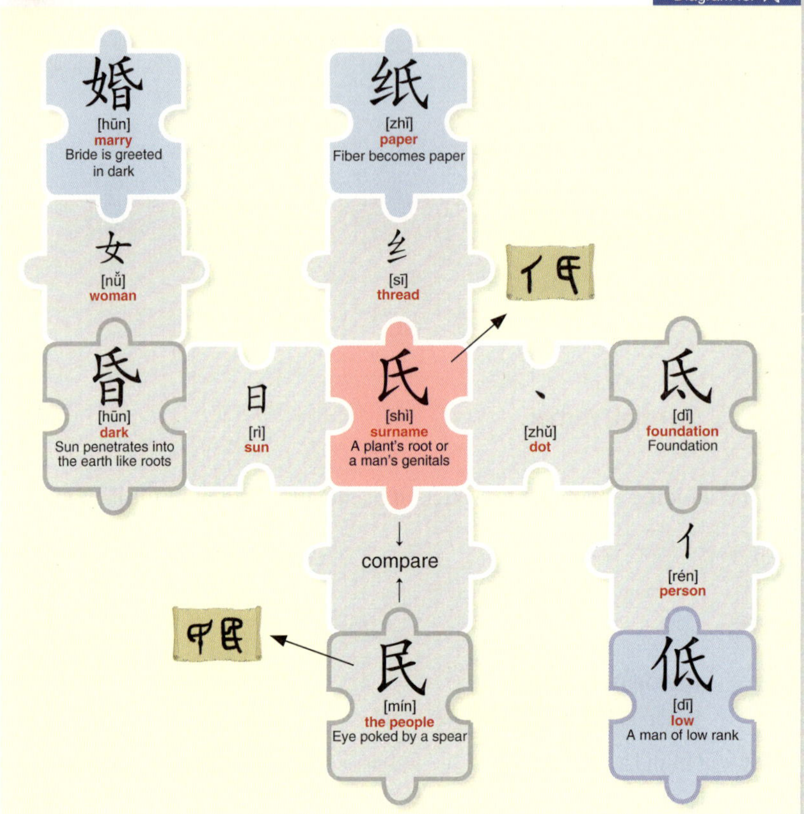

99

99

丿 厂 F 氏

氏 shì

surname

One cannot be sure, but the ancient text suggests the meaning 'surname' came from the fact that this character looks like a root or a man's genitals.

99a

纟 纟 纟 纟 纟 纟 纸

纸 zhǐ

paper

thread 纟[132] [sī] + root/surname 氏 [shì]

The root(氏), the main material paper is made of, is thread(纟). Paper was made with(氏) fiber and that is a thready(纟) substance.

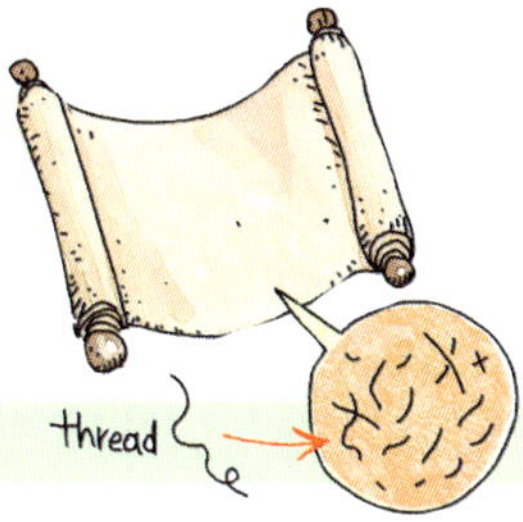

* China's Cai Lun(蔡伦, 50 AD~121) was the first man to make paper and he used flax fiber.

报纸[bàozhǐ] newspaper - 34a

99b 丿 亻 亻' 亻C 亻⺁ 低 低

低 dī

low

person 亻[70][rén] + foundation 氐 [dǐ]

'Base(氐)' implies 'below, the floor,' and a man(亻) whose social rank is below(氐) others is a 'low' person.

* When "氏[shì]" became 'surname' instead of 'genitals,' the Chinese added a dot(丶[233]) at the bottom of its character to mean "foundation 氐 [dǐ]."

降低[jiàngdī] reduce; lower - 58b

99c ㇕ ㇕ 尸 尸 民

民 mín

the people

War prisoners were made slaves by blinding them in one eye(目[11]) with a spear (矛[116]). But the meaning later changed to 'people.'

* The ancient character shows it's a spear(矛) poking an eye(目). This character is listed here because the radical of "民" is "surname 氏 [shì]" and has nothing to do with the meaning.

民族[mínzú] race; nation - 161a
农民[nóngmín] farmer; peasant - 130c
人民[rénmín] the people - 63
渔民[yúmín] fisherman - 185b

99d 丿 𠂆 ⺁ 氏 氏 昏 昏 昏

昏 hūn

dark

root/surname 氏 [shì] + sun 日[218][rì]

This character depicts the image of sunlight(日) penetrating deep into the earth like the roots(氏) of trees and has the meaning 'dark.'

99

99e

婚 hūn

marry

woman 女[96] [nǚ] + dark 昏 [hūn]

As sun sets and gets dark(昏), a bride(女) is greeted. This character illustrates the traditional wedding custom of the old China.

结婚[jié/hūn] marry; get married - 104b

100

耂

Diagram for 耂

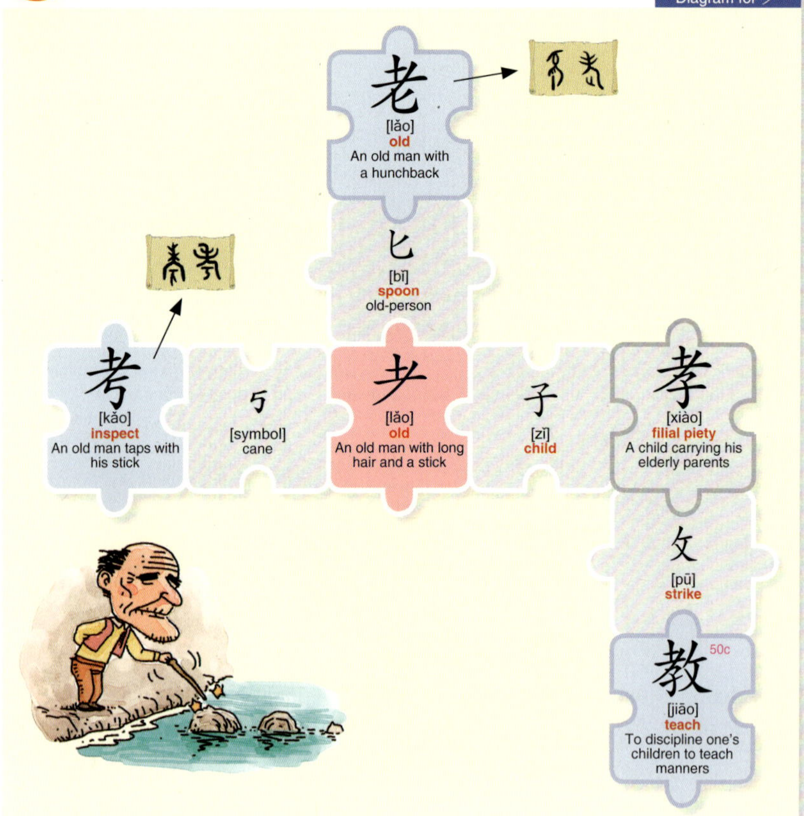

100 — 一 十 土 耂

耂
lǎo

old

An old man with a hunched back and long flying hair(丿) is using a stick to help him tread the ground(土[152]).

* This character is originally short for "old 老[100a][lǎo]." The word "ancient" illustrates that an old man (耂) with a hunched back and long hair is holding onto his walking stick(匕).

100a — 一 十 土 耂 耂 老

老
lǎo

old

old 耂 [lǎo] + old-person/spoon 匕[88][bǐ]

As "耂" cannot be used on its own, the Chinese added the character for 'old (匕)' to stress the meaning.

* "匕" is a mirror reflection of a person(人[63]) and is used to describe the elderly.

老师[lǎoshī] teacher (honorific) - 131e
老百姓[lǎobǎixìng] common people; ordinary people - 134a 208c
老人[lǎorén] old man (woman); the aged - 63

100

100b — 一 十 土 耂 耂 孝 孝

孝
xiào

filial piety

old 耂 [lǎo] + child 子[95][zǐ]

A filial son(子) is one who carries his old(耂) parents.

100c — 一 十 土 耂 耂 考

考
kǎo

inspect

old 耂 [lǎo] + cane 丂 [symbol]

A wary old(耂) man who uses his stick(丂) to tap and inspect where he is treading.

* Ancient text shows that the lower half is the crooked stick.

考试[kǎoshì] examination; test - 110b
考察[kǎochá] inspect; investigate - 126b

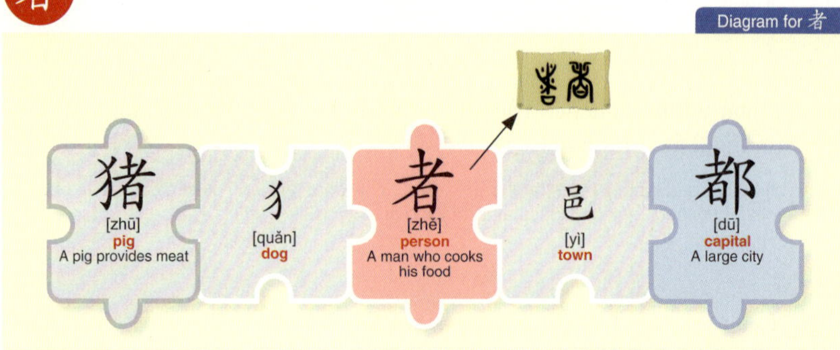

101 一 十 土 耂 耂 者 者 者

者 zhě person; -ist, -er (person)

This character describes someone cooking with a pot, and has nothing to do
with "old 耂[100][lǎo]." Only people are known to do that. Now, this character is
101 used after a verb or an adjective to describe a person or an object with certain
qualities.

或者[huòzhě] perhaps; maybe - 113d
读者[dúzhě] reader - 75d
记者[jìzhě] reporter; journalist - 82b

101a 一 十 土 耂 耂 者 者 者 者阝 都

都 dū/dōu capital / all

person 者 [zhě] + town 阝[147] → 邑[92d][yì]

A large village(邑) with many people who cook(者). To distinguish this word from a mere village(邑), the Chinese added "者" to say 'capital.'

* "Hill 阝 [fù]" on the right of a character means "邑."

首都[shǒudū] capital; metropolitan - 7

In a large city(邑), people(者) live all together.

连…都(也)[lián...dōu(yě... even…is/does… - 124c 84
他是个这么好的学生，所以我们都喜欢他。Such a good student is he that we all like him. - 84b 54b 63b 133a 93a 96c 46b 95a 208, 144a 63j 113b 145a 101a 140a 23c 84b

101b ノ 犭 犭 犭 犭 犭 犭 犭 猪 猪 猪

猪 zhū

pig

dog 犭[173] [quǎn] + person 者 [zhě]

A pig is an animal(犭) that provides meat to a person who cooks(者). This shows that pigs have provided us with food for many centuries.

* "犭" symbolizes an animal, the size of a large dog.

猪肉 pork - 101b 192

101

长

Diagram for 长

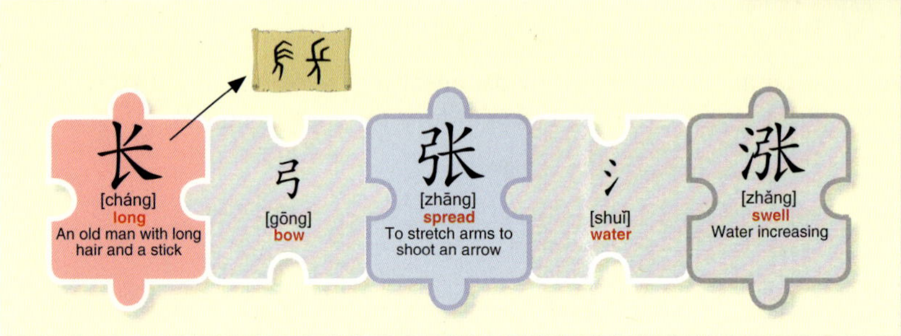

102

′ 一 ⺊ 长

长 cháng/zhǎng

long / elder; grow

Like "old 老[100a][lǎo]," this character also is an old man with long hair and a stick. But whereas "老" came to mean 'old,' "长" came to mean 'long.'

102 长期[chángqī] long term (period) - 44b

"长" describes long hair, but it also means 'an elder, to grow.'

校长[xiàozhǎng] schoolmaster; principal - 1d　增长[zēngzhǎng] increase; rise; grow - 152e

102a

ㄱ ㄱ 弓 弓′ 弓⺊ 弡 张

张 zhāng

spread

bow 弓[109][gōng] + long 长 [zhǎng]

To shoot an arrow, one must hold a bow(弓) and stretch out(长) the arms very tightly. This character is used to count items with flat surfaces like paper, leather, tables, beds.

紧张[jǐnzhāng] nervous tense; strained - 106b

102b

丶 丶 氵 氵ㄱ 氵ㄱ 氵弓 氵弓′ 氵弓⺊ 氵弡 涨

涨 zhǎng

swell

water 氵[202][shuǐ] + spread 张 [zhāng]

The water(氵) level swells as much as outstretched arms aiming a bow(张).

高涨[gāozhǎng] upsurge - 3

辛

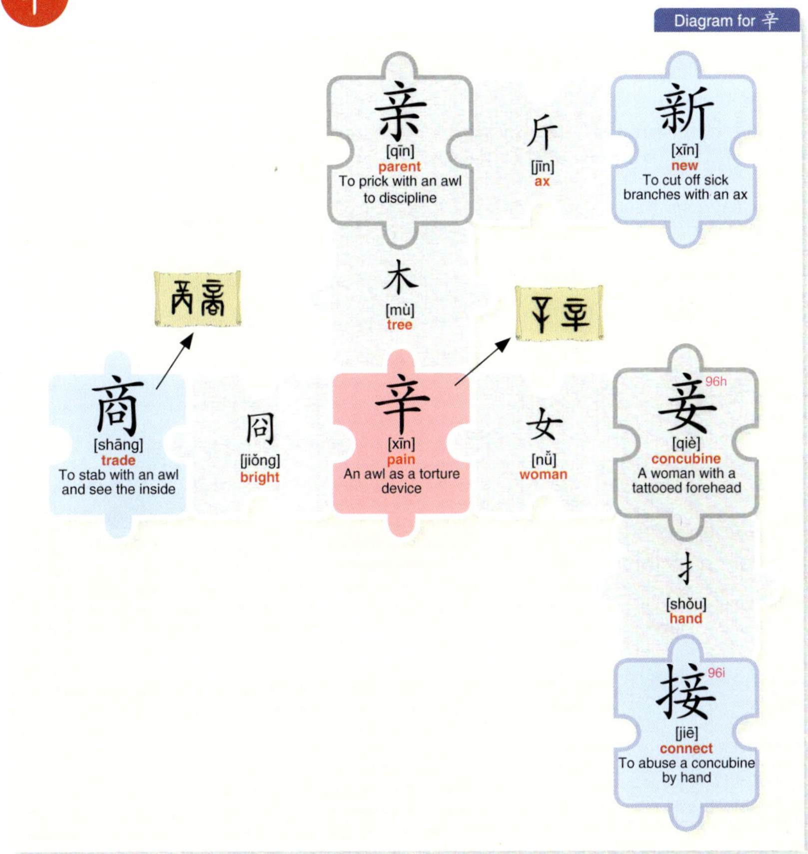

103

103

辛 xīn

pain; pungent

The shape of 'an awl, something long and sharp, a torture device' signifies pain. It also means 'spicy,' a taste that can be described as painful.

* The spicy taste is not felt by tastebuds on the tongue but by nerve endings that sense pain.

辛苦[xīnkǔ] hard; toilsome - 19d

103a

丶 亠 亠 立 立 亲 亲 亲 亲

亲 qīn

parent

awl/pain 立→辛 [xīn] + tree 木[210] [mù]

When a child goes wayward, a parent must discipline with an awl(辛) if required, to ensure that the child grows into good leader material(木). This character stresses the role of a parent.

* The traditional character(親) shows a parent looking out(見[13]) for the child and using an awl(立→辛) to discipline so the child grows(木) well.

父亲 [fùqīn] father - 98　　母亲 [mǔqīn] mother - 97
亲切 [qīnqiè] kind; cordial; intimate - 119b

103b

丶 亠 亠 立 立 亲 亲 亲 亲 亲 新 新 新

新 xīn

new

awl/pain 立→辛 [xīn] + tree 木[210] [mù] + ax 斤[118] [jīn]

If disciplining with an awl(辛) fails to help a child become something worthy(木), then one must take an ax(斤) to cut off the sick branches and help grow new ones.

新闻 [xīnwén] news - 10f
新鲜 [xīnxiān] fresh; new - 185a
新年 [xīnnián] New Year - 121a

103

103c

丶 亠 亠 亠 产 产 产 产 产 商 商 商

商 shāng

trade

awl/pain 立→辛 [xīn] + bright 冏[116a] [jiǒng]

To secure the best products, a merchant must stab with an awl(立→辛) and reveal(冏) the inside to check the quality.

* Ancient texts show this character as a combination of "辛" as an awl and "inner 内[64] [nèi]," which means stabbing with the awl(辛) reveals the inside(内).

商店 [shāngdiàn] store; shop - 127b　　商业 [shāngyè] commerce; trade - 223c

士

Diagram for 士

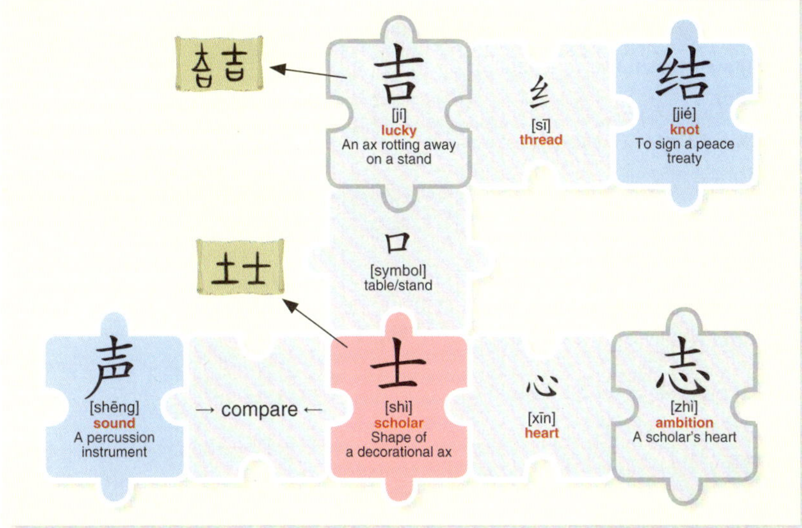

104

104 一 十 士

士 shì **scholar**

A decorational ax(士) shows authority. Only a scholar has enough knowledge to gain authority that comes with a title.

人士 [rénshì] personage; public figure - 63

104a 一 十 士 吉 吉 吉

吉 jí **lucky**

ax/scholar 士 [shì] + table/stand 口 [symbol]

An ax(士), a symbol of authority and also used as a weapon, is lying neglected on a stand(口). For the handle of an ax to rot away means there has been peace for many years, which is considered 'lucky.'

104b ㇑ ㇜ 纟 纟 纡 纡 纤 结 结

结 jié/jiē

knot / bear (fruit)

thread 纟[132][sī] + peace/lucky 吉 [jí]

To sign or agree to(纟) a peace(吉) treaty means to 'tie' two or more villages together.

* "纟" is used to tie or connect the parties.

结婚[jié/hūn] marry; get married - 99e
结果[jiéguǒ] bear fruit; result; outcome - 210g
总结[zǒngjié] summary - 16f
结束[jiéshù] finish; end - 211a
团结[tuánjié] unite; rally - 32c

This character also means 'to bear fruit' because a peace(吉) treaty that has been made(纟) signifies a period of no wars.

结实[jiēshi] solid; sturdy; fruition - 75a

104c 一 十 士 士 志 志 志

志 zhì

ambition

scholar 士 [shì] + heart 心[28][xīn]

104 The heart(心) of a scholar(士) that does not care for riches or titles but only for the realization of truth through continuous studies has a 'great goal' in mind.

同志[tóngzhì] comrade - 149b
意志[yìzhì] will - 21b

104d 一 十 士 韦 韦 吉 声

声 shēng

sound

frame 士 [symbol] + stone plate 尸 [symbol]

To make a sound by hitting a stone plate(尸) hanging on a frame(士). This character is used to count 'the number of sounds or times a sound was heard.'

* The traditional character(聲) shows an ear(耳[10a]) listening to the sound of a musical instrument (磬[qìng]) made with a thin stone plate(石[197]) that's played with a stick(殳[117]). The simplified character just shows a stone plate(尸) and a hanging frame(士).

声音[shēngyīn] voice; sound - 21
声调[shēngdiào] tone - 154
我喊了他两声。I called him twice. - 113b 114e 168a 84b 64b 104d
大声[dàshēng] loud; loudness - 74

壬

Diagram for 壬

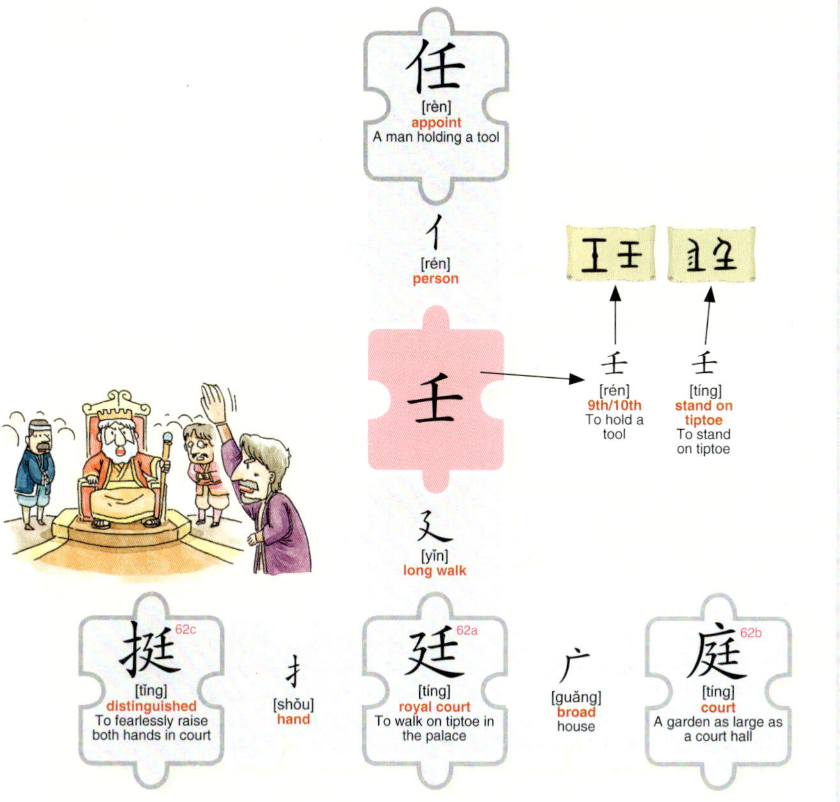

105

105

丿 二 千 壬

壬 rén/tíng 9th/10th / stand on tiptoe

Some say that this is the shape of someone holding the center of a tool(work 工[200][gōng]). It is also said that it's the shape of a flying shuttle. It's also the ninth out of ten Chinese calendar signs.

A character with the same shape as "壬[rén]" is "壬[tíng]," but this is the shape of a foot standing on tiptoe(止[53]) with the heel in the air.

* "壬[rén]" in "appoint 任[105a][rèn]" and "壬[tíng]" in "royal court 廷[62a][tíng]" are completely different characters that influence pronunciation.

105a ノ 亻 亻 仁 仟 任

任 rèn

appoint

person 亻[70] [rén] + holding tools/9th 壬 [rén]

A person(亻) holding(壬) the center of his tool is someone appointed to be in charge.

任何[rènhé] any; whatever - 17c　　责任[zérèn] responsibility - 186b

106

臣

Diagram for 臤

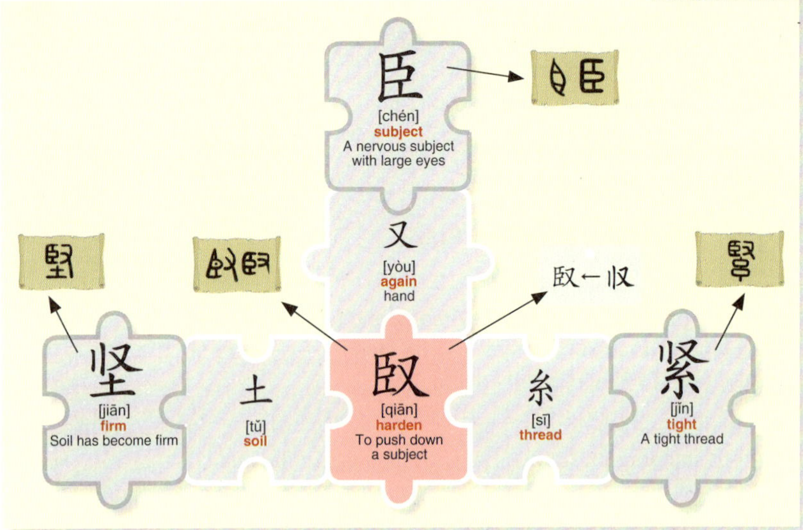

106 一 丅 丂 ㄢ 㔾 臣

臣 chén **subject**

This character is the side profile of a nervous person with eyes wide open. Subjects were not allowed to face the king directly, so they looked at him sideways, either with a lowered head or from a right angle. A nervous subject could not dare to relax and close his eyes in the king's presence.

大臣[dàchén] minister - 74

106a

臤 qiān **harden**

subject 臣 [chén] + hand/again 又[34][yòu]

A nervous subject with eyes wide open(臣) is being pushed down by a hand (又). This would freeze him in fear.

∗ In the simplified character, the subject(臣) becomes a knife(刂=刀[119]).

106b

紧 jǐn **tight**

harden 臤 [qiān] + thread 糸 = 纟[132][sī]

When a length of thread(糸) is as hard and stiff(臤) as a nervous subject(刂→臣) frozen stiff(臤) with pressure(又[34]), it means it has been pulled tight.

∗ The traditional character(緊) shows that the subject(臣) became a knife(刂=刀[119]).

紧张[jǐnzhāng] nervous tense; strained - 102a　　要紧[yàojǐn] important; essential - 170b

106c

坚 jiān **firm**

harden 臤 [qiān] + soil 土[152][tǔ]

The ground(土) becomes firm(臤) after the rain.

∗ The traditional character(堅) shows that the subject(臣) became a knife(刂=刀[119]).

坚持[jiānchí] persist in; stick to; adhere to - 42a　　坚定[jiāndìng] firm; steadfast - 54e

106

臣

Diagram for 监

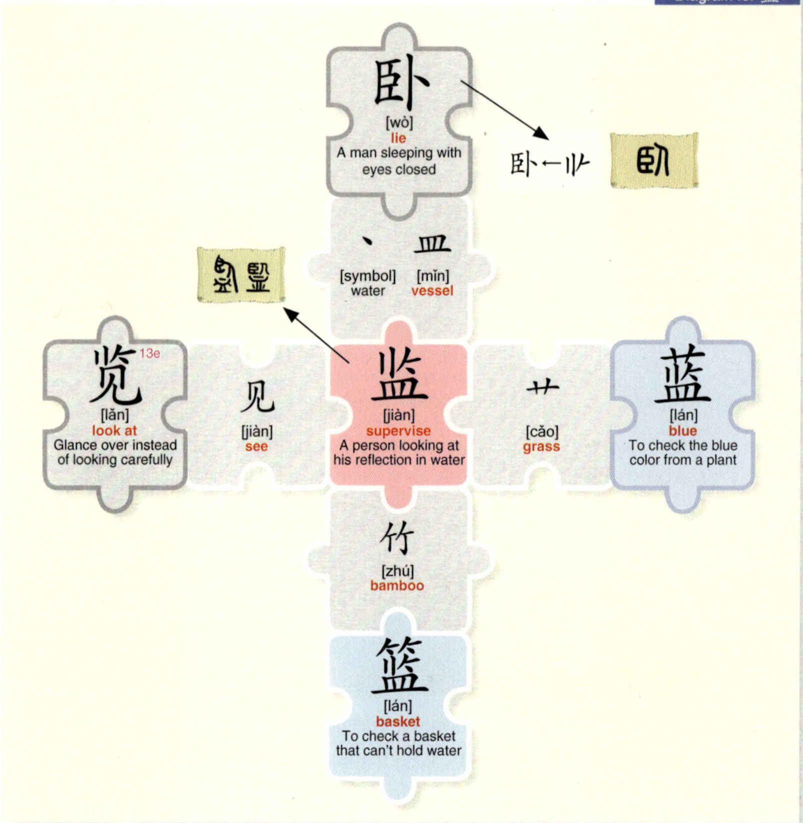

107

107 一 丅 丆 丂 亏 臣 臣 卧

卧 wò

lie

subject 臣[106] [chén] + person 卜[127] → 人[63] [rén]

A person(人) lying down to sleep is accentuated with "臣," an eye.

* The traditional character(臥) shows that "divination 卜 [bǔ]" is actually a variation of the character for person(人).

卧室 [wòshì] bedroom - 112a

107a

监 jiàn

supervise

subject 刂[119]→臣[106][chén] + person 𠂉→人[63][rén] + water 丶 [symbol] + vessel 皿[125b][mǐn]

Before mirrors were invented, people(人) looked at(臣) their reflections in a bowl(皿) of water(丶), which came to mean 'supervise or inspect.'

＊"臣" is the shape of eyes wide open.

＊The traditional character(監) shows that the subject(臣) became a knife(刂=刀[119]).

监视[jiānshì] keep watch on; surveillance - 13c

107b

蓝 lán

blue

grass 艹[207][cǎo] + supervise 监 [jiàn]

The blue dye was extracted from plants(艹). "监" is the pronunciation.

＊It's easier to remember this character of you think of "刂→臣[106]" as the blue eyes of a foreigner. Li Bai(李白, 701 AD~762), a famous poet of the Tang Dynasty was born between a rich Chinese man and a foreign woman and was said to have blue eyes.

蓝色 blue - 107b 68f

107

107c

篮 lán

basket

bamboo ⺮[216][zhú] + supervise 监 [jiàn]

"⺮" shows the basket is made of bamboo(⺮) and "监" is where the pronunciation comes from.

＊A plate(皿[125b]) made with bamboo(⺮) is actually a basket that cannot hold water.

打篮球[dǎlánqiú] play basketball - 31c 198b

篮球[lánqiú] basketball - 198b

王

Diagram for 王

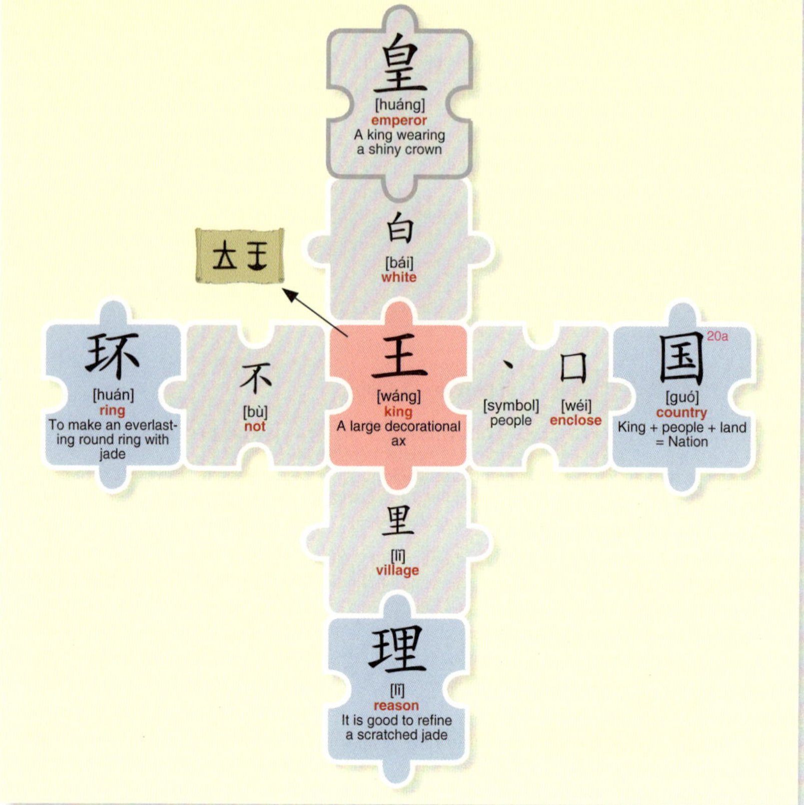

108

108 一 二 千 王

王 wáng

king

If a small ax symbolizing authority became "scholar 士[104][shì]," then a larger ax can mean substantial as in 'king.'

* The radical of "王" is "jade 玉[198][yù]," and when "玉" is used as part of another character, it changes into "王."

国王[guówáng] king - 20a

108a ′ ′ 白 白 白 白 皇 皇 皇

皇 huáng

emperor

white 白[134][bái] + king 王 [wáng]

A king(王) wearing a bright(白) shining crown is an 'emperor.'

皇后[huánghòu] empress - 18d

108b 一 二 千 王 𤣩 玑 玑 珂 理 理 理

理 lǐ

reason

jade 王→玉[198][yù] + village 里[151][lǐ]

It is only reasonable to refine a defective jade(玉) into a jewel instead of discarding it. "里" is where the character gets its pronunciation.

* Regardless of however much jade(玉) a village(里) can produce, it's still reasonable to refine them all and put them to use.

经理[jīnglǐ] manager; director - 132e
物理[wùlǐ] innate laws of things; physics - 49b
理发[lǐ/fà] haircut; hairdressing - 34f
道理[dàoli] principle; reason - 7a
处理[chǔlǐ] handle - 56b
总理[zǒnglǐ] premier; prime minister - 16f

108

108c 一 二 千 王 王一 玎 环 环

环 huán

ring; encircle

jade 王→玉[198][yù] + not 不[223a][bù]

This character depicts an image of producing a round ring with jade(玉). The shape of such a ring looks like the shape of a circulating circle without stops (不). The meaning of 'encircle' is also derived from it.

环境[huánjìng] environment; circumstances - 21d

Life

Life

War

Which events shaped the ancient societies? War probably affected people more than any other event, because it was a matter of life and death. Many Chinese characters are about war.

1. No war is fought without a weapon. Characters for 'arrow,' 'spear,' 'ax,' 'sword' and 'shield' are all part of more complicated characters.
2. Any nation going to war needs a secure supply line. Means of transportation such as carts and ships are important characters.
3. Before going to war, the ancient Chinese prayed to the gods. Characters for 'altar' and 'fortunetell ing' appear frequently.

Necessities of life

Regardless of which country you live, the three necessities that we all need are clothes, food, and a home.

1. Clothes are made with fabrics, and fabric are made with threads. These connections are reflected in Chinese characters. Fabrics were dyed to give their color, so there are many color-related characters, too.

2. From characters about cooked and uncooked rice to beans to "食," the shape of a bowl of rice covered with a lid. There are many characters regarding food.
3. Some characters describe the shape of a house, and some others describe the markings on a door.
   As many people lived in caves or mud huts, there are also many characters associated with hills.

Agriculture

Agriculture has been the very basis of human civilization since its beginning as it produces most basic foods for people.

1. This section will deal with characters related to land, such as crop fields and earth, as well as fire as people created fields by setting land on fire in the early days.
2. As agriculture developed, requirement of tools became evident. You will see that plow is used as a basic element of the character for many different symbols and meanings.
3. Harvested crops need vessels and plates to hold them. Many basic characters related to items like wine bottles, measuring cups, mesh bags, and covers will be covered in this section.

弓

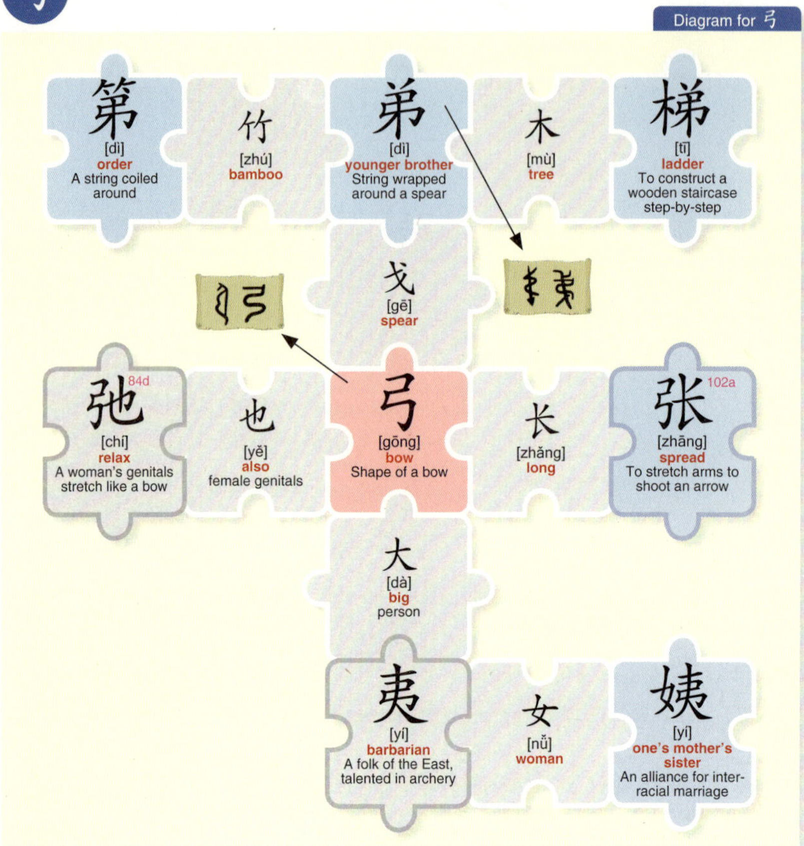

109

109

弓 gōng

bow

The most efficient weapon was the bow. This character takes the shape of a drawn bow.

109a

弟 dì

younger brother

spear 𢦏→戈 [gē] + coiled around/bow 弓 [gōng]

Meaning 'order' because it describes a string coiled around(弓) a spear(戈). This character also means 'younger brother' because there's a top and bottom to a coil.

* Ancient characters show that this "弟" character originally describes a string wrapped around(弓) a spear(戈), not a bow.

弟弟[dìdi] younger brother　　弟兄[dixiong] brothers - 72
兄弟[xiōngdì] brothers - 72

109b　丿 𠂉 𥫗 𥫗 𥫗 竺 笃 第 第 第 第

第 dì

order

bamboo 竹[216] [zhú] + younger brother 弟 [dì]

When "弟," the shape of a bow's drawstring coiled around something came to mean 'younger brother,' the Chinese combined it with the character for bamboo(竹) gave this character the meaning 'order.' It's also used as a prefix when counting.

第一[dìyī] the first - 223　　第一天 the first day - 109b 223 74b

109c　一 十 才 木 木 杙 栏 栏 档 梯 梯

梯 tī

ladder

tree 木[210] [mù] + order/younger brother 弟 [dì]

This letter depicts an image of wooden(木) staircase which is built up by placing stairs one-by-one(弟) to enable us to climb up and go to a higher place.

电梯[diàntī] elevator; lift - 157a

109d　一 ㇕ 彐 弓 弔 夷

夷 yí

barbarian

bow 弓 [gōng] + person/big 大[74] [dà]

This character signifies the alien people who used to live in the Eastern part of the old China. They were very good at archery(弓). It is interesting to note that the people of Goguryeo were horse-riding people(大) who were also talented in archery(弓). Goguryeo was a kingdom which was established in the eastern part of the old China in about 1st century B.C.

* The letter of Ju Mong, the founder's name of Goguryeo, means a person(大) who is very good at archery(弓).

109

109e ㇛ 㐅 女 女 妇 妇 妇 姨 姨

姨 yí

one's mother's sister

woman 女[96] [nǚ] + barbarian 夷 [yí]

In order to maintain peace, women(女) are brought from a uncivilized foreign country(夷) so as to form a marriage alliance. The meaning of one's mother's sister is derived out of this.

阿姨[āyí] auntie - 17e

110

弋

Diagram for 弋

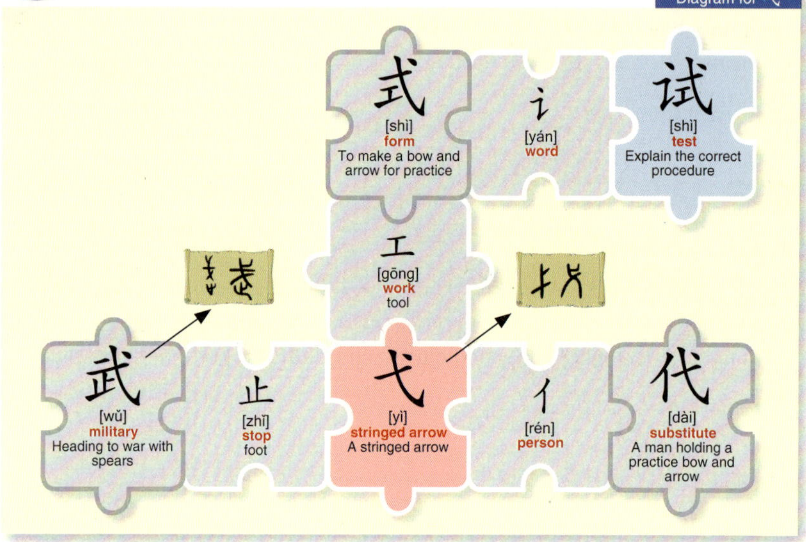

110 一 七 弋

弋 yì

stringed arrow

This character takes the shape of an arrow connected to the bow with a string used for shooting practice.

110a

一 二 亍 工 式 式

式
shì

form

stringed arrow 弋 [yì] + tool/work 工[200] [gōng]

A bow and arrow used for practice(弋) is made with tools(工). Even though they are only used for practice, they have to be made according to certain procedures.

方式[fāngshì] way; fashion; pattern - 160

110b

丶 讠 讠 讠 讠 讠 试 试

试
shì

test

word 讠=言[22] [yán] + form 式 [shì]

A test is to check whether one can explain(讠) or follow the correct procedures (式).

考试[kǎoshì] examination; test - 100c　　试验[shìyàn] experiment; test; trial - 67c

110c

丿 亻 仁 代 代

代
dài

substitute; historical period

person 亻[70] [rén] + stringed arrow 弋 [yì]

A person(亻) using a practice bow and arrow(弋) instead of one used in the war. Because the following era in history takes the place of the previous one, this character came to mean 'historical periods.'

代表[dàibiǎo] representative; delegate - 130b　　现代[xiàndài] modern times - 13d
古代[gǔdài] ancient times - 19

110

110d

一 二 亍 工 式 式

武
wǔ

military

spear 戈[113] [gē] + foot/stop 止[53] [zhǐ]

The feet(止) of men heading to war carrying spears (戈) is how the Chinese portrayed an army.

* This character shows that instead of a "stringed arrow 弋 [yì]," it's a spear with an extra stroke(戈) with a set of feet(止).

武器[wǔqì] weapon; arms - 172a

矢

Diagram for 矢

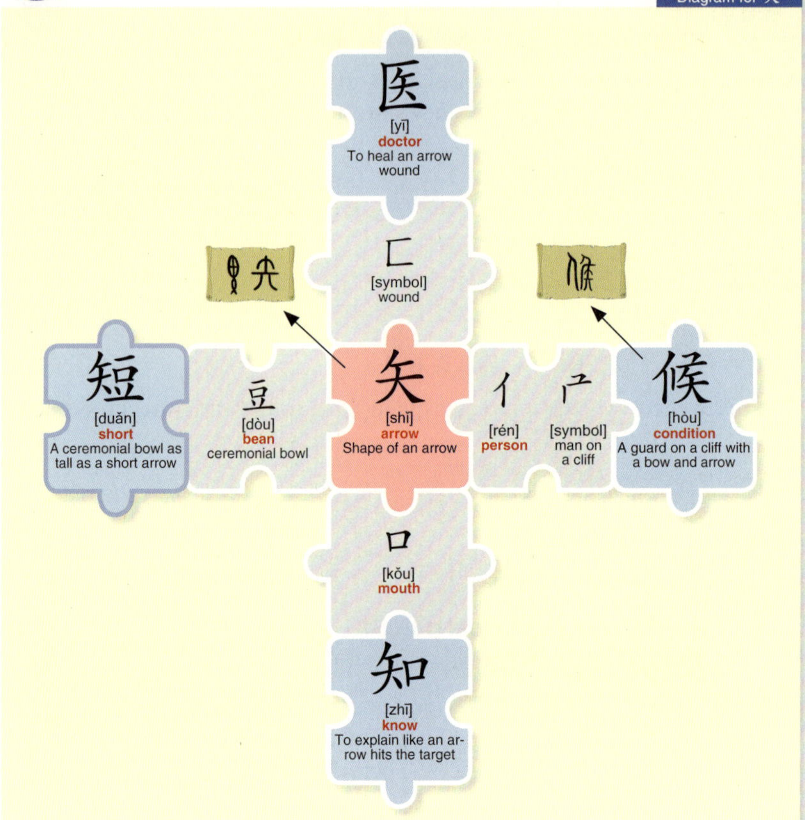

111

111

矢 shǐ **arrow**

The shape of an arrow including the head, body, and notch.

111a

医 yī **doctor**

wound 匸 [symbol] + arrow 矢 [shǐ]

A doctor is someone who pours alcohol on wounds(匸) caused by arrows(矢) to help them heal.

* The traditional character(醫) shows liquor(酉[162]) used to disinfect an open wound(匚) caused by an arrow(矢), then a splint(殳[117]) used to secure the body part.

医生[yīshēng] doctor - 208　　医院[yīyuàn] hospital - 73b

111b

丿 亻 亻 亻 亻 亻 亻 亻 侯 候

候 hòu

condition; wait; time

person 亻[70][rén] + man on a cliff ⺈ [symbol] + arrow 矢 [shǐ]

A guard(亻) hiding on the cliff(⺈) armed with a bow and arrows(矢) is checking the enemy's situation. To do so, he has to wait, which is where this character got its other meaning, 'time.'

* "⺈" is the simplified version of a man(⺈[68]) on a cliff(厂[148]).

时候[shíhou] time; moment - 42d
有时候[yǒushíhou] between times; occasionally - 39c 42d
气候[qìhòu] climate; weather - 204

111c

丿 𠂉 ⺈ 乍 矢 矢 知 知

知 zhī

know

arrow 矢 [shǐ] + mouth 口[16][kǒu]

'To know' about something means you can verbally(口) explain like how an arrow(矢) hits the bulls-eye.

知道[zhīdào] know; realize - 7a　　通知[tōngzhī] advise; notify; inform - 166b
知识[zhīshi] knowledge - 179b

111d

丿 𠂉 ⺈ 乍 矢 矢 矢 矢 知 短 短 短

短 duǎn

short

arrow 矢 [shǐ] + ceremonial bowl/bean 豆[140][dòu]

It can be said that a ceremonial bowl(豆) with legs is as 'short' or rather as tall as a short arrow(矢) is long.

* "豆" is the shape of a ceremonial bowl that has a stem or legs.

短期[duǎnqī] short term (period) - 44b

111

至

112

112

一 工 ㄊ 즈 주 至

至 zhì **arrive**

An arrow(矢[111]) that has been shot into the ground(土[152]) has reached its target.

* In the ancient days, a sacred arrow(矢) was shot and where it landed(一) was where they built important buildings or temples.

至今[zhìjīn] up to now - 66

112a

丶 丷 宀 宀 宀 宀 宀 宀 室

室
shì

room

house 宀[141][mián] + arrive 至 [zhì]

Tradition dictated that sacred arrows were shot and houses(宀) with rooms were built where the arrow landed(至).

* The Chinese believed in building and living in sacred locations.

教室[jiàoshì] classroom - 50c
办公室[bàngōngshì] office - 159b 93b
卧室[wòshì] bedroom - 107

112b

一 ㇀ ㇀ 互 乒 至 到 到

到
dào

arrive; to (a place)

arrive 至 [zhì] + knife 刂=刀[119][dāo]

An arrow that hits its mark(至) and a sword(刂) symbolizes war. To arrive (至) at the enemy camp armed with a sword(刀) gave the meaning 'to arrive, to go~.'

迟到[chídào] be late; arrive late - 91b
遇到[yùdào] encounter; run into; come across - 194c
从…到…[cóng...dào...] from… to - 63g
得到[dédào] get; obtain; gain - 40b
感到[gǎndào] feel; enter; sense - 114d

112c

丿 亻 亻 亻 亻 亻 亻 侄 倒 倒

倒
dǎo

fall

person 亻[70][rén] + arrive 到 [dào]

Soldiers(亻) who have reached(到) the enemy camp are felling the enemies.

打倒[dǎdǎo] overthrow; down with - 31c
倒了这棵树。This tree fell over. - 112c 168a 133a 210h 40d

112

戈

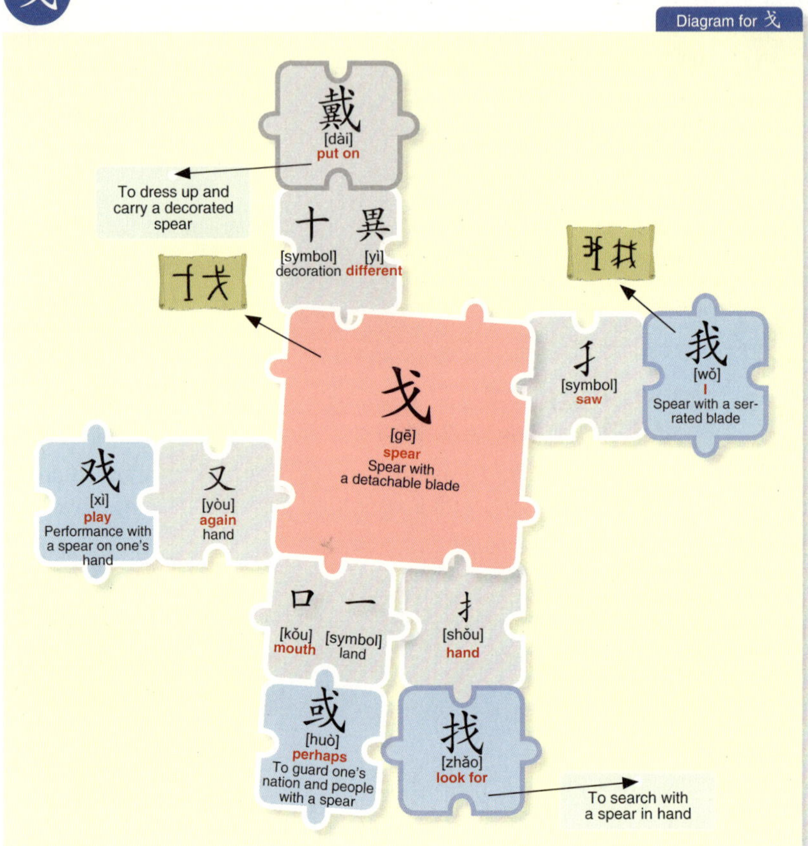

113

113

戈 gē

spear

The shape of a spear with a curved detachable blade.

113a

戴 dài

put on

decoration 十 [symbol] + spear 戈 [gē] + different 異→异(simplified) [yì]

To carry a spear with(戈) decorations(十) means to dress up for a important event, like a coronation. On such days, officials wore a special outfit, different(异) from their usual uniform.

* "异" describes a shaman wearing a ghost mask to a dance, which is unusual.

你把它戴去好了。You can wear that and go. - 69a 92b 88f 113a 94 96c 168a

113b 丿 二 于 手 我 我 我

我 wǒ

I; we

saw 扌 [symbol] + spear 戈 [gē]

This character originally meant 'saw' because of the serrated(扌) blade on the spear(戈), but later it meant 'me, us' because of the similar pronunciation.

* This character will be easier to remember if you think that a saw was a tool used during the war to make items for oneself.

我们[wǒmen] we - 145a

自我[zìwǒ] oneself; self; ego - 26

113c 一 寸 扌 扌 扎 找 找

找 zhǎo

look for; give change

hand 扌=手[31][shǒu] + spear 戈 [gē]

A soldier with a spear(戈) in his hand(扌) is searching for enemies in hiding. As one also has to calculate and search for small change, this character came to mean 'to give change.'

他找不着孩子了。He couldn't find the child. - 84b 113c 223a 11b 4c 95 168a
找他五块。To give him 5 yuan in change. - 113c 84b 226a 76b

113

113d 一 𠃌 ㄒ 可 可 式 或 或

或 huò

perhaps

spear 戈 [gē] + mouth 口[16][kǒu] + land 一 [symbol]

This character originally meant 'nation,' because spears(戈) are needed to protect the people(口) and the land(一). But, later it came to mean 'perhaps,' to reflect the worries of men who had left their families behind when they went to war.

* A mouth(口) is used to eat and speak and sometimes represents a living man.

或者[huòzhě] perhaps; maybe - 101

114

113e

ㄱ ㄡ 㕛 戏 戏 戏

戏 xì

play

hand/again 又[34] [yòu] + spear 戈 [gē]

This character symbolizes a person who is performing on stage as if he is fighting with an imitation spear(戈) on his hand(又). It means 'to play.'

* In order to differentiate this character with the character of "找[113c][zhǎo]," let us try to remember that it signifies the image of a performance on a stage where repeated(又) thrusts with a spear do not cause any death because it is a fake spear(戈).

游戏[yóuxì] game; play - 161b

戊

Diagram for 戊

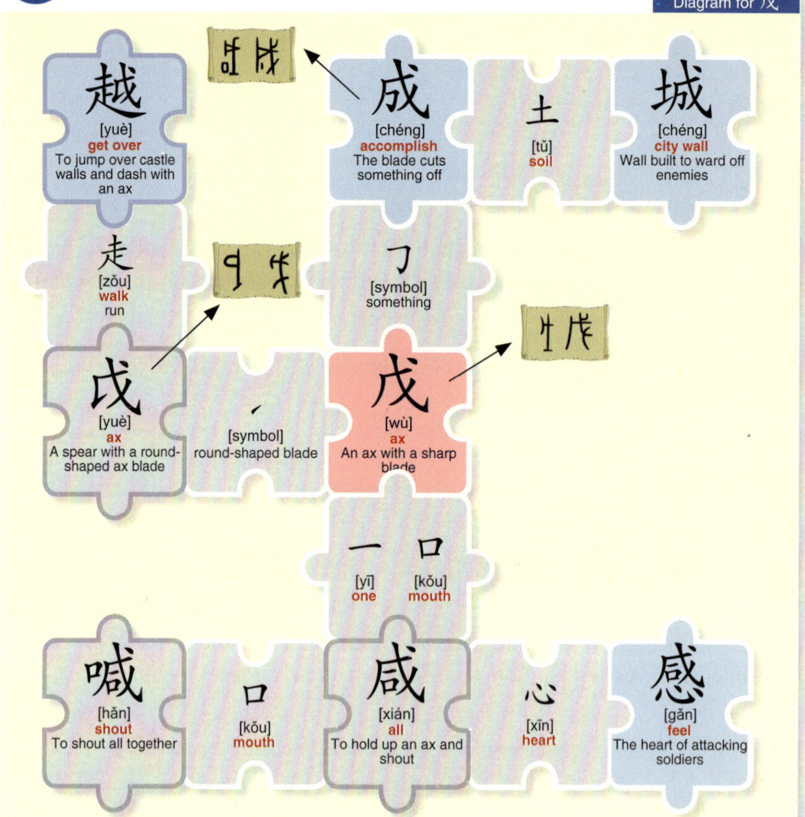

114 一 厂 戊 戊 戊

戊 wù ax

spear 戈 [gē] + line 丿[234] [piě]

Spears(戈) are thrust but axes with strong blades(丿) can chop off or be thrown. It is also the fifth of the ten calendar signs.

* "丿" has no meaning and can be interpreted in many ways.

114a 一 厂 万 成 成 成

成 chéng accomplish; become

ax 戊 [wù] + something ㄱ [symbol]

Something(ㄱ) has been cut off by the blade(丿) of an ax(戊). To accomplish at war means to cut off the opposing commander's head(ㄱ) with one's ax (戊).

成绩[chéngjì] result; record; achievement - 186c
变成[biànchéng] turn into; change into - 34c
成就[chéngjiù] achievement; accomplishment - 80b
成熟[chéngshú] ripe; mature - 3e
完成[wánchéng] complete - 73a

114b 一 十 土 圹 圹 坂 城 城 城

城 chéng city wall; city

soil 土[152] [tǔ] + accomplish 成 [chéng]

To build a wall with mud(土) brick around the city to fend off enemy soldiers who are trying to accomplish(成) their goal by invading.

城市[chéngshì] city; town - 131a

114c 一 厂 厂 斤 后 后 咸 咸 咸

咸 xián all

ax 戊 [wù] + one 一[223] [yī] + mouth 口[16] [kǒu]

Soldiers with axes(戊) shouting altogether in one(一) voice(口) as they attack.

114

114

114d

一 厂 厂 斤 后 后 咸 咸 咸 咸 感 感 感

感 gǎn

feel

all 咸 [xián] + heart 心[28] [xīn]

The heart, the emotion(心) of soldiers with axes shouting together(咸). A soldier in this situation feels everything from excitement to fear.

感冒[gǎnmào] catch cold; influenza - 11e
感到[gǎndào] feel; enter; sense - 112b
感谢[gǎnxiè] thank - 27c

114e

丨 口 口 口 口 吁 吁 呅 呅 咸 喊 喊

喊 hǎn

shout

mouth 口[16] [kǒu] + all 咸 [xián]

When the character for shouting(咸) came to mean 'all together,' the Chinese added a mouth(口) to make a new character to mean 'to shout.'

班长在前面喊口令。The class president shouted his order. - 119f 102 32a 221a 10 114e 16 86

114f

一 厂 戊 戊 戉

戉 yuè

ax

spear 戈[113] [gē] + round-shaped blade ㇃ [symbol]

"戊[wù]" is a character which is formed by the combination of a spear(戈) and a blade(丿). The character of "戉[yuè]" shows that the function of its spear has been improved as a more offensive weapon due to the round-shape blade of ax.

* Its ancient character clearly shows that there is an ax blade on the left side of the spear.

114g

一 + 土 丰 丰 走 走 走 走 越 越 越

越 yuè

get over; exceed

run/walk 走[53c] [zǒu] + ax 戉 [yuè]

This character symbolizes a soldier who jumps over castle walls and makes a dash(走) at the enemy with an ax(戉) as a weapon that has been much improved for offense.

戋

Diagram for 戋

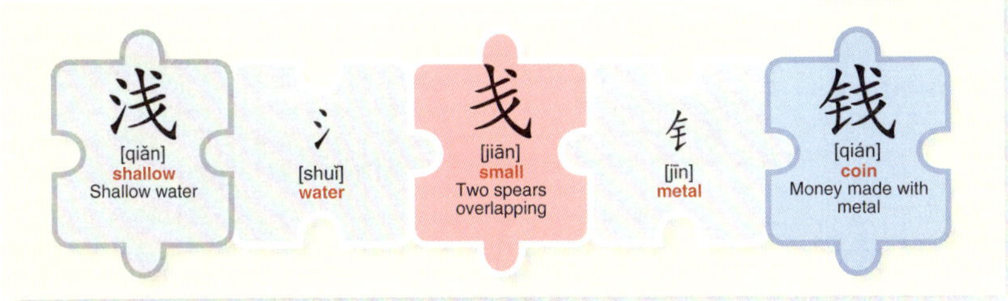

115

戋 jiān — small

A "spear 戈[113][gē]" is used to hurt or kill, so two written together means 'to injure.' It also means 'little, few' because spears pile up easily without taking up much space.

115a

钱 qián — coin; money

metal 钅=金[199][jīn] + small 戋 [jiān]

'Coins' are thin(戋) and flat pieces of metal(钅).

* The Qin(秦, 221~206 BC) was the first dynasty to unify China and build the Great Wall. The founding emperor gave orders to mint thin(戋) coins with holes in the middle with metal(金) and that was the beginning of the Chinese money system.

零钱[língqián] small change - 86c

115b

浅 qiǎn — shallow

water 氵[202][shuǐ] + small 戋 [jiān]

Little(戋) water(氵) means it's shallow.

这条小河水很浅。This tiny stream is very shallow. - 133a 56c 235 17d 201 14a 115b

115

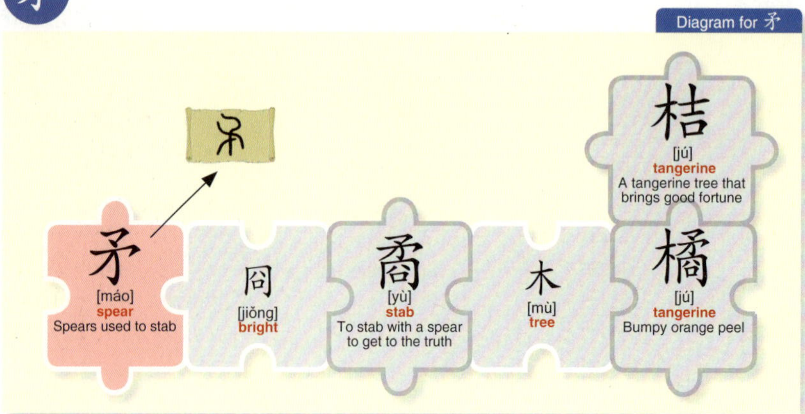

116

矛 máo

spear

116 A spear has a sharp tip like an awl, has a long handle, and is used to stab or pierce.

116a

矞 yù

stab

awl/spear 矛 [máo] + bright 冏[103c] [jiǒng]

To stab with a sharp awl(矛) to torture and reveal(冏) the truth.

* "冏" describes a window brightly lit with sunlight.

116b

橘 jú

tangerine

tree 木[210] [mù] + stab 矞 [yù]

The peel of an orange or tangerine is uneven, like it was poked(矞) with something sharp. This character describes an orange tree(木).

* Tangerines were considered otherwordly because of the taste and was offered only to the king and the gods. As the pronunciation for this character sounds similar to "lucky 吉[104a] [jí]," it's also considered an auspicious fruit. As a tree(木) that brings luck(吉), it's sometimes written as "桔[jú]."

橘子 [júzi] orange; tangerine - 95

殳

Diagram for 殳

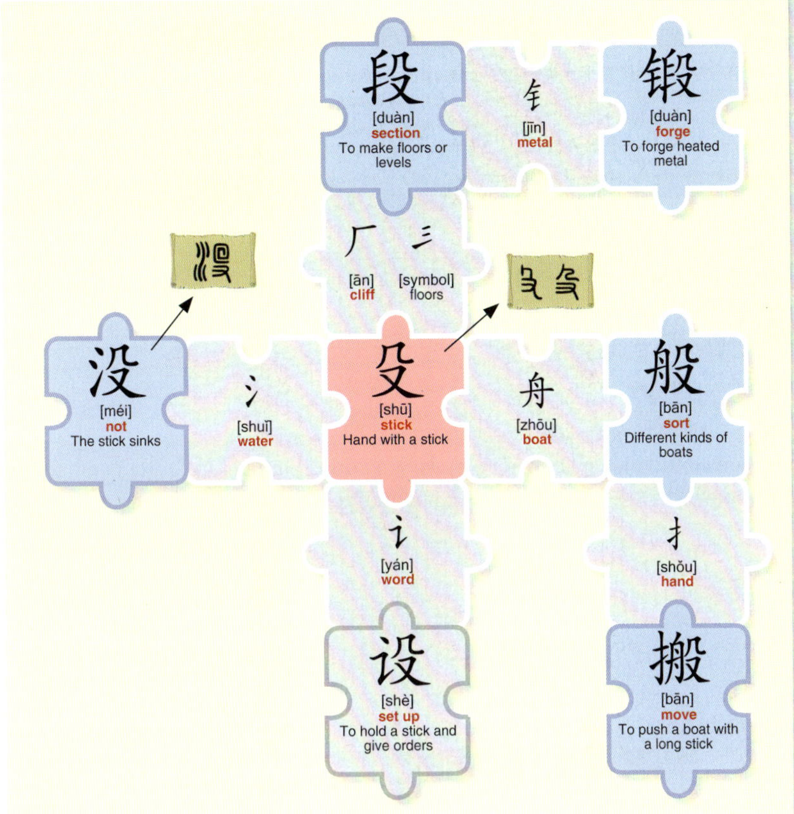

117

117

殳 shū

stick

This character is a hand(又[34]) holding a stick much like the body of a spear and means 'stick, strike.'

117a

段 duàn

section

cliff 厂[148] [ān] + floors 三 [symbol] + strike/stick 殳 [shū]

To divide a hill(厂) into sections, then use tools to beat(殳) the ground into levels(三). This character is used to describe sections or partitions of a secluded area, or pieces of thin and long objects.

手段[shǒuduàn] means; measure; method - 31
一段公路 a section of highway - 223 117a 93b 57a
一段时间 a period of time - 223 117a 42d 145c

117b

锻 duàn

forge

metal 钅=金[199] [jīn] + section 段 [duàn]

A blacksmith hits(殳) red-hot metals(钅) with a hammer to forge it and get rid of impurities. "段" is where this character gets the pronunciation.

* The stick(殳) in "段" indicates the beating action.

117

锻炼[duànliàn] temper; forge; train - 211d

117c

般 bān

sort

boat 舟[125] [zhōu] + stick 殳 [shū]

The type of boat(舟) differs depending on the shape of the sail or the oar(殳) used.

* Older boats were pushed along with a long stick(殳) instead of being rowed.

一般[yìbān] same as; sort; general - 223

117d

搬 bān

move

hand 扌=手[31] [shǒu] + sort 般 [bān]

To transport items in the kind(般) of boat that is pushed by a hand(扌) holding a long stick.

你把它搬过来吧。You move it over here. - 69a 92b 88f 117d 40f 212d 92c

117e ` 讠 讠' 讥 设 设

设 shè

set up

word 讠=言[22][yán] + stick 殳 [shū]

The man in charge is holding a baton(殳) while giving verbal(讠) orders to set up to construct a building.

建设[jiànshè] build; construct - 37b
设备[shèbèi] equipment; facility - 56a
设计[shè/jì] plan; design - 22b

117f ` ˎ 氵 氵' 汃 没 没

没 méi

not; not have

water 氵[202][shuǐ] + stick 殳 [shū]

A stick(殳) was thrown into the water(氵) to save a drowning man, but it was of no help and sunk. Such an item might as well 'not exists, not be of help.'

* The ancient character shows someone waving a hand(又[34]) asking for help, but who ends up drowning(回[20d]) in the water(氵).

没关系[méiguānxi] it doesn't matter - 45 132b
没意思[méiyìsi] boring; uninteresting - 21b 28a
没有[méiyǒu] not have - 39c

117

斤

Diagram for 斤

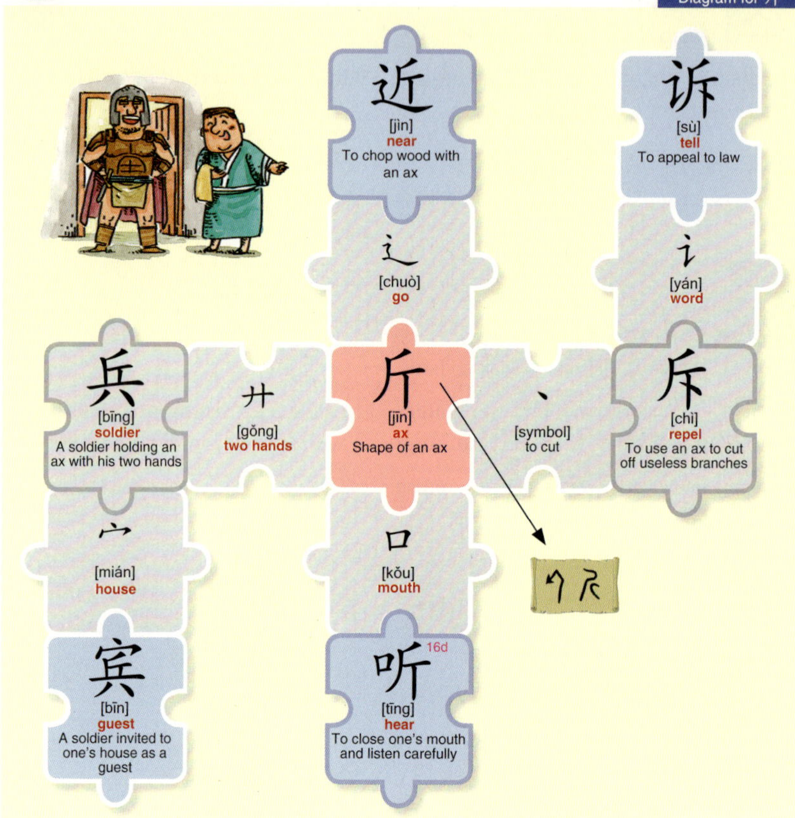

118

118　　　　丿 厂 斤 斤

斤 jīn	**ax**

An ax is used as a tool to chop up wood or a weapon to kill. The Chinese adopted this character to measure weight.

* One "斤" is 500 grams or 17.6 ounces.

公斤 [gōngjīn] kilogram (kg) - 93b
羊肉一斤多少钱? How much is 500 grams of mutton? - 171 192 223 118 222d 235a 115a

118a ㇒ 𠂆 𠂆 斤 䜣 䜣 近

近 jìn

near

ax 斤 [jīn] + go 辶[61] [chuò]

One stays near to his house or work site when taking an ax(斤) to go(辶) and chop firewood.

附近[fùjìn] vicinity; nearby - 41c 最近[zuìjìn] recently; lately - 10c

118b ㇒ 𠂆 𠂆 斤 斥

斥 chì

repel

ax 斤 [jīn] + to cut 丶 [symbol]

One must take an ax(斤) to cut off(丶) the useless branches when preparing timber for use. It implies that what is wrong must be repelled.

118c 丶 讠 讠 讠 讠 诉 诉

诉 sù

tell; complain

word 讠=言[22] [yán] + repel 斥 [chì]

To appeal(讠) to the law to abolish(斥) and prevent wrongdoings, one must 'tell, inform' what is going on.

告诉[gàosu] tell; let (make) know - 175d

118d ㇒ 𠂆 𠂆 斤 丘 乒 兵

兵 bīng

soldier

ax 斤 [jīn] + two hands 廾[43] [gǒng]

This character depicts the image of a brave soldier who is holding an ax(斤) with his two hands(廾).

118e 丶 丶 宀 宀 宀 宀 宀 宀 宾 宾

宾 bīn

guest

house 宀[141] [mián] + soldier 兵 [bīng]

This character depicts a soldier(兵) who has been invited to one's house(宀) as a guest on his way to the battlefield.

* The traditional character(賓) tells us about a Chinese custom that a guest invited(少 → 止[53]) to one's house(宀) is always treated as a precious treasure(貝[186]).

宾馆[bīnguǎn] hotel - 193c

118

119

刀

Diagram for 刀

119 ㇆ 刀

刀 dāo — **knife**

The shape of a knife with a handle.

刀子[dāozi] knife - 95

119a 丿 八 分 分

分 fēn — **divide; minute**

divide/eight 八[229] [bā] + knife 刀 [dāo]

To divide in half(八) with a knife(刀). A 'minute' is a division of time, a 'point' is a division of grades or levels, and 'fen' is the smallest denomination of Chinese currency. (1分 = 1/100元[73] = 1/10角[191])

* "八" means 'to be divided' because of the identical left and right shapes.

分钟[fēnzhōng] minute - 232b
部分[bùfen] part; section - 79f
十分[shífēn] fully; very; extremely - 231
得80分 score 80 marks - 40b 119a

119b 一 七 切 切

切 qiē/qiè

cut / correspond

seven 七[223d] [qī] + knife 刀 [dāo]

The shape of meat(七) cut up with a knife(刀).

* "七" is the shape of the cutting action, left-right, top-bottom.

Meat cut out(七) with a knife(刀) from one animal is 'identical.'

一切[yīqiè] all; everything - 223
亲切[qīnqiè] kind; cordial; intimate - 103a

119

119c 丶 ㇇ 衤 衤 衤 衤 初 初

初 chū

first

clothes 衤=衣[130] [yī] + knife 刀 [dāo]

The first thing one does when making clothes(衤) is to cut the fabric with a knife(刀).

* The first thing that God did after Adam and Eve ate the Forbidden fruit of good and evil was to make(刀) them clothes(衣). – Genesis 3:21

最初[zuìchū] first; prime; initial - 10c
初步[chūbù] first step; initial - 53a
初级[chūjí] elementary; primary; junior - 36g

119d

丶 ㅁ 口 号 另

另 lìng

other

mouth 口[16] [kǒu] + power 力[159] [lì] → knife 刀 [dāo]

To use a knife(刀) to separate the edible(口) meat from the bones means that the other parts are inedible.

* The character(另) was used with the same meaning in the ancient times

另外[lìngwài] other; another - 222a

119e

丶 ㅁ 口 号 另 另 别

别 bié

other; separate; don't

other 另 [lìng] + knife 刂=刀 [dāo]

When the character "另" came to mean 'other,' the Chinese decided to add another knife(刂) to it to mean 'different, to separate.' When the negative meaning of 'different' is stressed, it means 'don't do....'

* When "别" means 'other,' it is not followed with a quantifier. But when "另" is used to mean 'different,' a quantifier follows.

119

别人[biérén] other people; others - 63
特别[tèbié] special; especially - 42b
别的[biéde] other; else - 46b
别情。Feelings of separation. - 119e 135d
别忘了。Don't forget. - 119e 5a 168a

刀

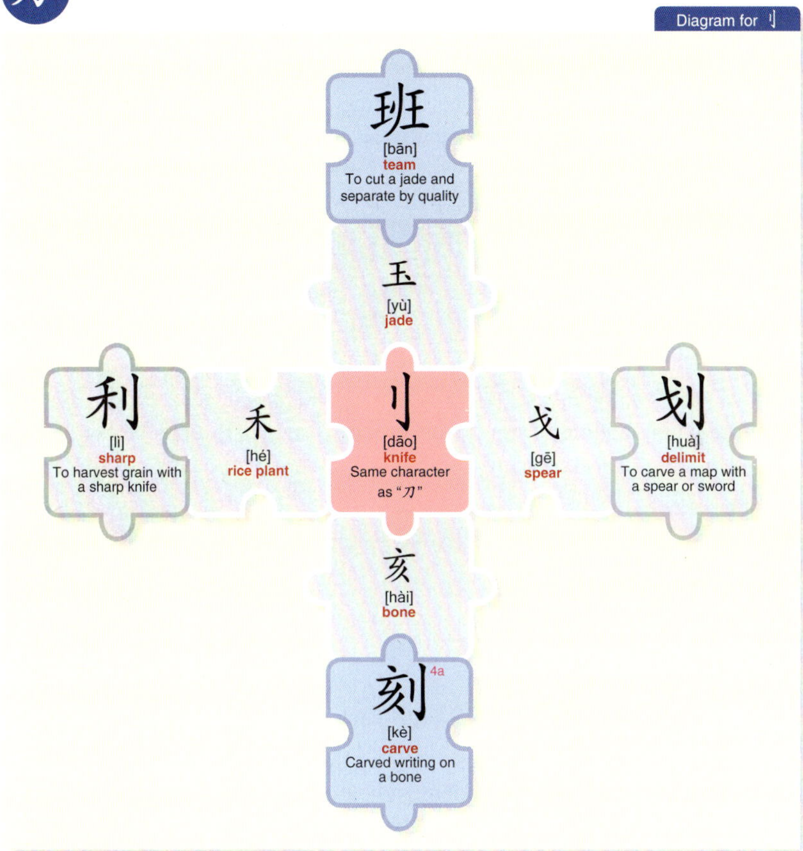

119

刂 dāo

knife

It's the same character as "knife 刀 [dāo]," but only takes this shape when part of a complicated character.

119

119f

一 二 千 王 王 玎 玎 玞 班 班

班 bān

team; class

jade 玉[198] [yù] + knife 刂=刀 [dāo]

This character describes someone dividing a jade(玉) with a knife(刂) and grouping the pieces according to quality. It means 'class, group.'

上班 [shàng/bān] go to work; go to the office - 223f
班长 [bānzhǎng] class monitor - 102
坐班 [zuò/bān] work in one's office during office time - 152b

119g

一 七 戈 戈 戈 划

划 huà

delimit

spear 戈[113] [gē] + knife 刂=刀 [dāo]

When planning action during a war, officers used sharp objects like a spear (戈) or a knife or sword(刂) to carve maps into wooden slabs or draw in the sand to 'delimit' boundaries.

计划 [jìhuà] plan; project - 22b

119h

一 二 千 千 禾 和 利

利 lì

sharp; advantage

rice plant 禾[139] [hé] + knife 刂=刀 [dāo]

Before using a knife(刂) to harvest rice(禾), the farmer has to make sure that it is indeed sharp. Harvest is considered advantageous for everyone.

利用 [lìyòng] use; utilize; make use of - 166
胜利 [shènglì] win; victory; triumph - 208a
流利 [liúlì] fluent; smooth - 202a
有利 [yǒulì] advantageous; beneficial; favourable - 39c

召

Diagram for 召

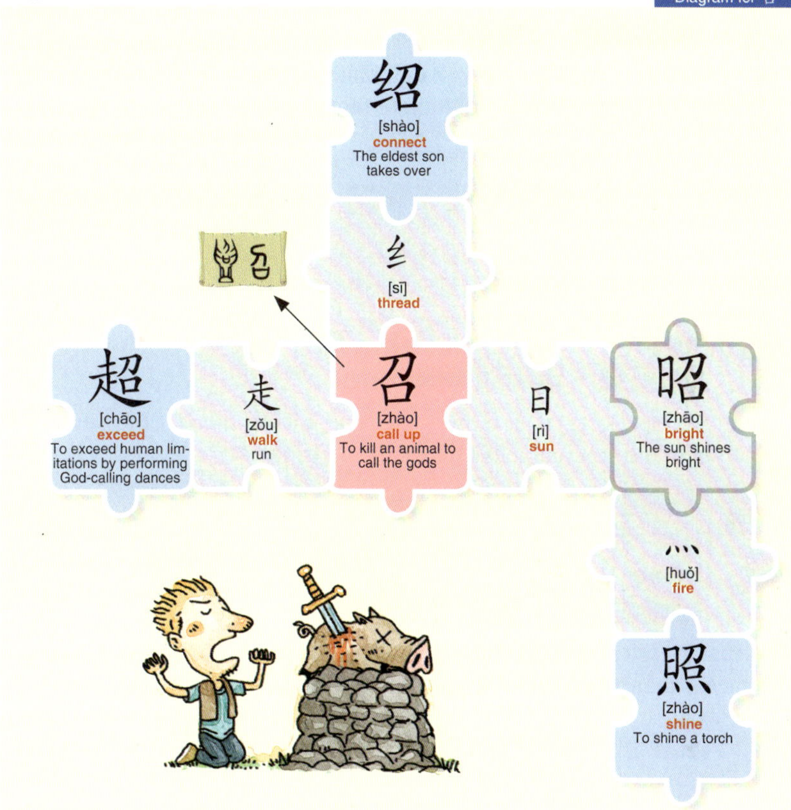

120

120 ㇆ 刀 刀 召 召

召 zhào

call up

knife 刀[119][dāo] + mouth 口[16][kǒu]

To kill an animal with a knife(刀) and call out(口) to the gods.

* The ancient character shows a man holding up his sacrifice to call the gods, but the modern character only shows the knife(刀) and a mouth(口) calling out to the gods.

召集[zhàojí] call together; convene - 178a

120

120a

丿 乡 纟 纫 纫 绍 绍 绍

绍 shào

connect

thread 纟[132] [sī] + call up 召 [zhào]

Through the act of calling God(召), the connection between the human beings and God is described with an addition of thread(纟).

* Thread(纟) is used to mean connection or continuance.

介绍 [jièshào] introduce; present - 63c

120b

丨 冂 日 日 日ㄱ 日刀 日刀 昭 昭

昭 zhāo

bright

sun 日[218] [rì] + call up 召 [zhào]

Figuratively speaking, it describes someone calling out(召) the sun(日) at night to light the area and make things more visible.

120c

丨 冂 日 日 日ㄱ 日刀 日刀 昭 昭 照 照 照 照

照 zhào

shine

bright 昭 [zhāo] + fire 灬 = 火[158] [huǒ]

This character describes a torch(灬) held to shine(昭) and light up the area. It also means to turn on(昭) lighting(灬) to take photos or film videos.

护照 [hùzhào] passport - 144f
照顾 [zhàogù] give consideration to; look after - 6d
照片 [zhàopiàn] photograph; picture - 215
照相机 [zhàoxiàngjī] camera - 11c 213
照相 [zhào/xiàng] take a picture - 11c

120d

一 十 土 丰 丰 走 走 起 起 起 超 超

超 chāo

exceed; super

run/walk 走[53c] [zǒu] + call up 召 [zhào]

This character depicts a shaman who is dancing and frequenting(走) the two different worlds of body and soul beyond the limitations of human faculties in order to call up(召) God.

超市 [chāoshì] supermarket - 131a

干

Diagram for 干

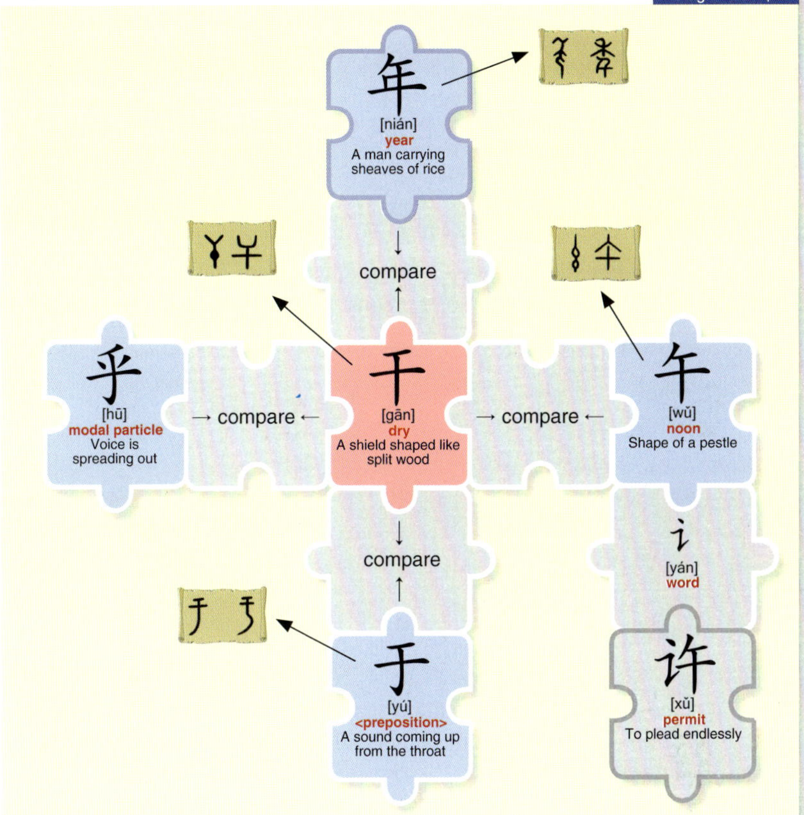

121

121 一 二 干

干 gān/gàn dry; clean / main part; do

The shape of a shield split at the top to defend and attack. This character is rarely used to mean a shield. Instead, it means 'dry,' which has the same pronunciation. It also means 'clean,' as something is usually dried after it's washed.

干净[gānjìng] clean; neat and tidy - 36b   干杯[gān/bēi] drink a toast; cheers - 223b

A plant with a stem that splits in two as it grows. A stem is an important part of a plant, so this character also means 'to do~, to work' at the center of something.

干部[gànbù] cadre - 79f
能干[nénggàn] able; capable; competent - 89b

121

121a

丿 𠂉 𠂉 𠂉 𠂉 年

年 nián

year

person 𠂉→人[63][rén] + rice plant 𠂇→禾[139][hé]

A man(人) carrying sheaves of rice(禾) reminds us of harvests. The Chinese harvest once a year, so this character means 'year.'

* Ancient texts show that this character's a combination of rice(禾) and a person(人).

去年[qùnián] last year - 94
年轻[niánqīng] young - 124b
明年[míngnián] next year - 218h
青年[qīngnián] youth; young people - 135
年级[niánjí] grade; year - 36g
今年[jīnnián] this year - 66
年纪[niánjì] age - 82c
新年[xīnnián] New Year - 103b

121b

丿 𠂉 二 午

午 wǔ

noon

This character depicts a pestle standing upright in a mortar which is used to grind grains into powder. When the sun shines directly above the center of the mortar, it is noon time.

* The ancient character shows that this is the shape of a mill with a mortar and a pestle under the roof of a building.

上午[shàngwǔ] ante meridiem (a.m.) - 223f
中午[zhōngwǔ] noon; midday - 232a
下午[xiàwǔ] post meridiem (p. m.) - 223g
午饭[wǔfàn] midday meal; lunch - 148b

121c

丶 讠 讠 讠 讠 许

许 xǔ

permit; maybe

word 讠=言[22][yán] + pestle/noon 午 [wǔ]

'Strike enough times and any tree will fall' is a popular adage. Like one pounding a pestle(午) endlessly, if one asks(讠) for permission enough times, one will get it. It also means 'maybe,' showing hope that endless(午) pleading(讠) might work.

许多 [xǔduō] many; much - 222d　　也许 [yěxǔ] perhaps; maybe - 84
允许 [yǔnxǔ] permit; allow - 71a

121d　　一 二 于

于 yú <preposition>

This character itself has no particular meaning, but it depicts the image of an open mouth in order to produce a sound necessary for making a script from the word. Currently, it is used as a 'preposition to describe place, time, direction and target.'

* Its shape is similar to the character 'shield, 干 [gān]' but the two letters have no relevance to each other in terms of meaning.

关于 [guānyú] concerning; regarding - 45　　终于 [zhōngyú] at last; finally - 206g

121e　　丿 𠂇 𠂤 乊 乎

乎 hū modal particle

This character depicts the image of calling somebody, when a voice starts to originate out of the throat and spreads out. It is used at the end of a sentence to express 'interrogative or exclamatory particle.'

几乎 [jīhū] almost; nearly - 213

平

Diagram for 平

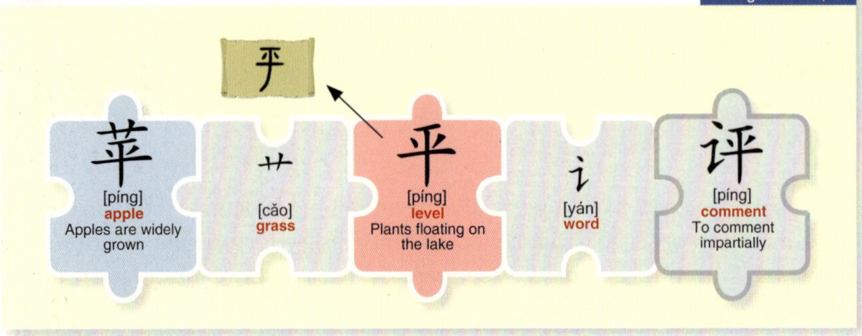

122

平 píng — level

A description of plants covering a lake's flat surface.

* Shirakawa Shizuka(白川静, 1910~2006), a Japanese scholar, says this character is the shape of woodchips flying as a man uses a plane(干) to shave a flat surface on a piece of wood(丷).

122 水平[shuǐpíng] horizontal; level - 201　　和平[hépíng] peace - 139a

122a

评 píng — comment

word 讠=言[22][yán] + level 平 [píng]

To comment or argue about something or someone with words(讠) that are impartial(平).

批评[pīpíng] criticize; criticism - 88b

122b

苹 píng — apple

grass 艹[207][cǎo] + level 平 [píng]

An apple is a fruit(艹) grown evenly(平) all around the world, so the Chinese decided to use this characteristic to describe it. This character is only used as part of the word "apple(苹果)."

* The apple is the most evenly(平) grown fruit(艹) in the world, meaning production is not limited to one area.

苹果[píngguǒ] apple - 210g

干

Diagram for 干

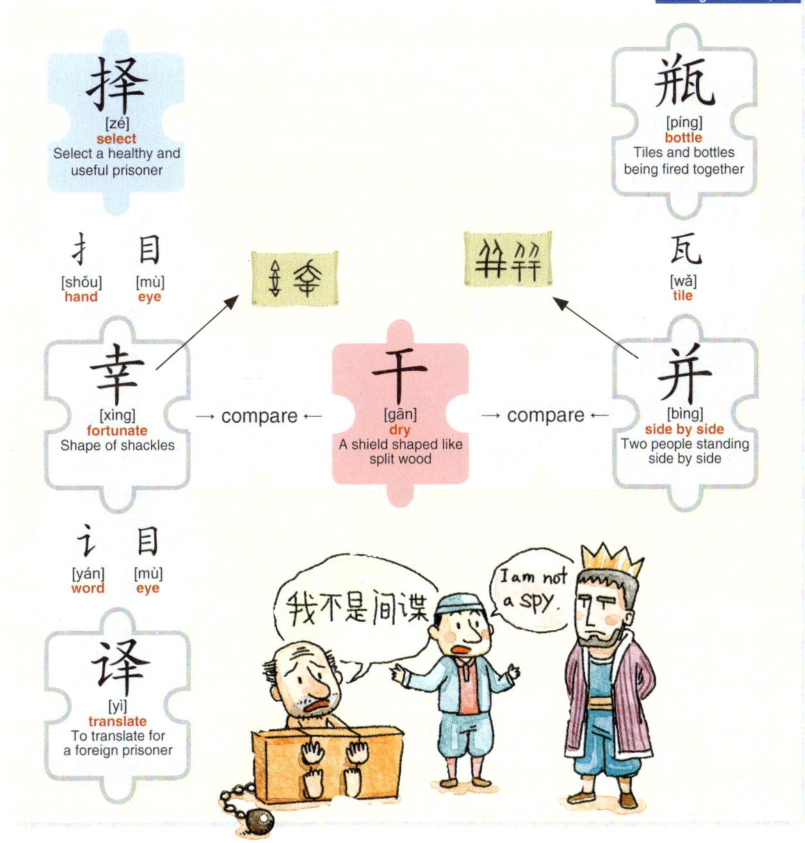

123

123 丶 丷 ⺌ 兰 兯 并

并 bìng	**side by side**

Two people(人[63] 人) are tied up(二) side by side so they do not part.

* This character is listed here only because "dry 干[121] [gān]" is its radical. There are no other connections.

并且[bìngqiě] and; also - 224

123a 丶 丷 丬 丷 ⺷ 并 并⺊ 瓶 瓶 瓶

瓶 píng

bottle

side by side 并 [bìng] + tile 瓦[146a] [wǎ]

To put bottles (ceramic ware) and tiles(瓦) into a kiln together(并) and fire them up.

* China was the first East-Asian country to use ceramics as everyday items.

瓶子[píngzi] bottle - 95   热水瓶[rèshuǐpíng] thermos; vacuum bottle - 158f 201

123b 一 十 土 圡 幸 幸 幸 幸

幸 xìng

fortunate

The shape of wooden shackles to restrain one's hands and feet. This character means 'to be lucky' that one is not in shackles.

* This character was made because in the ancient times, rulers threatened the people with imprisonment.

123 幸福[xìngfú] happiness; blessed - 126i   不幸[bùxìng] unfortunate; misfortune - 223a

123c 丶 讠 讠 译 译 译 译

译 yì

translate

word 讠=言[22] [yán] + peep 𠬤→睪 [yì]

"Peep 睪 [yì]" is a description of someone checking on a prisoner. This character means to check on a prisoner(睪), listen to his speech(讠), and to translate.

* "睪" is a combination of eyes(罒→目[11]) and shackles(幸) and means 'to check on a prisoner.'

翻译[fānyì] translate - 182b

123d 一 丨 扌 扌 扌 择 择 择

择 zé

select

hand 扌=手[31] [shǒu] + peep 𠬤→睪 [yì]

This character shows the image of examining(𠬤) the foreign prisoners and selecting a healthy and useful man for labor, with a gesture of one's hand(扌).

选择[xuǎnzé] select; choose - 71f

车

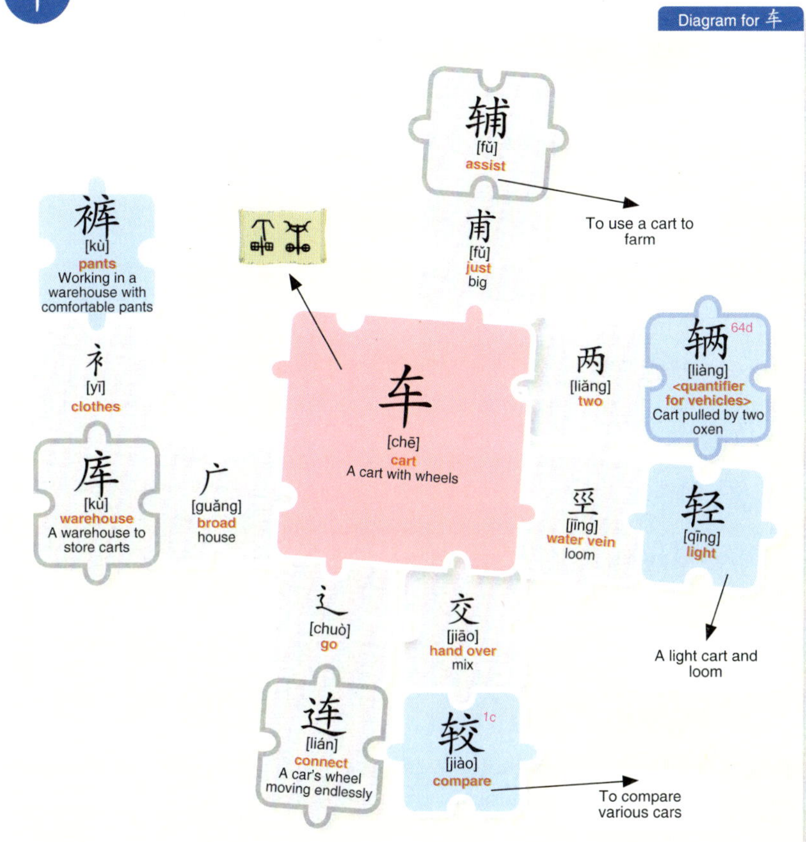

124

124

车 chē

cart; vehicle

The shape of a cart with wheels, drawn by horse or cattle. Now it means 'car.'

出租车 [chūzūchē] taxi; taxicab - 167a 139d
公共汽车 [gōnggòngqìchē] bus - 93b 43c 204a
车站 [chēzhàn] depot; station - 127c
电车 [diànchē] streetcar; trolley (car) - 157a
卡车 [kǎchē] truck - 128c
火车站 [huǒchēzhàn] train station - 158 127c
自行车 [zìxíngchē] bicycle - 26 60b
出租汽车 [chūzūqìchē] taxi; taxicab - 167a 139d 204a
火车 [huǒchē] train - 158
汽车 [qìchē] car; vehicle - 204a

124

124a

一 𠂇 𠂇 车 车 车 车 车 辅 辅 辅

辅 fǔ

assist

cart 车 [chē] + big/just 甫[166c] [fǔ]

To farm in a wide(甫) field, one needs a cart(车) to assist him.

* "甫" is a description of a wide field(田[154]) full of produce(屮[207]).

辅导[fǔdǎo] give guidance in study or training; tutor - 7b

124b

一 𠂇 𠂇 车 车 轻 轻 轻 轻

轻 qīng

light

cart 车 [chē] + loom/water vein 圣 → 巠[132e] [jīng]

The light movement of a cart's(车) wheels and the swift movement of a loom (巠).

* The right side of The traditional character(輕) is a variation of "巠," which is the original shape of a 'loom.'

年轻[niánqīng] young - 121a

124c

一 𠂇 𠂇 车 连 连 连

连 lián

connect

cart 车 [chē] + go 辶[61] [chuò]

A car(车) turns its wheels endlessly to go forward(辶). Something that never ends is 'connected or continuous.'

连…都(也)…[lián…dōu(yě)…] even…is/does… - 101a 84

连续[liánxù] continue - 75e

雨连着下了五天。It rained continuously for five days. - 205 124c 11b 223g 168a 226a 74b

124d

丶 亠 广 广 庄 库 库

库 kù

warehouse

house/broad 广[143] [guǎng] + cart 车 [chē]

A warehouse means a house(广) or place where carts(车) are stored.

124e　　` ｀ 礻 礻 礻 礻 礻 衤 裤

裤 kù

pants; trousers

clothes 衤＝衣[130] [yī] + warehouse 库 [kù]

In ancient times, most men and women used to wear skirts. Later, the modern type of pants(衤) became popular due to the introduction of combat fatigues in the 15th century. You may think about a person who is working in a warehouse(库) with comfortable pants(衤).

裤子 [kùzi] pants; trousers - 95

舟

Diagram for 舟

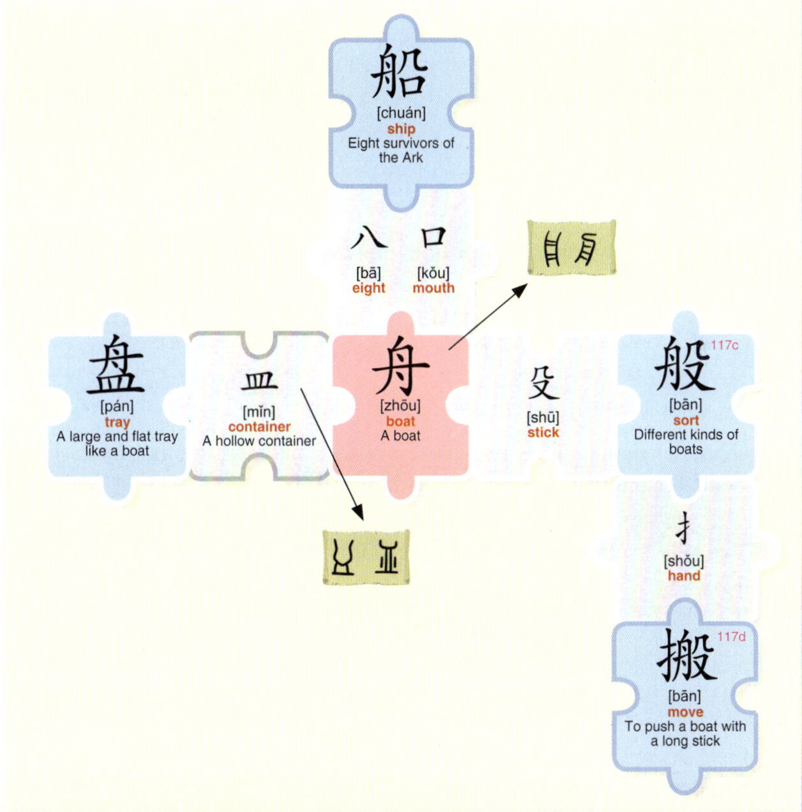

125

125

125 ′ 丿 ⺆ ⺆ 舟 舟

舟 zhōu

boat

A small boat made by carving out a whole piece of wood.

125a

船 chuán

ship

boat 舟 [zhōu] + eight 八[229] [bā] + mouth 口[16] [kǒu]

The Bible states that eight(八) people(口) survived in Noah's Ark(舟). This character seems to explain that, and means boats and ships of all sizes. - Genesis 7:13

* A mouth(口) is used to eat and speak and describes people.

乘船去大连。embark (on a ship) for Dalian - 88d 125a 94 74 124c

125b

皿 mǐn

container

This character shows an image of imitating a vessel which is hollow.

125c

盘 pán

tray; plate

boat 舟 [zhōu] + container 皿 [mǐn]

This character depicts the image of a tray or container(皿) that looks like a large boat(舟) and can contain various kinds of food.

盘子[pánzi] tray; plate - 95

示

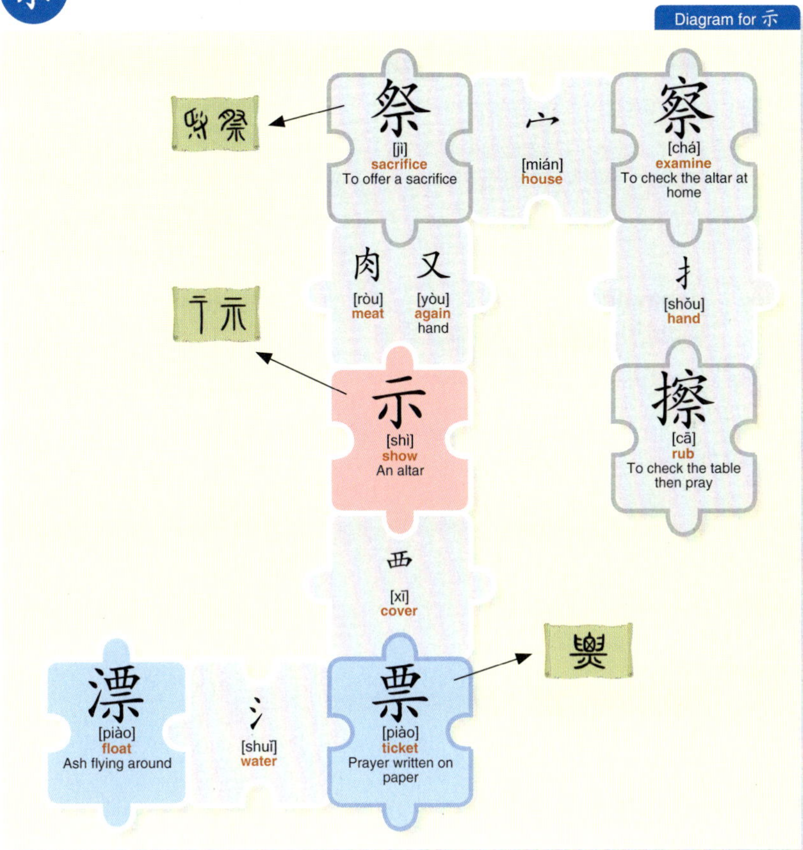

126

126 一 二 亍 亓 示

示 shì **show**

The shape of an altar used to offer sacrifices to gods. In return, the gods show the people something. When combined to become part of another character, it sometimes changes into "礻."

表示 [biǎoshi] show; express; indicate - 130b   指示 [zhǐshi] indicate; point out - 89a

126

126a 丿 ク タ タ タ⁷ 夗 奴 癶 祭 祭 祭

祭 jì

sacrifice

meat 月[221]→肉[192] [ròu] + hand/again 又[34] [yòu] + altar/show 示 [shì]

To have a sacrifice in which meat(肉) is offered(又) on an altar(示).

* "Moon 月 [yuè]" means "肉" when part of another character.
* "又" is a variation of 'hand,' used here because less strokes balance the character out.

126b 丶 丶 宀 宀 宀 宀 宊 宊 宊 宊 宊 宊 察 察

察 chá

examine

house 宀[141] [mián] + sacrifice 祭 [jì]

To check carefully if the offerings(祭) set up at home(宀) for the ancestors are appropriate.

* All East-Asian countries have set rules on which food is offered and where they are set on the table.

考察[kǎochá] inspect; investigate - 100c

126c 一 扌 扌 扌 扌 扩 扩 护 护 护 护 搽 搽 搽 擦 擦 擦

擦 cā

rub

hand 扌=手[31] [shǒu] + examine 察 [chá]

After checking the offerings(察), one prays for good fortune by rubbing their hands(扌) together.

126d 一 丆 丙 丙 两 西 西 覀 票 票 票

票 piào

ticket; banknote

cover 覀[170a] [xī] + altar/show 示 [shì]

To burn a written prayer in front of the altar(示) to ask for forgiveness or the covering(覀) of sins. Another piece of paper with much value is a 'ticket or paper money.'

* The ancient character shows someone using fire(火[158] [huǒ]) to burn the riches being held up (臼[43d] [jiù]) above the head(head/fontanel 囟[132h] [xìn]). Ash is light, which is why this character also means 'a note.'

邮票[yóupiào] (postage) stamp - 147d

126e

漂 piào

float

water 氵[202] [shuǐ] + written prayer/ticket 票 [piào]

Ash of the ceremonial prayer(票) flies around, and then lands and floats on water(氵).

漂亮 [piàoliang] pretty; beautiful - 3b

示

Diagram for 礻

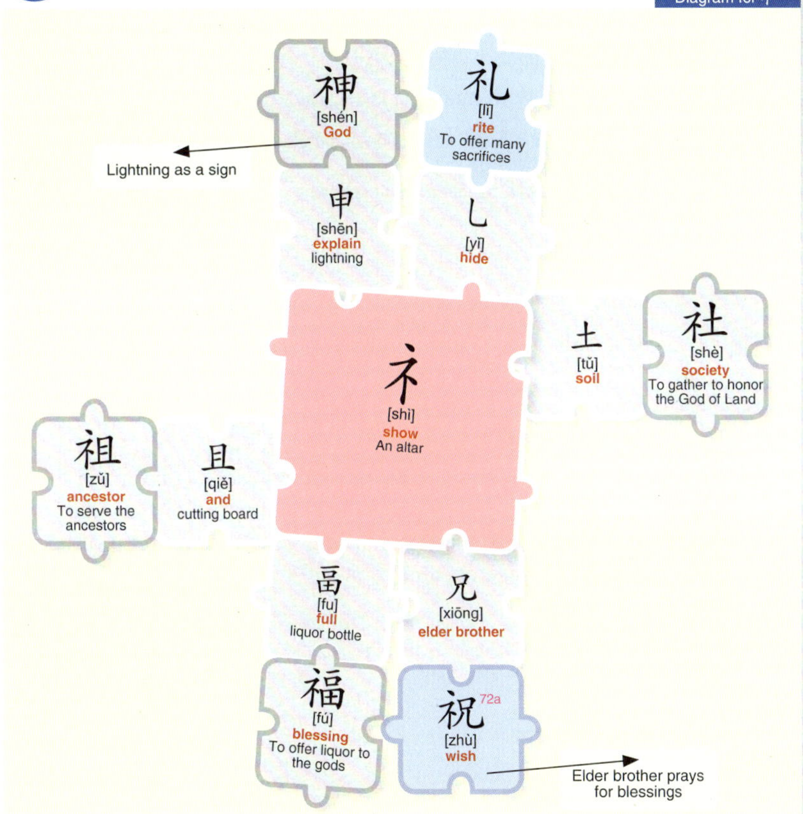

126

126

126f

丶 ㇇ 礻 礻 礻 初 初 衵 神

神 shén

God; supernatural; spirit

show 礻=示 [shì] + lightning/explain 申[157] [shēn]

This character means 'god, supernatural' because lightning(申) was considered a sign from the gods(礻) and was feared. It also means 'spirit' because gods are invisible and so are souls.

* "申" is the shape of lightning that spreads.

精神[jīngshén] spirit; mind - 135b　　神经[shénjīng] nerve - 132e

126g

丶 ㇇ 礻 礻 礼

礼 lǐ

rite; gift

altar/show 礻=示 [shì] + hide 乚[83e] [yǐ]

To have a ceremonial rite with many(乚) offerings on the altar(礻).

* The traditional character(禮) is a better description of an altar(示) overflowing(豊[fēng]→丰[209] [Simplified character]) with offerings.

* "乚" has no set meaning and can be interpreted depending on the character. Here, it gives the character its pronunciation.

礼物[lǐwù] gift; present - 49b　　礼堂[lǐtáng] assembly hall; auditorium - 150d

126h

丶 ㇇ 礻 礻 礻 社 社

社 shè

society

altar/show 礻=示 [shì] + soil 土[152] [tǔ]

In the agricultural society, soil(土) was considered sacred that made everything grow. This character describes people gathered in front of an altar(礻) to worship the God of Land(土). As this character describes a group of people gathered for a specific purpose, it came to mean 'society.'

社会[shèhuì] society - 66c

126i

丶 ㇇ 礻 礻 礻 礻 礻 礻 祁 福 福 福 福

福 fú

blessing

altar/show 礻=示 [shì] + liquor bottle/full 畐[163] [fu]

In the agricultural society, wine(畐) was a must on any altar(礻). That was because the foam from a fermented wine symbolizes a field rich with grain. To offer alcohol(畐) to the gods(礻) guaranteed a blessing.

* "畐" is the shape of a bottle of wine(酉[162]).

幸福[xìngfú] happiness; blessed - 123b	享福[xiǎng/fú] enjoy a happy life - 3c

126j

丶 ㇇ 才 礻 礻 礻冂 礻冃 礻月 祖

祖 zǔ

ancestor

altar/show 礻=示 [shì] + cutting board/and 且[224] [qiě]

To place a cutting board(且) full of meat on the altar(礻) as an offering to one's ancestors.

* "且" is the shape of a cutting board laden with meat on an altar.

祖国[zǔguó] mother country; one's country - 20a

126

卜

127

Diagram for 占

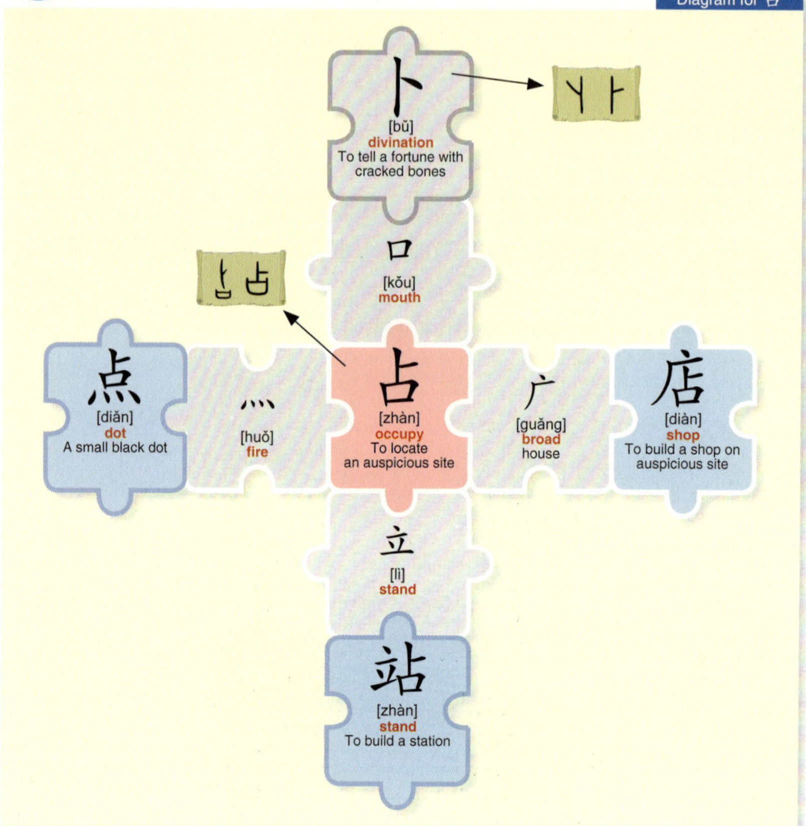

127 丨 卜

卜 bǔ

divination

When you drill a hole in a cow bone or tortoise shell then put it in a fire, it cracks. Back in the day the Chinese told fortunes based on them.

127a 丨 ⺊ ⺊ 占 占

占 zhàn

occupy

divination 卜 [bǔ] + mouth 口[16] [kǒu]

A description of someone being told(口) of an auspicious site through a fortunetelling(卜) and occupying the site.

占位子。To take a seat. - 127a 79c 95
占世界第一位。Rank first in the world. - 127a 207f 63d 109b 223 79c

127b

丶 亠 广 广 庐 庐 店 店

店 diàn

shop

house/broad 广[143] [guǎng] + occupy 占 [zhàn]

To occupy an auspicious site(占), construct a building(广) and open 'shop.'

* "广" is a house with one wall taken down, so think of a shop with a window-front to display products.

商店[shāngdiàn] store; shop - 103c
饭店[fàndiàn] hotel; restaurant - 148b
书店[shūdiàn] bookstore - 232d

127c

丶 亠 亠 立 立 立 站 站 站 站

站 zhàn

stand; station

stand 立[79] [lì] + occupy 占 [zhàn]

Description of the local government putting up(立) stations on a site they occupied(占) so officials could rest their horses or transfer to a new one while on official business. This is how 'bus stops or stations' were started.

火车站[huǒchēzhàn] train station - 158 124
车站[chēzhàn] depot; station - 124

127d

丨 ⺊ 占 占 占 占 点 点 点

点 diǎn

dot; little; snack

occupy 占 [zhàn] + fire 灬 = 火[158] [huǒ]

To make a character meaning 'dot,' the Chinese used the character for "fire 灬 [huǒ]" that makes ash, and combined it with "occupy 占 [zhàn]" to borrow the pronunciation. A dot is small, so this character means 'a little.' It also means 'a snack,' a small meal.

* The traditional character(點) can also imply that the fire(灬) is "black 黑[158d] [hēi]." Burning the bones black to tell a fortune(占) also influenced the meaning.

点心[diǎnxin] snack; refreshment - 28
点钟[diǎnzhōng] o'clock - 232b
一点儿[yīdiǎnr] a bit; a little - 223 71
差点儿[chàdiǎnr] slightly inferior to - 171b 71
特点[tèdiǎn] characteristic; distinguishing feature - 42b

127

卜

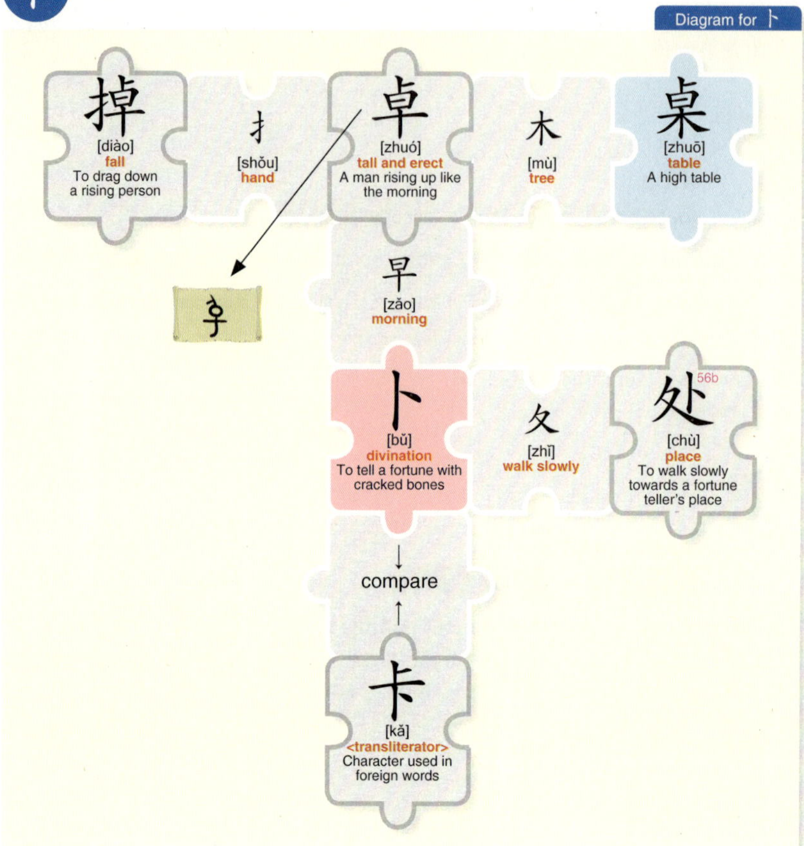

128

128

丨 ⺊ ⺊ 𠁣 占 卢 卓 卓

卓 zhuó

tall and erect

person 卜[127] →人[63][rén] + morning 早[128e][zǎo]

A great man(人) who rises up like the morning(早) sun is 'tall and erect.'

* The ancient character shows that the top section is not "divination 卜 [bǔ]" but person(人) rising like the morning(早).

128a

一 丨 扌 扌 扌 扌 扌 扌 扌 掉 掉

掉 diào

fall

hand 扌=手[31] [shǒu] + tall and erect 卓 [zhuó]

A group of people using hands(扌) to drag down or fell a prominent(卓) person.

128b

丨 卜 卜 卢 卢 卤 卓 卓 桌 桌

桌 zhuō

table

tall and erect 卓 [zhuó] + tree 木[210] [mù]

A high(卓) table made with wood(木).

桌子 [zhuōzi] table; desk - 95

128c

丨 卜 上 卡 卡

卡 kǎ

<transliterator>

up 上[223f] [shàng] + down 下[223g] [xià]

A combination of "上" and "下," this character has nothing to do with "divination 卜[127] [bǔ]" and is only used when writing the pronunciation of foreign words. 128

卡车 [kǎchē] truck - 124

兆

Diagram for 兆

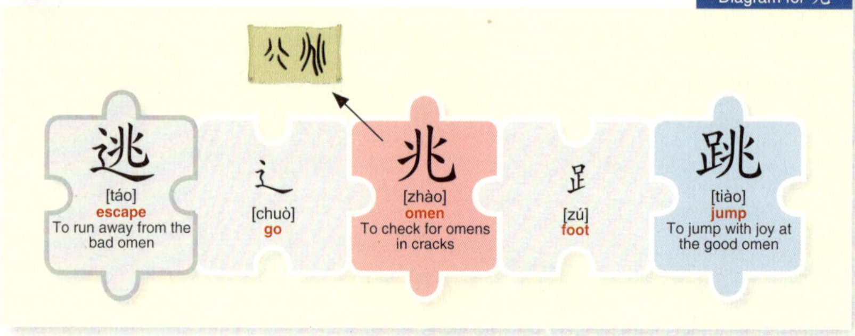

129

兆 zhào

omen

When you drill a hole in a cow bone or tortoise shell then put it in a fire, it cracks. This character means 'omen' and got its meaning in the similar way
129 to "divination 卜[127][bǔ]."

129a

跳 tiào

jump

foot ⻊=足[52] [zú] + omen 兆 [zhào]

The description of a man jumping up and down on his feet(⻊) when the fortuneteller mentions the good omen(兆).

跳舞[tiào/wǔ] dance - 58a

129b

逃 táo

escape

omen 兆 [zhào] + go 辶[61][chuò]

The description of a man running away(辶) at the news of a negative omen (兆).

逃跑[táopǎo] run away; escape - 47c

衣

Diagram for 衣

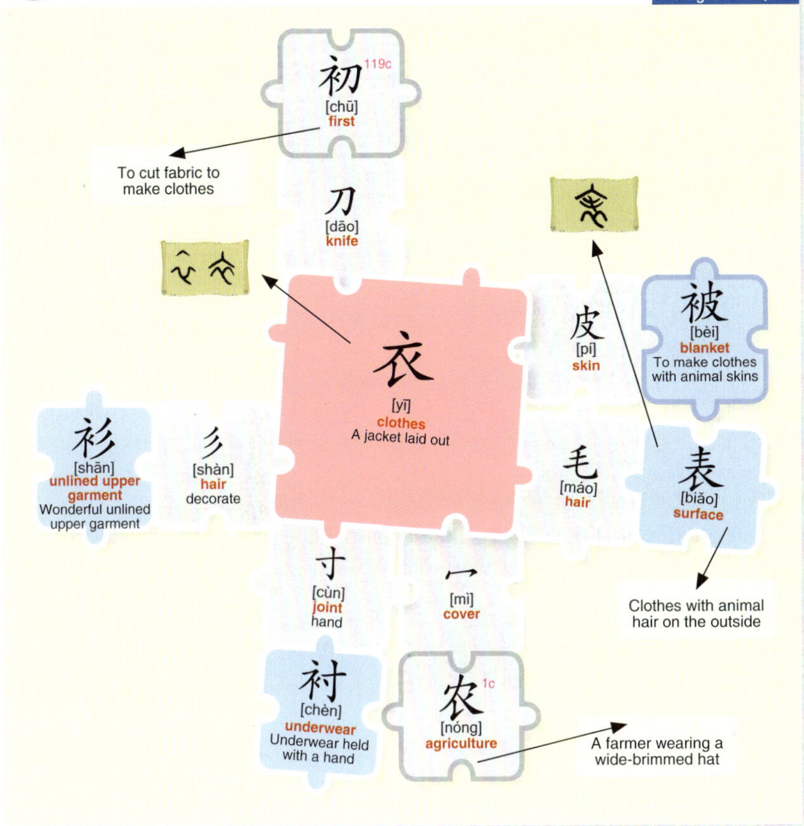

130

130 丶 亠 ナ 亡 衣 衣

衣 yī **clothes**

A jacket, an item of clothing, spread out on the floor. When combined to become part of another character, it sometimes changes into "衤."

衣服[yīfu] clothes - 34b
毛衣[máoyī] sweater - 188
雨衣[yǔyī] raincoat; waterproof - 205

130

130a

被 bèi

quilt; suffer; <passive indicator> 'by'

clothes 衤=衣 [yī] + skin 皮[189][pí]

If you wear clothes(衤) made with animals skins(皮), you look like you are swathed in a blanket. This character is also used as the preposition 'by' because the dead animal was stripped of its skin by the human beings. The subject that appears in front of "被" is a recipient of the action that follows.

* "皮" describes a hand(又[34]) stripping the skin.

被子[bèizi] quilt - 95
那本书已经被借出了。That book has been lent out now.
- 147e 210a 232d 82a 132e 130a 220a 167a 168a

130b

表 biǎo

surface

hair 毛[188][máo] + clothes 衣 [yī]

To make and wear clothes(衣) with the animal hair(毛) on the outside. It came to mean 'watch' because it is worn on the wrist and is very visible.

手表[shǒubiǎo] wrist watch - 31
表演[biǎoyǎn] perform - 136b
表扬[biǎoyáng] praise; commend - 219a
表示[biǎoshì] show; express; indicate - 126
表现[biǎoxiàn] show; express - 13d
代表[dàibiǎo] representative; delegate - 110c

130c

农 nóng

agriculture; farmer

cover 冖[169][mì] + clothes 𧘇→衣 [yī]

Farmers wear wide-brimmed hats(冖) and long-sleeved clothes(衣) to work.

* The traditional character(農) describes a man using a shell(辰[187]) to harvest grains(曲→禾[139]).

农村[nóngcūn] farm village; rural area - 40a
农民[nóngmín] farmer; peasant - 99c
农业[nóngyè] agriculture - 223c
农田[nóngtián] farmland; cropland - 154

130d

丶 ㇇ 衤 衤 衤 衤一 衬 衬

衬 chèn

underwear; lining

clothe 衤=衣 [yī] + hand/joint 寸[40] [cùn]

In order to create a character for 'underwear,' the phonetic sound of "joint 寸 [cùn]" is combined with "cloth 衤 [yī]."

* To easily understand this character, let us try to remember underwear which is a kind of clothes(衤) thin enough to hold with one hand(寸).

衬衫[chènshān] shirt; blouse - 130e

130e

丶 ㇇ 衤 衤 衤 衤' 衫 衫

衫 shān

unlined upper garment

clothe 衤=衣 [yī] + decorate/hair 彡[8] [shàn]

This letter signifies 'unlined upper garment(衤).' The sound of "hair 彡 [shàn]" is combined to its original meaning.

* For easy recollection of the character, you may think about a person who wears a wonderful(彡) unlined upper garment shirts(衤).

衬衫[chènshān] shirt; blouse - 130d

131

巾

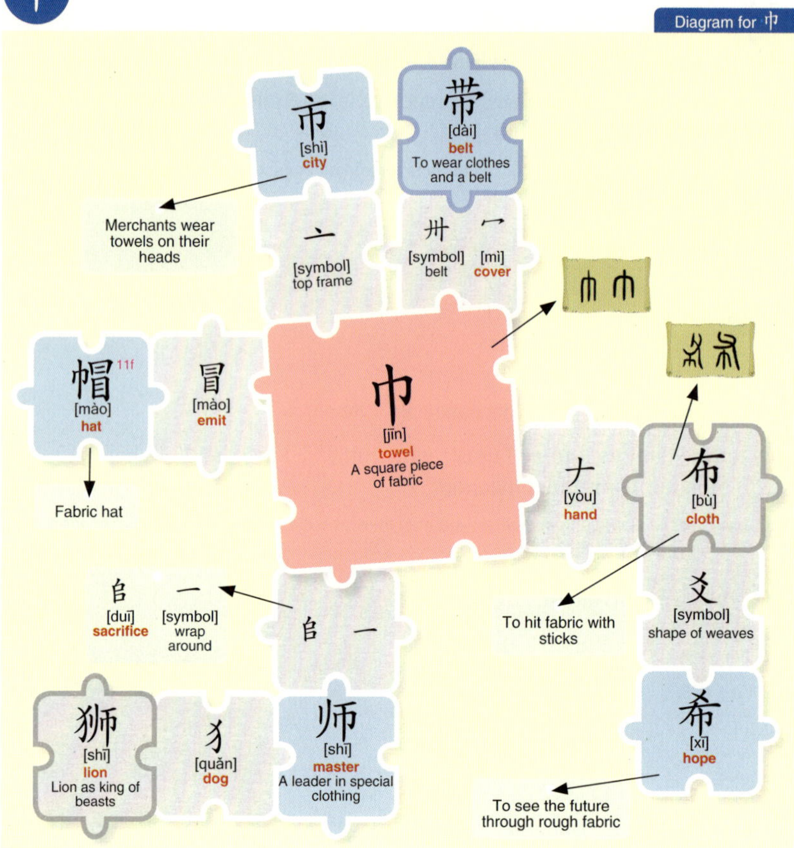

131 丨 冂 巾

巾 jīn	**towel**

A towel is a square piece of fabric used to wipe hands.

毛巾 [máojīn] towel - 188

131a 丶 亠 亣 市 市

市 shì	**city**

top frame 亠 [symbol] + towel 巾 [jīn]

Back in the day, shop signs were pieces of fabric(巾) hanging from a horizontal pole with a top frame(亠) and markets were full of them. A place with many markets is a 'city.'

超市[chāoshì] supermarket - 120d
城市[chéngshì] city; town - 114b
市场[shìchǎng] market; market place - 152a

131b 一 十 卄 卅 卌 卌 带 带 带

带 dài

belt; carry

belt 卅 [symbol] + cover 冖[169] [mì] + towel 巾 [jīn]

'To cover(冖) one's body with fabric(巾) and wear a belt(卅)' is where the character for 'belt' came from. People attached things to their belt 'to carry' around.

磁带[cídài] magnetic tape - 197b
地带[dìdài] zone; region; belt - 84a

131c 一 ナ 𠂇 右 布

布 bù

cloth; spread

hand ナ[39] [yòu] + towel 巾 [jīn]

To spread cloth(巾) under a flat stone and beat it with handheld(ナ) sticks. Fabric treated that way became flat, like it was ironed, so this character also means 'to spread.'

* The ancient character shows that "ナ" is the shape of a hand holding a stick. China and also Korea used sticks to beat and flatten fabric.

131

131d

希 xī

hope

shape of weaves 𠂔 → 爻 [symbol] + towel 巾 [jīn]

Rough fabrics(巾) like hemp cloth have what seems like holes(爻) because the strands are coarse. Such fabrics are transparent and when one can see his future so clearly, he can have 'hope.'

希望[xīwàng] hope; wish - 5c

131e

师 shī

master

sacrifice 刂 → 𠂤[193] [duī] + wrap around 帀 [zā]

A leader wearing a ceremonial outfit(帀) is officiating a ceremony and holding up the offering(𠂤), i.e., a piece of meat.

* The traditional character(師) shows that the offering(𠂤) has taken a shape similar to a knife(刂[119]).
* "帀[zā]" describes a large piece of fabric(巾) wrapped around a body.

131

老师[lǎoshī] teacher (honorific) - 100a
师傅[shīfu] master; master worker - 166e
教师[jiàoshī] teacher - 50c

131f

狮 shī

lion

dog 犭[173] [quǎn] + master 师 [shī]

The leader(师) of all animals(犭) would be the lion.

* "犭" means an animal the size of a large dog.

狮子[shīzi] lion - 95

纟

Diagram for 纟

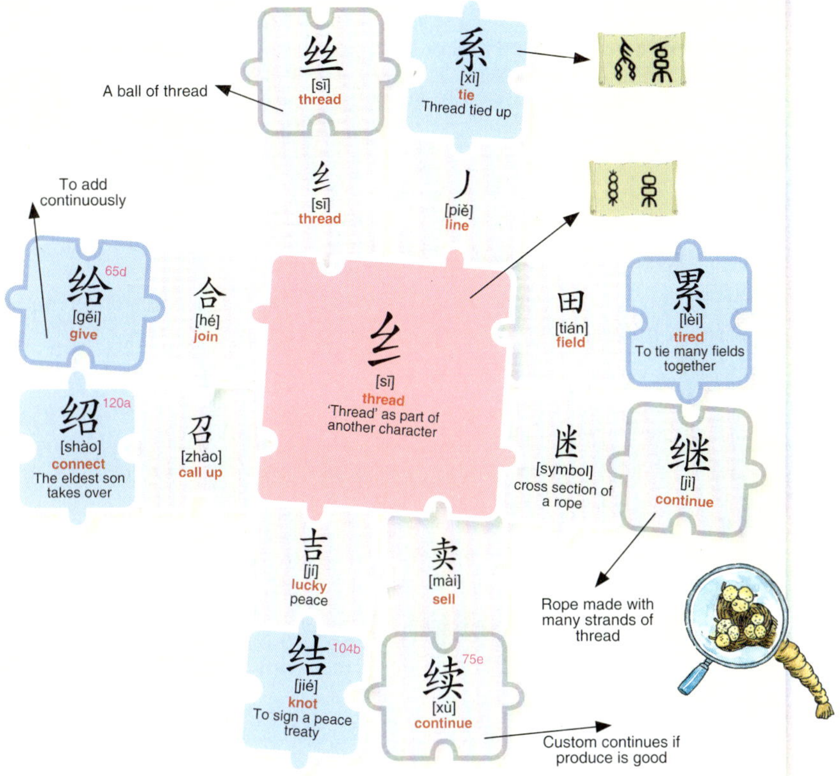

132

132

纟
sī

thread

This character replaces "thread 丝[132a][sī]" when used as part of a more complicated character. When used as such, "纟" means the character has something to do with 'tying or connecting,' typical thread-like characteristics.

* When this character is placed at the center, The traditional character(糸) is used.

132

132a

丿 ㄠ 纟 丝 丝 (stroke order)

丝 sī

thread

The shape of a neatly rolled ball or a tangled mess of thread.

丝毫[sīháo] (not) in the least - 188b

132b

系 xì

tie; department

line 丿[234] [piě] + thread 糸=纟 [sī]

A piece of thread(糸) connected to(丿) another piece. As a connection implied similarities, this character came to mean 'department.'

* "丿" has no set meaning and can be interpreted in many ways.

没关系[méiguānxi] it doesn't matter - 117f 45

关系[guānxi] relation - 45

联系[liánxi] contact; connect - 10e

132c

累 lèi

tired

field 田[154] [tián] + thread 糸=纟 [sī]

A description of many fields(田) tied together with thread(糸). A farmer who owns much land would be tired.

* The traditional character(纍) shows three rice paddies(田) tied(糸) together.

我累得再也走不动了。I was too tired to walk any further.
- 113b 132c 40b 149a 84 53c 223a 159d 168a

132d

继 jì

continue

thread 纟 [sī] + cross section of a rope 㡭 [symbol]

"㡭" is a description of the cross section of a rope made with many strands of thread(纟). A thick rope(㡭) made with a huge quantities of threads(纟) is used to tie things together.

* The traditional character(繼) shows that separate strands of thread(糸) were connected to make the rope.

继续[jìxù] continue - 75e

纟

Diagram for 纟

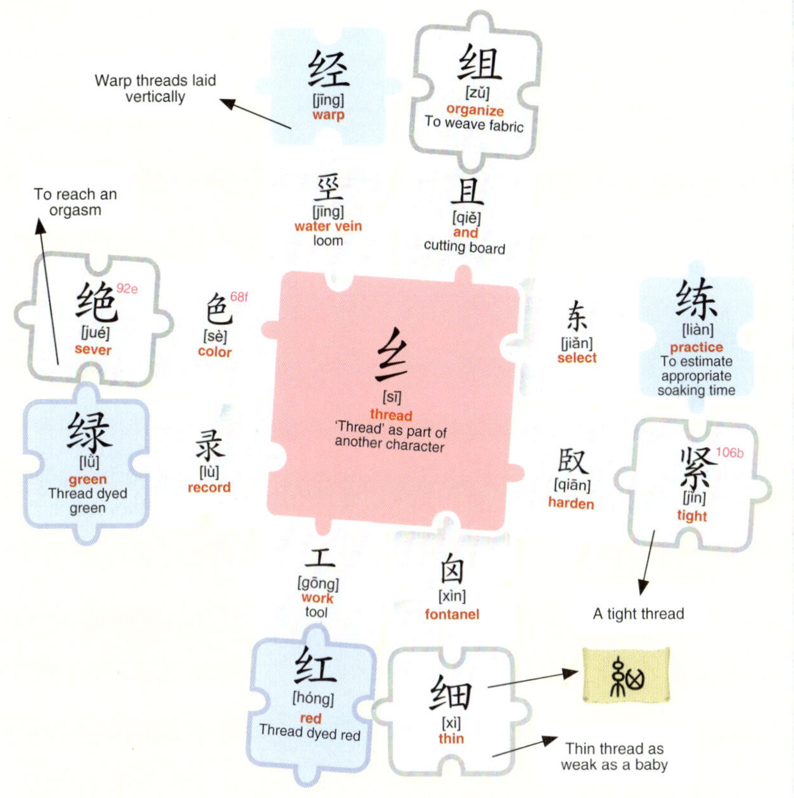

132e

纟 纟 纟 纟 纟 经 经 经

经
jīng

warp; pass through

thread 纟 [sī] + loom/water vein 𢀖 → 坙[124b] [jīng]

Threads(纟) laid vertically on a loom(坙) are called 'warp threads.' It also means 'to pass through,' because the shuttle on the loom carries the weft thread that is laid horizontally through these wrap threads.

* The right-hand side of The traditional character(經) is a variation of "坙," which originally was shaped after a loom.

已经[yǐjīng] already - 82a
经常[jīngcháng] daily; constantly - 150c
经过[jīngguò] pass; go through - 40f
经理[jīnglǐ] manager; director - 108b

经济[jīngjì] economy; economic - 133c　　经验[jīngyàn] experience - 67c

132f　　丿 ㇜ 纟 纟 纟 纟 纟 组

组 zǔ

organize

thread 纟 [sī] + cutting board/and 且[224] [qiě]

"且"is a description of a cutting board with slices of meat piled on it and means 'layers of.' Weaving is the result of thread(纟) being layered together (且). This character also means 'to organize.'

组织[zǔzhī] organization; organize - 179a

132g　　丿 ㇜ 纟 纟 纟 纟 纟 练

练 liàn

practice

thread 纟 [sī] + select 东=柬[221c] [jiǎn]

To make silk, the thread(纟) has to be extracted from the silkworm's cocoon and this is done by soaking them in boiling water. The time has to be estimated(东) correctly and that requires much practice.

132

* This character can also be interpreted to mean 'to make the thread soft and whiter.'

练习[liànxí] practice; exercise - 182a　　熟练[shúliàn] skilled; practised; proficient - 3e

132h　　丿 ㇜ 纟 纟 纟 纟 纟 细

细 xì

thin; delicate

thread 纟 [sī] + fontanel 田[154] → 囟[28a] [xìn]

New thread(纟) is thin and delicate, like a baby whose hole in the skull(囟) still has not fused.

* The ancient characters shows that "field 田 [tián]" is a variation of "囟," which is the hole in a newborn baby's skull that disappears when the skullbones fuse.

细心[xìxīn] careful; attentive - 28

132i　　丿 ㇜ 纟 纟 纟 红

红 hóng

red; popularity

thread 纟 [sī] + tool/work 工[200] [gōng]

The Chinese dyed fabric or threads(纟) and this character meaning 'red' gets its pronunciation from "工." Red was believed to bring good fortune, so this character also means 'to be popular.'

* "工" is a tool but also a sacrificial artifact. It will be easier to remember 'red' if you think of blood on a sacrificial tool.

红茶[hóngchá] black tea - 207b 红旗[hóngqí] red flag; red banner - 44c

132j 纟 纟 纟 纟 纟 纟 纾 纾 绿 绿 绿

绿 lǜ

green

thread 纟 [sī] + record 录[203a] [lù]

The Chinese dyed fabric or threads(纟) and this character meaning 'green' gets its pronunciation from "录."

* "录" describes the action of poking a hole in a tree. Most plants are 'green.'

132

Diagram for 文

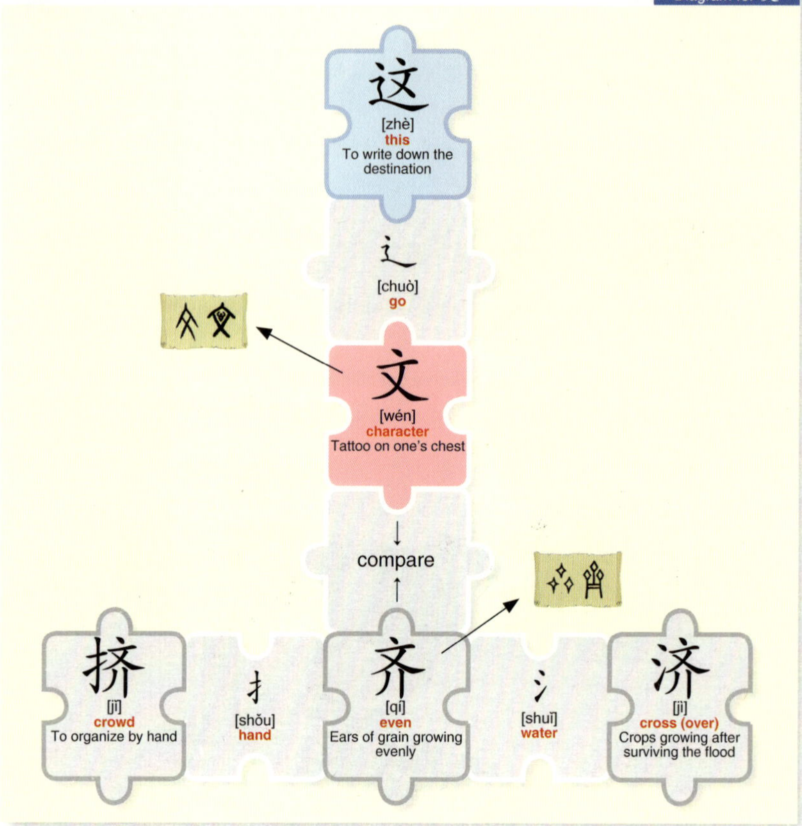

133

133　　丶 亠 ナ 文

文 wén　character; script

A man with a tattoo on his chest(乂), which is below the head(亠[1][tóu]). Chinese characters began as rough tattoo-like drawings, so this character means 'character, writing.'

文化[wénhuà] culture - 70a	课文[kèwén] text - 210i
文学[wénxué] literature - 95a	文学家[wénxuéjiā] Trecentist; litterateur - 95a 174a
文艺[wényì] literature and art - 83b	文章[wénzhāng] article; essay - 21a
中文[zhōngwén] the Chinese language - 232a	

133a 丶 亠 ナ 文 `文 汶 这

这 zhè

this

character 文 [wén] + go 辶[61][chuò]

This describes someone putting a location in writing(文) in order to get there (辶). With writing, one can explain as if the destination is close by, so this character means 'this.'

* The traditional character(這) means one uses words(言[22]) to help find(辶) a location.

这个[zhège] this one - 63b
这么[zhème] this way; like this - 93a
这样[zhèyàng] like this; this way - 171a
这里[zhèlǐ] here - 151
这些[zhèxiē] these - 88h

133b 丶 亠 ナ 文 齐 齐

齐 qí

even

Ears of grain are growing in neat and even lines.

* This character has nothing to do with "character 文 [wén]" and is used as a radical.

整齐[zhěngqí] orderly; neat; even - 54a
一齐[yīqí] at the same time; in unison - 223

133c 丶 丶 氵 氵 汁 汶 浐 济 济

济 jì

cross (over); benefit

water 氵[202][shuǐ] + even 齐 [qí]

This character describes a neat row of crops(齐) growing well after surviving a drought or a flood(氵). To survive a hardship means that one has 'crossed over,' and survival or taking a risk usually brings 'profit.'

经济[jīngjì] economy; economic - 132e

133d 一 十 扌 扌 扩 扩 挞 挤 挤

挤 jǐ

crowd; squeeze

hand 扌=手[31][shǒu] + even 齐 [qí]

To use hands(扌) to organize(齐) something. One can store much more when well organized, so this character also means 'full.' Putting hands(扌) side by side(齐) to push down one something means 'to squeeze.'

小猪挤在一起取暖。The young pigs crowded against one another for warmth. - 235 101b 133d 32a 223 53d 10b 33b
把水挤掉。squeeze the water out - 92b 201 133d 128a

133

白

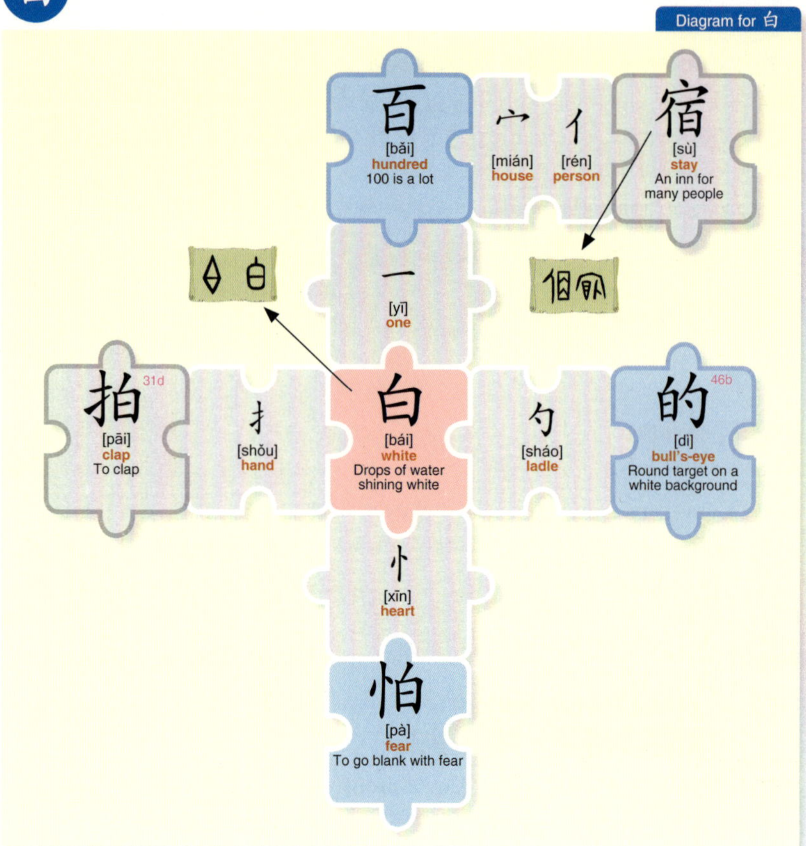

134

134 ノ 亻 白 白 白

白 bái — **white**

A drop of water reflecting the sun(日[218]) and shining(丶) white. In ancient times, the Chinese revered the color white, so it also means 'best.'

明白[míngbai] clear; obvious - 218h
白菜[báicài] Chinese cabbage - 33e
白天[báitiān] daytime - 74b

134a

一 丆 丆 百 百 百

百 bǎi

hundred; 100

one 一[223] [yī] + best/white 白 [bái]

The number one(一) combined with the best(白) means '100.'

老百姓[lǎobǎixìng] common people; ordinary people - 100a 208c

134b

丶 丶 宀 宀 宀 宀 宀 宀 宿 宿 宿

宿 sù

stay

house 宀[141] [mián] + person 亻[70] [rén] + hundred 百 [bǎi]

An inn or a hotel is a house(宀) where many(百) people(亻) can stay the night.

* The ancient characters explain that "百" is the shape of a mat used for sleeping on, and that this character is the shape of a house(宀) with sleeping mats(百) for people(亻).

宿舍[sùshè] dormitory; living quarters - 168c

134c

丶 丶 忄 忄 忄 怕 怕 怕

怕 pà

fear

heart 忄=心[28] [xīn] + white 白 [bái]

When you are very afraid(忄), your mind goes blank(白) and you cannot think.

* "心" describes emotions and represents fear.

害怕[hài/pà] be afraid; be scared - 209d　可怕[kěpà] fearful; dreadful; horrible - 17

134

青

Diagram for 青

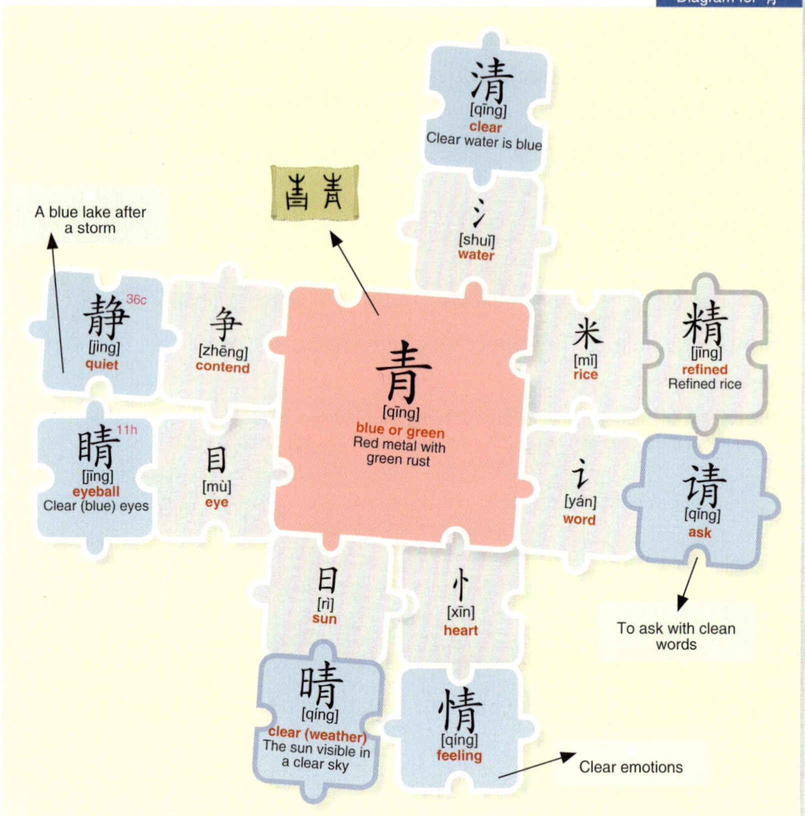

135

135

一 = 丰 主 青 青 青 青

青 qīng

blue or green

Green rust appearing(生[208]) on a red(冃→丹) metal like copper.

* The ancient characters shows that this is a combination of "be born 生 [shēng]" and "red 丹 [dān]."
* "丹" describes a well(井[228]) dug within a structure to stop it from caving in from which red minerals (丶) like copper were extracted.

青年[qīngnián] youth; young people - 121a　　年青[niánqīng] young - 121a

135a ` ﹅ 氵 氵 氵 氵 汢 清 清 清 清

清 qīng

clear

water 氵[202][shuǐ] + blue 青 [qīng]

When sunlight hits clear water, the infrared rays and red lights are absorbed and only the blue lights are reflected. So the clearer the water(氵) the bluer (青) it is.

清楚[qīngchu] clear; understand - 55a

135b

精 jīng

refined

rice 米[138][mǐ] + blue 青 [qīng]

Blue water symbolizes clarity and blue(青) rice(米) means it is clean to eat. This character also means 'refined.'

精彩[jīngcǎi] brilliant; splendid; wonderful - 8b

精神[jīngshén] spirit; mind - 126f

135c

请 qǐng

ask

word 讠=言[22][yán] + blue 青 [qīng]

Blue water symbolizes clarity and blue(青) words(讠) mean 'clear' speech. When making a request, one must be polite.

请假[qǐng/jià] ask for leave - 34k

请问[qǐngwèn] ask (formal) - 145b

请柬[qǐngjiǎn] a letter of invitation - 211c

请求[qǐngqiú] ask; request - 203b

135d

情 qíng

feeling

heart 忄=心[28][xīn] + blue 青 [qīng]

Blue water symbolizes clarity and a blue(青) heart(忄) means one's emotions are not complicated. When one is not confused, one's 'feelings or emotions' are strong.

事情[shìqing] affair; matter; thing - 36d

热情[rèqíng] passion; ardor; fervor - 158f

情况[qíngkuàng] circumstances; situation - 72b

爱情[àiqíng] love (between man and woman); affection - 34e

135

135e 丨 冂 冃 日 日一 日二 日丰 日主 日青 晴 晴 晴

晴 qíng

clear (weather)

sun 日[218] [rì] + blue 青 [qīng]

The sun(日) shines in a cloudless blue(青) sky when the weather is clear.

今天看上去是个晴天。Looks like a fine day today. - 66 74b 11a 223f 94 54b 63b 135e 74b

135

黄

Diagram for 黄

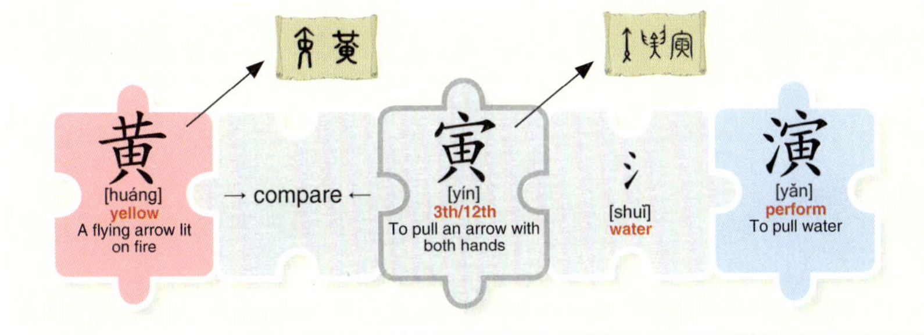

136 一 十 艹 芏 芇 芢 苗 黄 黄 黄 黄

黄 huáng — yellow

Some scholars say that "矢[111][shǐ]," "寅[136a][yín]," and "黄" all symbolize an arrow. We are not sure with the modern character, but an arrow lit on fire then shot across the night sky looks "黄," yellow.

黄色 yellow - 136 68f

136

136a 丶 丷 宀 宀 宀 宫 宫 宙 宙 寅 寅

寅 yín — 3th/12th

At first, it represented an arrow, but later took the shape of two hands and now means 'to pull.' It's also the third sign of the Chinese zodiac.

136b 丶 丶 氵 氵 氵 氵 氵 氵 浐 浐 淙 演 演 演

演 yǎn — perform

water 氵[202][shuǐ] + pull/3th 寅 [yín]

To 'pull(寅) water(氵)' means to make it flow. A performance is something that should flow naturally.

表演[biǎoyǎn] perform - 130b　　演出[yǎnchū] perform - 167a

食

Diagram for 食

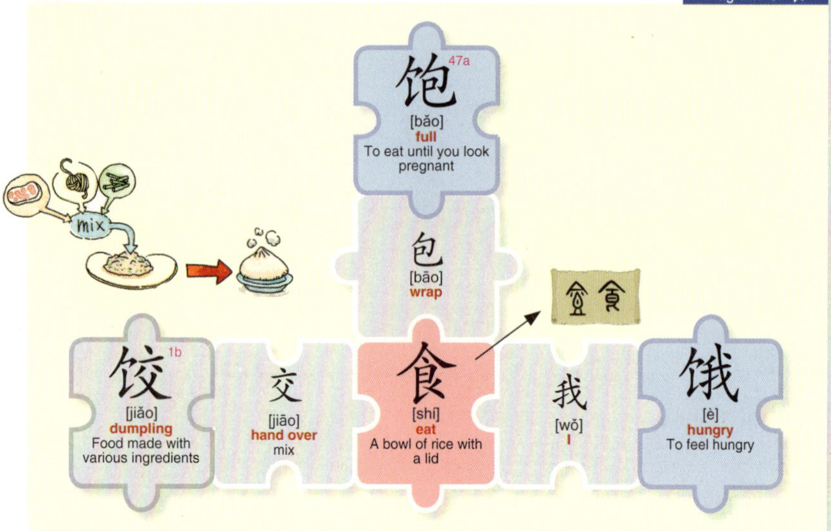

137

137

食 shí

eat; food

A bowl of food(艮) and a lid(亼[65]) to keep it warm means 'food, to eat.' When used as part of a character, it changes to "饣."

* The ancient characters show that "艮" in the "食" character has nothing to do with "to look back 艮[14] [gěn]."

食堂 [shítáng] dining hall; mess hall; cafeteria - 150d　　食物 [shíwù] food - 49b

137a

饿 è

hungry; starve

eat 饣= 食 [shí] + I 我[113b] [wǒ]

You cannot tell if someone else is hungry unless you ask. You(我) feel hungry when it's time to eat(饣).

他觉得非常饿。He felt very hungry - 84b 13a 40b 181 150c 137a

米

Diagram for 米

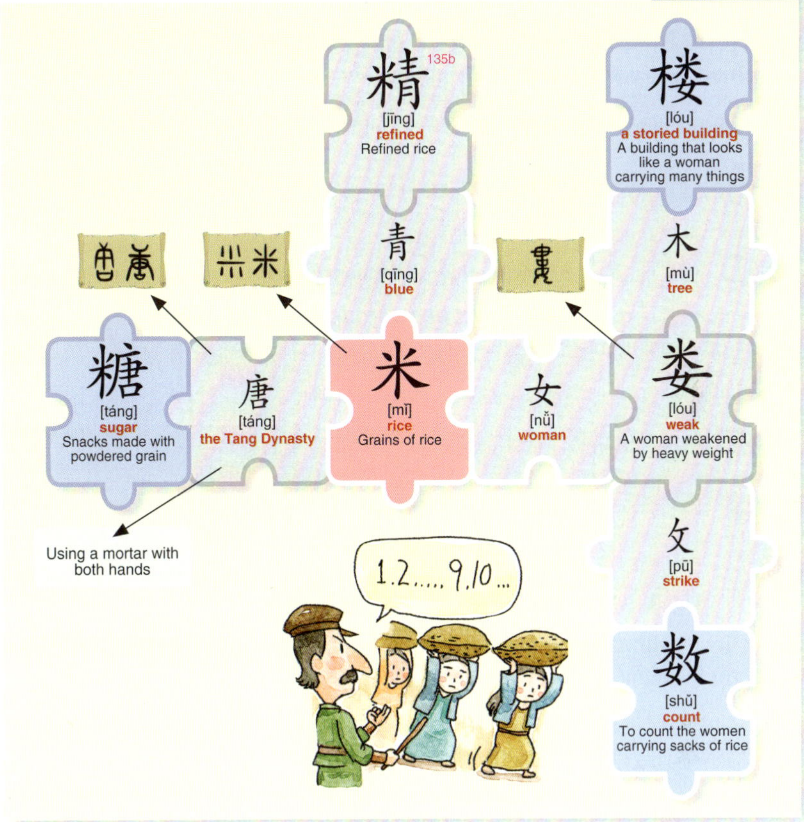

138

138

丶 丷 丬 半 米 米

米 mǐ

rice; meter

The shape of rice grains that were milled. Because of the similar pronunciation, it means 'meter.'

米饭[mǐfàn] (cooked) rice - 148b　　玉米[yùmǐ] corn - 198

这座山有3500米高。The mountain is 3500 meters high. - 133a 152c 195 39c 138 3

138

138a

丶 丷 丷 䒑 半 米 类 娄 娄

娄 lóu

weak

rice 米 [mǐ] + woman 女[96][nǚ]

A woman(女) who is always carrying heavy sacks of rice(米) becomes weak.

*The traditional character(婁) describes a woman carrying a lot of things on her head.

138b

一 十 才 木 木 木' 杧 栏 栏 柈 楼 楼 楼

楼 lóu

a storied building; floor

tree 木[210][mù] + rice 米 [mǐ] + woman 女[96][nǚ]

A wooden(木) building that looks like a woman(女) carrying sacks of rice(米) on her head has many floors.

* The Forbidden City is China's most famous wooden structure.

办公楼 office building - 159b 93b 138b　　教学楼 teaching building - 50c 95a 138b

138c

丶 丷 丷 䒑 半 米 类 娄 娄 娄' 数 数 数

数 shǔ/shù

count / number

rice 米 [mǐ] + woman 女[96][nǚ] + strike 攵[50][pū]

An official with a baton in his hand(攵) is counting the number of rice(米) sacks the women(女) carry on their heads.

* "攵" is the shape of a hand(又[34]) holding a stick(丨).

你去数一下有几辆车。Go and check to see how many cars there are.
- 69a 94 138c 223 223g 39c 213 64d 124

This character is derived from a shape of counting the number like one, two, three… and came to mean 'count the number.'

数学[shùxué] mathematics - 95a　　数字[shùzì] numeral - 95b

138d

丶 亠 广 户 户 庐 庚 庚 唐 唐

唐 táng

the Tang Dynasty (618-907)

To hold the pestle(庚[gēng]) in hand(彐[36]) and grind whatever is in the mortar (口). It later meant the 'Tang Dynasty.'

* The ancient character shows both hands holding the pestle. That is why "mouth 口[16][kǒu]" is not actually a person's mouth but a mortar.

138e

糖 táng

sugar; candy

rice 米 [mǐ] + pounding/Tang Dynasty 唐 [táng]

One can make snacks or sweets with grains(米) powdered in a mortar(唐).

单糖 simple sugar; monosaccharide - 231c 138e
白糖 white sugar - 134 138e
冰糖 rock candy; sugar candy - 206a 138e

禾

139

Diagram for 禾

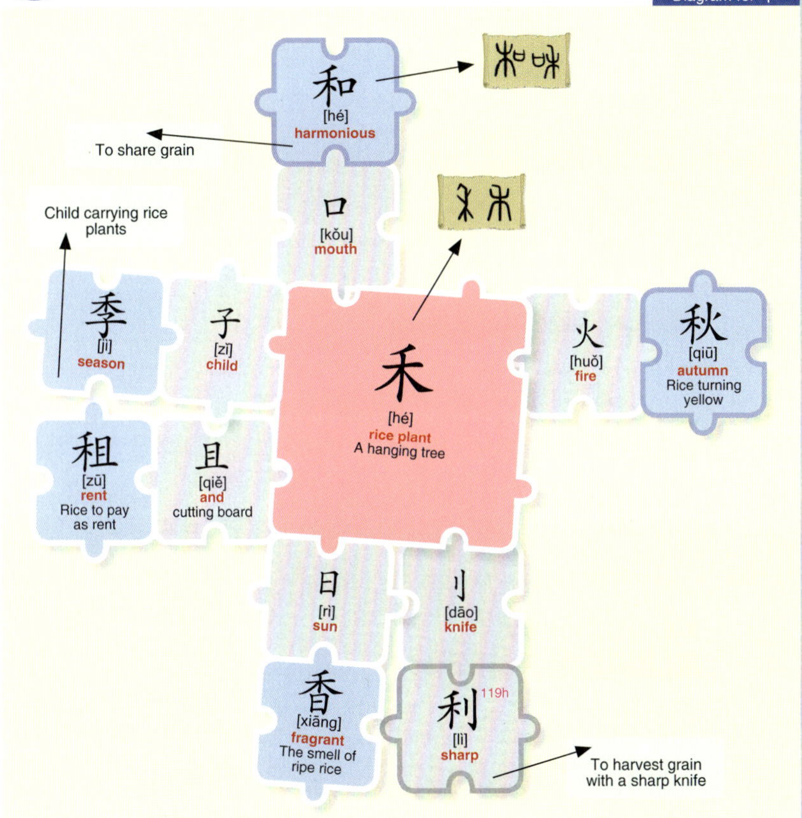

139 丿 二 千 千 禾

禾 hé — rice plant

A rice stalk is a kind of a tree(木[210]) that hangs its head(丿) as it ripens.

* An Asian saying goes, "The riper the rice, the lower it bows." It means the more one knows, the humbler he is. This shows how Asians thought rice stalks bowed.

139a 丿 二 千 千 禾 禾 和 和

和 hé — harmonious; and; with

rice plant 禾 [hé] + mouth 口[16][kǒu]

People living in harmony are willing to share food(口) made with their harvest(禾). This character came to mean 'with…, together with….'

* The ancient character describes someone blowing(口) a pipe or a flute(龠→禾) and meant that music had to be harmonious.

暖和[nuǎnhuo] warm; nice and warm - 33b   和平[hépíng] peace - 122

139

139b 丿 二 千 千 禾 禾 禾' 秒 秋

秋 qiū — autumn; fall

rice plant 禾 [hé] + fire 火[158][huǒ]

Rice(禾) fields that are catching fire(火) is another way of saying the rice is ripe and almost ready to harvest. This also means it is autumn.

* Asians liken the autumn rice(禾) paddies to a field that caught fire(火).

秋天[qiūtiān] autumn; fall - 74b

139c 丿 二 千 千 禾 禾 香 香 香

香 xiāng — fragrant; savory

rice plant 禾 [hé] + sun 日[218][rì]

On sunny(日) days around harvest time, the fragrance of ripe rice(禾) is everywhere. Food that smell nice usually taste good.

香蕉[xiāngjiāo] banana - 207c
这饭真香! This rice is really appetizing. - 133a 148b 12c 139c

139d

租 zū

rent

rice plant 禾 [hé] + cutting board/and 且[224] [qiě]

Sheaves of rice(禾) stacked in a corner to pay as rent looks like meat on a chopping board(且) ready to be offered to the gods.

* "且" describes a chopping board covered in pieces of meat.

出租车 [chūzūchē] taxi; taxicab - 167a 124   出租汽车 [chūzūqìchē] taxi; taxicab - 167a 204a 124

139e

季 jì

season

rice plant 禾 [hé] + child 子[95] [zǐ]

In autumn, the harvest season of the year, a child(子) is picking up ears of rice (禾) and carrying a sheaf of rice(禾).

季节 [jìjié] season; time - 85g

140

豆

Diagram for 豆

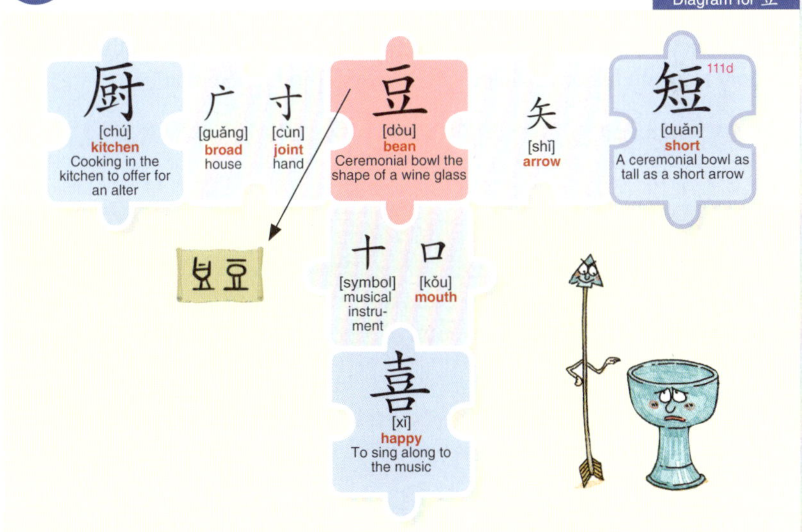

140

140 一 丆 𠫓 𠮷 豆 豆 豆

豆 dòu

bean

A ceremonial bowl or altar has a stem or legs like a wine glass. The shape is like that of a bean.

豆腐 [dòufu] bean curd - 41b

140a 一 十 士 吉 吉 吉 吉 吉 壴 壴 喜 喜

喜 xǐ

happy

instrument name 壴[51b] [zhǔ] + mouth 口[16] [kǒu]

"壴" is a musical instrument(十) on the altar(豆), signifying an instrument used in ceremonies. To sing(口) along with the music played by it(壴) means you are happy.

喜欢 [xǐhuan] like; enjoy - 23c

140b 一 厂 厂 厂 厂 厂 厂 厂 厂 厨 厨 厨

厨 chú

kitchen; cook

house/broad 厂→广[143] [guǎng] + altar/bean 豆 [dòu] + hand/joint 寸[40] [cùn]

This character signifies the image of a competent cook who is cooking in the kitchen(广) with his or her hands(寸) to offer food at the altar(豆).

厨房 [chúfáng] kitchen - 144b

宀

Diagram for 宀

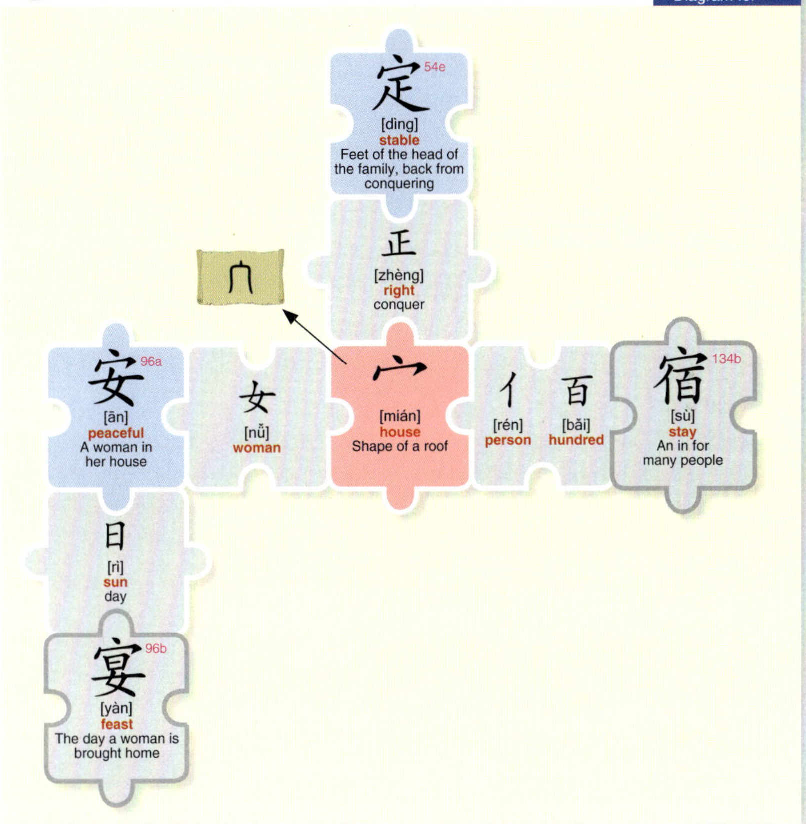

141

141 丶 冖 宀

宀 mián

house

A house, represented by its roof. When part of another character, it gives the meaning of a house where people live.

穴

Diagram for 穴

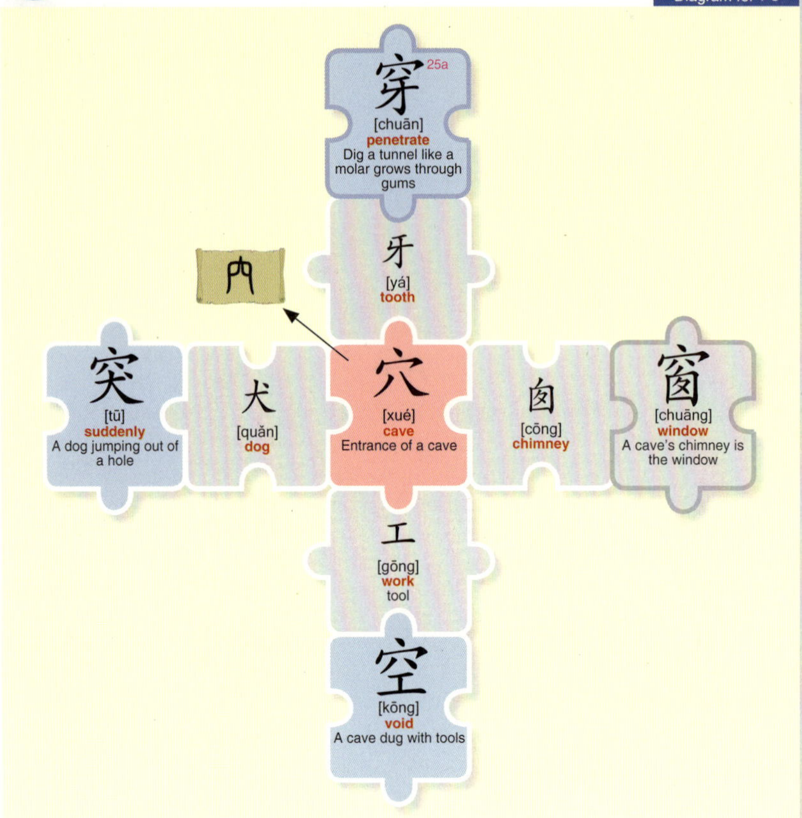

142

142

丶 丷 宀 穵 穴

穴 xué

cave

house 宀 [mián] + eight 八[229] [bā]

Back in the day, many people used caves as houses(宀). This character depicts the entrance to the cave(八).

* "八" is an open entrance.

142a 丶 丷 宀 宀 穴 穴 空 穸 穸 窗 窗 窗

窗 chuāng

window

cave 穴 [xué] + chimney 囱 [cōng]

Caves(穴) do not have windows, so people made chimneys(囱) instead.

* "囱" is a square hole(口[symbol]) through which fire(火[158]) and ash escaped. Think of a chimney (口) as a hole in the back(fall behind 夂[56][zhǐ]) for smoke to escape.

窗户 [chuānghu] window - 144

142b 丶 丷 宀 宀 穴 穴 空 空

空 kōng

void; air

cave 穴 [xué] + tool/work 工[200][gōng]

An empty cave(穴) dug out with tools(工). An empty space is only filled with air.

空调 [kōngtiáo] air-condition - 154b
空气 [kōngqì] air; atmosphere - 204
空间 [kōngjiān] space; room; blank - 145c

142

142c 丶 丷 宀 宀 穴 穴 空 穻 突 突

突 tū

suddenly

cave 穴 [xué] + dog 犬[172][quǎn]

A dog(犬) suddenly jumping out of a cave-like(穴) hole and surprising a person.

突然 [tūrán] sudden - 158e
突出 [tū/chū] protrude; project - 167a

广

Diagram for 广

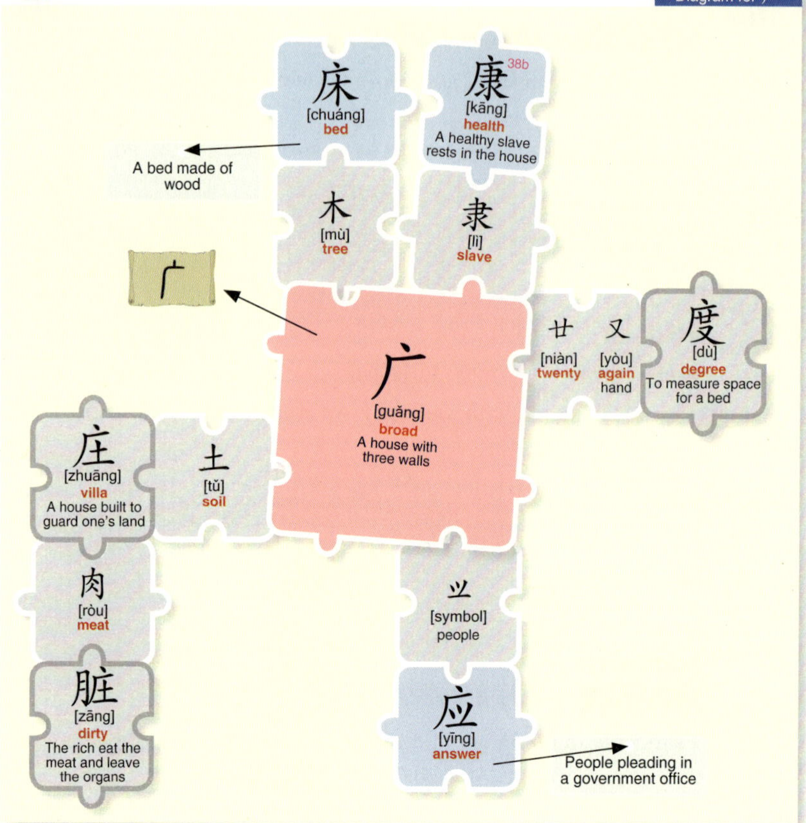

143

143

丶 亠 广

广 guǎng

broad

Offices in old palaces and buildings had one wall torn down where the king or officials would sit. This character describes a house with three walls, which would be wide.

广播[guǎngbō] broadcast - 183b
广场[guǎngchǎng] square; public square - 152a

143a

丶 亠 广 庄 庄 床 床

床 chuáng

bed

house/broad 广 [guǎng] + tree 木[210] [mù]

The Chinese slept in beds whereas the Koreans and Japanese slept on the floor. A wooden(木) structure within a house(广) would be the bed.

起床[qǐ/chuáng] get up; rise - 53d　　机床[jīchuáng] lathe; machine tool - 213a

143b

丶 亠 广 广 庐 庐 庐 庐 度

度 dù

degree

house/broad 广 [guǎng] + twenty 廿[50d] [niàn] + hand/again 又[34] [yòu]

To use a hand(又) to measure many sides(廿) of a large house(广) to judge how much space there is.

* "廿" is two "ten 十[231] [shí]" overlapping.

态度[tàidu] manner; bearing - 74d　　高度[gāodù] altitude; high degree - 3

143c

丶 亠 广 广 広 应 应

应 yīng

answer; should

house/broad 广 [guǎng] + people 㐅 [symbol]

In an office with three walls(广), the people(㐅) are pleading their case. When the people ask, the official must help, so this came to mean 'to answer, one should~.'

* The traditional character(應) shows that an official in his office(广) must treat the people(亻[70]) as gently as if they are small birds(隹[178]) with all his heart(心[28]). Three characters(亻, 隹, 心) have been reduced to dots(丶).

应该[yīnggāi] should; ought to; must - 4b　　答应[dāying] answer; reply; respond - 65b
应当[yīngdāng] should; naturally - 150e　　响应[xiǎngyìng] respond; answer - 150a

143

143d 丶 亠 广 庄 庄 庄

庄 zhuāng

villa; village

house/broad 广 [guǎng] + soil 土[152] [tǔ]

A villa is an extra house(广) the rich built to watch over their land(土) in the countryside. This character came to mean 'village' because the hired farmers lived around the villa.

村庄 [cūnzhuāng] village; hamlet - 40a

143e 丿 月 月 月 月` 月` 肚 肚 脏 脏

脏 zàng/zāng

viscera / dirty

meat 月[221] → 肉[192] [ròu] + villa 庄 [zhuāng]

The rich occupants of the villa(庄) slaughtered an animal to eat the meat(肉) and left the internal organs for the villagers to eat. This gave this character the meaning 'dirty.'

* "Moon 月 [yuè]" as part of another character usually means "肉."

143

心脏 [xīnzàng] heart - 28
衣服脏。The clothes are dirty. - 130 34b 143e

户

Diagram for 户

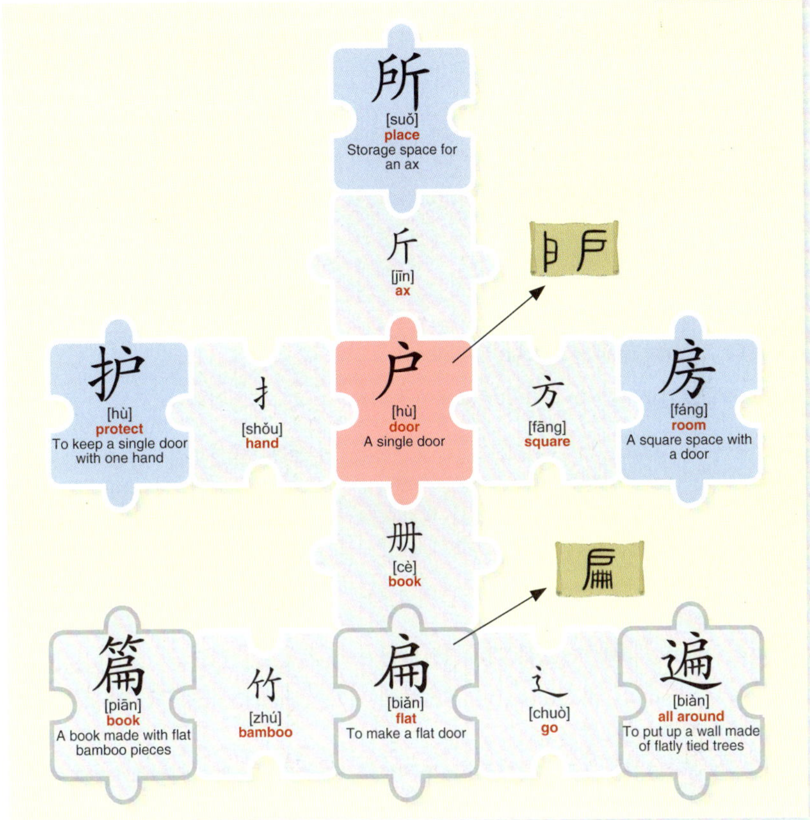

144

144

户 hù **door**

Small huts or storage rooms had a single door, smaller than the larger double doors(门).

窗户 [chuānghu] window - 142a

144a

丶 厂 戶 戶 戶' 所 所 所

所 suǒ

place

door 户 [hù] + ax 斤[118] [jīn]

A storage room is a place with a single door(户) where farming tools such as an ax(斤) are kept.

所以 [suǒyǐ] so; therefore - 63j 所有 [suǒyǒu] own; possess; have - 39c
研究所 [yánjiūsuǒ] research institute - 197d 230a

144b

丶 亠 ㇇ 户 户 户 房 房

房 fáng

room; house

door 户 [hù] + square 方[160] [fāng]

A square(方) area with a single door(户) is a room or a house.

房间 [fángjiān] room - 145c 厨房 [chúfáng] kitchen - 140b
房子 [fángzi] house; building - 95

144

144c

丶 亠 ㇇ 户 户 肩 扁 扁 扁

扁 biǎn

flat

door 户 [hù] + book 冊 → 册[217] [cè]

A door(户) usually made by tying branches together to make a flat slab, just like bamboo books(册).

* Bamboo books: Before paper was invented, the Chinese tied flat pieces of bamboo together.

144d

丶 亠 ㇇ 户 户 肩 扁 扁 扁 褊 遍 遍

遍 biàn

all around

flat 扁 [biǎn] + go 辶[61] [chuò]

Not only did the Chinese tie branches together(扁) to make doors, they did the same to make fences to go all around(辶) their houses. This character is also used to count the 'number of actions.'

这本书我看过五遍。I read this book five times. - 133a 210a 232d 113b 11a 40f 226a 144d

144e

篇 piān

book; piece

bamboo 竹[216][zhú] + flat 扁 [biǎn]

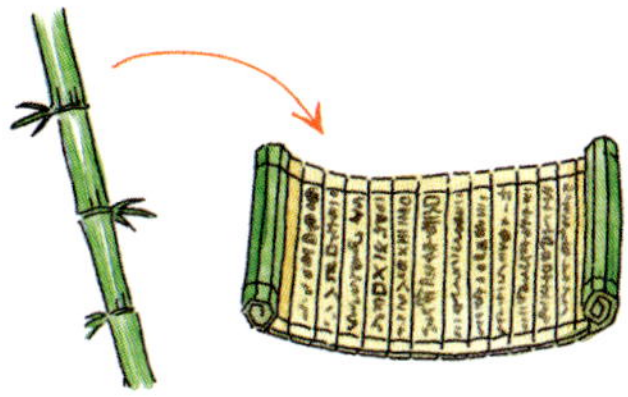

Before paper was invented, flat(扁) slabs of bamboo(竹) were tied together to make books. This character is also used to 'count the number of sentences.'

一篇文章 a piece of writing - 223 144e 133 21a

144f

护 hù

protect

hand 扌=手[31][shǒu] + door 户 [hù]

This character depicts an image of a petty poor person who is protecting his one-door(户) house with his hands(扌).

护照 [hùzhào] passport - 120c

门

Diagram for 门

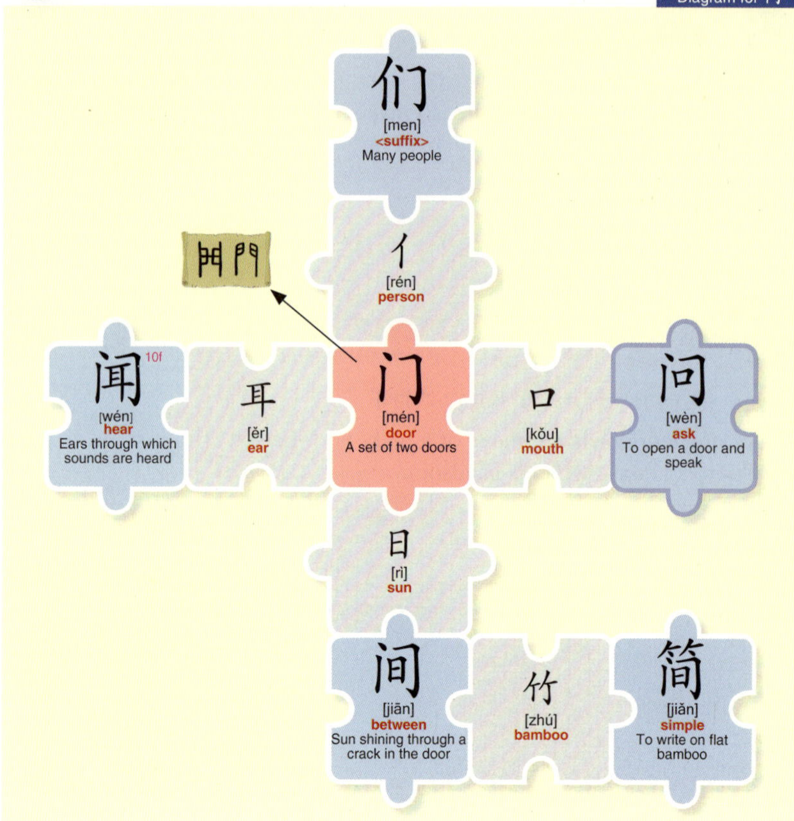

145

145 丶 丨 门

门 mén **door**

Palaces and large houses had doors that came in a set of two, unlike a "single door 户[144] [hù]."

门口 [ménkǒu] entrance; doorway - 16 部门 [bùmén] department; branch; section - 79f

145a 丿 亻 亻 仃 们

们 men

<suffix>

person 亻[70][rén] + door 门 [mén]

"门" is a door that is only complete as a set of two, so this character is a suffix showing plural usage of people(亻). It is always used after a pronoun or noun indication a person.

我们[wǒmen] we - 113b
人们[rénmen] people - 63
她们[tāmen] they (female) - 84c
咱们[zánmen] we - 26a
你们[nǐmen] you (plural) - 69a
他们[tāmen] they - 84b
它们[tāmen] they (thing) - 88f

145b 丶 丨 门 门 问 问

问 wèn

ask

door 门 [mén] + mouth 口[16][kǒu]

To open a door(门) and ask(口) if he is at the right house.

问题[wèntí] question; problem - 54d
请问[qǐngwèn] ask (formal) - 135c
访问[fǎngwèn] visit - 160a
问好[wèn/hǎo] send one's regards to - 96c

145

145c 丶 丨 门 门 问 间 间

间 jiān

between; room

door 门 [mén] + sun 日[218][rì]

This describes the sun(日) shining through a space in the door (门). It came to mean 'room,' the space between two walls and is also a quantifier used to count the number of rooms.

房间[fángjiān] room - 144b
洗手间[xǐshǒujiān] restroom; toilet - 71e 31
之间[zhījiān] between; among - 83d
一间教室。One classroom. - 223 145c 50c 112a
时间[shíjiān] time; hour - 42d
中间[zhōngjiān] center; between - 232a
空间[kōngjiān] space; room; blank - 142b

145d 丿 𠂉 ⺮ ⺮ 竹 竹 竹 竹 筒 筒 简 简 简

简 jiǎn

simple

bamboo 竹[216][zhú] + between 间 [jiān]

Before paper was invented, sentences were simple because the Chinese wrote on tiny spaces(间) of flat bamboo(竹).

简单[jiǎndān] simple - 231c

瓦

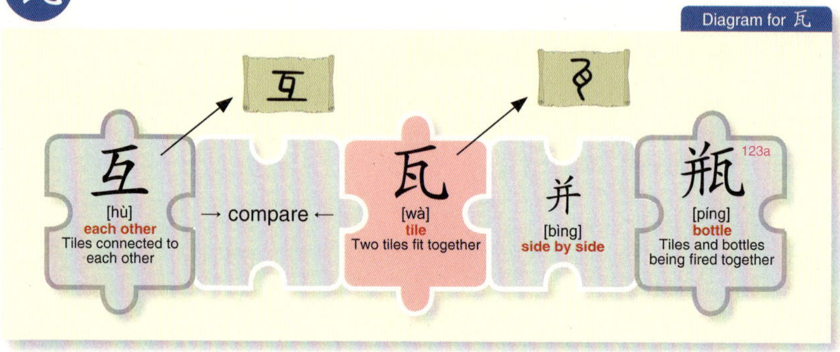

146

互 hù — each other

Roofing tiles are made in such a way that they fit together. This character describes two tiles fit together.

146 互相[hùxiāng] mutual; each other - 11c　　相互[xiānghù] mutual; each other - 11c

146a

瓦 wà — tile

When the shape of two tiles fitting together "互[hù]" came to mean 'each other,' the Chinese added a dot(丶) to stress the meaning 'tile.'

瓦解[wǎjiě] disintegrate; fall to pieces - 175c

阝

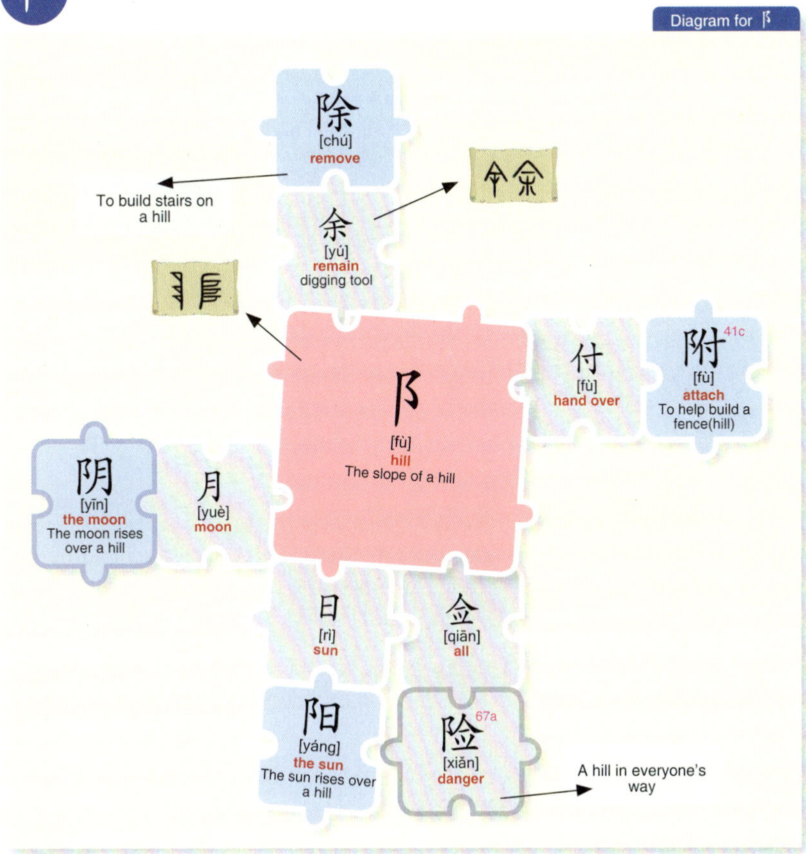

147

147

阝 fù **hill**

This character describes the slope of a hill. When used on the left of a character it means 'hill,' but when used on the right it means "town 邑[92d][yì]."

147a 阝 阝 阝 阝 阝 阝 阝 阝 除

除 chú

remove

hill 阝 [fù] + digging tool/remain 余 [yú]

To use tools(余) to carve stairs in a hill(阝) to make it easier to climb. This character came to mean 'to eliminate' because stairs in a steep hill eliminate much of the hard work.

* The ancient character shows that "余" is the shape of a tool with a sharp end used to dig up plants by the roots.

除了 [chúle] except - 168a
除了…以外 [chúle...yǐwài] except for; but for - 168a 63j 222a

147b 阝 阝 阝 阝 阳 阳

阳 yáng

the sun

hill 阝 [fù] + sun 日[218] [rì]

This describes the sun(日) rising above a hill(阝). This character, in particular, depicts the sun to symbolize "Yang," an opposing force of "Yin," which is the most important energies in Oriental philosophy. Therefore it means 'clear, bright, summer, man.'

太阳 [tàiyáng] the sun - 74c

147c 阝 阝 阝 阴 阴 阴

阴 yīn

the moon; cloudy

hill 阝 [fù] + moon 月[221] [yuè]

This describes the moon(月) rising above a hill(阝), and symbolizes "Yin" as explained in the above character "阳." This character means 'cloudy, dark, winter, woman.'

昨天是阴天。It was cloudy yesterday. - 234c 74b 54b 147c 74b

147

阝

Diagram for 阝

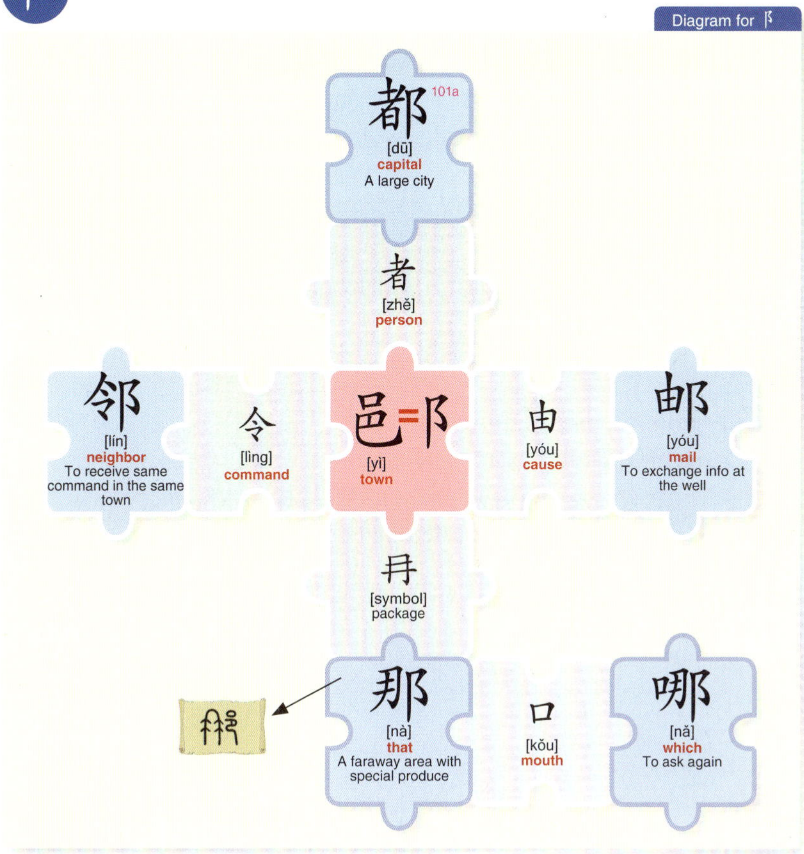

147

147d

邮 yóu

mail

well/cause 由[156] [yóu] + town 阝→邑[92d] [yì]

The village(邑) well(由) was the best place for the women to exchange information and gossip. That's how this character came to mean 'mail.'

* "由" is interpreted to mean 'well' because it's the shape of a deep water tank.

电子邮件[diànzǐyóujiàn] E-mail - 157a 95 175a
邮局[yóujú] post office - 91a
邮票[yóupiào] (postage) stamp - 126d

147e 丁 ヨ ヨ 尹 那 那

那 nà

that

package 尹→冄 [symbol] + town 阝→邑[92d][yì]

The left half of this character(冄) is a bundle of goods tied up and folded in half for easy transport. A faraway place(邑) with special produce(冄) was referred to as 'that' place.

那个[nàge] that one - 63b
那里[nàli] there; that place - 151
那么[nàme] that way; like that - 93a
那些[nàxiē] those - 88h
那样[nàyàng] of that kind; like that - 171a

147f 丨 冂 口 叮 叮 呁 呁 哪 哪

哪 nǎ/na

which; what / <modal particle>

mouth 口[16][kǒu] + that 那 [nà]

'Which, what' is how you start a question(口) when you don't know what 'that thing(那)' the other person referring to is.

147 It's also used as a modal particle at the end of a sentence to show surprise.

* When the syllable before this character ends with a 'n,' "哪[na]" is used instead of "啊[17f][a]" because of the pronunciation.

哪里[nǎlǐ] where - 151
哪个[nǎge] which - 63b
你小心哪！You be careful! - 69a 235 28 147f

147g ノ 人 人 今 令 令阝 邻

邻 lín

neighbor

command 令[86][lìng] + town 阝→邑[92d][yì]

The neighbors living in the same town(邑) receive the same command(令) from one single leader.

邻居[línjū] neighbor - 90g

厂

Diagram for 厂

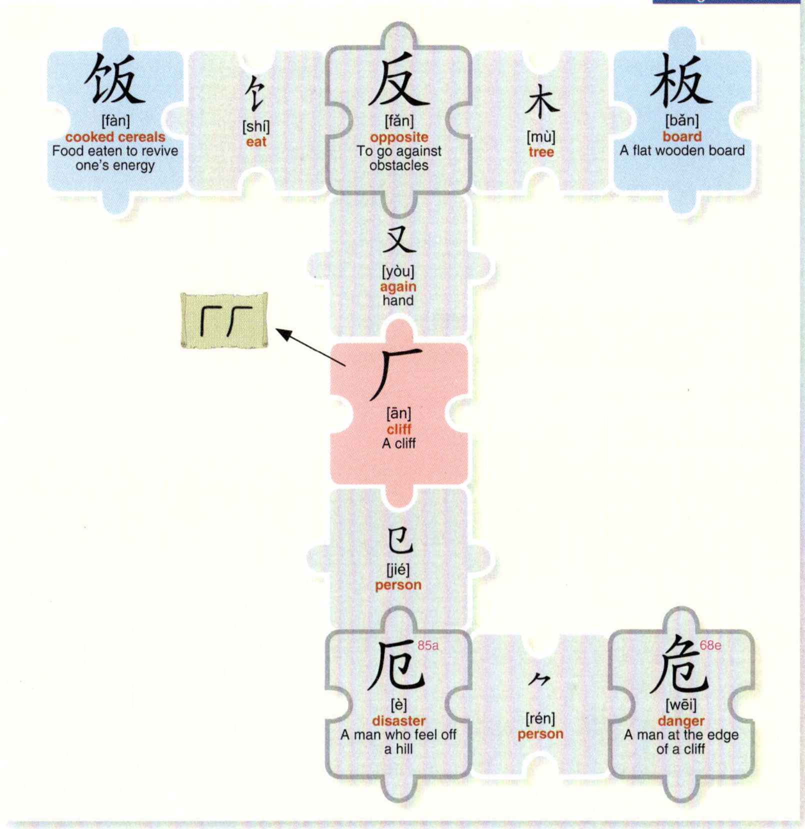

148

148

一 厂

厂 ān/chǎng

cliff / factory

A cliff with stones jutting out at the edge.

A factory is a place where material or complete products are stacked like cliffs(厂).

* When part of another character, it usually means 'cliff' and when used alone it usually means 'factory.'

工厂 [gōngchǎng] factory - 200

148a 一 厂 万 反

反 fǎn

opposite

cliff 厂 [ān] + hand/again 又[34] [yòu]

To put one's hand(又) against the cliff(厂) to overcome it and oppose the effect.

反对[fǎnduì] oppose - 40c
反映[fǎnyìng] reflect; mirror - 77b
违反[wéifǎn] violate - 190c

148b 丿 𠂊 饣 饣 饤 饭 饭

饭 fàn

cooked cereals; meal

eat 饣 = 食[137] [shí] + opposite 反 [fǎn]

One eats(饣) three meals a day to recover(反) one's energy.

* In Asia this character usually refers to cooked rice.

饭馆[fànguǎn] restaurant - 193c
米饭[mǐfàn] (cooked) rice - 138
饭店[fàndiàn] hotel; restaurant - 127b
晚饭[wǎnfàn] supper; dinner - 68b
午饭[wǔfàn] midday meal; lunch - 121b
早饭[zǎofàn] breakfast - 218e

148

148c 一 十 才 木 木 杉 杤 板

板 bǎn

board

tree 木[210] [mù] + opposite 反 [fǎn]

If you take a piece of wood(木) and flatten it on both sides, then you have a board that can be used even when flipped over(反).

黑板[hēibǎn] chalkboard; blackboard - 158d

冂

Diagram for 冂

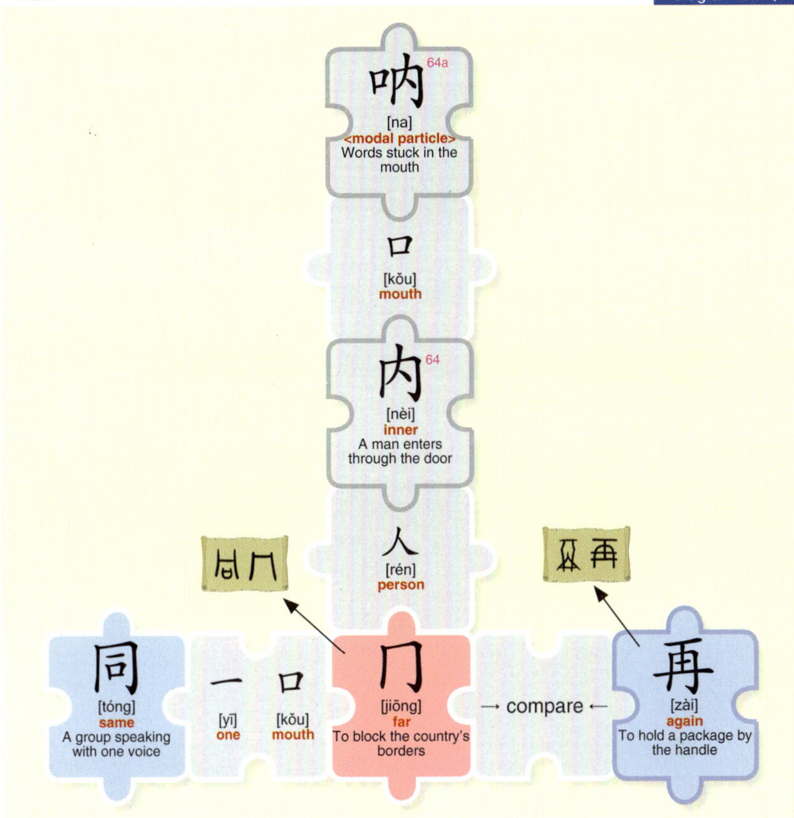

149

149

丨 冂

冂 jiōng

far

When a border crossing is closed, it becomes one boundary that is just too far away and impossible to cross.

* When used as part of another character, it's usually for the shape, not the meaning.
* This is a different character from "door 门[145] [mén]."

149a 一 丁 冂 再 再 再

再 zài

again

handle 丅 [symbol] + package 冉 [symbol]

This character means 'again' because it is the shape of a package(冉) being held up by the handle(丅).

再见[zàijiàn] good-bye; see you again - 13

149b 丨 冂 冂 同 同 同

同 tóng

same

boundary/far 冂 [jiōng] + one 一 223 [yī] + mouth 口 16 [fǎn]

To speak in one(一) voice(口) means it is the same group(冂).

* "冂" is a boundary, so think of this as a group within the same boundaries.

同学[tóng/xué] be in the same school - 95a
同意[tóngyì] agree - 21b
不同[bùtóng] not alike; different - 223a
同志[tóngzhì] comrade - 104c
同事[[tóng/shì] colleague; work together - 36d
相同[xiāngtóng] identical; same - 11c
同时[tóngshí] at the same time - 42d

149

向

Diagram for 尚

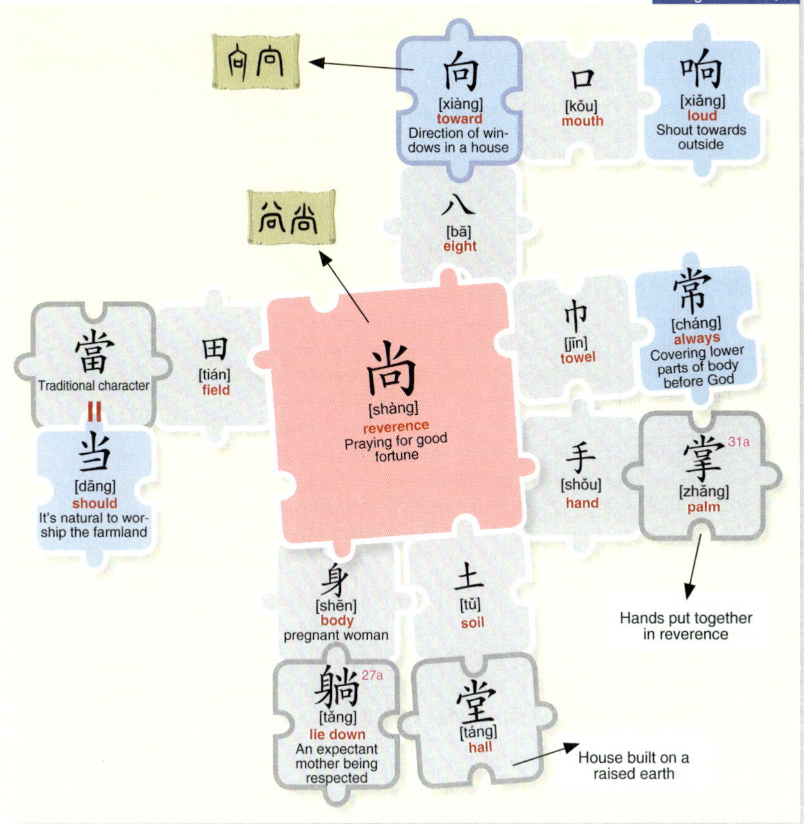

150

150

丿 丨 门 向 向 向

向 xiàng

toward; face

house 宀[141] [mián] + windows 口 [symbol]

Signifies looking/facing towards the windows(口) inside a house(宀).

* "mouth 口[16] [kǒu]" symbolizes a 'window' in this case.

方向 [fāngxiàng] direction - 160

150

150a

丨 ㄇ 口 口' 叮 咛 咛 响 响

响 xiǎng

loud

mouth 口[16] [kǒu] + towards 向 [xiàng]

One yells(口) loudly towards the window(向) as a sense of someone is felt outside.

* "口" plays a role of yelling in this case.

影响[yǐngxiǎng] influence; affect - 2d　　响应[xiǎngyìng] respond; answer - 143c

150b

丨 ⺌ ⺌ 忄 尚 尚 尚 尚

尚 shàng

reverence

eight ソ→八[229] [bā] + towards 向 [xiàng]

Symbolizes an act of praying for blessings or fortunes from heaven(八) to(向) God, which came to mean reverence.

* "八" symbolizes 'fortunes or blessings descending from heaven.'

高尚[gāoshàng] noble; lofty - 3

150c

丨 ⺌ ⺌ ⺌ 𫩏 𫩏 尚 尚 常 常 常

常 cháng

always

reverence 尚 [shàng] + towel 巾[131] [jīn]

Signifies covering of lower body(巾) when one goes to worship(尚), which is always required to show the respect.

* Reproductive organs were not to be shown in public when approaching God as it symbolized creation.

非常[fēicháng] extraordinary; unusual - 181　　经常[jīngcháng] daily; constantly - 132e
常常[chángcháng] frequently; often - 13

150d

丨 ⺌ ⺌ ⺌ 𫩏 𫩏 尚 尚 堂 堂 堂

堂 táng

hall

reverence 尚 [shàng] + soil 土[152] [tǔ]

Meaning of hall is derived from the ancient practices of building a house or building on top of highly raised(尚) earth(土) to prevent water damage from rain.

* "尚" also contains meaning of 'to raise.'

食堂[shítáng] dining hall; mess hall; cafeteria - 137
礼堂[lǐtáng] assembly hall; auditorium - 126g

150e 丨 ⺌ ⺌ 当 当 当

当 dāng

should; work as; serve as

reverence ⺌→尚 [shàng] + field ヨ→田[154] [tián]

Fields(田) in agriculture that produce crops should be worshipped/revered (尚). It has the meaning 'working for/serving as.' Sometimes it is used as a preposition to signify and emphasize the importance of time and location of any particular event.

* Traditional character(當) combines "田" and "尚," which is simplified into the current version.

当然[dāngrán] natural; naturally - 158e
应当[yīngdāng] should - 143c
当公共汽车司机 work as a bus driver - 150e 93b 43c 204a 124 18e 213a
当时 at that time - 150e 42d
当场 on the spot - 150e 152a

150

里

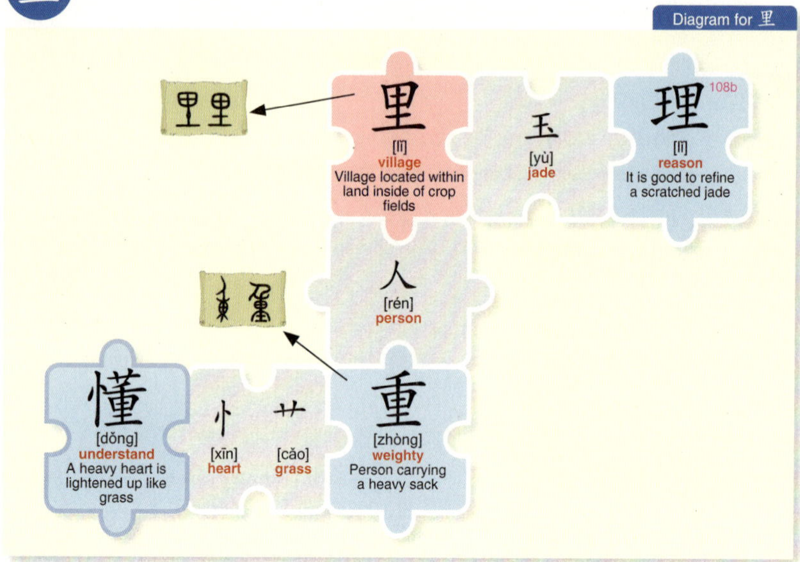

151

151 丨 冂 日 曰 甲 甲 里

里 lǐ village; unit of length / in; inside

A village is located in land(土[152]) close to crop fields(田[154]). The character is also used as a unit of distance in terms of measuring the distance from the village to the field.

公里[gōnglǐ] kilometre (km) - 93b

Meaning of 'inside' is derived from the fact that the village is located inside the farmland.

* The traditional character(裏) meaning inside uses "里" as a phonetic symbol to signify " inside of clothing(衣)."

里边[lǐbian] inside - 61a
哪里[nǎlǐ] where - 147f
那里[nàli] there; that place - 147e
这里[zhèlǐ] here - 133a

151a

丿 二 千 㐄 㐄 旨 旨 重 重

重 zhòng

weighty

person 千→人[63][rén] + sack/east 里→東→东[211][dōng]

Signifies a person(人) carrying a heavy sack(东) on his back.

* "东" signifies a sack with both ends tied up; the ancient character (the inscriptions on bones and tortoise carapaces) clearly shows sack(东) together with man(人).

重要[zhòngyào] important; significant - 170b
重大[zhòngdà] great; weighty - 74
重视[zhòngshì] attach importance to - 13c

151b

丶 丶 忄 忄 忄 忄 忄 忄 忄 忄 懂 懂 懂 懂 懂

懂 dǒng

understand

heart 忄=心[28][xīn] + grass 艹[207][cǎo] + weighty 重 [zhòng]

When someone understands my heavy(重) heart(忄), it becomes light like grass(艹).

* "supervise 董 [dǒng]" is used as a pronunciation guide to signify a good management of heavy(重) load of goods, so that it looks light like grass(艹).

懂得[dǒngde] understand - 40b

151

土

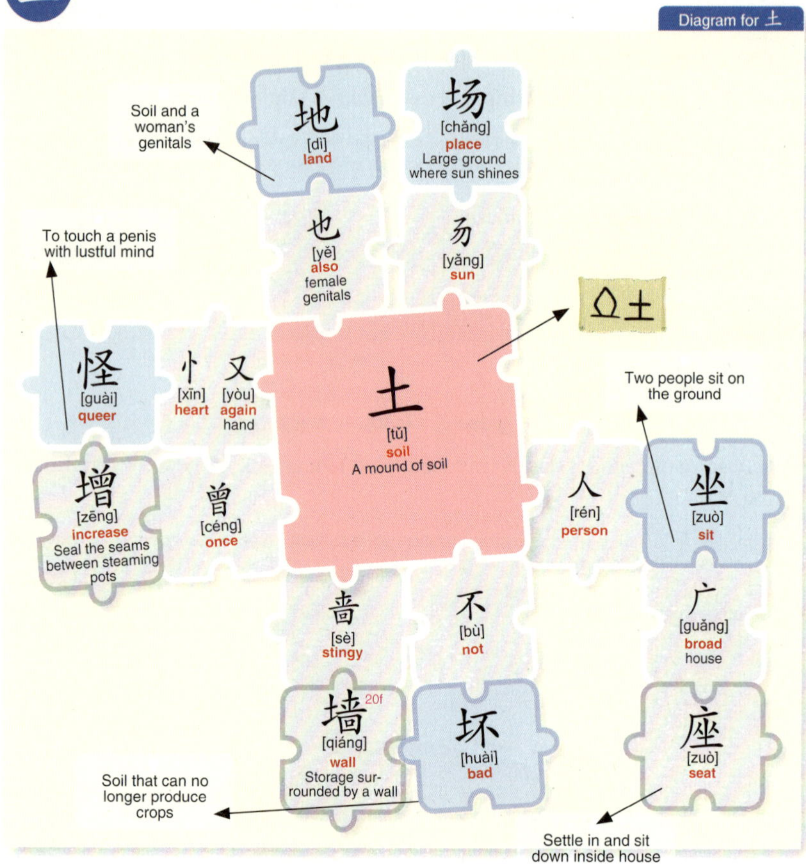

152

152 一 十 土

土
tǔ

soil

Signifies a mound of earth or soil. Also came from the model of male penis made from earth.

152a 一 十 土 场

场
chǎng

place

soil 土 [tǔ] + sun 昜=昜[219] [yáng]

A large ground(土) with sunlight shining upon it(昜) provides a suitable place for people to gather and hold events. Since many events took place in such places, it was also used as a unit to count the number of various events such as literary activity, entertainments, and sports.

机场[jīchǎng] airport - 213a
操场[cāochǎng] playground - 180a
广场[guǎngchǎng] square; public square - 143
市场[shìchǎng] market; market place - 131a
一场球赛[yī chǎng qiú sài] a ball game - 223 152a 198b 206d

152b

丿 人 𠆢 从 从 丛 坐

坐 zuò

sit

person 人[63] [rén] + soil 土 [tǔ]

Signifies two people(人) sitting down on ground(土) to have a chat.

坐班[zuò/bān] work in one's office during office time - 119f

152c

丶 亠 广 广 庐 库 庳 庳 座 座

座 zuò

seat

house/broad 广[143] [guǎng] + sit 坐 [zuò]

Signifies a person who is comfortably seated(坐) inside a house(广). Used also as a unit to count items that are relatively large and firmly seated.

* "broad 广" symbolizes a large house with an open wall on side.

讲座[jiǎngzuò] a course of lectures - 228a
座位[zuòwèi] seat; place - 79c
一座桥[yī zuò qiáo] a bridge - 223 152c 78c

152d

一 十 土 圹 圹 坏 坏

坏 huài

bad

soil 土 [tǔ] + not 不[223a] [bù]

Soil(土) produces plants which serve as most essential elements for easily available food chain in the ecological world. When the soil as such has turned bad, it can no longer(不) produce such plants or crops.

坏处[huàichu] harm; disadvantage - 56b
破坏[pòhuài] destroy; ruin - 189a

152

152e 一 十 土 扌 扌' 扩 圹 圹 坳 坳 坳 埠 增 增 增

增 zēng

increase

soil 土 [tǔ] + stacked dual pot steamer/once 曾[229b] [céng]

Signifies act of sealing the seams using clay(土) between two steaming pots(曾) to increase its heat efficiency.

* "曾" symbolizes a steamer, with 'water-boiling pot (日)' on bottom, 'perforated pot to receive steam (罒)' on top, and finally steams exiting(丷) from the top.

增加[zēngjiā] increase; raise - 159g
增长[zēngzhǎng] increase; rise; grow - 102

152f 丶 丷 忄 忆 怄 怪 怪 怪

怪 guài

queer

heart 忄=心[28] [xīn] + hand/again 又[34] [yòu] + male penis/soil 土 [tǔ]

152 Out of an image of having a lustful mind(忄) and touching a penis(土) with one's hands(又), the meaning of 'queer' is derived.

奇怪[qíguài] strange; odd - 18

圭

Diagram for 圭

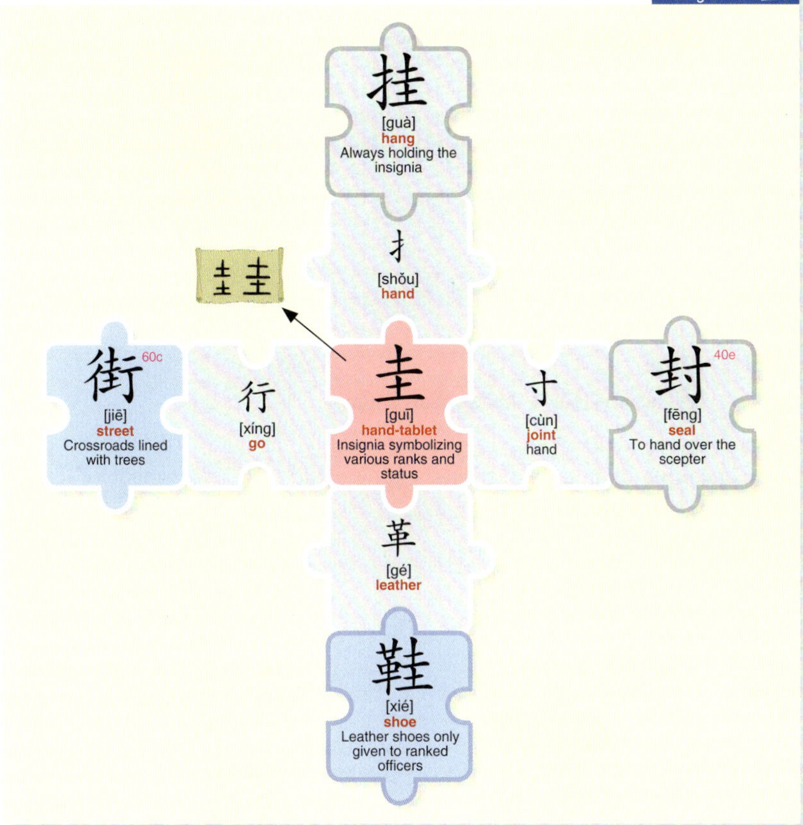

153

153

一 十 土 圭 圭 圭

圭
guī

hand-tablet

Symbolizes a small traditional insignia which is rectangular in shape. It is made from jade or wood (therefore a small tablet) that was used as an appointment certificate and also as marks that distinguished various ranks of government officers.

* Although this has no relation to "soil 土[152][tǔ]," it's covered here due to its similar shape and the fact that it takes "土" as its radical.

153a 一 丨 扌 扌一 扌十 扌土 扌土 挂 挂

挂 guà

hang

hand 扌=手[31][shǒu] + hand-tablet 圭 [guī]

King's servants and officers always held(扌) onto the insignia tablets(圭) in handling national affairs – almost as if the insignia(圭) is hanging from the hands(扌).

挂号[guà/hào] register - 16c

153b 一 十 廿 廿 廿 芇 芇 苩 革 革一 革十 革土 鞋 鞋 鞋

鞋 xié

shoe

leather 革[189b][gé] + hand-tablet 圭 [guī]

Officers and servants who are given the insignia tablet(圭) (therefore a prestigious position in the office) from the king could wear shoes made of leather (革).

* In the ancient China, leather shoes were only allowed to be worn by nobles whereas commoners could only afford to wear them during their wedding ceremony.

153

高跟鞋。high-heeled shoes; high heels - 3 14c 153b

田

Diagram for 田

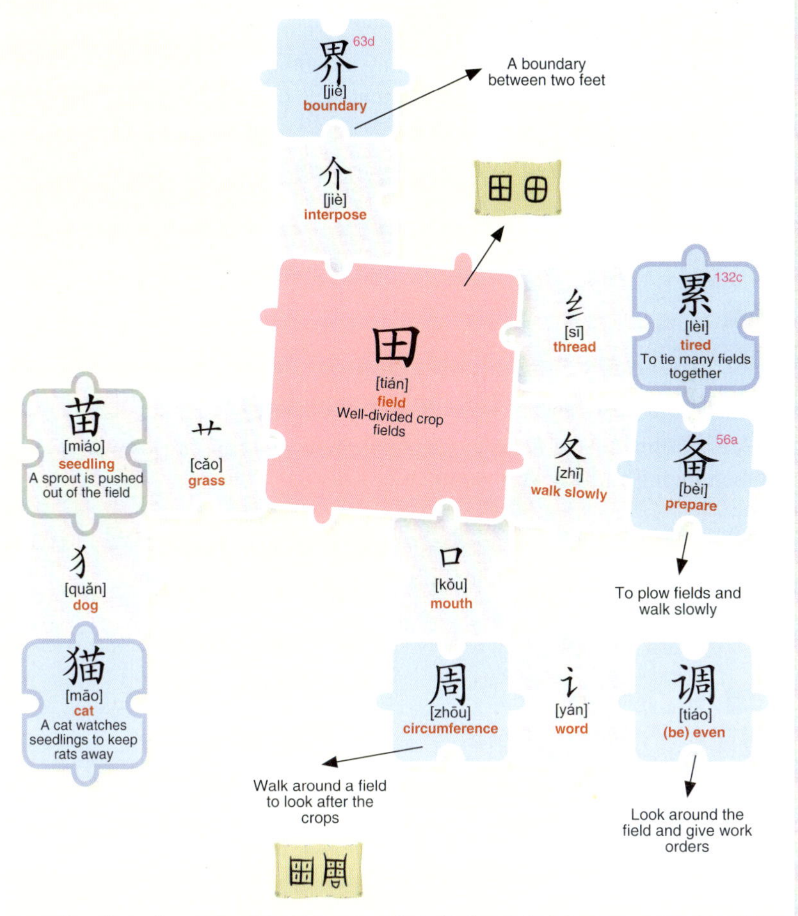

154

154

丨 冂 曰 田 田

田 tián **field**

Signifies crop fields that are clearly divided by drains and mounds (banks).

农田 [nóngtián] farmland; cropland - 130c

154

154a 丿 冂 月 円 用 用 周 周

周 zhōu

circumference; week; cycle

field 用→田 [tián] + mouth 口[16] [kǒu]

Signifies act of regularly circling or going around the circumference (bounds) of the field(田) to take care of crops that will become food for the mouth (口).

* Ancient bone-letters show dots(丶) inside a field(田), signifying regularly- maintained -fields that help crops(丶) to grow well.

周末[zhōumò] weekend - 210b   周围[zhōuwéi] surroundings - 190b

154b 丶 讠 讠 订 订 订 调 调 调 调

调 tiáo/diào

(be) even / investigate; tone

word 讠=言[22] [yán] + circumference 周 [zhōu]

Signifies circling(周) of fields to see or investigate if crops are growing evenly, and then giving various work orders by words(讠).

空调[kōngtiáo] air-condition - 142b

Also came to mean tone whether or not the tone of voice is even.

声调[shēngdiào] tone - 104d   调查[diàochá] investigate - 224c

154c 一 艹 艹 艹 节 苗 苗 苗

苗 miáo

seedling; sprout

grass 艹[207] [cǎo] + field 田 [tián]

This character has the image of a sprout(艹) which is coming up out of the field(田) in the spring.

154d 丿 犭 犭 犭 犭 犭 犭 猫 猫 猫 猫

猫 māo

cat

dog 犭[173] [quǎn] + seedling 苗 [miáo]

This character has the image of a cat(犭) that keeps watching the seedlings(苗) to be sown in the spring time in order to keep the rats away from a granary.

* "犭" is used as a stroke meaning an animal which is as big as a dog.
* "苗[miáo]" is used as a phonetic element to express 'meowing' of a cat.

熊猫[xióngmāo] panda; bearcat - 89c

由

Diagram for 甶

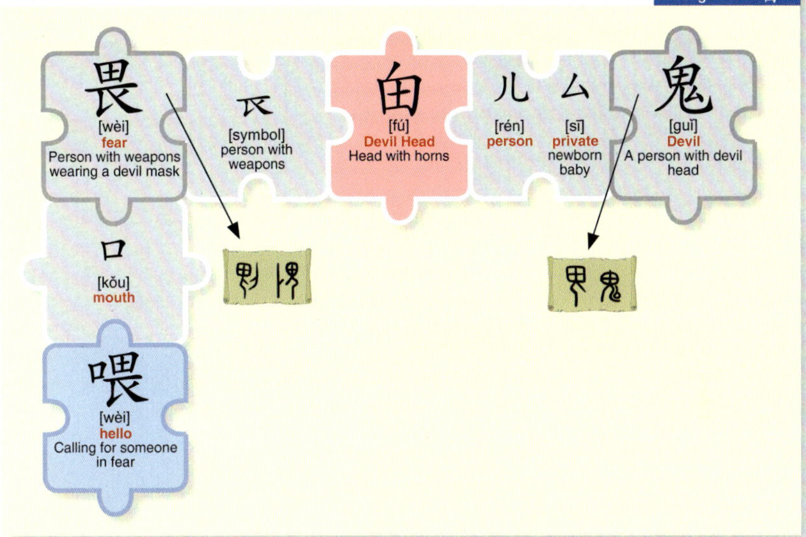

155

155

甶 fú

Devil Head

Signifies a head of the devil that has horns(丶) on top of its head(田).

* Has no relation to "field 田[154][tián]." It has been, however, covered here due to similar shape while it uses "田" as its radical.

155a

鬼 guǐ

Devil

devil head 甶 [fú] + person 儿[71][rén] + newborn baby/private 厶[93][sī]

A person(儿) with a devil's head(甶), together with a newborn baby(厶) sacrificed as offering, combined to mean the devil.

* The ancient character shows a person(儿) wearing a devil mask(甶).

搞鬼[gǎo/guǐ] play tricks - 3a

155b

丶 冂 日 田 田 甼 畏 畏 畏

畏 wèi

fear

devil head 田→甶 [fú] + person with weapons 𧘇 [symbol]

Symbolizes a person wearing a devil's mask(甶) with weapons(𧘇). Imagine how scary and fearful that would be at night.

* Ancient character shows a person(儿[71]) with a devil mask(甶) holding weapons(刀[119]) on hand – a fearful stance.

155c

丨 口 口 口' 口冂 口日 口田 口田 口甼 口畏 口畏 喂

喂 wèi

hello; hey

mouth 口[16] [kǒu] + fear 畏 [wèi]

Signifies calling(口) out to someone – Hello? Anyone? – in fear(畏) when walking about at night and feeling something eerie. Now it is used to get attention of someone or when answering the phone.

喂，你去哪儿？Hey, where are you going? - 155c 69a 94 147f 71
喂，请问你是谁呀？Hello, who's speaking, please? - 155c 135c 145b 69a 54b 178b 25b

155

由

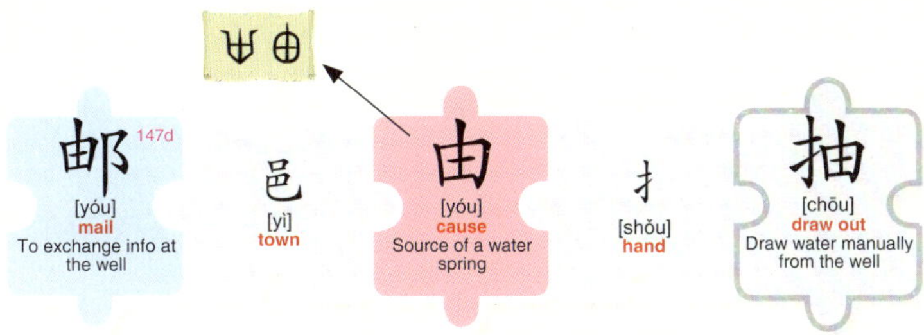

156 丨 冂 冃 由 由

由 yóu

cause

Symbolizes a deep well with water springs – a source or cause of water for people.

* Has no relation to "field 田[154] [tián]," but is covered here due to similar shape and it uses "田" as its radical.

156

自由 [zìyóu] freedom - 26

156a 一 十 扌 扌 扣 扣 抽 抽

抽 chōu

draw out

hand 扌=手[31] [shǒu] + underground water well/cause 由 [yóu]

Signifies the act of drawing water by hand(扌) from an water well(由).

抽象 [chōuxiàng] abstract - 174b

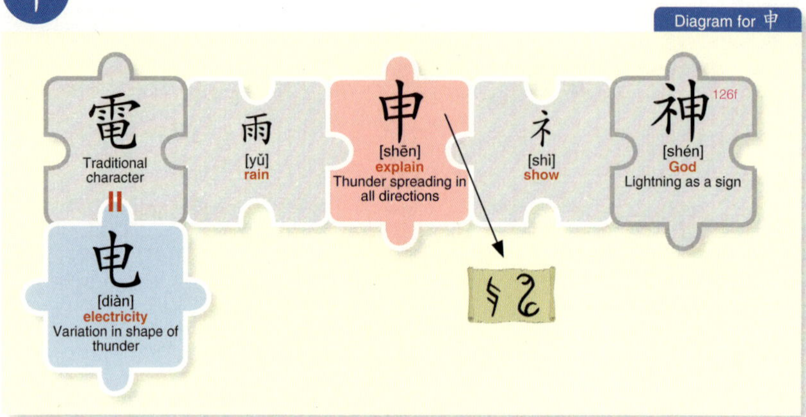

157

申 shēn

explain

157 Symbolizes thunder that spreads out to all directions. Came to mean explain as in explaining your opinion or will to all directions.

* Has no relation to "field 田[154] [tián]" but is covered here due to similar shape and it uses "田" as its radical.

157a

电 diàn

electricity

As the character "申[shēn]" came to mean 'explain,' the character is also given a slight twist to restore meaning of thunder. Used now as the term for electricity as thunder is electrical discharge in the atmosphere.

* Traditional character(電) signifies thunder(电) mostly occurring during rain(雨[205]).

打电话[dǎdiànhuà] make a (phone) call - 31c 24b
电视[diànshì] television; TV - 13c
电梯[diàntī] elevator; lift - 109c
电车[diànchē] streetcar; trolley (car) - 124
电话[diànhuà] telephone - 24b
电脑[diànnǎo] computer - 192c
电影[diànyǐng] film; movie - 2d
电子邮件[diànzǐyóujiàn] E-mail - 95 147d 175a
电灯[diàndēng] electric light (lamp) - 158a

火

Diagram for 火

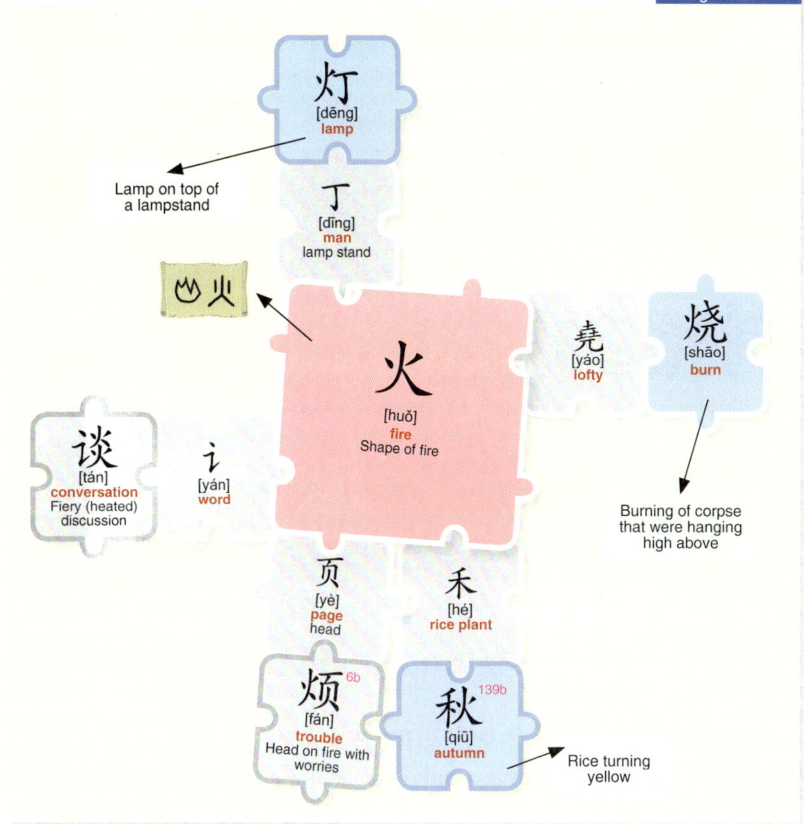

158

丶 丷 火 火

火 huǒ **fire**

A simple representation of fire as a shape.

* Fire is being covered in this section as in the old days crop fields were created by burning down mountains and fields.

火车站[huǒchēzhàn] train station - 124 127c   火车[huǒchē] train - 124

158a

灯 dēng

lamp

fire 火 [huǒ] + lamp stand/man 丁[225] [dīng]

Signifies a lamp fire(火) burning on top of a lampstand(丁).

* Traditional character(燈) shows fire(火) raised up high(登[59a]) – thus "man 丁 [dīng]" can be said to represent a lampstand.

电灯[diàndēng] electric light (lamp) - 157a

158b

烧 shāo

burn

fire 火 [huǒ] + lofty 尧 [yáo]

Signifies burning(火) of enemy's corpse which is hung high(尧) to create fear.

* "lofty 尧 [Yáo]" signifies a scene that an enemy is killed by spear(戈[113]) and its corpse is hanged high(towering 兀[170] [wù]) for the purpose of public display.

发烧[fā/shāo] have a fever; have a temperature - 34f

158

158c

谈 tán

conversation

word 讠=言[22] [yán] + flame/scorching 炎 [yán]

A heated discussion or conversation is initiated as words(讠) come together in fiery or scorching fashion(炎).

* "炎" stacked two fires(火) on top of each other to signify intense burning.

会谈[huìtán] talks - 66c

谈话[tán/huà] conversation; talk - 24b

火

Diagram for 灬

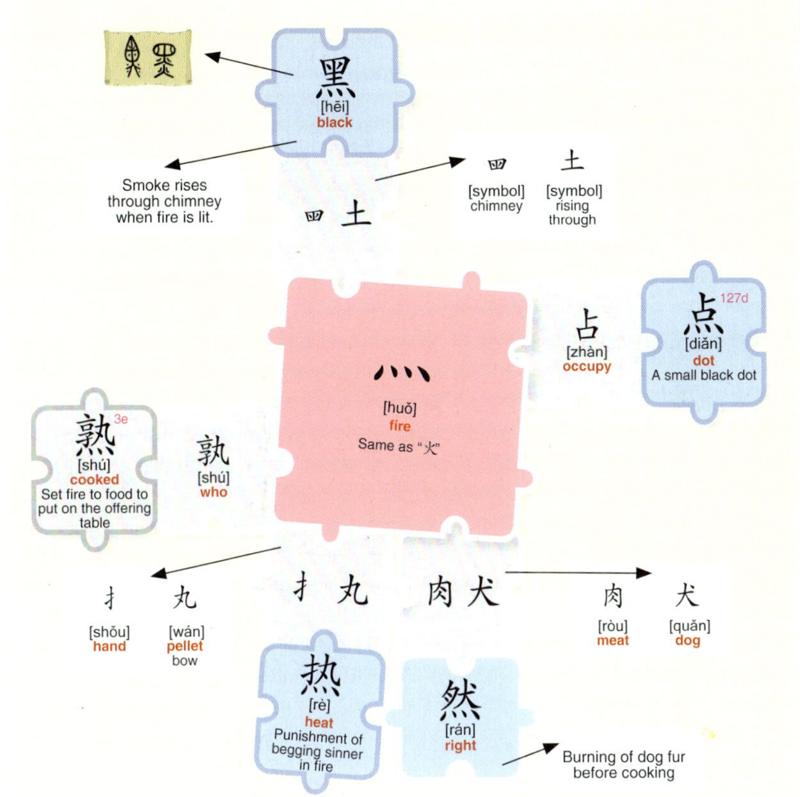

158

158

灬
huǒ

fire

A variation of character fire "火[huǒ]," used only in combination with other characters.

158d

丨 ㄇ ㄇ ㄇ 四 四 甲 里 里 里 黑 黑

黑
hēi

black

chimney 罒 [symbol] + rising through 土 [symbol] + fire 灬 = 火 [huǒ]

Fire(灬) causes black smoke to rise into chimney(罒) and exit(土), turning everything near it into charcoal black.

* The bronze inscription, one of the ancient Chinese scripts depicts fire(灬) causing chimney to turn black.

黑板[hēibǎn] chalkboard; blackboard - 148c

158e

丿 ク タ 夕 夕 夕 夕 夕 夕 然 然 然

然
rán

right; so

meat 月[221] → 肉[192] [ròu] + dog 犬[172] [quǎn] + fire 灬 = 火 [huǒ]

The fur is removed by burning(灬) prior to cooking dog(犬) meat(肉). It was then rightly so that such cooked dog meat would appear in ceremonial tables and offerings.

* Dog meat was an exquisite delicacy that always appeared in large ceremonies and offerings in the old dynasties of China.

* When "moon 月 [yuè]" combines with other characters, it becomes to mean "肉."

158

当然[dāngrán] natural; naturally - 150e
然后[ránhòu] then; after that; afterwards - 18d
虽然[suīrán] though; although - 184a
突然[tūrán] sudden - 142c
忽然[hūrán] suddenly - 49a

158f

一 十 扌 扌 执 执 执 执 热 热

热
rè

heat

hand 扌 = 手[31] [shǒu] + bow/pellet 丸[230c] [wán] + fire 灬 = 火 [huǒ]

Signifies the act of punishing a sinner by using the high heat of fire(灬) although a sinner is begging(丸) for mercy with two hands(扌).

* "丸" symbolizes a person bent down completely to bow.

热情[rèqíng] passion; ardor; fervor - 135d
热爱[rè'ài] ardently love - 34e
热水瓶[rèshuǐpíng] thermos; vacuum bottle - 201 123a

力

Diagram for 力

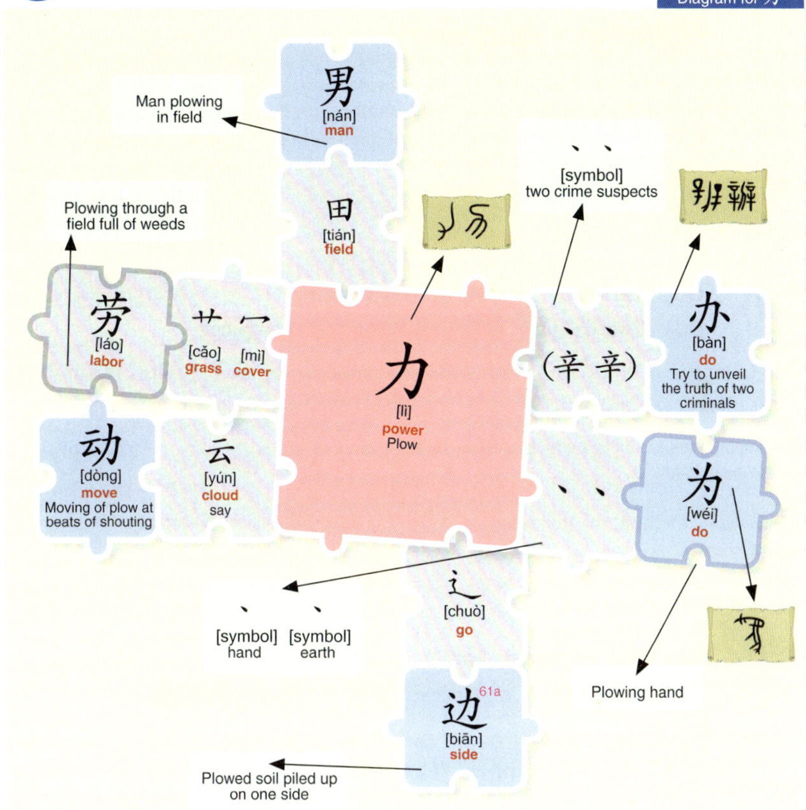

159

フ 力

力
lì

power

Symbolizes plow, a critical tool in agriculture. Power is needed to pull the plow in fields.

努力 [nǔ/lì] try hard; strive - 96f
风力 [fēnglì] wind power - 213c
能力 [nénglì] ability; capacity; capability - 89b

159

159a 丨 冂 冃 冊 田 男 男

男 nán

man

field 田[154] [tián] + plow/power 力 [lì]

Signifies a man working in the field(田) using plows(力) at the time of agrarian society.

男人[nánrén] man - 63

159b フ 力 力 办

办 bàn

do; manage

plow/power 力 [lì] + two crime suspects 丶丶 [symbol]

The meaning of to do or to manage is driven as if a plow(力) digs through the heart of two crime suspects(丶 丶) to unveil their true intentions.

* Traditional character(辦) shows a plow(力) between two neck-cuffs(pain 辛[103][xīn]) that signify criminal suspects.

办法[bànfǎ] method; means; way - 94b　　办公室[bàngōngshì] office - 93b 112a

159c 丶 丿 为 为

为 wéi/wèi

do; act / support; for

hand 丶 [symbol] + plow/power 力 [lì] + earth 丶 [symbol]

Signifies the act of plowing(力), as the earth(丶) is being plowed by the hand (丶) that's holding onto the plow(力).

* Ancient character shows training of elephants(象) by hand(爫) in order to do hard works.

认为[rènwéi] think; consider - 63a　　以为[yǐwéi] think; believe; consider - 63j

Plow(力) plays an important role of plowing earth(丶). But the main function of plow is to support humans. That is what is expressed by hand(丶) to hold with.

为什么[wèishénme] why - 231a 93a　　因为[yīnwèi] because - 74e
为了[wèile] for - 168a

159d

一 二 云 云 动 动

动 dòng

move

say/cloud 云[227] [yún] + plow/power 力 [lì]

Signifies a cow moving with plow(力) at the shouting(云) command of a man.

* Traditional character(動) shows moving of a plow(力) to distribute seeds inside a heavy(重[151a]) sack.

运动[yùndòng] motion; movement - 227a
活动[huódòng] activity - 24c
推动[tuīdòng] push forward - 31f
动物[dòngwù] animal - 49b
劳动[láodòng] labor - 159e

159e

一 十 艹 艹 艹 劳 劳

劳 láo

labor

grass 艹[207] [cǎo] + cover 冖[169] [mì] + plow/power 力 [lì]

Meaning of labor is derived from the act of plowing(力) in order to renew a field covered(冖) in weeds(艹).

* Traditional character(勞) shows a servant plowing(力) late through the night, laminated by open fire(火[158]).

劳动[láodòng] labor - 159d
劳驾[láojià] excuse me - 159h

力

159

159f ノ ク 夂 夅 务

务 wù

strive; affair

walk slowly 夂[56][zhǐ] + plow/power 力 [lì]

One needs to apply force – or to strive – in order to slowly move(夂) the plow (力) ahead. Meaning of work or affair is derived from the fact that farmers put such effort into their daily work.

* Traditional character(務) shows soldiers holding onto spears(矛[116]), and walking slowly ahead (夂) with all their power(力).

服务员 [fúwùyuán] service staff - 34b 186h
服务 [fúwù] serve - 34b
业务 [yèwù] business - 223c

159g ㇆ 力 ⺈ 加 加

加 jiā

add

plow/power 力 [lì] + mouth 口[16][kǒu]

Farmers using all their physical power into plowing(力) of the field, shouting or singing(口) from their mouth(口) add more power(力) to each stroke or push they need to give.

参加[cānjiā] take part in; participate in - 8c 增加[zēngjiā] increase; raise - 152e
更加[gèngjiā] still more - 35c

159h ㇆ 力 ⺈ 加 加 驾 驾 驾

驾 jià

ride

add 加 [jiā] + horse 马[176][mǎ]

A horse(马) is ready to be ridden when its saddles are properly put on(加) – now also became meaning of to drive, to fly or to sail.

劳驾[láojià] excuse me - 159e

159i 丨 口 口 叻 叻 叻 咖 咖

咖 kā

<transliterator>

mouth 口[16][kǒu] + add 加 [jiā]

Used to politely reject something by words(口) when someone gives you something(加) – now used on transliteration of foreign words such as Coffee (咖啡).

咖啡[kāfēi] coffee - 181b

159j 一 厂 历 历

历 lì

experience

barn/factory 厂[148][chǎng] + plow/power 力 [lì]

A harvest year is complete when the plow(力) is returned to the shed(厂) – and when the year is complete, you gain another share of experience from it.

* Traditional character(歷) shows stockpiling of harvested crops(禾[139]) in the shed(厂), and looking back on the steps(止[53]) one took over the past year.
* "厂" signifies shed or barn as if the crops are piled up high.

历史[lìshǐ] history - 35 经历[jīnglì] experience - 132e

159

方

Diagram for 方

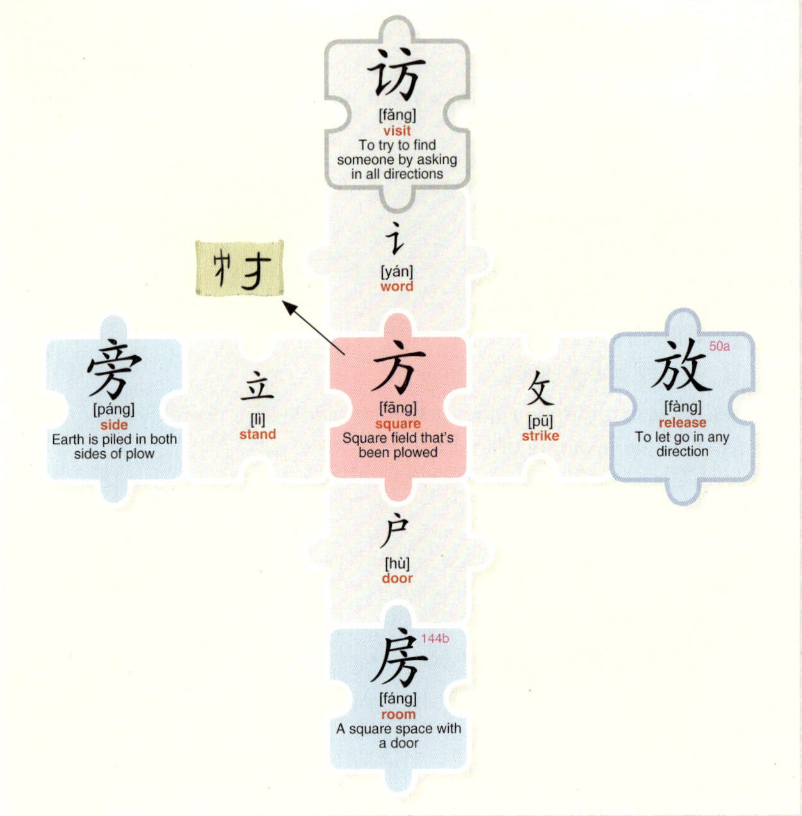

160

丶 亠 亢 方

160

方 fāng

square; direction

A variation on the shape of a plow(方) – a field is square shape after proper plowing. Also signifies direction as square has points facing to all four directions.

北方[běifāng] north; northern region - 88c	地方[dìfang] area; place - 84a
方便[fāngbiàn] convenient - 35d	方法[fāngfǎ] method; means; way - 94b
方面[fāngmiàn] aspect; side; field - 10	方向[fāngxiàng] direction - 150

160a

丶 讠 讠 讠 访 访

访
fǎng

visit

word 讠=言[22][yán] + direction/square 方 [fāng]

Signifies the act of visiting a famous teacher or doctor by asking(讠) around in all directions(方) one can think of.

访问[fǎngwèn] visit - 145b

160b

丶 亠 亠 立 立 产 产 产 旁 旁

旁
páng

side

stand 立[79][lì] + plow/square 方 [fāng]

Earth is dug up and piled(立) to each side of a plow(方).

旁边[pángbiān] lateral; side - 61a

160

斿

Diagram for 斿

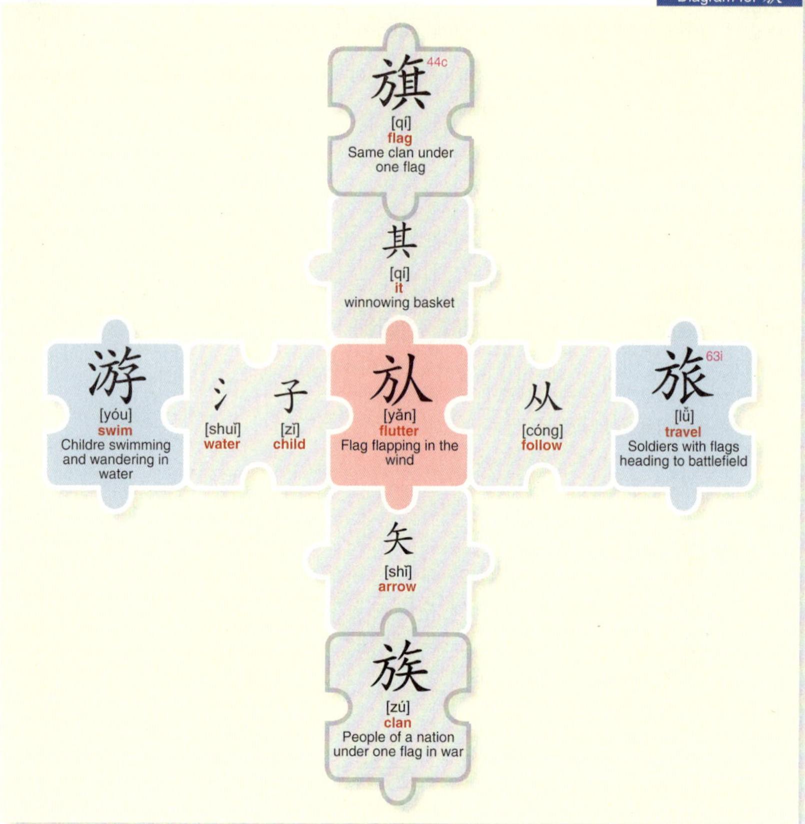

161

161 ˋ 亠 亣 方 方 斿

斿 yǎn

flutter

square 方 [fāng] + waving flag 人 [symbol]

Signifies a rectangular(方) flag(人) flapping or fluttering in the wind.

* Although the right side looks same as a person "人[63] [rén]," it symbolizes a flapping flag. Its shape can change(𠂉) when combined with other characters.

161a 丶 亠 方 方 方 方 方 方 方 旌 旌 族

族 zú

clan

flutter 方→㫃 [yǎn] + arrow 矢[111] [shǐ]

Waving flag(㫃) and arrow(矢) signify war. When people are gathered under one flag(㫃) in a time of war, it means " the people are from same tribe or clan of long generations sharing same culture and language."

民族[mínzú] race; nation - 99c

161b 丶 丶 氵 氵 氵 汸 汸 汸 沩 游 游 游

游 yóu

swim; wander

water 氵[202] [shuǐ] + flutter 方→㫃 [yǎn] + child 子[95] [zǐ]

Signifies children(子) swimming or wandering in water(氵), under the protection of flag(㫃) or adults.

* Pronunciation is affected by the character "斿[yóu]" which signifies children(子) playing and wandering under the waving flag(㫃).

旅游[lǚyóu] trip; travel - 63i	游泳[yóu/yǒng] swim - 201b
游戏[yóuxì] game; play - 113e	游览[yóulǎn] go sightseeing - 13e

161

酉

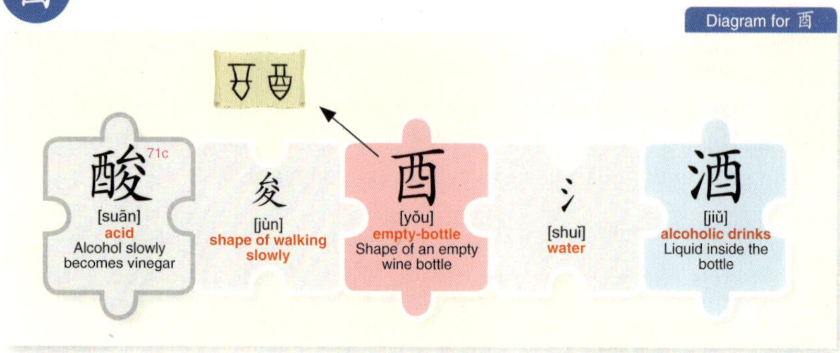

162 一 丆 丙 丙 两 西 酉

酉 yǒu

empty-bottle

Meaning of an empty wine bottle is derived from the shape of traditional vessel that held wine.

162

162a 丶 丶 氵 氵 汀 沂 沔 洒 洒 酒

酒 jiǔ

alcoholic drinks

water 氵 202 [shuǐ] + empty-bottle 酉 [yǒu]

An empty bottle(酉) is filled with wine (or alcohol in general) in the form of liquid(氵).

啤酒 [píjiǔ] beer - 215d

畐

Diagram for 畐

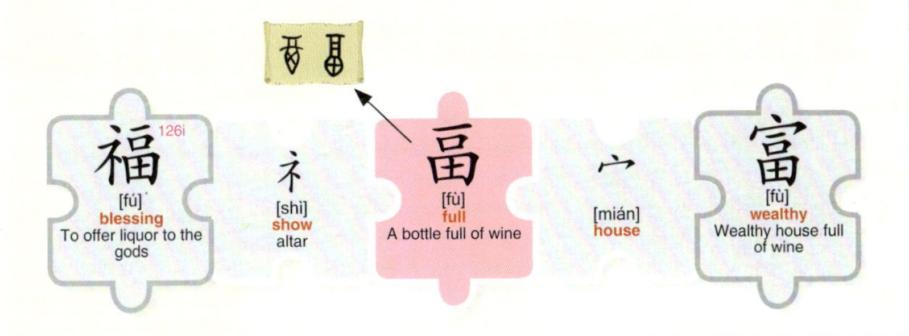

163

畐 fù **full**

Symbolizes a bottle(酉[162]) full of wine.

163a

富 fù **wealthy**

house 宀[141] [mián] + full 畐 [fù]

A household(宀) owning a lot(畐) of wine or alcohol could only mean a rich or wealthy family.

丰富 [fēngfù] abundant; rich; plentiful - 209

163

斗

Diagram for 斗

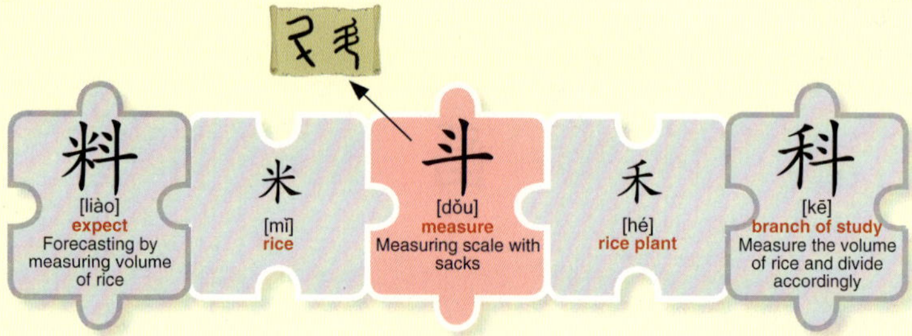

164 、 ⺀ 亠 斗

斗 dǒu/dòu

measure / fight

Symbolizes the shape of a measuring scale, with sacks on side to hold and measure the volume of grain. Used as a unit of grain volume.

164

* 100升 = 10斗 = 1石[197].

Traditional character(鬥) looks completely different. But it has the same sound, and is used to mean 'fight.' Keep in mind that the intonation changes in this case.

斗争[dòuzhēng] fight; struggle - 36a

164a ˊ 二 千 千 禾 禾 禾 禾 科

科 kē

branch of study

rice plant 禾[139][hé] + measure 斗 [dǒu]

Harvested rice(禾) is measured with a measuring scale(斗) and is divided to each purpose such as tax, rent, and distribution of seeds. Became to signify the unit of division in tasks or study, or partitioning of tasks in an organization or institute.

* For example, science is a systematically divided(科) study of nature for easier understanding (学).

科学[kēxué] science - 164a
科研[kēyán] scientific research - 197d
科长[kēzhǎng] section chief (manager) - 102

164b 丶 丷 䒑 半 米 米 米 米 料 料

料 liào

expect

rice 米[138][mǐ] + measure 斗 [dǒu]

One can forecast or expect how long the rice will last by measuring(斗) the volume of rice(米).

材料[cáiliào] material - 32b

网

Diagram for 网

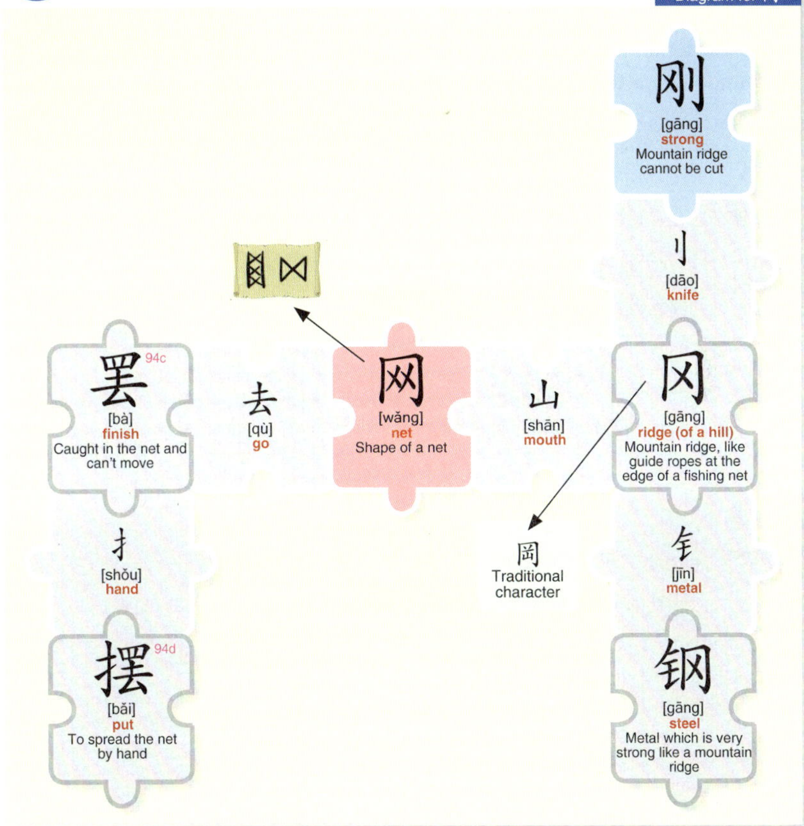

165

165

165

丨 冂 冂 冈 冈 网

网
wǎng

net

Symbolizes a net to catch birds or fish. Sometimes changes shape to "罒" for visual appearance when combined with other characters.

上网[shàngwǎng] be on the internet - 223f　　网球[wǎngqiú] tennis - 198b

165a

丨 冂 冂 冈

冈
gāng

ridge (of a hill)

fishing net 网 [wǎng] + mountain 山[195] [shān]

A mountain(山) has ridges that connect one mountain to another just like a fishing net(网) is surrounded by a thicker edge or guide ropes.

* The traditional character(岡) depicts how the two characters, 'fishing net(网)' and 'mountain(山)' are combined.

165b

丨 冂 冂 冈 冈 刚

刚
gāng

strong; just

ridge 冈 [gāng] + knife 刂=刀[119] [dāo]

Ridges(冈) are thick and strong, and are difficult to cut even with a sharp knife(刂). Used also as an adverb meaning just.

刚才[gāngcái] just now; a moment ago - 32

165c

丿 𠂉 𠂉 乍 钅 钆 钔 钢 钢

钢
gāng

steel

metal 钅=金[199] [jīn] + ridge 冈 [gāng]

Steel is a very strong metal(钅), just like the ridges(冈) of mountains or guide ropes of fishing nets.

钢笔[gāngbǐ] fountain pen - 188a

用

Diagram for 用

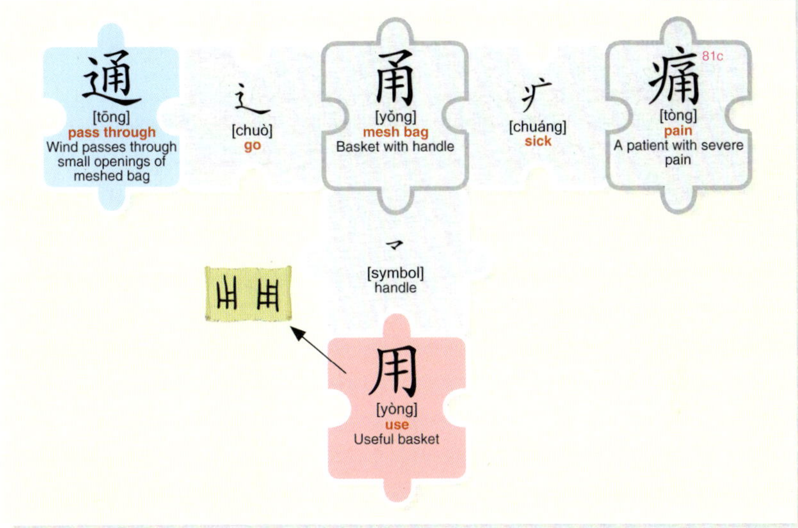

166

丿 冂 月 月 用

166

用
yòng

use

Symbolizes the shape of a traditional basket which can be conveniently used for containing things or agricultural crops.

作用 [zuòyòng] action; effect - 234b
利用 [lìyòng] use; utilize; make use of - 119h
耐用 [nàiyòng] durable - 9a
不用 [bùyòng] need not - 223a
使用 [shǐyòng] make use of; use - 35b

166a

甬
yǒng

mesh bag

handle ㇇ [symbol] + use 用 [yòng]

As "用" is used as a verb to use, a small handle(㇇) is added on top of basket(用) to restore the meaning of basket or meshed bag.

166b ㇇ ㇇ 乛 乃 乃 予 甬 甬 诵 诵 通

通 tōng

pass through

mesh bag 甬 [yǒng] + go 辶[61] [chuò]

Wind can pass through(辶) the holes of mesh basket(甬).

普通话[pǔtōnghuà] Mandarin (common speech of the Chinese language) - 79g 24b
通过[tōngguò] pass; pass through - 40f　通知[tōngzhī] advise; notify; inform - 111c

166

用

Diagram for 甫

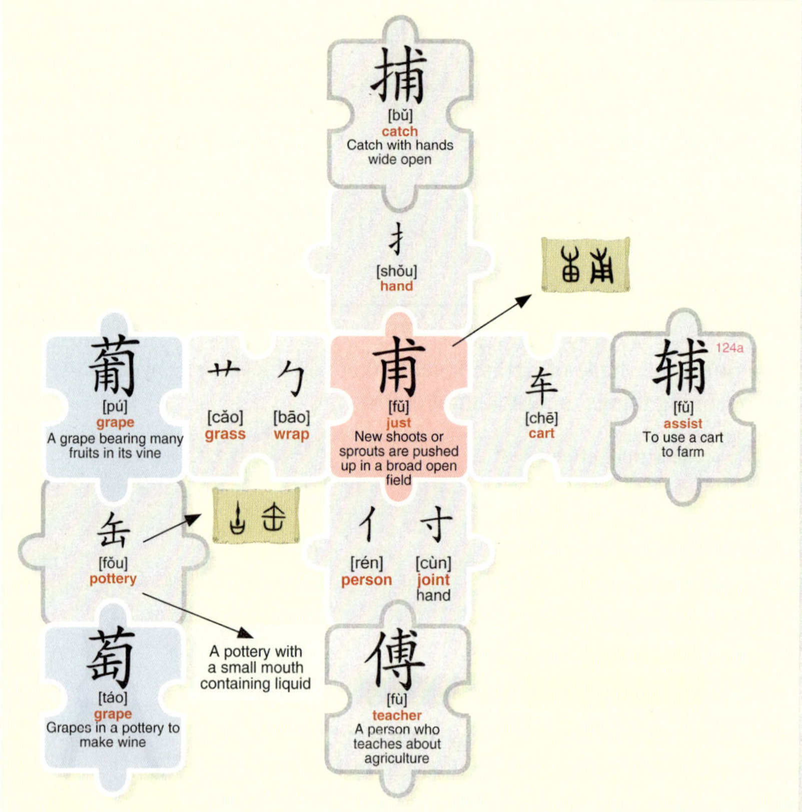

166c 一 丆 冂 冃 冃 甫 甫

甫 fǔ

just

Vegetables just started to spring their young sprouts(屮[207]) in a large field. Such broad open field has brought about a meaning of 'big, many.'

* This character belongs to this section because the radical is "用 [yòng]," but it has nothing to do with its meaning.

166d 一 十 扌 扌 扩 扪 捎 捎 捕 捕

捕 bǔ

catch

hand 扌=手[31] [shǒu] + big/just 甫 [fǔ]

Symbolizes the act of catching an animal with hands(扌) wide(甫) open.

逮捕 [dàibǔ] arrest; apprehend - 38a

166e 丿 亻 亻 亻 伂 伂 佰 俌 俌 傅 傅 傅

傅 fù

teacher

person 亻[70] [rén] + many/just 甫 [fǔ] + hand/joint 寸[40] [cùn]

A teacher is a person(亻) who teaches or gives hands to(寸) you on how to farm in order to yield lots(甫) of harvest. It tells us that 'agriculture' has its long history in human civilization because it brings about the staple food necessary for their survival.

师傅 [shīfu] master; master worker - 131e

166f 一 十 艹 艹 芍 芍 芍 苚 萄 萄 葡 葡

葡 pú

grape

grass 艹[207] [cǎo] + wrap 勹[46] [bāo] + many/just 甫 [fǔ]

This character illustrates the image of a grape vine which is covered by its creeping(勹) vines(艹) with many(甫) fruits hanging on them.

葡萄 [pútáo] grape - 166h

166

166g　　丿 𠂉 𠂉 午 缶 缶

缶 fǒu

pottery

This character symbolizes a pottery which is used to contain liquid. Its belly is a bit bulged and has a small mouth. The container was used, in ancient times, as a percussion instrument.

166h　　一 十 廾 艹 芍 芍 芍 苟 萄 萄 萄

萄 táo

grape

grass 艹[207] [cǎo] + wrap 勹[46] [bāo] + pottery 缶 [fǒu]

This character portrays the image of making wine in pottery(缶). The wine is made from clusters of grapes grown in a grapevine covered with its creeping (勹) vines(艹).

葡萄 [pútáo] grape - 166f

166

凵

Diagram for 凵

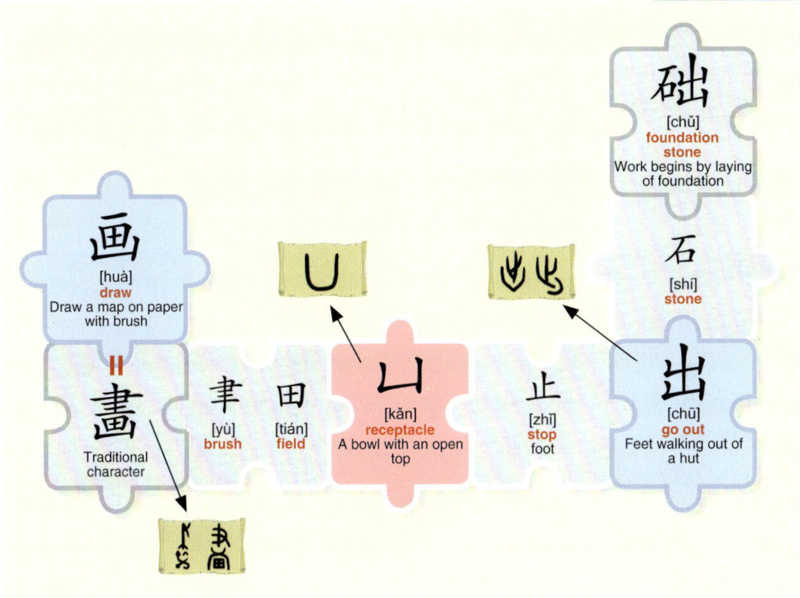

167

167 乚 凵

凵 kǎn **receptacle**

A character with variable interpretations, which can either mean an open mouth bowl or an open-top vessel.

167a 乚 凵 屮 出 出

出 chū **go out**

foot/stop 止[53][zhǐ] + receptacle 凵 [kǎn]

According to the ancient character (called "inscriptions on bones and tortoise carapaces"), it signifies the symbol of feet(止) walking out of a hut(凵).

出租车[chūzūchē] taxi; taxicab - 139d 124
出发[chūfā] set out; start off - 34f
出去[chūqu] go out; get out - 94
演出[yǎnchū] perform - 136b
出现[chūxiàn] appear; emerge; turn up - 13d
出来[chūlái] come out - 212d
出租汽车[chūzūqìchē] taxi; taxicab - 139d 204a 124

167b 一 ア 不 石 石 矼 砑 砷 础 础

础 chǔ

foundation stone

stone 石[197][shí] + go out 出 [chū]

Building of a house begins(出) by laying out foundation stones(石).

* The ancient character "出" signifies the first step toward outside from inside; therefore can mean a beginning.

基础[jīchǔ] base; foundation - 44a

167c 一 厂 戸 币 币 亩 画 画

画 huà

draw, paint

brush 一→聿[37][yù] + field 田[154][tián] + drawing paper 凵 [symbol]

Signifies drawing or painting of a map(田) or a picture on a canvas(凵) with a brush(聿).

* Traditional character(畫) shows painting of a map(田) on a paper(一) with a brush(聿).

画儿[huàr] picture - 71 画报[huàbào] illustrated magazine; pictorial - 34a

167

亅

Diagram for 亅

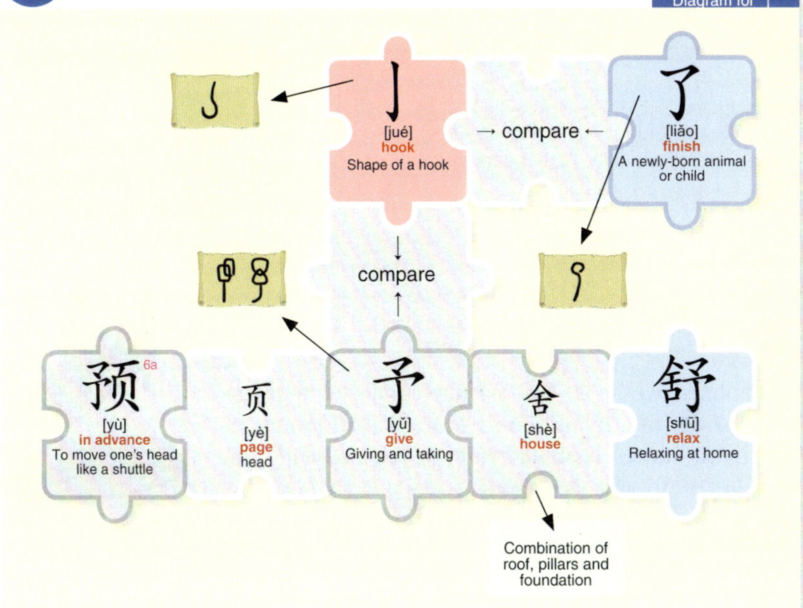

168

168 亅

亅 jué

hook

It is called a hook due to its bent shape at the end. Can be used only when combined with other characters.

* " 亅 " is covered here as it is a tool to make a mesh basket or net.

168a ㇇ 了

了 liǎo/le

finish; know / <particle>

Symbolizes a child or baby animal that is just finished being born. To finish something also means to understand or know its overall process.

* Mentioned here as " 亅 [jué]" is its radical.

了解 [liǎojiě] understand - 175c

With change of pronunciation, it is also used to signify an end of action, or as a particle to signal a new change due to completion.

除了[chúle] except - 147a　　为了[wèile] for - 159c
除了…以外[chúle...yǐwài] except for; but for - 147a 63j 222a
…极了[jíle] extremely - 36h
今天来了一封信。A letter arrived today. - 66 74b 212d 168a 223 40e 22a
天黑了，今天去不成了。It's dark already, and so I cannot go today. - 74b 158d 168a, 66 74b 94 223a 114a 168a

168b　　㇇ ㇇ 子 予

予 yǔ

give

Symbolizes two hooks that are interconnected together, or the shape of a flying shuttle in traditional looms. As the shuttle moves back and forth to release string, the meaning of 'to give' is derived.

给予[jǐyǔ] give - 65d

168

168c　　丿 人 𠆢 亼 仐 仐 舍 舍

舍 shè

house

roof 人 [symbol] + pillars 干 [symbol] + stone 口 [symbol]

A house is built on a foundation stone(口) by standing pillars(干) and roof (人) on top.

* Breaks down into "person 人[63] [rén]," "dry 干[121] [gān]" and "mouth 口[16] [kǒu]," but has no actual relation to them.

宿舍[sùshè] dormitory; living quarters - 134b

168d　　丿 丿 𠂉 𠂉 亼 仐 仐 舍 舍 舒 舒 舒

舒 shū

relax

house 舍 [shè] + shuttle/give 予 [yǔ]

As a flying shuttle(予) on a loom releases strings from a bundle, tensions are unwinded in a house(舍) so one can relax.

舒服[shūfu] comfortable - 34b　　舒适[shūshì] comfort; comfortable - 24d

冖

Diagram for 冖

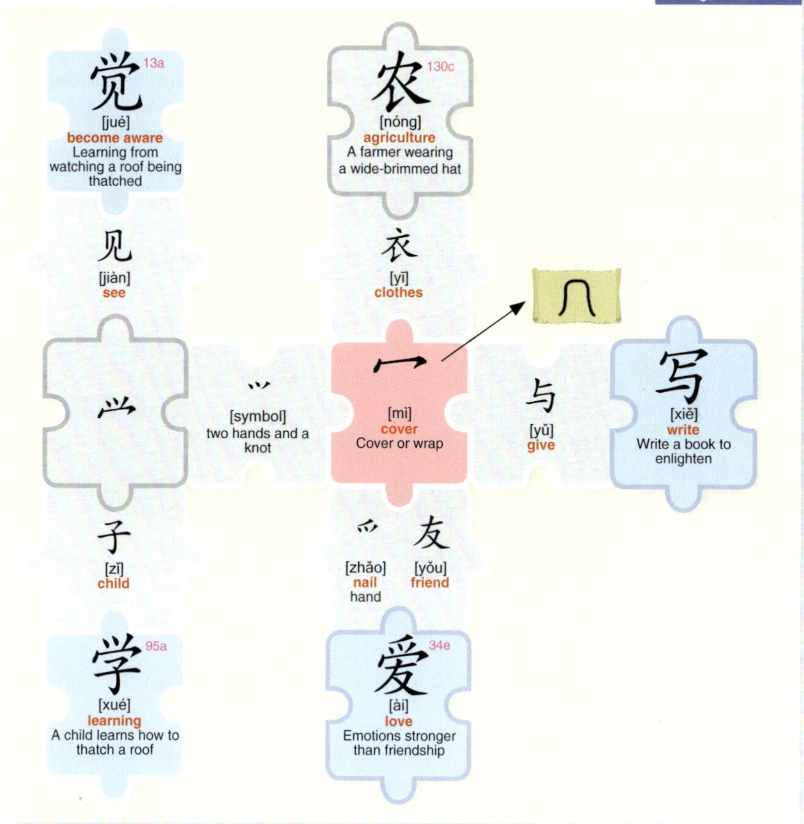

169

169

冖 mì **cover**

Symbolizes a cloth or wrap to cover food or goods.

169a　　　　　　　　　　　　　　　　　　　　　　　　　　　　　　　　　　　　　　, ⺈ ⺈ 写 写

写
xiě

write

cover 冖 [mì] + give 与 [yǔ]

Writing a book and passing(与) it to someone can enlighten people and also can help escape from the 'cover(冖) of ignorance.'

* Traditional character(寫) shows a nest(宀[141]) of a magpie bird(舃[xì]) which looks the same as if it was transcribed regardless of where it is. The meaning of write is derived from this apparent copying.

听写 [tīngxiě] dictate; dictation - 16d

170

西

Diagram for 西

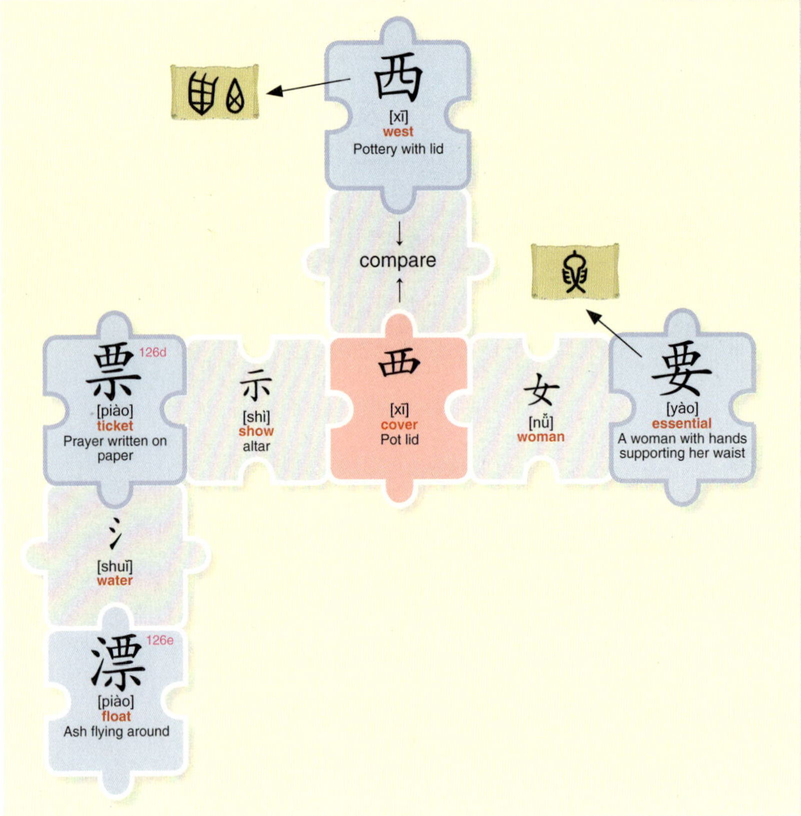

170 一 丆 丙 丙 西 西

西 xī

west

Symbolizes a pottery with a dark brown glaze that holds water, with a lid on top. Borrowed to mean the concept of west since the pronunciation is same. Also can mean a 'thing' as an essential utensil like a bag(东[211]) that can be found anywhere.

* Ancient version of this character clearly shows a lid being added on top of a pottery.

东西[dōngxi] thing - 211	西瓜[xīguā] watermelon - 33f
西边[xībiān] west side - 61a	东西 east and west - 211 170

170a 一 丆 丙 丙 覀 覀

覀 xī

cover

Simple form of a cover used to close bottles or pots.

170b 一 丆 丙 丙 覀 覀 要 要 要

要 yào

essential; must; need

cover 覀 [xī] + woman 女[96][nǚ]

A woman(女) is standing while supporting her waist with two hands(覀→臼[43d]); derived to mean essential, must or need as the waist is the most critical part in a body.

* Ancient version of this character shows "覀" as shape of two hands, "both hands 臼[126d][jiù]."

需要[xūyào] need - 9b	要求[yāoqiú] ask; demand - 203b
重要[zhòngyào] important; significant - 151a	主要[zhǔyào] main; major - 233c
不要[bùyào] don't - 223a	要是[yàoshi] if; suppose; in case - 54b

Nature

Nature

Animals

Animals play a very important role in food chain where humans reside on top.

1. Land animals which are most friendly with humans, such as sheep, dog, pig and cow, appear as basic characters.
2. Other animals include birds – whose flight fascinated mankind for years – as well as insects and fish. Shellfish also plays an important role as it was used for currency in ancient times.
3. Animal by-products such as fur, skin, horn and meat are also used as basic characters.

Natural scenery

Mountains and natural resources including animals are the key components of the nature. Humans needed tools to manage such resources. Water, grass and trees provide the most basic source of food to the natural food chain. The characters in this section will show how these components play role as basic characters.

Heavenly bodies

All things on earth are affected by the movement of heavens. Therefore, it is very natural to have the symbol of heavens to become a basic character. This section will explain how the basic characters from sun and moon are combined to form new characters and meanings, along with their background.

Miscellaneous

As the last steps in the formation of the basic characters, there are numbers and codes. Codes were used to convey meanings that were difficult to express with shapes. You will find additional numbers that were skipped before, and the basic strokes '丨, 丶, 丿' which are just symbols (codes) without specific meaning.

Try to understand the background and process of how these strokes are incorporated into the basic characters.

羊

Diagram for 羊

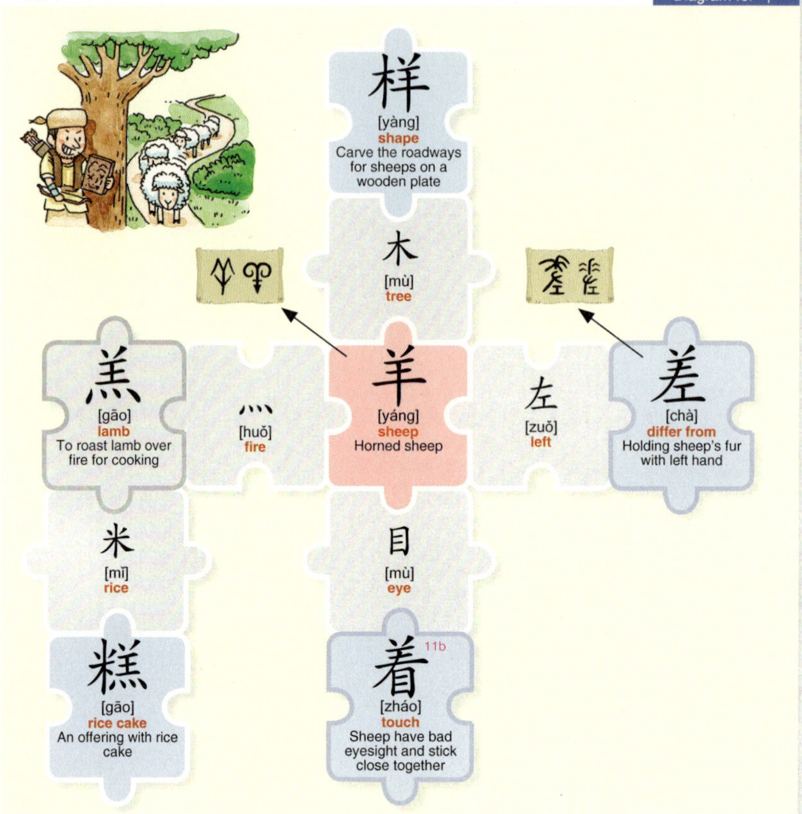

171

171 丶 丷 䒑 䒑 兰 羊

羊 yáng **sheep**

Symbolizes a sheep with horns when one looks at it from the front.

羊肉 [yángròu] mutton - 192

171a 一 十 才 木 木 木 杧 栏 栏 样

样 yàng **shape**

tree 木[210] [mù] + sheep 羊 [yáng]

Sheeps tend to remember their ways and always follow them; humans first hunted sheep(羊) by waiting for the herd on their return path. The shape of the return path is then drawn on a wooden plate(木) for easier hunt.

* Traditional character(樣) shows waterways(水[201]) or landscapes(羊) drawn on a wooden(木) plate.

怎么样[zěnmeyàng] how - 234d 93a	一样[yīyàng] the same; equally; alike - 223
那样[nàyàng] of that kind; like that - 147e	样子[yàngzi] appearance; shape - 95
怎样[zěnyàng] how - 234d	这样[zhèyàng] like this; this way - 133a

171b

差 chà

differ from; wanting

sheep 羊 [yáng] + left 左[39a][zuǒ]

While holding the sheep(羊) on the left hand(左) to shear the fur, the length of the fur differs from one part of sheep to another. This character is derived from such meaning, "different or running short."

* Ancient character shows holding of crops(禾[139]) with the left(左) hand to signify that even crops from the same field are of different lengths.

差不多[chàbuduō] almost; nearly; just about - 223a 222d
差点儿[chàdiǎnr] slightly inferior to - 127d 71

171

171c

羔 gāo

lamb

sheep 羊 [yáng] + fire 灬=火[158][huǒ]

This character portrays the image of roasting and cooking a baby lamb(羊) over fire(灬) for a holy offering. Lamb meat is mild, fine-textured and good for digestion. Especially, a year-old baby lamb is delicious and is treated as high-quality food.

171d

糕 gāo

rice cake

rice 米[138][mǐ] + lamb 羔 [gāo]

This character depicts the image of offering rice cake(米) onto an alter like lamb(羔). During the agriculture era, rice cake became an important food used as an offering for important memorial services.

蛋糕[dàngāo] cake - 55b

犬

Diagram for 犬

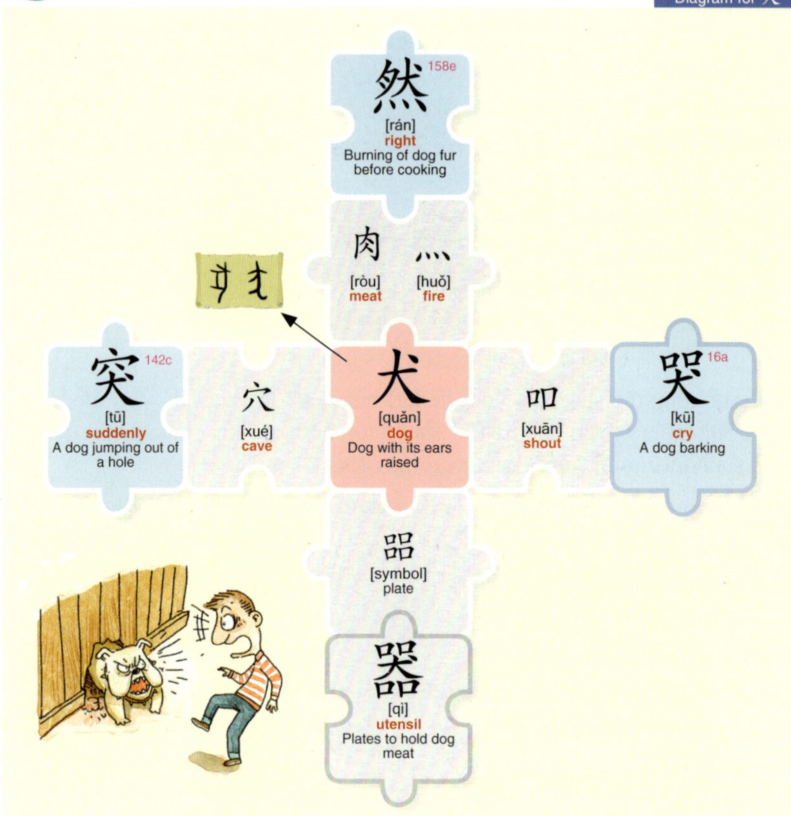

172

172 一 ナ 大 犬

犬
quǎn

dog

Symbolizes a dog with its ears(丶) raised.

172a

丶 ㇆ 口 ㅁ ...器 (stroke order)

器 qì

utensil

plate 㗊 [symbol] + dog 犬 [quǎn]

Symbolizes the shape of plates(㗊) that held dog meat(犬) used in ceremonies and sacrifices.

∗ Dog meat was an essential part of ceremonies and events.

机器 [jīqì] machine - 213a　　武器 [wǔqì] weapon; arms - 110d

犭

Diagram for 犭

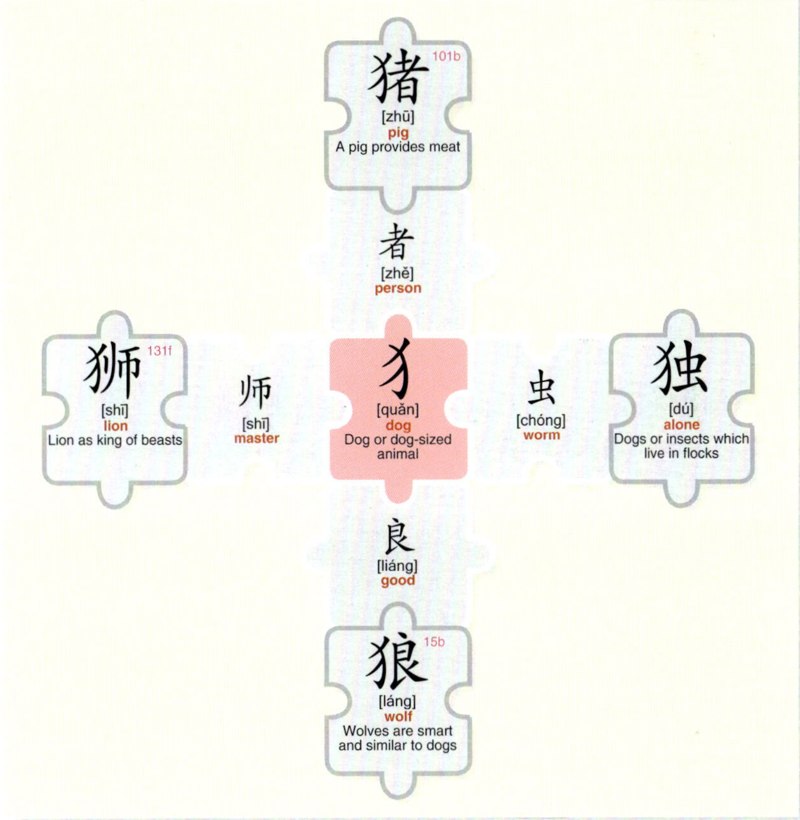

173

173 丿 犭 犭

犭 quǎn

dog

Used only in combination with other characters to replace dog “犬” or to symbolize a small dog-sized animal.

173a 丿 犭 犭 犭 犭 犭 独 独 独

独 dú

alone

dog 犭 [quǎn] + worm 虫[184] [chóng]

Among dogs(犭) or group of insects(虫) which live in flocks, there is always a leader standing alone in the center.

174

豕

Diagram for 豕

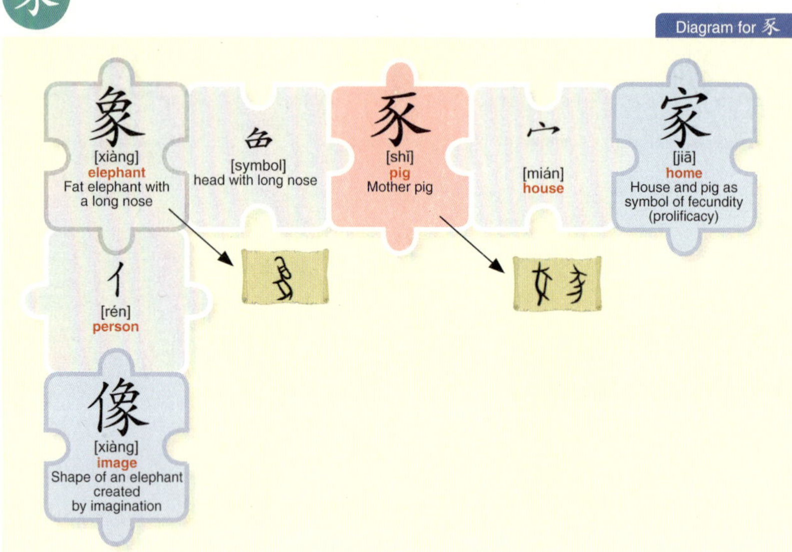

174

豕 shǐ — pig

Symbolizes a well-fed pig lying sideways to milk her young one.

174a

家 jiā — home; …ist

house 宀 141 [mián] + pig 豕 [shǐ]

Combination of house(宀) and pig(豕) which gives plentiful birth. It came to mean a family. This character shows a kind of Chinese humor in favor of prolificacy. Used also as an ending of someone in a specific profession, as in "~ist" in pianist.

* A pig produces 8 to 12 babies in a single birth.

大家[dàjiā] great master; authority - 74
国家[guójiā] country; state; nation - 20a
家庭[jiātíng] family - 62b
文学家[wénxuéjiā] Trecentist; litterateur - 133 95a

174b

象 xiàng — elephant; shape

head with long nose ⺈ [symbol] + pig 豕 [shǐ]

An elephant has a head with long nose(⺈) and a fat body(豕) like a pig. Also means shape as an elephant was more of an exotic imaginary creature to the people of the northern China where Chinese characters originated.

抽象[chōuxiàng] abstract - 156a

174c

像 xiàng — image; be like

person 亻 70 [rén] + elephant 象 [xiàng]

Ancient Chinese people(亻) in the northern area could only imagine how a shape of an elephant(象) would look like. The meaning of 'likeness' is also derived from the similar shape of an "imaginary elephant" being close to the actual one due to its uniqueness.

好像[hǎoxiàng] seem; be like - 96c
录像[lù/xiàng] picture recording; videotape - 203a
肖像[xiàoxiàng] portrait - 235c

牛

Diagram for 牛

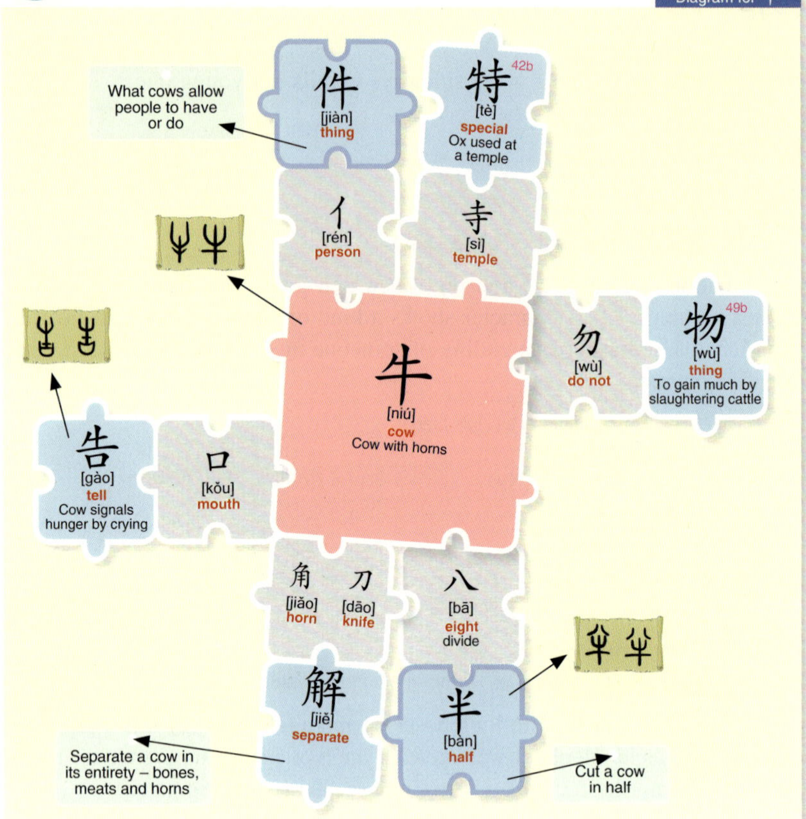

175

175 丿 𠂉 𠂉 牛

牛 niú **cow**

Symbolizes a cow with horns looked at from the front.

牛奶[niúnǎi] (cow's) milk - 96d

175a 丿 亻 亻 仁 仁 件

件 jiàn **thing; <quantifier>**

person 亻[70] [rén] + cow 牛 [niú]

Cows(牛) allowed people(亻) to do many things, from plowing to providing meat and carcasses as a sacrifice. Used as a unit of countable affairs, cloths or goods from the emphasis on meaning of 'things.'

电子邮件[diànzǐyóujiàn] E-mail - 157a 95 147d
条件[tiáojiàn] condition; qualification - 56c
事件[shìjiàn] event; incident - 36d
一件事 one task - 223 175a 36d
一件衣服 one item of clothing - 223 175a 130 34b

175b

丶 丷 丷 ⺷ 半

半 bàn

half

divide/eight 八[229] [bā] + cow 牛 [niú]

Signifies a cow(牛) which is being butchered and cut in half(八). A cow is considered as an animal which makes many good things possible.

* "八" is a symbol of symmetry in half, signifying to divide.

半天[bàntiān] half of the day - 74b
半岛[bàndǎo] peninsula - 177c
半导体[bàndǎotǐ] semiconductor - 7b 29b
半拉[bànlǎ] half - 79a
半夜[bànyè] midnight; half of a night - 222b

175c

ノ ク 勹 角 角 角 角 角' 角" 角刀 角刃 解 解

解 jiě

separate; understand

horn 角[191] [jiǎo] + knife 刀[119] [dāo] + cow 牛 [niú]

This character depicts a scene that a cow(牛) is butchered by a knife(刀) and came into completely separate parts such as the meat, bones and even its horns(角). Also came to mean 'understand' by understanding everything in its entirety by dividing them into such smaller parts.

解决[jiějué] solve - 76a
了解[liǎojiě] understand - 168a
解放[jiěfàng] liberate - 50a
解答[jiědá] answer; solve - 65b

175d

ノ ⺈ 𠂉 生 牛 告 告

告 gào

tell

cow 牛 [niú] + mouth 口[16] [kǒu]

Two theories exist for this: ① a signpost(⺧) is put up to warn people of dangerous traps(口), or ② a cow(牛) crying(口) to signal and tell the owners that it's hungry.

告诉[gàosu] tell; let (make) know - 118c
报告[bàogào] inform; report - 34a

175

马

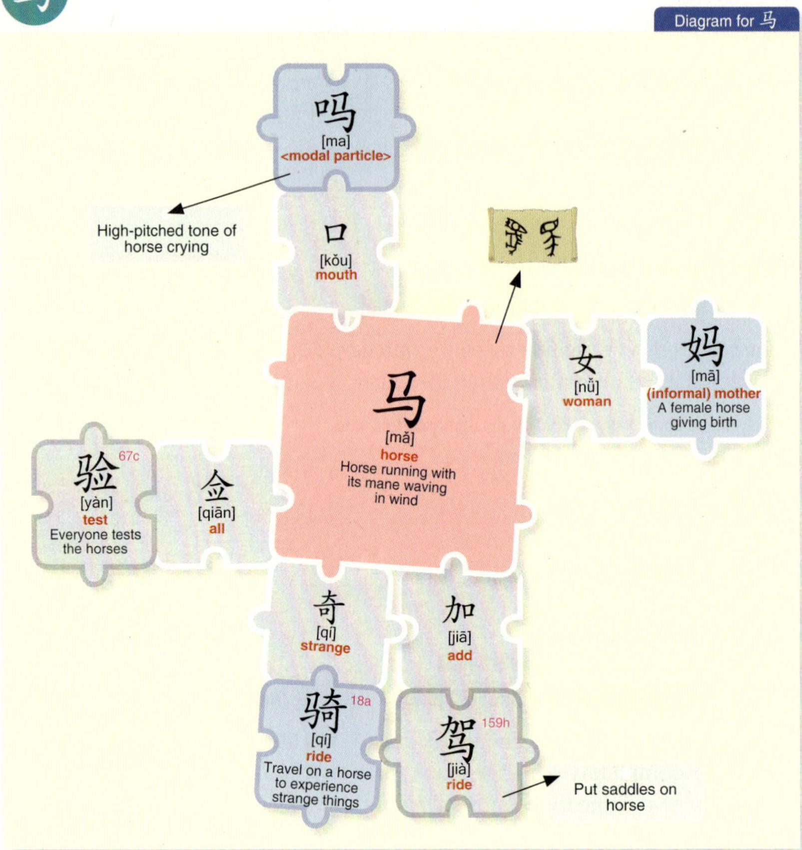

176

176

㇇ 马 马

马 mǎ

horse

A symbol of a horse running fast with four feet(一) and its mane waving in the wind.

马上[mǎshàng] at once; immediately - 223f　　马路[mǎlù] street; road - 57a

176a 丨 ㄇ 口 口⁷ 吗 吗

吗 ma

<modal particle>

mouth 口[16][kǒu] + horse 马 [mǎ]

Used as a postpositional particle to form a question, in a sense that a high tone(马) is formed when speaking(口) a question.

* Try to imagine a high-pitched sound of a horse as the question(马) mark.

你有时间吗? Do you have some time? - 69a 39c 42d 145c 176a
你吃饭了吗? Did you eat? - 69a 16b 148b 168a 176a

176b ㄑ 女 女 女⁷ 妈 妈

妈 mā

(informal) mother

woman 女[96][nǚ] + horse 马 [mǎ]

Meaning of mother is formed by combining woman(女) with "马" as pronunciation guide.

* Remember that horses(马) give birth to only one foal like human mothers(女) do most times whereas cows or sheeps often give more than one offspring in a single birth.

妈妈[māma] mom; mommy

176

鸟

Diagram for 鸟

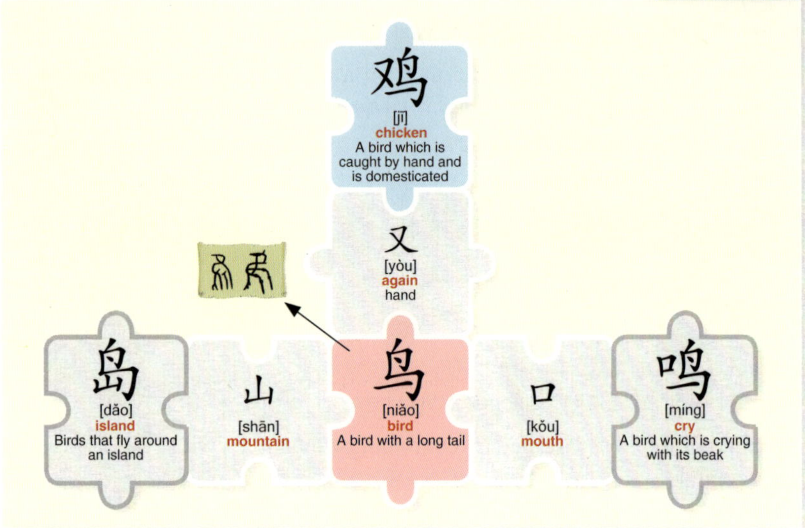

177

177

鸟 niǎo

bird

Symbolizes a bird with a long tail, beak and legs.

177a

鸡 jī

chicken

hand/again 又[34] [yòu] + bird 鸟 [niǎo]

Signifies a bird(鸟) caught in hand(又), or domesticated – i.e. Chickens.

鸡蛋 [jīdàn] (hen's) egg - 55b

177b

鸣 míng

cry

mouth 口[16] [kǒu] + bird 鸟 [niǎo]

Signifies a bird(鸟) crying with its beak(口). This character is used to mean cry of birds, animals or insects.

177c

岛 dǎo

island

bird 鸟 [niǎo] + mountain 山[195] [shān]

A small island as a small mountain(山) in middle of the sea has lots of birds (鸟) flying around freely.

* Or, can also be thought as birds(鸟) being able to freely approach islands(山).

半岛 [bàndǎo] peninsula - 175b

隹

178

Diagram for 隹

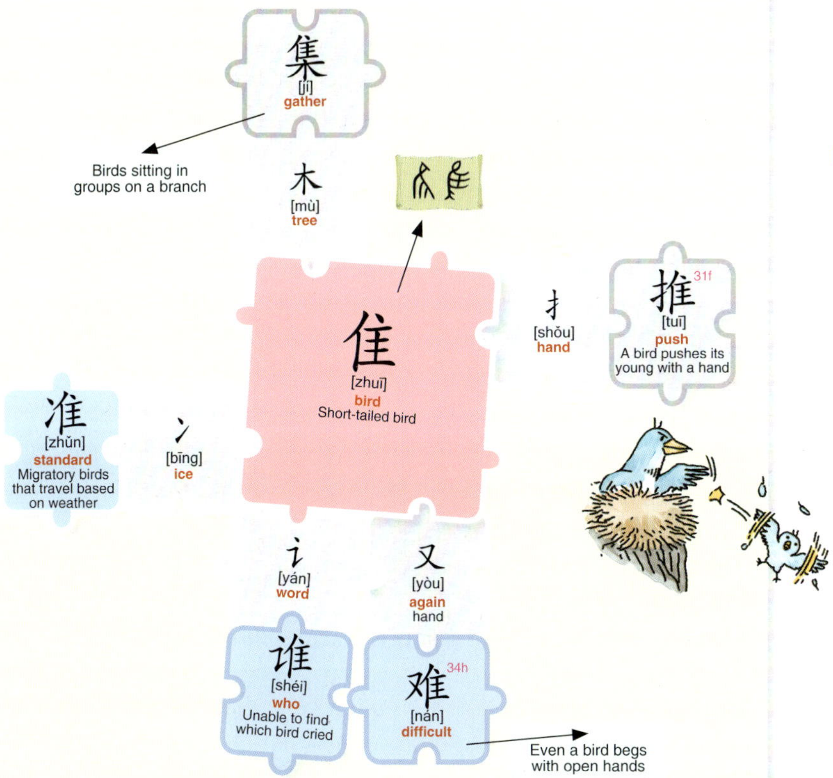

178

丿 亻 亻 亻 亻 亻 隹 隹

隹 zhuī

bird (short-tailed)

Signifies a small bird which looked at from its side. While "鸟[177][niǎo]" is used to and signify long-tailed and larger birds, this character is a general term to mean 'short-tailed and smaller birds.'

178a

丿 亻 亻 亻 亻 亻 亻 隹 隹 隹 隹 集

集 jí

gather

bird 隹 [zhuī] + tree 木[210][mù]

Symbolizes small birds(隹) gathered onto a branch of a tree(木) and chatting or chirping.

集合[jíhé] gather; assemble - 65a
集中[jízhōng] concentrate - 232a
召集[zhàojí] call together; convene - 120

178b

丶 讠 讠 讠 讠 讠 讠 谁 谁 谁

谁 shéi

who

word 讠= 言[22][yán] + bird 隹 [zhuī]

It is hard to find who cried(讠) out when a group of small birds(隹) sit together.

您找谁? Who are you looking for? - 69b 113c 178b

178c

丶 冫 冫 冫 冫 冫 冫 冫 准 准

准 zhǔn

standard

ice 冫[206][bīng] + bird 隹 [zhuī]

When temperatures fall below a given or standard temperature such as freezing(冫) point, migratory birds(隹) prepare to fly away to warmer territories.

* Traditional character(準) shows water(氵[202]) which always remain perfectly horizontal, and a falcon(falcon 隼 [sǔn]) that always flies at a fixed height when looking for a prey – a standard in height and shape.

准备[zhǔnbèi] prepare - 56a
准时[zhǔnshí] punctual; on time - 42d

178

只

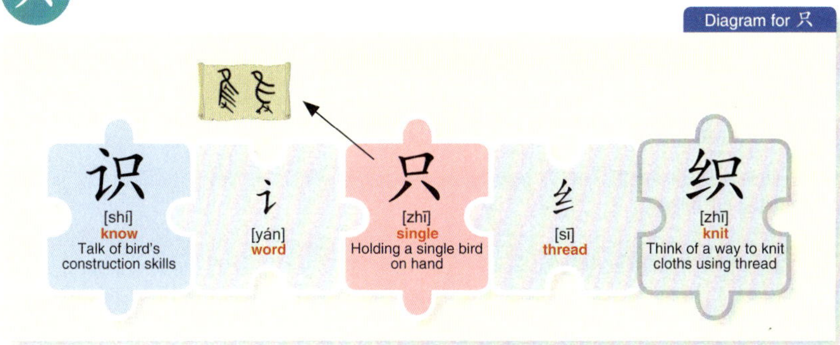

179

只 zhī/zhǐ

single / only

mouth 口[16][kǒu] + hand/again 八→又[34][yòu]

Symbolizes only one bird (represented by "口" instead of "隹[178]"), being held on one hand(又). Used as unit to count a single item in a given pair, or when counting animals or ships.

* Traditional character(隻) clearly shows holding of one bird(隹) on hand(又). 179

一只鞋 one shoe - 223 179 153b
一只鸟 a bird - 223 179 177
一只小船 a boat - 223 179 235 125a

Also signifies the word "just," in the sense of holding just one bird(隹) in hand(又).

只好[zhǐhǎo] have to; be forced to - 96c
只是[zhǐshì] merely; only; just - 54b
只有[zhǐyǒu] only; alone - 39c

179a

织 zhī

knit

thread 纟[132][sī] + a bird/single 只 [zhī]

Symbolizes how one can imagine the way to knit a piece of clothing using threads(纟) by looking at a bird(只) which builds its nest by knitting small branches together.

* Traditional character(織) shows knitting of a clothing by threads(糸) per direction of a clay plate(clay 戠 [shì]).

组织[zǔzhī] organization; organize - 132f

179b

` 讠 讠 订 识 识 识

识
shí

know

word 讠=言[22] [yán] + a bird/single 只 [zhǐ]

Symbolizes an act of explaining through words(讠) how a bird(只) builds its nest to let others know.

* Traditional character(識) shows passing of knowledge written on clay plates(clay 戠 [shì]) by words(言) of mouth.

认识[rènshi] recognize; know - 63a 知识[zhīshi] knowledge - 111c

179

喿

Diagram for 喿

180 丶 ㇆ 口 ㇐ 𠮛 吕 吕 品 品 品 喿 喿 喿

喿 sào

cry

birds 品 [symbol] + tree 木[210][mù]

Symbolizes singing or crying of birds(品) sitting on a tree branch(木).

* "品" represents a group of birds, each "mouth 口[16][kǒu]" replacing "隹[178]."

180a 180 一 十 扌 扌 扌 扌 扌 扌 扌 扌 扌 扌 操 操 操 操

操 cāo

hold; exercise

hand 扌=手[31][shǒu] + cry 喿 [sào]

Symbolizes an act of trying to catch birds by hand(扌) because they are too loud (喿). Also signifies that one needs to practice or exercise in order to catch a bird by hands.

操场[cāochǎng] playground - 152a

180b 丶 丶 氵 氵 氵 氵 氵 氵 氵 氵 氵 氵 澡 澡 澡 澡

澡 zǎo

bathe

water 氵[202][shuǐ] + cry 喿 [sào]

Birds singing on the tree branch(喿) jump into the water(氵) to bathe themselves. Birds are known to keep a high standard of hygiene. They always try to keep their feathers cleaned and sometimes bathing in sands to drop off parasites.

洗澡[xǐzǎo] have a bath; wash - 71e

非

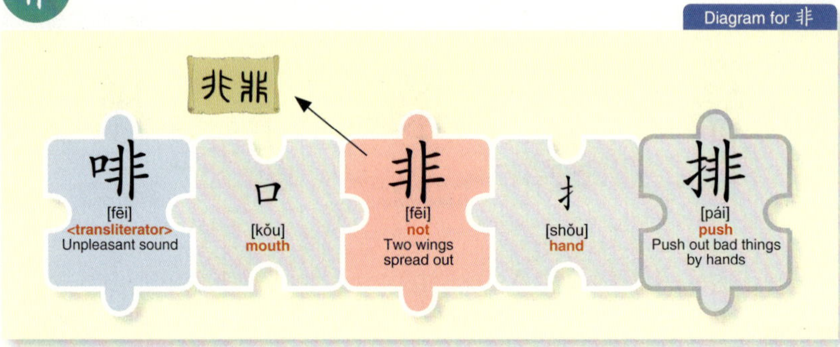

181

非 fēi

not

Symbolizes a bird spreading its wings wide; each wing, when spread out, will not meet the other wing. Therefore it is used as negation.

181 非常[fēicháng] extraordinary; unusual - 150c

181a

排 pái

push; arrange

hand 扌=手[31][shǒu] + not 非 [fēi]

Signifies pushing of bad or incorrect(非) things by hands(扌). Also has meaning of arranging things that are out of order(非) into proper order.

安排[ānpái] arrange - 96a
排斥[páichì] exclude - 118b
排球[páiqiú] volleyball - 198b
排列[páiliè] arrange - 30b

181b

啡 fēi

<transliterator>

mouth 口[16][kǒu] + not 非 [fēi]

Originally meant to 'signify' snoring, which is an uncomfortable(非) sound (口) made during sleep. Now used as a transliterator to write words from foreign languages such as coffee(咖啡).

咖啡[kāfēi] coffee - 159i

羽

Diagram for 羽

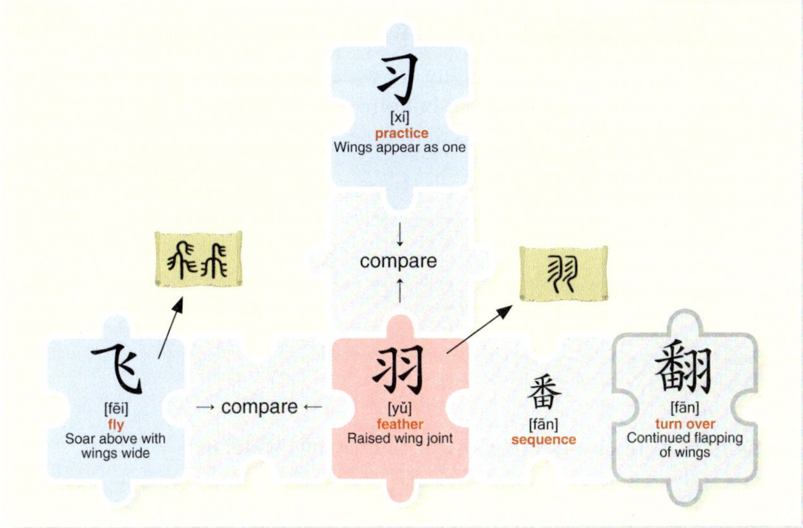

182

182 ㇆ ㇆ 习 羽 羽 羽

羽 yǔ **feather**

Symbolizes a bird with its wings raised high to show its feathers.

羽毛球[yǔmáoqiú] badminton - 188 198b

182a ㇆ ㇆ 习

习 xí **practice**

Symbolizes a baby bird practicing to fly so hard that its two wings(羽) become looking like one(习).

学习[xuéxí] study; learn - 95a
复习[fùxí] review - 56d
练习[liànxí] practice; exercise - 132g
习惯[xíguàn] habit; be used to - 186f
预习[yùxí] prepare lessons before class - 6a

182b

翻
fān

turn over; rummage

sequence 番[183a][fān] + feather 羽 [yǔ]

A bird is continuously(番) flapping its wings(羽), resulting in wings being turned over as it flaps from top to bottom. Also signifies rummaging, as one needs to search over and under to find something.

* "番" signifies footprints(釆) of animals printed one after another on a field(田).

翻译[fānyì] translate - 123c

182c

飞
fēi

fly

Symbolizes a big bird flying above with its wings wide open.

飞机[fēijī] airplane - 213a

183

釆

Diagram for 番

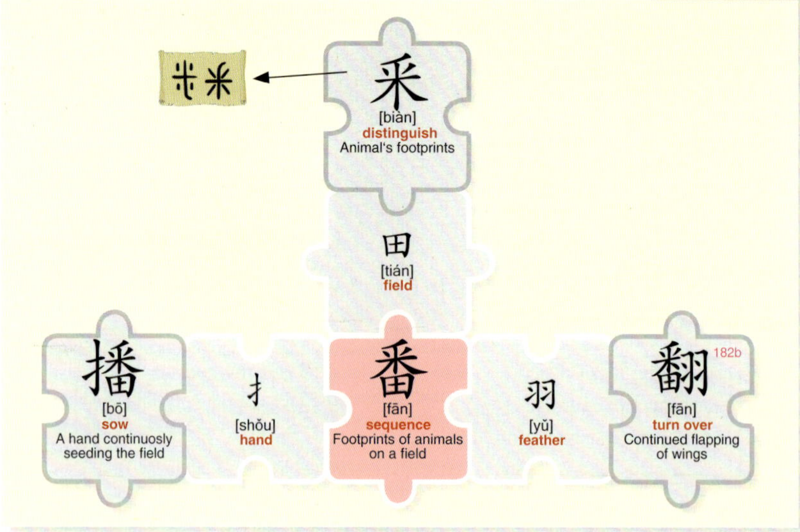

183 一 ㇀ ㇀ 亠 平 平 釆

釆 biàn

distinguish

Symbolizes a footprint, which can be used to distinguish what the animal was by looking at it.

* Used only as a combination to add meaning to other characters.

183a

番 fān

sequence

footprints/distinguish 釆 [biàn] + field 田[154] [tián]

Signifies footprints(釆) of animals printed one after another on a field(田).

183b

播 bō

sow

hand 扌= 手[31] [shǒu] + sequence 番 [fān]

Signifies continued(番) seeding(扌) or sowing of crops, one after another, on a field(田). Also used as meaning for broadcast, as electro-magnetic waves are seeded onto the air. 183

* Hands(扌) represent the act of seeding in this case.

广播[guǎngbō] broadcast - 143

虫

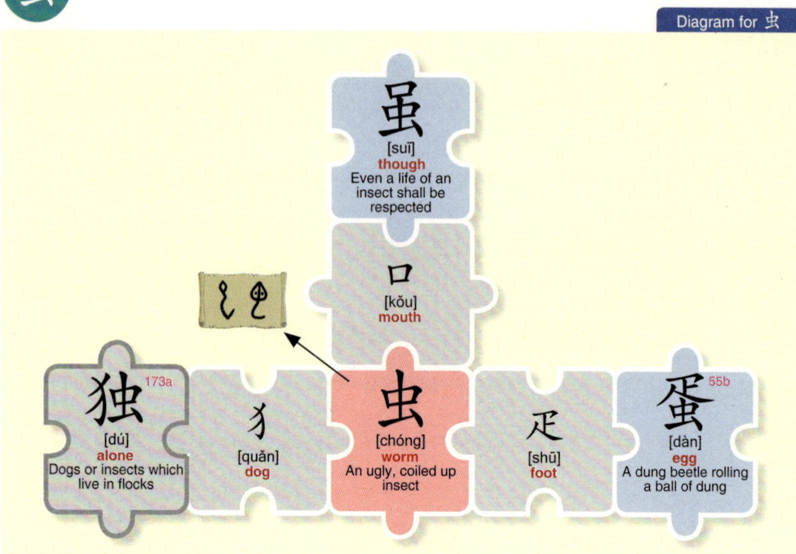

184

184 丨 冂 口 中 虫 虫

虫 chóng **worm**

Symbolizes a snake coiled up on the ground. Used to describe any insects, long or short.

虫子[chóngzi] insect; worm; bug - 95

184a 丨 冂 口 口 吕 吕 咠 虽 虽

虽 suī **though**

mouth 口[16][kǒu] + worm 虫 [chóng]

Life, symbolized by mouth(口), is written together with insect(虫), to mean that life should not be disregarded even though it is only a life of an insect.

虽然[suīrán] though; although - 158e

鱼

Diagram for 鱼

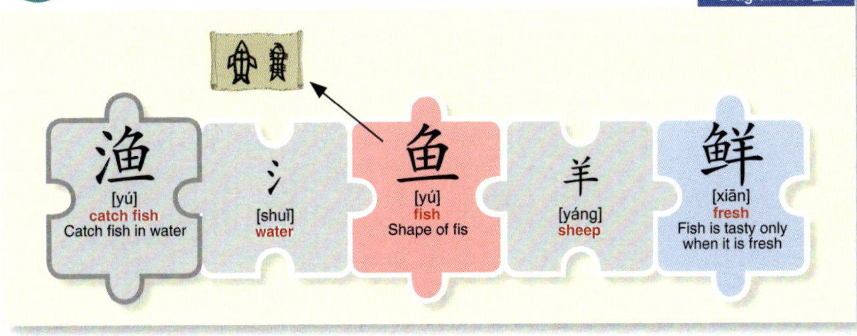

185 ノ ク 𠂊 各 各 角 角 鱼

鱼 yú

fish

Head(⺈), body(田) and tail(一) are combined together to form a fish.

我不太喜欢吃鱼。I am not a big fan of eating fish. - 113b 223a 74c 140a 23c 16b 185

185

185a ノ ク 𠂊 各 各 角 角 鱼 鱼 鱼' 鱼' 鲜 鲜 鲜

鲜 xiān

fresh

fish 鱼 [yú] + sheep 羊[171] [yáng]

Fish(鱼) caught for purposes of eating can go bad very easily; only when it's fresh, it can be delicious like meat of lamb(羊).

* Lamb(羊) has been known as a delicacy due to the fibre being very thin and soft.

新鲜[xīnxiān] fresh; new - 103b　　鲜花[xiānhuā] fresh flower; flower - 70b

185b 丶 丶 氵 氵 氵 氵 泊 泊 洵 渔 渔

渔 yú

catch fish

water 氵[202] [shuǐ] + fish 鱼 [yú]

One can catch fish(鱼) in waters(氵) like the river or the ocean.

渔民[yúmín] fisherman - 99c

贝

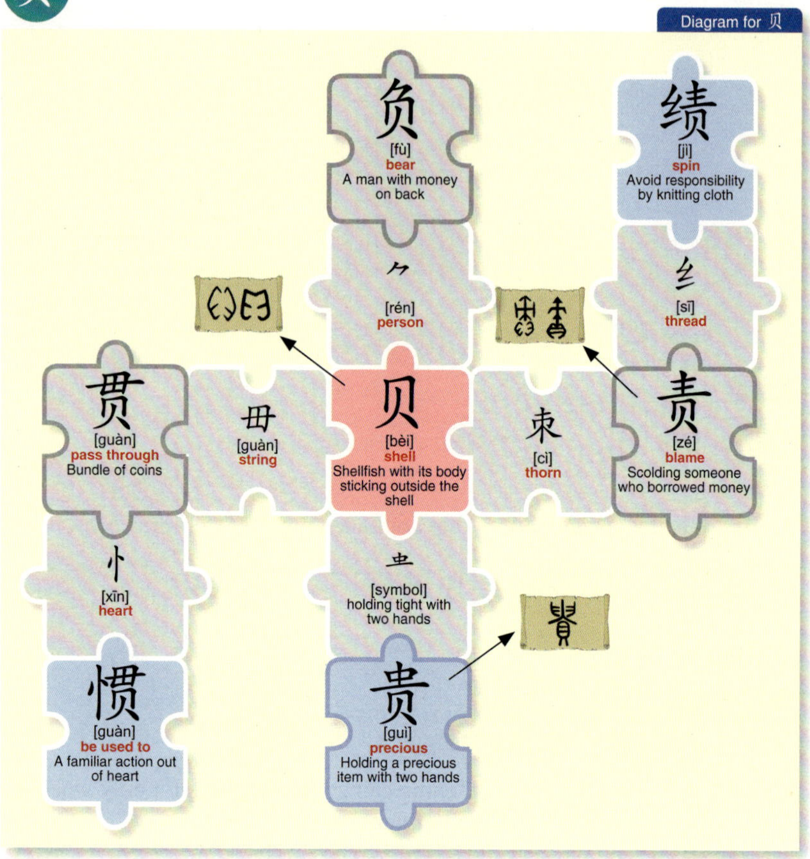

186

186 丨 冂 贝 贝

贝
bèi

shell

The body(人) of shellfish is sticking out from its shell(冂). Purple-colored shellfish(贝) back in Yin(殷) and Jiu(周) Dynasties were used as currency by the inhabitants of the region.

* Due to its shape, sometimes also used as a replacement for "鼎[dǐng]," a pot with three feet.

186a ノ ク 个 各 贠 负

负 fù

bear; bear debt

person ⺈[68] [rén] + currency/shell 贝 [bèi]

Symbolizes a person(⺈) bearing a sack of money(贝) on his back. Money signifies Debt.

负责[fùzé] in charge of - 186b

186b 一 二 キ 主 丰 青 青 责

责 zé

blame

thorn 主→朿[cì] + currency/shell 贝 [bèi]

Act of blaming or scolding is represented by a thorn(朿) towards an indebted who owes money(贝).

* The ancient version of the character shows the top part as a variation of "朿," meaning the thorn on a tree(木[210]).

负责[fùzé] in charge of - 186a 责任[zérèn] responsibility - 105a

186c 乙 纟 纟 纟 纟 纟 纟 纟 纟 绩 绩

186

绩 jì

spin (thread); achievement

thread 纟[132] [sī] + blame 责 [zé]

Represents the entire process of knitting a cloth by spun threads(纟). Cloth was traded as valuable material and was used to pay tax or debt in place of certain responsibilities(责). It also allowed people to achieve their goal by being a valuable source of funds.

成绩[chéngjì] result; record; achievement - 114a

186d 丶 口 口 中 虫 中 冉 贵 贵

贵 guì

precious

holding tight with two hands 虫 [symbol] + currency/shell 贝 [bèi]

Symbolizes grabbing of a precious, high-priced(贝) item with two hands (虫).

贵姓[guìxìng] (honorific) family name; surname; last name - 208c

186e

贯 guàn — pass through

thread 毌 [guàn] + currency/shell 贝 [bèi]

Signifies a bundle of coins(贝) created by passing through(毌) a piece of thread through the hole in the middle.

* Qin Shi Huang(秦始皇, 259~210 BC) of the Qin dynasty(秦, 221~206 BC) had unified the mainland China for the first time and built the Great Wall. He also created metal coins with hole in the middle. This became the standard form of all Chinese currency.

* "毌" symbolizes a coin with string passing through the middle.

> 一贯[yīguàn] consistent - 223

186f

惯 guàn — be used to

heart 忄=心[28] [xīn] + pass through 贯 [guàn]

A habit is an action which someone does without thinking, thus from the heart(忄), by being used to do a same action for a long period of time; i.e put-

ting many coins into one bundle by passing through(贯) strings in each one of them.

> 习惯[xíguàn] habit; be used to - 182a

贝

Diagram for 贝

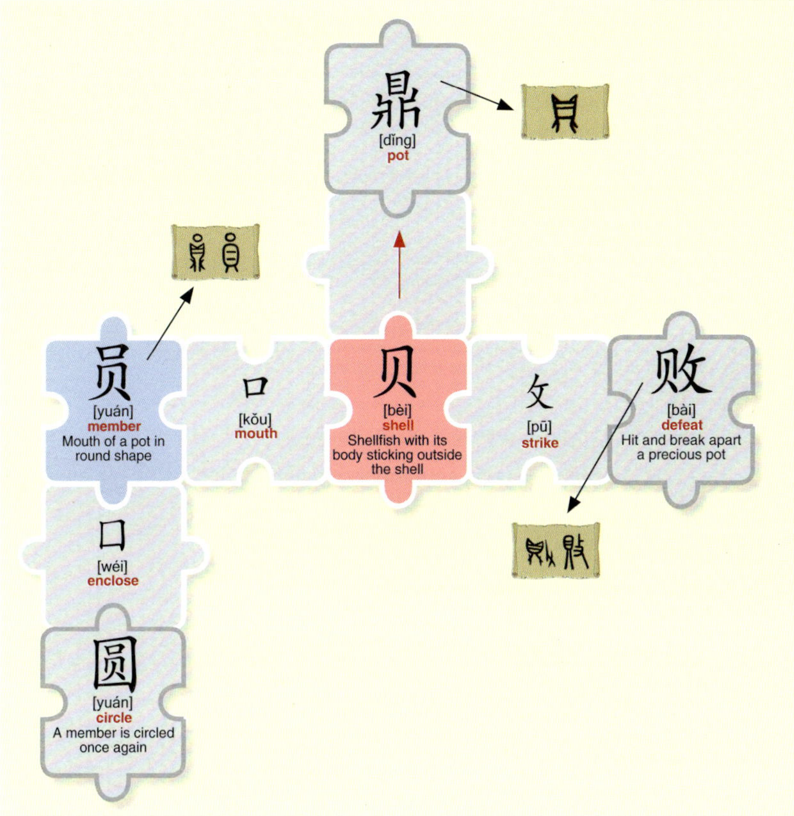

186

186g

败 bài

defeat

shell 贝 [bèi] → pot 鼎 [dǐng] + strike 攵 50 [pū]

In the ancient China, pots with decorated feet were used as a symbol of royals that was used in many special ceremonies. When defeated in war, enemies would destroy such pots(鼎) with heavy maces(攵).

* "鼎" is present on the ancient character, which is replaced with "贝" to simplify writing.

* In the ancient times of China, a variety of Chinese scripts were engraved on bronze-made bells or tripodal cauldrons. They were called "Bronze inscriptions."

打败[dǎ/bài] defeat; beat - 31c

186h 丶 ㄇ ㄇ 尸 吕 员 员

员 yuán

member

mouth 口[16][kǒu] + shell 贝 [bèi] → pot 鼎 [dǐng]

Used to signify circle from the shape of the mouth(口) in a pot(鼎). Now became to mean a member (as in "someone inside the circle(员)") or someone who takes part in a group.

* "鼎" is present on the ancient character, which is replaced with "贝" to simplify writing.

服务员 [fúwùyuán] service staff - 34b 159f	教员 [jiàoyuán] teacher - 50c
技术员 [jìshùyuán] technician - 51a 210f	委员 [wěiyuán] committee member - 96j

186i 丨 冂 冂 冂 冃 冃 冐 圎 圆 圆

圆 yuán

circle

enclose 囗[20][wéi] + member 员 [yuán]

When "员 [yuán]" became to mean a member or a person in a group, an encirclement "囗" is added to restore the meaning of circle or round.

186

辰

Diagram for 辰

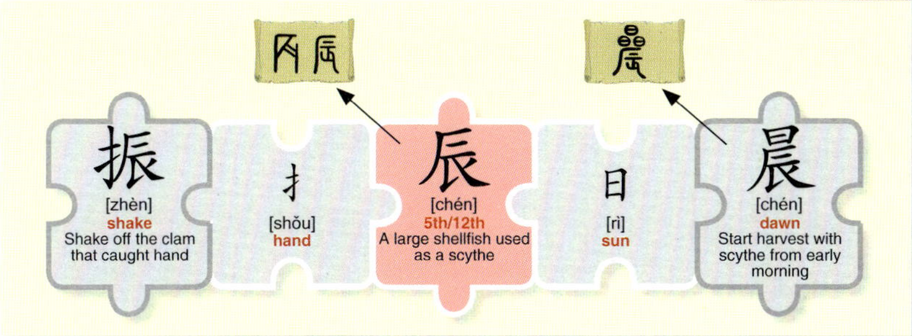

187 一 厂 厂 尸 尻 辰 辰

辰 chén **5th/12th**

The ancient script (called "inscriptions on bones and tortoise carapaces") shows a large clam with its body sticking out. The clam, with its large and strong shell, was used as a scythe in ancient times when harvesting. It is now defined as the fifth order of the twelve Chinese zodiacs. 187

187a 丨 冂 日 日 旦 尸 尸 戸 尼 晨 晨

晨 chén **dawn**

sun 日[218] [rì] + sickle/5th 辰 [chén]

Symbolizes a farmer starting his harvest with scythe(辰) since early in the morning when stars(日→晶) are still up.

* The ancient character shows three stars of light(晶) being made in the night instead of current sun (日).

早晨 [zǎochén] (early) morning - 218e

187b 一 十 扌 扩 扩 扩 护 振 振 振

振 zhèn **shake**

hand 扌=手[31] [shǒu] + clam/5th 辰 [chén]

Symbolizes a person shaking off the large clam(辰) that caught his hand(扌).

振动 [zhèndòng] vibrate; oscillate - 159d

毛

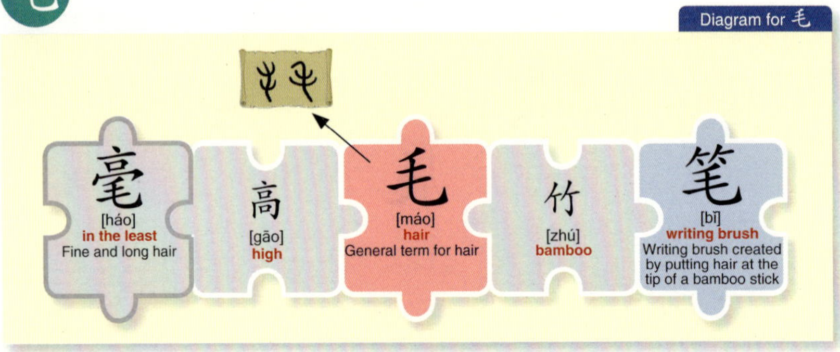

188

毛 máo

hair

Refers to any type of hair, be it human, animals, plants or even on fruits. Also used as unit of currency in modern China. (1毛 = 1/10元[73])

188 毛病[máobìng] fault; defect; illness - 81a
毛巾[máojīn] towel - 131
毛衣[máoyī] sweater - 130
羽毛球[yǔmáoqiú] badminton - 182 198b

188a

笔 bǐ

writing brush

bamboo 竹[216][zhú] + hair 毛[máo]

Symbolizes a brush for writing, created by attaching animal hair(毛) at the tip of a bamboo(竹) straw. Now used to refer to any stylus or writing tools including pen and pencil.

* The traditional character(筆) is a combination of brush(聿[37]) and bamboo(竹).

铅笔[qiānbǐ] (lead) pencil - 199a
钢笔[gāngbǐ] fountain pen - 165c

188b

毫 háo — in the least

high 高[gāo] + hair 毛 [máo]

Symbolizes fine and long(高) hair(毛), which is also used to mean not in the least – a negation to stress something even like a fine hair is not there at all.

* Simplified form of "高" is stressing length here.

毫无[háowú] not in the least - 80c　　丝毫[sīháo] (not) in the least - 132a

皮

Diagram for 皮

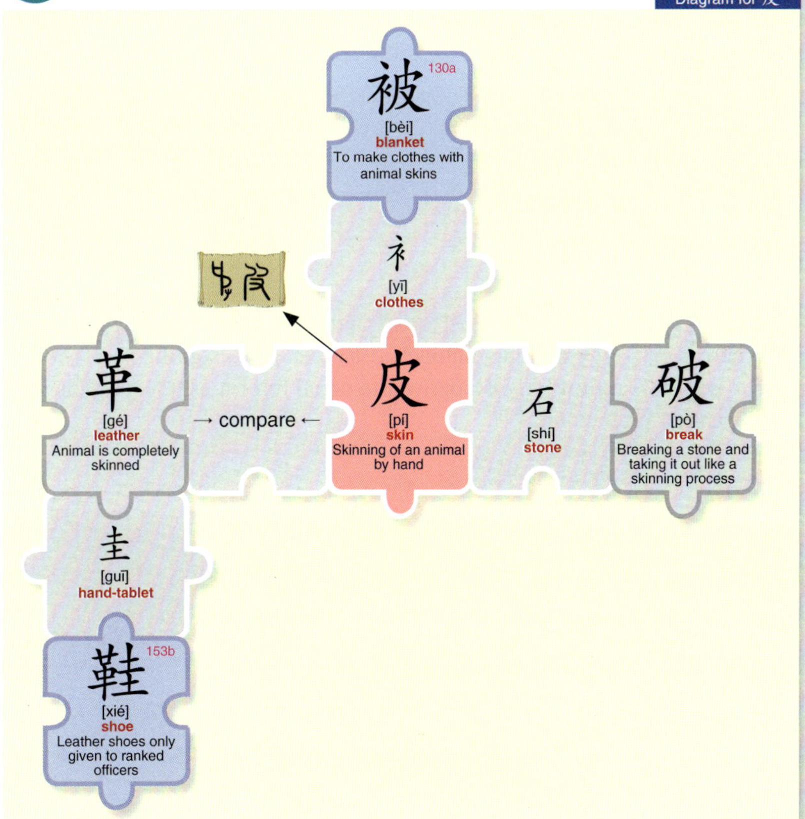

189

189 一 厂 广 皮 皮

皮 pí

skin

Symbolizes skinning of an animal using hand(又) tools, meaning unprocessed raw skin of animal.

皮革[pígé] leather; hide - 189b

189a 一 丆 丆 石 石 石⁻ 矿 矽 砂 破

破 pò

break

stone 石[197][shí] + skin 皮 [pí]

Symbolizes a stone(石) being broken apart and taken away like a skinning(皮) process with hand tools.

破坏[pòhuài] destroy; ruin - 152d

189b 一 十 艹 廿 廿 芇 芇 苎 革

189 **革** gé

leather; reform

An animal is cut in shape of "十[231][shí]" and its skin is removed completely. Whereas "皮[pí]" signifies untouched leather, "革" signifies a processed leather with furs removed. Also derived to mean reform as a leather changes its shape after processing.

改革[gǎigé] reform; reformation - 50b

韦

Diagram for 韦

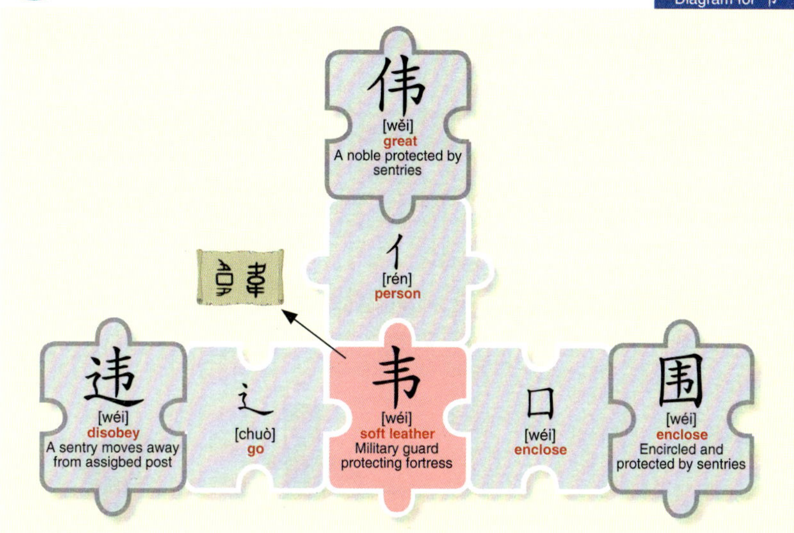

190 一 二 彐 韦 190

韦 wéi **soft leather**

The ancient character signifies an act of sentries crossing each other on duty by their two feet(止[53]) directing to the opposite. It also looks like an act of tanning soft hide which is stretched out by the two feet(止) each facing the opposite direction.

* By the present character, try to imagine an act of sentries holding their arms(韦) or a heavy tool (韦) which is used for tanning hide.

190a 丿 亻 亻 亻 伟 伟

伟 wěi **great**

person 亻[70][rén] + sentry/soft leather 韦 [wéi]

Only a person(亻) of great power may have sentries(韦) protecting him.

伟大[wěidà] great; mighty - 74

190b 丨 冂 冂 冃 冃 周 围

围 wéi

enclose

enclose 口[20] [wéi] + sentry/soft leather 韦 [wéi]

A castle is secured by enclosing(口) it with many sentries(韦).

周围 [zhōuwéi] surroundings - 154a

190c 一 二 亏 韦 韦 讳 违

违 wéi

disobey

sentry/soft leather 韦 [wéi] + go 辶[61] [chuò]

A sentry(韦) who moves away(辶) from his assigned post is disobeying the order.

违反 [wéifǎn] violate - 148a

191 角

Diagram for 角

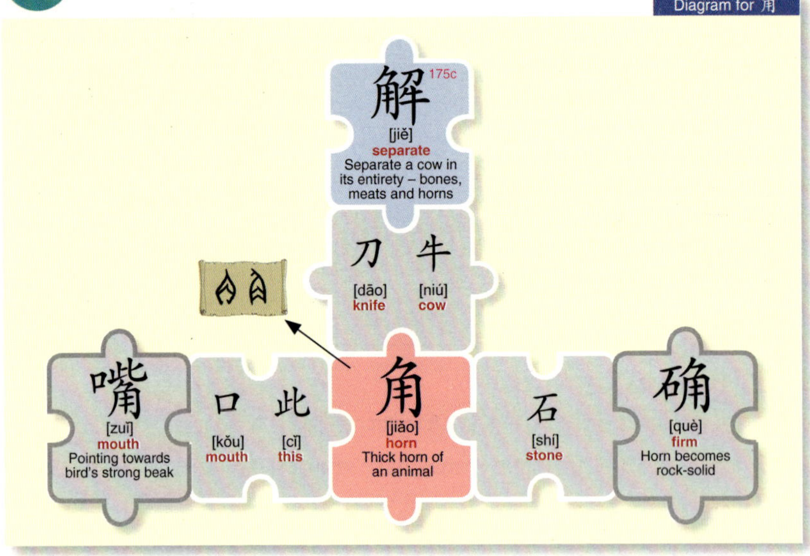

191 丿 ⺈ ⺈ 𠂊 角 角 角 角

角 jiǎo — horn; angle; quarter

Symbolizes thick horns present in animals as in cows and sheep. The angles of such horns are all different, and also became to mean a quarter (1/4). Due to its similar pronunciation, it is also used as an auxiliary unit of currency in China. (1角 = 1/10元[73] = 10分[119a])

191a

确 què — firm

stone 石[197][shí] + horn 角 [jiǎo]

The horns(角) of a deer are soft when they are growing, but become firm and strong like a stone(石) as time goes by.

* Deer's horn usually starts growing around April or May and is covered under fur-covered skin. The inside of horn is soft because it contains many blood vessels.

确实[quèshí] certain; true - 75a　　正确[zhèngquè] exactness; correct - 54

191b

嘴 zuǐ — mouth

mouth 口[16][kǒu] + this 此[88g][cǐ] + horn 角 [jiǎo]

Symbolizes pointing(此) towards the beak(口) of a bird, which is strong and protruded like a horn(角). Used when referring to things which are similar to a mouth in role or shape.

* "此" is a demonstrative pronoun, stressing the fact that "嘴" is used when pointing the mouth, as well as being a pronunciation guide.

嘴巴[zuǐba] cheek; mouth - 92a　　山嘴 the spur of a hill - 195 191b

191

肉

Diagram for 肉

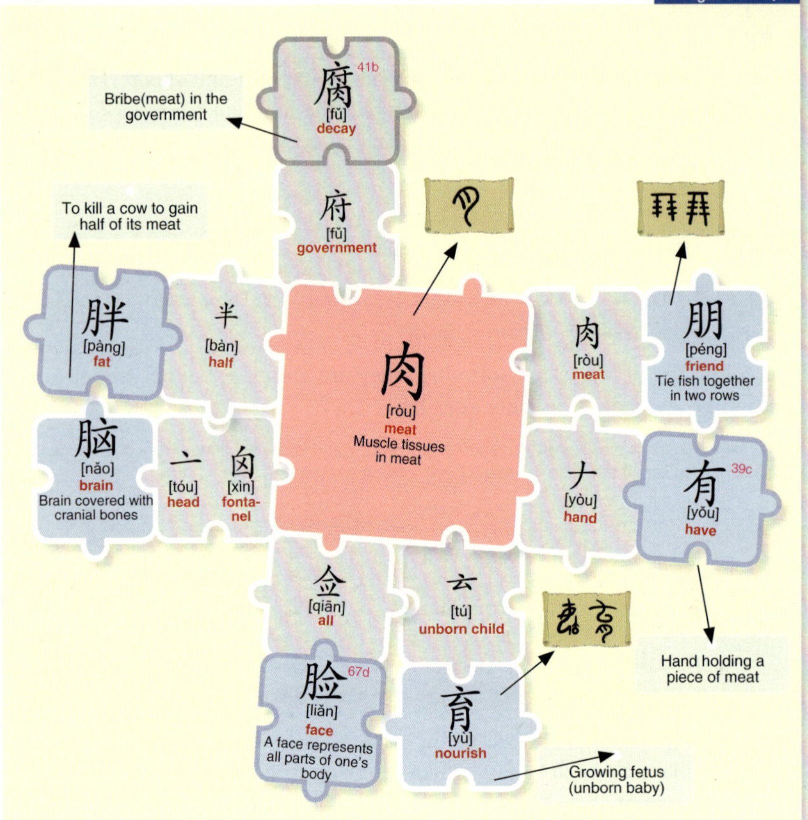

192

192

丨 冂 内 内 肉 肉

肉
ròu

meat; flesh

Represents the shape of tissues(仌) that appear when a meat is cut(冂).

* Changes into "moon 月[221] [yuè]" in most cases when combined with other characters.

羊肉 [yángròu] mutton - 171	牛肉 beef - 175 192

192a 丿 刀 月 月 刖 朋 朋 朋

朋 péng

friend

meat 月[221]→肉 [ròu] + meat 月→肉 [ròu]

Two similar-sized fish(肉) are tied together to form a two-row bundle of fish, representing people who share similar ideas becoming friends.

朋友[péngyou] friend - 34d　　小朋友[xiǎopéngyǒu] children - 235 34d

192b 丶 亠 𠫓 𠫓 产 育 育 育

育 yù

nourish

child 𠫓[202a][tú] + meat 月[221]→肉 [ròu]

This character comes from "growing." A child(𠫓) is nourished when his or her body grows in flesh(肉).

* "𠫓" is an upside-down form of "child 子[95][zǐ]," with identical meaning.

体育[tǐyù] sports; physical education - 29b　　教育[jiàoyù] education - 50c

192c 丿 刀 月 月 月` 月亠 月𠆢 脑 脑 脑

脑 nǎo

brain

meat 月[221]→肉 [ròu] + head 亠[1][tóu] + fontanel 㐫→囟[132h][xìn]

This character shows the image of brain in our head(亠), one of the most important organs in our human body(肉), covered(㐫) with cranial bones.

* We look at its traditional character(腦), "㐫" is a changed form of "囟[xìn]". A fontanel is a crown of a newly-born child's head. It has a very mild membrane pulsing whenever a baby breathes.

电脑 [diànnǎo] computer - 157a

192d 丿 刀 月 月 月' 月'' 月𠃊 月⺷ 胖

胖 pàng

fat

meat 月[221]→肉 [ròu] + half 半[175b][bàn]

In the old agricultural society, people used to kill a cow which was used for pulling a cart and for plowing. It was for deriving the meat(肉) out of it to offer for memorial rites. Killing of cow is considered as an action of great sacrifice with a special meaning because the half(半) of something great should be sacrificed to get something more important. Later on, the meaning of 'fat' was derived from its original meaning 'great.'

* "半[bàn]" is a scene of action where a cow (牛[175]) is slaughtered and halved(八[229]) into the two portions.

* When we look at a fat or overweight person, we may think, "how good it would be if he or she lost the half(半) of his or her flesh(肉)."

192

𠂤

Diagram for 𠂤

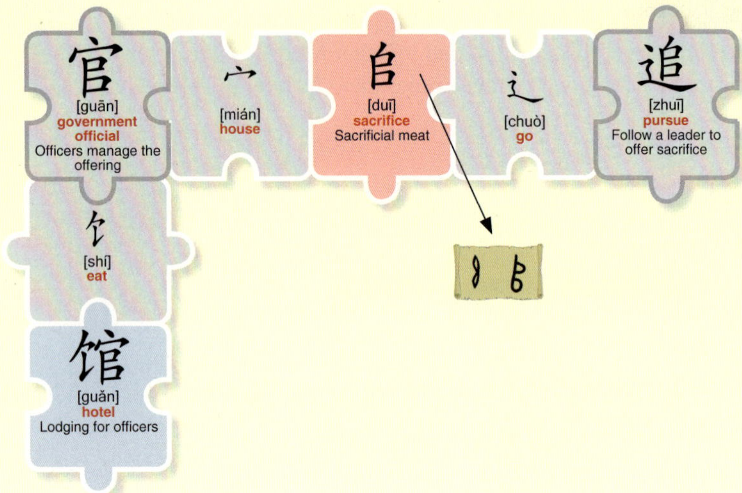

193

193

𠂤 duī

sacrifice

Symbolizes a piece of sacrificial meat used for ceremonies.

* The ancient character depicts shape of a meat, but this character is not used by itself.

193a

追 zhuī

pursue

sacrifice 𠂤 [duī] + go 辶[61] [chuò]

Symbolizes people pursuing(辶) a leader to offer sacrifice(𠂤) to God.

追求[zhuīqiú] pursue; seek - 203b

193b

官 guān

government official

house 宀[141] [mián] + sacrifice 㠯→𠂤 [duī]

Sacrificial offering was a major national event in ancient Chinese dynasties; government officials(宀) then managed the offering(𠂤) used in such events.

法官[fǎguān] judge - 94b

193c

丿 𠂉 饣 饣 饣 饣 饣 饣 饣 馆 馆

馆 guǎn

hotel

eat 饣=食[137][shí] + government official 官 [guān]

Symbolizes a place where travelling government officials(官) can rest and eat (饣), which in turn became to mean a public place used for official purposes. Due to the similar purpose, also became to mean hotels or lodges in general.

饭馆[fànguǎn] restaurant - 148b
图书馆[túshūguǎn] library - 206f 232d
旅馆[lǚguǎn] hotel - 63i
宾馆[bīnguǎn] hotel - 118e
大使馆[dàshǐguǎn] embassy - 74 35b

193

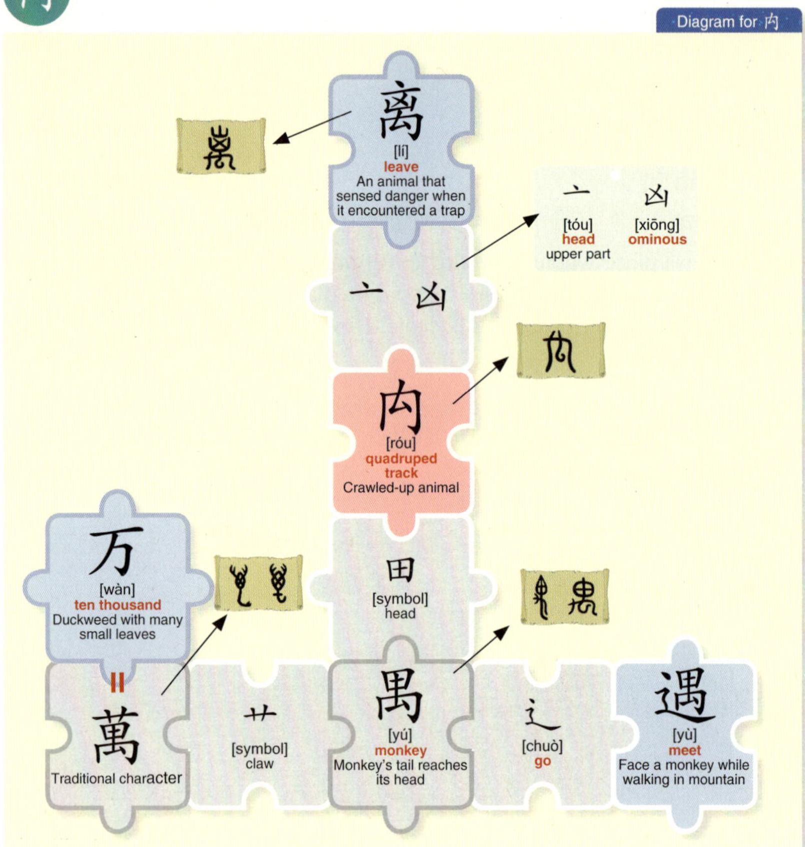

194

194

禸 róu — quadruped track

Symbolizes a rear shape of an animal crawled up with its tails rolled, or footprints of animals. It can also be used as an element to mean beast when combined with other characters.

194a

离 lí

leave

upper part/head 亠[1] [tóu] + ominous 凶 [xiōng] + beast/track 禸 [róu]

An animal(禸) feels something wrong(凶) after finding a trap with a camouflage covering(亠) while it's walking. It then leaves the place immediately – also derived to mean move away from a particular place or time.

* "凶" signifies a trap(凵) with an X-shaped(乂) opening, representing something that fell in.

离开 [líkāi] leave; depart from - 43a   脱离 [tuōlí] break away; secede - 72e

194b

禺 yú

monkey

head 田 [symbol] + beast/track 禸 [róu]

A long-tailed monkey(禸) sitting down has its tail reaching all the way up to its head(田).

194c

遇 yù

meet

monkey 禺 [yú] + go 辶[61] [chuò]

A person meets a monkey(禺) while walking in mountain trails(辶). Monkeys have always been animals very close to Chinese people over the history, like the popular book "The Journey to the West."

* The Journey to the West is an epic novel written by Wu Cheng'en(吴承恩, 1500 AD~1582) and published in the 1590s during the Ming Dynasty(明,1368 AD~1644), and is based on the true story about a monk travelling to India and bringing back a copy of Buddhist scripture.

遇到 [yù/dào] encounter; run into; come across - 112b

194d

万 wàn

ten thousand

Symbolizes duckweed which lives on water and has countless number of small leaves – then becoming to mean ten thousand.

* Traditional character(萬) represents a scorpion, with two claws(艹) and long tail(禺) that strikes its prey with poison. Since arthropods like scorpions are known to have many feet, it later became to mean ten thousand. Adding "worm 虫[184] [chóng]" back into this character(萬) restores the meaning of "scorpion 虿→蠆(Trad.) [chài]."

山

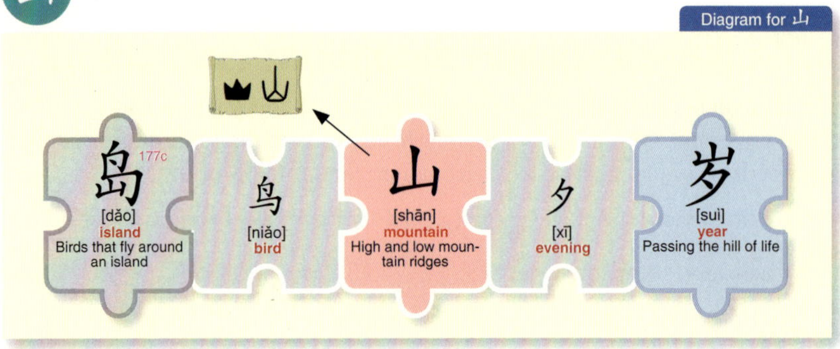

195 丨 山 山

山 shān

mountain

Represents a mountain with summit and ridges in different heights.

爬山[páshān] mountain climbing - 33c   山谷[shāngǔ] mountain valley - 196

195

195a 丨 山 山 岁 岁 岁

岁 suì

year

mountain 山 [shān] + evening 夕[222] [xī]

Evening(夕) represents the end of a day – signifies passing of a high mountain(山) in a trek of life and finalizing(夕) the past year.

我今年十三岁了。I am thirteen years old. - 113b 66 121a 231 223e 195a 168a

谷

Diagram for 谷

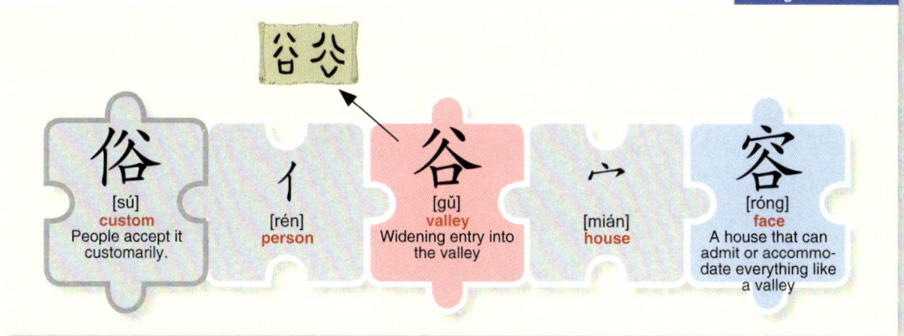

196

谷 gǔ

valley

valley 仌 [symbol] + mouth 口[16] [kǒu]

Symbolizes an entrance(口) of a valley(仌) which gets wider as it accepts more water down the way.

山谷[shāngǔ] mountain valley - 195 **196**

196a

容 róng

admit; face

house 宀[141] [mián] + valley 谷 [gǔ]

Symbolizes a house(宀) that is as big as a valley(谷) and can admit any amount of water that flows into it. Also derived to mean face, as a face can accept and react to all kinds of situations.

* The shape itself resembles a smiling face.

容易[róngyì] easy - 49c　　内容[nèiróng] content; substance - 64

196b

俗 sú

custom

person 亻[70] [rén] + valley 谷 [gǔ]

Like a valley(谷) which accepts all waters, customs represent something that's been customarily accepted(谷) and passed for long generation of people(亻).

风俗[fēngsú] custom - 213c

石

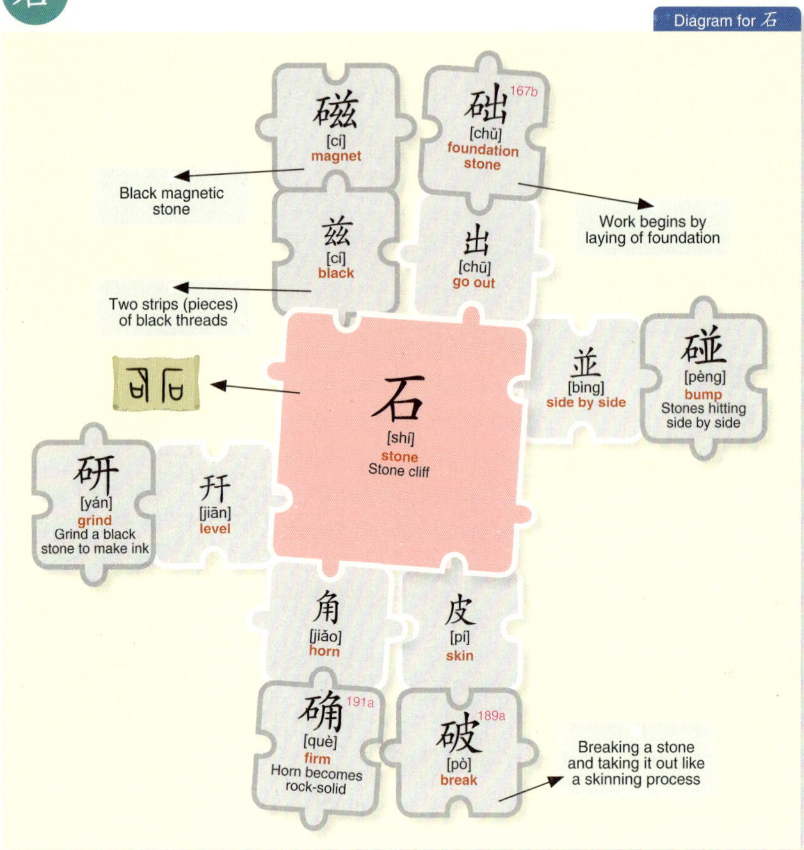

197

197 一 丆 不 石 石

石 shí **stone**

Derived to mean stone by symbolizing large boulders(口) forming cliffs(丆→厂[148]).

化石 [huàshí] fossil - 70a

197a

兹 cí

black

black 玄 [xuán] + black 玄 [xuán]

This character signifies the meaning of "dark" by the two strips of black thread(玄).

* The radical "玄" is a shape of turning over "thread 纟[132][sī]," and came to mean "dark" because it doesn't look thin.

197b

磁 cí

magnet

stone 石 [shí] + black 兹 [cí]

Symbolizes how a magnetic stone(石) is colored in black(兹).

磁带[cídài] magnetic tape - 131b

197c

碰 pèng

bump

stone 石 [shí] + side by side 並 [bìng]

197

Stones(石) that fall from cliffs have different lengths to hit the ground based on their weight and size; ultimately, only the similar-sized stones(石) will bump into each other side by side(並).

* "並" represents two people standing(立) side by side, same as "并[123][bìng]."

碰见[pèng/jiàn] meet (unexpectedly); bump into - 13

197d

研 yán

grind; research

stone 石 [shí] + level 幵 [jiān]

Chinese traditional ink was made by grinding a black stone(石) on top of inkstone(幵) with water. This character is derived to mean research, in the sense that academic research began by writing texts.

* "幵" symbolizes two shields(干[121]) put together in the front to make it flat.

研究[yánjiū] research - 230a　　科研[kēyán] scientific research - 164a

玉

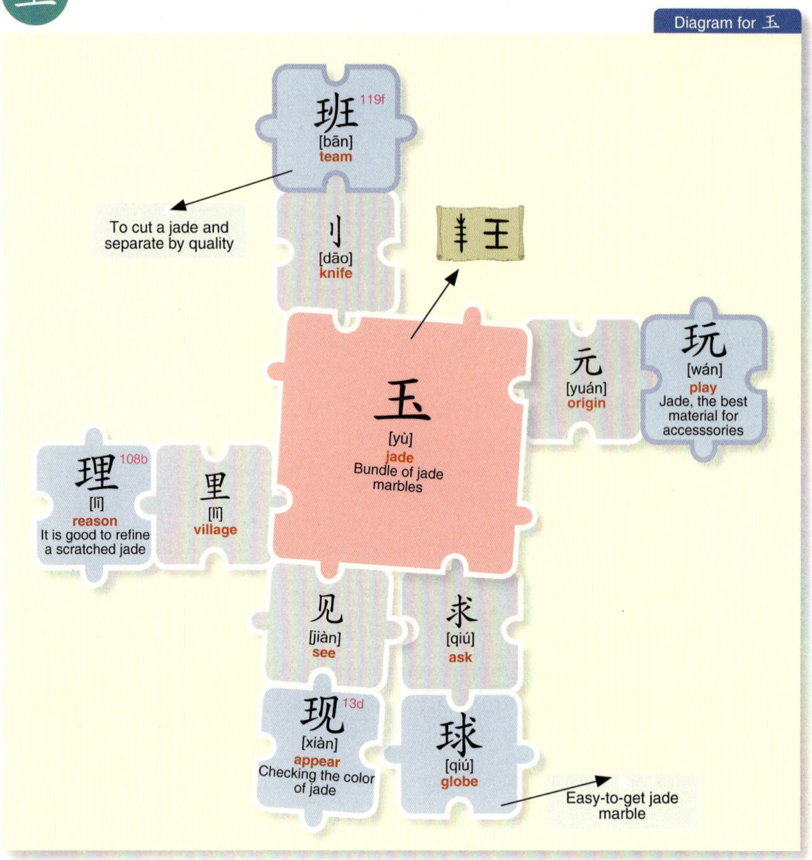

198

198 一 二 干 王 玉

玉 yù **jade**

A few jade marbles are made into a bundle by passing threads(丶) into the center hole.

* Usually changes its shape to "king 王[108][wáng]" when combined with other characters.

玉米[yùmǐ] corn - 138

198a　一 二 千 王 王˙ 王˙ 玗 玩

玩 wán

play

jade 王[108] → 玉 [yù] + origin 元[73] [yuán]

Symbolizes the fact that jade(玉) was the best(元) material to create women's favorite playing accessories.

* Chinese people started to make jade since the early stone ages. Jade has been used to be used as accessories since 500 B.C.

开玩笑[kāiwánxiào] joke; make fun of - 43a 78a　　玩儿[wánr] play - 71

198b　一 二 千 王 王˙ 玗 玗 玗 球 球 球

球 qiú

globe

jade 王[108] → 玉 [yù] + ask 求[203b] [qiú]

Jade(玉) marbles or globes were the most popular and easy-to-get(求) jade items in the ancient times.

打篮球[dǎlánqiú] play basketball - 31c 107c　　踢足球[tīzúqiú] play football - 49d 52
篮球[lánqiú] basketball - 107c　　排球[páiqiú] volleyball - 181a
月球[yuèqiú] the moon - 221　　足球[zúqiú] soccer; football - 52

198

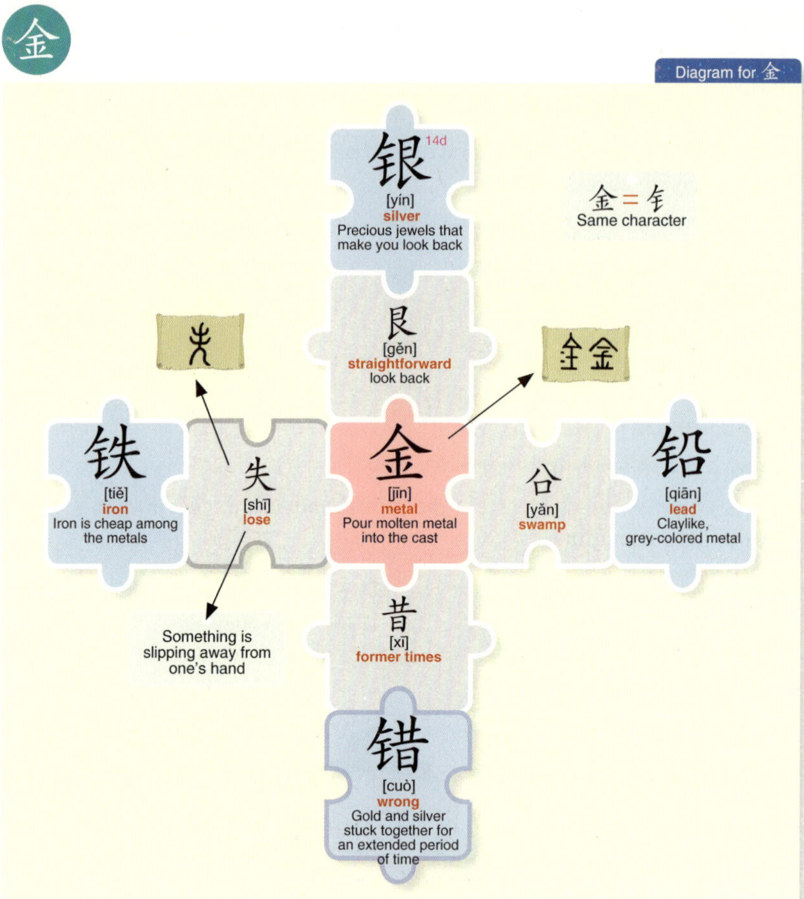

199 丿 人 亼 今 今 全 余 金

金 jīn

metal; gold

Metals(丶) taken from earth(土[152]) were melted and poured into the cast (亼[63f]). As well, became to represent gold as the first valuable metal – beautiful, easy to manipulate, does not rust – that attracted human attention.

* Gold is actually the earliest of metals to be used by humans, it first being used in Mesopotamia around 3.000 B.C.

合金[héjīn] alloy; compound metal - 65a

199a ノ 𠂉 𠂉 𠂉 钅 钅 钅 钅 铅 铅

铅 qiān — lead

metal 钅=金[jīn] + swamp 㕣 [yǎn]

Symbolizes lead, a metal(钅) with blueish grey color like a swamp(㕣).

* "㕣" represents clays opening up(八) and sucking in everything like a mouth(口) – when something falls into a swamp it becomes very difficult to take it out. See "公[93b]."

铅笔[qiānbǐ] (lead) pencil - 188a

199b ノ 𠂉 𠂉 𠂉 钅 钅 钅 钅 钅 钅 错 错 错

错 cuò — wrong

gold/metal 钅=金[jīn] + former times 昔[220][xī]

If gold(钅) and silver are stuck together for an extended period of time(昔), their materials start to flow to each other and mix. Such mix is considered wrong and inauspicious to happen to pure gold.

* In fact, gold(钅) and silver will diffuse into each other when left in contact for too long(昔).

不错[bùcuò] correct; right; not bad - 223a　错误[cuòwù] wrong; mistake; error - 22e

199

199c ノ 𠂉 𠂉 生 失

失 shī — lose

This character depicts an image of something which is slipping away from under one's hand(手[31]), and the meaning of 'to lose' is derived from it.

199d ノ 𠂉 𠂉 𠂉 钅 钅 钅 钅 铁 铁

铁 tiě — iron

metal 钅=金[jīn] + lose 失 [shī]

Iron is most used by the human beings. It is cheap(失) and easily available (失) among the metals(钅).

* Let us try to think that the character "lose 失 [shī]" has been changed to indicate the negative meaning.

地铁[dìtiě] subway; metro - 84a

工

Diagram for 工

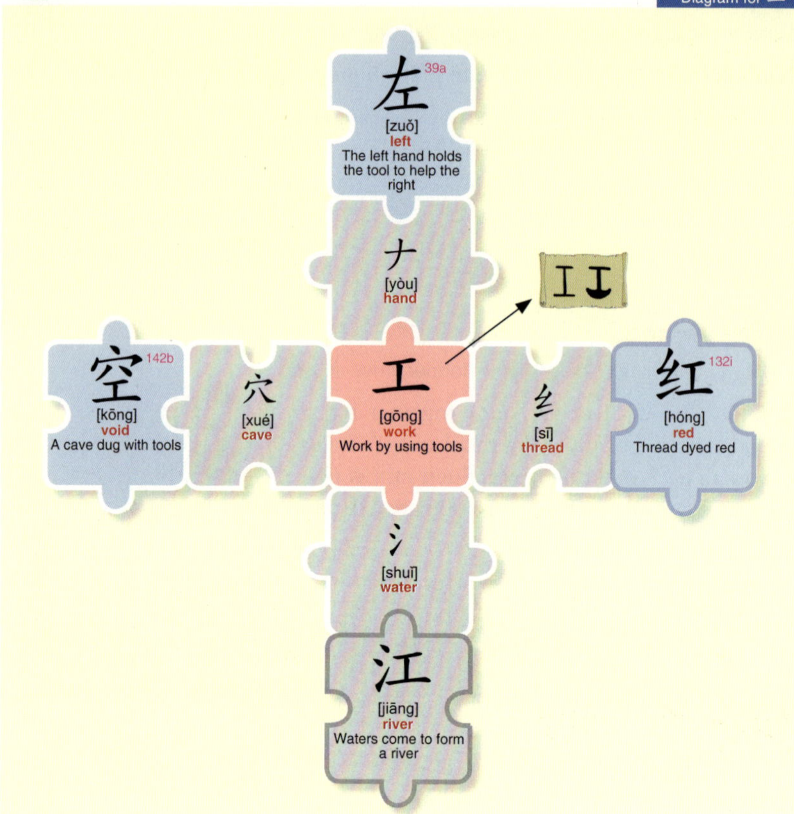

200

200 一 丅 工

工 gōng **work**

Symbolizes a tool used to make things or while performing sacrifice – work in general.

工作[gōngzuò] job; work - 234b
工厂[gōngchǎng] factory - 148
工人[gōngrén] worker; workman - 63
工业[gōngyè] industry - 223c
罢工[bà/gōng] strike; walk out - 94c

200a 丶 冫 氵 氵 汀 江

江 jiāng

river

water 氵[202] [shuǐ] + work 工 [gōng]

Small streams(氵) come together to form(工) a large river.

世界上最长的江是哪条江? Which river is the longest river in the world?
- 207f 63d 223f 10c 102 46b 200a 54b 147f 56c 200a

水

201

Diagram for 水

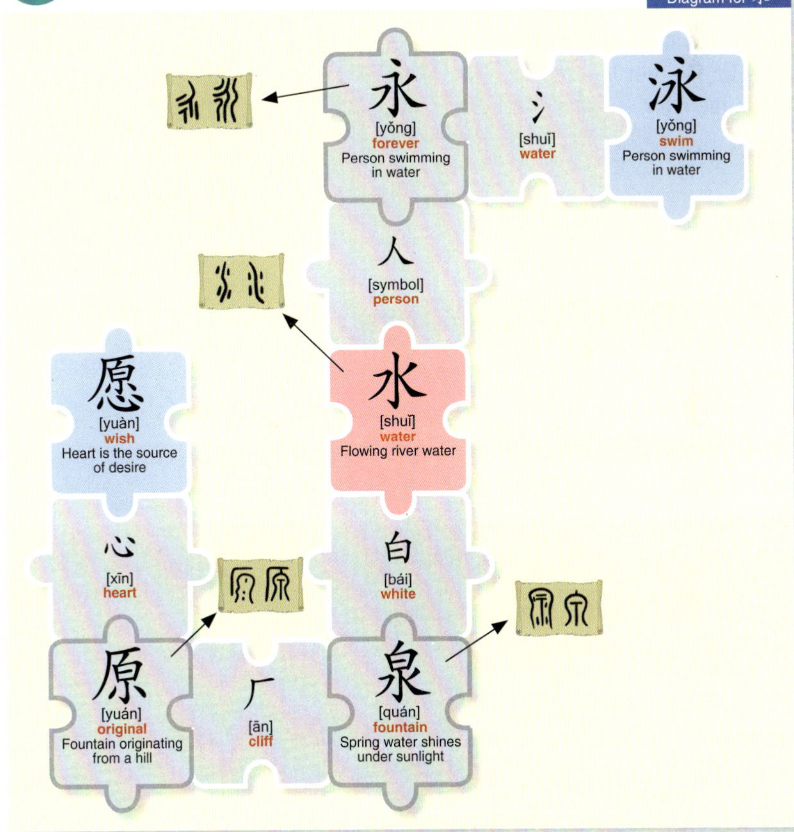

201

201

丨 亅 水 水 (stroke order)

水 shuǐ

water

Symbolizes water by representing water flowing in rivers(水).

水果[shuǐguǒ] fruit - 210g
水平[shuǐpíng] horizontal; level - 122
汽水[qìshuǐ] carbonated drinks; soda (pop) - 204a
热水瓶[rèshuǐpíng] thermos; vacuum bottle - 158f 123a

201a

永 yǒng

forever

person 丶→人[63] [symbol] + water 水 [shuǐ]

The character was initially used to symbolize a person(丶 →人) swimming in river(水), but later derived to mean forever as in things floating endlessly down the river.

永远[yǒngyuǎn] forever - 73d

201b

泳 yǒng

swim

water 氵[202] [shuǐ] + forever 永 [yǒng]

As "永" came to mean forever, water(氵) is added to restore the meaning of swimming.

游泳[yóu/yǒng] swim - 161b

201c

泉 quán

fountain

white 白[134] [bái] + water 水 [shuǐ]

Water(水) springing in fountain between stones is shining(白) under sunlight.

201d

原 yuán

original

cliff 厂[148] [ān] + fountain 泉 [quán]

All rivers originate from a small source fountain(泉) in between boulders located in high grounds(厂).

* Note that the water(水) below "泉" is simplified into "small 小[235][xiǎo]."

原来[yuánlái] original; former - 212d　　原谅[yuánliàng] excuse; forgive - 2b

201e　　一 厂 厂 厂 历 历 历 原 原 原 原 愿 愿 愿

愿 yuàn

wish

original 原 [yuán] + heart 心[28][xīn]

Signifies how human desire or wish originates(原) from the heart(心).

愿意[yuànyi] be willing; be ready - 21b　　愿望[yuànwàng] desire; wish - 5c

氵

Diagram for 氵

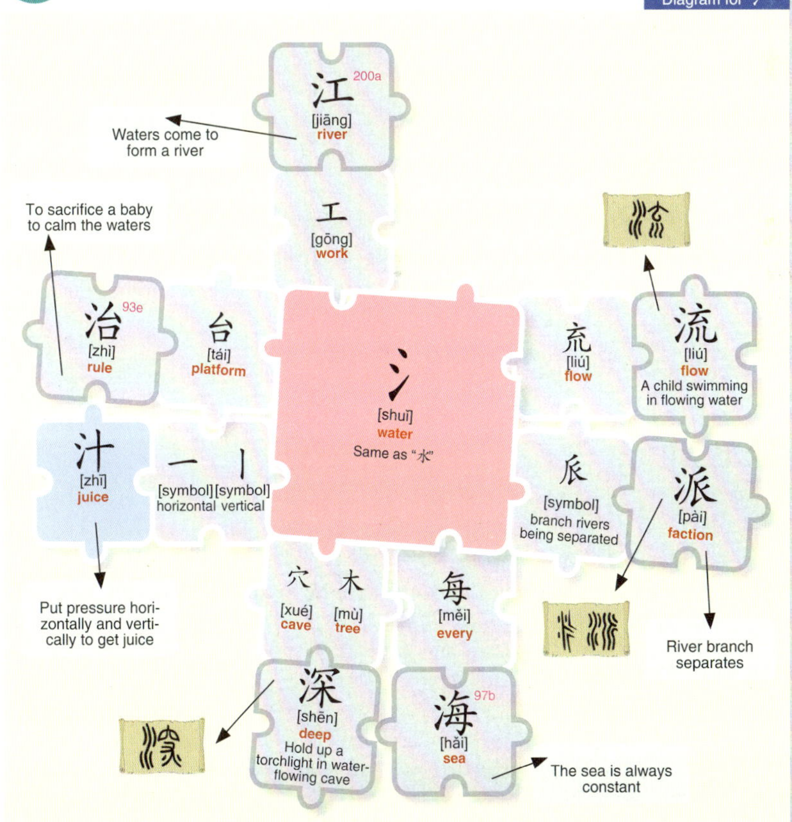

202

202

氵 shuǐ **water**

A different form of "water 水[201][shuǐ]" which is used only in combination with other characters.

202a

流 liú **flow**

water 氵[shuǐ] + flow 㐬 [liú]

"㐬[liú]," which symbolizes a child playing in flowing water, is not used by itself. Therefore water(氵) is added to restore the original meaning of water flowing.

* "㐬" symbolizes a child(𠫓[192b][tú]) swimming in flowing water(stream 川 [chuān]).

交流[jiāoliú] exchange; interchange - 1a　　流利[liúlì] fluent; smooth - 119h

202b

派 pài **faction; dispatch**

water 氵[shuǐ] + branch rivers being separated 𠂢 [symbol]

Symbolizes small branch rivers separating(𠂢) from the main stream(氵), which came to mean factions or the act of dispatching someone to another place.

教派 religious sect - 50c 202b
你是谁派来的? Who dispatched you here? - 69a 54b 178b 202b 212d 46b

202c

深 shēn **deep**

water 氵[shuǐ] + cave 穴 → 穴[142][xué] + tree 木[210][mù]

Symbolizes a man holding(又[34]) torch fire(火[158]) inside a deep, dark cave (穴) with water(氵) flowing on the floor.

* "木" is a changed form of person holding(又) a fire(火).

深刻[shēnkè] deep; profound - 4a　　深入[shēnrù] go deep into - 63e

202d

汁 zhī

juice

water 氵[shuǐ] + horizontal 一 [symbol] + vertical 丨 [symbol]

This character depicts the image of putting pressure horizontally(一) and vertically(丨) in order to squeeze juice(氵) from fruit.

果汁[guǒzhī] fruit juice - 210g

氺

Diagram for 氺

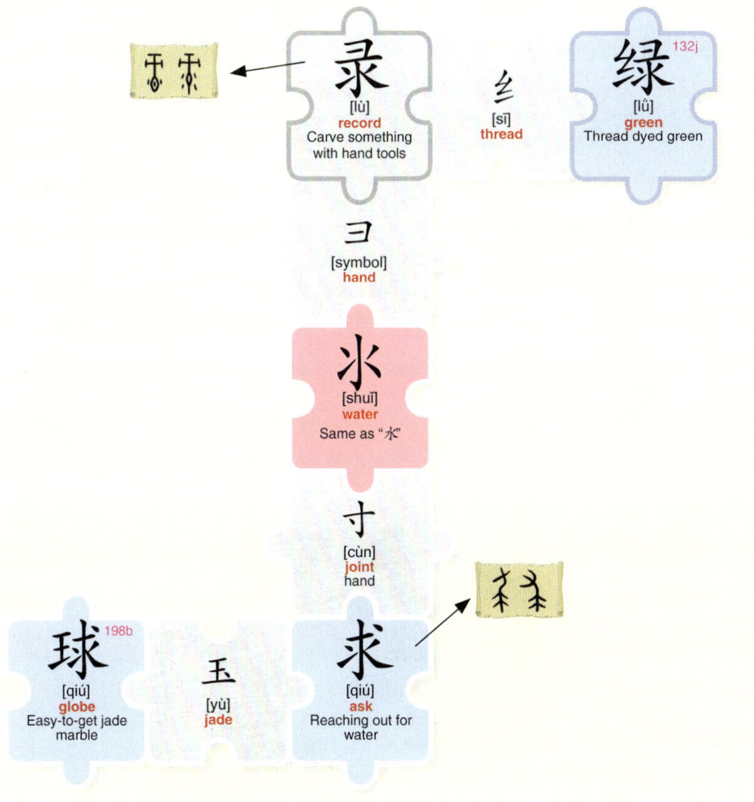

203

丨 丬 丬 氺 氺

203 **203**

氺 shuǐ — water

A different form of "water 水[201][shuǐ]" which is used only in combination with other characters. Occurrence is rare.

203a ㇇ ㇇ 彐 寻 寻 寻 录 录

录 lù — record

hand ヨ → ヨ[36][symbol] + water 氺 [shuǐ]

Ancient inscriptions show carving or recording something on woods by hand (ヨ), and "氺" does not seem to suggest water but rather wood particles spraying outward during carving.

录音[lù/yīn] sound recording - 21
记录[jìlù] record - 82b
录像[lù/xiàng] picture recording; videotape - 174c

203b 一 十 寸 才 求 求 求

求 qiú — ask; seek

hand/joint 寸[40][cùn] + water 氺 [shuǐ]

Symbolizes hands(寸) to get water(氺) – therefore meaning to seek or ask for water.

* The ancient character shows a hand(寸) reaching out in order to find valuable medicines.

要求[yāoqiú] ask; demand - 170b
请求[qǐngqiú] ask; request - 135c
乞求[qǐqiú] beg for - 83a
追求[zhuīqiú] pursue; seek - 193a

气

Diagram for 气

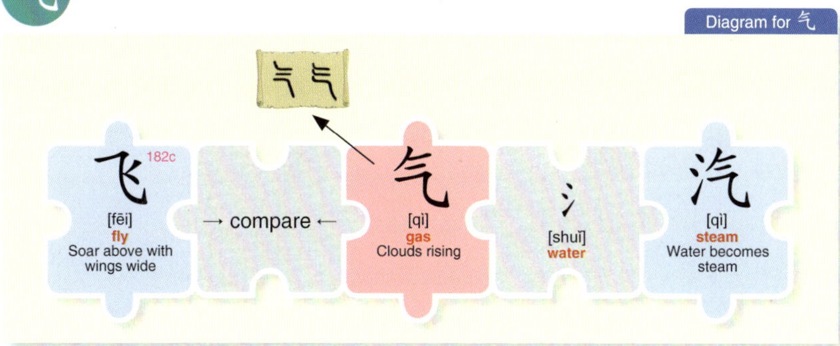

204

气 qì

gas; air; energy

Symbolizes clouds or water vapor rising up in the air – derived to mean air or gas in general, or a term for energy.

不客气[búkèqi] impolite; you're welcome - 223a 57b　天气[tiānqì] weather - 74b 204
生气[shēng/qì] get angry - 208　客气[kèqi] polite; courteous - 57b
空气[kōngqì] air; atmosphere - 142b
暖气[nuǎnqì] central heating; heating installation - 33b
气候[qìhòu] climate; weather - 111b

204a

汽 qì

steam

water 氵[202] [shuǐ] + gas 气 [qì]

Water(氵) becomes form of air(气) – steam – and rises upward.

公共汽车[gōnggòngqìchē] bus - 93b 43c 124　出租汽车[chūzūqìchē] taxi; taxicab - 167a 139d 124
汽车[qìchē] car; vehicle - 124　汽水[qìshuǐ] carbonated drinks; soda (pop) - 201

雨

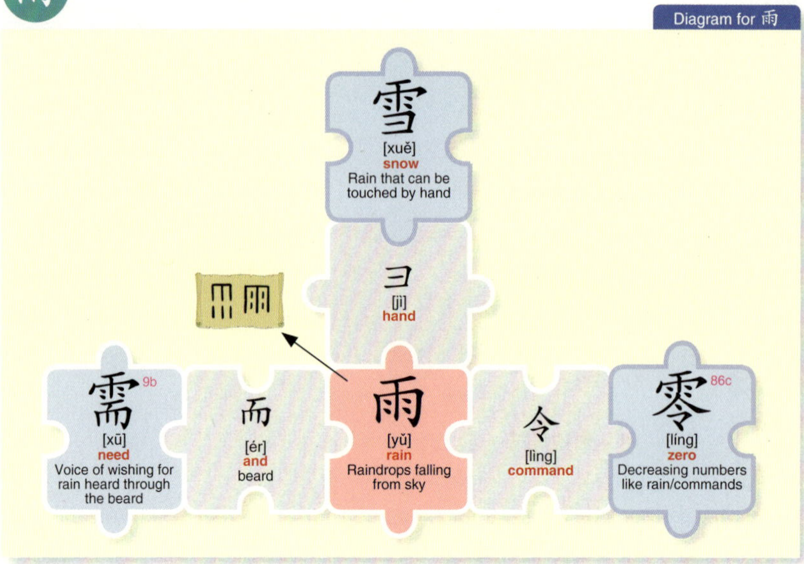

205

205 一 丆 门 帀 币 雨 雨 雨

雨 yǔ

rain

Combination of raindrops(丶) falling(巾) from the sky(一) – meaning rain.

下雨[xiàyǔ] rain - 223g　　雨衣[yǔyī] raincoat; waterproof - 130

205a 一 丆 门 帀 币 雨 雨 雨 雪 雪 雪

雪 xuě

snow

rain 雨 [yǔ] + hand 彐[36] [jì]

A somewhat poetic expression; snow is a form of rain(雨) that can be touched by hand(彐).

雪花[xuěhuā] snowflake - 70b

Diagram for 冫

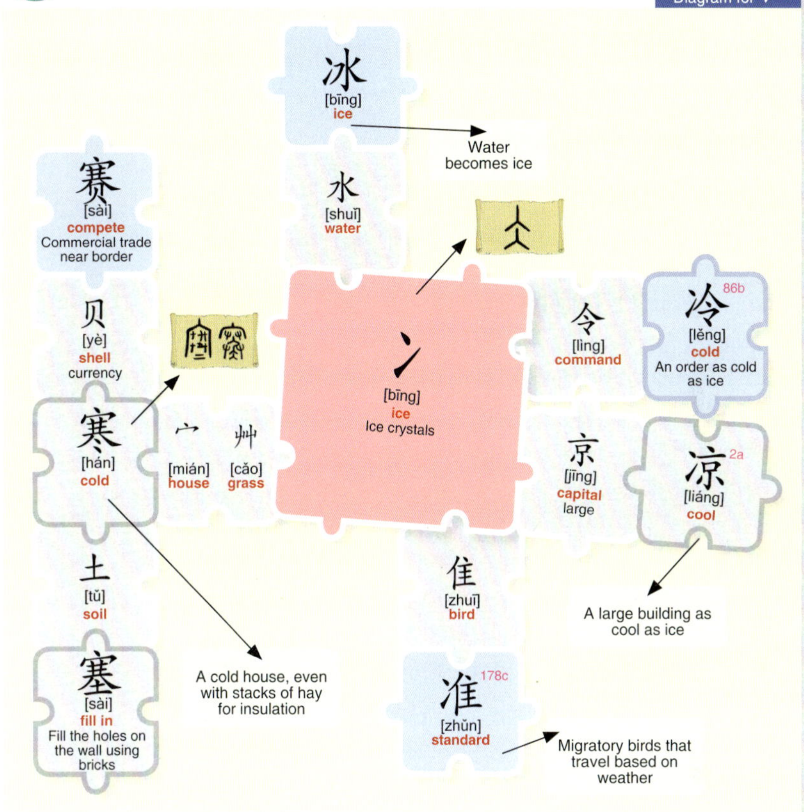

206

206

冫
bīng

ice

The ancient character used to describe ice by putting together two shapes of ice crystals. Modern reform simplified the crystal into a simple dot(丶), and is used only in combination with other characters to add meaning of coldness or freezing.

206

206a

丶 冫 冫 汌 沙 冰

冰 bīng

ice

ice 冫 [bīng] + water 水[201] [shuǐ]

As temperature drops below zero, water(水) becomes ice(冫).

冰箱[bīngxiāng] icebox; refrigerator - 216a　　滑冰[huá/bīng] ice skating - 29a

206b

丶 丶 宀 宀 宀 宀 宑 宑 宑 寒 寒 寒

寒 hán

cold

house 宀[141] [mián] + grass 艹[207] → 艸 [cǎo] + ice 冫 [bīng]

Symbolizes how ice(冫) cold wind still blows into a house(宀), even when the inside is insulated by stacks of hay(共→茻).

* The ancient character shows a person(人[63]) shivering in cold(冫) wind, in the midst of hay(茻) put inside of house(宀).

寒假[hánjià] winter vacation - 34k　　寒冷[hánlěng] cold; frigid - 86b

206c

丶 丶 宀 宀 宀 宀 宑 宑 宑 寒 寒 寒 塞

塞 sài

fill in; fort

house 宀[141] [mián] + grass 艹[207] → 艸 [cǎo] + soil 土[152] [tǔ]

Bricks, created by mixing hays(共→茻) with clay(土), are used to fill in the gaps and holes in a house(宀). Derived to mean fort, as forts fill in and guard the nation's border to protect people inside.

206d

丶 丶 宀 宀 宀 宀 宑 宑 宑 寒 寒 寒 寨 赛

赛 sài

compete

fort 塞 [sài] + currency/shell 贝[186] [bèi]

A border fortress(塞) between two nations attracts merchants and traders to buy and sell goods from each nation. Symbolizes how people are trying to compete in order to earn the money(贝).

* Instead of "土[152]" in the bottom of character, "塞," the character "贝" meaning money is inserted.

比赛[bǐsài] match; contest; game - 88a

冫

Diagram for 冬

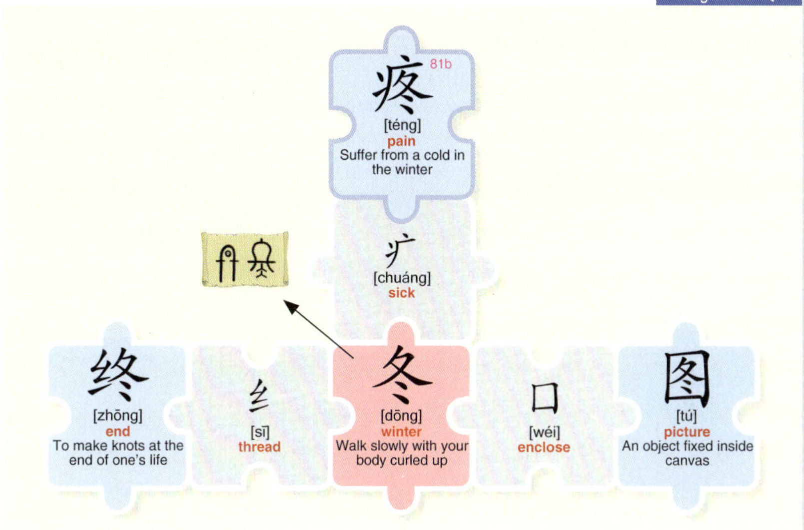

206e ノ ク 夂 冬 冬

冬 dōng

winter

walk slowly 夂[56][zhǐ] + ice 冫 [bīng]

In the bitter cold(冫) of winter, people tend to curl up and walk slow(夂).

* Its ancient character has an image of knots made at both ends of a thread. It describes 'winter' because everything ends its growth in the season of winter.

冬天[dōngtiān] winter - 74b

206f 丨 冂 冂 冈 冈 图 图 图

图 tú

picture

enclose 口[20][wéi] + winter 冬 [dōng]

Symbolizes a picture or a drawing, by an object enclosed(口) inside a canvas and staying still as if frozen(冬).

* "冬" depicts a situation that all things are frozen in winter meaning the stoppage or discontinuation of life.

地图[dìtú] map - 84a
企图[qǐtú] attempt; seek; try - 53b
图书馆[túshūguǎn] library - 232d 193c

206g

终 zhōng

end

thread 纟[132] [sī] + winter 冬 [dōng]

The character, "冬[dōng]" used to mean 'to end or to finish' by making knots at the ends of thread, but its meaning was transformed into its original meaning 'winter' by addition of a thread(纟).

终于[zhōngyú] at last; finally - 121d

207

艹

Diagram for 艹

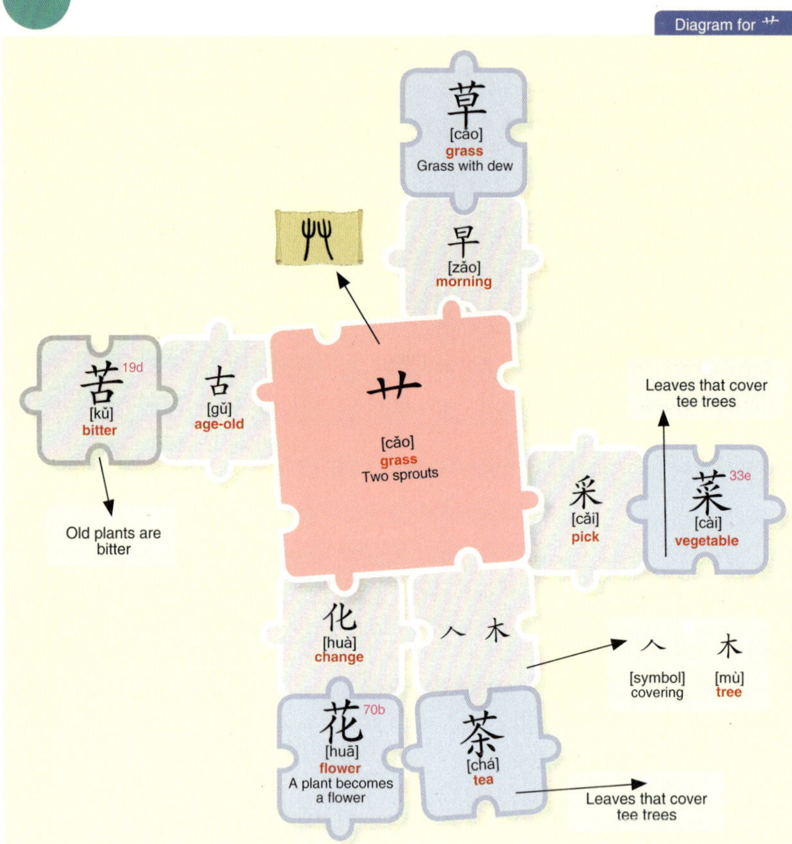

207

一 十 艹

艹 cǎo grass

Simplified form of sprouts or grass(艸) formed by combining two sprouts(屮). Used only in combination with other characters and usually placed on top of a character.

207a

一 十 艹 艹 节 芇 苜 莒 草

草 cǎo grass

grass 艹 [cǎo] + morning 早[218e] [zǎo]

Grass(艹) on the field shining with the morning sun(早).

草地[cǎodì] lawn - 84a　　草原[cǎoyuán] grassland - 201d

207b

一 十 艹 ⺾ 艾 苂 苓 茶 茶

茶 chá tea

grass 艹 [cǎo] + covering 𠆢 [symbol] + tree 木[210] [mù]

Symbolizes the making of tea by processing leaves(艹) that cover(𠆢) the tea trees(木).

* Tea originates from the Szechuan(四川) region of China, and spread to all other regions.
* Part below "艹" is a variation of "余[147a]." Take note of how either side stokes of "木" are separated.

红茶[hóngchá] black tea - 132i

207

艹

Diagram for 艹

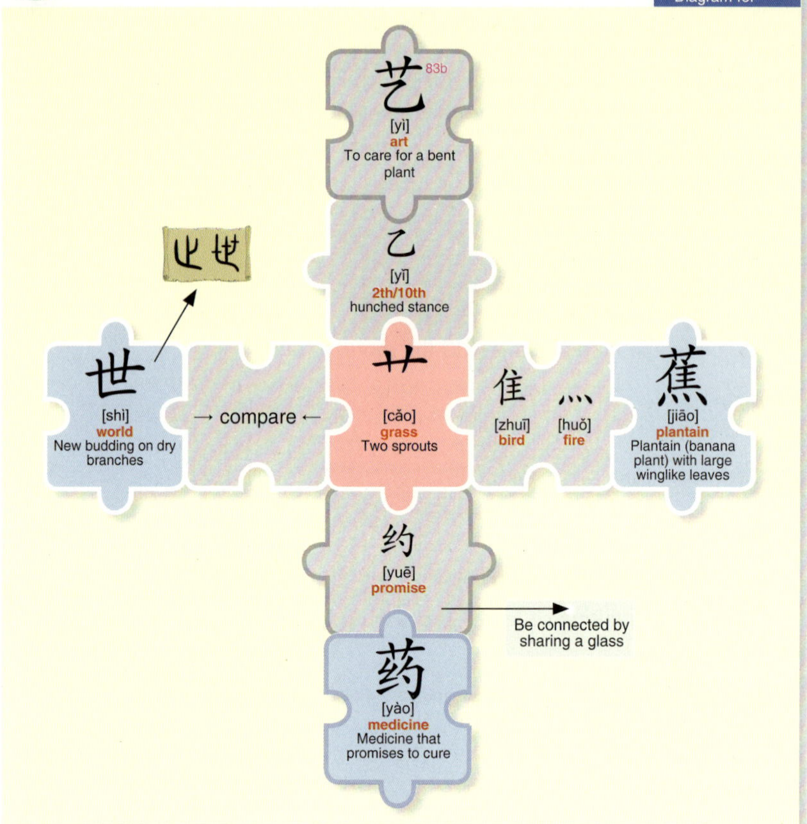

207

207c

蕉 jiāo

plantain

grass 艹 [cǎo] + bird 隹[178] [zhuī] + fire 灬 = 火[158] [huǒ]

Plantain is a perennial plant with a soft grasslike(艹) stem and large leaves like wing of a bird(隹). As years pass, the stems above ground may die(灬) out but the root still survives. Also refers to banana, a type of plantain plant.

* "灬" has a meaning to destroy something by burning; therefore adds meaning of death to plantain's stems and leaves.

香蕉 [xiāngjiāo] banana - 139c

207d 纟 纟 纟 约 约 约

约 yuē

promise

thread 纟[132][sī] + ladle 勺[46a][sháo]

Symbolizes a ceremony of sharing a glass of wine(勺) with a promise to be together for the rest of life, thereby connecting(纟) the bride and groom in a covenant.

* Sharing of wine in Chinese traditional weddings signifies a promise, an act originating from a blessing for many children.

约会[yuēhuì] appointment - 66c

207e 一 十 艹 艹 艺 艺 药 药 药

药 yào

medicine

grass 艹 [cǎo] + promise 约 [yuē]

A doctor hands out natural medicine(艹) to a patient with promise(约) that it will cure him or her. The meaning of this character is derived from such a situation.

* In Chinese medicine, most ingredients are herbs and plants(艹).

中药[zhōngyào] Chinese medicine - 232a

207f 一 十 廿 廿 世

世 shì

world; lifetime

Symbolizes new sprouts(屮) budding out on a dry branch in spring, signifying the beginning of life in a new world.

世界[shìjiè] world - 63d　　世纪[shìjì] century - 82c

207

生

Diagram for 生

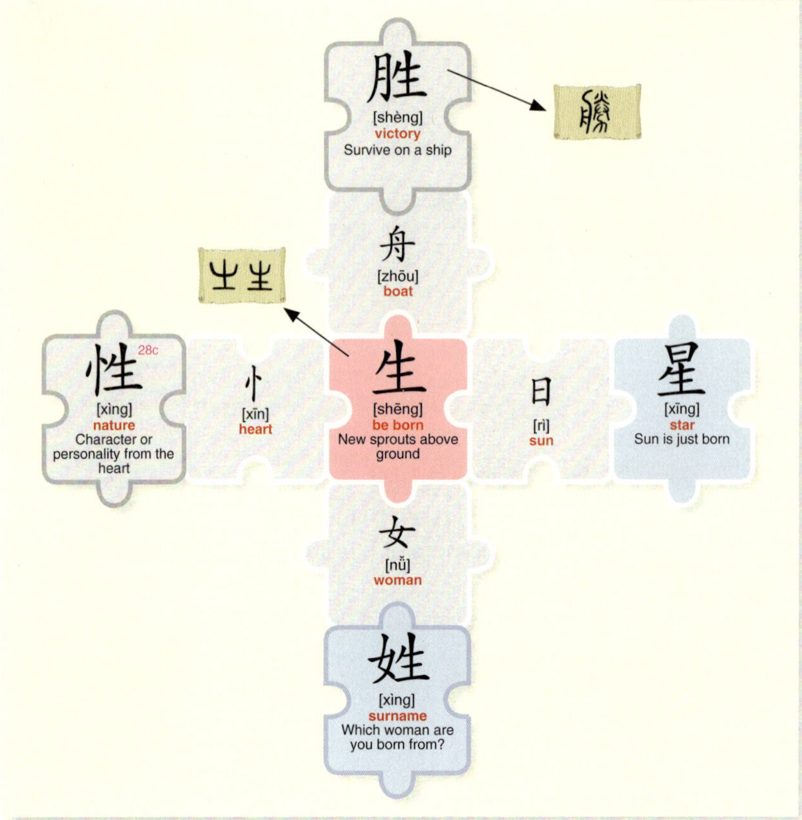

208

208 ノ 𠂉 𠂉 牛 生

生 shēng **be born; life**

New sprouts(屮[207]) start growing above ground(土[152]) – representing birth and life.

先生[xiānsheng] teacher - 71d
学生[xuésheng] student - 95a
医生[yīshēng] doctor - 111a
生病[shēng/bìng] get sick - 81a
生日[shēngrì] birthday - 218
生气[shēng/qì] get angry - 204
发生[fāshēng] happen; occur; arise - 34f
留学生[liúxuéshēng] student studying abroad - 87d 95a

生产[shēngchǎn] produce - 8d
生词[shēngcí] new word - 18f
生活[shēnghuó] live; life - 24c
先生[xiānsheng] teacher - 71d

208a

胜 shèng

victory

boat 月[221]→舟[125][zhōu] + life/be born 生 [shēng]

Victory is achieved if you are alive(生) on a battleship(舟) with nowhere to run.

* The ancient character shows fierce(力[159]) fighting of men with torchlights(火[158]) on their hands on a ship(舟), stressing that victory is achieved through a hard battle.

胜利[shènglì] win; victory; triumph - 119h
名胜[míngshèng] scenic spot - 222c

208b

星 xīng

star

sun 日[218][rì] + be born 生 [shēng] 208

Stars are represented as a baby sun(日) which was just born(生).

星期[xīngqī] week - 44b
星期日[xīngqīrì] Sunday - 218

208c

姓 xìng

surname

woman 女[96][nǚ] + be born 生 [shēng]

Back in the ancient maternal society, a person was given a surname that identified which woman(女) he or she was born(生) from.

贵姓[guìxìng] (honorific) family name; surname; last name - 186d
老百姓[lǎobǎixìng] common people; ordinary people - 100a 134a
姓名[xìngmíng] full name - 222c

丰

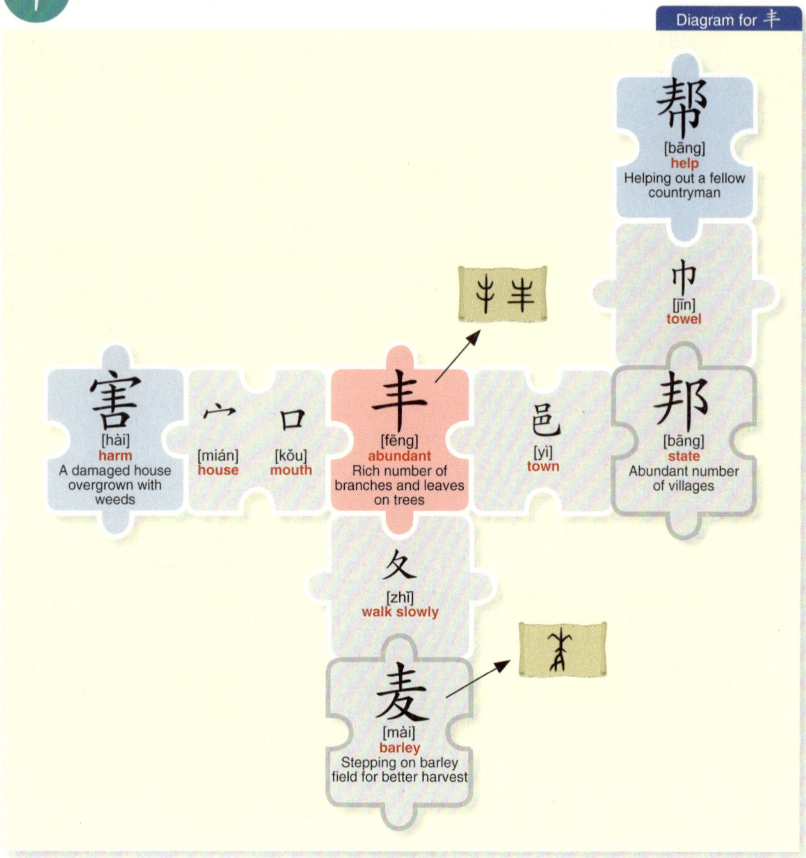

209

209 一 二 三 丰

丰 fēng

abundant

Signifies how leaves and branches are abundant in trees.

丰富 [fēngfù] abundant; rich; plentiful - 163a

209a 一 二 三 丰 丰⺋ 邦

邦 bāng

state

abundant 丰 [fēng] + town 阝[147] → 邑[92d] [yì]

Signifies that there are an abundant(丰) number of villages(邑) in which they form together to create a nation or state.

* When "hill 阝[fù]" is placed on right side of a character, it means the same as "邑."

联邦[liánbāng] federation; union - 10e

209b

一 二 三 丰 丰 邦 邦 帮 帮

帮 bāng

help

state 邦 [bāng] + towel 巾[131] [jīn]

Symbolizes how people of the same nation(邦) come together to help each other with towels(巾) wrapped around their head in times of distress.

帮助[bāngzhù] help; assist - 224b　　帮忙[bāng/máng] help - 5b

209c

一 二 十 キ 主 声 麦

麦 mài

barley

abundant 丰 [fēng] + walk slowly 夂[56] [zhǐ]

When growing barley, the field must be stepped (treaded) in order to prevent young barley sprouts from freezing to death. This is symbolized by slowly walking(夂) on the barley field for an abundant(丰) harvest later year. 209

小麦[xiǎomài] wheat - 235

209d

丶 丶 宀 宀 宀 宇 宝 宝 害 害

害 hài

harm

house 宀[141] [mián] + abundant 丰 [fēng] + mouth 口[16] [kǒu]

This letter has the image of cursing with one's mouth(口) wishing that the house(宀) of one's enemy would be overgrown(丰) with weeds. Although the enemy's house is located far away and beyond the reach of one's hands, its overgrown weeds may indicate that the enemy may have already been damaged.

害怕[hài/pà] be afraid; be scared - 134c

木

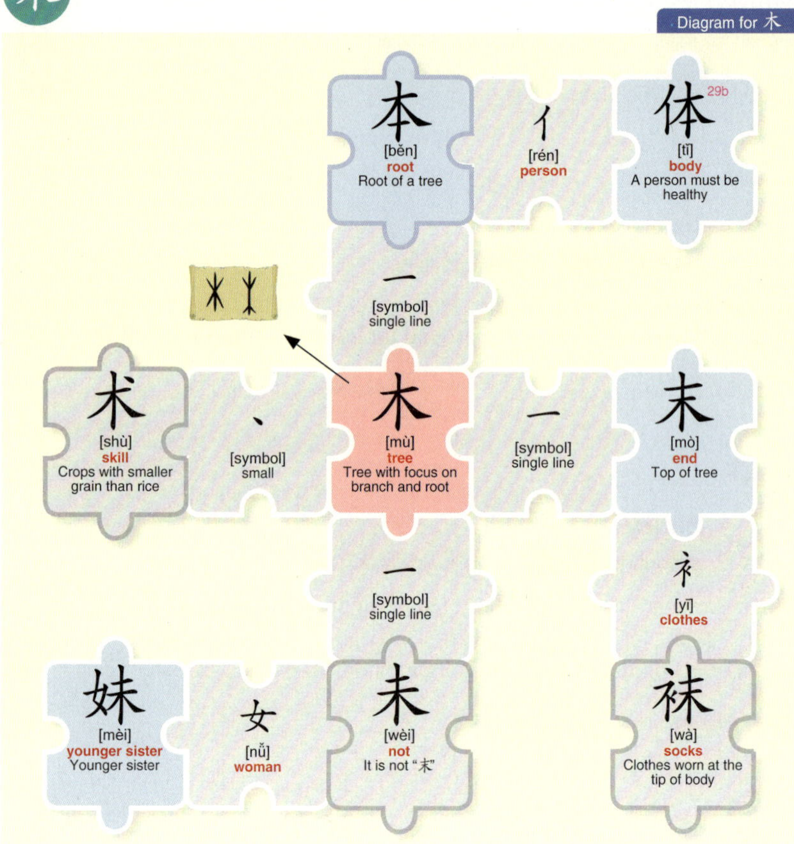

210

210 一 十 才 木

木 mù **tree**

Symbolizes a tree by combining branches(一), root(八), and the stem(丨).

树木[shùmù] tree - 40d

210a 一 十 才 木 本

本 běn **root; book**

tree 木 [mù] + single line 一 [symbol]

A horizontal line(一) is added into the bottom of "木" to emphasize its root. Also signifies book, in a sense that a book is the root of knowledge.

本子[běnzi] book; notebook - 95
课本[kèběn] textbook - 210i
根本[gēnběn] root; fundamental - 14b
基本[jīběn] basic - 44a
本领[běnlǐng] ability; capability; skill - 6c

210b

一 二 干 末 末

末 mò

end

a long line 一 [symbol] + tree 木 [mù]

A horizontal line(一) is added into top of "木" to emphasize that location is the end.

周末[zhōumò] weekend - 154a

210c

丶 ラ 衤 衤 衤 衤一 衤二 衤+ 衤未 袜

袜 wà

socks

clothes 衤=衣[130] [yī] + end 末 [mò]

Socks are clothing(衤) which you wear on the very tip(末) of your body.

袜子[wàzi] socks; stockings - 95

210d

一 二 十 未 未

未 wèi

not

a short line 一 [symbol] + tree 木 [mù]

A shorter horizontal line(一) is added into top of "木" to emphasize that the growth is not yet finished. The tree is, therefore, not great in size, but rather small trees that are still growing.

未来[wèilái] future - 212d

210e

㇛ 女 女 女一 女二 女+ 妹 妹

妹 mèi

younger sister

woman 女[96] [nǚ] + not 未 [wèi]

Signifies a younger sister, who is not(未) above you among siblings(女).

妹妹[mèimei] younger sister

210

210

210f

一 十 才 木 术

术
shù

skill

tree 木 [mù] + small 丶 [symbol]

Originally it used to signify millet, a crop(木) that has smaller(丶) grain than rice. Millet is a crop that is easy to grow even on barren land of considerable size; therefore, it required skills to manage millet growing.

* Traditional character(術) shows a crossroad(行 60b) in a large millet(术) field, signifying that skills were used to create roads to make growing crops easier.

技术[jìshù] technique; skill; art - 51a   艺术[yìshù] art - 83b

木

Diagram for 木

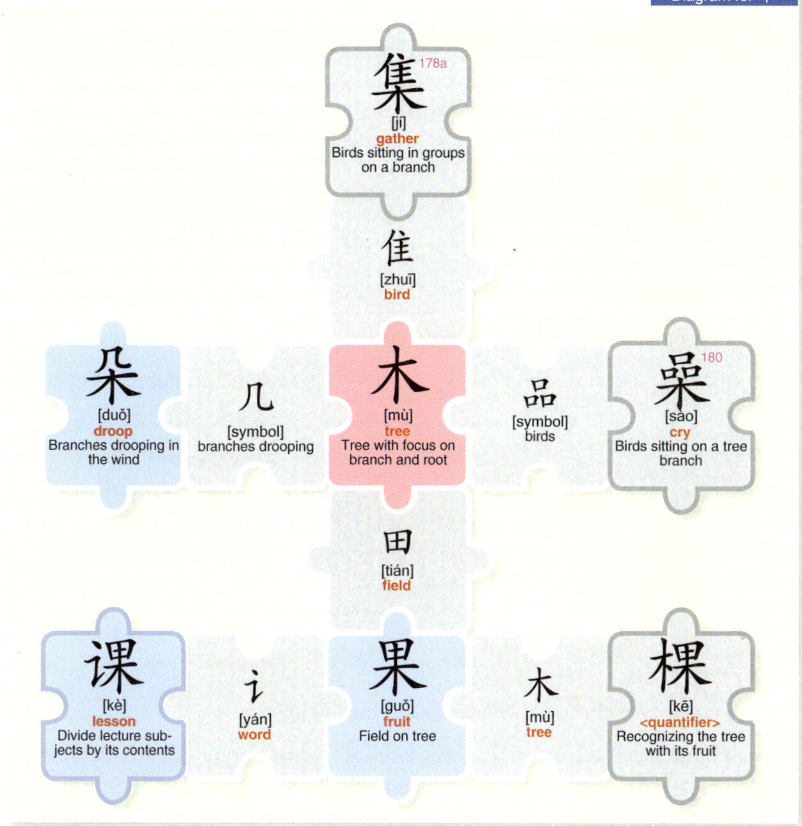

210

210g 丶 冂 日 日 旦 甲 果 果

果 guǒ

fruit

field 田[154] [tián] + tree 木 [mù]

A crop field(田) hanging from trees(木) signifies fruits hanging from tree branches.

苹果[píngguǒ] apple - 122b
水果[shuǐguǒ] fruit - 201
果汁[guǒzhī] fruit juice - 202d
如果[rúguǒ] if; in case; in the event of - 96g
结果[jiéguǒ] bear fruit; result; outcome - 104b

210h

一 十 才 木 朩 朩ㄇ 朩ㄇ 朩巴 梩 椢 椢 棵

棵 kē

<quantifier>

tree 木 [mù] + fruit 果 [guǒ]

Symbolizes naming of a fruit tree(木) by looking at what fruit(果) it bears; now used as a unit to count trees or plants.

我种下了五棵树。I planted five trees. - 113b 232c 223g 168a 226a 210h 40d

210i

丶 讠 讠ㄱ 讠ㄇ 讠ㄇ 讠巴 讵 课 课 课

课 kè

lesson

word 讠=言[22][yán] + fruit 果 [guǒ]

Symbolizes division of subjects or lessons based on the content(果) of a lecture(讠).

* "果" signifies a fruit of learning, with emphasis on its contents, in this character.

课本[kèběn] textbook - 210a

课文[kèwén] text - 133

上课[shàng/kè] attend class - 223f

下课[xià/kè] finish class - 223g

210

210j

丿 几 朵 朵 朵 朵

朵 duǒ

droop

branches drooping 几 [symbol] + tree 木 [mù]

This character depicts the image of a tree (木) whose branches are waving and drooping(几) in the wind. It sometimes means 'ear' because of the image of a drooping ear lobe. It is also used as 'units to count flower, cloud or anything similar to them.'

* The upper stroke "几" and the stroke "table 几[213][jī]" have the same shape, but no relevance to each other in terms of their meanings.

耳朵[ěrduo] ear - 10a

东

Diagram for 東

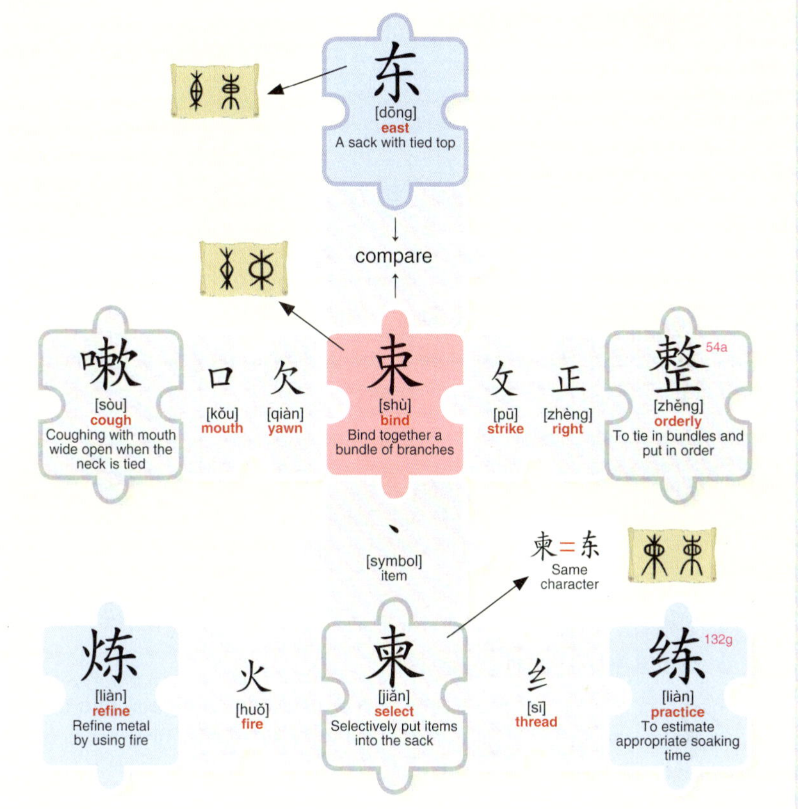

211 一 𠂇 左 车 东

东 dōng **east**

Symbolizes a sack(小) with its mouth tied(𠀁) up. East, an abstract concept of direction, was something difficult to represent by symbols, and so this character was taken due to its identical pronunciation. Used together with "west 西[170] [xī]," which was a very common type of pottery that can be seen in any directions, to mean things in general.

* Ancient character (inscription on bones and tortoise carapaces) on clearly shows the top of a sack being tied up.

东西[dōngxi] thing - 170　　东边[dōngbiān] east side - 61a　　东西 east and west - 211 170

211a

束 shù

bind

tree 木[210] [mù] + bundle 口 [symbol]

Symbolizes how tree(木) branches are tied and bound(口) together for easier transportation.

结束[jiéshù] finish; end - 104b

211b

嗽 sòu

cough

mouth 口[16] [kǒu] + bind 束 [shù] + yawn 欠[23] [qiàn]

Symbolizes an animal coughing with its mouth(口) wide(欠) open when hunters or butchers tie(束) its neck with string.

* "欠" signifies mouth wide open.

咳嗽[késou] cough; tussis - 4d

211

211c

柬 jiǎn

select; letter

bind 束 [shù] + item 丶 [symbol]

Only necessary items(丶) are selected when packing(束) things into a sack. Also derived to mean letter, in a sense that only selected words are actually written down when writing a formal letter.

* "柬" simplies into "东" when combined with other characters.

请柬[qǐngjiǎn] a letter of invitation - 135c

211d

炼 liàn

refine

fire 火[158] [huǒ] + select 东 = 柬 [jiǎn]

Impurities can be selectively(柬) removed by melting a metal with fire(火) – the process of refining metal.

锻炼[duànliàn] temper; forge; train - 117b

林

Diagram for 林

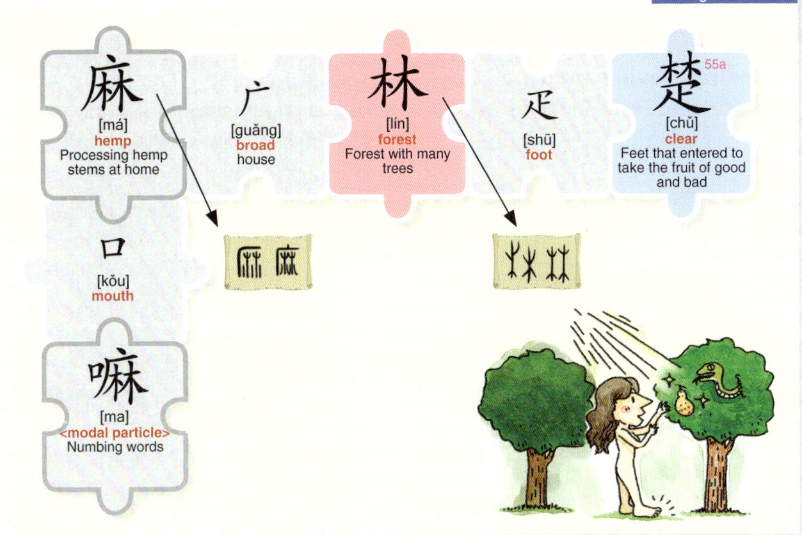

212

212

一 十 才 木 木 村 村 林

林
lín

forest

tree 木[210] [mù] + tree 木 [mù]

Two trees(木) are combined to symbolize forest.

树林[shùlín] wood; grove - 40d

212a

丶 亠 广 广 庁 庁 庁 庁 府 麻 麻

麻
má

hemp; numb

house/broad 广[143] [guǎng] + skin of hemp stem 朩 [děng]

Symbolizes women processing the bark(朩) of hemp stems to produce strings in a house(广). Hemp leaves and flowers also contain anesthetic substance, which led into meaning for numbness.

* Hemp was produced around 2,800 B.C in China to obtain fibre and strings.
* Ancient character shows "林"(木[210]) as a shape of hemp bark(朩) being taken off.

麻烦[máfan] troublesome; inconvenient - 6b

212b 丨 ㄇ 口 口` 口ˉ 吖 吖 听 吘 味 咻 嘛 嘛 嘛

嘛 ma

<modal particle>

mouth 口[16] [kǒu] + numb/hemp 麻 [má]

Symbolizes saying words(口) that can numb(麻) people – signifying something is numbingly clear to everyone. Used as modal particle at the end of sentences to emphasize previous statements such as "reasoning, justice or morality and facts."

不会就学嘛。If you can't do it, you should learn it. - 223a 66c 80b 95a 212b

木

212

Diagram for 木

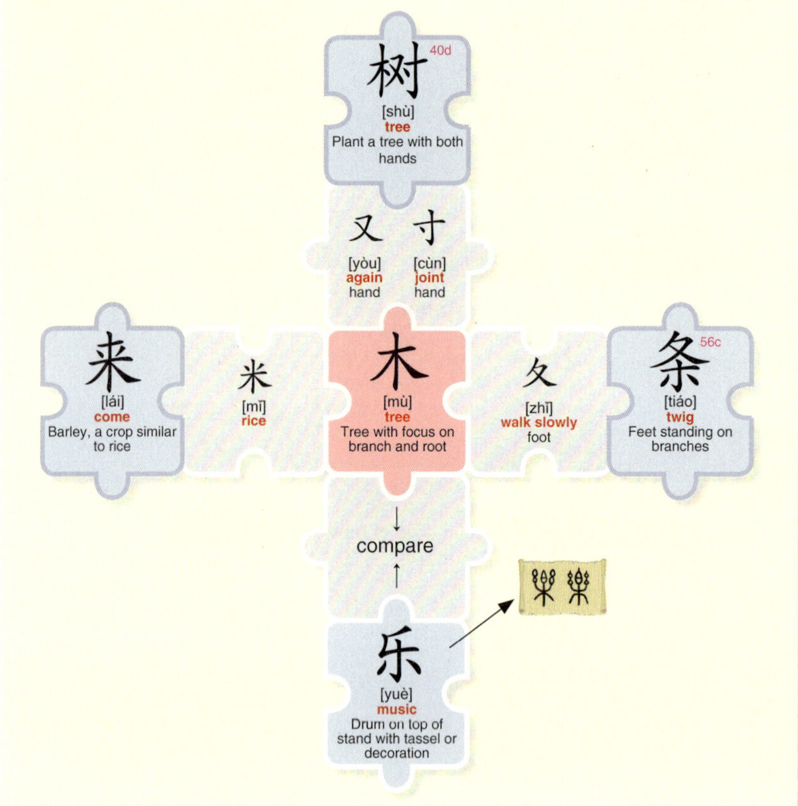

212c

丆 𠂉 乐 乐 乐

乐
yuè/lè

music / pleasure

drum with tassel 𠂆 [symbol] + stand 朩 [symbol]

Music is symbolized by a drum(𠂆) with decoration standing on a drumstand(朩).

* Traditional character(樂) shows drum(白) with string(絲[132a]) decoration standing on dumstand(朩).

音乐[yīnyuè] music - 21

Also derived to mean joy or pleasure in playing with decorated drum(𠂆) on a drumstand(朩).

快乐[kuàilè] happy; joyful; cheerful - 28d
乐观[lèguān] optimistic; sanguine - 13b

212d

一 丆 冖 立 平 来 来

来
lái

come

tree 木[210][mù] + rice 米[138][mǐ]

212

Symbolizes barley, which is a crop(木) similar to rice(米). Barley bears its grain in spring after long winter, signifying that long-sought spring is coming with barley.

* Imagine how the ancient people waited for spring to come during harsh winters when they had no food.

出来[chūlái] come out - 167a
回来[huílái] return; come back - 20d
进来[jìnlái] come in - 228b
上来[shànglái] begin; start - 223f
原来[yuánlái] original; former - 201d
过来[guòlái] come over - 40f
将来[jiānglái] the future - 214a
起来[qīlái] stand up; sit up - 53d
下来[xiàlái] come down - 223g

几

Diagram for 几

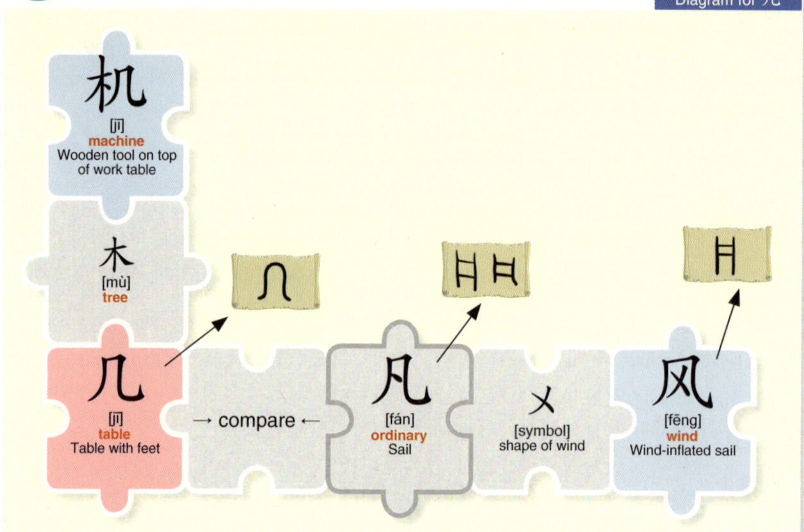

213 **213** 丿 几

几 jī/jǐ — table / a few; how many

Symbolizes a small table with its feet stretched out.

* Discussed here as the meaning is related with wood.

> 几乎 [jīhū] almost; nearly - 121e

Also means a few, or when forming a question to ask how many of something exists.

* For easier memorization, think of students studying math on a table.

> 今天几号? What's the date today? - 66 74b 213 16c

213a 一 十 才 木 机 机

机 jī — machine

tree 木[210] [mù] + table 几 [jī]

A machine made of wood(木) is placed on top of work table(几).

飞机[fēijī] airplane - 182c
手机[shǒujī] cell phone; mobile phone - 31
司机[sījī] driver; chauffeur - 18e
机器[jīqì] machine - 172a
机场[jīchǎng] airport - 152a
机会[jīhuì] chance; opportunity - 66c
照相机[zhàoxiàngjī] camera - 120c 11c

213b 丿 几 凡

凡 fán **ordinary**

Symbolizes the shape of a sail on a boat that gives power through wind. Derived to mean ordinary, as wind is a very ordinary source of power that exists everywhere.

平凡[píngfán] ordinary - 122

213c 丿 几 风 风

风 fēng **wind**

sail/ordinary 凡 [fán] + shape of wind 㐅 [symbol]

Symbolizes the shape of a fully inflated(㐅) sail(凡) with strong wind.

213

刮风[guāfēng] blow (of the wind) - 24a
风浪[fēnglàng] wind and waves; storm - 15a
风俗[fēngsú] custom - 196b
风景[fēngjǐng] scenery; landscape - 2c
风力[fēnglì] wind power - 159

丬

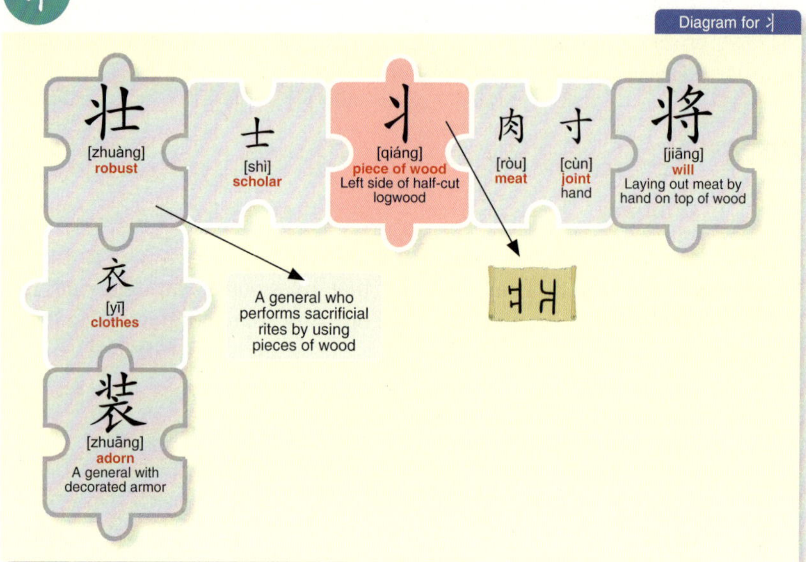

214

214 丶 冫 丬

丬 qiáng — piece of wood

Symbolizes a flat side of a half-cut logwood, which came to simply mean a piece of wood.

214a

将 jiāng — will

piece of wood 丬 [qiáng] + meat 夕[222] → 月[221] → 肉[192] [ròu] + hand/joint 寸[40] [cùn]

Symbolizes a general laying out of pieces of sacrificial meat(肉) onto a piece of wood(丬) by hand(寸). The sacrificial ceremony was for blessing of victory in the future – wishing that victory will happen.

* Traditional character(將) shows "evening 夕 [xī]" is in fact a simplified form of moon(月), which is a different form of meat.

* When intonation changes to "jiàng," it becomes meaning of general who performs such ceremonies in war.

将来[jiānglái] the future - 212d　　将要[jiāngyào] will; shall - 170b

214b 丶 冫 丬 丬一 丬十 壮

壮 zhuàng

robust

piece of wood 丬 [qiáng] + scholar 士[104] [shì]

Symbolizes the strong stance of a general(士) who performs ceremonies during war using pieces of wood(丬).

* "士" is a representation of an axe, a symbol of authority of a general.

健壮[jiànzhuàng] healthy and strong; robust - 37c

214c 丶 冫 丬 丬一 丬十 壮 壮 壮 壮 些 奘 装 装 装

装 zhuāng

adorn; install

robust 壮 [zhuàng] + clothes 衣[130] [yī]

A general who performs wartime ceremonies(壮) is wearing an adorned armor(衣). Meaning of to install is derived from the act of decorating such armor.

他装起老人来了。He is dressing up like an old man. - 84b 214c 53d 100a 63 212d 168a
他正装着电灯。He is installing a light right now. - 84b 54 214c 11b 157a 158a

215

片

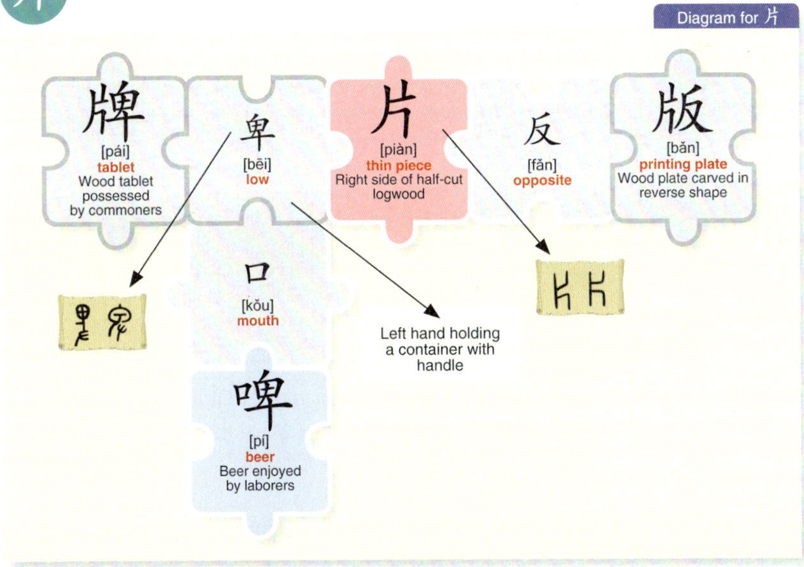

215 丿 丿 𠂆 片

片 piàn — thin piece

Opposite of "丬[214][qiáng]," this symbolizes the right side of a log, meaning a thin piece. Also used as a unit to count thin or flat items.

照片[zhàopiàn] photograph; picture - 120c　　片面[piànmiàn] unilateral; one-sided - 10
一片儿面包 a slice of bread - 223 215 71 10 47

215a 丿 丿 𠂆 片 片 片 版 版

版 bǎn — printing plate

thin piece 片 [piàn] + opposite 反[148a][fǎn]

Symbolizes a wood(片) printing plate that's been carved in reverse(反) shape to print on paper.

出版[chūbǎn] publish - 167a

215

215b ノ 丿 冂 白 白 甶 卑 卑

卑 bēi — low

container with handle 甶 [symbol] + left hand 𠂇 [symbol]

The meaning low is derived from the fact that left hand(𠂇) is regarded low in China, which also holds an everyday item like a container with handle(甶).

* Part on the bottom that looks similar to "ten 十[231][shí]" is a reversed form of "hand 𠂇[39][yòu]" signifying the left hand.

自卑[zìbēi] feel oneself inferior - 26

215c 丿 丿 𠂆 片 片 片 片 片 片 牌 牌 牌

牌 pái — tablet

thin piece 片 [piàn] + low 卑 [bēi]

Symbolizes a small wooden(片) tablet used for identification, which was given out to everyone including commoners of low(卑) status.

牌子[páizi] plate; sign - 95

215d

啤 pí

beer

mouth 口[16][kǒu] + low 卑 [bēi]

Synthesized to write Beer, a foreign word(口), by adding "卑" as pronunciation guide.

* Think of how beer is most commonly enjoyed(口) by laborers(卑).

啤酒[píjiǔ] beer - 162a

竹

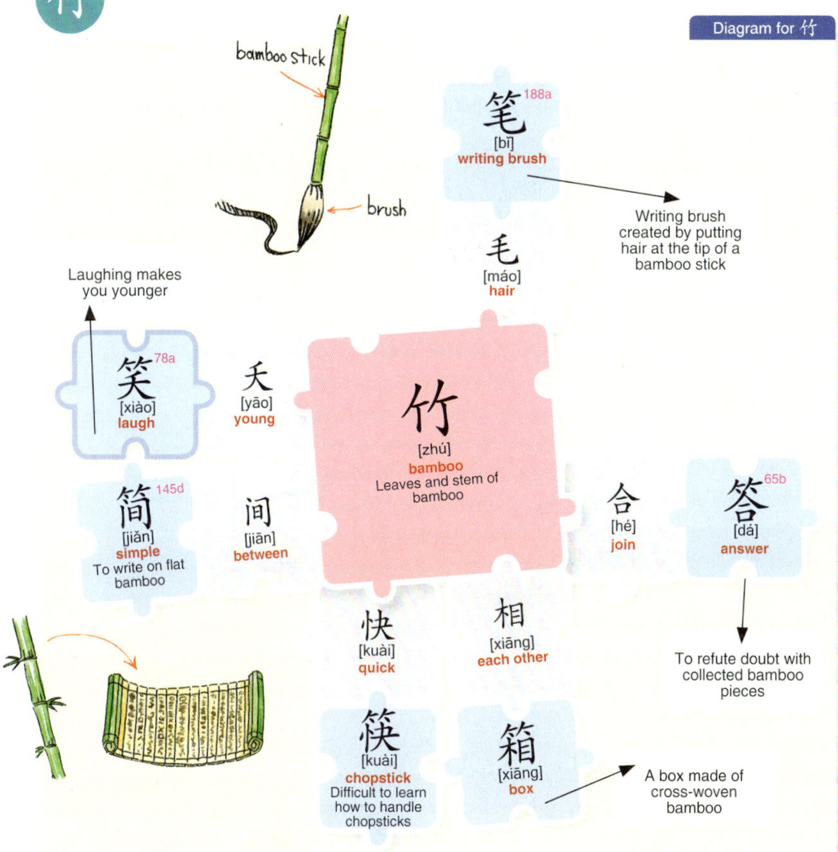

216

216

216

竹 zhú

bamboo

Symbolizes a simplified form of bamboo. Bamboo is used in China as a symbol of longevity due to its long life and evergreen nature, as well as having same pronunciation as wish "祝[72a][zhù]."

竹子[zhúzi] bamboo - 95

216a

箱 xiāng

box

bamboo 竹 [zhú] + each other 相[11c][xiāng]

Bamboo is light and easy to bend, but it is not easily breakable. This character portrays a box which is made by processing and cross-weaving(相) bamboo (竹).

冰箱[bīngxiāng] icebox; refrigerator - 206a
行李箱[xínglǐxiāng] suitcase; trunk (boot) - 60b 95c

216b

筷 kuài

chopstick

bamboo 竹 [zhú] + quick 快[28d][kuài]

In most countries in the East Asia, people eat food with chopsticks which are made of thin wood. This character is made by combining 'bamboo(竹)' which is raw material to make chopsticks, and the sound element "快[kuài]."

* For easier recollection of this character, let us try to think about bamboo-made chopsticks which are difficult to learn how to handle quickly(快).

筷子[kuàizi] chopstick - 95

册

Diagram for 册

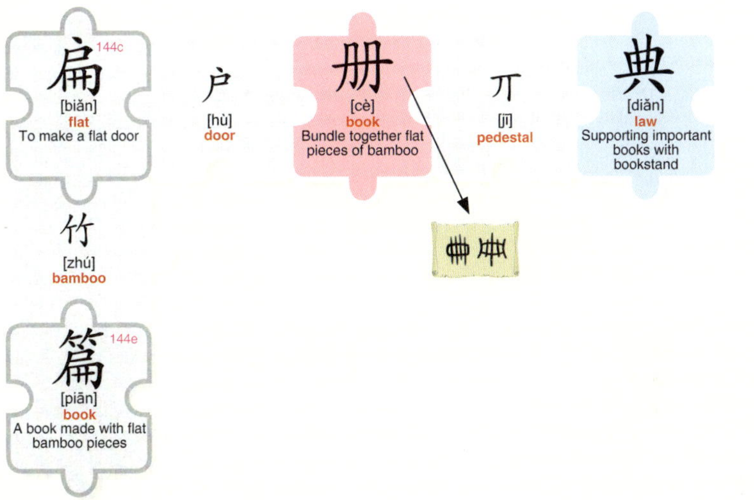

217

丿 刀 川 刖 册 217

册 cè

book

Symbolizes bamboo books(册), created by bundling together thinly cut plates of bamboo(竹[216]).

* Before paper was invented, bamboo plates(册) were used to write on.

注册[zhùcè] register; log-in - 233e

217a

丶 冂 冂 巾 曲 曲 典 典

典 diǎn

law; ceremony; dictionary

book 曲→册[cè] + pedestal 丌[12c][jī]

Symbolizes putting important books(册) on national ceremonies or law on bookstands(丌). Meaning of dictionary is also derived from the fact that dictionaries contain all such important writings in one place.

* "丌" symbolizes a supporting stand.
* Although "册, 冊, 曲" look different, they are currently used as same meaning.

字典[zìdiǎn] dictionary - 95b　　词典[cídiǎn] dictionary - 18f

日

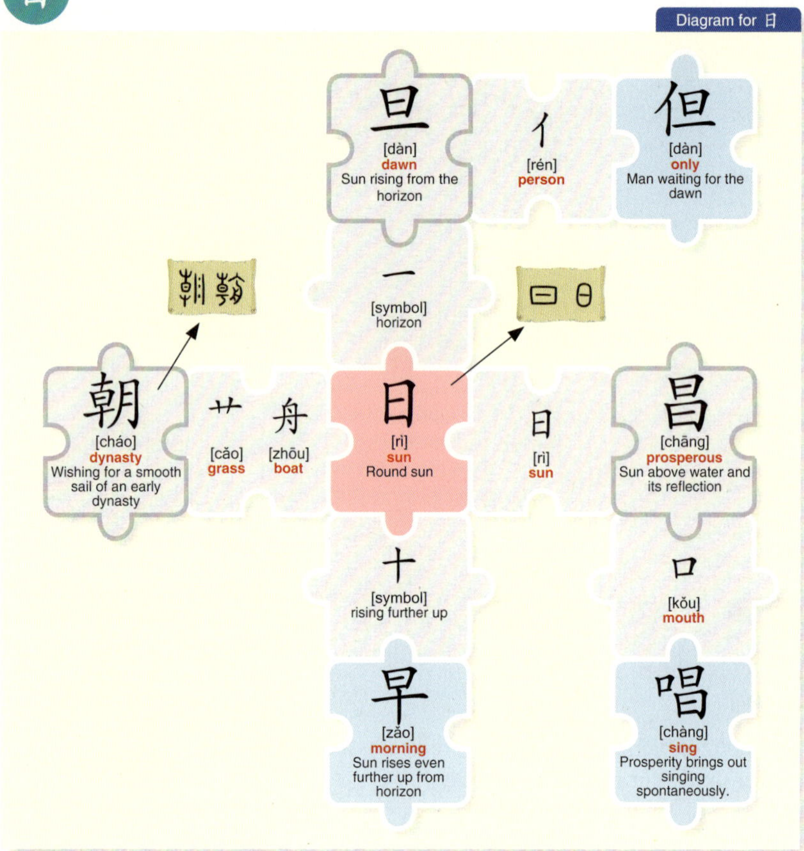

218

218 丨 冂 日 日

日
rì

sun; day

Symbolizes the round sun, also signifying day – a cycle of the sun.

生日 [shēngrì] birthday - 208
日语 [rìyǔ] Japanese (language) - 226c
星期日 [xīngqīrì] Sunday - 208b 44b
节日 [jiérì] festival; holiday - 85g
日子 [rìzi] day; date - 95

218a

丶 冂 日 日 旦

旦
dàn

dawn

sun 日 [rì] + horizon 一 [symbol]

Dawn arrives as the sun(日) rises just above the horizon(一).

218b

丿 亻 亻 亻 但 但 但

但
dàn

only; but

person 亻[70] [rén] + dawn 旦 [dàn]

Man(亻) can but only wait for the dawn(旦) to arrive, and there is nothing else he can do.

但是[dànshi] but; however - 54b
不但[bùdàn] not only - 223a

218c

丶 冂 日 日 旦 昌 昌 昌

昌
chāng

prosperous

sun 日 [rì] + sun 日 [rì]

Symbolizes sun(日) above the horizon and its reflection in water. The sun(日) will get stronger and brighter as it rises, giving the meaning of prosperous.

218

218d

丨 口 口 口 口 口 口 口 唱 唱 唱

唱
chàng

sing

mouth 口[16] [kǒu] + prosperous 昌 [chāng]

When everything goes well(昌), people start to sing spontaneously with their mouths(口).

唱歌[chànggē] sing a song - 17b
我唱给你们听。Let me sing you a song. - 113b 218d 65d 69a 145a 16d

218e

丶 冂 日 日 旦 早

早
zǎo

morning

sun 日 [rì] + rising further up 十 [symbol]

Sun(日) rises further up(十) from the dawn "旦[dàn]," to start morning.

早上[zǎoshang] morning - 223f
早晨[zǎochén] (early) morning - 187a
早饭[zǎofàn] breakfast - 148b

218f

一 十 𠂇 古 古 吉 直 卓 𠦝 朝 朝 朝

朝
cháo

dynasty; toward

grass 艹[207] [cǎo] + sun 日 [rì] + boat 月[221] → 舟[125] [zhōu]

Originally meant as a morning sun(日) rising above the grass(艹) field. In the bronze inscription, however, ship(舟) was added to imply a smooth voyage – symbolizing a wish for a smooth(舟) sailing of a newly-established dynasty. Also derived to mean facing toward something, as people of a nation always faced the kingdom of a dynasty.

* The ancient character shows that "moon 月 [yuè]" used in "朝" actually looks like "舟."

那个窗户朝东。The window faces to the east. - 147e 63b 142a 144 218f 211

日

218

Diagram for 日

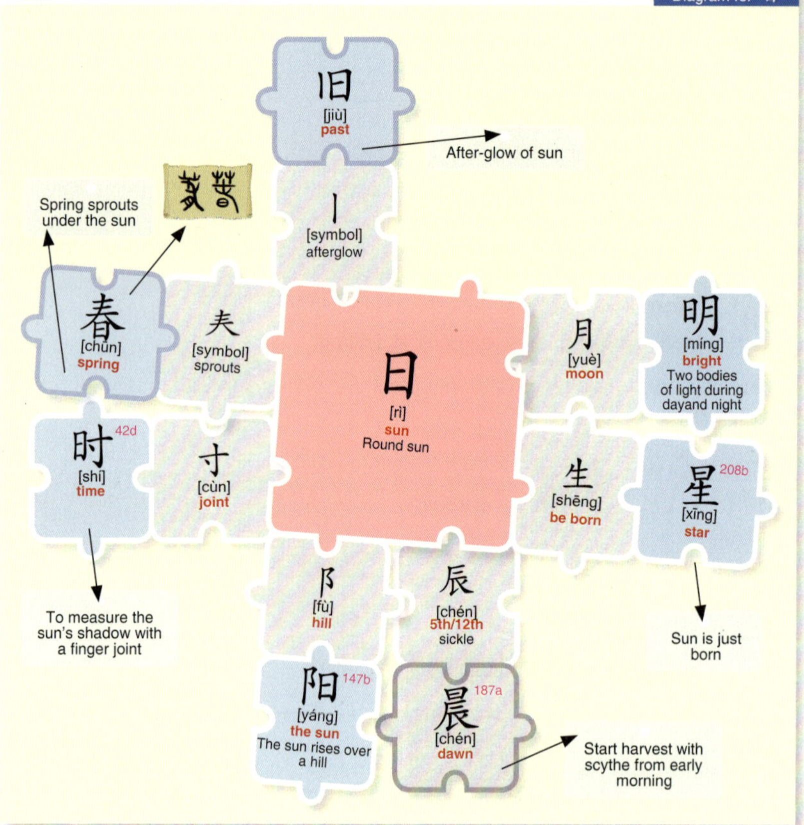

218g

丨 ㇼ 㐄 旧 旧

旧
jiù

past

afterglow 丨 [symbol] + sun 日 [rì]

Symbolizes the sun(日) being slightly overlapped, representing the afterglow of the past sun with a simple symbol(丨).

旧衣服 used (old) clothes - 218g 130 34b

218h

丨 冂 日 日 明 明 明 明

明
míng

bright; next

sun 日 [rì] + moon 月[221] [yuè]

Sun(日), light of the day, and the moon(月), light of the night, are combined to signify brightness. Also signifies wishing for a bright future to come next.

明天[míngtiān] tomorrow - 74b
明白[míngbai] clear; obvious - 134
说明[shuōmíng] explain; illustrate - 72d
聪明[cōngming] intelligent; bright; clever - 16g
明年[míngnián] next year - 121a

218

218i

一 二 三 夫 夫 夫 春 春 春

春
chūn

spring

sprouts 夫 [symbol] + sun 日 [rì]

Symbolizes sprouts(夫) budding out as spring comes with stronger sunlight (日).

* The ancient character shows "夫" as a group of sprouts(屮[207]).

春天[chūntiān] spring (season) - 74b
春节[chūnjié] Spring Festival (Chinese New Year) - 85g

易

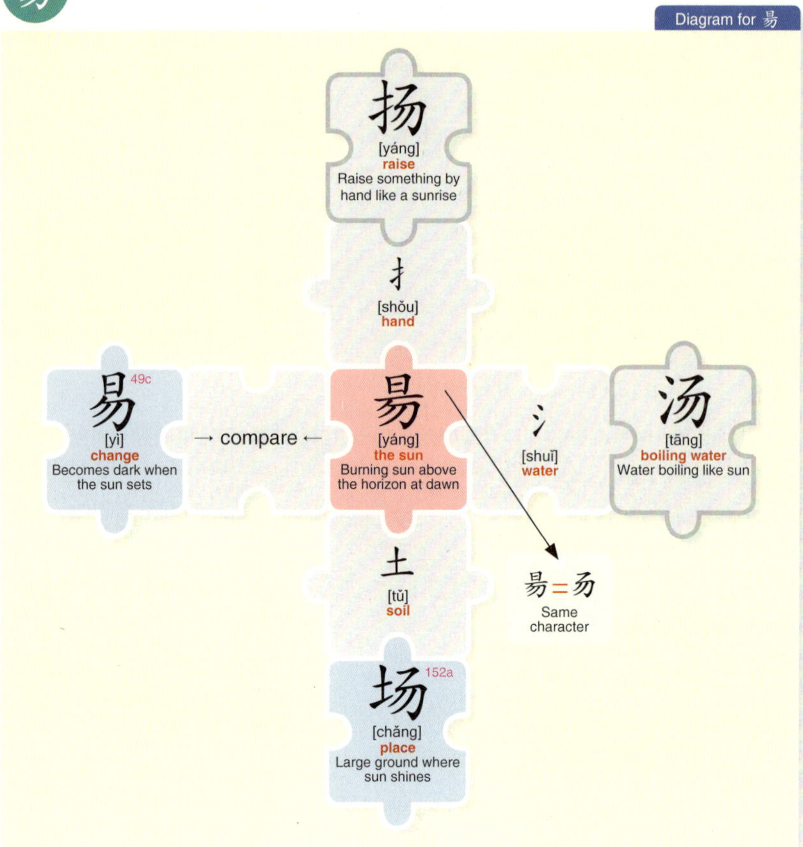

219

219

丨 冂 日 日 旦 旦 昜 昜 昜

昜
yáng

the sun

dawn 旦[218a][dàn] + haze/do not 勿[49][wù]

At dawn(旦), the edge of just-risen sun burns in haze(勿). This is the ancient version of the sun "阳[147b][yáng]," and changes into "𠃓" when combined with other characters.

* When "勿" is used in relation to a non-living thing, it can symbolize haze.

* Be careful not to confuse this with "change 易[49c][yì]."

219a

一 扌 扌 扚 扬 扬

扬
yáng

raise

hand 扌=手[31] [shǒu] + the sun 𠃓=昜 [yáng]

Symbolizes raising something by hand(扌) like a sun(𠃓) rising above the horizon.

表扬 [biǎoyáng] praise; commend - 130b   发扬 [fāyáng] develop; promote - 34f

219b

丶 冫 氵 氵 汅 汤

汤
tāng

boiling water

water 氵[202] [shuǐ] + the sun 𠃓=昜 [yáng]

Symbolizes water(氵) boiling like a fierce sun(𠃓). Also refers to soup in general.

我们喝了一些鸡汤。We had some chicken soup. - 113b 145a 48c 168a 223 88h 177a 219b

219

昔

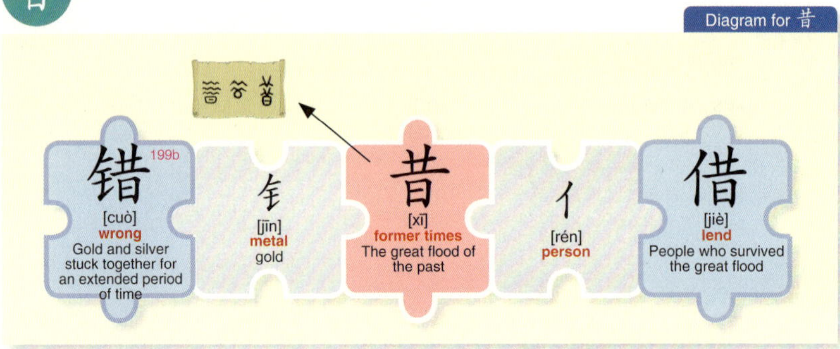

220 一 十 卄 土 芈 昔 昔 昔

昔 xī

former times

overflowing 龷 [symbol] + day/sun 日[218] [rì]

220 The largest disaster humans remember in history is the great flood (variation of "水[201]"), in which everyone on earth was wiped out except the 8 family members of Noah. It is believed that character symbolizes the past or the former days(日) of the flood(龷). Refer to Genesis 6:13~7:24 in the Bible.

* Ancient inscriptions actually show an overflowing water and sun(日), representing the particular day.

220a 丿 亻 亻 仁 仆 伫 借 借 借 借

借 jiè

lend; borrow

person 亻[70] [rén] + former times 昔 [xī]

The family of Noah, people(亻) who survived the great flood in past(昔), would not have lived if they had not followed God's words. Their lives are basically borrowed from God.

我要借书。I want to borrow some books. - 113b 170b 220a 232d

月

Diagram for 月

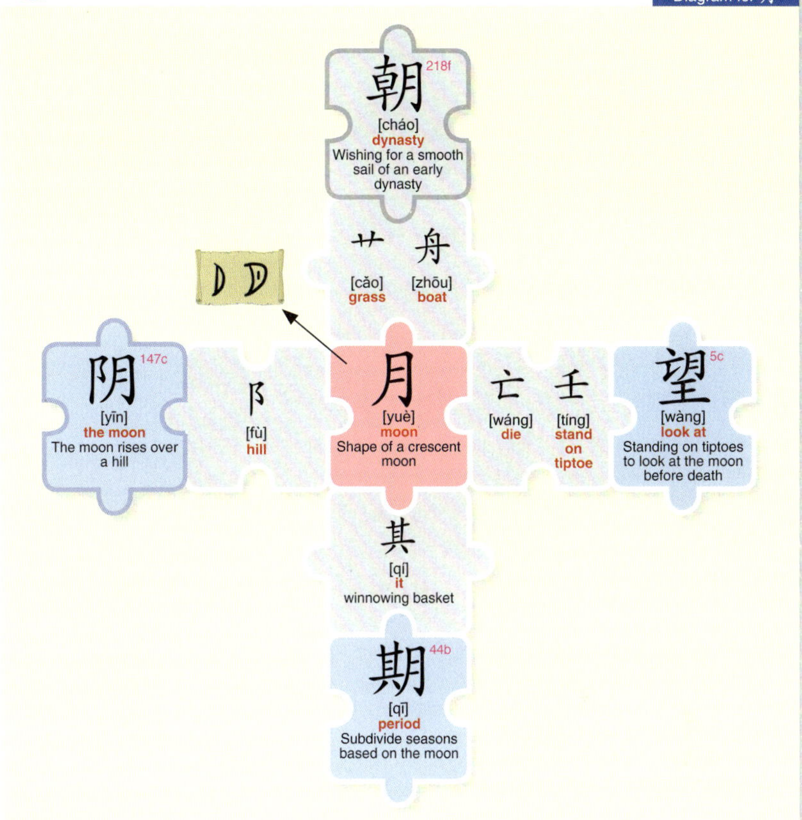

221

221 丿 刀 月 月

月 yuè

moon; month

Symbolizes the shape of the crescent or half moon. When combined with other characters, it means "meat 肉[192][ròu]" or sometimes "boat 舟[125][zhōu]."

月亮[yuèliang] moon - 3b　　月球[y5uèqiú] the moon - 198b

221

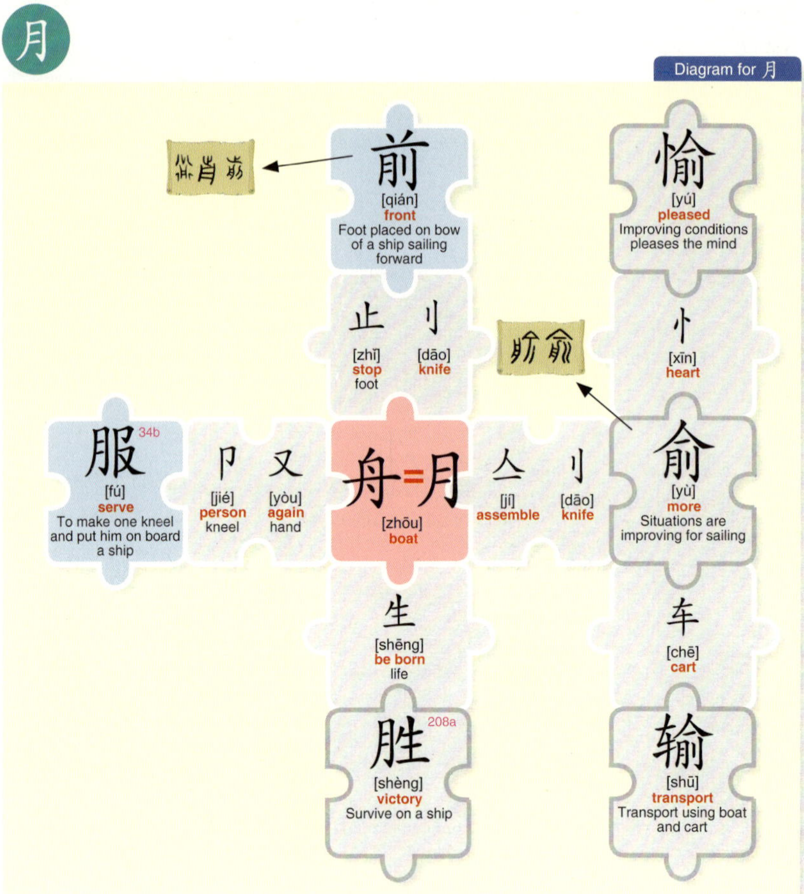

221a

前 qián

front

foot/stop 䒑→止[53][zhǐ] + boat 月→舟[125][zhōu] + knife 刂=刀[119][dāo]

Symbolizes feet(止) of a man standing on the bow – or the front – of a ship (舟) sailing forward(刂) on water.

* Sword(刂) is used here to symbolize water being spilt into sides when a ship sails forward.

* The ancient character (called "the inscriptions on bone and tortoise carapaces") shows a feet(止) of a person standing on bow a ship(舟) moving(行[60b]) forward.

前面 [qiánmian] front; ahead - 10 以前 [yǐqián] before; formerly - 63j

从前[cóngqián] before; formerly - 63g
目前[mùqián] at the present time - 11
前边[qiánbiān] in front; ahead - 61a

221b

丿 人 𠂉 个 亼 合 俞 俞 俞

俞 yù

more

assemble 亼[65][jí] + boat 月→舟[125][zhōu] + knife 刂=刀[119][dāo]

The collective(亼) circumstances are getting better for a ship(舟) to sail forward(刂).

221c

丶 丷 忄 忄 忄 忄 忄 愉 愉 愉 愉 愉

愉 yú

pleased

heart 忄=心[28][xīn] + more 俞 [yù]

Signifies a pleased mind(忄) as winds and conditions get better(俞).

愉快[yúkuài] cheerful; pleasant - 28d

221d

一 𠂇 𠂇 车 车 轮 轮 轮 输 输 输 输 输

输 shū

transport

cart 车[124][chē] + more 俞 [yù]

Signifies transportation of goods using boats and carts(车) as winds and conditions get better(俞).

运输[yùnshū] transport - 227a

221

夕

Diagram for 夕

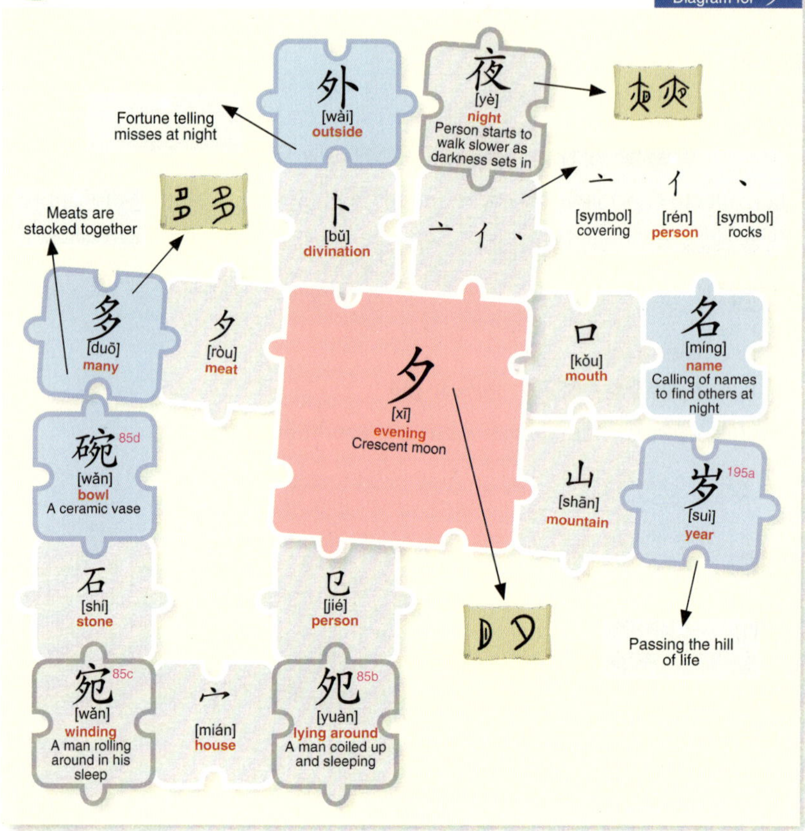

222 ノ ク 夕

夕 xī **evening**

Symbolizes the shape of a crescent moon, signifying evening.

222a ノ ク 夕 夘 外

外 wài **outside**

evening 夕 [xī] + divination 卜[127] [bǔ]

Fortune-telling(卜) at night(夕) causes both teller and spirits into exhaustion to miss (as in outside of truth) their telling.

除了…以外[chúle...yǐwài] except for; but for - 147a 168a 63j
外边[wàibian] outside - 61a
外国[wàiguó] foreign country - 20a
外语[wàiyǔ] foreign language - 226c
另外[lìngwài] other; another - 119d

222b 丶 亠 广 广 疒 疒 夜 夜

夜 yè

night

covering 亠 [symbol] + person 亻[70][rén] + walk slowly 夂[56][zhǐ] + rocks 丶 [symbol]

A person(亻) is walking(夂) slowly in dark night(亠) to avoid rocks(丶) in the road.

* In the ancient script called "the bronze inscription", it is also described as a moon(夕) inside armpit (丶) of a person(大[74]), which is the most dark place in a human body.

半夜[bànyè] midnight; half of a night - 175b
夜晚[yèwǎn] night - 68b

222c 丿 ク 夕 夕 名 名

名 míng

name

evening 夕 [xī] + mouth 口[16][kǒu]

In the middle of a dark night(夕), one must call(口) out names of others to find or recognize them.

名字[míngzi] name - 95b
有名[yǒumíng] famous; well-known - 39c
报名[bào/míng] enroll; enlist; enter one's name - 34a
名胜[míngshèng] scenic spot - 208a
姓名[xìngmíng] full name - 208c

222d 丿 ク 夕 夕 多 多

多 duō

many

meat 夕→月[221]→肉[192][ròu] + meat 夕→月→肉 [ròu]

Many pieces of meat(肉) are stacked together to describe meaning of many. Also used as a suffix at the end of quantifiers to represent the unknown remaining amount.

* The ancient character shows "夕" is in fact meat, instead of crescent moon.

多少[duōshao] how much; how many - 235a
多么[duōme] how; what - 93a
许多[xǔduō] many; much - 121c
差不多[chàbuduō] almost; nearly; just about - 171b 223a
50多岁 over fifty years old - 222d 195a

222

一

Diagram for 不

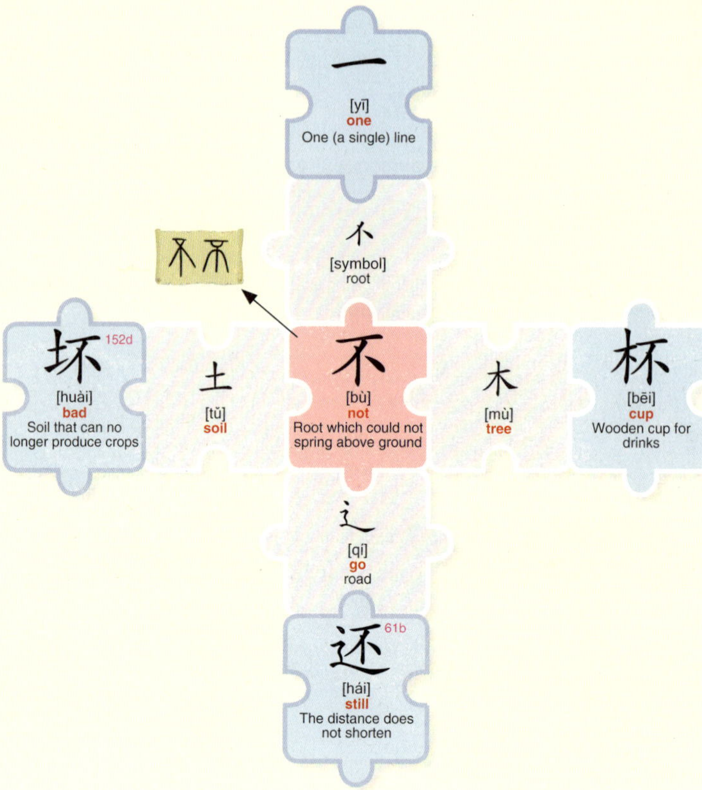

223

223 一

一 yī

one; 1

One line is stroked to represent number 1.

第一[dìyī] the first - 109b	一起[yīqǐ] in the same place; together - 53d
一般[yìbān] same as; sort; general - 117c	一边[yìbiān] one side - 61a
一定[yídìng] fixed; established; regular - 54e	一共[yīgòng] altogether - 43c
一会儿[yīhuìr] a little while - 66c 71	一样[yīyàng] the same; equally; alike - 171a
一直[yīzhí] straight; continuously - 12	

一边…一边…[yībiān...yībiān...] Two actions taking place simultaneously - 61a
(他们一边工作一边学习。They work and learn at the same time. - 84b 145a 200 234b 95a 182a)
一点儿[yìdiǎnr] a bit; a little - 127d 71
一…就…[yī...jiù...] as soon as; directly - 80b
一块儿[yīkuàir] at the same place; together - 76b 71
一切[yīqiè] all; everything - 119b
一下[yīxià] one time; once - 223g
一些[yìxiē] some; a few; a little - 88h

223a

一 ア 不 不

不 bù

not; no

ground /earth 一 [symbol] + root 个 [symbol]

Root(个) of plants will not spring above ground(一). Used as negation.

* "不" is shown here as "one 一 [yī]" is the radical for this character.

不客气[búkèqi] impolite; you're welcome - 57b 204
对不起[duìbuqǐ] I'm sorry - 40c 53d
不错[bùcuò] correct; right; not bad - 199b
不但[bùdàn] not only - 218b
不久[bùjiǔ] soon; before long - 68g
不如[bùrú] not as good as; not equal to - 96g
不同[bùtóng] not alike; different - 149b
不要[bùyào] don't - 170b
不用[bùyòng] need not - 166

223

223b

一 十 才 木 木 杉 杯 杯

杯 bēi

cup

tree 木[210] [mù] + not 不 [bù]

A meaning of drinking cup (for alcohol) is derived from wooden(木) cups used by people with "不" added as pronunciation guide.

* Remember how Chinese made toasts: when they toast(干杯), they empty(不) the glass and show the bottom of the glass(木).

杯子[bēizi] cup; glass - 95
干杯[gān/bēi] drink a toast; cheers - 121

一

Diagram for 一

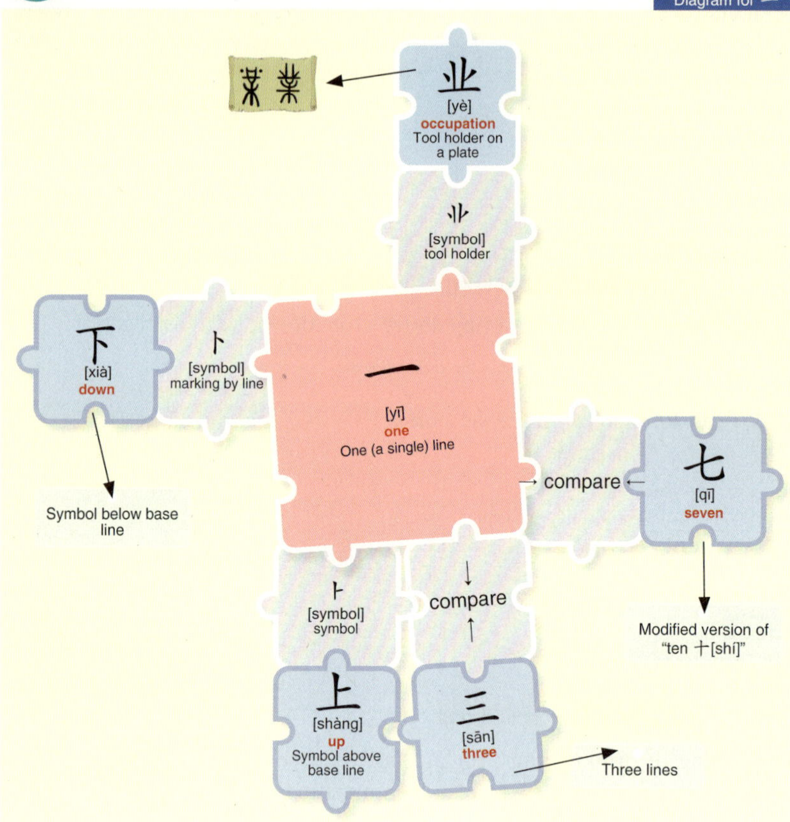

223

223c

业
yè

occupation

tool holder 丬 [symbol] + supporting plate 一 [symbol]

A tool holder(丬) is placed on top of a supporting plate(一), derived to mean occupation or work.

* The ancient character shows a musical instrument under a hanger(业), representating a task that needs to be learnt.

作业[zuòyè] homework; work - 234b
工业[gōngyè] industry - 200
农业[nóngyè] agriculture - 130c
商业[shāngyè] commerce; trade - 103c
业务[yèwù] business - 159f

223d 一七

七 qī **seven; 7**

Lower part of "ten 十[231] [shí]" is bent to represent number 7, a little less than 10.

223e 一 二 三

三 sān **three; 3**

Three strokes of lines are used to represent number 3.

223f 丨 ⺊ 上

上 shàng **up**

symbol ⺊ [symbol] + base line 一 [symbol]

A symbol(⺊) above a line serving as base(一). Can be used differently as verb. See below for usage examples.

上午[shàngwǔ] ante meridiem (a.m.) - 121b
上班[shàng/bān] go to work; go to the office - 119f
晚上[wǎnshang] (in the)evening; (at)night - 68b
早上[zǎoshang] morning - 218e
上网[shàngwǎng] be on the internet - 165
上课[shàng/kè] attend class - 210i
上去[shàngqù] go up; upward - 94
马上[mǎshàng] at once; immediately - 176
上边[shàngbian] upside - 61a
上来[shànglái] begin; start - 212d
上学[shàng/xué] go to school - 95a

223g 一 丁 下

下 xià **down**

base line 一 [symbol] + marking by line ⺊ [symbol]

A symbol(⺊) below a line serving as base(一). Opposite of "up 上 [shàng]," and can be used differently as verb. See below for usage examples.

下午[xiàwǔ] post meridiem (p. m.) - 121b
下边[xiàbian] below; under - 61a
下来[xiàlái] come down - 212d
一下[yīxià] one time; once - 223
下雨[xiàyǔ] rain - 205
下课[xià/kè] finish class - 210i
下去[xiàqù] go down; descend - 94

224

224 丨 冂 月 月 且

且 qiě **and**

Meat is piled in layers on a cutting board(一) for the honoring of ancestors. As layers of meat are laid one after the other, meaning of and is derived from here.

* "且" is shown here as "one 一[223][yī]" is the radical for this character.

而且[érqiě] not only … but (also); and that - 9　　并且[bìngqiě] and; also - 123

224a

㇛ 女 女 如 如 如 姐 姐

姐 jiě

elder sister

woman 女[96] [nǚ] + cutting board/and 且 [qiě]

Signifies an elder sister, who is a woman(女) in family whose age is "put on" as in pile of meat on cutting board(且).

小姐[xiǎojiě] young lady; miss - 235　　姐姐[jiějie] elder sister

224b

丨 ㄇ 月 月 且 助 助

助 zhù

help

cutting board/and 且 [qiě] + power 力[159] [lì]

Meaning of to help is derived as people pile together their efforts(力) like the meat on the cutting board(且).

帮助[bāngzhù] help; assist - 209b

224c

一 十 才 木 木 杏 杏 杏 查

查 chá

investigate

tree 木[210] [mù] + cutting board/and 且 [qiě]

One needs to investigate whether woods(木) are straight enough to be piled or stacked together – as in the meat on cutting board(且) – to make a raft of timber.

* The lower character "旦[218a] [dàn]" depicts the shape of a cutting board(且) if we look at it ancient script.
* The ancient script of "查" has its original meaning of "timber (or log) raft."

检查[jiǎnchá] inspect; examine - 67b　　调查[diàochá] investigate - 154b

224d

丶 丶 冖 宀 宁 宜 宜 宜

宜 yí

suitable

house 宀[141] [mián] + cutting board/and 且 [qiě]

Signifies an act of honoring the ancestors in a home(宀), which is considered appropriate and suitable, with the meat piled on a cutting board(且).

便宜[piányi] cheap; inexpensive - 35d

224

224e

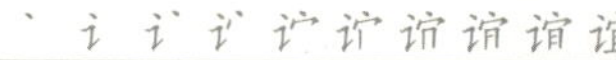

谊 yì

friendship

word 讠=言[22] [yán] + suitable 宜 [yí]

Friendship between two close friends can become stronger when appropriate (宜) words(讠) are used politely.

友谊[yǒuyì] friendship - 34d

丁

225

Diagram for 丁

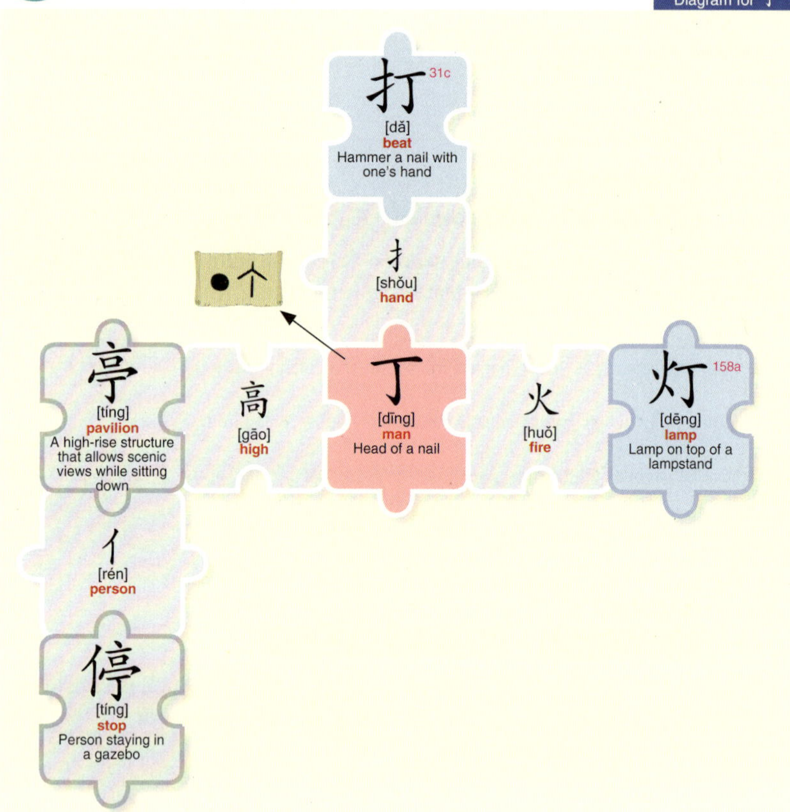

225 一丁

丁 dīng

man

Signifies head(一) of a nail(亅). A bigger head means easier to drive the nail; consequently, meaning of a man is derived as his head(一) is grown with power to spare(亅) in work.

* "丁" is shown here as "one 一[223][yī]" is the radical for this character.

225a 亠亣亣亣亯亯亯亭

亭 tíng

pavilion

high 高[3][gāo] + nail/man 丁 [dīng]

Signifies a gazebo, that is built to rise high(高) on a scenic area that allows one to sit down(丁) and enjoy.

* "丁" contains meaning to nail down something and 'stabilize,' which came to mean to sit down firmly on a place.

* The bottom part of character "高" is omitted to keep the artistic balance in composition.

亭子[tíngzi] pavilion - 95

225

225b 亻亻亻亻亻亻亻亻亻亻停

停 tíng

stop; stay

person 亻[70][rén] + pavilion 亭 [tíng]

Signifies a person(亻) stopping by/staying inside a gazebo(亭) built in a beautiful scenic area.

停止[tíngzhǐ] stop; halt - 53

Diagram for 二

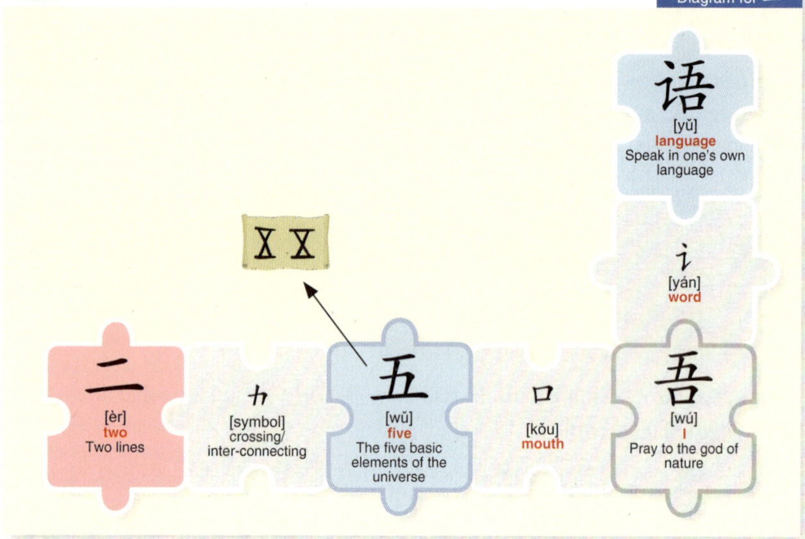

226

226

二 èr

two; 2

Two lines are stroked horizontally to signify number two.

226a

五 wǔ

five; 5

heaven and earth 二 [symbol] + crossing/inter-connecting 𠄠 [symbol]

The two horizontal lines(二) signifying heaven and earth is inter-connected (𠄠) to represent the universe. It was believed that the universe contained five basic elements.

* The ancient character shows an "X-shaped" interconnect between two lines(二).

* In the oriental philosophy of Yin(阴[147c]) and Yang(阳[147b]), there are five basic natural elements that maintain the natural world: water(水[201]), fire(火[158]), wood(木[210]), metal(金[199]), and earth(土[152]).

226b
一 丁 五 五 吾 吾 吾

吾
wú

I; we

five 五 [wǔ] + mouth 口[16] [kǒu]

Signifies an act of wishing(口) for well-being of myself (I) or ourselves (we) to the god of nature who governs the five(五) basic elements of nature

* "口" here signifies the role of mouth in wishing/praying.

226c
丶 讠 讠 订 讦 讦 语 语 语

语
yǔ

language

word 讠=言[22] [yán] + I 吾 [wú]

Signifies an act of prayer(讠) to a deity in one's own(吾) language.

汉语[hànyǔ] Chinese (language) - 34g
法语[fǎyǔ] French (language) - 94b
日语[rìyǔ] Japanese (language) - 218
英语[yīngyǔ] English (language) - 77a
语言[yǔyán] language - 22
词语[cíyǔ] words; expressions; terms - 18i
口语[kǒuyǔ] spoken language - 16
外语[wàiyǔ] foreign language - 222a
语法[yǔfǎ] grammar; syntax - 94b

226

Diagram for 云

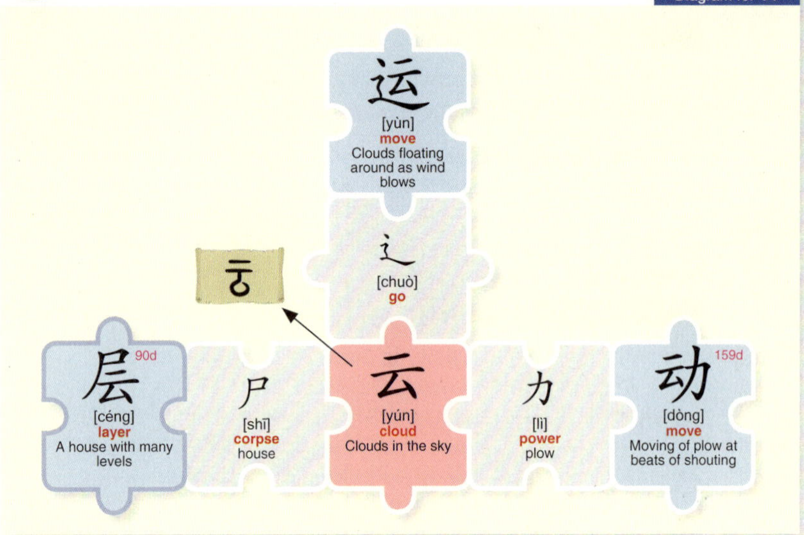

227

227 一 二 云 云

云 yún **cloud; say**

Signifies clouds floating in the sky. A floating cloud can also predict rain, which then also came to mean to say.

* "云" is shown here as "two 二[226][èr]" is the radical for this character.

227a 一 二 云 云 运 运 运

运 yùn **move**

cloud 云 [yún] + go 辶[61][chuò]

Signifies a cloud(云) floating(辶) around, or moving, as wind blows.

运动[yùndòng] motion; movement - 159d　　运输[yùnshū] transport - 221d

井

Diagram for 井

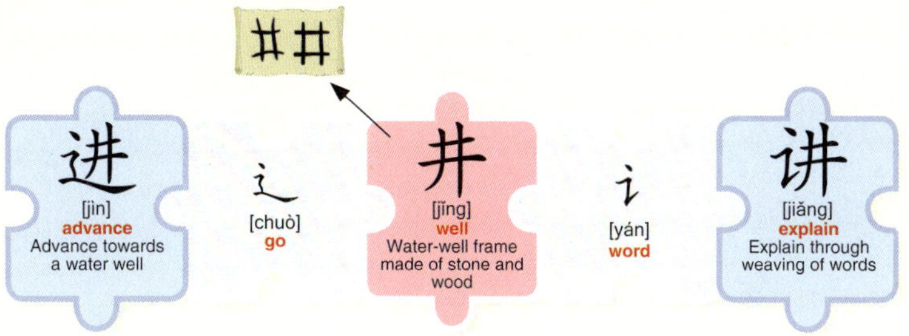

228 一 二 ≠ 井

井 jǐng

well

Signifies the frame of a waterwell, created by weaving together stone and wood materials and digging downward.

* "井" is shown here as "two 二[226] [èr]" is the radical for this character.

228

228a 丶 讠 讠 讠 讲 讲

讲 jiǎng

explain

word 讠=言[22] [yán] + well 井 [jǐng]

As one can build a well(井) by weaving together stones and woods, an explanation can be given by weaving(井) of words(讠).

讲话[jiǎng/huà] speak; talk - 24b　　讲座[jiǎngzuò] a course of lectures - 152c

228b 一 二 ≠ 井 井 讲 进

进 jìn

advance

well 井 [jǐng] + go 辶[61] [chuò]

Signifies a thirsty man in the heat running(辶) or advancing towards a well (井).

进来[jìnlái] come in - 212d　　进去[jìnqù] go in; get in; enter - 94

进行[jìnxíng] progress; advance - 60b

八

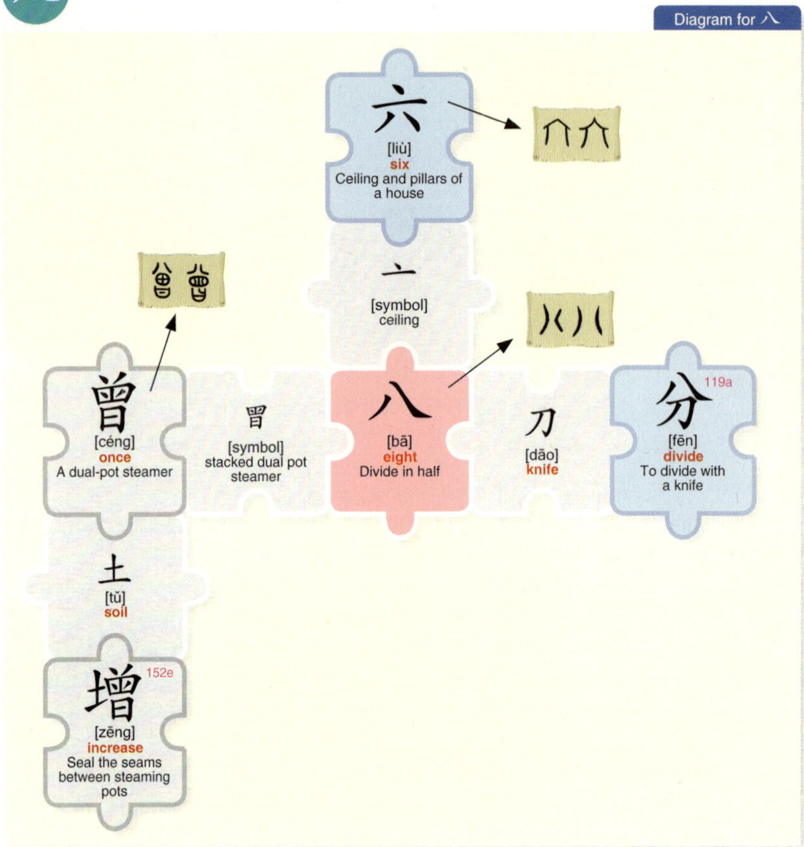

229

229 ノ 八

八
bā

eight; 8

Shaped as two matching lines in opposite, means to divide. Currently means number 8, derived from a number that can be continuously divided(八).

* When written upside down(` '), it signifies 'heavenly blessing.'

229a 丶 亠 六 六

六 liù

six; 6

Originally meant a shape of house with ceiling(亠[1]) and pillars(八), but later became to mean number 6.

* The ancient form of this letter shows shape of ceiling(宀[141]) as than the current version(亠).

229b 丶 丷 丷 㣺 ... 曽 曽 曾 曾

曾 céng

once

eight 丷→八 [bā] + stacked dual pot steamer 曾 [symbol]

This character signifies an act of steam-vaporising(八) from the top of a stacked dual-pot steamer which consists of a water-boiling pot(曰) on bottom and a holed steam-receiving pot(罒) on top. Doubles as meaning of "at early" or "already" as the water is already boiling if steams are shooting out from top.

* The character shaped like eight "八" symbolizes exiting steam.

不曾 [bùcéng] never - 223a

229

九

Diagram for 九

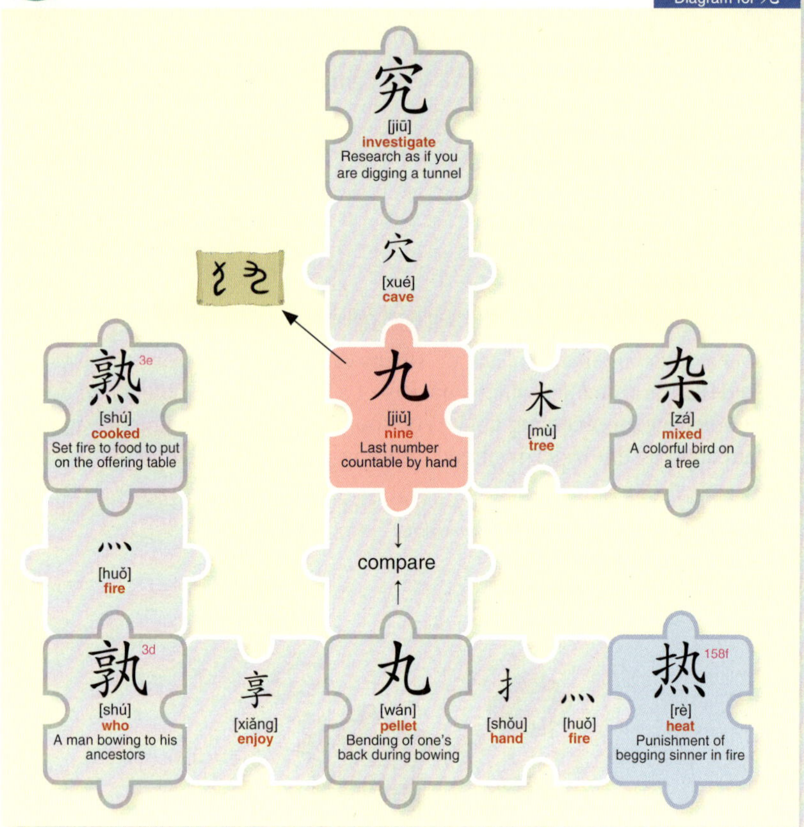

230

230 丿 九

九
jiǔ

nine; 9

Signifies number 9 by representing the edge of hand(ナ[39]) in bent(乚) form, meaning the last(乚) decimal number countable by hand.

230a

丶 丷 宀 穴 穴 穷 究

究 jiū

investigate

cave 穴[142][xué] + nine 九 [jiǔ]

Signifies research or investigation as in digging a deep(九) hole(穴).

* Nine "九" being the last digit in decimal system reinforces meaning of depth.

研究[yánjiū] research - 197d　　研究所[yánjiūsuǒ] research institute - 197d 144a

230b

丿 九 九 杂 杂 杂

杂 zá

mixed

nine 九 [jiǔ] + tree 木[210][mù]

Signifies a bird with feathers with many(九) different colors mixed, sitting on a tree(木).

* The traditional character(雜) depicts a bird(隹[178]) wearing a cloth(衣[130]) of mixed colors on a tree (木).

复杂[fùzá] complicated - 56d　　杂技[zájì] acrobatics - 51a

230

230c

丿 九 丸

丸 wán

pellet

When bowing, person's back takes a round shape like an egg or pellet.

* Has no relation to character "九[jiǔ]," meaning number nine.

十

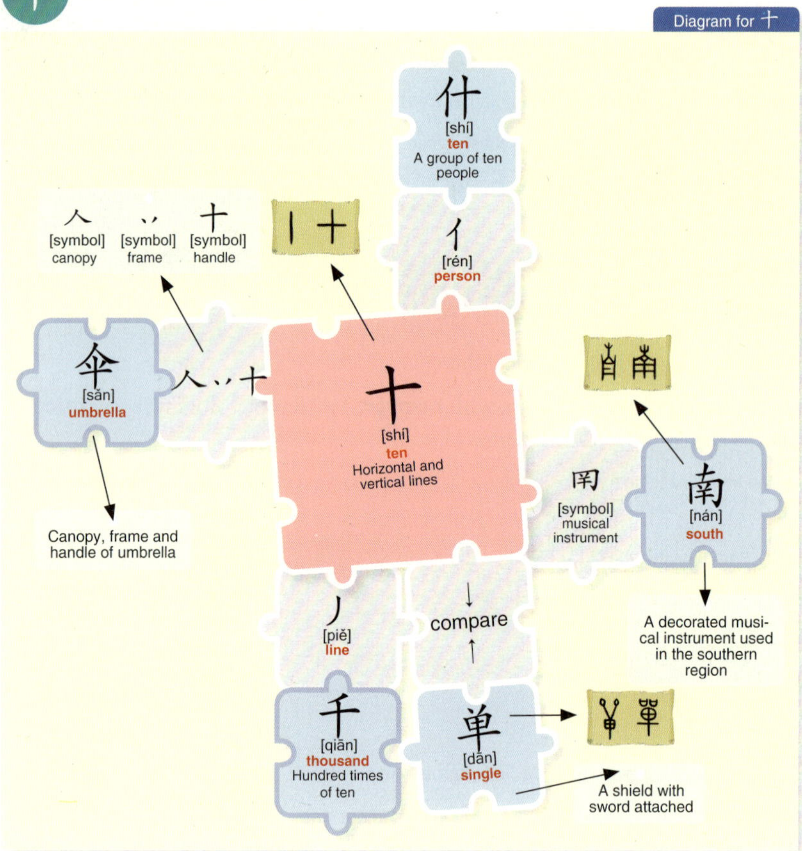

231

231 一 十

十 shí

ten; 10

The number 10 was originally written as single vertical line(丨) but later added a horizontal line to reduce confusion.

十分 [shífēn] fully; very; extremely - 119a

231a

丿 亻 亻 什

什
shí/shén

ten; assorted

person 亻[70][rén] + ten 十 [shí]

Signifies ten(十) of different people(亻) forming a group. Also means number 10 when dealing with fractions or multiples of numbers.

什九。Nine tenths (9/10) - 231a 230 什百。Tenfold or hundredfold. - 231a 134a

When pronounced as "shen," the character becomes an indivisible unit of a language.

什么[shénme] what - 93a 为什么[wèishénme] why - 159c 93a

231b

一 十 𠂇 冇 冇 冇 冇 南 南

南
nán

south

hanger decorations 十 [symbol] + musical instrument 𢆉 [symbol]

A clear-sounding percussion instrument(𢆉) with hanging decorations(十) used in southern China, which eventually became to mean south.

* Certain tribes in the southern China still have a traditional instrument called "南."

南边[nánbian] south side - 61a 南方[nánfāng] south - 160

231c

丶 丷 𠂉 冂 冃 旦 甾 单

单
dān

single

A sword is added on the traditional double-edged Chinese shield(shield/dry 干[121][gān]), allowing the wearer to hunt with only single apparatus as the shield now doubles as offensive weapon.

菜单[càidān] menu; bill of fare - 33e 简单[jiǎndān] simple - 145d

231d

丿 二 千

千
qiān

thousand

line 丿[234][piě] + ten 十 [shí]

Number ten "十" is given an additional line(丿) to signify a hundred times of itself – one thousand.

* "丿" does not have specific definition and can be adapted to many different definitions.

231

千万 [qiānwàn] ten million; by all means - 194d

231e

伞 sǎn

umbrella

canopy 人 [symbol] + frame 丷 [symbol] + handle 十 [symbol]

This character reflects the image of an unfolded umbrella which consists of canopy(人), frame(丷) and handle(十).

232 丨

Diagram for 丨

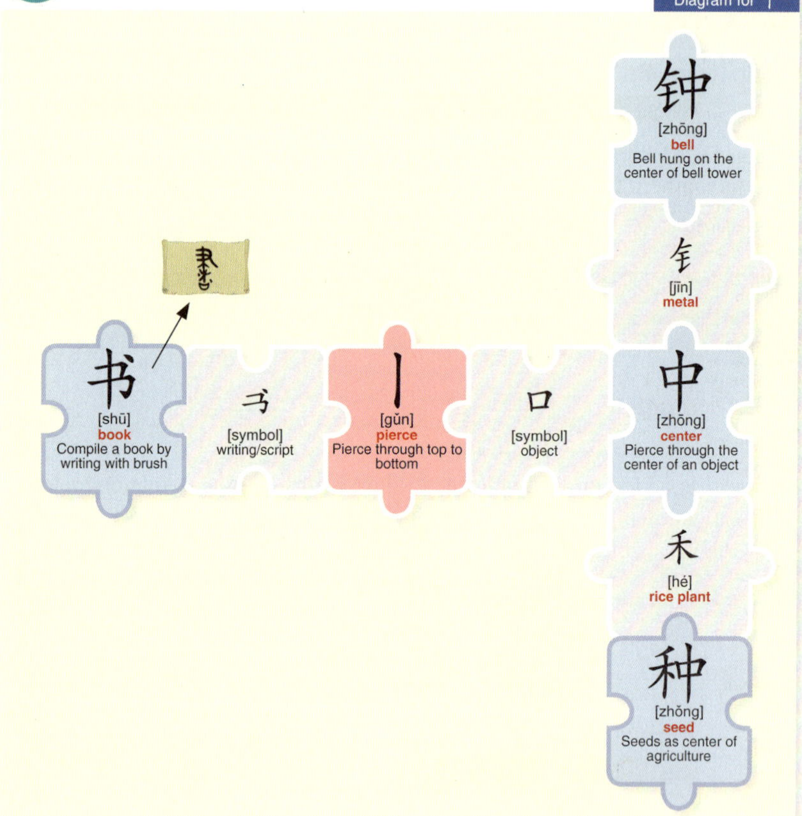

232 丨

丨 gǔn **pierce**

Signifies action of striking/piercing vertically from top to bottom.

232a 丨 冂 口 中

中 zhōng **center**

object 口 [symbol] + piercing/penetrating 丨 [gǔn]

This character describes an object(口) which is pierced(丨) in the middle or center. It also means that China is the center of the world. Works also as a meaning of "currently being" or "continuing" when placed after a verb, in the sense of being in the middle of an action. In this case, the character "exist 在[32a][zài]" is placed before the verb.

中国[Zhōngguó] China - 20a
中午[zhōngwǔ] noon; midday - 121b
中间[zhōngjiān] center; between - 145c
中文[zhōngwén] the Chinese language - 133
中学[zhōngxué] middle school - 95a
集中[jízhōng] concentrate - 178a
第二号大桥在建设中。The Bridge No. 2 is currently being constructed.
- 109b 226 16c 74 78c 32a 37b 117e 232a

232

232b ノ ケ ケ 乍 钅 钅 钔 钔 钟

钟 zhōng **bell; clock**

metal 钅=金[199][jīn] + center 中 [zhōng]

Signifies a metal(钅) bell being hung on the center(中) of the bell tower. In the olden days, the bell tower of town offices also served as clocks.

分钟[fēnzhōng] minute - 119a
点钟[diǎnzhōng] o'clock - 127d
钟头[zhōngtóu] hour - 75

232

232c

丶 二 千 禾 禾 禾 和 和 种

种 zhǒng

seed; species

rice plant 禾[139][hé] + center 中 [zhōng]

Seeds of crops, which can be stored and transported, is the central(中)part of cultivating crops(禾). As well, a same seed will always yield a same crop – thereby also doubling as the meaning of species.

各种[gèzhǒng] every kind - 57
种植[zhòngzhí] plant; grow - 12a
种子[zhǒngzi] seed - 95

232d

乛 马 书 书

书 shū

book

writing/script 马 [symbol] + brush 丨 [symbol]

Signifies writing of characters(马) using brush(丨), which ends up becomes a complete book.

* The traditional character(書) is formed by inking the brush(聿[37]) in the Chinese palette(曰[symbol]) and writing with it.

图书馆[túshūguǎn] library - 206f 193c
读书[dúshū] read; study - 75d
书包[shūbāo] schoolbag; satchel - 47
书店[shūdiàn] bookstore - 127b

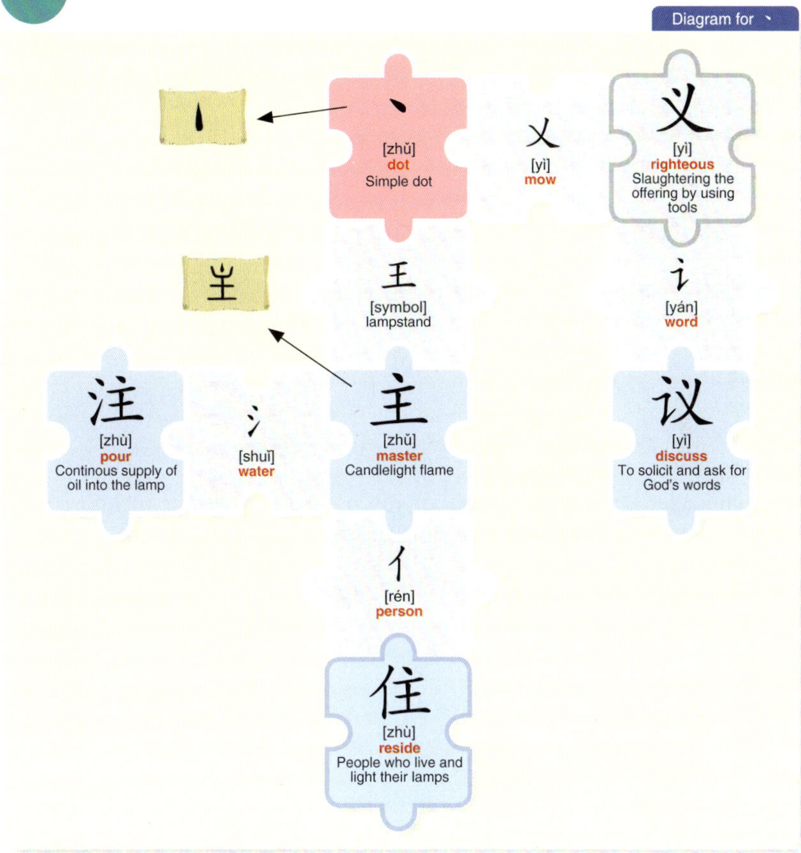

233

233

丶 zhǔ

dot

A simple dot. Used often as a symbol of a specific character in simplification process of traditional characters into simplified versions.

233

233a

`丿乂义`

义 yì

righteous; meaning

offering 丶 [symbol] + mow 乂 [yì]

This character symbolizes the action of knocking down(乂) a sacrifice(丶) with a tool to offer to a deity. Through such a sacrifice ritual to ask for God's will, the meaning of 'righteous, meaning' is derived.

* "Mow 乂 [yì]" indicates an act of cutting grass or plants or of killing a live animal by "X."
* Traditional version(義) is formed by slaughtering the sheep(羊[171]) with a sawtoothed spear(我[113b]).

意义[yìyì] meaning; significance - 21b

233b

`讠讠讠议议`

议 yì

discuss

word 讠=言[22][yán] + righteous 义 [yì]

This character depicts the image of discussing(讠) together to know what God's intention(义) is and also what is a right way(义) to do.

会议[huìyì] meeting; conference - 66c

233c

`丶亠亠丰主`

主 zhǔ

master

flame 丶 [symbol] + lampstand 王 [symbol]

Signifies flame(丶) that burns on top of lampstand(王), derived to mean the master as the flame is the center of all objects and beings in darkness.

* The character may look identical to the character "king 王[108][wáng]," but has no relation to any meaning of king or royalty.

主要[zhǔyào] main; major - 170b
主意[zhǔyi] plan; idea - 21b
主张[zhǔzhāng] assert; maintain; opinion - 102a

233d ノ イ イ' 亻亠 仁 仠 住

住 zhù

reside

person 亻[70] [rén] + lamp/master 主 [zhǔ]

Meaning of to reside/to live is formed by the people(亻) or residents who light their lamps(主) at night.

住院[zhù/yuàn] be in hospital - 73b

233e 丶 丶 氵 氵 氵 汴 注 注

注 zhù

pour; concentrate

water 氵[202] [shuǐ] + lamp/master 主 [zhǔ]

Signifies pouring of oil(氵) into the lamp(主) to keep it. The character also doubles as to concentrate, as you continuously pour your attention into a single affair like you do with oil and its lamp.

注意[zhùyì] pay attention to; take note of - 21b
注册[zhùcè] register; log-in - 217
注射[zhùshè] inject; get a shot - 27b

233

234

Diagram for 乍

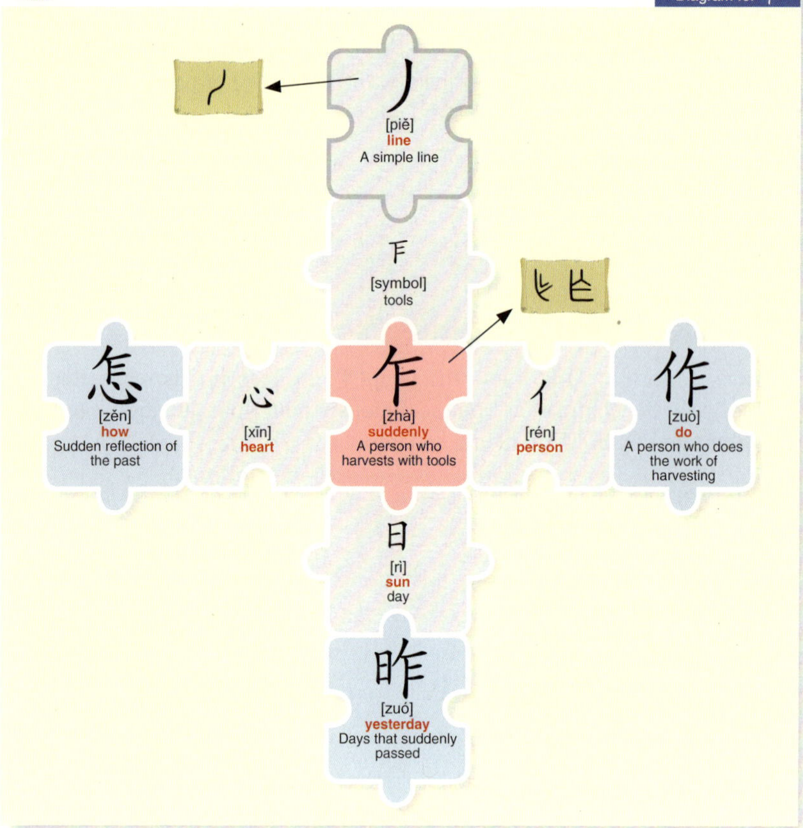

234 丿

丿 piě **line**

A shape of simple line stroked from upper right to lower left. Can be interpreted in many different ways without a solid definition.

234a ノ 𠂉 亇 乍 乍

乍 zhà **suddenly**

Signifies a person(𠂉→人[63]) harvesting the crops using tools(𠂇). Crops are harvested suddenly, after spending a year to grow.

* The reason for introducing "乍" here is due to the fact "丿[piě]" is a radical in this case.

234b 丿 亻 亻' 亻𠂉 竹 作 作

作 zuò

do

person 亻[70][rén] + suddenly 乍 [zhà]

The character "乍," which signifies a person harvesting with tools, is used to mean "sudden"; by adding the subject person(亻) it reinforces the meaning of to do.

工作[gōngzuò] job; work - 200
作业[zuòyè] homework; work - 223c
作用[zuòyòng] action; effect - 166

234c 丨 冂 日 日 日' 日𠂉 昨 昨 昨

昨 zuó

yesterday

day/sun 日[218][rì] + suddenly 乍 [zhà]

As the old saying goes, time flies – and it really does feel fast. Meaning of yesterday is formed from the day(日) that passed all of a sudden(乍).

昨天[zuótiān] yesterday - 74b

234d 丿 𠂉 乍 乍 乍 乍 怎 怎 怎

怎 zěn

how

suddenly 乍 [zhà] + heart 心[28][xīn]

A question of how is formed when you suddenly(乍) reflect in your heart(心) the events of your past, and start asking yourself questions.

* "心" signifies the condition of one's heart, as in an emotion or character at that moment.

怎么[zěnme] how - 93a
怎么样[zěnmeyàng] how - 93a 171a
怎样[zěnyàng] how - 171a

234

Diagram for 小

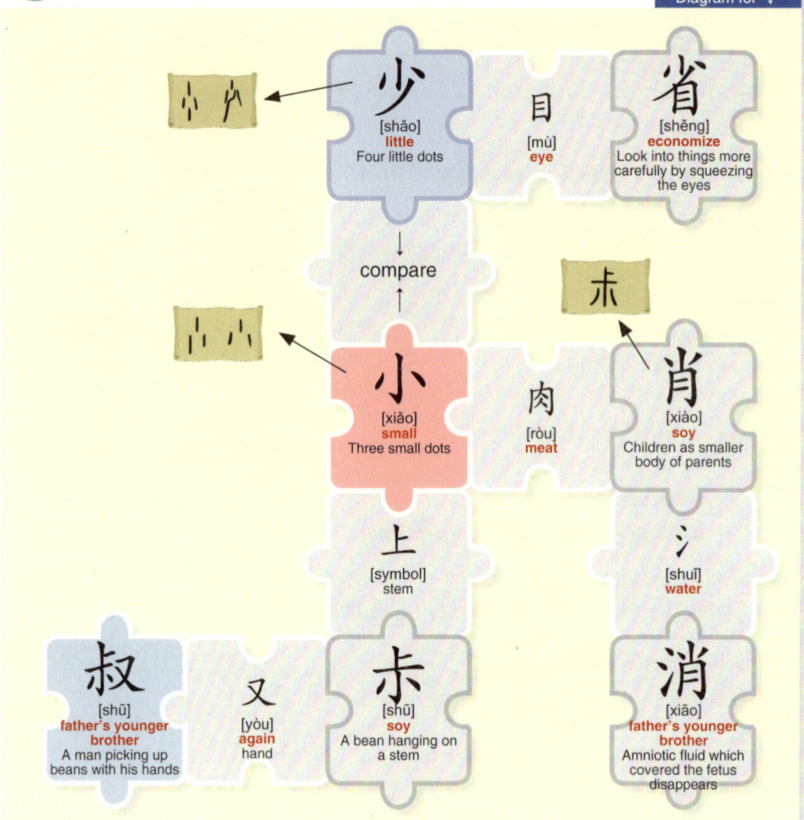

235

235 亅 小 小

小 xiǎo **small**

Signifies group of three small dots(丶).

小姐[xiǎojiě] young lady; miss - 224a
小时[xiǎoshí] hour - 42d
小心[xiǎoxīn] be careful - 28
小孩儿[xiǎoháir] child; kid - 4c 71
小朋友[xiǎopéngyǒu] children - 192a 34d

235a

丨 ⺌ 小 少

少 shǎo

little

Signifies group of four little dots(丶).

多少 [duōshao] how much; how many - 222d 不少 [bùshǎo] not a little; quit a few - 223a

235b

丨 ⺌ ⺌ 少 少 省 省 省 省

省 shěng

economize; province

little 少 [shǎo] + eye 目[11] [mù]

This signifies the act of bringing objects into focus – in order to have a better, more careful look into – by squeezing(少) the eyes(目). One can then economize by looking into things more carefully. Doubles as meaning for a province or district, which is an administrative division of a nation which allows rulers to look more carefully into the people.

* In fact, when you squeeze(少) your eyes(目) to focus on something distant, the eyebrows will force the iris to close down, increasing the field of depth and helping you to see better.

节省 [jiéshěng] economize; save - 85g 广东省 Guangdong province - 143 211 235b 235

235c

丨 ⺌ ⺌ 𣥂 肖 肖 肖

肖 xiào

resemble

small 小 [xiǎo] + meat 月[221] → 肉[192] [ròu]

A child is described as a small(小) body(肉) – signifying resemblance with his/her parents.

肖像 [xiàoxiàng] portrait - 174c

235d

` ゛ 氵 氵' 氵'' 氵"' 氵' 消 消 消

消 xiāo

disappear; news

water 氵[202] [shuǐ] + resemble 肖 [xiào]

A child who takes after his/her parents(肖) is born when the amniotic fluid (氵) bursts and disappears. As well, contains dual meaning of continuously-changing "news" as the fetal fluid is continuosly formed and disappears in a life cycle of human child.

消息[xiāoxi] news - 26b 取消[qǔxiāo] cancel - 10b

235e

丨 ⺊ 上 𠂇 未 尗

尗 shū

soy

stem 上 [symbol] + bean 小 [symbol]

The ancient script has the image of a small bean(小) hanging on a stem(上).

235f

丨 ⺊ 上 𠂇 未 尗 叔 叔

235

叔 shū

father's younger brother

soy 尗 [shū] + hand/again 又[34] [yòu]

During the ancient times of hunting and agriculture, men used to hunt and perform labor like plowing. This character depicts the image of a father's younger brother who is too young to do such a hard work but is engaged in an easier work like bean(尗) picking with his hands(又).

叔叔[shūshu] father's younger brother

A concluding remark

The fact that you are reading this probably means that you have an interest in Chinese characters and a knowledge that almost rivals that of a scholar. Now is the time to reveal how Chinese characters were made and share the purpose of this book. Doing so will help you approach the thousands of new Chinese characters you will come across with an objective but inquisitive mind.

How the Chinese characters were made?

- Pictograms : The origin of Chinese characters are the pictograms of items the ancient Chinese used to communicate with. A tree's branches (一), roots(八), and trunk(丨) became the character "tree 木 [mù]." Once you know their origins, the 300 odd Chinese pictograms shouldn't be so hard to memorize.
- Codes : Codes were used to convey meanings that were difficult to do so with shapes. For example, a long horizontal stroke(一) on the top of a tree (木) to emphasize the end of something came to mean "end 末 [mò]."
  There are about 130 such characters. If you remember they are made based on pictograms, these also should be easy to remember.
- Ideograms : As time passed, pictograms and codes were combined to make new characters. For example, a person(亻) leaning against a tree(木) means "rest 休 [xiū]." There are about 1,000 such Ideograms. Once you know the pictograms and codes these characters are based on, they shouldn't be such a threat.
- Combined characters : The meanings of Ideograms can be memorized based on the characters they are composed of, but remembering the pro nunciation is a whole new matter. So the ancient Chinese made new char acters by borrowing the meaning of one and the pronunciation of another and combining them. For example, they combined "clothes 衤 [yī]" and "end 末 [mò]" to make "socks 袜 [wà/mò]." About 97% of all Chinese characters were made this way.
- In addition to the above-mentioned characters, there are "derivative cognates (reciprocal meaning)" and "Rebus(or phonetic loan or borrowed characters)." They have, however, slight variations in meaning or pronunciation, and therefore shouldn't need much effort to remember.

Basic characters as the backbone

We can tell that all ideograms, combined characters, "derivative cognates (reciprocal meaning)" and "Rebus (or phonetic loan or borrowed character)" were made with pictograms and codes. So if we know all the characters that are pictograms and codes, then we can easily deduce the meaning, which is a unique quality of Chinese characters.

Xu Shen(许慎, 30 AD~124), a Han Dynasty scholar and the author of the first Chinese language dictionary Shuowen Jiezi(说文解字), selected 540 basic characters. Scholars from countries that still use Chinese characters, namely China, Korea, and Japan, selected 200 of them and called them 'radicals.' But there are some basic characters that are not radicals, so including those, there are about 250 basic characters in the Chinese language.

That's it. All languages have a basic form, and Chinese is, of course, no exception. English has the 26-letter alphabet while Korean has 24 vowels and consonants and Japanese has 50 letters. Remember those basics and you can learn the language. 250 basic Chinese characters sounds daunting, but it shouldn't be. English, Korean, and Japanese are phonetic languages, so just because you can read and write doesn't mean you understand. But Chinese characters are ideograms with meaning and with memorizing come understanding.

Most Chinese characters combined

Most Chinese characters are combined characters which are relatively easy to understand because the basic characters that form the whole convey both meaning and pronunciation.

Wang Anshi(王安石, 1021 AD~1086), one of the Eight Giants of the Tang (唐) and Song(宋) Dynasties' literary world suggested that within a combined character, the part that gave its meaning also gave its pronunciation. This is only natural because when making a combined character, the scholar would first look for a character with a similar pronunciation. Let's take a previous example, the character "socks 袜 [wà/mò]." The Chinese combined "clothes 衤 [yī]" for the meaning and "end 末 [mò]" for the pronunciation to describe socks (袜), clothes(衤) for a part at the end(末) of one's body. Isn't that fascinating!

Of course, not all combined characters are like that. Some combined characters have parts that are included only for the pronunciation. For example, to make "狼[láng]," the character for 'wolf,' the Chinese combined "dog 犭 [quǎn]" and borrowed the pronunciation from "good 良 [liáng]." Searching for the seemingly invisible or nonsensical connection might help you memorize these kinds of characters. "狼[láng]" means a wolf(犭) has a good(良) head. In other words, this character means a wolf is smart. The Native Americans acknowledged this and believed wolves to be sacred animals. This book is a compilation of such stories and explanations that are sure to help you remember Chinese characters.

How to enjoy the hidden meanings of Chinese character

Now that you know how Chinese characters were formed and why this book was written, we should consider how to apply the characters you have learned so far.

In most cases, this book provides only one English word as the meaning to one given Chinese character. But as is the case with any language, most characters have multiple meanings. Especially so for pictograms, because their meanings change depending on the situation and the reason they are used in a combination. For example, this book explains that "对[duì]" is "Two persons are holding up candles with their hands(又, 寸) to talk to each other to see if they have the right person for whom they have been looking. It came to mean 'to…' by its image 'facing toward each other or face-to-face.'" Because of that, "对" can mean 'to face, right/correct, to answer, mutually/face to face, pair/couple.' It will be much easier to remember the origin of a character and use that to learn the other derivative meanings.

Each time you come across a new, more complicated Chinese character, you'll notice you're breaking them down into smaller components. In most cases, one component will give you the pronunciation and the others will help you deduce the meaning. Keep that fact in mind when studying any Chinese character. Think about the why such components were put together to make a new character and the size of your vocabulary will know no bounds.

Hanyu Pin'yin index

r

s

t

Z

Index of Base Characters

When looking for Chinese characters in a dictionary without knowing its Pin'yin, one must use the radical-based index to find a specific character. However this can be a difficult task to perform in the early stages of learning. This index includes the base characters that form part of a composite character that will enable readers to find a correct character based on its base. Those that are printed in blue in the list of characters are either radicals or used as base characters. You can find more characters based on these with counting on the total number of strokes.

1 stroke

2 strokes

3 strokes

4 strokes

4
strokes

5 strokes

6 strokes

7
strokes

8 strokes

9 strokes

10 strokes

11 strokes

12 strokes

13 strokes